PHILIP'S

STREET ATLAS

UNRIVA
DETAIL
BEST-SE
ATLAS RANGE*

C000088431

NAVIGATOR
BRISTOL & BATH

BATH AND NORTH EAST SOMERSET, NORTH SOMERSET AND SOUTH GLOUCESTERSHIRE

www.philips-maps.co.uk

Published by Philip's a division of Octopus Publishing Group Ltd
www.octopusbooks.co.uk
Carmelite House,
50 Victoria Embankment,
London EC4Y 0DZ
An Hachette UK Company
www.hachette.co.uk

First edition 2022
BABDA

ISBN 978-1-84907-601-2

© Philip's 2022

Map data

This product includes mapping data licensed from Ordnance Survey® with the permission of the Controller of Her Majesty's Stationery Office. © Crown copyright 2022. All rights reserved. Licence number 100011710.

CONTENTS

III	**Key to map symbols**
IV	**Key to map pages**
VI	**Route planning**
VIII	Major administrative and Postcode boundaries
1	**Street maps** at 3½ inches to 1 mile
141	**Street maps of Bristol and Bath city centres** at 7 inches to 1 mile
144	**Index** of towns, villages, streets, hospitals, industrial estates, railway stations, schools, shopping centres, universities and places of interest

Key to map symbols

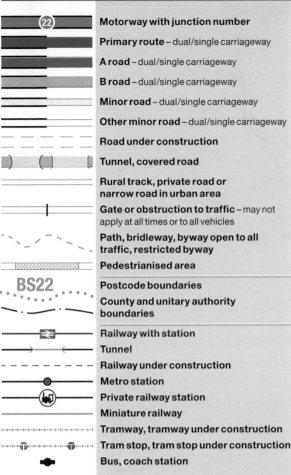

(22)	Motorway with junction number
	Primary route – dual/single carriageway
	A road – dual/single carriageway
	B road – dual/single carriageway
	Minor road – dual/single carriageway
	Other minor road – dual/single carriageway
	Road under construction
	Tunnel, covered road
	Rural track, private road or narrow road in urban area
	Gate or obstruction to traffic – may not apply at all times or to all vehicles
	Path, bridleway, byway open to all traffic, restricted byway
	Pedestrianised area
BS22	**Postcode boundaries**
	County and unitary authority boundaries
	Railway with station
	Tunnel
	Railway under construction
	Metro station
	Private railway station
	Miniature railway
	Tramway, tramway under construction
	Tram stop, tram stop under construction
	Bus, coach station

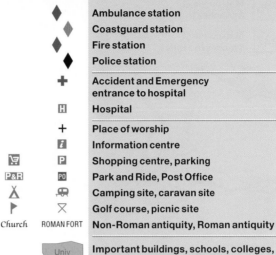

◆	**Ambulance station**
◆	**Coastguard station**
◆	**Fire station**
◆	**Police station**
✚	**Accident and Emergency entrance to hospital**
H	**Hospital**
+	**Place of worship**
i	**Information centre**
P	**Shopping centre, parking**
P&R PO	**Park and Ride, Post Office**
Å ⛟	**Camping site, caravan site**
▶ ✕	**Golf course, picnic site**
Church ROMAN FORT	**Non-Roman antiquity, Roman antiquity**
Univ	**Important buildings, schools, colleges, universities and hospitals**
	Woods, built-up area
River Medway	**Water name**
	River, weir
	Stream
	Canal, lock, tunnel
	Water
	Tidal water

58 87 246 **Adjoining page indicators and overlap bands** – the colour of the arrow and band indicates the scale of the adjoining or overlapping page (see scales below)

The dark grey border on the inside edge of some pages indicates that the mapping does not continue onto the adjacent page

The small numbers around the edges of the maps identify the 1-kilometre National Grid lines

Abbreviations

Acad	**Academy**	Meml	**Memorial**
Allot Gdns	**Allotments**	Mon	**Monument**
Cemy	**Cemetery**	Mus	**Museum**
C Ctr	**Civic centre**	Obsy	**Observatory**
CH	**Club house**	Pal	**Royal palace**
Coll	**College**	PH	**Public house**
Crem	**Crematorium**	Recn Gd	**Recreation ground**
Ent	**Enterprise**		
Ex H	**Exhibition hall**	Resr	**Reservoir**
Ind Est	**Industrial Estate**	Ret Pk	**Retail park**
IRB Sta	**Inshore rescue boat station**	Sch	**School**
		Sh Ctr	**Shopping centre**
Inst	**Institute**	TH	**Town hall / house**
Ct	**Law court**	Trad Est	**Trading estate**
L Ctr	**Leisure centre**	Univ	**University**
LC	**Level crossing**	W Twr	**Water tower**
Liby	**Library**	Wks	**Works**
Mkt	**Market**	YH	**Youth hostel**

Enlarged maps only

	Railway or bus station building
	Place of interest
	Parkland

The map scale on the pages numbered in blue is 3½ inches to 1 mile
5.52 cm to 1 km • 1 : 18 103

0	¼ mile	½ mile	¾ mile	1 mile

0	250m	500m	750m	**1km**

The map scale on the pages numbered in red is 7 inches to 1 mile
11.04 cm to 1 km • 1 : 9 051

0	220yds	440yds	660yds	½ mile

0	125m	250m	375m	**500m**

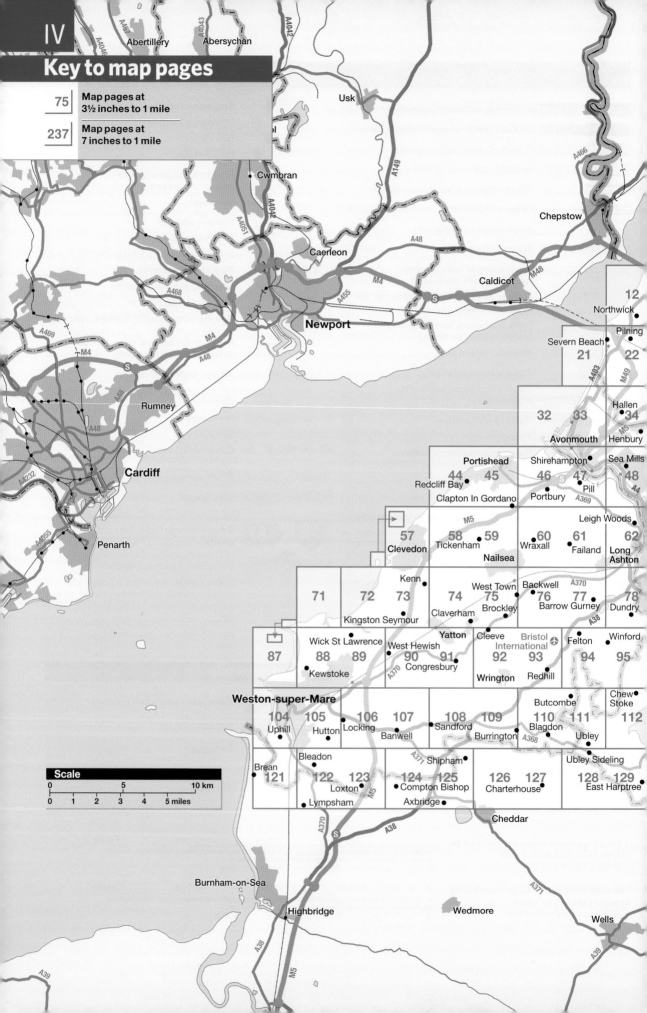

Key to map pages

| 75 | Map pages at 3½ inches to 1 mile |
| 237 | Map pages at 7 inches to 1 mile |

Abertillery Abersychan

Usk

Cwmbran

Chepstow

Caerleon

A48

Caldicot

Newport

12

Northwick

Severn Beach Pilning

21 22

Rumney

32 33 Hallen 34

Avonmouth Henbury

Portishead Shirehampton Sea Mills

44 45 46 47 48

Redcliff Bay Pill

Clapton In Gordano Portbury

Cardiff

Leigh Woods

57 58 59 60 61 62

Clevedon Tickenham Wraxall Failand Long Ashton

Nailsea

Penarth

Kenn West Town Backwell

71 72 73 74 75 76 77 78

Claverham Brockley Barrow Gurney Dundry

Kingston Seymour

Wick St Lawrence Yatton Cleeve Bristol International Felton Winford

87 88 89 90 91 92 93 94 95

Kewstoke West Hewish Congresbury Wrington Redhill

Weston-super-Mare Butcombe Chew Stoke

104 105 106 107 108 109 110 111 112

Uphill Hutton Locking Sandford Blagdon Ubley

Banwell Burrington

Bleadon Shipham Ubley Sideling

Brean 121 122 123 124 125 126 127 128 129

Loxton Compton Bishop Charterhouse East Harptree

Lympsham Axbridge

Cheddar

Burnham-on-Sea

Wedmore Wells

Highbridge

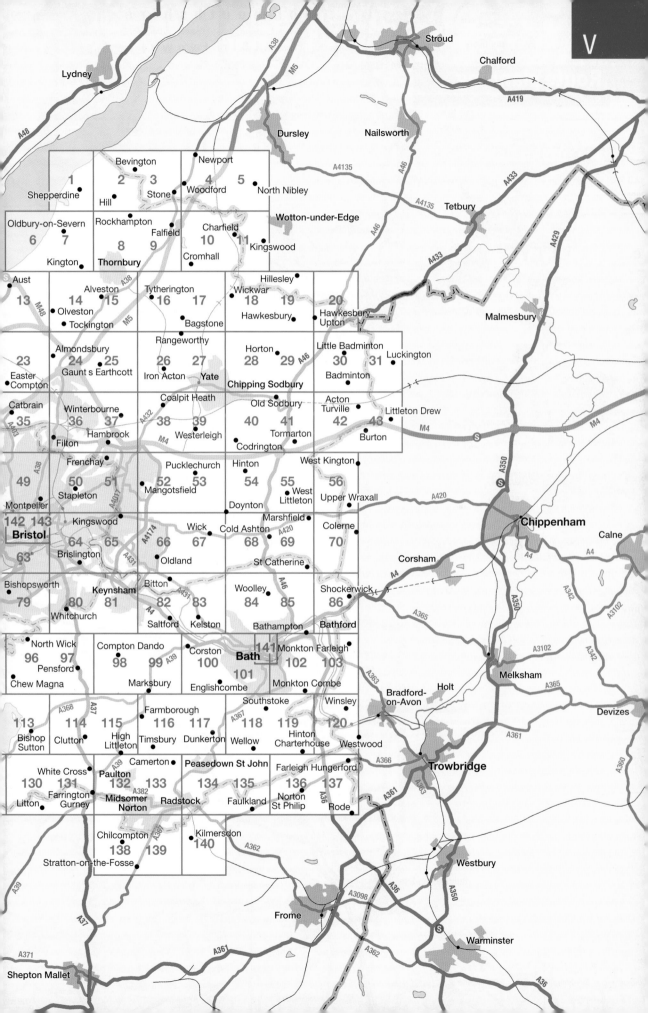

Lydney

Stroud

Chalford

A419

A48

M5

Dursley

Nailsworth

A4135

A46

A4135

Tetbury

A433

A429

Malmesbury

1	Bevington 2	3	Newport 4	5
Shepperdine	Hill	Stone	Woodford	North Nibley

Wotton-under-Edge

| Oldbury-on-Severn 6 | 7 | Rockhampton 8 | Falfield 9 | Charfield 10 | 11 |

Kington Thornbury Cromhall Kingswood

Aust

| S 13 | Alveston 14 | 15 | Tytherington 16 | 17 | Wickwar Hillesley 18 | 19 | Hawkesbury 20 |

M48 Olveston Tockington Bagstone Hawkesbury Upton

M5

Rangeworthy

| 23 | Almondsbury 24 | 25 | 26 | 27 | Horton 28 | 29 | Little Badminton 30 | 31 |

Easter Compton Gaunt's Earthcott Iron Acton Yate Chipping Sodbury Badminton Luckington

A46

Catbrain

Coalpit Heath Old Sodbury Acton Turville Littleton Drew

| 35 | Winterbourne 36 | 37 | 38 | 39 | 40 | 41 | 42 | 43 |

A463 Filton Hambrook Westerleigh Codrington Tormarton Burton

A432 M4 A4 M4

Frenchay Pucklechurch Hinton West Kington

| 49 | 50 | 51 | 52 | 53 | 54 | 55 | 56 |

Montpelier Stapleton Mangotsfield Doynton West Littleton Upper Wraxall

A38 A4017 A420 A350

Kingswood Marshfield S

| 142 | 143 | 64 | 65 | 66 | 67 | 68 | 69 | 70 |

Bristol Wick Cold Ashton Colerne Chippenham Calne

63 Brislington Oldland St Catherine A4 A4

A431 A4174 A420

Bishopsworth Keynsham Bitton Woolley Shockerwick Corsham

| 79 | 80 | 81 | 82 | 83 | 84 | 85 | 86 |

Whitchurch Saltford Kelston Bathampton Bathford A365 A3102 A342 A3102

North Wick Compton Dando Corston Monkton Farleigh Melksham Devizes

| 96 | 97 | 98 | 99 | 100 | 141 101 | 102 | 103 |

Pensford Bath Holt

Chew Magna Marksbury Englishcombe Monkton Combe Bradford-on-Avon

A368 A37 A39 Southstoke Winsley A363

| 113 | 114 | 115 | 116 | 117 | 118 | 119 | 120 |

Bishop Sutton Clutton High Littleton Timsbury Dunkerton Wellow Hinton Charterhouse Westwood

Camerton Peasedown St John Farleigh Hungerford Trowbridge

Paulton

| 130 | 131 | 132 | 133 | 134 | 135 | 136 | 137 |

White Cross Farrington Gurney Midsomer Norton Radstock Faulkland Norton St Philip Rode

Litton A382 A36 A361 A363

Chilcompton Kilmersdon

| 138 | 139 | 140 |

Stratton-on-the-Fosse A362 A3098 A36

Frome

Westbury

A371 A37 A361 A362 A350 S A36

Shepton Mallet Warminster

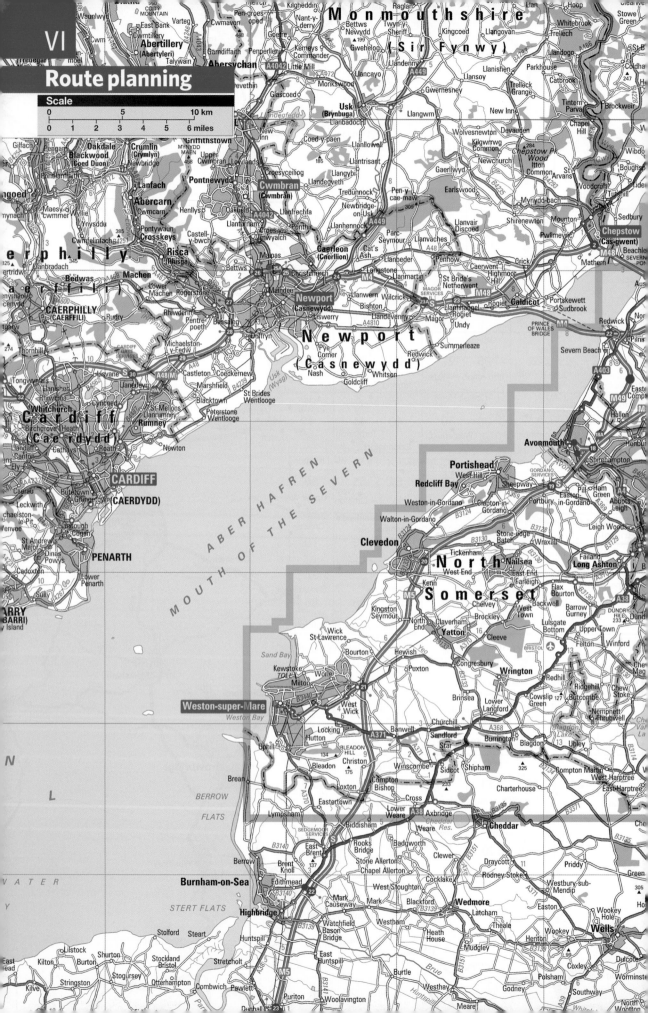

Gloucestershire STREET ATLAS

Gloucestershire STREET ATLAS

A B C D E F

8

7

97

GL13

6

White House

Severn Way

Chapel House

Manor Farm

The Laurels

5

96

PH

Shepperdine Farm

North Ham Corner

4

Shepperdine Farm

River Severn

Shepperdine

Brickhouse Farm

3

Shepperdine Withybed

BS35

95

GL13

Harestreet La

SHEPPERDINE RD

Jobscreen Farm

Lowgoods Farm

2

Oldbury Power Station (decommissioned)

Knight's Farm

HILL LA

Mast

1

STONEYARD LA

94

60 A B 61 C D 62 E F

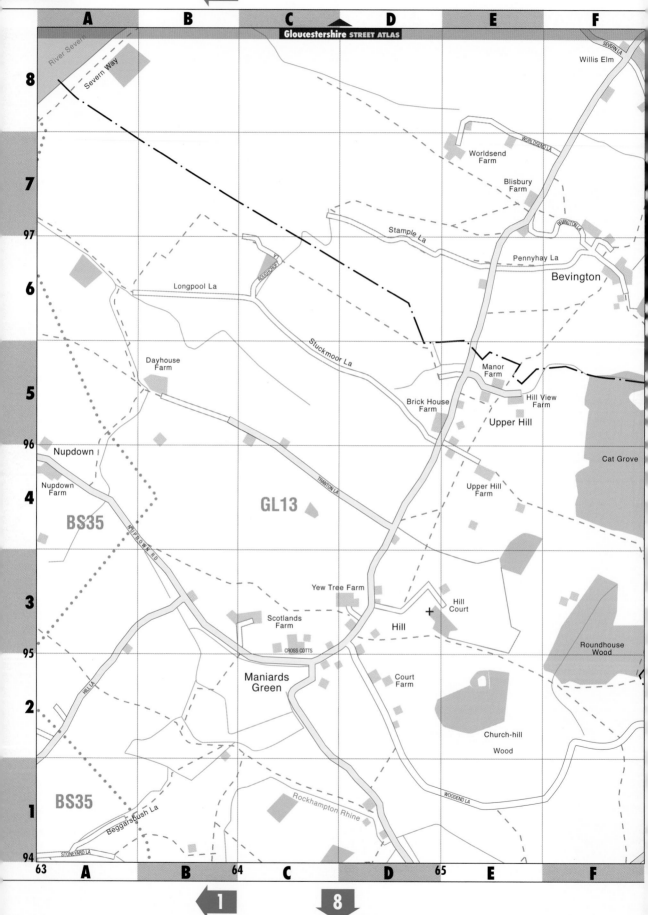

A   B   C   D   E   F

8

7

97

6

5

96

4

3

95

2

1

94

River Severn

Severn Way

Willis Elm

Worldsend Farm

WORLDSEND LA

Blisbury Farm

SEVERN LA

Stample La

BEVINGTON LA

Pennyhay La

Bevington

Longpool La

ROUGHCROFT

Stuckmoor La

Manor Farm

Dayhouse Farm

Brick House Farm

Hill View Farm

Upper Hill

Nupdown

Cat Grove

Nupdown Farm

Upper Hill Farm

BS35

KILPDOWN RD

TRANTON LA

GL13

Yew Tree Farm

Hill Court

Scotlands Farm

Hill

Roundhouse Wood

CROSS COTTS

Court Farm

Maniards Green

HILL LA

Church-hill Wood

BS35

Beggarsbush La

Rockhampton Rhine

WOODEND LA

STONEYARD LA

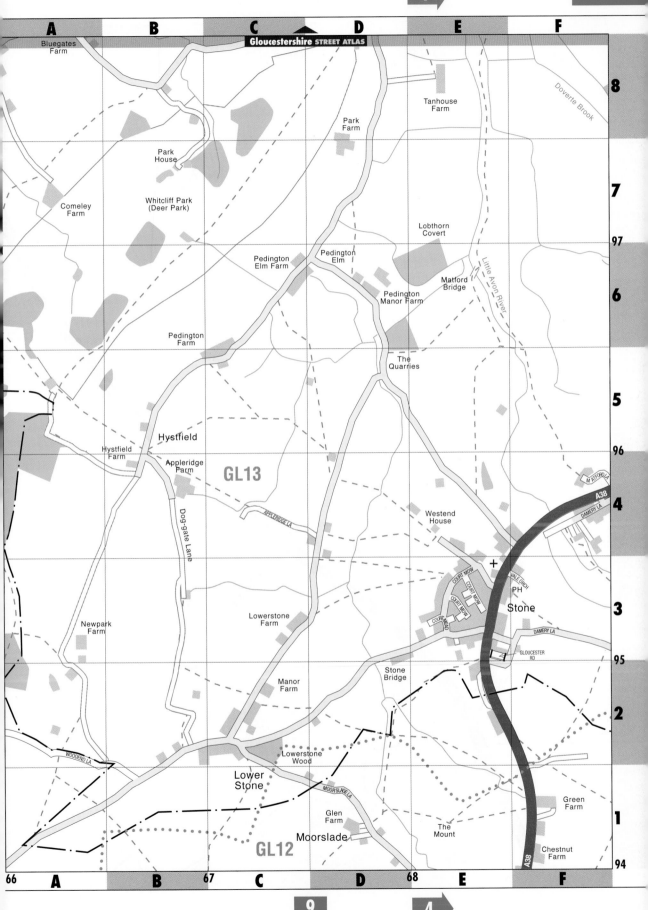

Gloucestershire STREET ATLAS

A   B   C   D   E   F

8

Doverte Brook

Bluegates
Farm

Tanhouse
Farm

Park
Farm

Park
House

7

Whitcliff Park
(Deer Park)

Comeley
Farm

97

Lobthorn
Covert

Pedington
Elm

6

Pedington
Elm Farm

Matford
Bridge

Pedington
Manor Farm

Little Avon River

Pedington
Farm

The
Quarries

5

Hystfield

96

Hystfield
Farm

Appleridge
Farm

GL13

M ATFORD LA

A38

DAMERY LA

APPLERIDGE LA

Westend
House

4

Dog-gate Lane

COURT MDW

COURT MDW

VALE ORCH

PH

Stone

COURT MDW

Lowerstone
Farm

COURT MEAD

3

Newpark
Farm

DAMERY LA

GLOUCESTER
RD

95

Manor
Farm

Stone
Bridge

2

WOODEND LA

Lowerstone
Wood

Green
Farm

Lower
Stone

MOORSLADE LA

Glen
Farm

The
Mount

1

Moorslade

Chestnut
Farm

GL12

A38

94

66   A   B   67   C   D   68   E   F

8

Newport

PH

Hotel

Greenways

Goldwick
Farm

CROSSWAYS

Baynhamcourt
Farm

COCKSHUTE LA

7

Oakleaze
Farm

Dowrie Brook

Hogsdown
Farm

97

6

GL13

HAYCROFT LA

Lower
Wick

GL11

Manor
Farm

Swanley
Farm

Lowerwick
Farm

SWANLEY LA

Swanley

Middle
Wick

5

Woodfordgreen
Farm

Whitehall
Farm

Middlewick
Farm

96

A38

Woodford

PH

Michaelwood
Farm

Wick
Bridge

Harold's
Brake

4

DAMERY LA

Damery
Wks

Mast

MULE ST

Michaelwood
Service Area

Sweetbrier
Brake

Woodford
Farm

3

Middle Mill
Farm

DAMERY LA

95

Furzeground
Wood

Michaelwood Lodge
Farm

2

Micheal Wood

GL12

DAMERY LA

Little Avon River

Crockley's
Farm

Damery

1

Damery
Bridge

Iron Mill Grove

94

Daniel's Wood

M5

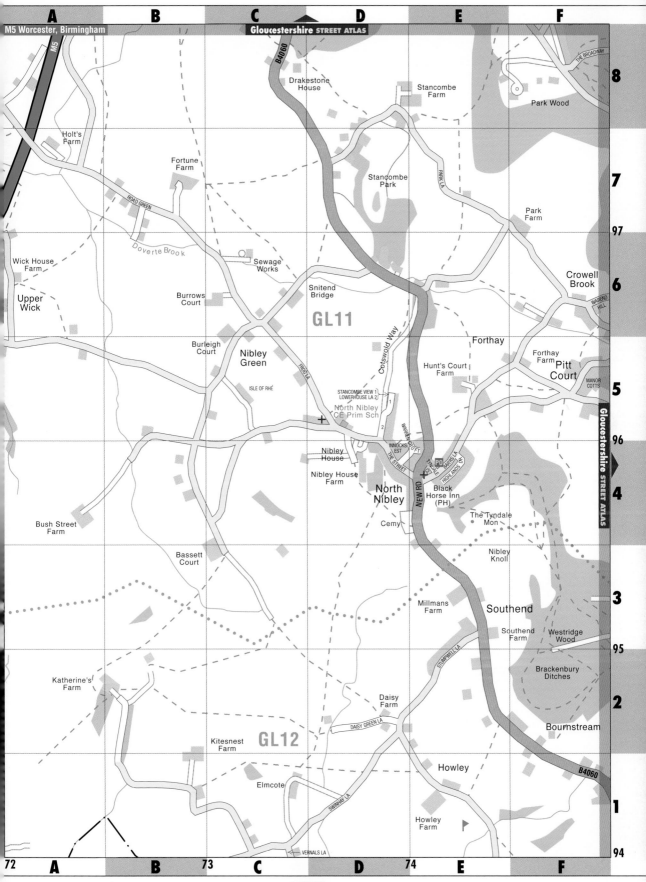

Gloucestershire STREET ATLAS

Cowhill
Warth

Pillhead
Gout

Lower
Farm

MANOR FARM LA

Littleton Warth

Ind
Est

Cophills La

North
Field

BS35

Severn Way

Thornmead
Gout

Littleton Rhine

Lower Corston
Farm

BRICK
COTTS

Rushen
Gout

Rusholme

Rushen La

Littleton-upon-
Severn

Village
Farm

PH

Sewage
Works

Potato
Tump

Bushy
Brake

River Severn

A B C D E F

8 7 93 6 5 92 4 3 91 2 1 90

57 58 59

A B C D E F

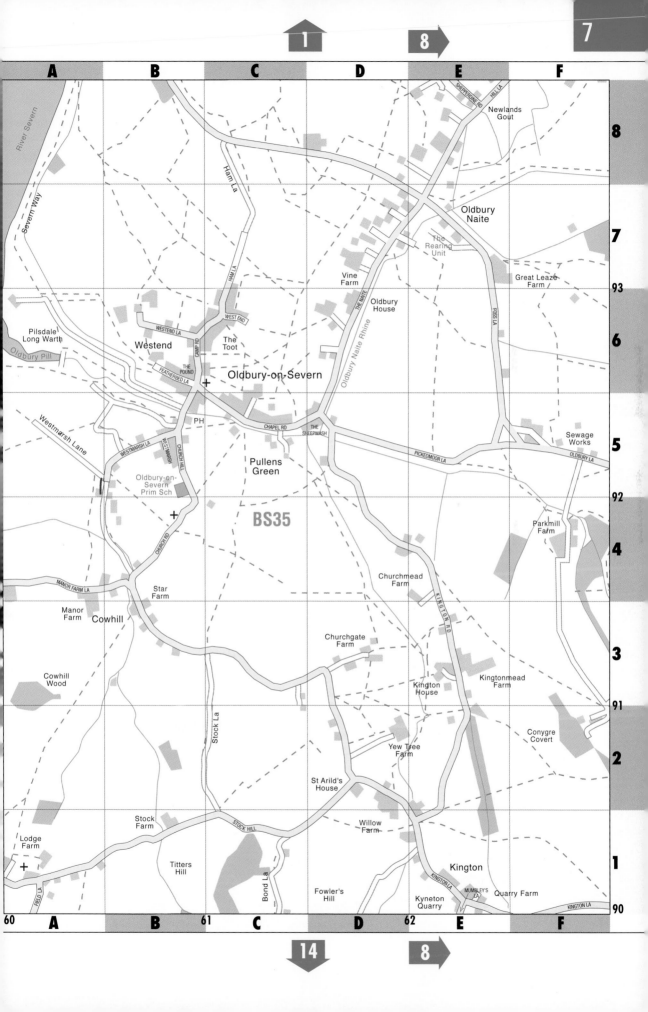

A B C D E F

8

GL13

Northfield Lane

Northfields

The Old Rectory

Rockhampton Rhine

Lodge Farm

7

CHURCH VIEW

Rockhampton

Court Farm

The Hollies

Pennywell Farm

93

Henridge Hill

The Firs

6

Rockhampton Rhine

Yew Tree Farm

Newton

Luce's Farm

Groves Tully

5

Pound Mill Farm

Maypole Farm

Pound Mill Bsns Ctr

Oak Farm

Duckhole

Horse La

Catsbrain La

Longman's Grove

92

Spring Farm

Lower Morton

BS35

Manor Farm

4

1 SWALLOWTAIL CL
2 SPECKLED WOOD RD
3 MEADOW BROWN CL
4 PURPLE EMPEROR RD
5 MARBLED WHITE CL

Morton House

Park Farm

Upper Morton

GLOUCESTER RD

Mile End Farm

Morton

B4061

The Knapp

3

Manorbrook Prim Sch

Knapp Farm

91

THORNBURY

The Castle Sch

Shailing Sch

2

Thornbury Castle

St Mary's CE Prim Sch

Crossways House

Crossways

Yewtree Farm

Whitewall La

Beechacres

Christ the King RC Prim Sch

New Siblands Sch

GL12

1

Cerny

The Castle Sch Sixth Form Ctr

Thornbury

Crossways Jun & Inf Schs

B4061

HIGH ST

The Plain

90

A B C D E F

63 64 65

B1
1 QUAKER CT
2 ST JOHN ST
3 PULLINS GN
4 CRISPIN LA
5 SAW MILL LA
6 ST MARYS WAY
7 SILVER ST
8 ST MARY ST
9 ROCKLEASE
10 GROVESEND RD
11 BUCKINGHAM PAR
12 GLOUCESTER TERR

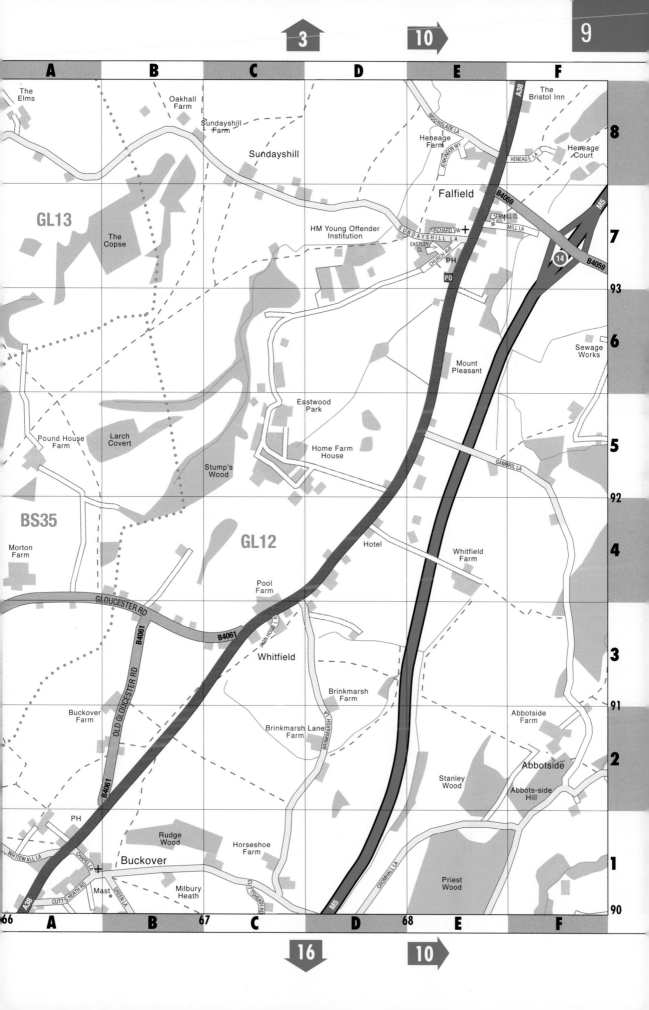

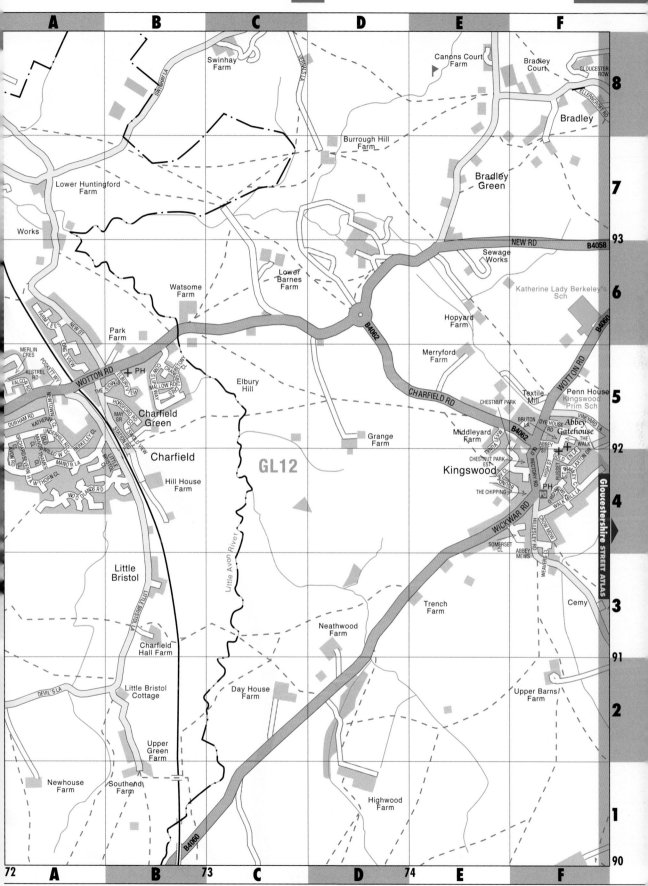

M48 Chepstow, Newport

M48

Severn Road
Bridge

Footpath/Cycle Way

Mast •

Toll

Severn Way

Aust
Cliff

PASSAGE RD

New House
Farm

Old
Passage

Old Passage
House

Aust Warth

River Severn

Cake Pill

MILL HILL LA

A403

Foss Ditch

Cake Pill
Gout

Asnum
Copse

Severn Way

Lords Rhine

Bilsham Rhine

Northwick Pig
Farm

BS35

Bilsham
Farm

EASTFIELD LA

AUST RD

Laural
Farm

Church
Farm

Northwick

Mill
Farm

SEVERN RD

B4055

Manor
Farm

BILSHAM LA

DANGER
AREA

NORTHWICK RD

Holm Rhine

Red
Lodge

Rifle Range

North Worthy
Farm

Severn
Lodge Farm

NEW PASSAGE RD

BLANDS
ROW

B4064

**New
Passage**

A403

B4055

M4

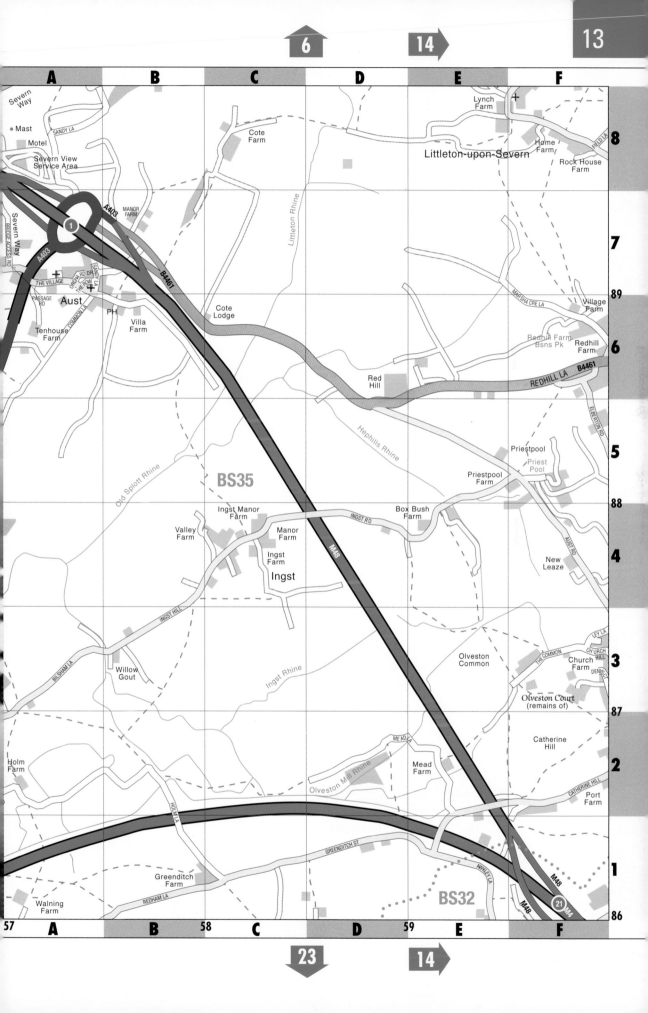

A **B** **C** **D** **E** **F**

8

Sacks Hill
Cole's Brake
JUBILEE WAY
Beech Farm
KINGTON LA
Bond Lane

Stonage Field
Works
Hay Wood

7
Henley Hill
BS35
Mumbleys Plat
MUMBLEYS HILL
Kington Grove
CH

89
Elberton Court Farm
Fierypits Brake
SWEETWATER LA
Mumbleys Farm
VILLAGE FARM
Haywood Farm
Gate Farm
MUMBLEYS LA

6
ROADS AT ELBERTON
B4461
Brocketty Brake
VATTINGSTONE LA
Marlwood Sch
Elberton
Camp Farm
Vinyards Brake
HADDRELL CT 1
BRIDGE HO 2
VATTINGSTONE HO 3
B4461

5
Alveston Down
STRODE GDNS
BUSH CT

88
Home Farm
Hazel Farm
ROSEWOOD AVE
WEST VIEW

4
FOXHOLES LA
Old Down
Stroud Common
Upper Hazel
BRIDLE WAY
CLIVE GDNS

ELBERTON RD
VICARAGE LA
Olveston CE Prim Sch
THE CRESCENT
PUMP LA
GREENHILL LA

3
CHURCH HILL
PH
Olveston
Fernhill Cottage
The Down House
ALVESTON RD
THE DOWN
THE INNER DOWN
PH
HAZEL LA
Lower Hazel

DENYS CT
Little Down
Sheepcombe Brake
MERRYWOOLES
A38

87
GREEN CT
ORCHARD RISE
HAW LA
OLD DOWN HILL
Tockington Hill
BS32
BRIARLEAZE
PH

2
Eastcombe Hill
Tockington Manor Sch
Sheepcombe Farm
B4427
CHURCH RD
UPPER TOCKINGTON RD
TOCKINGTON GN
POOL CNR
WASHINGPOOL HILL RD
Home Farm
Willis Brake
GLOUCESTER RD
Rudgeway

THE ELMS
MANOR PK
PH
MANOR CL
Tockington
RUDGWAY PK

1
Port Farm
HARDY LA
MILL LA
LOWER TOCKINGTON RD
Tockington Mill Rhine
Gorse Covert
Oakleaze
SILVER HILL BRAKE
WASHINGPOOL HILL
A38

86

A **B** **C** **D** **E** **F**
60 61 62

A **B** **C** **D** **E** **F**

A38

Garden Ctr

Lodge Farm

GREEN LA

Acorn Farm

Corbets

8

Mast

CUTTSHEATH RD

Hope Farm

CROMHALL LA

M5

Priest Wood

Trapwell Bridge

RECTORY LA

Cuttsheath

Jones's Wood

BS35

Barmer's Land Farm

Baden Hill

7

NEW RD

Quarry

89

TYTHERINGTON RD

WOODLANDS RD

WOODLANDS

Tytherington Hill

Stidcot

6

Quarry

STOW HILL RD

THE JAYS

STOWELL HILL RD

BADEN HILL RD

Lower Hill Farm

STIDCOT LA

Pendicks Farm

Stidcot Farm

Ashworthy Farm

The Castle

THE ORCHARD

Stidcot Plat

Stidcot

5

PH

WEST ST

DUCK ST

PO

THE NURSERIES

NUT FIE

Tytherington

Newhouse Farm

STIDCOTE LA

Summer Bridge

M5

Brook Farm

West Street Farm

ITCHINGTON RD

SOUTHLANDS

Mill Farm

88

4

GL12

BAGSTONE RD

B4058

3

Moorleaze

Ladden Brook

87

B4058

2

Lower Farm

Hotel

BAGSTONE RD

BS35

BS37

Rangeworthy

WOTTON RD

PH

1

LATTERIDGE LA

Stockhill Cottage

Cemy

CHURCH LA

Rangeworthy CE Prim Sch

86

66 **A** **B** 67 **C** **D** 68 **E** **F**

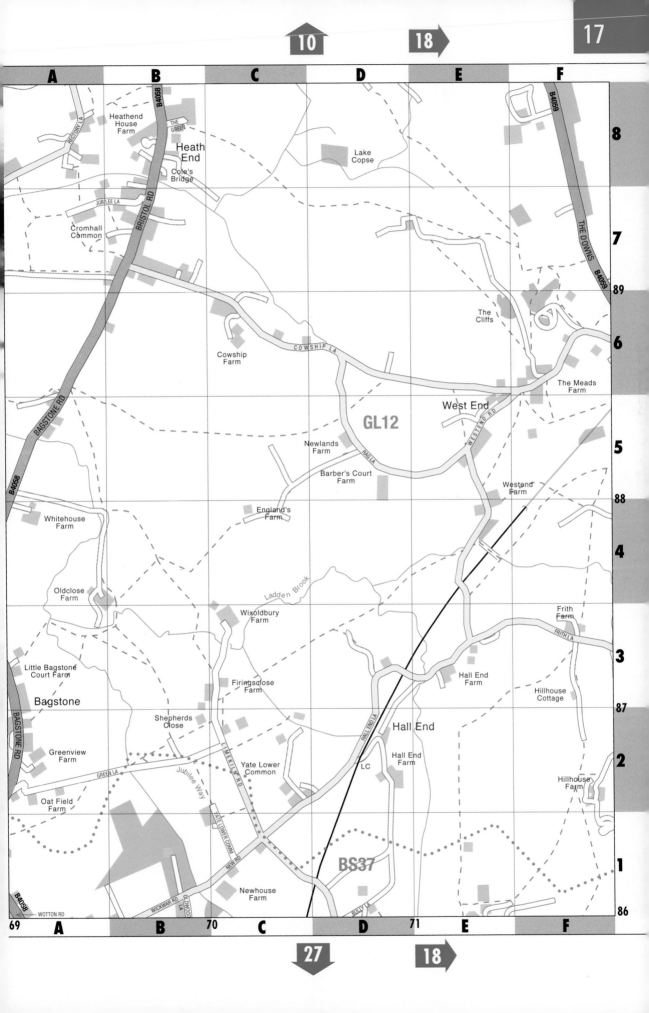

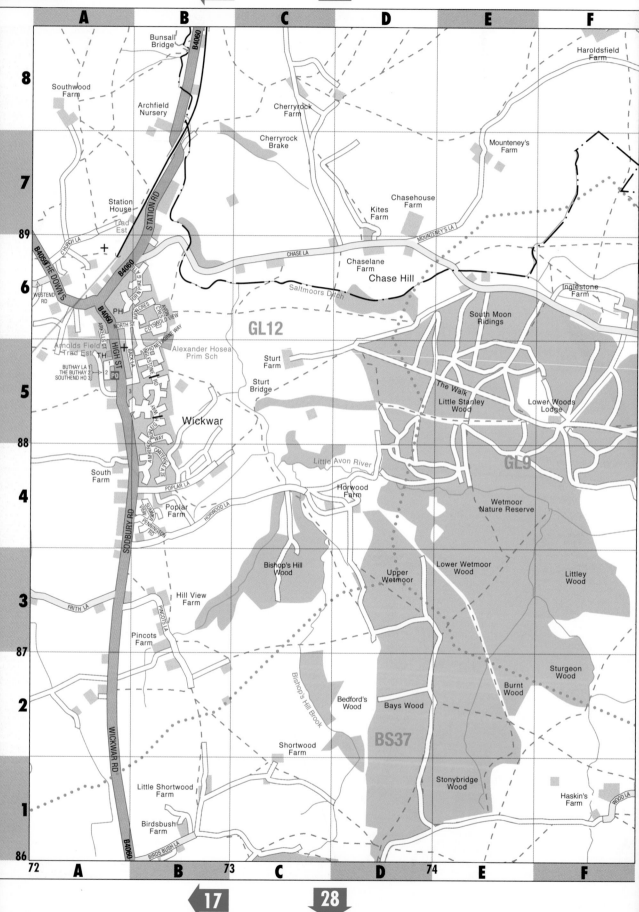

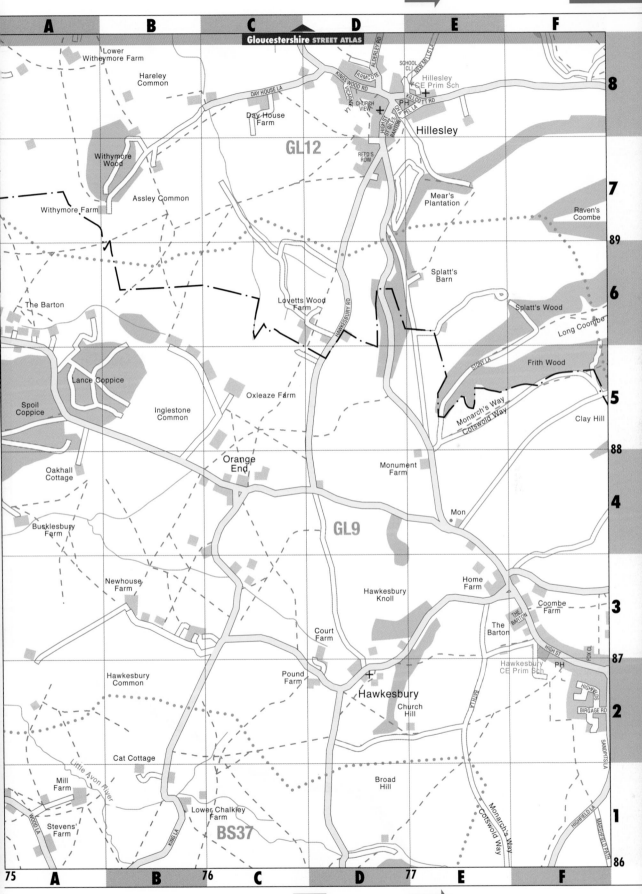

Gloucestershire STREET ATLAS

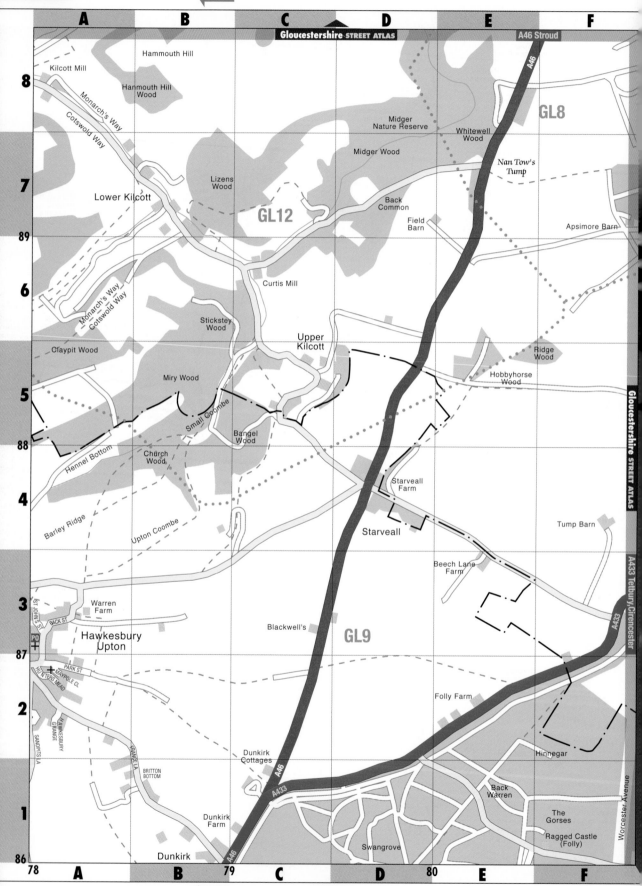

Gloucestershire STREET ATLAS

A46 Stroud

GL8

A B C D E F

8

Kilcott Mill

Hammouth Hill

Hanmouth Hill Wood

Monarch's Way

Cotswold Way

Midger Nature Reserve

Whitewell Wood

Midger Wood

Nan Tow's Tump

7

Lower Kilcott

Lizens Wood

GL12

Back Common

Apsimore Barn

89

Field Barn

6

Monarch's Way Cotswold Way

Curtis Mill

Stickstey Wood

Upper Kilcott

Ridge Wood

Claypit Wood

Miry Wood

Hobbyhorse Wood

5

Small Coombe

Bangel Wood

Hennel Bottom

Church Wood

Starveall Farm

88

Barley Ridge

Upton Coombe

Starveall

Tump Barn

4

Beech Lane Farm

3

Warren Farm

BACK ST

Hawkesbury Upton

Blackwell's

GL9

87

PARK ST

HUNTERS MEAD

MAYPOLE CL

Folly Farm

2

HAWKESBURY GRANGE

GRANGE LA

BRITTON BOTTOM

SANDPITS LA

Dunkirk Cottages

Hinnegar

A46

A433

Back Warren

1

Dunkirk Farm

The Gorses

Ragged Castle (Folly)

Swangrove

Worcester Avenue

86

78 A B 79 C D 80 E F

Gloucestershire STREET ATLAS

A433 Tetbury,Cirencester

A B C D E F

Herefordshire & Monmouthshire STREET ATLAS | M4 Newport, Cardiff

M4

Prince of Wales Bridge

M4

8

The Binn Wall

7

BEACH RD

B4064

BEACH AVE

85

RUSTIC PK

PO

STATION RD

Severn Beach

RIVERSIDE PK

6

BS35

5

84

SHINGLEA

A403

4

River Severn

Severn Way

CENTRAL AVE

Severn View Ind Pk

3

SEVERN RD

BS10

New Pill Gout

Works

83

Chittening Warth

Red Hung

2

ARTHUR BALL WAY

Power Station

1

BS11

A403

Stup Pill

Crook's Marsh

82

51 A B 52 C D 53 E F

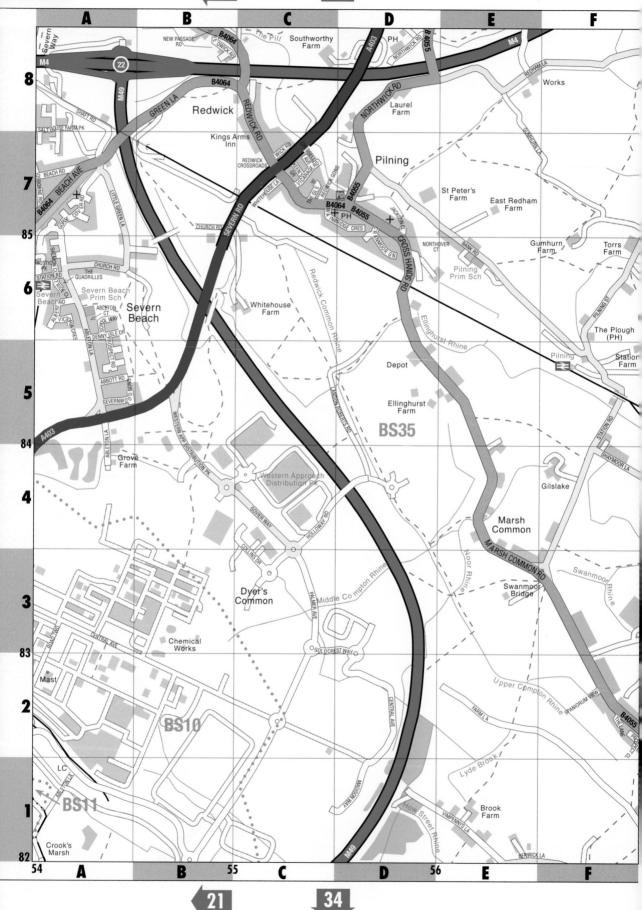

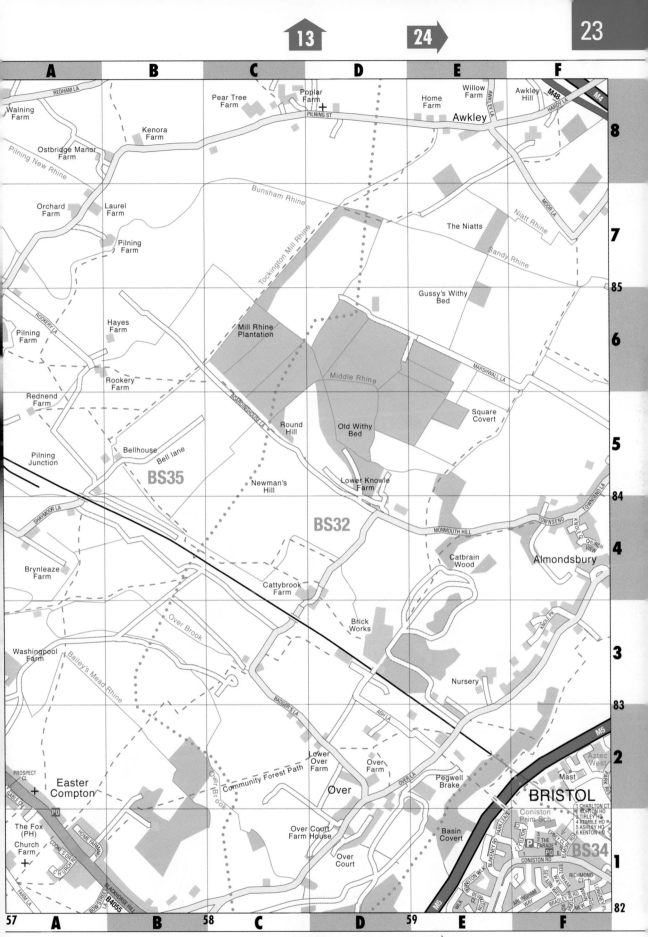

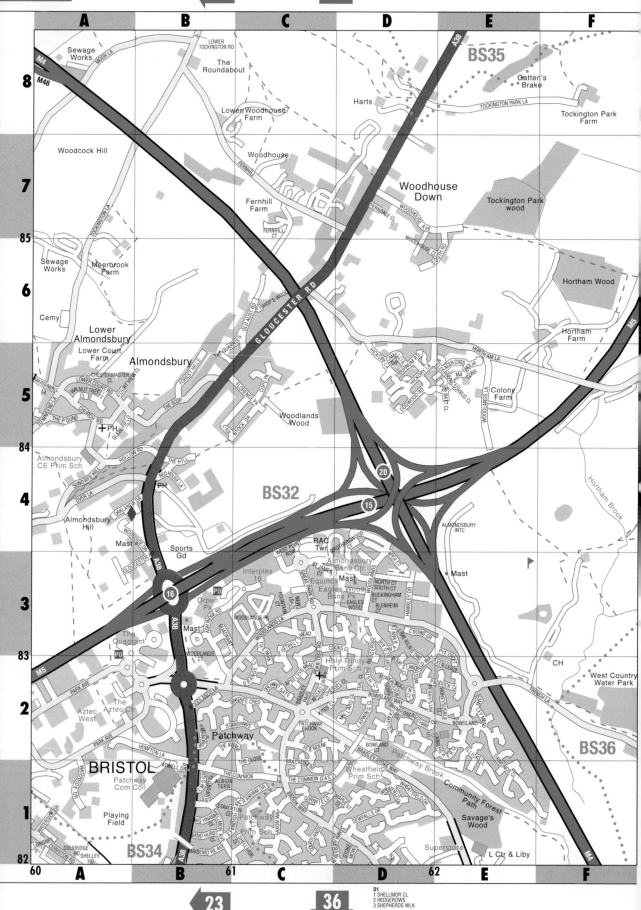

A B C D E F

8
7
85
6
5
84
4
3
83
2
1
82

60 A 61 B C 62 D E F

BS35

Gatten's Brake

Tockington Park Farm

M4
M48
M48
Sewage Works
MOOR LA
LOWER TOCKINGTON RD
The Roundabout
Lower Woodhouse Farm
Harts
TOCKINGTON PARK LA

Woodcock Hill
Woodhouse
FERNHILL
Woodhouse Down
Tockington Park wood

FERNHILL
Fernhill Farm
FERNHILL CT
FERNDALE CL
WOODHOUSE AVE
WOODHOUSE SOUTH RD

Sewage Works
Meerbrook Farm
TOCKINGTON LA
OLD AUST RD
BISHOP'S WOOD
GLOUCESTER RD
Hortham Wood

Cemy
Lower Almondsbury
THE QUADRATE
Hortham Farm

Lower Court Farm
Almondsbury
FOREST HILLS
HICKORY LA
CAME LA
VIBURNUM RD
MAGNOLIA
HORTHAM LA
Colony Farm

CHESTERMASTER CL
COURT VIEW CL
THE SCOP
FLORENCE PK
COPSE PK
Woodlands Wood
HICKORY CT
DOGWOOD RD
FRAISER CRES
SORBUS CL
BATT CL
MAGNOLIA
WOODLANDS LA
WOODMANS

MARSHWALL LA
WALNUT TREE
LOWER COURT CL
CRANATOCK DR

Almondsbury CE Prim Sch
TOWNSEND LA
THE POUND
CHURCH RD
PH
GLEBE FIELD
HOLLOW RD
THE HILL

Almondsbury Hill
SUNDAY'S HILL
OVER LA
RED HOUSE LA
PH
BS32
20
15
Hortham Brook
Almondsbury INTC

Mast
OAKLANDS DR
WOODSIDE DR
Sports Gd
WEST POINT ROW
RAC Twr
BROTHERWOOD
Mast

GLOUCESTER DR
A38
Interplex 16
GREAT PARK RD
Almondsbury Bsns Ctr
ST JAMES CT
Eagles Wood Bsns Pk
NORTH CT
SOUTH CT
KEX GR
Mast

16
A38
Orpen Pk
PO
ASH RIDGE RD
WOODLANDS PK
NEW LEAZE
FOUNTAIN CT
Equinox
Mast
EAGLES WOOD
BUCKINGHAM CT
BLENHEIM CT
HAWKLEY DR
CROWS GR

The Quadrant
PO
Mast
QUADRANT
WOODLANDS CT
WOODLANDS LA
STREL'S MEAD
NEW LEAZE
BEAR TREE RD
COOKS CL
RUSH CL
PYE CROFT

Aztec West
The Aztec Ctr
PARK AVE
GRANGE CL
ORCHARD GATE
APSELEY'S MEAD
BRADLEY
FOXGLOVE
PADDOCK CL
OXEN LEAZE
CH
West Country Water Park

PARK AVE
BARTREE CRES
STANSHAWS CL
Patchway
Holy Trinity Prim Sch
KITES CL
BOWLAND WAY
PRIMROSE
PRESHAM
HOMESTEAD
BOWSLAND
Sch
TRENCH LA
BS36

HEMPTON LA
THE AVENUE
Patchway
FERNDENE
BRADLEY STOKE WAY
Patchway Brook
Community Forest Path

BRISTOL
Patchway Com Coll
ATWELL DR
THE GLOSE
BRACKEN DENE
Wheatfield Prim Sch
WHEATFIELD RD
WHEATFIELD DR
ELLICKS CL
ORMONDS CL

Playing Field
THE COMMON
ALBION TERR
The Common (East)
CORNFIELD CL
SAXON WAY
Savage's Wood

WATERSIDE DR
COLERIDGE RD
SHELLEY RD
BS34
A38
PATCHWAY CE PRIM SCH
DEWFALLS DR
Superstore
L Ctr & Liby

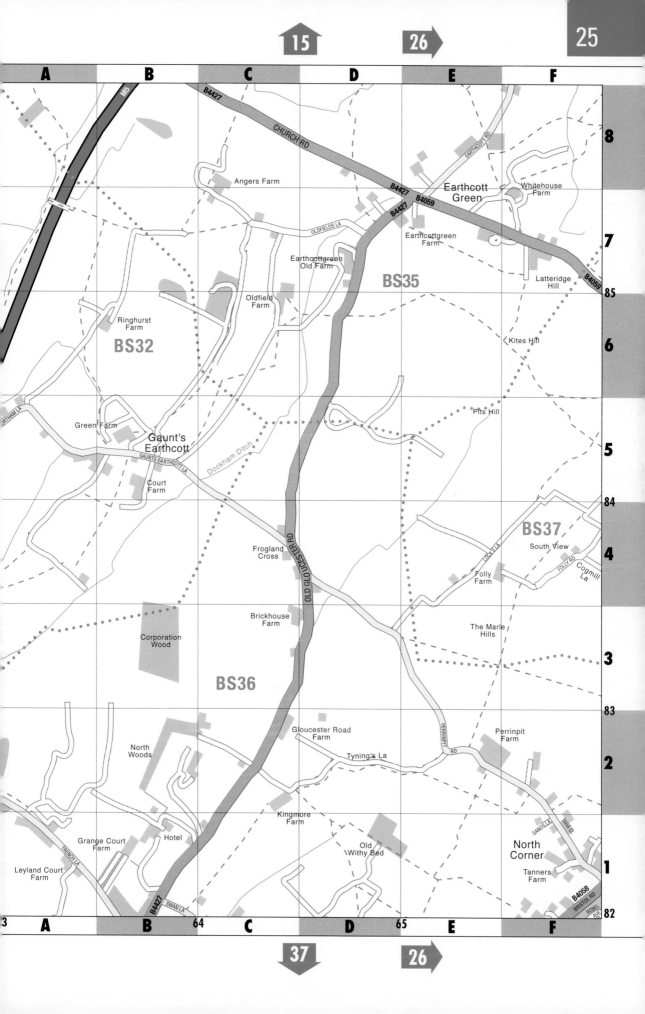

25
16

A B C D E F

8
7
85
6
5
84
4
3
83
2
1
82

BS35

Lower Lark's Farm

LARK'S LA

LATTERIDGE LA

Dowells Farm

Patch Elm Farm

PATCH ELM LA

Mudgedown Farm

Northend Farm

B4059

CHAINGATE LA

Chaingate House

WOTTON RD

Ladden Bows Bridge

LATTERIDGE RD

Latteridge

HOLLY RD

Two Pools Farm

Backfield Farm

LC

Acton Court

Sheephouse Farm

Ladden Brook

BS37

Acton Lodge

Hill House

B4059

B4058

B4058

B4059

Laddenside Farm

Elm Farm

LC

THE GREEN

PH

LATTERIDGE RD

PARK ST

Iron Acton

PH

HIGH ST

PH

WOTTON RD

HOLLY HILL

Isle of Rhee

YATE RD

B40

Cogmill La

BRISTOL RD

STATION RD

Iron Acton CE Prim Sch

Iron Acton CE Prim Sch

Algars Manor

LC

CHILWOOD CL

ALGARS DR

Robins Wood

NIBLEY LA

Lavenham Farm

River Frome

Brake Farm

83

Cog Mill Farm

FRAMPTON END RD

Tubb's Bottom

BS36

PH

B4058

Frampton Cotterell

CONIFER

MILL LA

Chestnut Farm

A432

BADMINTON RD

A43

Cemy

Mayshill

WESTERN AVE

CHURCH RD

SCHOOL RD

66 A B 67 C D 68 E F 82

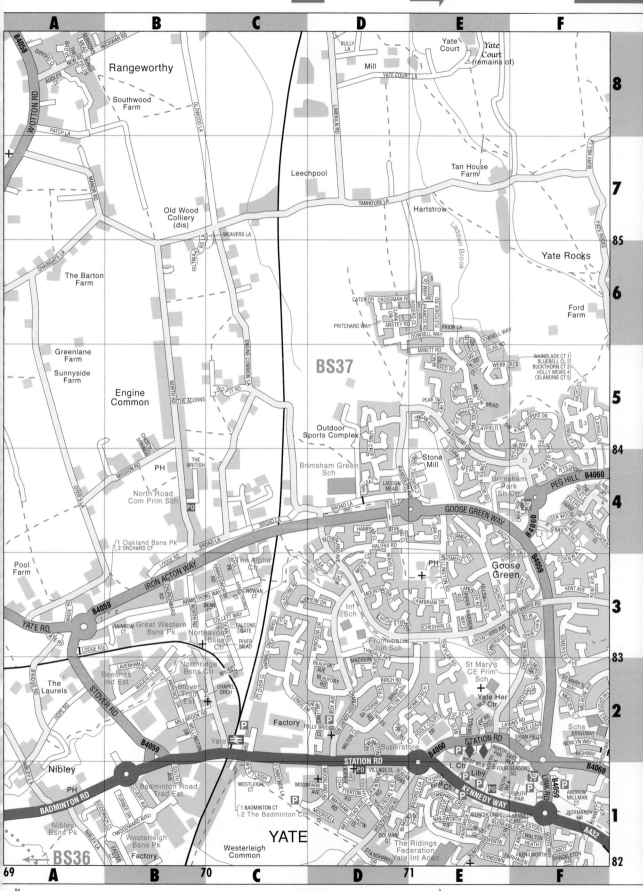

A B C D E F

8
7
85
6
5
84
4
3
83
2
1
82

Rangeworthy

Southwood Farm

The Barton Farm

Greenlane Farm

Sunnyside Farm

Engine Common

Pool Farm

The Laurels

Nibley

Nibley Bsns Pk

BS36

Old Wood Colliery (dis)

WEAVERS LA

The British

North Road Com Prim Sch

1 Oakland Bsns Pk
2 ORCHARD CT

IRON ACTON WAY

Rainbow Great Western Bsns Pk

Northavon Bsns Ctr

Beeches Ind Est

Northridge Bsns Ctr

Stover Trad Est

CHAPEL ORCH

Badminton Road Trad Est

Westleigh Bsns Pk Factory

Westerleigh Common

YATE

1 BADMINTON CL
2 The Badminton Ctr

Leechpool

TANHOUSE LA

BS37

Outdoor Sports Complex

Brimsham Green Sch

Stone Mill

Broad La

The Alpha Ctr

Fromebank Jun Sch

Factory

Yate

Superstore

STATION RD

Mill

Yate Court

Yate Court (remains of)

YATE COURT LA

Tan House Farm

Hartstrow

Yate Rocks

Ford Farm

WAINBLADE CT 1
BLUEBELL CL 2
BUCKTHORN CT 3
HOLLY MEWS 4
CELANDINE CT 5

CATER DR
CROSSMAN RD

PRITCHARD WAY

Goose Green

GOOSE GREEN WAY

PEG HILL
B4060

Brimsham Park Sh Ctr

St Mary's CE Prim Sch

Yate Her Ctr

Schs Ridgeway

STATION RD
NORTH EAST
Four Seasons Sq
L Ctr Liby

KENNEDY WAY

The Ridings Federation Yate Int Acad

Andrew Millman Ct

B4060
A432

F4
1 CORBETT CL
2 PARTRIDGE CL
3 HAMPSHIRE WAY
4 GREENWAYS RD
5 BLACKBERRY CL

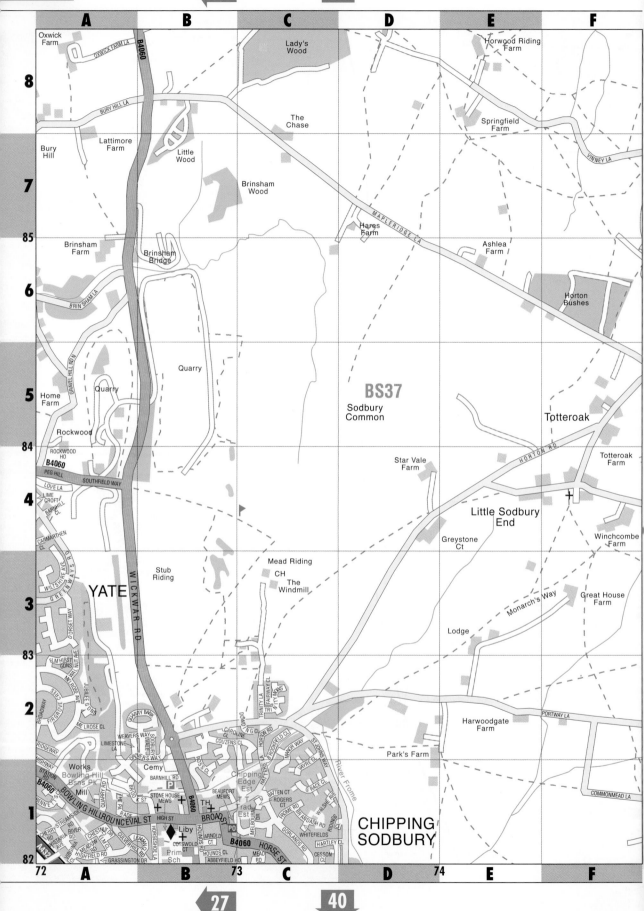

A B C D E F

8

Oxwick
Farm

OXWICK FARM LA

B4060

BURY HILL LA

Lady's
Wood

The
Chase

Horwood Riding
Farm

Springfield
Farm

VINNEY LA

Bury
Hill

Lattimore
Farm

Little
Wood

Brinsham
Wood

7

85

Brinsham
Farm

Brinsham
Bridge

Hares
Farm

MAPLERIDGE LA

Ashlea
Farm

BRIN SHAM LA

6

GRAVEL HILL RD N

Horton
Bushes

Home
Farm

Quarry

Quarry

Quarry

Rockwood

BS37

Sodbury
Common

Totteroak

5

84

ROCKWOOD
HO

B4060

PEG HILL

SOUTHFIELD WAY

LOVE LA

LIME
CROFT

BARNHILL
CL

Star Vale
Farm

HORTON RD

Totteroak
Farm

Winchcombe
Farm

4

CARMARTHEN
CL

WICKWAR RD

Greystone
Ct

Little Sodbury
End

YATE

Stub
Riding

Mead Riding
CH
The
Windmill

Monarch's Way

Great House
Farm

Lodge

3

83

WILTSHIRE AVE
GREENWAYS RD
DORSET WAY

ELMHIRST
GDNS

Harwoodgate
Farm

PORTWAY LA

2

BROADWAY
FIR GROVE CRES
JUBILEE GDNS
MELROSE AVE
RIDGEWAY
HIGHWAY

QUARRY BANK
WEAVERS WAY
LIMESTONE LA
SPOONER S WAY
SODBURY ST

Caroline
CT
COUZENS CL

TRINITY LA
FAIRWAY CL

Park's Farm

River Frome

COMMONMEAD LA

Works
Bowling Hill
Bsns PK
Mill

Cemy

STONE HOUSE
MEWS

BEAUFORT
MEWS

Chipping
Edge
Est

MANOR WAY
ST JOHNS WAY
JAYRE CT

1

B4060

STATION RD
BENNE

BOWLING HILLROUNCEVAL ST

BARNHILL RD

P

THE PARADE

BRO

HIGH ST

HORSESHOE LA

BROAD ST

TH

Liby

Prim
Sch

HOUNDS

COTSWOLD
CT

ARNOLD
CT

B4060

HORSE ST

MELBOURNE

FREDERICK CT
HORTON RD

ROSS CL

BATTEN CT
Rogers
CT
FROME CT

BRANDASH RD

RACE CL

WALSHE AVE

WHITEFIELDS

HARTLEY CL

GORLANDS RD

CESSON
CL

MEAD
RD

CHIPPING
SODBURY

82

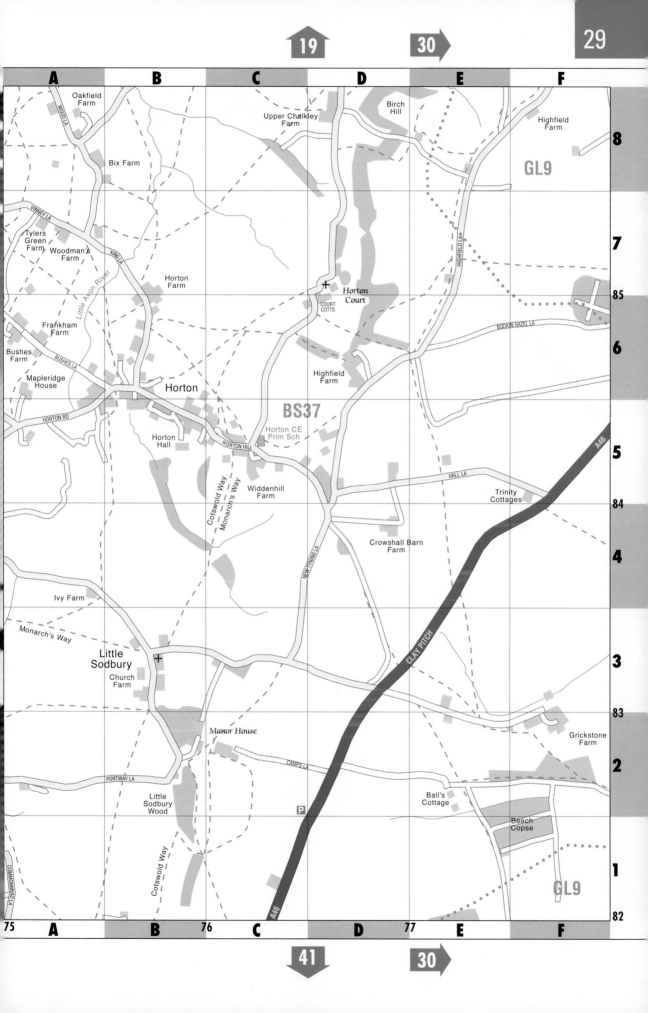

A B C D E F

8

GL9

7

85

6

BS37

5

84

4

3

83

2

1

GL9

82

75 A B 76 C D 77 E F

Oakfield Farm

WOOD LA

Bix Farm

Upper Chalkley Farm

Birch Hill

Highfield Farm

VINNEY LA

Tylers Green Farm

Woodman's Farm

KING LA

Horton Farm

Horton Court

HIGHFIELD LA

COURT COTTS

Frankham Farm

Little Axon River

BODKIN HAZEL LA

Bushes Farm

BUSHES LA

Mapleridge House

Horton

Highfield Farm

HORTON RD

Horton Hall

HORTON HILL

Horton CE Prim Sch

Cotswold Way

Monarch's Way

Widdenhill Farm

HALL LA

Trinity Cottages

A46

Crowshall Barn Farm

NEW TYNING LA

Ivy Farm

Monarch's Way

CLAY PITCH

Little Sodbury

Church Farm

Manor House

CAMPS LA

Grickstone Farm

PORTWAY LA

Ball's Cottage

Little Sodbury Wood

P

Beech Copse

COMMONMEAD LA

Cotswold Way

A46

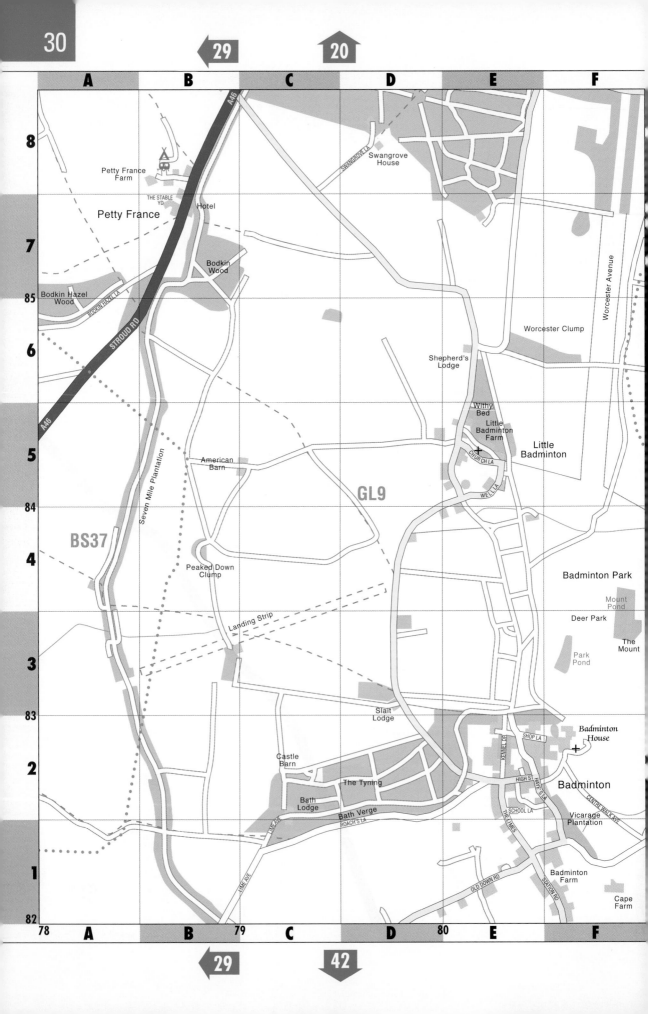

29
20

A **B** **C** **D** **E** **F**

8

Petty France Farm

THE STABLE YD

Petty France

Hotel

Swangrove House

SWANGROVE LA

7

Bodkin Wood

85

Bodkin Hazel Wood

BODKIN HAZEL LA

Worcester Clump

Worcester Avenue

6

STROUD RD

Shepherd's Lodge

A46

Withy Bed

Little Badminton Farm

Little Badminton

5

American Barn

Seven Mile Plantation

CHURCH LA

WELL LA

GL9

84

BS37

4

Peaked Down Clump

Badminton Park

Mount Pond

Deer Park

The Mount

Landing Strip

3

Park Pond

83

Slait Lodge

Badminton House

Castle Barn

SHOP LA

2

The Tyning

Bath Lodge

HIGH ST

Badminton

HAVE S LA

Vicarage Plantation

CENTRE WALK AVE

Bath Verge

ROACH'S LA

SCHOOL LA

THE LIMES

STATION RD

1

LIME AVE

Badminton Farm

OLD DOWN RD

Cape Farm

82

78 **A**   **B** 79 **C**   **D** 80 **E**   **F**

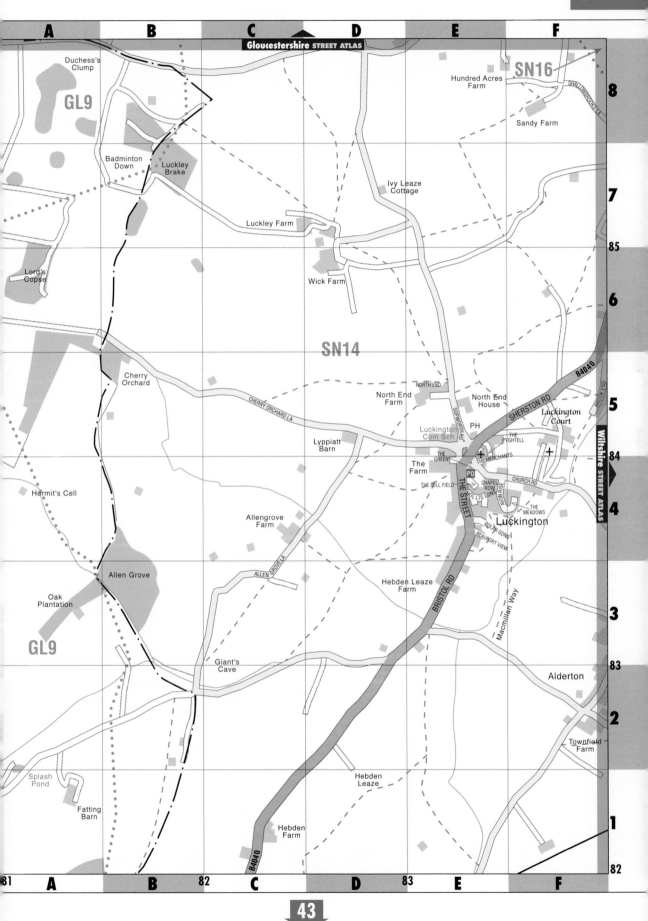

SN16

GL9

Duchess's Clump

Badminton Down

Luckley Brake

Lord's Copse

Hundred Acres Farm

Sandy Farm

SHALLOWBROOKS LA

Ivy Leaze Cottage

Luckley Farm

Wick Farm

SN14

Cherry Orchard

CHERRY ORCHARD LA

North End Farm

NORTH END

North End House

SHERSTON RD

B4040

Luckington Court

PH

Luckington Com Sch

SOPWORTH RD

BROOK END

THE PYGHTELL

Lyppiatt Barn

THE MERCHANTS

THE GREEN

The Farm

THE BELL FIELD

PO

CHAPEL ROW

MON RISE

CHURCH RD

THE MEADOWS

Hermit's Cell

Allengrove Farm

HOLLIS GDNS

THE STREET

COLN GDNS

BEAUFORT VIEW

Luckington

Wiltshire STREET ATLAS

Allen Grove

ALLEN GROVE LA

Oak Plantation

Hebden Leaze Farm

BRISTOL RD

Macmillan Way

GL9

Giant's Cave

Alderton

Splash Pond

Fatting Barn

Hebden Leaze

Townfield Farm

Hebden Farm

B4040

81   82   83   82

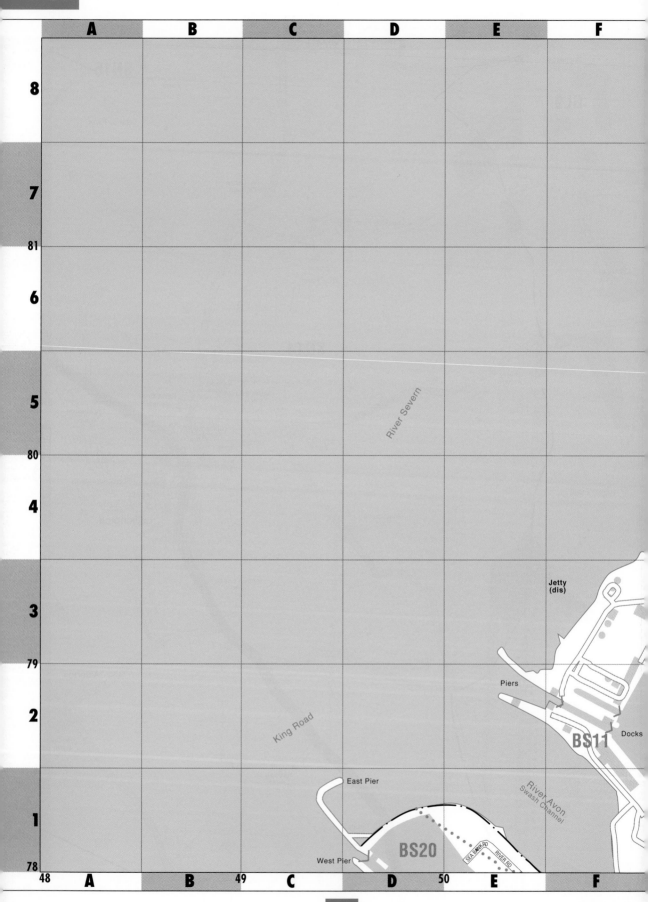

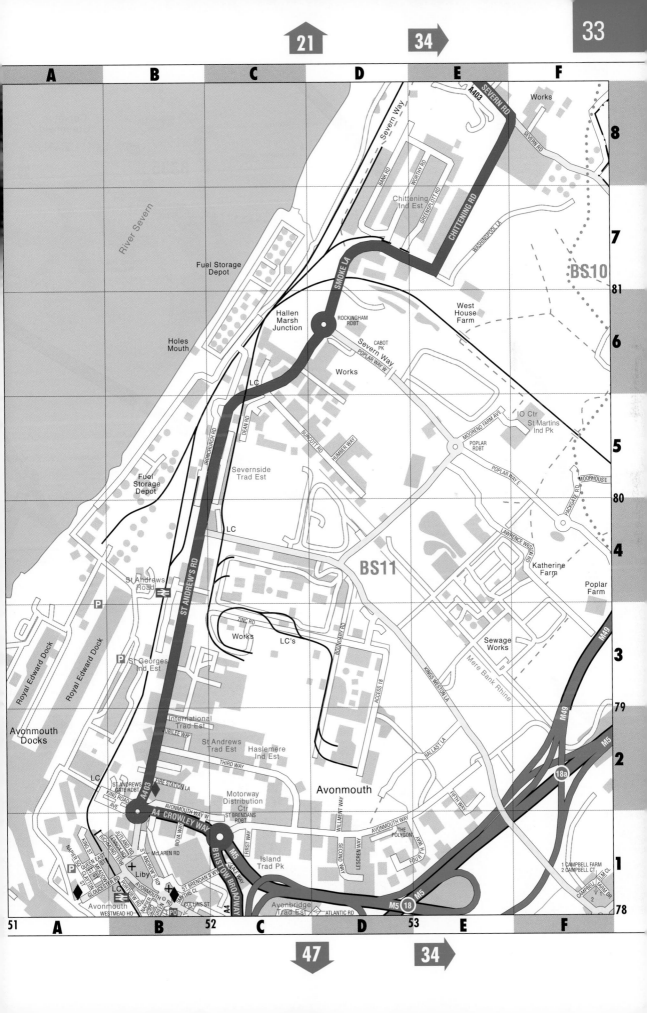

27

D7
1 MINSTER CT
2 FOUNTAIN CT
3 MONKS HO
4 FRIARS HO
5 ABBEY HO
6 PRINKNASH CT

40

E8
1 The Ridings' Federation
Yate Int Acad

39

YATE

BS36

Says Court Farm

Say's Wood

Beech Hill

Elm Farm

Rodford

Westerleigh Common

Westerleigh Rd

Dodmoor Farm

Westerleigh

BS37

Brook Farm

Jorrocks Ind Est

Brice's Farm

Mill House Farm

Kidney Hill

Sunnybank

Abattoir

Dewshill Wood

Cliff Farm

Crem

Leigh Farm

Leigh La

Westerleigh Hill Farm

Mast

Westerleigh Hill

Grove Farm

Besom La

Pool Farm

Wapley Rank

Wapley Bushes

Wapley Common

Cliff Farm

Chescombe Farm

Wychwell Farm

Church Farm

Beanwood Farm

Bean Wood

Bush's Farm

Wapley Hill

Wapley

Beanwood Pk (Cvn Site)

B4465

Wayleaze

B4465

Burbarrow La

Gorse Covert

BS16

BS16

BS16

Westerleigh Common

Abbotswood Prim Sch

Wellesley Prim Sch

Culverhill Sch

Kingsgate Park

Raysfield Inf & Jun Schs

Heron Way

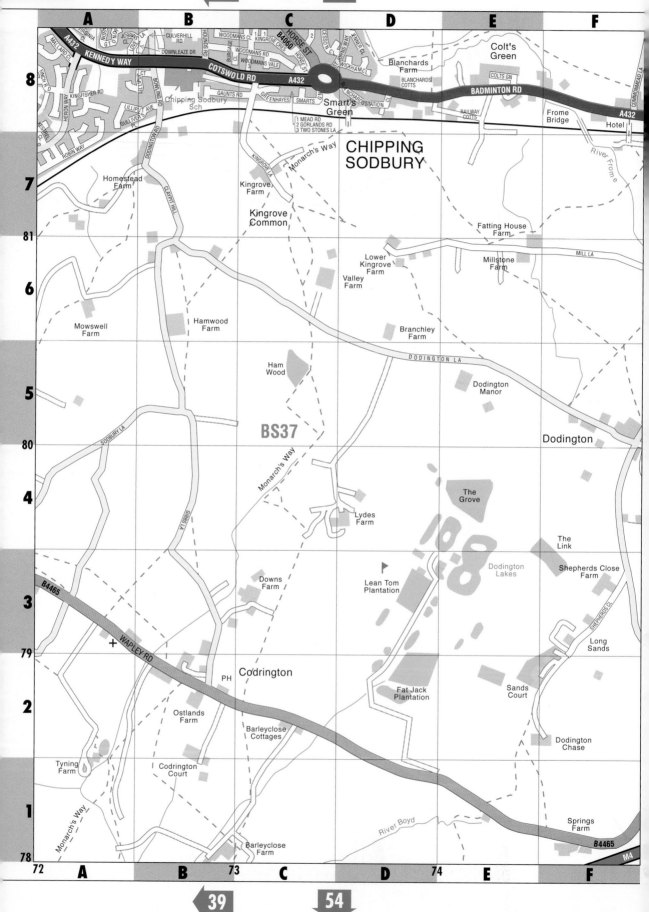

CHIPPING SODBURY

Colt's Green

Blanchards Farm
BLANCHARDS COTTS

KENNEDY WAY

COTSWOLD RD
A432

BADMINTON RD
A432

Chipping Sodbury Sch

GAUNTS RD

GREENHAYES

SMARTS

Smart's Green

1 MEAD RD
2 GORLANDS RD
3 TWO STONES LA

RAILWAY COLTS

Frome Bridge

Hotel

River Frome

Monarch's Way

Homestead Farm

CLAYPIT HILL

DODINGTON RD

Kingrove Farm

KINGROVE LA

Kingrove Common

Fatting House Farm

MILL LA

Lower Kingrove Farm

Millstone Farm

Valley Farm

BS37

Mowswell Farm

Hamwood Farm

SODBURY LA

Branchley Farm

DODINGTON LA

Ham Wood

Dodington Manor

Dodington

GIBBS LA

Monarch's Way

The Grove

Lydes Farm

The Link

Shepherds Close Farm

Dodington Lakes

Downs Farm

Lean Tom Plantation

SHEPHERDS CL

Long Sands

B4465

WAPLEY RD

PH

Codrington

Fat Jack Plantation

Sands Court

Dodington Chase

Ostlands Farm

Barleyclose Cottages

Tyning Farm

Codrington Court

Monarch's Way

River Boyd

Springs Farm

B4465

M4

Barleyclose Farm

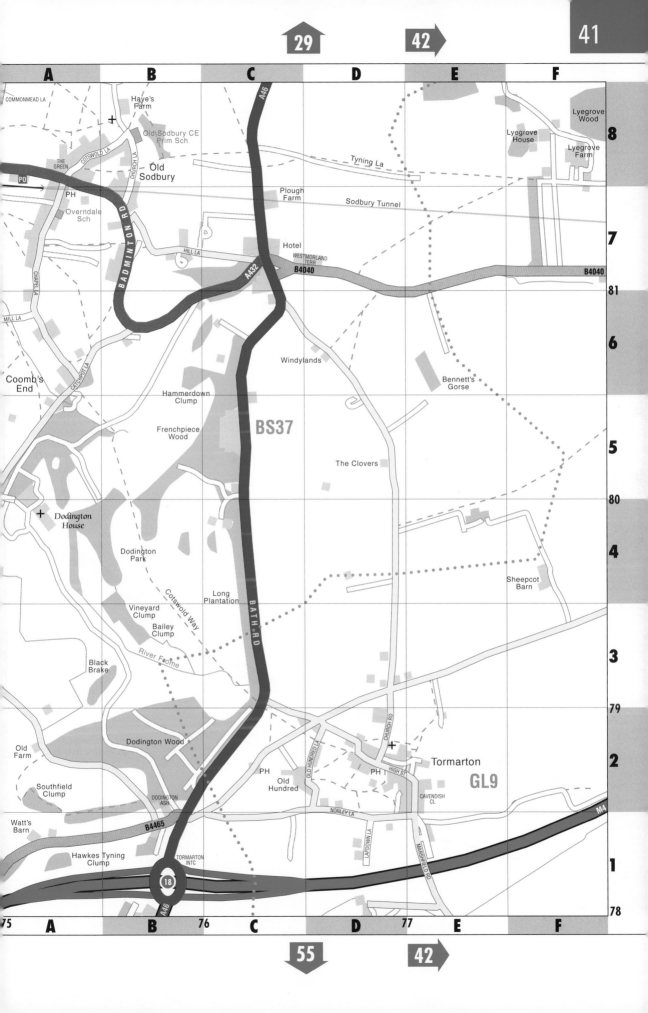

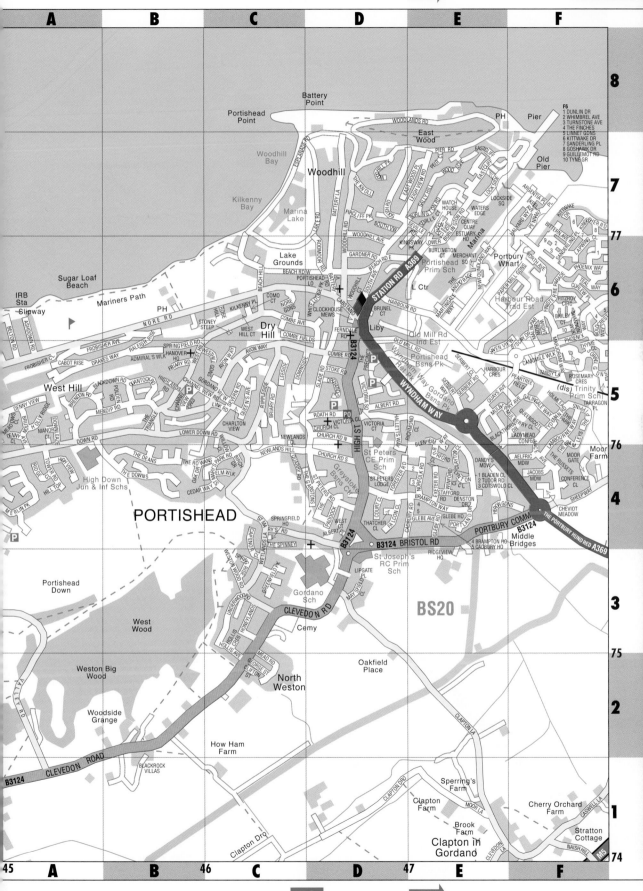

8

King Road

BS 11

Nelson Point

River Avon

River Quay

The Royal Portbury Dock

Gordano Quay

RIVER RD

GORDANO RD

7

Drove Rhyne

Sewage Works

St George's Quay

ST GEORGE'S RD

SHEEPHOUSE CVN PK

Marsh Lane Ind Est

BJORMANS WAY

77

WREN

KINGFISHER RD

SPARROW LA

GDNS

FIELDFARE AVE

PHOENIX WAY

STONECHAT GREEN

REDPOLL

THE MARTLINS

WAGTAIL GDNS

Portbury Wharf

BUNTING LA

THE DROVE

MARSH LA

REDLAND AVE

6

THE FINCHES

GOLDCREST WAY

ROBIN PL

ROWEL RD

SORREL GDNS

Atherton House

WHARF LA

SHEEPWAY LA

ROYAL PORTBURY DOCK RD

FIRST AVE

GARONOR WAY

GORDANO WAY

5

SHEEPWAY

Sheepway

Sheepway Gate Farm

Elm Tree Farm

Portbury Way

BANYARD RD

BRADLEY RD

Drove Rhyne

ROYAL PORTBURY DOCK RD

76

BS20

ELM TREE PK

(dis)

4

Cole Acre

STATION RD

THE PORTBURY HUNDREDS

A369

M5

19

Gordano Service area

MARTCOMBE RD A369

Portbury

PRIORY RD

Priory Farm Trad Est

STATION RD

PH

PRIORY WLK

The Priory (remains of)

CHURCH LA

HIGH ST

St Mary's CE VA Prim Sch

Longlands Wood

3

Conygar Hill

FORGE END

BRITTAN PL

MILL LA

HILLSIDE

Bulling's Wood

75

MILL CL

The Mount

Caswell Cross

CASWELL LA

Upper Caswell Farm

Rifle Range

FAILAND LA

Honor Farm

2

Lower Caswell House

CASWELL HILL

Prior's Wood

PORTBURY LA

Oakham Farm

COOMBE LA

1

CHARLTON DR

BS48

Birch Wood

Budding's Wood

BS8

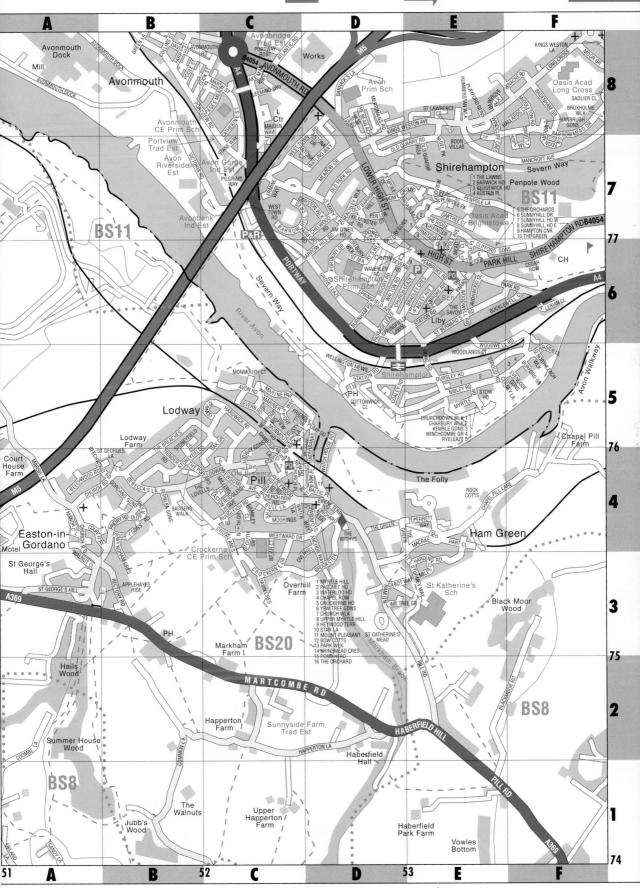

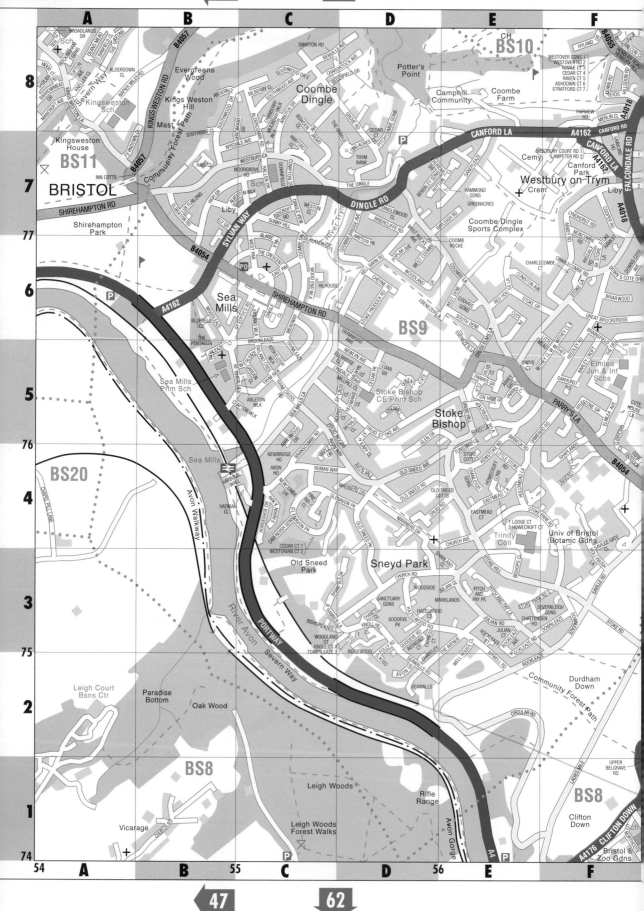

A7
1 WESTMINSTER CL
2 CARLTON HO
3 CARLTON CT
4 IVY LODGE
5 BELLEVUE COTTS
6 WESTBURY MEWS

B6
1 CRANFORD CT
2 BLANDFORD CL
3 ST PETER'S WLK
F1
1 ASHLEY CT
2 CARY CT

3 CARR HO
4 WINKWORTH PL
5 COREY CL
6 LANGSDOWN HO
7 DAVEY TERR
8 NEWFOUNDLAND ST
9 FRANKLYN LA

10 DERMOT ST
11 CAIRNS' CRES
12 LOWER ASHLEY RD
13 GORDON RD
14 MARY CARPENTER PL

35

F2
1 SOMMERVILLE RD S
2 ASHLEY COURT RD
3 BALMORAL MANS
4 FALKLAND RD
5 CUMBERLAND GR
6 Ashley Trad Est

50

F2
7 ASHLEY GROVE RD
8 Minto Road Ind Ctr
9 MINTO RD
10 Parkway Trad Est
11 LYNMOUTH RD
12 NEWLAND HTS

F4
1 CARLTON CT
2 COULSON HO
3 ATHENA CT

49

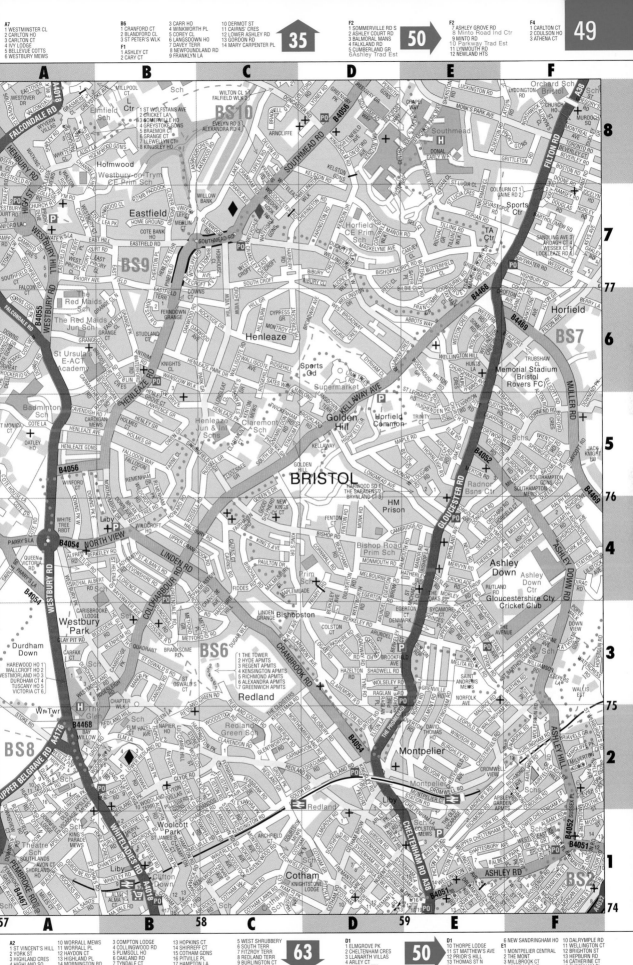

57

A2
1 ST VINCENT'S HILL
2 YORK ST
3 HIGHLAND SQ
4 HIGHLAND CRES
5 RICHMOND DALE
6 RICHMOND DALE
7 QUARRY STEPS
8 SUTHERLAND PL

10 WORRALL MEWS
11 WORRALL PL
12 HAYDON CT
13 HIGHLAND PL
14 MORNINGTON RD
15 ANGLESEA PL
16 NORMANTON RD
B1
1 KING'S PARADE AVE
2 GROSVENOR CT

3 COMPTON LODGE
4 COLLINGWOOD RD
5 PLIMSOLL HO
6 OAKLAND RD
7 TYNDALE CT
8 IMPERIAL RD
9 WHATLEY CT
10 CLIFTON METRO
11 Clifton Down Sh Ctr
12 GEORGE CT

13 HOPKINS CT
14 SHIRREFF CT
15 COTHAM GDNS
16 FRYVILLE PL
17 HAMPTON LA
B2
1 FERNLEIGH CT
2 LOWER REDLAND MEWS
3 EAST SHRUBBERY
4 SHRUBBERY COTTS

5 WEST SHRUBBERY
6 SOUTH TERR
7 FITZROY TERR
8 REDLAND TERR
9 BURLINGTON CT
10 GREENWAY HO

63

D1
1 ELMGROVE PK
2 CHELTENHAM CRES
3 LLANARTH VILLAS
4 ARLEY CT
5 ARLEY COTTS
6 HILLSIDE HO
7 VICTORIA CT
8 VICTORIA GDNS
9 FREMANTLE LA

50

D1
10 THORPE LODGE
11 ST MATTHEW'S AVE
12 PRIOR'S HILL
13 THOMAS ST N
D2
1 PROSPECT PL
2 BROOKFIELD LA
3 BROOKFIELD RD
4 GILLHAM HO
5 ELTON MANS

6 NEW SANDRINGHAM HO
E1
1 MONTPELIER CENTRAL
2 THE MONT
3 MILLBROOK CT
4 ARMIDALE AVE
5 ARMIDALE COTTS
6 PICTON MEWS
7 WOODMANCOTE RD
8 NORRISVILLE RD
9 BARNABAS ST

10 DALRYMPLE RD
11 WELLINGTON CT
12 BRIGHTON ST
13 HAMPDEN RD
14 CATHERINE CT
15 SYDENHAM CT
16 NINE TREE HILL
17 DOVE ST
18 ARMADA HO
19 ARMADA PL

← 49

36

↑

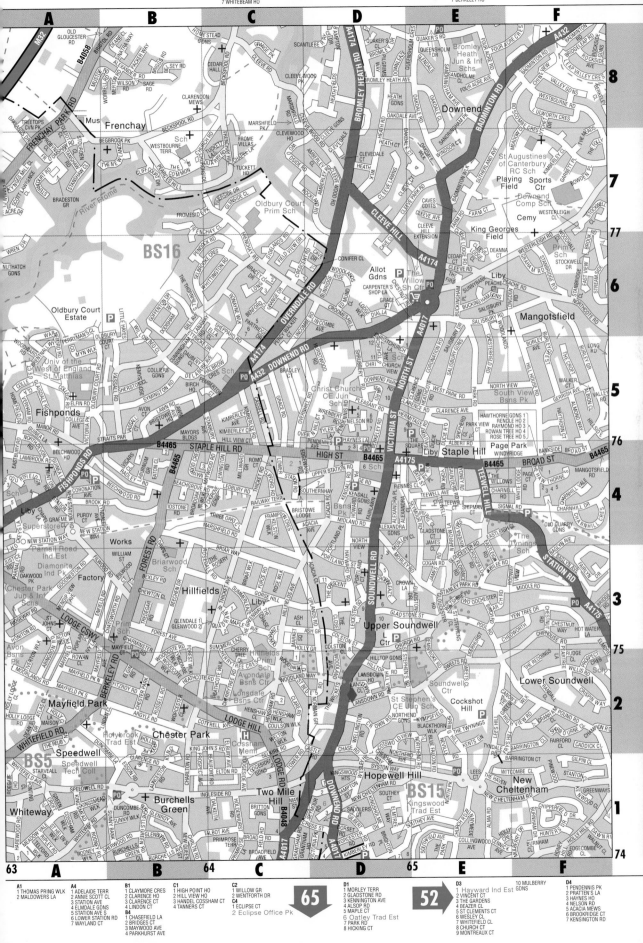

C6
1 URFORDS DR
2 SHIMSEY CL
3 BRIDGES DR
4 GRANGEWOOD CL
5 HORNBEAM CL
6 SYCAMORE HO
7 WHITEBEAM HO

D5
1 BRITANNIA CT
2 OVERHURST CT
3 GARTON CL
4 PLEASANT HO
5 PENDENNIS HO
6 SHRUBBERY CT
7 BERKELEY HO

8 NELSON HO
9 PAMELA HO
10 JOHN WESLEY CT
11 ORCHARD COTTS
12 VICARAGE COTTS

52

A7
1 WAKEFORD RD
2 WESTBOURNE CL

C7
1 MEADOWSWEET RD
2 FOXGLOVE RD
3 WALNUT WAY
4 PRIMROSE WAY
5 YARROW CL
6 CARNATION RD

51

38

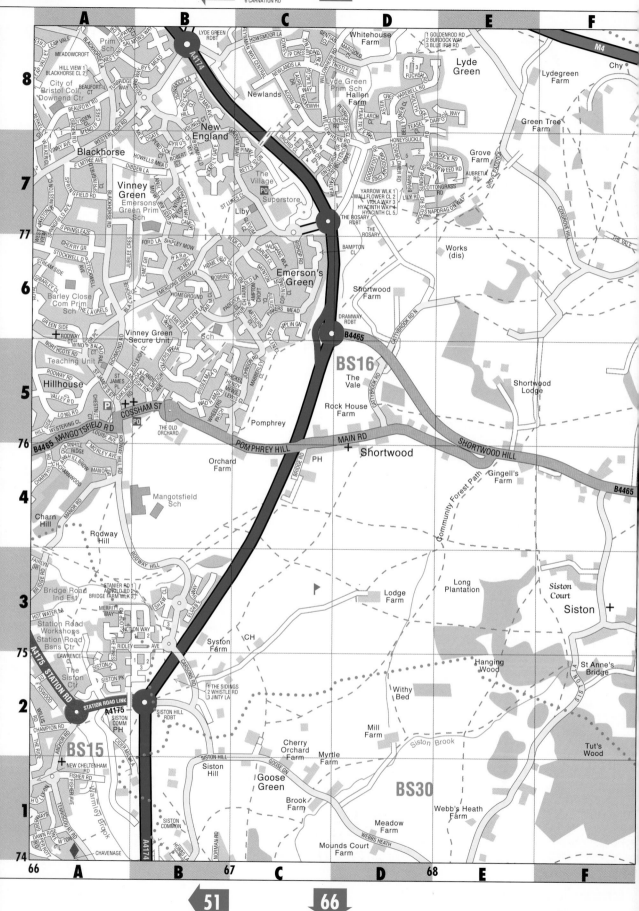

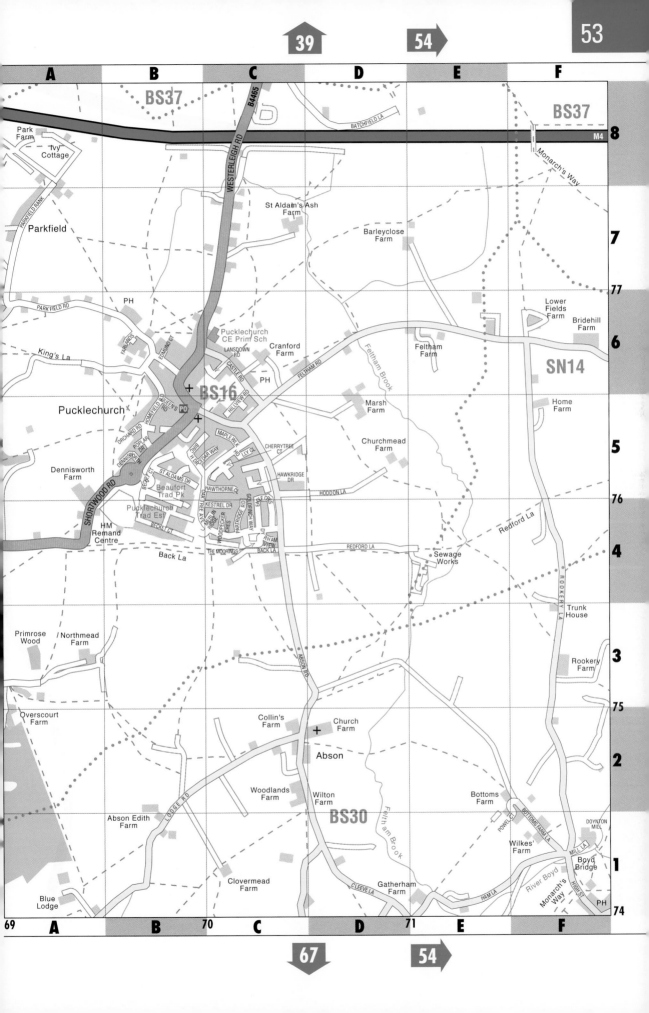

A B C D E F

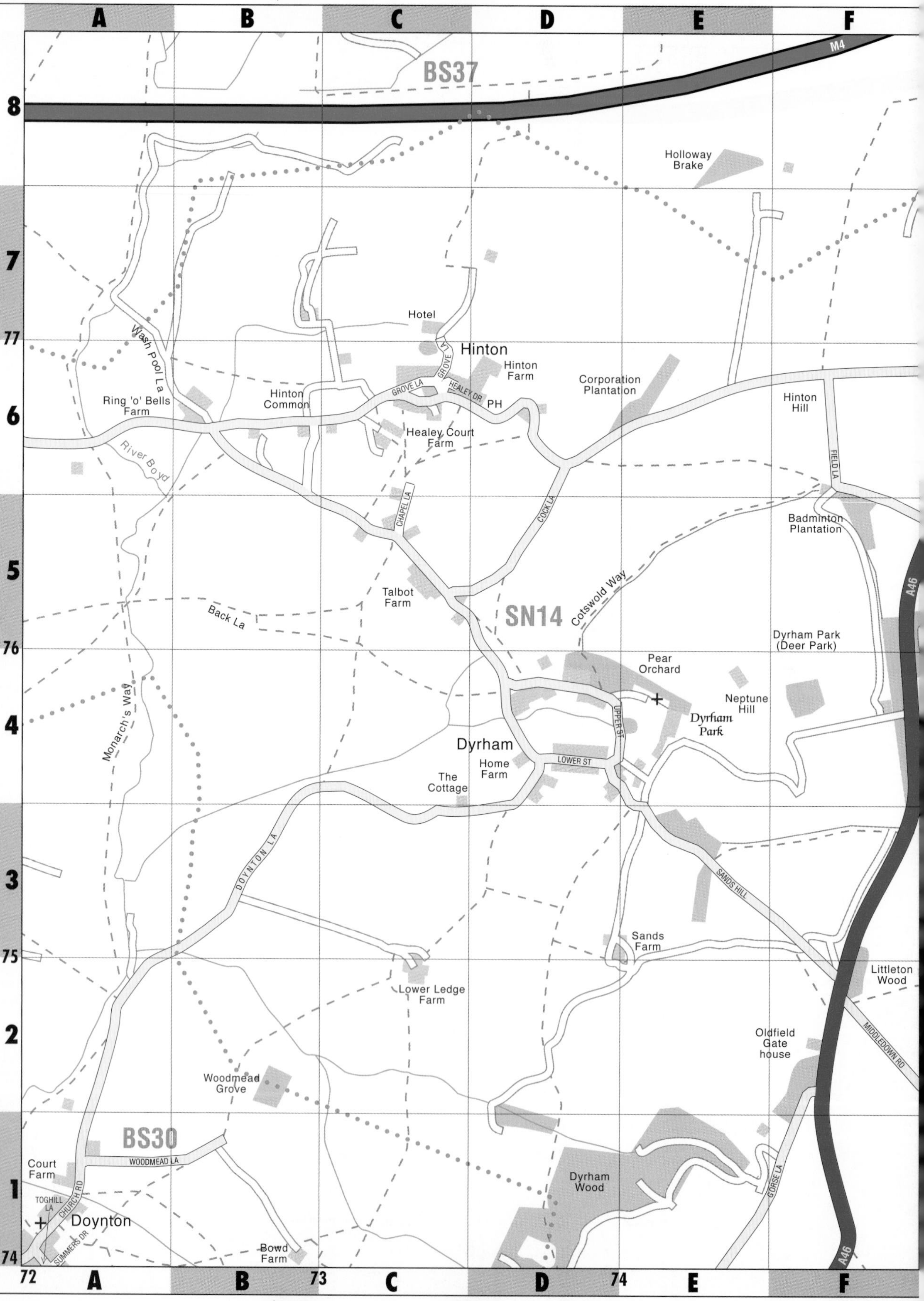

BS37

M4

8

Holloway
Brake

7

77

Hotel

Wash Pool La

Hinton

Hinton
Farm

Corporation
Plantation

Ring 'o' Bells
Farm

Hinton
Common

GROVE LA

HEALEY DR

PH

Hinton
Hill

FIELD LA

6

River Boyd

Healey Court
Farm

CHAPEL LA

COCK LA

Badminton
Plantation

A46

5

Back La

Talbot
Farm

SN14

Cotswold Way

Dyrham Park
(Deer Park)

76

Pear
Orchard

Neptune
Hill

Monarch's Way

4

Dyrham

UPPER ST

Dyrham
Park

Home
Farm

LOWER ST

The
Cottage

DOYNTON LA

SANDS HILL

3

Sands
Farm

75

Littleton
Wood

Lower Ledge
Farm

MIDDLEDOWN RD

2

Oldfield
Gate
house

Woodmead
Grove

BS30

Court
Farm

WOODMEAD LA

CHURCH RD

Dyrham
Wood

GORSE LA

1

TOGHILL LA

Doynton

SUMMERS DR

Bowd
Farm

A46

74

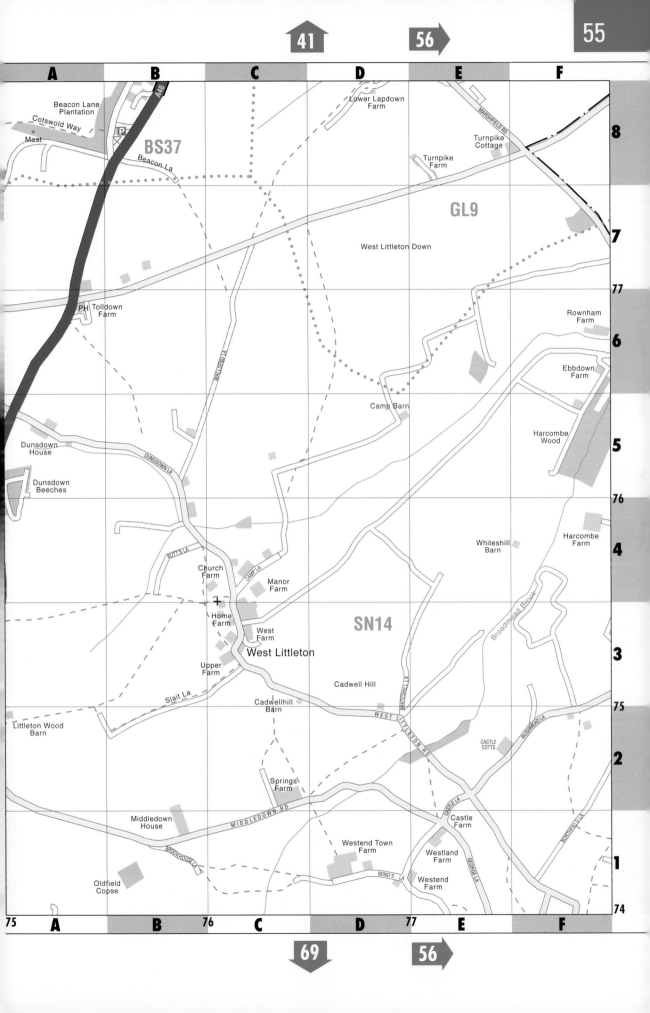

A   B   C   D   E   F

GL9

8

Kington Down Farm

Fox Covert

West Kington

Down Farm

Brook Farm

HOLLOWAY HILL

DRIFTON HILL

7

SHIRE HILL

77

Mill House

Latimer Farm

Broadmead Brook

6

Hazel Grove

Shirehill Farm

Lower Shirehill Farm

Gunning's Wood

SN14

5

76

4

TORMARTON RD

Hillcrest Farm

Maggs Farm

Plough Farm

New Homestead Farm

THE CREST

Rushmead Farm

3

Mountain Bower

Highfield Cottage

RUSHMEAD LA

Downthorns Farm

75

NORTHFIELD LA

Martor Ind Est

2

Culverslade

DOWN RD

Upper Wraxall

Home Farm

Hillcrest Farm

PH

A420

Upper Farm

1

Cemy

A420 Chippenham

The Shoe

Northfield House

74

78   A   B   79   C   D   80   E   F

Wiltshire STREET ATLAS

8

7

73

6

5

72

4

3

71

2

70

Margaret's Bay

Blackhill Sands

BS21

Back Hill

Castle Hill

West Wood

Ladye Point

Walton Castle

Castle Farm

CH

Ladye Bay

Sports Ctr

Swiss Valley

B3124

B3124

Walton Cliff

Walton St Mary

Clevedon Sch

Walton Cliff

High Cliff

WELLINGTON TERR

Wellington Ct 1
Beaufort Ct 2
St Christopher's Ct 3
Edgarley Ct 4
St Martins 5

New Park Ho

HILL RD

Pier

Clevedon Bay

Alexandra Ct 1
Coity Pl 2
Coppice Mews 3
Beach Mews 4
Woodlands Rd 5
Seavale Mews 6
Six Ways 7
Hallam Ct 8
St Clements Ct 9
Pembroke Ct 10
Oaklands 11

B3130

1 Averill Ct
2 Bellevue Mans
3 Bellevue Ct
4 Archer Ct
5 Lindon Ct

Dial Hill

St Nicholas Park Chantry
CE VC Prim Sch

Strawberry Hill

All Saints East Clevedon CE Prim Sch

Court Hill

ELTON RD

B3124

TICKENHAM RD

B3130

CLEVEDON

Salthouse Bay

1 WESTERN CT
2 CHAPEL CT
3 OVERSTABLES LA
4 THE TRIANGLE CTR
5 THE TRIANGLE

EAST CLEVEDON TRIANGLE

East Clevedon

OLD ST

B3130 OLD DAIRY CT

Salthouse Point

Clevedon Min Rly

Recn Gd

Hangstone Hill

OLD CHURCH RD

B3130

Liby

B3133 GREAT WESTERN RD

Clevedon Com

Northern Path

CROSSMAN WLK

M5

Church Hill

West End

B3133

MOOR LA

Hither Green Ind Est

20

B3133

Moor La

Wain's Hill

Recn Gd Sports Ctr Five Bsns Ctr

KENN RD

Yeo Moor Prim Sch

Wrangle Farm Gn

Superstore

The Chaffins The Penns

Blind Yeo

Prim Sch

B3133

M5

Blind Yeo

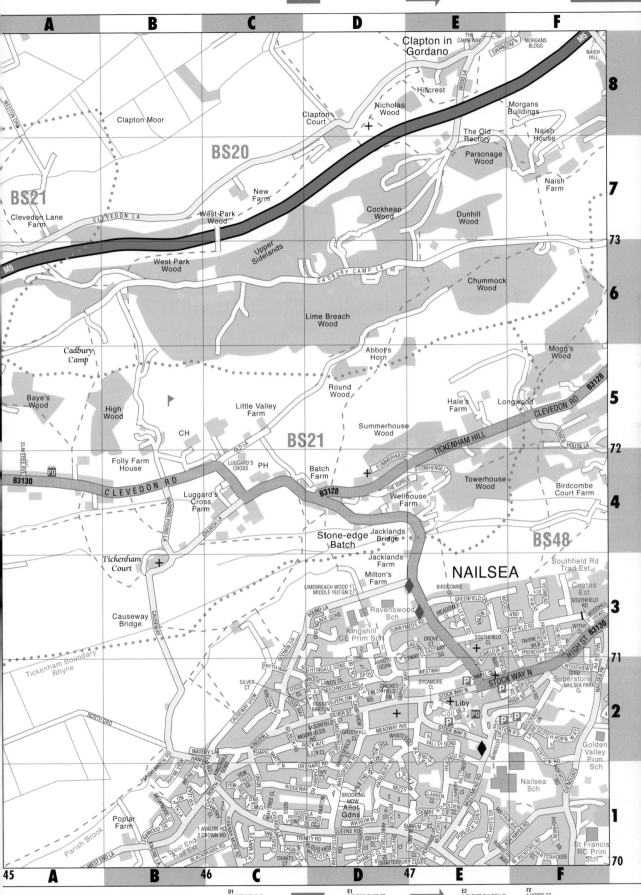

Clapton in Gordano

8

BS20

BS21

7

73

6

5

72

4

BS48

NAILSEA

3

71

2

1

70

D1
1 MIZZYMEAD CL
2 BEAUFORT GDNS
3 AMBERLEY GDNS
4 CLAREMONT GDNS
5 DOWNLAND CL
6 DORCHESTER CL

E1
1 FARMHOUSE CT
2 BRENDON GDNS
3 MENDIP CL
4 SELWORTHY GDNS
5 DUNSTER GDNS
6 BIDDISHAM CL

E2
1 CHRIST CHURCH CL
2 CLEVEDON WLK
3 SOMERSET SQ
4 COLLIERS WLK
5 CROWN GLASS PL
6 VALLEY CL
7 FARMHOUSE CL

F2
1 HOBBS CT
2 FRIENDSHIP GR
3 SCOTS PINE AVE
4 HAWTHORN WAY
5 SCOTCH HORN CL
6 BLACKTHORN WAY

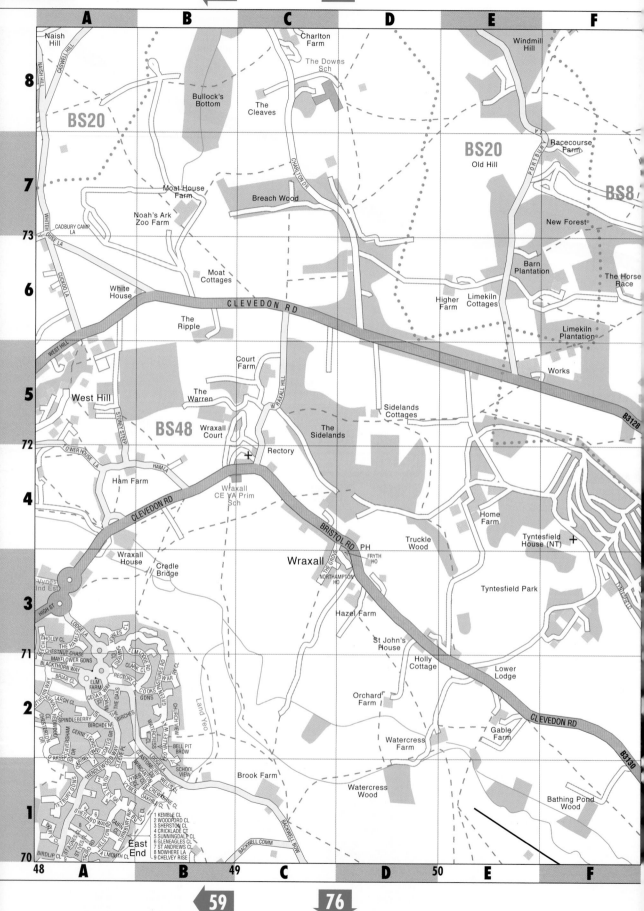

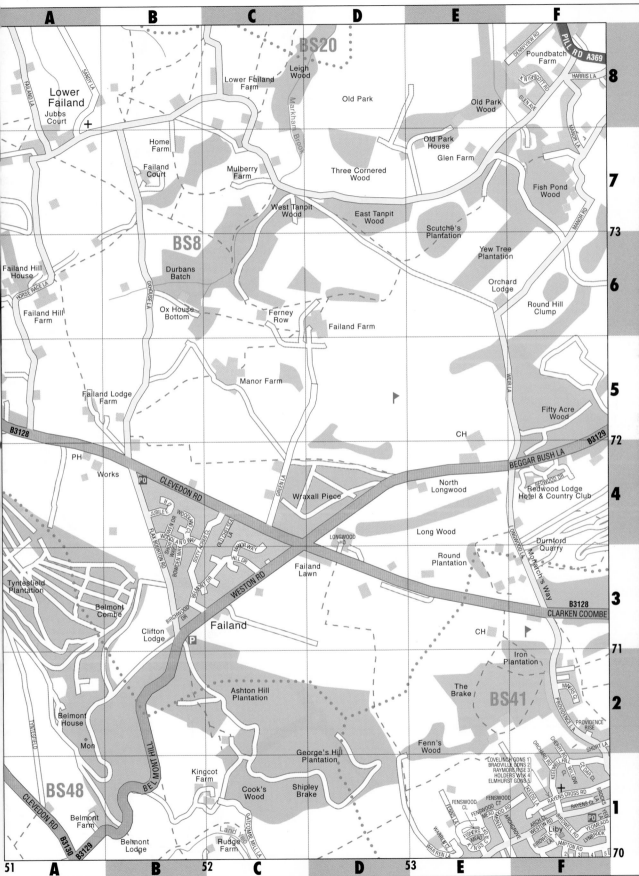

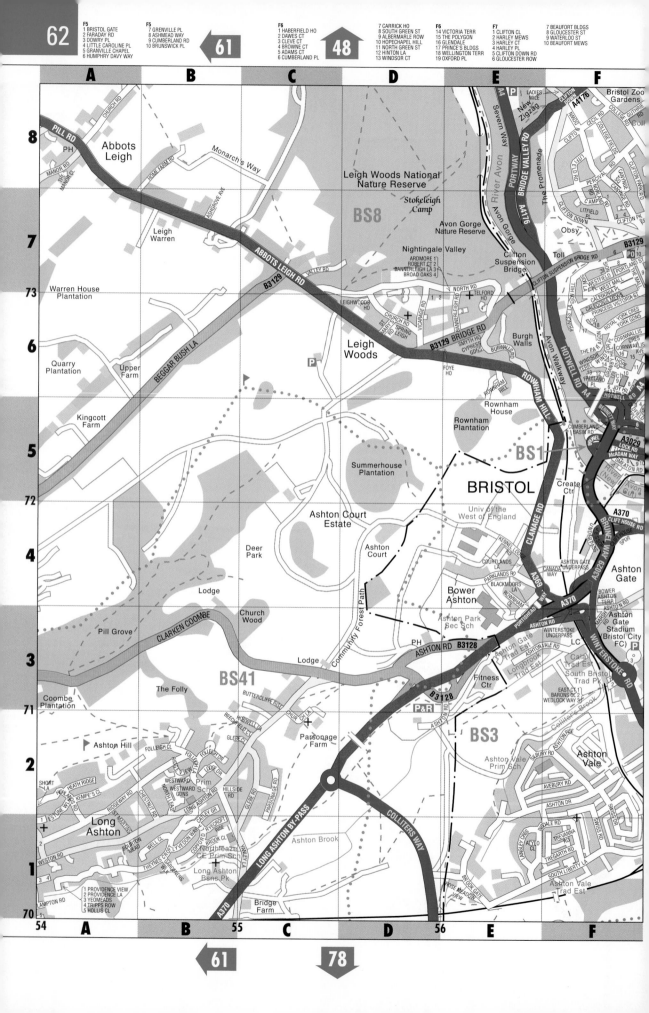

62

F5
1 BRISTOL GATE
2 FARADAY RD
3 DOWRY PL
4 LITTLE CAROLINE PL
5 GRANVILLE CHAPEL
6 HUMPHRY DAVY WAY

F5
7 GRENVILLE PL
8 ASHMEAD WAY
9 CUMBERLAND RD
10 BRUNSWICK PL

◄ **61**

F6
1 HABERFIELD HO
2 DAWES CT
3 CLEVE CT
4 BROWNE CT
5 ADAMS CT
6 CUMBERLAND PL

48

7 CARRICK HO
8 SOUTH GREEN ST
9 ALBEMARLE ROW
10 HOPECHAPEL HILL
11 NORTH GREEN ST
12 HINTON LA
13 WINDSOR CT

F6
14 VICTORIA TERR
15 THE POLYGON
16 GLENDALE
17 PRINCE'S BLDGS
18 WELLINGTON TERR
19 OXFORD PL

F7
1 CLIFTON CL
2 HARLEY MEWS
3 HARLEY CT
4 HARLEY PL
5 CLIFTON DOWN RD
6 GLOUCESTER ROW

7 BEAUFORT BLDGS
8 GLOUCESTER ST
9 WATERLOO ST
10 BEAUFORT MEWS

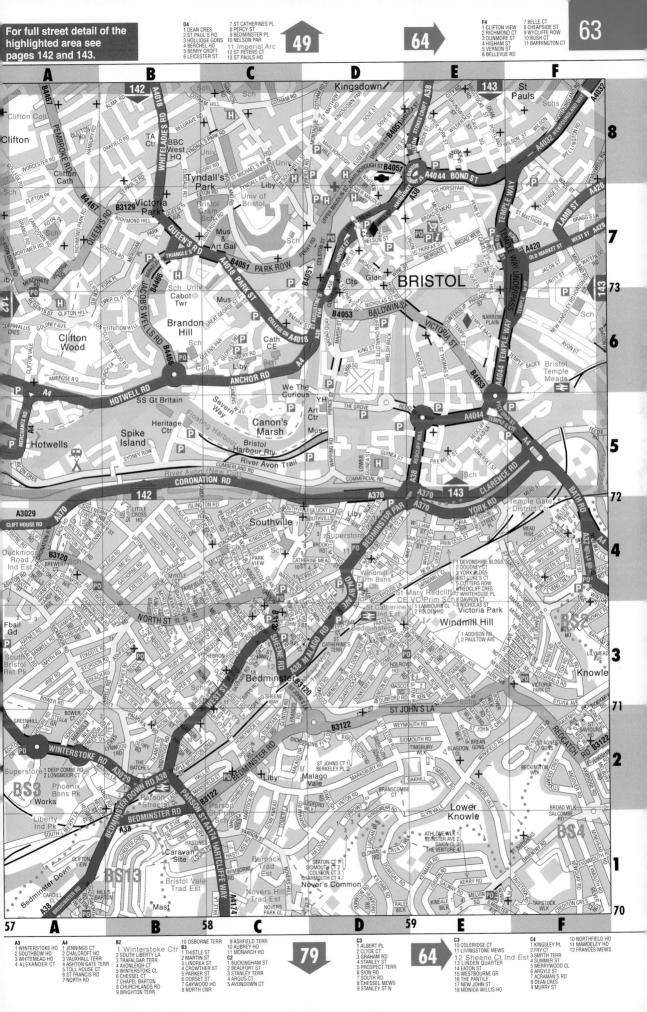

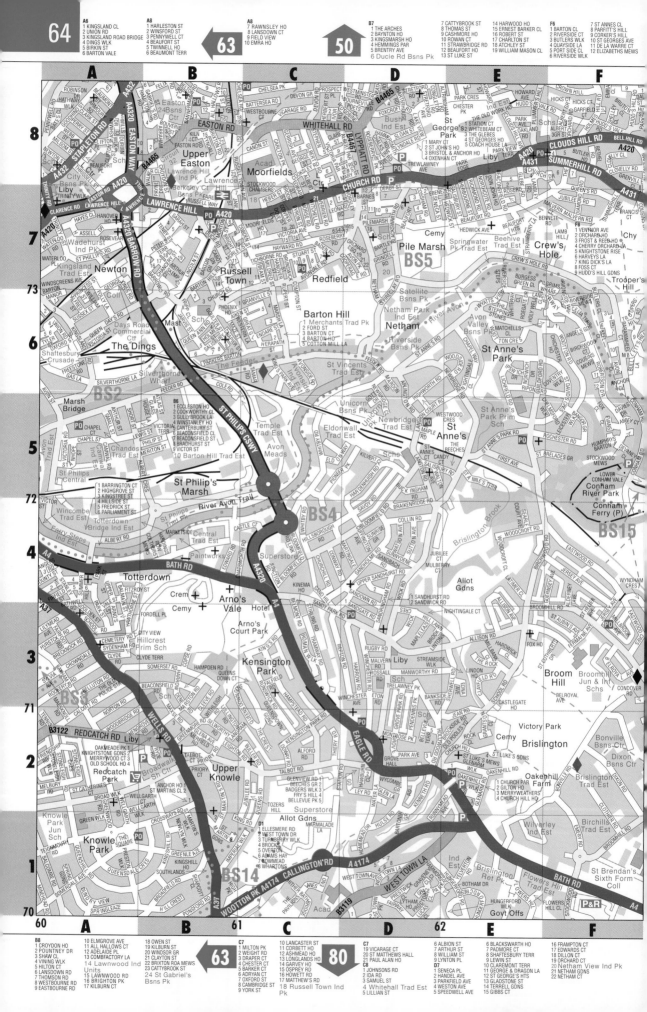

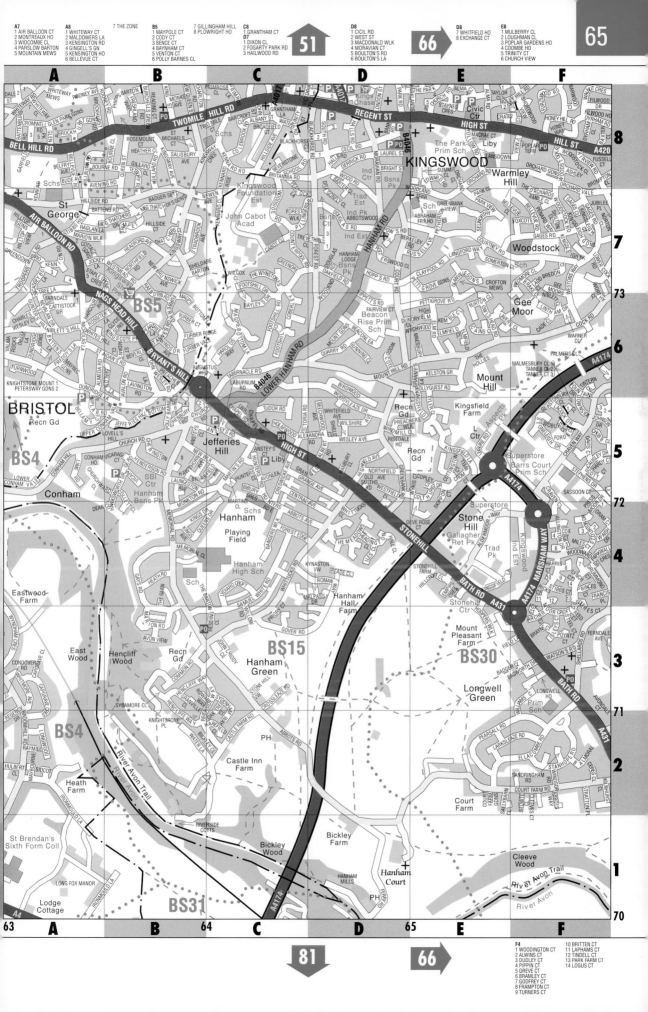

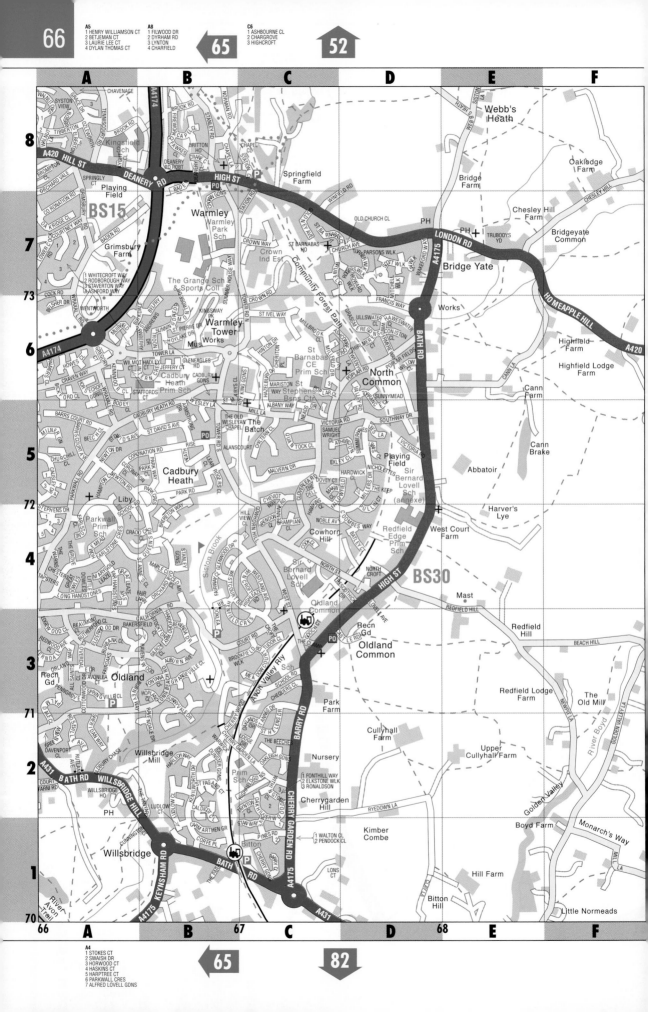

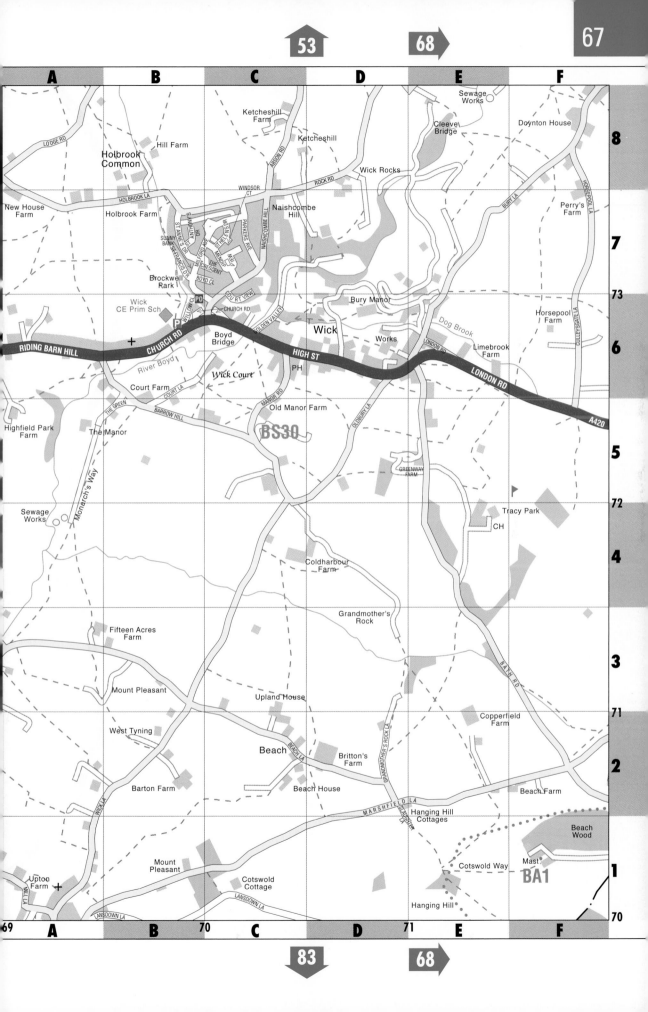

A

Perrymans Cl

Rectory Farmhouse

Doynton

Beech Farm

TOGHILL LA

WATERY LA

8

Babwell Farm

TOGHILL LA

7

Woodlands Farm

B

73

BS30

Toghill Grove

P

6

Highways

TOG HILL

CHIPPENHAM RD

Toghill House Farm

Toghill Barn Farm

GORSE LA

Shrubbery Farm

PH

Pennsylvania

Sandy Tyning

A46

Oldfield Farm Cottages

8

PH

THE FOLLY

A420

Cold Ashton

The Lynch

HYDE'S LA

TOGHILL LA

A420

Toghill Farm

5

Uplands

Tog Hill

St John's Wood

SN14

Shapland's Farm

COTSWOLD WAY

GREEN WAY LA

72

Tracy Cottage Farm

4

FREEZINGHILL LA

Hamswell Farm

Hamswell House

Hill Farm

Nimlet

Henley Hill

Freezing Hill

Lower Hamswell

Vine Cottage

Henley Tyning Farm

LEIGH LA

3

Parkfield Farm

HALL LA

Lilliput Farm

Nimlet Hill

HALL LA

HALL LA

71

Noade's Leaze Farm

Rushmead Wood

BA1

2

Battlefields

Torney's Court Farm

Manor Farm

GLOUCESTER RD

Tadwick

TADWICK LA

Sir Bevil Grenville's Mon

1

Goudie's Farm

Manor Farm

A46

70

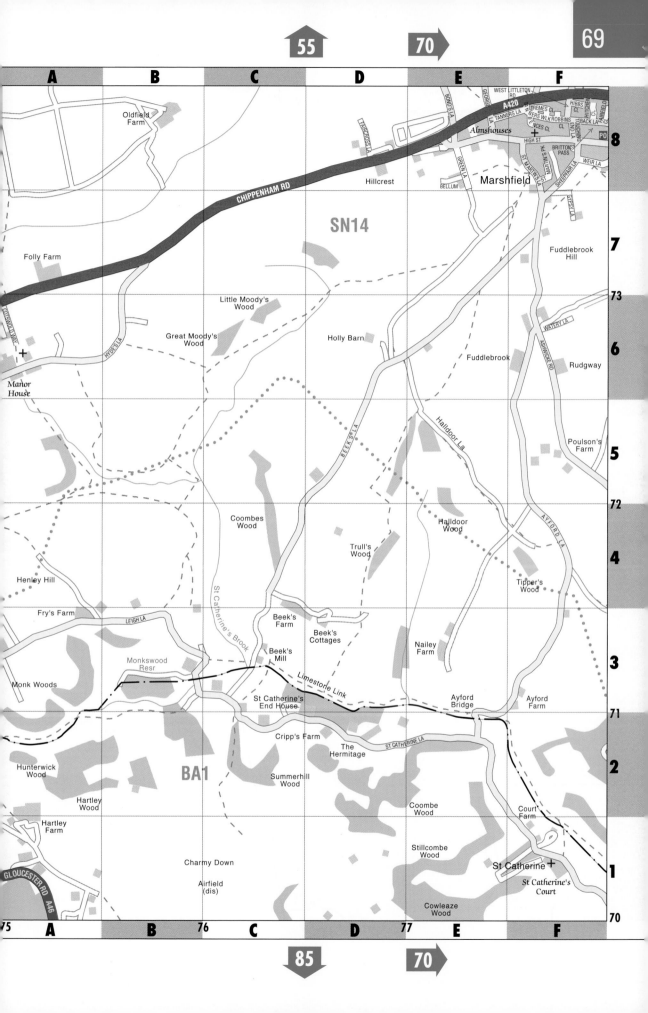

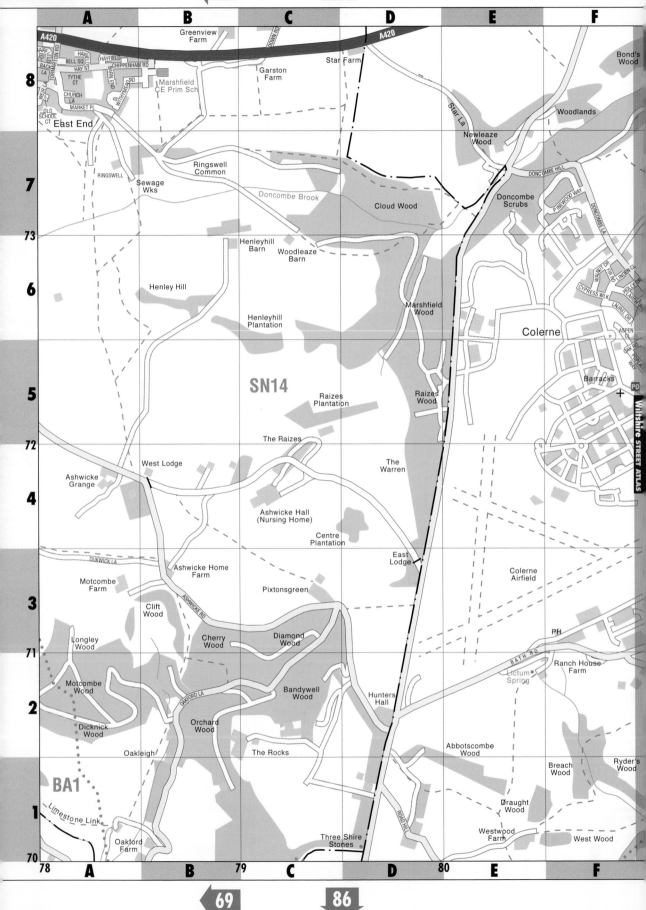

A · B · C · D · E · F

8

7

73

6

5

72

4

3

71

2

1

70

A420
Greenview Farm
A420
Star Farm

TORRINGTON RD
HAYFIELD
BELL SQ
HAY ST
TYTHE CT
CHURCH LA
MARKET PL
BACK LA
WEIR LA
OLD SCHOOL CT
CHIPPENHAM RD
BARN END
WITHY MEAD RD
HAYFIELD
Marshfield CE Prim Sch
Garston Farm
Star La
Bond's Wood
Woodlands
East End
Ringswell
Sewage Wks
Ringswell Common
Doncombe Brook
Cloud Wood
Newleaze Wood
Doncombe Scrubs
Doncombe Hill
PINEWOOD WAY
DONCOMBE LA
Henleyhill Barn
Woodleaze Barn
WALNUT DR
FIR RD
LINDEN CL
CYPRESS WLK
LAUREL DRI
HOLLY DRI
MULBERRY CL
Henley Hill
Henleyhill Plantation
Marshfield Wood
Colerne
ASPEN CL
OAK RD
POPLAR WAY
SN14
Raizes Plantation
Raizes Wood
Barracks
PO
Wiltshire STREET ATLAS
The Raizes
West Lodge
The Warren
Ashwicke Grange
Ashwicke Hall (Nursing Home)
Centre Plantation
East Lodge
Colerne Airfield
DUKWICK LA
Ashwicke Home Farm
ASHWICKE RD
Pixtonsgreen
Motcombe Farm
Clift Wood
PH
Longley Wood
Cherry Wood
Diamond Wood
BATH RD
Ranch House Farm
Lictum Spring
Motcombe Wood
OAKFORD LA
Bandywell Wood
Hunters Hall
Dicknick Wood
Orchard Wood
Abbotscombe Wood
Breach Wood
Ryder's Wood
Oakleigh
The Rocks
ROAD HILL
Draught Wood
BA1
Limestone Link
Three Shire Stones
Westwood Farm
West Wood
Oakford Farm

78 · A · 79 · B · C · 80 · D · E · F

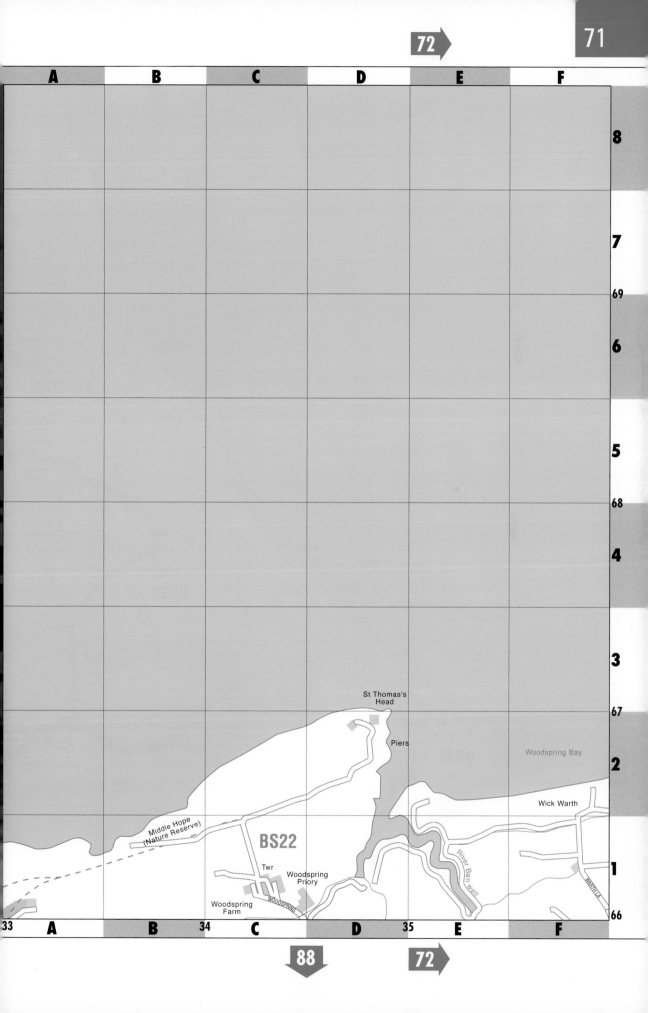

A   B   C   D   E   F

8

7

69

6

5

68

4

3

67

St Thomas's
Head

Piers

Woodspring Bay

2

Wick Warth

Middle Hope
(Nature Reserve)

BS22

Twr

Woodspring
Priory

River Banwell

1

WARTH LA

Woodspring
Farm

WOODSPRING

66

71

A B C D E F

8

7

69

6

5

68

4

3

67

2

1

66

36 A B 37 C D 38 E F

71
89

Dowlais Ditch

Kingston Pill

Seawall Farm

Hook's Ear

Treble House Farm

BACK LA

Sewage Works

Channel View Farm

BS21

MIDDLE LA

MIDDLE LA

Broadstone Rhyne

Broadstone Farm

BROADSTONE LA

Wharf Farm

BS22

HAM LA

Ham Farm

New House Farm

Ham Rhyne

Pool Farm

Sewage Works

MUDDY LA

BS22

Yeo Bank Farm

Mendip View Farm

YEO BANK LA

Mill Leaze Rhyne

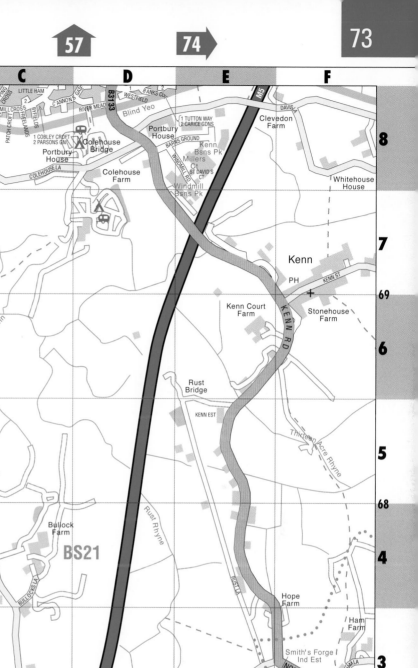
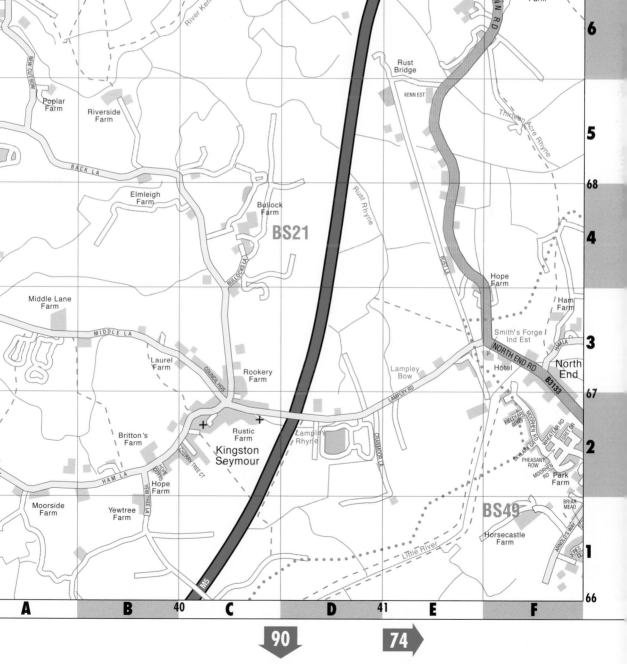

A B C D E F

8
7
69
6
5
68
4
67
3
2
66
1

CLEVEDON

Dowlais Farm
Dorsal Farm
Stileway Bsns Pk
CH
Masts

LONGACRE
OAKLEY
SMOKSWOOD
BAKER CL
STRODE RD
CATE MEAD
THE HYDE
CHIPPING CROSS
MILL CROSS
PATCH CROFT
BYFIELDS
FREELANDS
LITTLE HAM
C ANNON'S GATE
RIVER MEAD
B3133
WESTFIELD
BANKS CL
Blind Yeo
DAVIS

1 COBLEY CROFT
2 PARSONS GN
Portbury House
Colehouse Bridge

Portbury House
1 TUTTON WAY
2 CARICE GDNS
Clevedon Farm

BARNS GROUND
Kenn Bsns Pk
Millers Ct
ST DAVID'S CT
WINDMILL RD
Whitehouse House

Colehouse LA
Colehouse Farm
Windmill Bsns Pk

Lower Farm
Southfield Farm

LOWER STRODE RD
River Kenn

Kenn
PH
KENN ST

Kenn Court Farm
Stonehouse Farm

NEW CUT BOW

KENN RD

Poplar Farm
Riverside Farm

Rust Bridge

Thirteen Acre Rhyne

BACK LA

KENN EST

Elmleigh Farm
Bullock Farm

BS21

Rust Rhyne

BULLOCKS LA

Middle Lane Farm

RUST LA

Hope Farm
Ham Farm

MIDDLE LA

Smith's Forge Ind Est
HAM LA
North End
NORTH END RD
B3133

Laurel Farm
Rookery Farm

COUNCIL HOS

Lampley Bow
Hotel

LAMPLEY RD

Britton's Farm
Rustic Farm
Kingston Seymour
Lampley Rhyne

CHERRY TREE CT
JONES CROFT
CRANMOOR LA

FIELDFARE GDNS
MOORHEN RD
WHEATEAR RD
EGRET DR
Park Farm
SKYLARK RD
PHEASANT ROW
MOORHEN RD

Hope Farm
Moorside Farm
Yewtree Farm

HAM LA
YEW TREE LA
LO BANK LA

BS49
BRIAR MEAD

Horsecastle Farm
Little River
ARNOLD'S WAY
JONES CL

M5

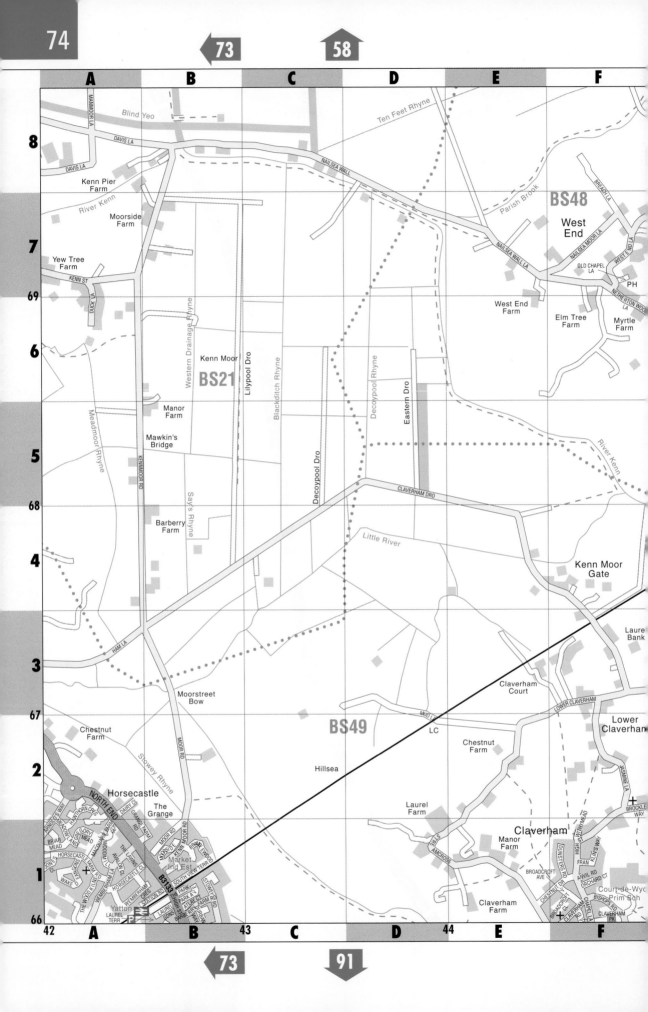

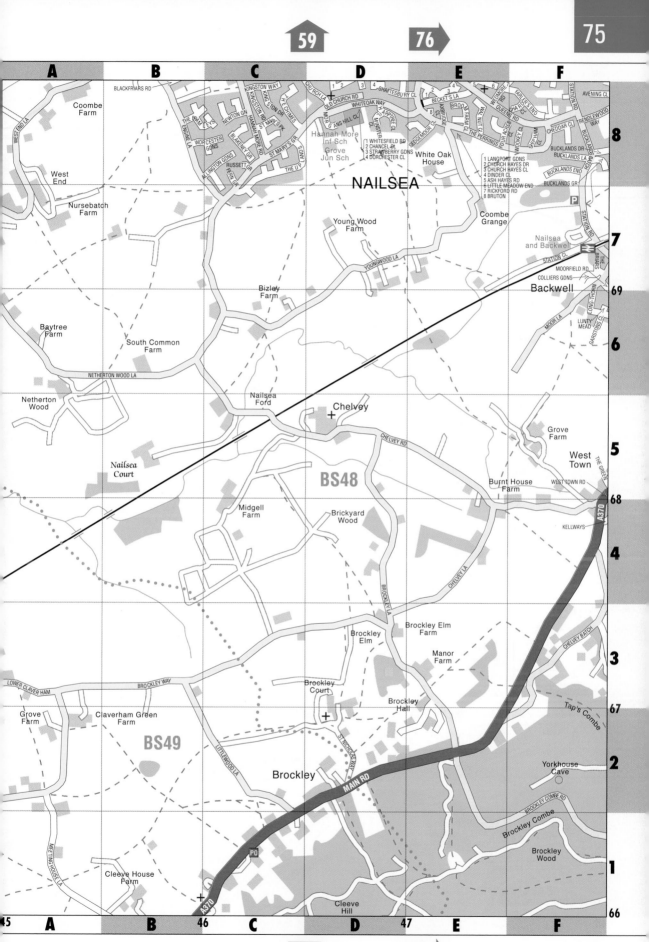

A B C D E F

8

Birdlip Cl
Fowey Cl
Avening Cl
Buckland's View
Buck Lanes View
Dibden's Farm
Schrubbets Farm
Cider House
Backwell Common
Depot
LC
Flax Bourton CE Prim Sch
Priory Farm
Church Lane End
Church La

7

Combe Side
Moorside Farm
The Croft
Woolleys Farm
Hunts Farm
Backwell Green
Backwell House
Backwell
Farleigh
Chapel Hill
George Cl
Stancombe La
Castle Cl
Rice Cl
Main Rd
The Grange
Bourton Combe
A370
Flax Bourton
Parsons Mead

69

Moor La
Station Rd
Westfield Rd
Westmaven Cl
Meadow Cl
Backwell Sch
Fairfield Mead
Linem Way
Unicombe Cl

6

West Leigh Inf Sch
Westfield Dr
Mariners Cl
Mariners Dr
The Crescent
Orchard Dr
Ctr
Liby
Farleigh Rd
Fairfield Sch
Backwell Down
Farleigh Combe Manor
Cherry Wood
Bourton Combe

5

Rushmoor La
Bramley Dr
PO
West Town Rd
St Andrews Rd
St John Sq
Summerlands
Dark La
Backwell
Backwell CE Sch
Church La
Church Town
Quarry
Backwell Hill Rd
BS48
Quarry
The Conygar

68

Kelway
Pit Ln
Robinson Cl
Rope Wlk
Karen Cl
Oakleigh Cl
Hill
Dale Rd
Hillside Rd
A370
PH
The Green
Church Town
Cheston Combe
Water Catch Farm

4

Chelvey Farm
Pit La
Quarry
Backwell Hill
The Spinney

3

Chelvey Batch
Mast
Backwell Hill House
Hyatt's Wood
Hyattswood Farm

67

Home Farm
Backwell Hill
Long La
Quarry
Hyatts Wood Rd

2

Healls Scars
Spinnings Rd
Edson's Farm
Oatfield Pool

1

Brockley Wood
Brockley Combe Rd
The Batch
Willis's Batch
Downside Rd
The Batch
Oatfield Farm
Oatfield Wood
Oxfield

66

Warren Plantation
Downside House Farm
Downside

48 A B 49 C D 50 E F

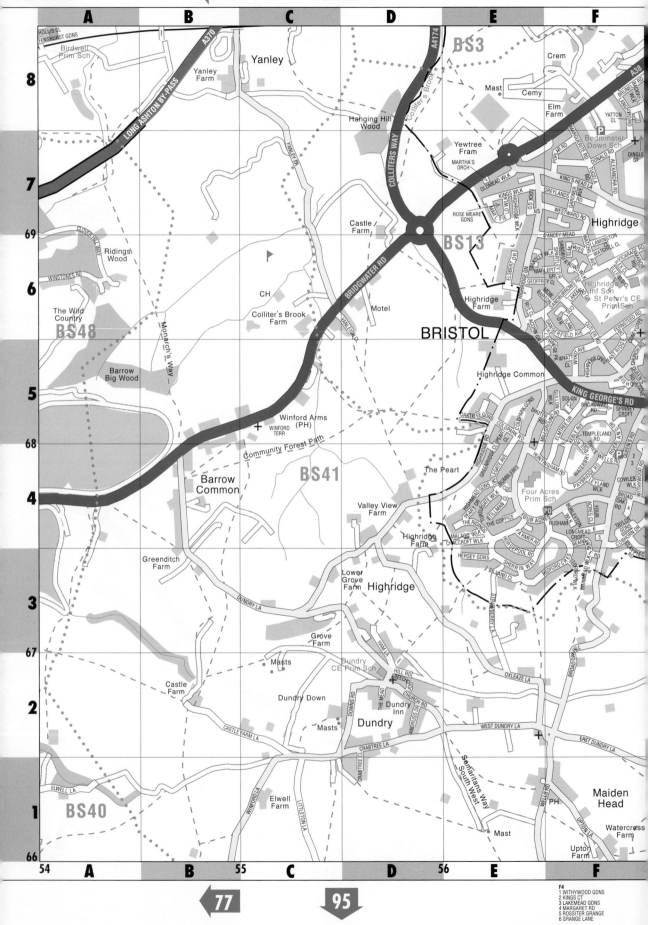

A B C D E F

8

7

69

6

BS48

5

68

4

3

67

2

1

BS40

66

Long Ashton By-Pass
A370
Yanley
Yanley Farm
Hollis Cl
Fenshurst Gdns
Birdwell Prim Sch

BS3
Crem
Mast
Cemy
Elm Farm
A38
Brunel Way
Langford Rd
Yatton Cl
Dingle Ct

Colliters Way
Colliter's Brook
Hanging Hill Wood
Yewtree Fram
Martha's Orch
Oldmead Wlk
Kings Wlk
Highbridge Wlk
Rose Meare Gdns

Castle Farm
BS13
Highridge
King's Head La
Westward Rd
D'Ancey Mead
Lamington Cl
Vicarage Rd

Bridgwater Rd
Motel
Highridge Farm
BRISTOL
Highridge Inf Sch
St Peter's CE Prim Sch
Fernstead Rd

Ridings Wood
Winstones Rd
CH
Colliter's Brook Farm

The Wild Country
BS48
Monarch's Way
Barrow Big Wood

Highridge Common
King George's Rd
Oaktree Gdns
Broadwall Rd
Spinney Croft

Winford Arms (PH)
Winford Terr
Community Forest Path
BS41

The Peart
Four Acres Prim Sch
Cowleb Wlk
Broad Oak Cl

Barrow Common
Valley View Farm
Highridge Farm
Malago Wlk
Chalcroft Wlk
The Ridings
The Coppice
Four Acres
Farmer Rd
Rusham
Longmead Croft
Taylor Gdns
Common Dr

Greenditch Farm
Lower Grove Farm
Highridge
Hersey Gdns
Sherrin Wy
Billand Cl
Redford Cres
Strawberry La

Dundry La
Grove Farm
Masts
Dundry CE Prim Sch
Hill Rd
Oxleaze La
Broad Oak Hill

Castle Farm
Dundry Down
Masts
The Mead
Dundry Inn
Dundry
West Dundry La
East Dundry La

Castle Farm La
Downs Rd
Church Rd
Andruss Dr
Crabtree La

Elwell La
BS40
Winford Rd La
Elwell Farm
Littleton La
Crabtree Cl

Samaritans Way South West
Wells Rd
PH
Maiden Head
Watercress Farm
Mast
Upton Farm

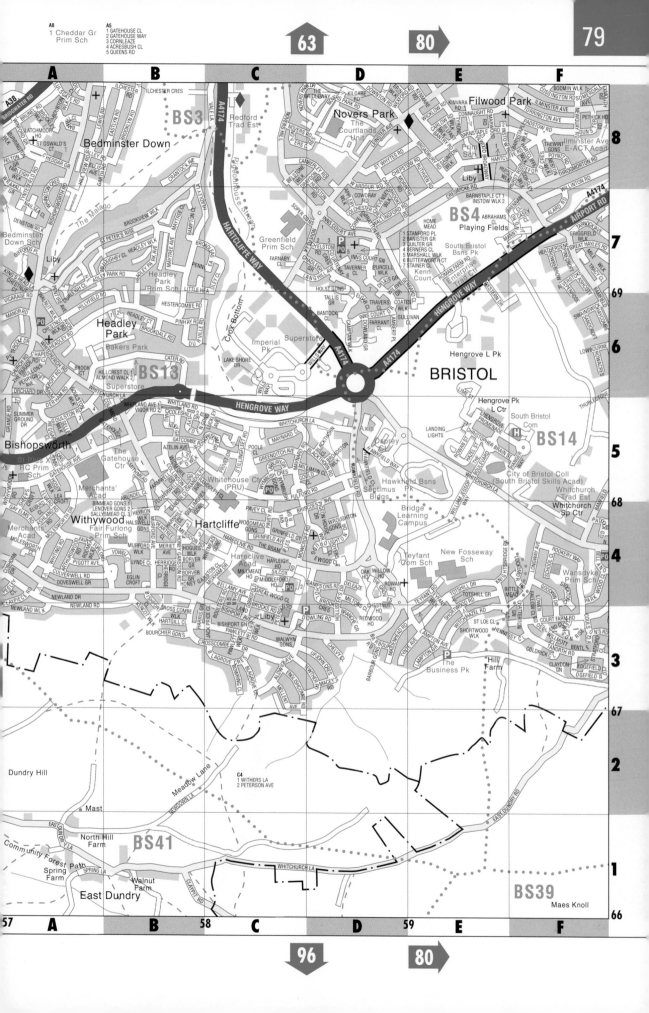

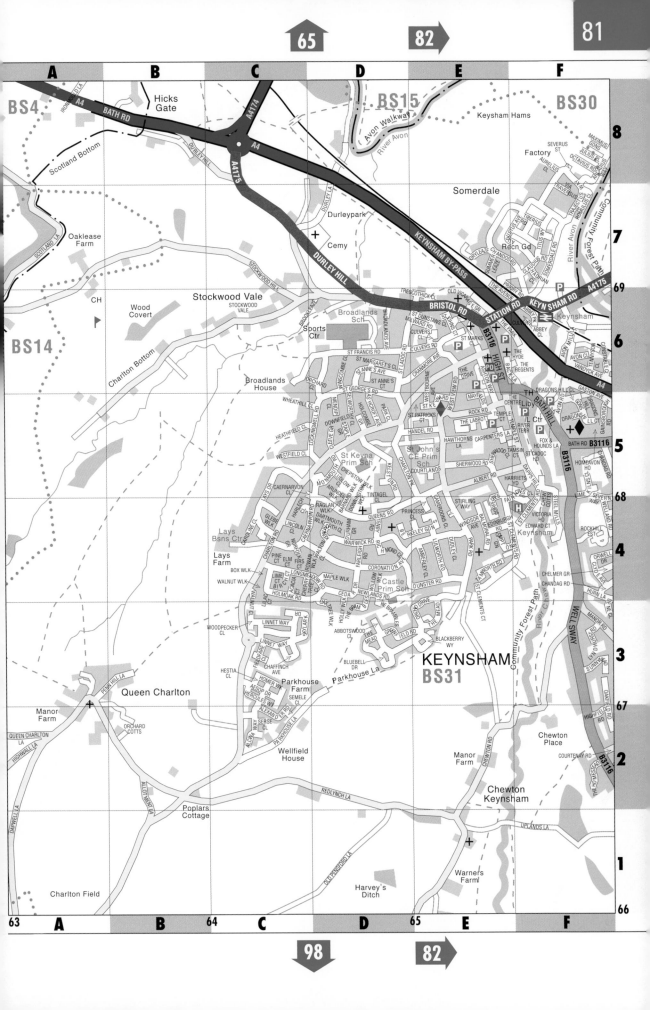

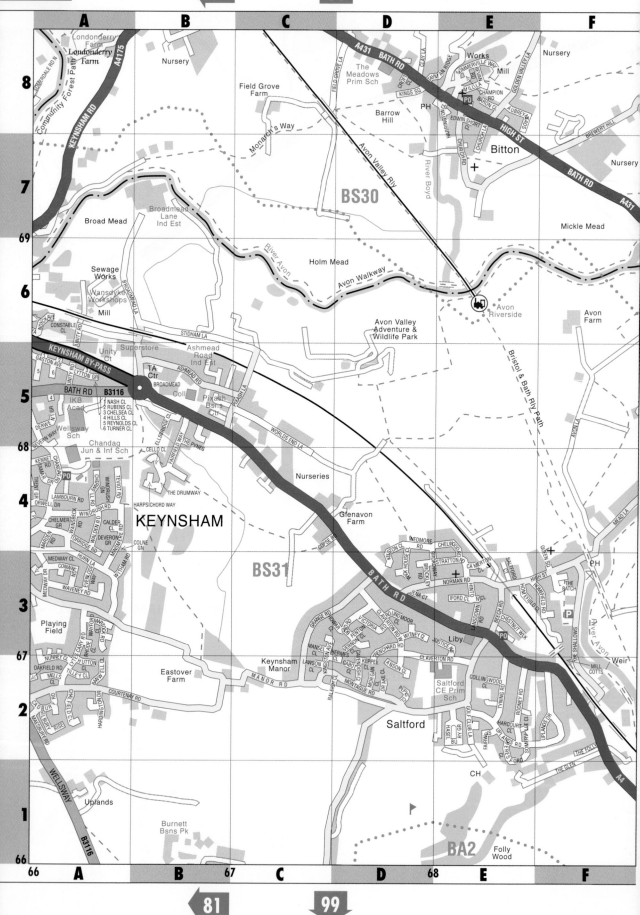

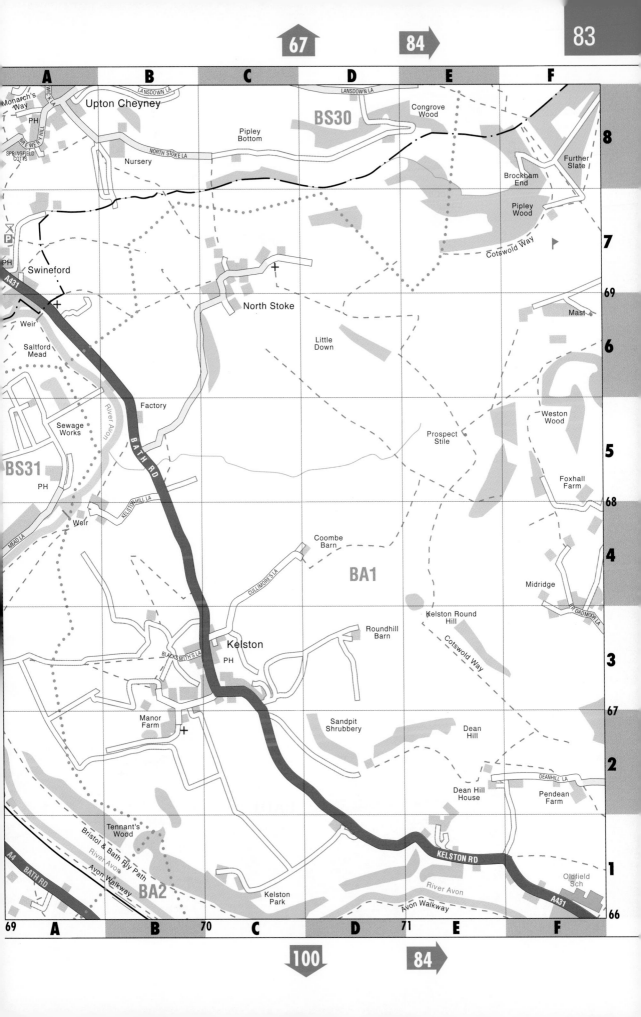

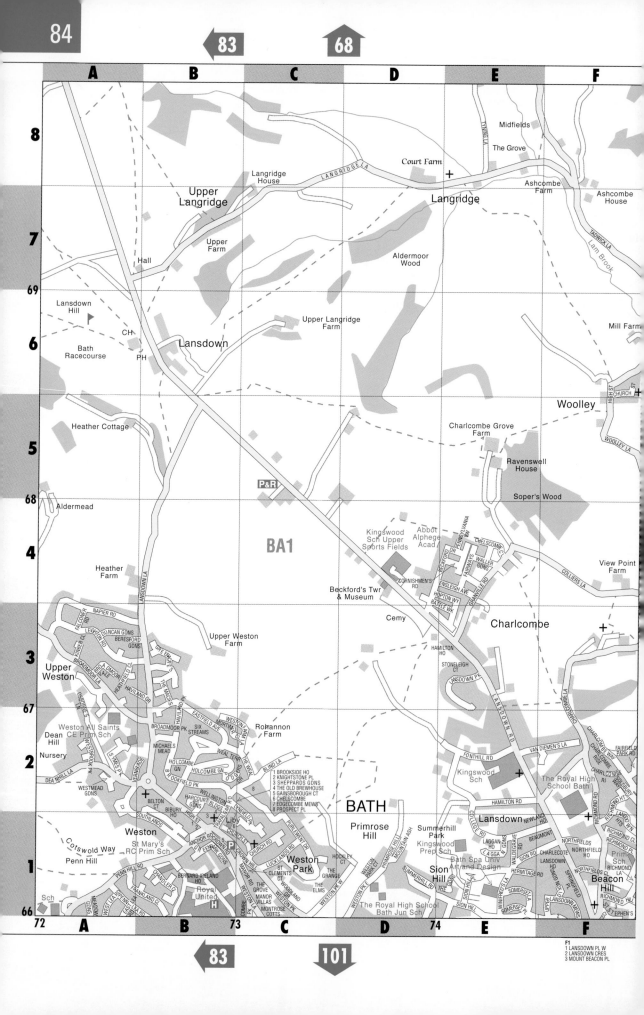

A B C D E F

8

Midfields
The Grove
Court Farm
Langridge
Ashcombe Farm
Ashcombe House
Langridge House
Upper Langridge
LANGRIDGE LA
TADWICK LA
Lam Brook
TYNING LA

7

Upper Farm
Hall
Aldermoor Wood

69

Mill Farm
Lansdown Hill
CH
Upper Langridge Farm
Lansdown
Bath Racecourse
PH

6

Woolley
HIGH ST
CHURCH
WOOLLEY LA
Charlcombe Grove Farm
Heather Cottage
Ravenswell House
Soper's Wood

5

68

Aldermead
P&R

BA1

Kingswood Sch Upper Sports Fields
Abbot Alphege Acad
PENNSYLVANIA W
CHELSCOMBE C
View Point Farm
COLLIERS LA

4

Heather Farm
LANSDOWN LA
BECKFORD DR
FAIRWAYS
WALLER GDNS
ENSLEIGH AVE
GRANVILLE RD
Beckford's Twr & Museum
CORNISHMEN'S RD
HOPTON WY
BATTLE WK
Cemy
Charlcombe
HAMILTON HO
STONELEIGH CT
LANSDOWN PK

3

Upper Weston
NAPIER RD
FALCONER RD
LEIGHTON RD
DUNCAN GDNS
BERESFORD GDNS
KIMBER RD
BROADMOOR LA
BROCK LE
DMOOR
HEATHBRAE CL
HAVILAND GR
GRE ENB
Upper Weston Farm
CHARLCOMBE LA
LANSDOWN RD

67

Weston All Saints CE Prim Sch
Dean Hill
Nursery
DEA DHILL LA
WESTBROOK PK
OSPRING S
LYNES PK
BROADMOOR PK
MICHAELS MEAD
HOLCOMBE GN
THE MALLS
HAVILAND
EASTFIELD AVE
MORTIMER CL
SIX STREAMS
WESTON LA
HIGH ST
THE WEAL
Rohannon Farm
FONTHILL RD
VAN DIEMEN'S LA
Kingswood Sch
CHARLCOMBE RISE
CHARLCOMBE WAY
FAIRFIELD PARK RD

2

WESTMEAD GDNS
BELTON CT
BIBURY HO
HARCOURT BLDGS
TRAFALGAR RD
HIGH ST
HOLCOMBE GN
BROOKFIELD PK
WELLINGTON RD
WEAL TERR
PURDO'S
LONGFIELD
BLIND LA
1 BROOKSIDE HO
2 KNIGHTSTONE PL
3 SHEPPARDS GDNS
4 THE OLD BREWHOUSE
5 GAINSBOROUGH CT
6 CHELSCOMBE
7 EDGECOMBE MEWS
8 PROSPECT PL
BATH
Primrose Hill
Summerhill Park
Kingswood Prep Sch
Bath Spa Univ Art and Design
HAMILTON RD
COLLEGE RD
Lansdown
NEWLAND
BEAUMONT
LAGGAN GA GGA
WALDEGRAVE RD
CHARLECOTE
LANSDOWN HO
NORTHFIELDS
Northfield HO
The Royal High School Bath
RICHMOND LA
RICHMOND RD
RICHMOND PL
Prim Sch
Richmond
Beacon Hill

1

Cotswold Way
Penn Hill
St Mary's RC Prim Sch
Weston
ANCHOR RD
BERNARD IRELAND HO
Royal United
H
CHANDLER CL
FRANKLAND CL
PENN HILL RD
WEST LA
REDFERN CL
MEADOW
CROWN HILL
CHURCH RD
MANOR RD
WESTON PK
Weston Park
LUCKLANDS RD
THE GRANGE
MANOR VILLAS
MONTROSE COTTS
ST CLEMENTS CT
WOODLAND
HOCKLEY CT
THE ELMS
PRIMROSE HILL
MOUNTAIN ASH
SUMMERHILL RD
Sion Hill
SION HILL PL
HERMITAGE RD
WINIFRED'S LA
SOMERSET
UPPER LANSDOWN MEWS
SPRINGFIELD PL
ST STEPHEN'S RD
Richmond

66

Sch
MEADOWS
The Royal High School Bath Jun Sch

A   73   B   C   D   74   E   F

F1
1 LANSDOWN PL W
2 LANSDOWN CRES
3 MOUNT BEACON PL

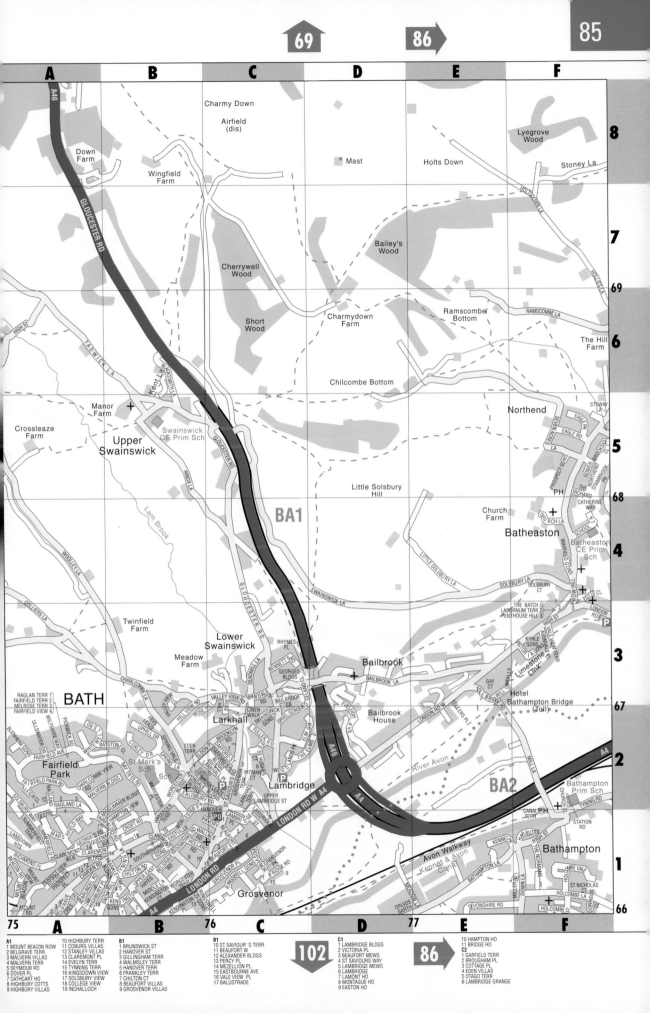

A1
1 MOUNT BEACON ROW
2 BELGRAVE TERR
3 MALVERN VILLAS
4 MALVERN TERR
5 SEYMOUR RD
6 DOVER PL
7 CATHCART HO
8 HIGHBURY COTTS
9 HIGHBURY VILLAS
10 HIGHBURY TERR
11 COBURG VILLAS
12 STANLEY VILLAS
13 CLAREMONT PL
14 EVELYN TERR
15 TYNNING TERR
16 KINGSDOWN VIEW
17 SOLSBURY VIEW
18 COLLEGE VIEW
19 INCHALLOCH

B1
1 BRUNSWICK ST
2 HANOVER ST
3 GILLINGHAM TERR
4 WALMSLEY TERR
5 HANOVER TERR
6 FRANKLEY TERR
7 CHILTON CT
8 BEAUFORT VILLAS
9 GROSVENOR VILLAS

B1
10 ST SAVIOUR'S TERR
11 BEAUFORT W
12 ALEXANDER BLDGS
13 PERCY PL
14 MEZELLION PL
15 EASTBOURNE AV
16 VALE VIEW PL
17 BALUSTRADE

C1
1 LAMBRIDGE BLDGS
2 VICTORIA PL
3 BEAUFORT MEWS
4 ST SAVIOURS WAY
5 LAMBRIDGE MEWS
6 LAMBRIDGE
7 LAMONT HO
8 MONTAGUE HO
9 EASTON HO

10 HAMPTON HO
11 BRIDGE HO
C2
1 GARFIELD TERR
2 BROUGHAM PL
3 COTTAGE PL
4 EDEN VILLAS
5 OTAGO TERR
6 LAMBRIDGE GRANGE

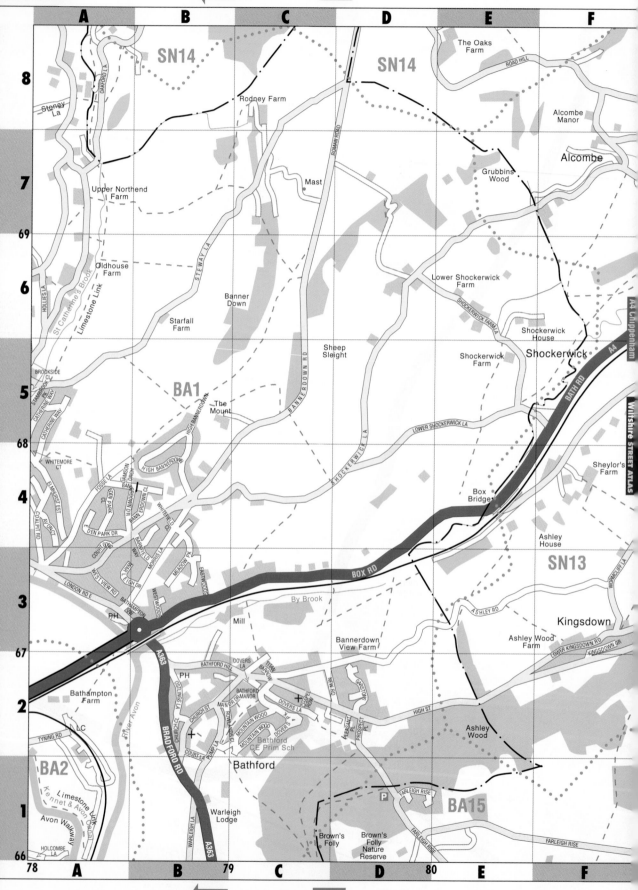

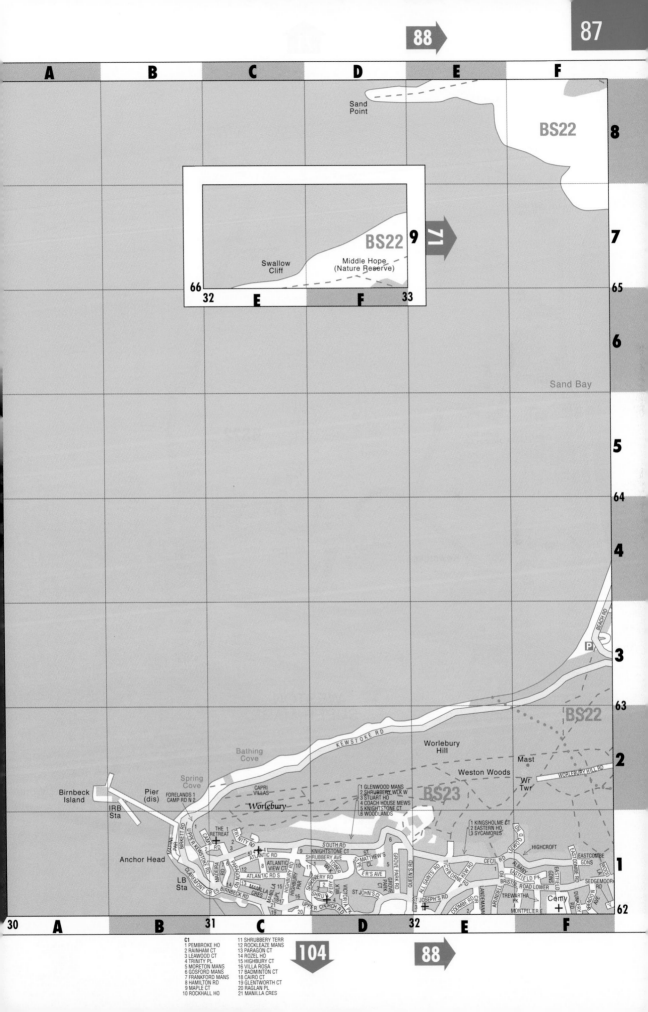

A   B   C   D   E   F

Sand Point

BS22   8

BS22 9 LL   7

Swallow   Middle Hope
Cliff   (Nature Reserve)

66   65

32   E   F   33

6

Sand Bay

5

64

4

BEACH RD

P   3

BS22   63

KEWSTOKE RD   Worlebury
                        Hill   Mast   2

Bathing   Weston Woods   Wr
Cove   Twr   WORLEBURY HILL RD

Spring   CAPRI   1 GLENWOOD MANS
Cove   VILLAS   2 SHRUBBERY WLK W   BS23
Birnbeck   Pier   FORELANDS 1   3 STUART HO
Island   (dis)   CAMP RD N 2   Worlebury   4 COACH HOUSE MEWS
                                                        5 KNIGHTSTONE CT
IRB   6 WOODLANDS   1 KINGSHOLME CT
Sta   THE 1   2 EASTERN HO
                      RETREAT   3 SYCAMORES
                           1   SOUTH RD ST   HIGHCROFT   EASTCOMBE
            TRINITY RD   3   KNIGHTSTONE CT MATTHEW'S   GDNS
                           2   ATLANTIC RD   9   CL   CECIL RD   ALBANY
Anchor Head   5   5 GROVE   EASTFIELD PK
                              ATLANTIC   10 11 TOWER R'S AVE PARK QUEEN'S RD   1
                              VIEW CT S   WLK   RD   BRISTOL ROAD LOWER   SEDGEMOOR
LB   13   ATLANTIC RD S 12 SHRUBBERY RD   ST JOHN'S   ST JOSEPH'S RD   RD
Sta   15   16 14 ST JOHN'S C   MONTPELIER E Cemy   62

30   A   B   31   C   D   32   E   F

C1
1 PEMBROKE HO   11 SHRUBBERY TERR
2 RAINHAM CT   12 ROCKLEAZE MANS
3 LEAWOOD CT   13 PARAGON CT
4 TRINITY PL   14 ROZEL HO
5 MORETON MANS   15 HIGHBURY CT
6 GOSFORD MANS   16 VILLA ROSA
7 FRANKFORD MANS   17 BADMINTON CT
8 HAMILTON RD   18 CAIRO CT
9 MAPLE CT   19 GLENTWORTH CT
10 ROCKHALL HO   20 RAGLAN PL
                       21 MANILLA CRES

F2
1 COTMAN WLK
2 WESTWOOD CL
3 BLACKMOOR
4 APPLEDORE
5 BAMPTON
6 KENNFORD
7 KNIGHTSTONE PL

A B C D E F

8
7
65
6
5
64
4
3
63
2
1
62

BS21
Tutshill Ear
Yeo Bank Farm
River Yeo
Oldbridge River
Sluice Farm
Hippisley's Farm
Bourton
Manor Farm
New Ear La
Wick Road
Manor Farm
New Ear La
The Round Pond
The Lawns
A370
BS24
Haybow Farm
Doubleton Farm Cotts
Rolstone
Stuntree Farm
West Rolstone Rd
Poplar Farm
Rolstone Farm
Way Wick

Lower Wick Farm
Warth La
Middle La
Ducks La
Icelton Farm
East Town Rhyne
Icelton
Appleton Farm
Council Hos.
Wick Rd
Cedar Farm
East-town Farm
Rose Court
Cypress Farm
Wick St Lawrence
Yeo Bank La
Hoopers La
Dolecroft La
M5
Banfield Farm
Ebdon Court Farm
Ebdon
Ebdon Farm
1 Foxglove Cl
2 Lavender Cl
3 Yarrow Ct
Ebdon Lane Farm
Court Farm
Willow Farm
BS22
Ebdon La
Oxhouse Ind Est
Lynchmead Farm
Com Prim Sch
WESTON-SUPER-MARE
Castle Batch
Brimbleworth Farm
St Georges
The Burrows
River Banwell
1 Spencer Dr
2 Rudhall Gn
Priory Com Sch
Ind Est
PO
Superstores
Queensway Ctr
Commercial Way
Bristol Rd
Bristol Road Bridge
B3440
New Bristol Rd
Park Way
Worle
B3440
Somerset Ave
West Wick
Red Lodge Bsns Pk
21
A370
Haybow
Poplar Farm
Rolstone
1 Sunnybank Ct
2 Apple Farm La
3 Weston Gateway Tourist Pk
4 Blackburn Way
5 Westley Ms
6 Barker Cl
Sunnybank Way
Hedge Cl
West Wick
Scot Elm Dr
M5

A2
1 KENNFORD
2 ST CLEMENTS CT
3 KINGSWEAR
4 BAMPTON
5 CREDITON
6 FENITON
7 INSTOW
8 IVYBRIDGE
9 HONITON
10 EXBOURNE
11 COLYTON
12 DALWOOD
13 DOWLAND
14 HARTLAND
15 EBDEN LO

B4
1 WELLARD CL
2 TYLER GN
3 TREMLETT MEWS
4 GARNER CT
5 WAINWRIGHT CL
6 EMLYN CL
7 THE SAFFRONS

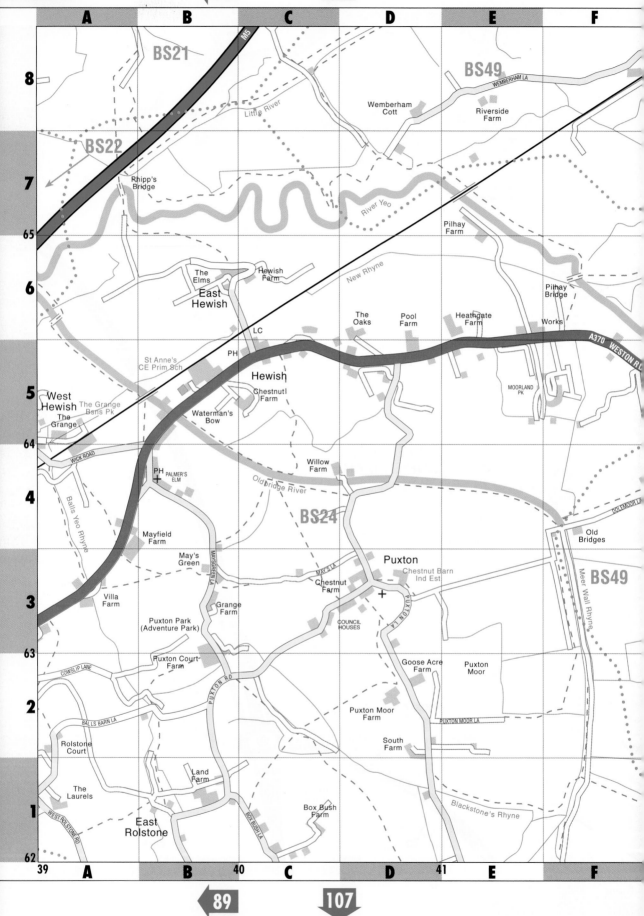

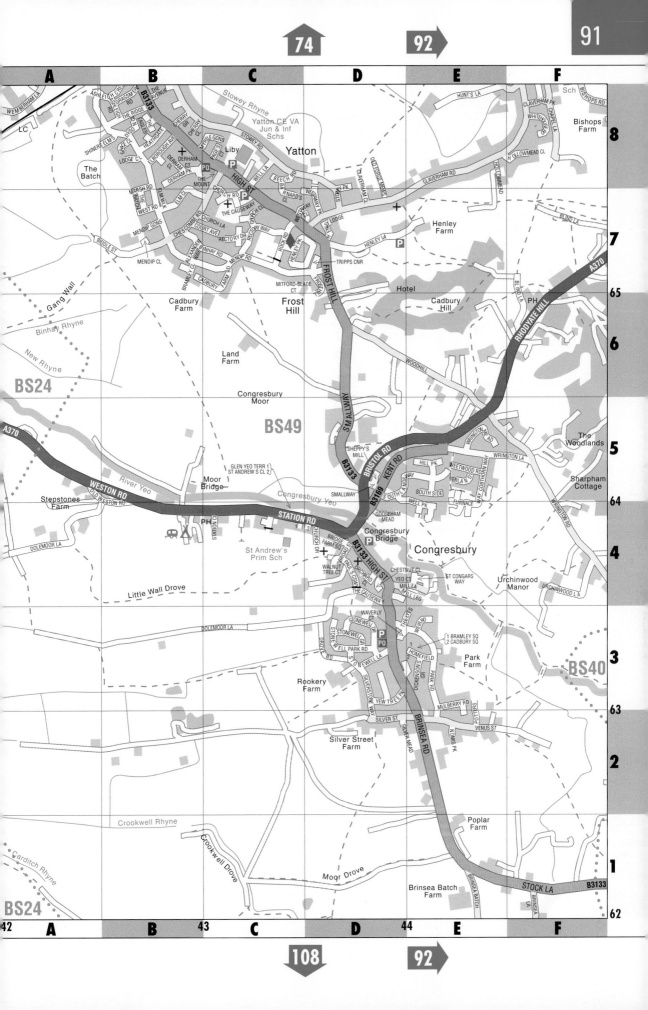

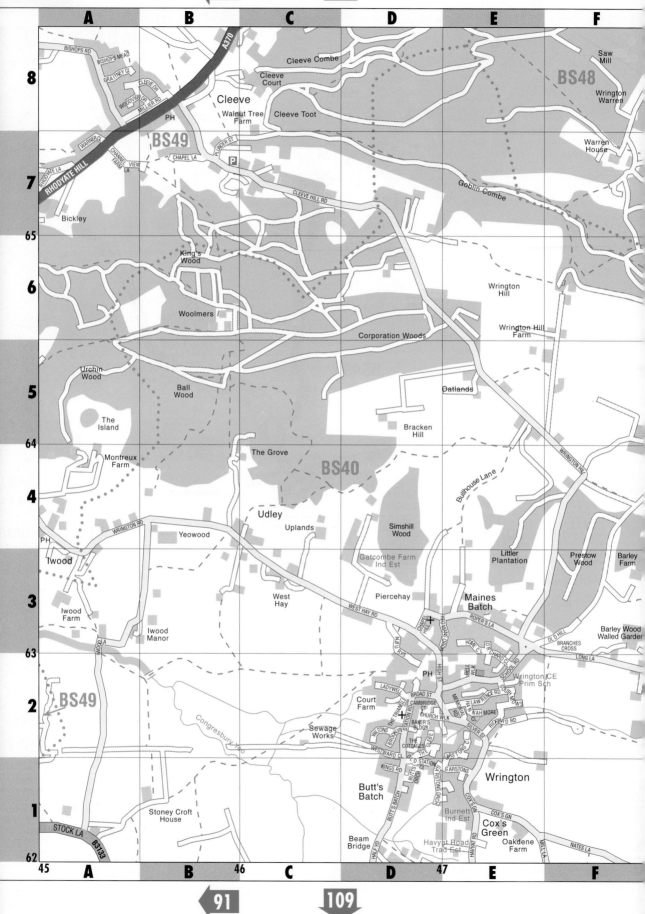

A B C D E F

8

BISHOPS RD
BISHOPS MEAD
GRATTNEY CL
WOODVIEW DR
MILLIER RD

Cleeve Combe
Cleeve Court
Cleeve

Saw Mill

BS48

Wrington Warren

Walnut Tree Farm
Cleeve Toot

Warren House

BS49

CLEEVE DR
CHANNEL FARM
VIEW LA
CHAPEL LA
PLUNDER ST
P
PH

7

RHODYATE HILL
RHODYATE LA
WARNER CL

Cleeve Hill Rd
Goblin Combe

Bickley

65

King's Wood

6

Woolmers

Wrington Hill

Corporation Woods

Wrington Hill Farm

Urchin Wood

5

Ball Wood

Oatlands

The Island

Bracken Hill

64

Montreux Farm

The Grove

BS40

Bullhouse Lane

4

Udley

Uplands

Simshill Wood

Littler Plantation

Prestow Wood

Barley Farm

PH
Twood

WRINGTON RD

Yeowood

Gatcombe Farm Ind Est

Piercehay

Maines Batch

ROPER'S LA

3

Iwood Farm

West Hay

WEST HAY RD

CHAPEL HILL
BROAD HILL
HOME CL
OLD HILL
BRANCHES CROSS

Barley Wood Walled Garden

Iwood Manor

WOOD LA

HIGH ST
CHARD CL RD
SCHOOL RD
LONG LA
Wrington CE Prim Sch

63

BS49

LADYWELL
BROAD ST
PH
MEADOW CL
LAWRENCE RD
RICKYARD RD

2

Congresbury Yeo

Court Farm
THE TRIANGLE
CAMBRIDGE CT
CHURCH WLK
SILVER ST
WAH MORE

Sewage Works

BAKER'S BLDGS
THE COTTAGES

WILTONS
BROOKLYN
STATION RD
WESTWARD CL
OLD STATION CL
GARSTONS ORCH
GARSTONS

Wrington

1

Stoney Croft House

BUTT'S BATCH
KINGS RD
BUTT'S BECH
HALF YD
HAVYAT RD
COX'S GN
Burnett Ind Est
Cox's Green

Butt's Batch

STOCK LA
B3133

Beam Bridge

Havyat Road Trad Est

Oakdene Farm

MILL LA
NATES LA

62

45 A 46 B C 47 D E F

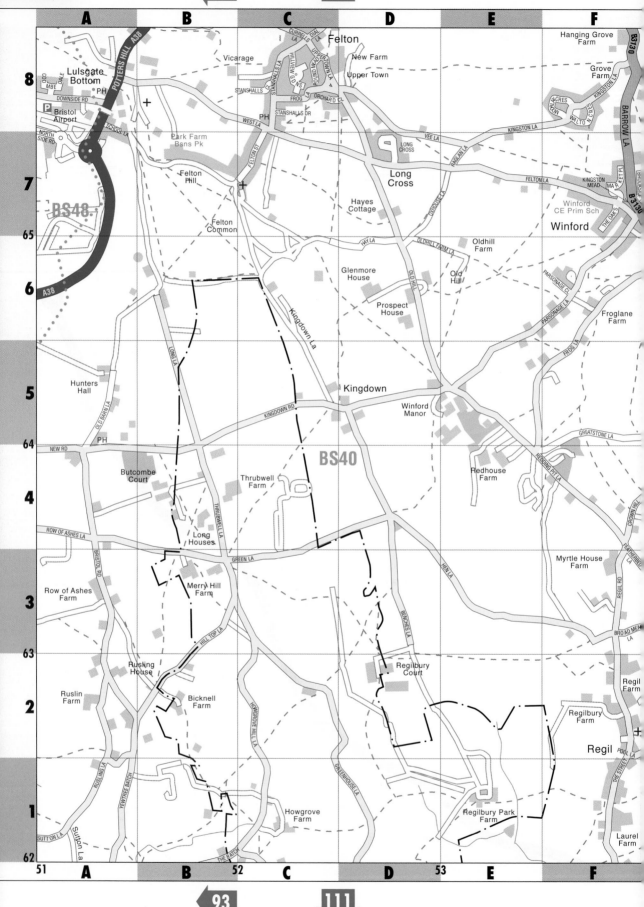

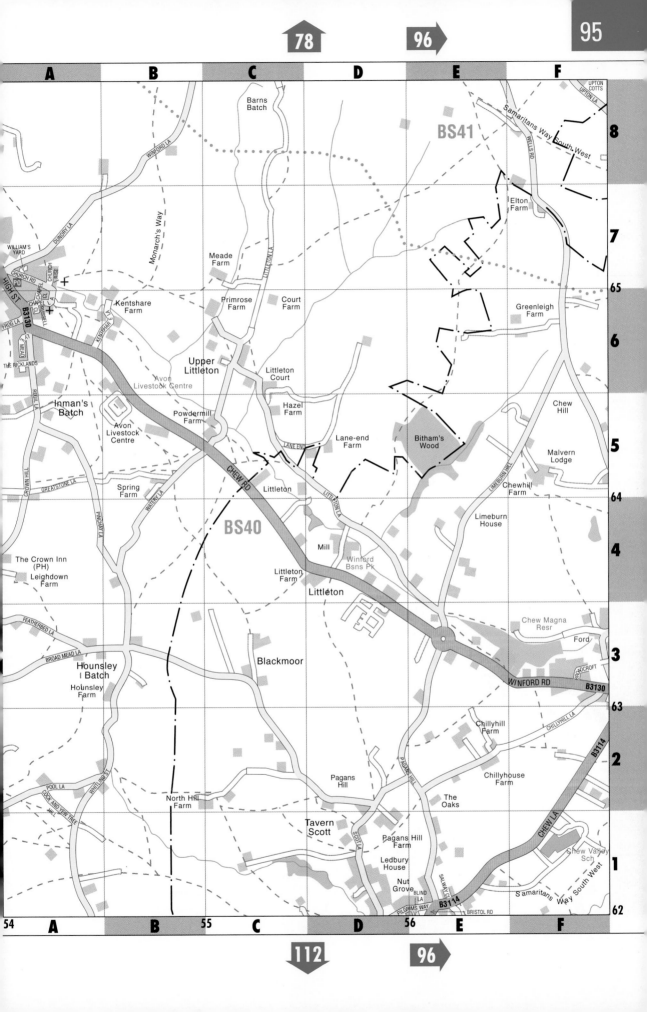

95
79

A B C D E F

8

Waterloo Farm

North Wick

Rattledown Farm

BS41

Yewtree Farm

Model Farm

Maes Knoll Farm

7

Manor Farm

NORTHWICK RD

NORTON LA

Norton Malreward Court

65

Community Forest Path

Norton Hawkfield

6

Samaritans Way South West

Whistley Wood

5

Wr Twr

NORTON LA

64

Blacklands

BS40

BS39

4

North Chew Farm

Halfway Farm

B3130

BUTHAM LA

CHEW HILL

NUTGROVE LA

Fairfield House

NORTH ELM LA

Chew Magna

Stanton Court

3

Chew Magna Prim Sch

STONELEIGH

The Rookery

SPRATTS BRIDGE

SPEARLEAZE

SILVER ST

STREAMSIDE

BUTHAM LA

THE BATCH

NORTON CL

LOWER BATCH

NORTH CHEW TERR

Mill Place

Rosedale

Church Farm

BATTLE LA

HARFORD SQ

PO

CHEW COURT FARM

River Chew

SANDY LA

PH

63

WINFORD RD

CHEW LA

B3114

HIGH ST

CHEW ST

MADAM'S PADDOCK

SOUTH PAR

THE CHALKS

PH

P

PINE CT

Mill

STANTON RD

Bridge Farm

SANDY LA

PH

Tun Bridge

TUNBRIDGE RD

TUNBRIDGE CL

DUMPERS LA

Paradise

TYNING LA

UPPER STANTON

2

Chota Castle

Tunbridge Farm

Vicarage

DENNY LA

PITT'S LA

MOORLEDGE RD

Stanton Drew

BROMLEY RD

HIGHFIELDS

THE DRIVE

THE CRESCENT

1

Roundhill Farm

MOORLEDGE LA

Moorledge

Moorledge Farm

62

95
113

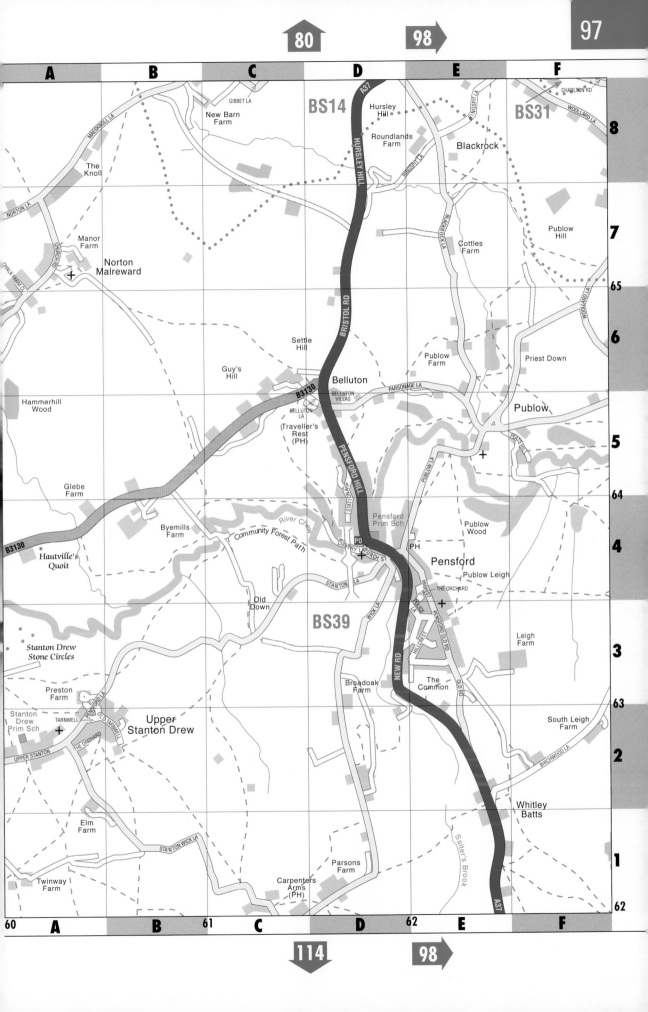

A B C D E F

8

7

65

6

64

5

4

3

63

2

1

62

BS14

BS31

BS39

CHARLTON RD
WOOLLARD LA

Hursley
Hill

Roundlands
Farm

Blackrock

Publow
Hill

Cottles
Farm

Priest Down

Publow
Farm

Publow

Publow
Wood

Publow Leigh

Leigh
Farm

South Leigh
Farm

Whitley
Batts

GIBBET LA

New Barn
Farm

The
Knoll

Manor
Farm

Norton
Malreward

Settle
Hill

Belluton

BELLUTON
VILLAS

BELLUTON
LA

Traveller's
Rest
(PH)

Guy's
Hill

Hammerhill
Wood

Glebe
Farm

Byemills
Farm

Hautville's
Quoit

Community Forest Path

River Chew

Old
Down

Pensford
Prim Sch

PO

PH

Pensford

THE ORCHARD

The
Common

Broadoak
Farm

Stanton Drew
Stone Circles

Preston
Farm

Stanton
Drew
Prim Sch

Upper
Stanton Drew

Tarnwell

Elm
Farm

Twinway
Farm

Carpenters
Arms
(PH)

Parsons
Farm

Salter's Brook

NORTON LA
CHURCH RD
CHALK FARM CL
MAESDOWN LA

BRISTOL RD
HURSLEY HILL
A37

PENSFORD HILL
CHURCH ST
STANTON LA
WICK LA
NEW RD
HILLCREST
HIGH ST
POUND LA
PENSFORD OLD RD
OLD RD
PUBLOW LA
PARSONAGE LA
BLACKROCK LA
KINGSPIT LA
WOOLLARD LA OLD RD
BEAK'S HILL
BIRCHWOOD LA

B3130
B3130

PENSFORD LA
OLD TARNWELL
THE ORCHARD
UPPER STANTON
STANTON WICK LA

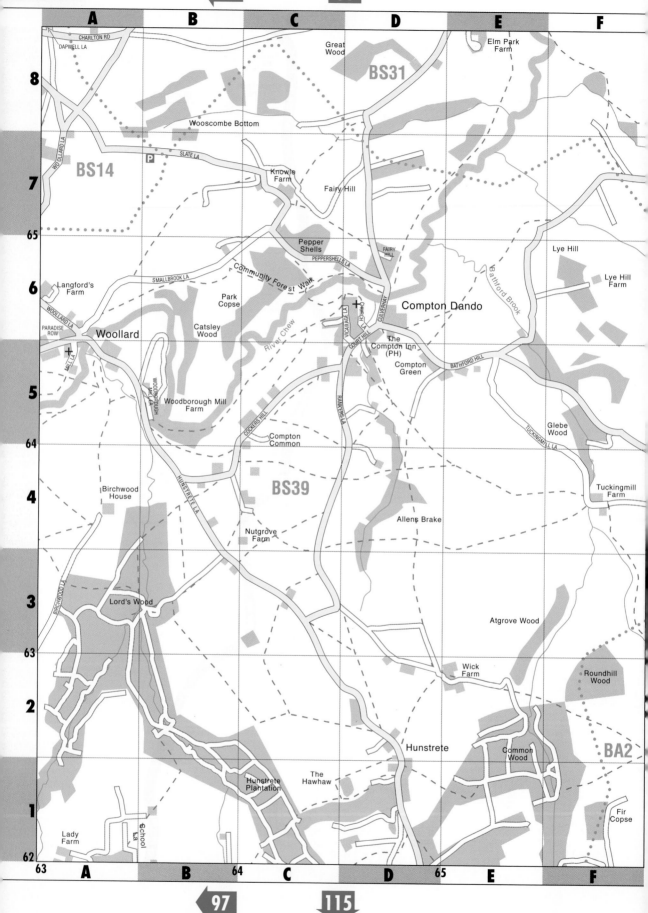

A B C D E F

8

CHARLTON RD
DAPWELL LA

Great
Wood

BS31

Elm Park
Farm

Wooscombe Bottom

7

BS14

SLATE LA

P

Knowle
Farm

Fairy Hill

Lye Hill

65

Pepper
Shells

FAIRY
HILL

PEPPERSHELLS LA

Lye Hill
Farm

SMALLBROOK LA

Community Forest Walk

Bathford Brook

6

Langford's
Farm

Park
Copse

WOOLLARD LA

Compton Dando

River Chew

Catsley
Wood

VICARAGE LA

CHURCH

CULVERWAY

PARADISE
ROW

Woollard

The
Compton Inn
(PH)

Compton
Green

BATHFORD HILL

MILL LA

WOODBOROUGH MILL LA

Woodborough Mill
Farm

COCKERS HILL

RANKERS LA

TUCKINGMILL LA

Glebe
Wood

5

64

Compton
Common

Tuckingmill
Farm

HUNSTRETE LA

BS39

4

Birchwood
House

Allens Brake

BIRCHWOOD LA

Nutgrove
Farm

Atgrove Wood

3

Lord's Wood

Roundhill
Wood

63

Wick
Farm

2

Hunstrete

Common
Wood

BA2

SCHOOL LA

Hunstrete
Plantation

The
Hawhaw

1

Lady
Farm

Fir
Copse

62

63 A B 64 C D 65 E F

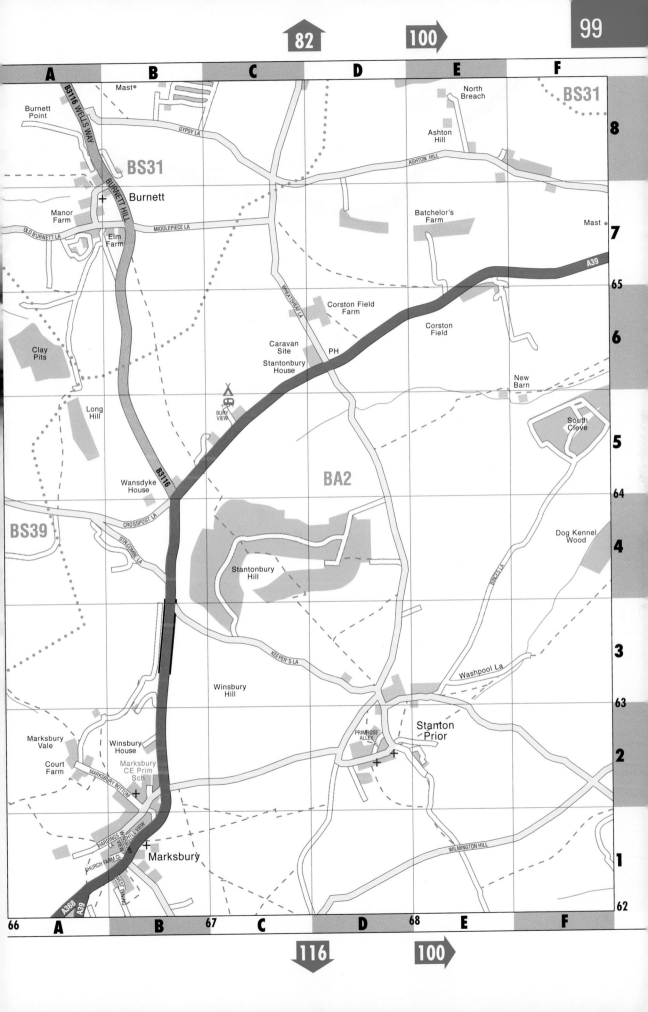

BS31

BA1

A4

BATH RD

New Bridge

PH
P&R

NEWBRIDGE RD

A431
KELSTON RD

A4

HOMEMEAD

BRISTOL RD

Newton Bridge

Avon Walkway

Avon Walkway

LOWER BRISTOL RD

A36

CORSTON LA

GOOLD CL

Corston

THE ORCHARD

THE BARTON

LOWER FARM LA

THE PADDOCK

MEADLANDS

COTTON MEAD

A4

A36

CARRSWOOD VIEW

BRISTOL RD

ASHTON HILL

Church Farm Bsns Pk

WELLS RD

PO

A39

A4

Camp Site

Seven Acre Wood

BROOK COTTS

Long Shrub

PH

Corston Brook

WALING LA

65

Woodenhouse Covert

CHURCH COTTS

VILLAGE RD

WORKSHOP LA

PO

Home Farm

PENNYQUICK

Mill

PENNYQUICK VIEW

RED AS PK

REDL

DAV CRES

CLEEV GN

RED AV PK

HINTON CL

6

Newton Park

Newton St Loe

CLAYS GULLY

Clays End

NEWTON RD

CAMELEY GN

CAMELEY GN

SHAW'S WAY

CORSTON DR

CLAYSEND

BLOYCE CL

TANNERS WLK

LONG A3 CL

B DYCE CL

Sch

Bath Spa University Coll (Newton Park Campus)

P

KEPPELS GATE

Claysend Farm

PENNYQUICK HILL

SHERIDAN RD

GARRICK RD

WEDGWOOD RD

POOL MEAD RD

PO

5

Park Wood

ALEC RICKETTS CL 1
KELSTON VIEW 2
POOLE HO 3
GARRE HO 4

64

St Loc's Castle

BA2

Newton Brook

Whiteway

MORRIS CL

WHITEWAY RD

WASHPOOL LA

4

Haycombe Farm

Whistling Copse

Ashery Gully

Crem

Cemy

TWELVE O'CLOCK LA

Park Farm

HAYCOMBE LA

3

Pennsylvania Farm

Nursery

63

WILMINGTON HILL

Wilmington Farm

Manor Farm

RECTORY FARM LA

Tithe Barn

INN OX GR

2

Englishcombe

Wilmington

Wilmington La

1

62

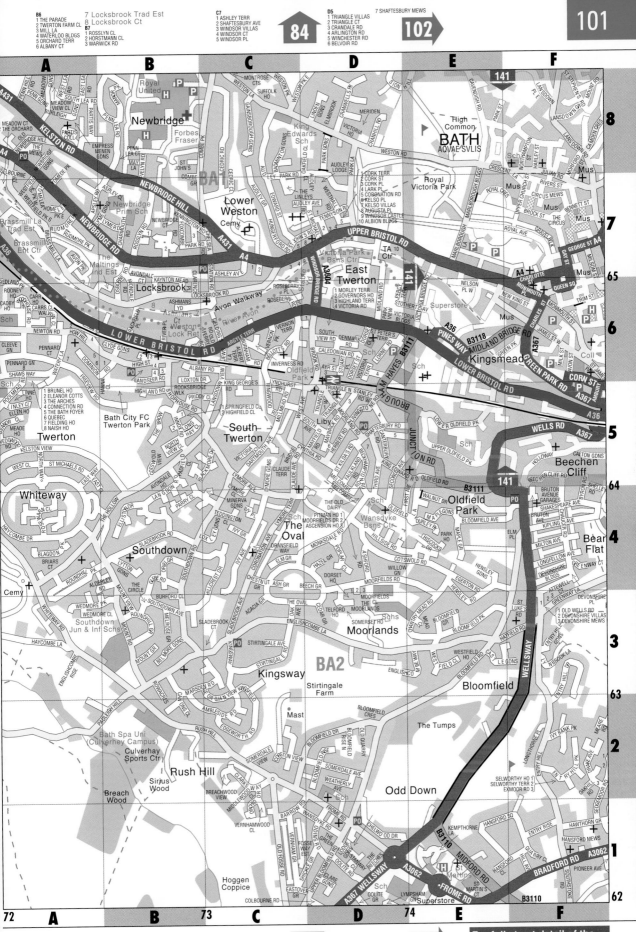

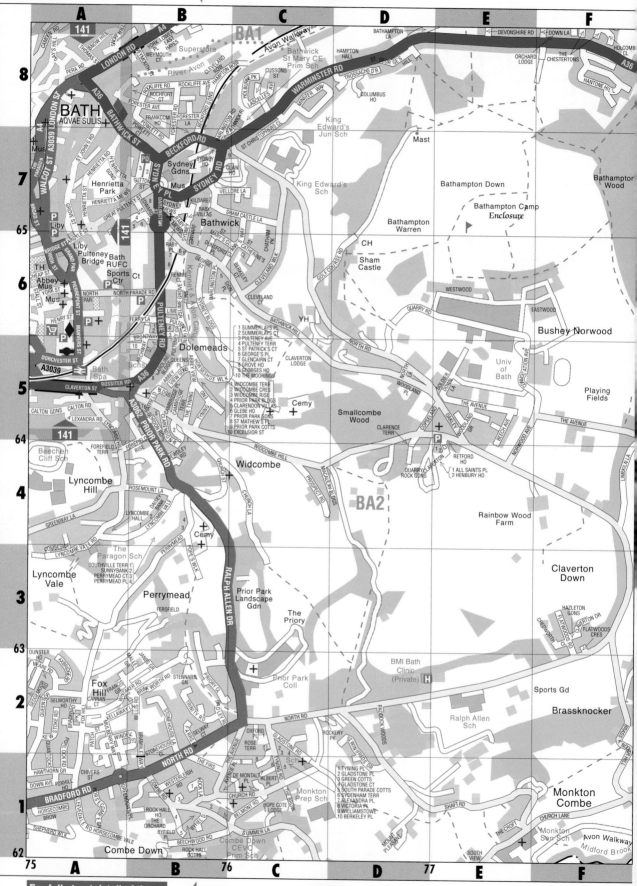

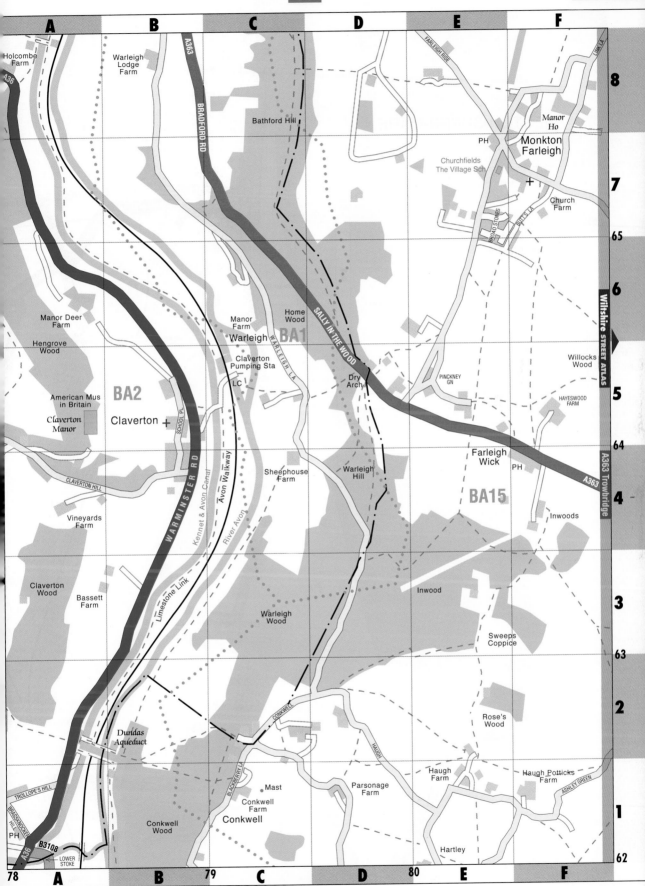

87

121

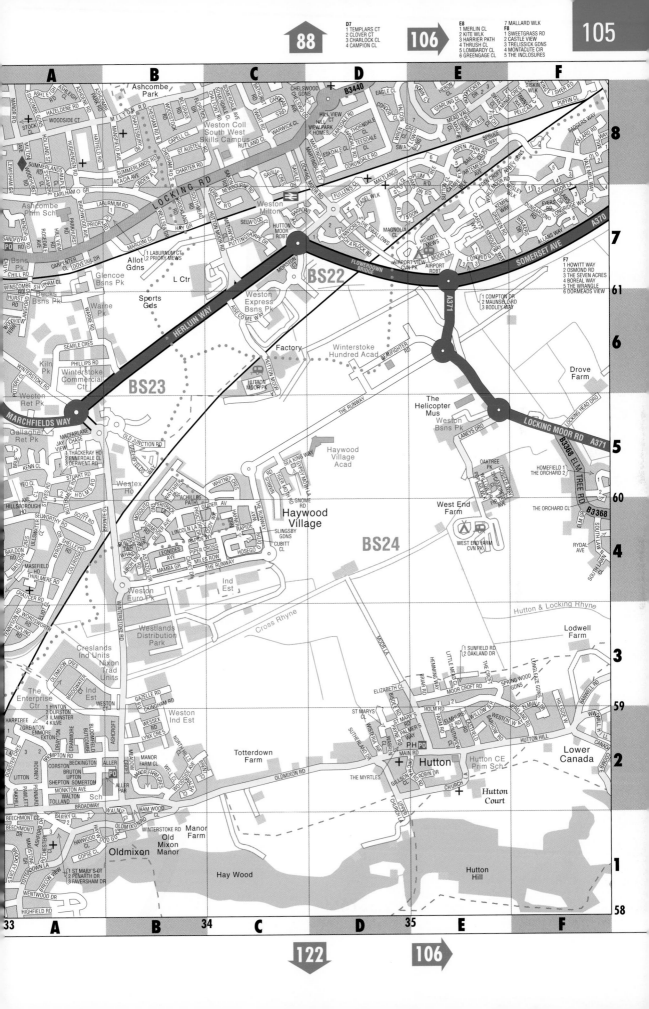

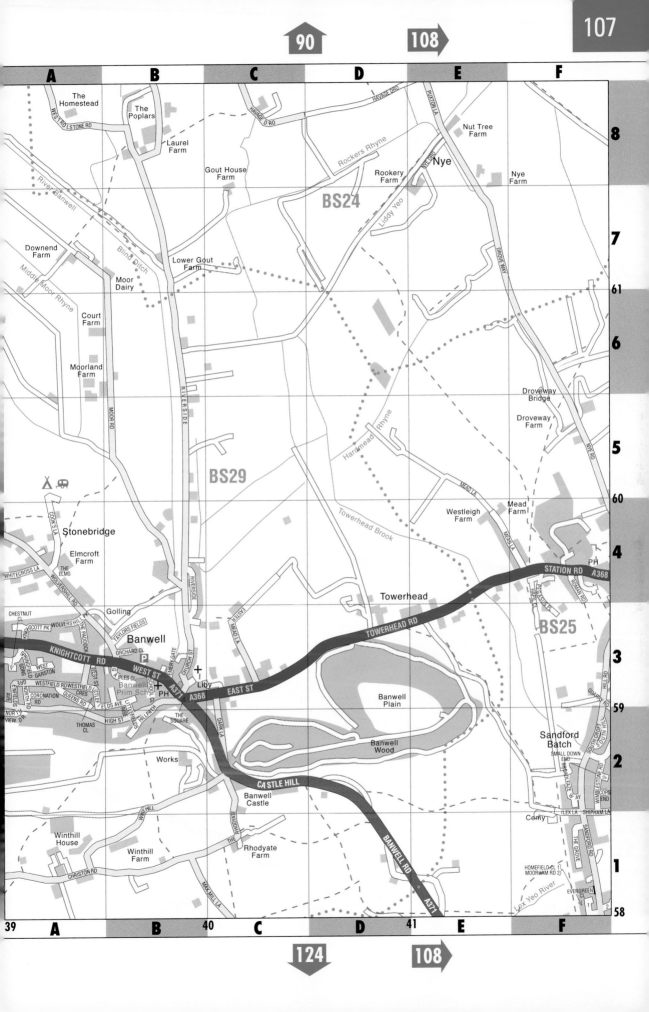

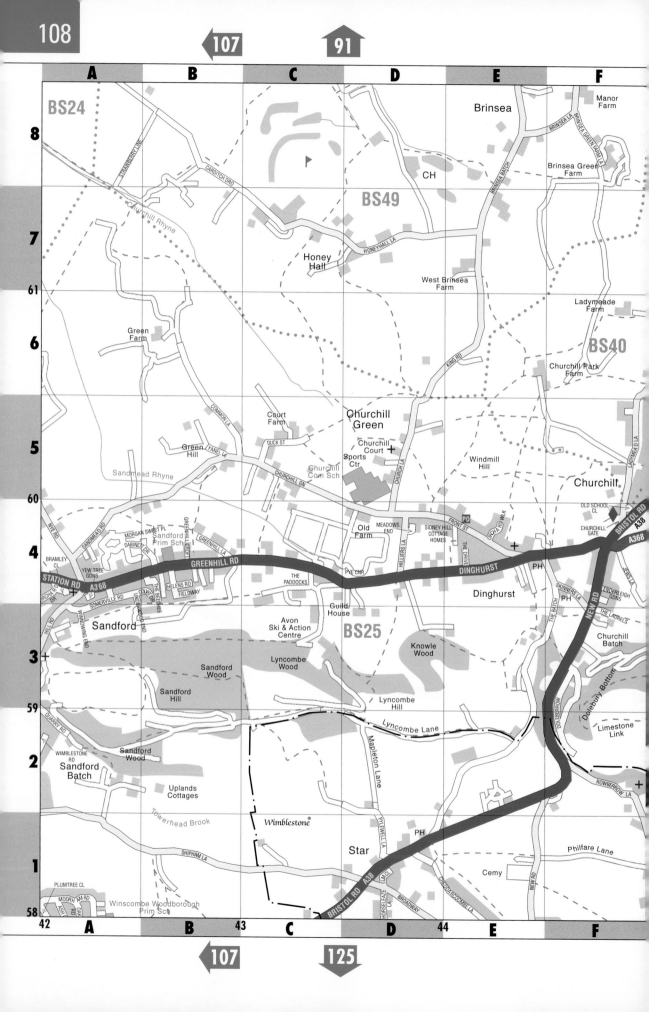

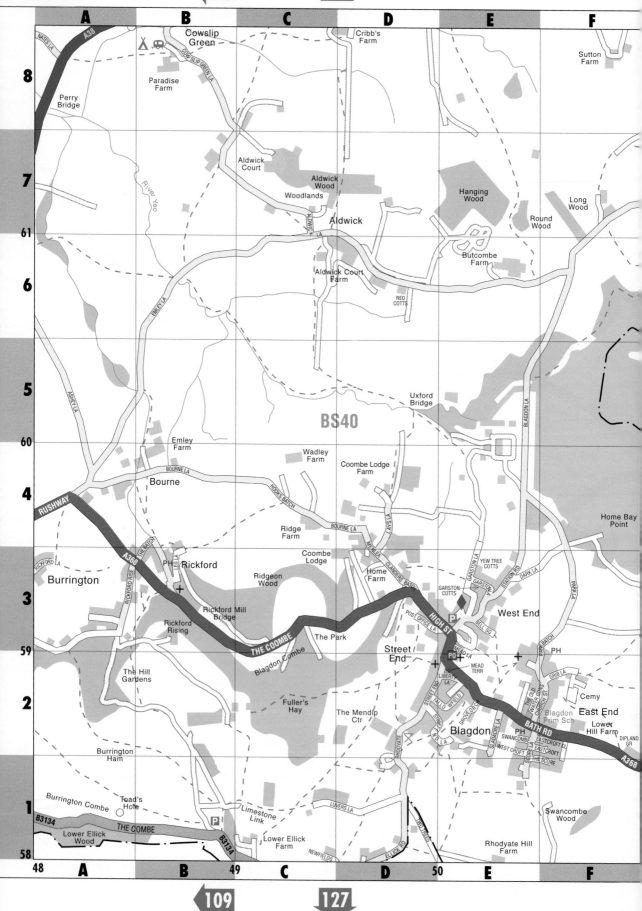

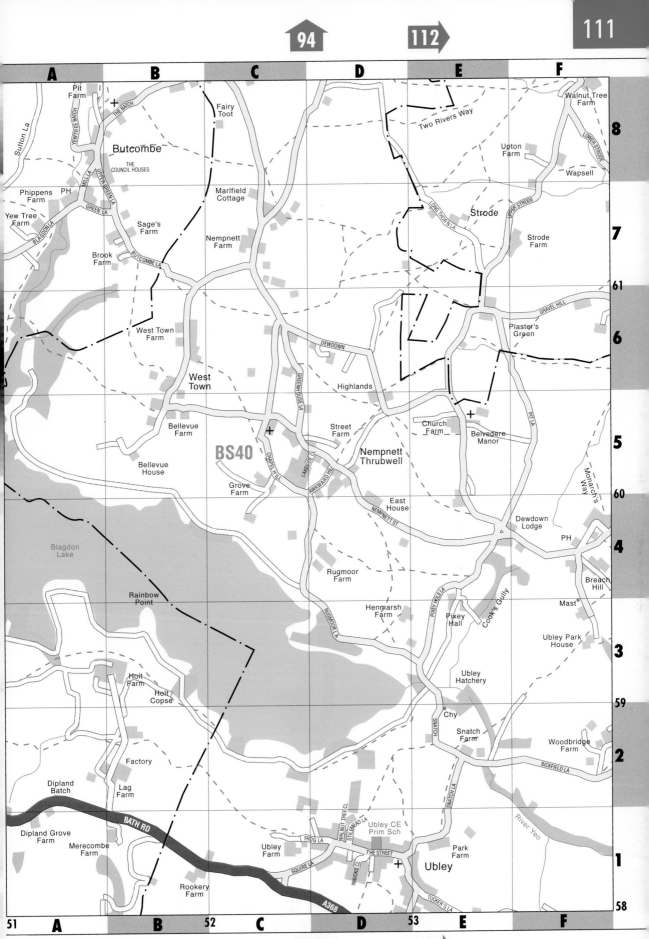

Pit Farm
THE BATCH
YEW TREE BATCH
Fairy Toot
Butcombe
THE COUNCIL HOUSES
Sutton La
MILL LA
Phippens Farm
PH
GREEN LA
Marlfield Cottage
UPPER GREEN LA
Yew Tree Farm
BLAGDON LA
Sage's Farm
Nempnett Farm
Brook Farm
BUTCOMBE LA

Two Rivers Way
Walnut Tree Farm
Upton Farm
LOWER STRODE
Wapsell
Strode
UPPER STRODE
LONG THORN LA
Strode Farm

61

West Town Farm
West Town
DEWDOWN
Highlands
GRAVEL HILL
Plaster's Green

6

Bellevue Farm
GREEN DUSE LA
Street Farm
Church Farm
PIT LA
Belvedere Manor

5

BS40
CHAPEL HILL
LAKESIDE CL
AWKWARD HILL
Nempnett Thrubwell

Bellevue House
Grove Farm
NEMPNETT ST
East House
Dewdown Lodge
PH
Monarch's Way

60

Blagdon Lake
Rugmoor Farm
RUGMOOR LA
Breach Hill
Mast

4

Rainbow Point
Henmarsh Farm
PIXEY POLE LA
Pixey Hall
Cook's Gully
Ubley Park House

3

Holt Farm
Holt Copse
Ubley Hatchery

59

Chy
SNATCH
Snatch Farm
Woodbridge Farm

Factory
BICKFIELD LA

2

Dipland Batch
Lag Farm
Merecombe Farm
BATH RD
Dipland Grove Farm
WALNUT TREE CL
STILE MEAD LA
FROG LA
Ubley CE Prim Sch
SNATCH LA
Park Farm
River Yeo

Ubley Farm
SQUIRE LA
INNICKS CL
THE STREET
Ubley

1

Rookery Farm
A368
TUCKER'S LA

58

111
95

| A | B | C | D | E | F |

8

The Knoll

Lower Strode

Lower Strode Farm

Church Farm

Scot La
PH
Church La
The Cedars
Pilgrims Way

Chew Stoke CE Prim Sch

Webbs Mead

Mill La

Quarry Hay

Works

B3114

Chew Stoke

PO
Chapel

Bristol Rd

Bilbie Cl
Bilbie Rd
Bushy Thorn Rd

Wally Court Rd

Fairseat Workshops

Walley La

7

Manor Farm

Gravel Hill

Shoreditch

Wallis Farm

Stoke Hill House

Scotfield La

Breach Hill La

Stoke Hill

Woodford Hill

Perry House Farm

Lower Strode

Monarch's Way

61

Rose Cottage

Woodford Lodge

6

Stoke Villice

Obelisk

BS40

Rookery Farm

Manor Farm

Caple La

Breach Hill Comm

5

Kings Hill La

Nunnery Copse

60

Breach Hill Common

Breach Hill

4

Herons Green Farm

Herons S Green La

Chew Valley Lake

Monarch's Way

Herons Green

P

Herons Green Bay

Moreton Point

BS39

3

Moreton La

59

Moat Farm

2

Villice La

Bickfield Farm

Bickfield La

Stratford La

1

River Yeo

Summerlea Farm

Oldbarn La

B3114

A368

58

| 54 | A | B | 55 | C | D | 56 | E | F |

111
129

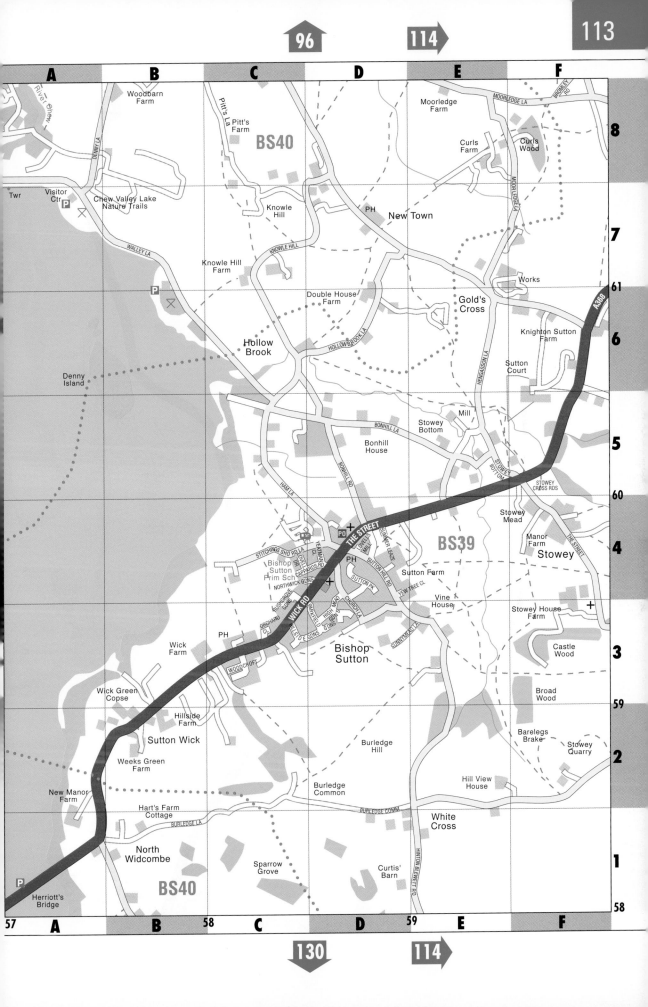

113
97

A　B　C　D　E　F

8

STANTON WICK LA

Stanton Wick

CHELWOOD RDBT

A37

A368

Bromley Farm

Curl's Farm

Utcombe Farm

Chelwood House Hotel

Park Farm

7

Stanton Wick Farm

Fry's Bottom

FRY'S BOTTOM

A368

61

Round Hill

Salter's Brook

Red Hill

Breach

6

FEATHERED LA

Folly Wood

Honey Gaston

BS39

North End Farm

THE FLAT

5

Folly Farm Nature Reserve

North End

60

Dowling's Wood

Taylor's Farm

KING LA

LONG YEAR LA

LOWER BRISTOL RD

4

Cinderlands Brake

Tynemoor Wood

Hill Farm

3

Tynemore Farm

Warwick Arms (PH)

UPPER BRISTOL RD

WARWICK GDNS

TYNINGS

TYNINGS WAY

ROGERS CL

BROOMHILL LA

MAYPOLE CL

Clutton Prim Sch

BIRCHILL CL

BATCH LA

GREENRIDGE

Greensbrook

THE MEAD

FURN EACHHILL LA

COOKS HILL

STAT

PO

MOORSFIELD

Clutton

MAYNARD TERR

NANNY HURN'S LA

59

Sleight Farm

Cholwell Farm

Cholwell House

Church Farm

CHURCH SQ

KINGS DN MDW

VALLEY VIEW

VENUS LA

CARLTON

2

Cholwell

New Cholwell Farm

CHOLWELL COTTS

Bendalls Bridge

Willow Farm

MARSH LA

Limestone Link

Paul Wood

Temple Cloud

THE SQUARE

BRANDOWN CL

TEMPLE INN LA

GOLDNEY VIEW

GOLDNEY WAY

GREYFIELD

1

PAULWOOD RD

PH

OAKLANDS

CHARD RD

TEMPLE OWN

MEAD RD

GOLDNEY WAY

FIELD GARDENS RD

HAM CL

FAIRVIEW

PAULMONT RISE

ASHMEAD

ELM VIEW

A37

Cameley CE Prim Sch

58

60　A　61　B　C　D　62　E　F

113
131

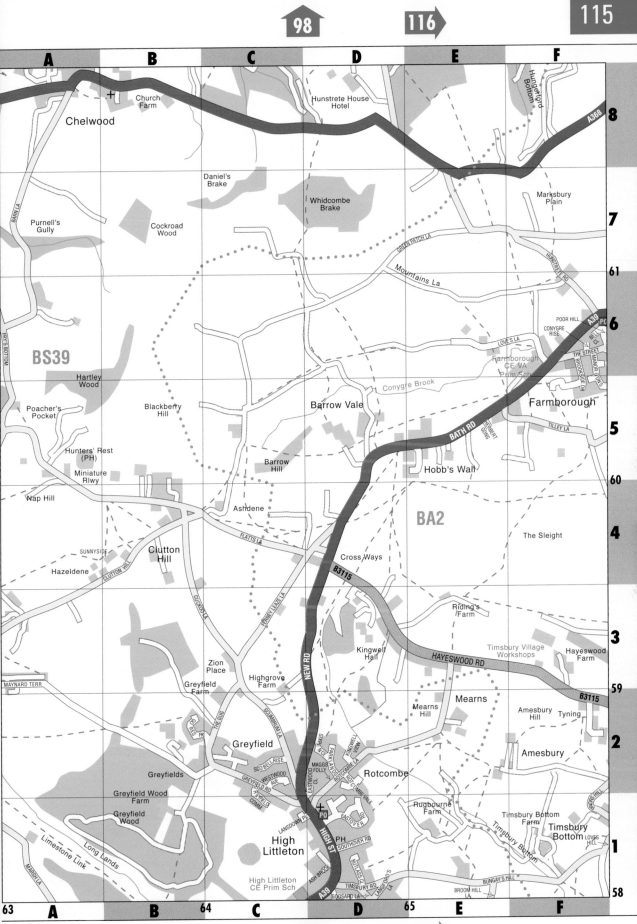

A   B   C   D   E   F

8

A368

A39

Beech Tree Farm

The Brendons

PRISTON LA

Priston New Farm

MARKSBURY LA

Pendown Hill

Pottern

Pottern Brake

Marksbury Plain

MOLLIFREND LA

Mollifrend House

7

PH

BATH RD

Old Inn

Conygre Brook

61

Sewage Works

PRISTON LA

FARMBOROUGH LA

A39

6

Castle Farm

Priest Barrow

POOR HILL

BRIDGE GDNS

BELLIFANTS

FERENBERGE CL

THE STREET

MEADWAY

CHURCH

THE BATCH

PH

Farmborough

RECTORY CL

THE MEAD

TILLEY CL

TILSBURY RD

Long Wood

MANOR GDNS

Tilley Farm

Tilley

TILLEY LA

5

BA2

Farmborough Common

60

FOUNDRY COTTS

Wallmead House Farm

Lammas Field Farm

Priston Wood

PRISTON LA

4

Wallmead Farm

Wall Mead

THE WOODLANDS

BLOOMFIELD RD

Bloomfield

NORTHFIELD

B3115

BLOOMFIELD

UPPER FURLONG

LIPPIATT LA

Tunley Farm

OVERDALE

3

Sleight Farm

BLOOMFIELD AVE

Crocombe

CROCOMBE LA

CROCOMBE

THE MEAD

St Mary's CE Prim Sch

BLOOMFIELD PARK RD

THE GLEBE

The Sleight

LANSDOWN VIEW

59

SUNNYSIDE GDNS

B3115 HAYESWOOD RD

THE AVENUE

NORTH RD

LANSDOWN CRES

PARKWAY LA

PH

TUNLEY HILL

2

Tyning

PRIORS HILL

ST MARY'S CL

PITFOUR TERR

NEWMANS LA

GILBERT RD

RECTORY

HOME FIELD

Hook

PARKWAY

Meadgate East

SCUMBRSET FOLLY

OTSTON

Hook Hill

Meadgate West

WEEKESLEY LA

Bengrove Wood

CHURCH RD

SOUTH RD

SOUTH VIEW

1 Bakers Par

PH

Loves Hill Farm

PRIORS HILL

SOXY

BARTHOLOMEW ROW

HILLVIEW

The Folly

CAMERTON RD

Sheep House Farm

Timsbury

1

Timsbury Bottom

LOVES HILL

LAUREL GDNS

GREENVALE CL

GREENVALE DR

ST JOHNS RD

MILL LA

RADFORD HILL

Meadgate Farm

WEEKESLEY LA

RED HILL

Limestone Link

ORCHARD COTTS

WHITEHOUSE RD

Lynch House

Greenvale

Cam Brook

NEW PIT COTTS

BRIDGE PLACE RD

WICK LA

58

66   A   B   67   C   D   68   E   F

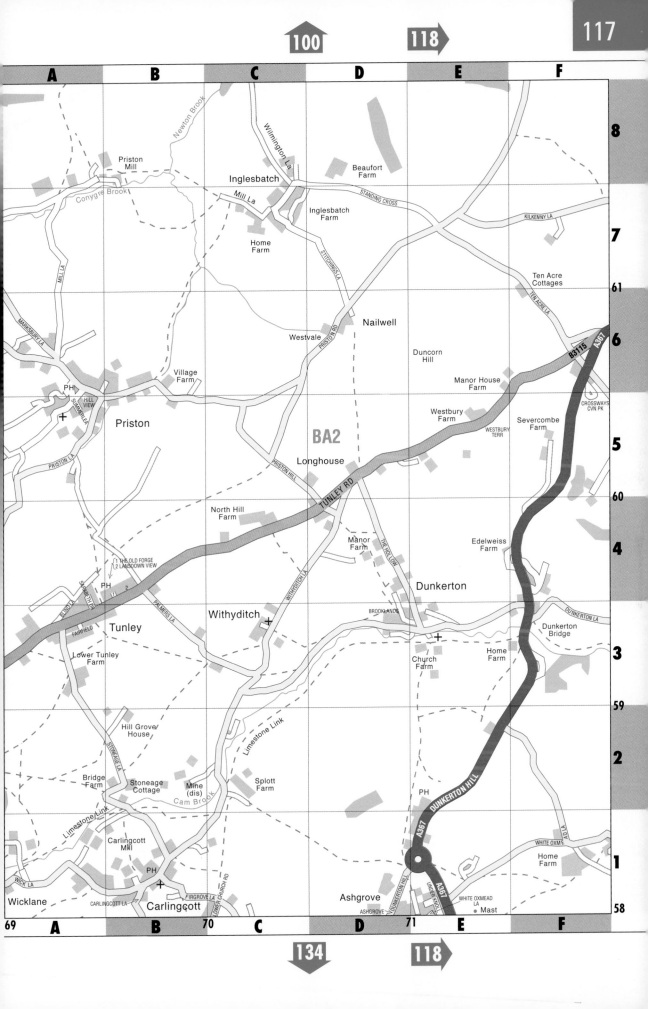

117 101

A B C D E F

8

Middle Wood

Vernham Wood

BRISTOL VIEW 1
UPPER BLOOMFIELD RD 2
BURNT HOUSE COTTS 3
FOSSE WAY EST 4

OLD FOSSE RD
WELLSWAY

LYMPSHAM GN

Three Ways Sch

MIDFORD RD

B3110

MENDIP GDNS
WELL RD
FULLERS WAY
CRANMORE
RIDGE GREEN

St Gregory's RC Sch

Odd Down

Kilkenny La

Woodleaze

CARDINAL CL
POPLAR RD
GREGORY GN
EULIS MANOR RD
HEATHER DR
HOLLY DR
MEADOW RD
ALDER WAY
SPRUCE WAY
HAZEL WAY
Mast

Nurseries

SOUTHSTOKE LA
OLD SCHOOL HILL
CRANLEIGH

A367

BURNT HOUSE RD
Sulis Manor

VICTORIA COTTS

PACK HORSE LA

P&R

Southstoke
PH
COURTMEAD

7

Down Wood

Works

Hodshill

HODSHILL

61

West Wood

COMBE HAY LA
WOODFLE HILL

Rowley Wood

A367

Fortnight Farm

6

Fosse Farm

Engine Wood

Week Farm

Limestone Link

Anchor Farm

5

Rowley House

Rowley Farm

ROWLEY FARM LA
ANCHOR LA

BROWNEY LA

Cemy
PH

60

Rainbow Wood

THE LOWER LA
BACKY HILL

Dunnyham Brake

Upper Twinhoe Farm

DUNKERTON LA

Manor House Farm

Cam Brooke

Combe Hay

Tut's Wood

Brake Wood

Middle Twinhoe

4

BA2

Upper Twinhoe

Limestone Link

Underdown Wood

3

Twinhoe Green

59

TWINHOE LA

2

BATH HILL

Manor Farm

FARM LA

White Ox Mead Farm

Upper Hayes

BILL'S HILL
Church Farm

1

CROSSWAYS LA

WEAVERS ORCH
HIGH ST
THE SQUARE
STATION RD
RAILWAY LA
MILL HILL
FORD RD

Wellow

St Julian's CE Prim Sch

HUNGERFORD TERR
HENLEY VIEW

Wellow Brook

58

72 A 73 B C 74 D E F

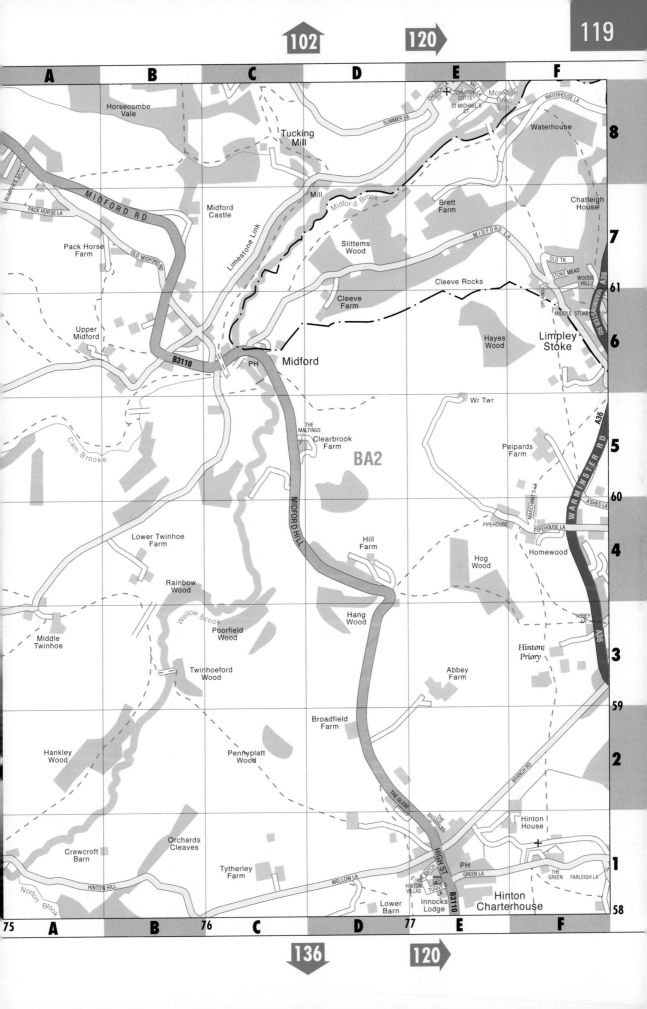

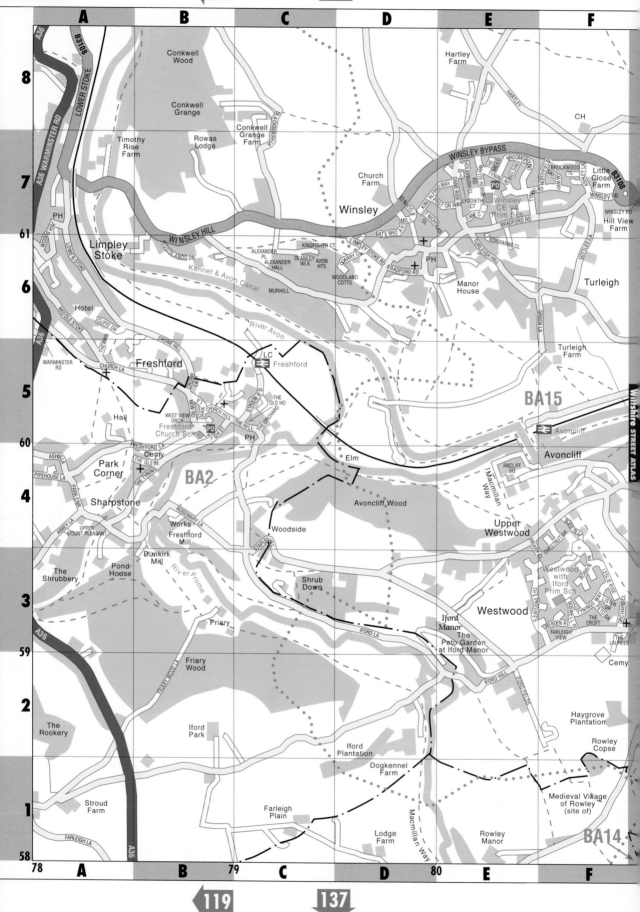

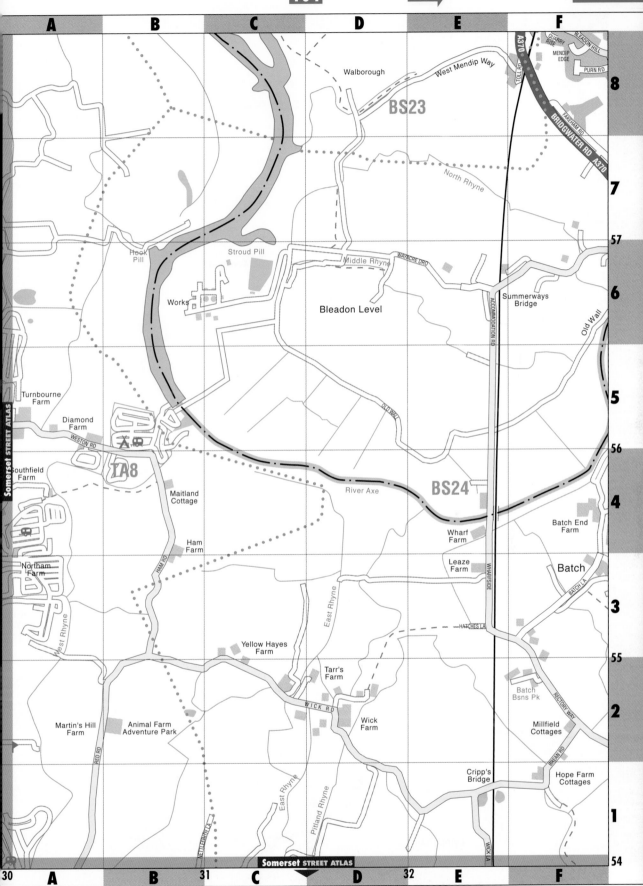

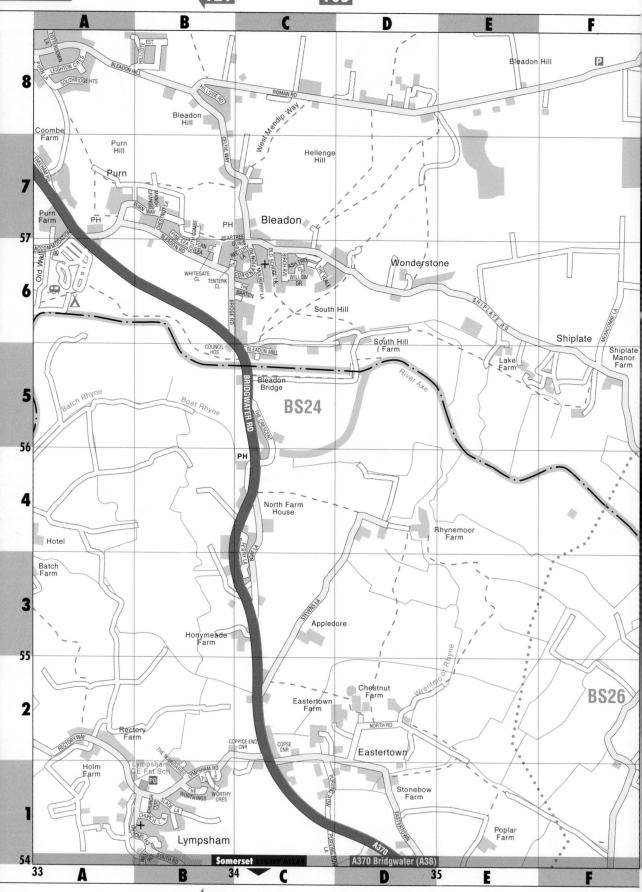

A B C D E F

8

TOTTERDOWN LA
PURN LA
LEIGHTON CRES
SOUTHRIDGE HTS
BLEADON HILL
HILLCOTE EST
HILLSIDE RD
ROMAN RD
Bleadon Hill
P

Coombe Farm
Bleadon Hill
West Mendip Way
Hellenge Hill

7
EXENHAM RD
Purn Hill
Purn
PH
Purn Farm
PURN WAY
MANOR GRANGE LA
CHESTNUT LA
COOMBE
PINE LEA
BLEADON RD
SOUTH FERN LEA
PEARTREE GDNS
PH
Bleadon
Wonderstone

57
ACCOMMODATION
Old Way
RECTORY LA
WHITEGATE CL
TENTERK CL
CORONA
OLD SCHOOL LA
MULBERRY LA
BIRCH AVE
ASH TREE CL
WILLOW DR
THE VEALE
SHIPLATE RD
Shiplate

6
THE BARTON
BRIDGE RD
South Hill
MEARCOMBE LA
Shiplate Manor Farm

COUNCIL HOS
BLEADON MILL
South Hill Farm
Lake Farm

5
Batch Rhyne
Boat Rhyne
BRIDGWATER RD
THE CRESCENT
Bleadon Bridge
BS24
River Axe

56
PH

4
Hotel
North Farm House
Rhynemoor Farm

Batch Farm
FERRY LA
THE BACK

3
STEVENS LA
Appledore

Honymeade Farm
Wrentmo or Rhyne

55
Chestnut Farm
BS26

2
Rectory Farm
Eastertown Farm
NORTH RD
Eastertown

COPPICE END CNR
COPSE CNR
PURVING ROW
Stonebow Farm

1
Holm Farm
RECTORY WAY
THE BOUNDARIES
Lympsham CE Est Sch
PO
LYMPSHAM RD
THE WORTHINGS
SLADE LA
WORTHY CRES
CHURCH CL RD
CHURCH LA
EASTERTOWN LA
Poplar Farm

Lympsham
WEST RD
SOUTH RD
COOMBE LA
A370
A370 Bridgwater (A38)

54
Somerset
33 A 34 B C 35 D E F

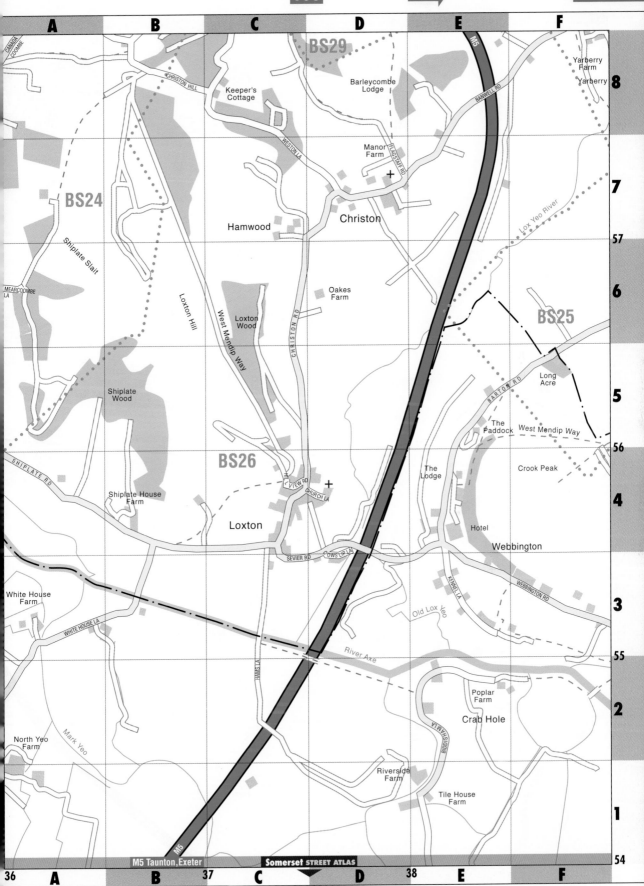

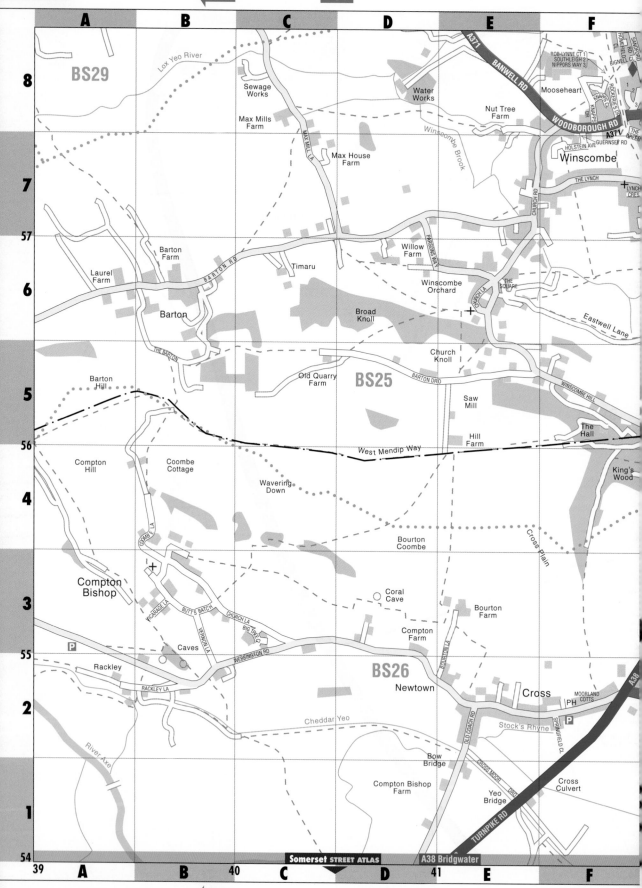

A B C D E F

BS29

Lox Yeo River

Sewage Works

8

Max Mills Farm

Max House Farm

Max Mill La

Winscombe Brook

Water Works

A371 BANWELL RD

WOODBOROUGH RD

ROB-LYNNE CT 1
SOUTHLEIGH 2
NIPPORS WAY 3

Mooseheart

Nut Tree Farm

HOLSTEIN AVE GUERNSEY RD

Winscombe

A371

THE GREEN

7

THE LYNCH

LYNCH CRES

57

Barton Farm

Timaru

Barton Rd

Willow Farm

Winscombe Orchard

PARSONS WAY

THE SQUARE

CHURCH RD

Laurel Farm

6

Barton

THE BARTON

Broad Knoll

Church Knoll

BARTON DRO

CHURCH LA

Eastwell Lane

WINSCOMBE HILL

Barton Hill

Old Quarry Farm

BS25

Saw Mill

Hill Farm

The Hall

5

West Mendip Way

56

Compton Hill

Coombe Cottage

Wavering Down

Bourton Coombe

Cross Plain

King's Wood

4

COOMBE LA

Compton Bishop

Coral Cave

Bourton Farm

3

VICARAGE LA

BUTT'S BATCH

CHURCH LA

BIG TREE CL

VERNON LA

Compton Farm

BOURTON LA

55

P

Caves

WEBBINGTON RD

BS26

MOORLAND COTTS

A38

Rackley

RACKLEY LA

Newtown

Cross

PH

2

Cheddar Yeo

OLD COACH RD

Stock's Rhyne

SPRINGFIELD CL

P

River Axe

Bow Bridge

CROSS MOOR DRO

Cross Culvert

1

Compton Bishop Farm

Yeo Bridge

TURNPIKE RD

54

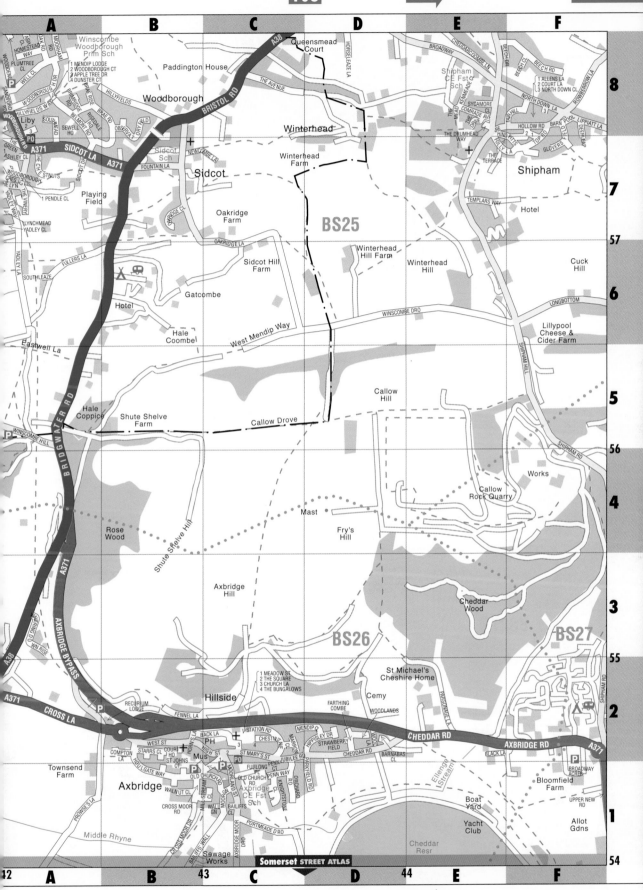

8

ROWBERROW LA

Holloway La

Riding Sch

Rowberrow Warren

LIPPIATT LA

7

Blackdown Farm

Black Down

57

BS25

6

Longbottom Farm

LONGBOTTOM

West Mendip Way

Longbottom

Tyning's Farm

Trots Corner

5

Tyning's Gate

BS40

GB Cave

56

Long House Barn

Tyning's Gate

Ashridge Farm

Charterhouse Farm

4

WARRENS HILL RD

Race Track (Vehicular)

The Perch

Milkway Barn

Piney Sleight Farm

SHIPHAM RD

Batts Combe Quarry

3

BS27

55

Piney Sleight

Batt's Coombe

Fore Cliffs

2

Chelm's Coombe

Structural Test Ctr

B3135

THE CLIFFS

Warrens Hill

Horseshoe Bend

Cheddar Gorge

AXBRIDGE RD

VENNS GATE

Hamfield Farm

WARREN'S HILL

TH SHOLD

P

Cheddar Cliffs

Samaritans Way South West

Cliff Plantation

West Mendip Way

1

UPPER NEW RD

B3135

Round Oak Farm

THE CHESTNUTS 1 MENDIP VILLAS 2

OAK RD

MEWSWELL DR

THE BAR RD

HANT

KENT ST

WARREN'S SQ

P

54

A371 Wells Shepton Mallet

CUFIC LA

Somerset STREET ATLAS

35

45 A **B** **46** C **D** **47** E **F**

West Twin Brook

East Twin Brook

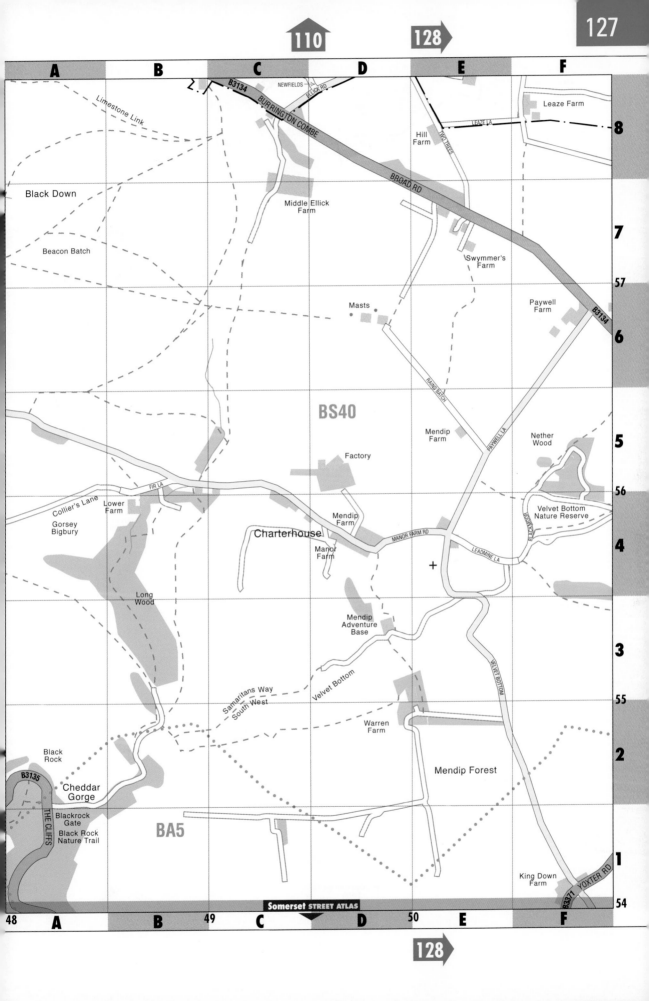

A　B　C　D　E　F

8

B3134
NEWFIELDS
ELLICK RD
Leaze Farm
LEAZE LA
Hill
Farm
TWO TREES
BURRINGTON COMBE
BROAD RD

Limestone Link

7

Black Down
Middle Ellick
Farm
Swymmer's
Farm

Beacon Batch

Paywell
Farm
B3134

57

Masts
BS40
RAINS BATCH
PAYWELL LA

6

Mendip
Farm
Nether
Wood

5

Factory

Mendip
Farm

FIR LA
Collier's Lane
Lower
Farm
Charterhouse
Manor
Farm
MANOR FARM RD
LEADMINE LA
BLACKMOOR LA
Velvet Bottom
Nature Reserve

56

Gorsey
Bigbury

+

4

Long
Wood
Mendip
Adventure
Base
VELVET BOTTOM

3

Samaritans Way
South West
Velvet Bottom

55

Warren
Farm

Black
Rock
Mendip Forest

2

B3135
Cheddar
Gorge
THE CLIFFS
Blackrock
Gate
Black Rock
Nature Trail
BA5

King Down
Farm
B3371
YOXTER RD

1

54

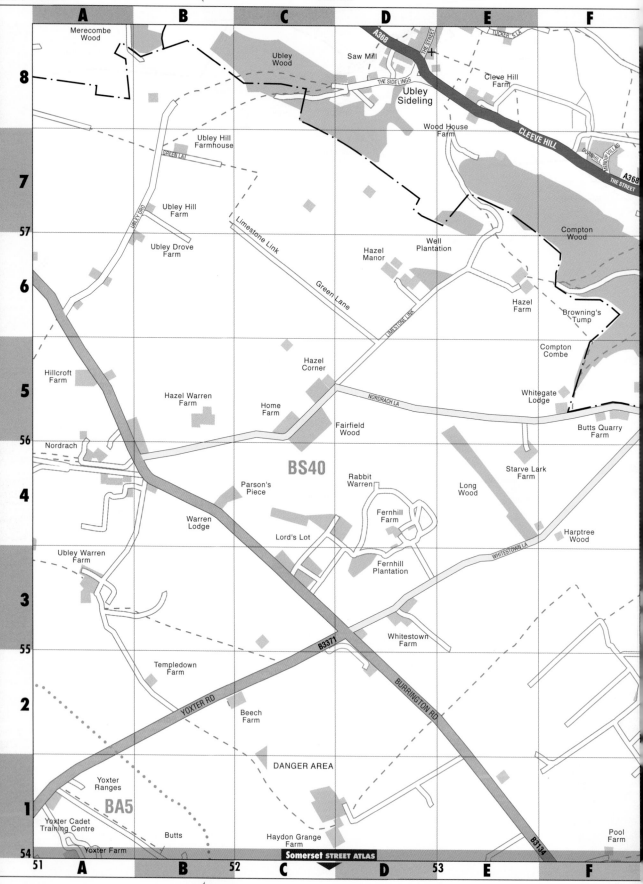

A   B   C   D   E   F

8

Merecombe Wood

Ubley Wood

Saw Mill

A368   THE STREET

Ubley Sideling

TUCKER ST

Cleve Hill Farm

THE SIDELINGS

Wood House Farm

CLEVE HILL

BARNHILL VILL'S
MENDIP VILL'S

A368

A368
THE STREET

Ubley Hill Farmhouse

GREEN LA

7

57

Ubley Hill Farm

UBLEY DRO

Limestone Link

Compton Wood

Ubley Drove Farm

Green Lane

Hazel Manor

Well Plantation

Hazel Farm

Browning's Tump

6

Limestone Link

Compton Combe

Hazel Corner

Home Farm

Hillcroft Farm

Hazel Warren Farm

NORDRACH LA

Whitegate Lodge

5

Fairfield Wood

Butts Quarry Farm

56

Nordrach

BS40

Rabbit Warren

Starve Lark Farm

Parson's Piece

Long Wood

Harptree Wood

4

Warren Lodge

Fernhill Farm

Lord's Lot

WHITESTOWN LA

Ubley Warren Farm

Fernhill Plantation

3

55

Whitestown Farm

B3371

Templedown Farm

BURRINGTON RD

YOXTER RD

Beech Farm

2

DANGER AREA

Yoxter Ranges

1

BA5

Yoxter Cadet Training Centre

Haydon Grange Farm

B3134

Pool Farm

Butts

54

Yoxter Farm

51   A   B   52   C   D   53   E   F

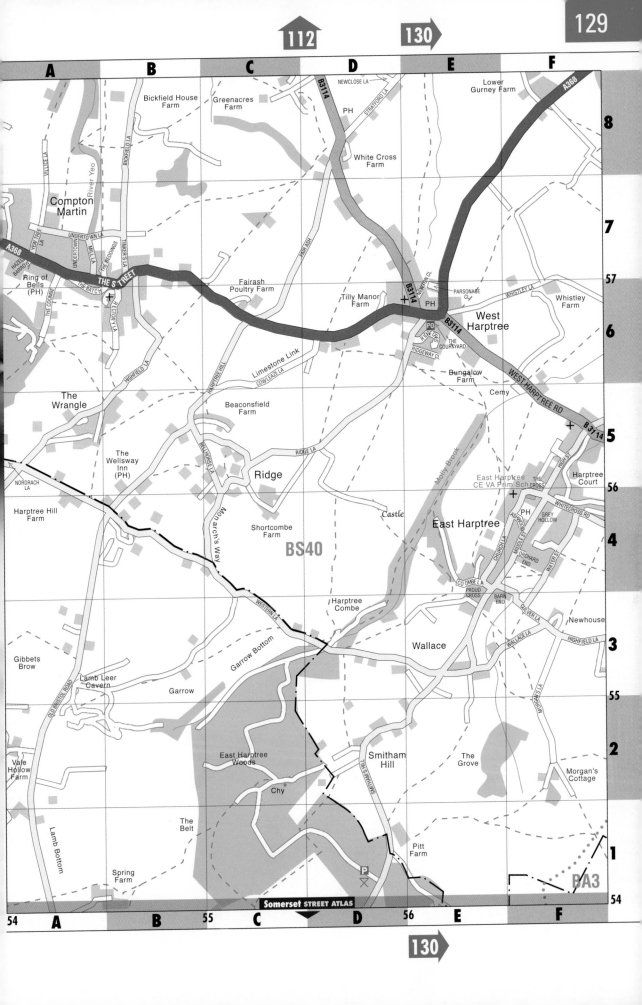

A B C D E F

8
7
57
6
5
56
4
55
3
2
1
54

NEWCLOSE LA
STRATFORD LA
Lower
Gurney Farm
A368

Bickfield House
Farm

Greenacres
Farm

B3114

PH

White Cross
Farm

VILLICE LA
River Yeo
BICKFIELD LA

Compton
Martin

YEW TREE LA
UNDERTOWN LA
MILL LA
THE REDDINGS
TINKERS LA

HAZEL BARROW
A368

UNDERTOWN LA
THE S TREET
Ring of
Bells
(PH)

THE BATCH
THE COOMBE
RECTORY LA
HIGHFIELD LA

FAIR ASH

Fairash
Poultry Farm

B3114
Newton CL

PARSONAGE CL

WHISTLEY LA

Whistley
Farm

Tilly Manor
Farm

PH

West
Harptree

PO

RIDGE CRSS
THE
COURTYARD
RIDGEWAY CL

B3114

WEST HARPTREE RD

B3114

The
Wrangle

HARPTREE HILL
Limestone Link
COW LEAZE LA

Beaconsfield
Farm

Bungalow
Farm

Cemy

NORDRACH
LA

The
Wellsway
Inn
(PH)

BRIDLE PATH LA

Ridge

RIDGE LA

Molly Brook

East Harptree
CE VA Prim Sch

HIGH ST

Harptree
Court

THE
CROSS

Harptree Hill
Farm

Monarch's Way

Shortcombe
Farm

BS40

Castle

East Harptree

PH

WHITECROSS RD

GREY
HOLLOW

CHURCH LA
ASHGROVE RD
MILL LA
ORCHARD
END
WATER ST

Harptree
Combe

COOMBE LA
PROUD
CROSS

BARN
END

OLIVER LA

WALLACE LA

Newhouse

HIGHFIELD LA

Gibbets
Brow

Lamb Leer
Cavern

OLD BRISTOL ROAD

WESTERN LA

Garrow Bottom

Garrow

Wallace

MORGAN'S LA

55

Vale
Hollow
Farm

Lamb Bottom

East Harptree
Woods

Chy

Smitham
Hill

THE PRIALLIMS

The
Grove

Morgan's
Cottage

The
Belt

Spring
Farm

P

Pitt
Farm

BA3

A B C D E F
54 55 56

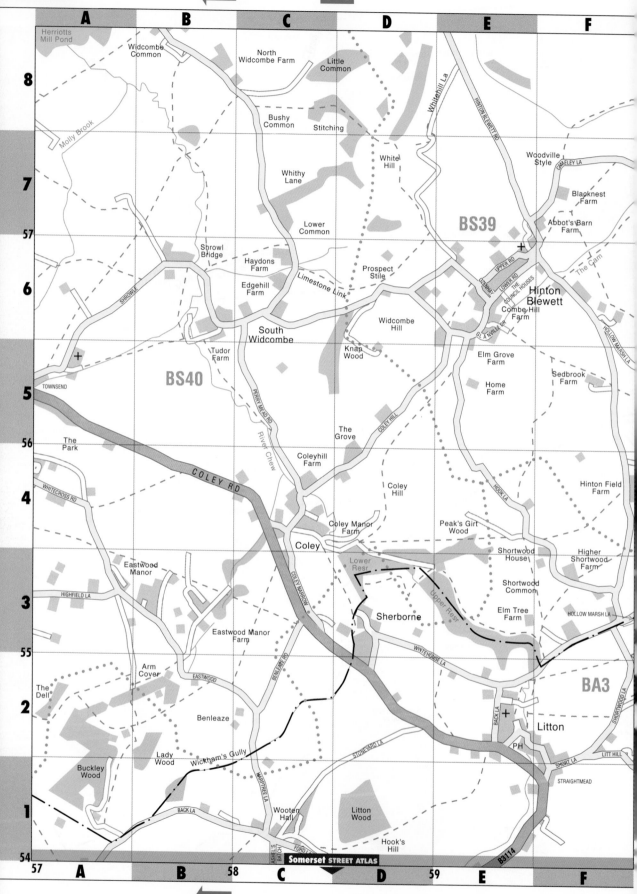

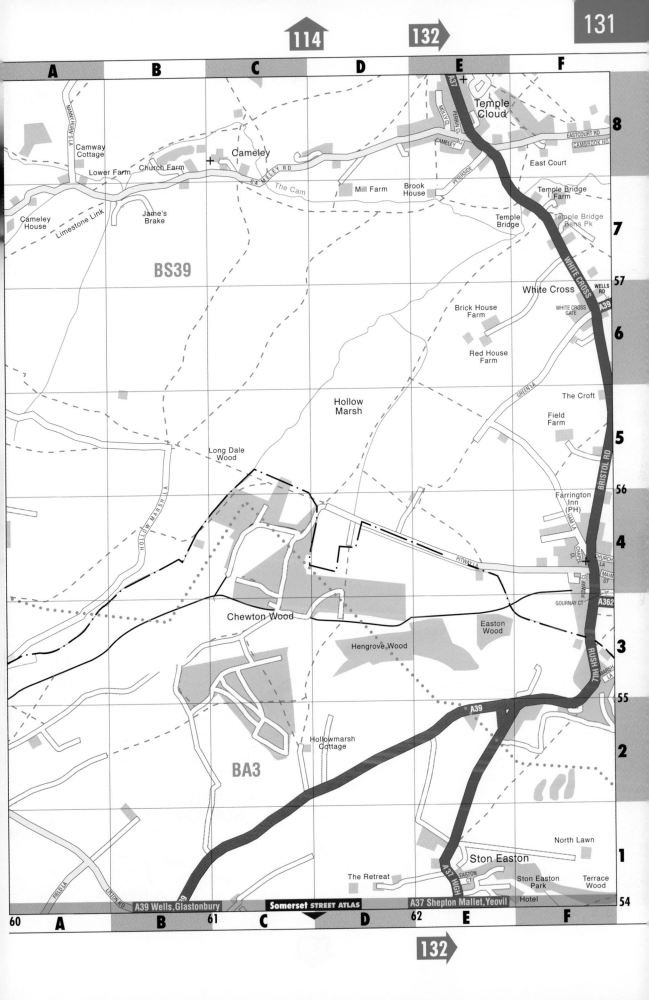

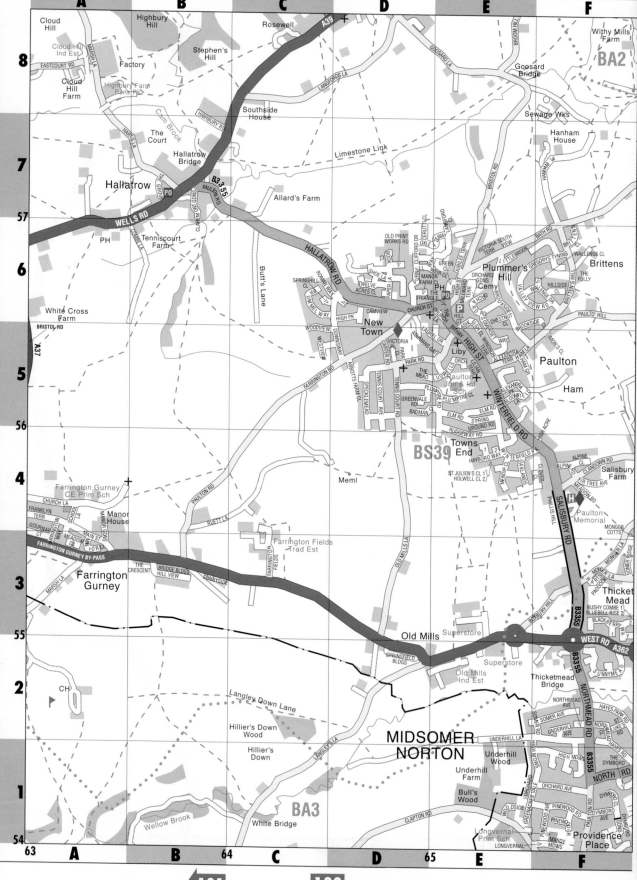

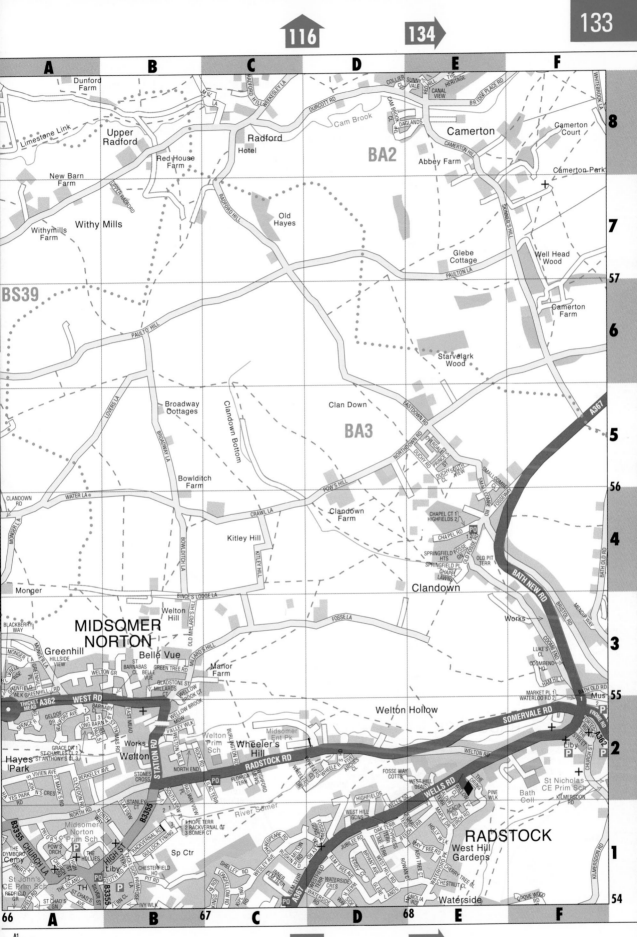

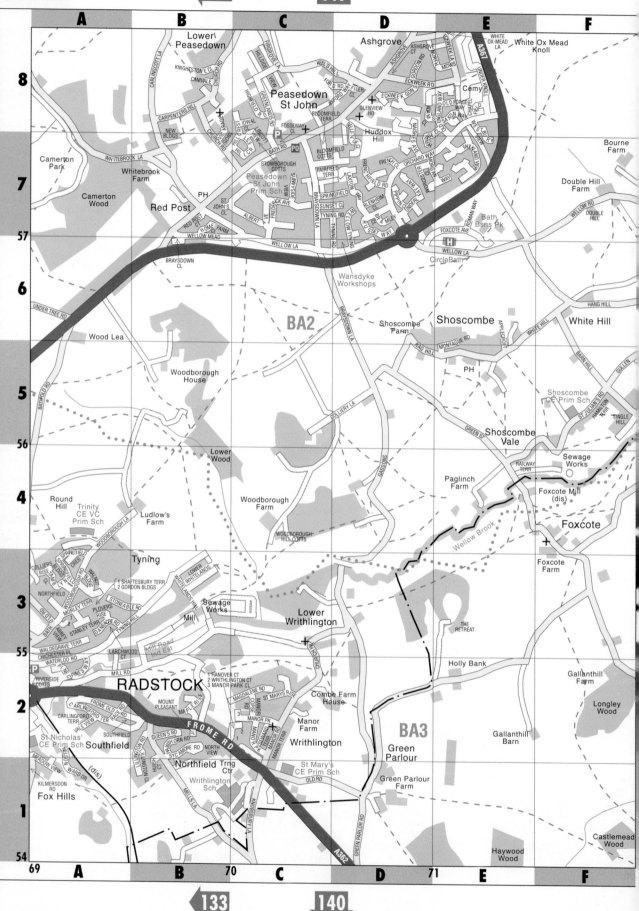

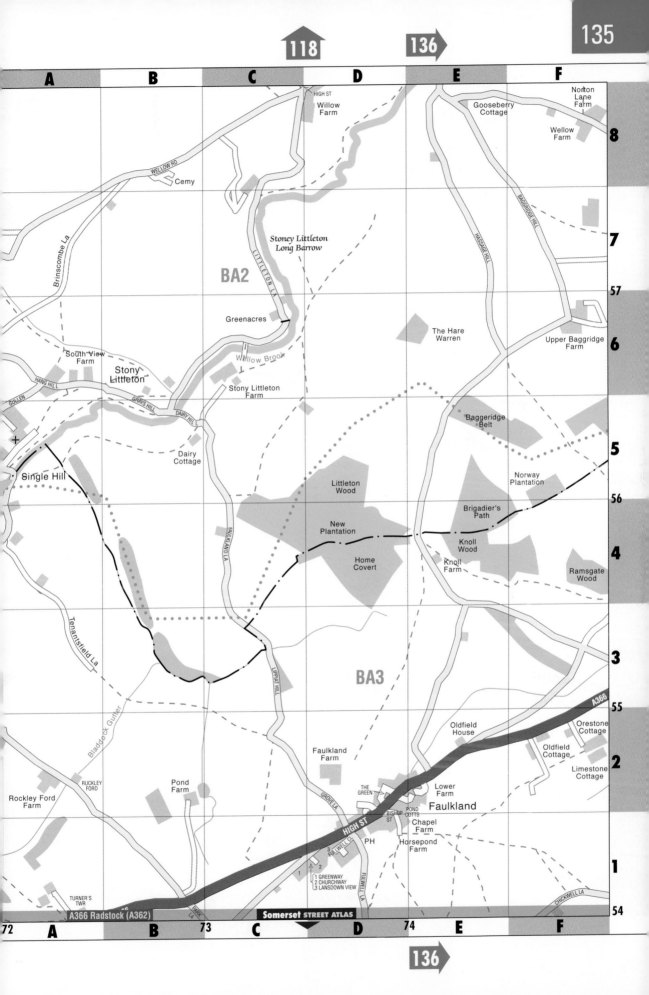

A B C D E F

8
7
57
6
5
56
4
3
55
2
1
54

HIGH ST
Willow Farm
Norton Lane Farm
Gooseberry Cottage
Wellow Farm

WELLOW RD
Cemy
BAGGRIDGE HILL
HASSAGE HILL

Stoney Littleton Long Barrow
BA2
LITTLETON LA
Brinscombe La

Greenacres
The Hare Warren
Upper Baggridge Farm

Wellow Brook
South View Farm
Stony Littleton
HANG HILL
GRAYS HILL
DAIRY HILL L
Stony Littleton Farm
Baggeridge Belt

GULLEN
Dairy Cottage
Norway Plantation

Single Hill
Littleton Wood
Brigadier's Path

New Plantation
Knoll Wood
56

FAULKLAND LA
Home Covert
Knoll Farm
Ramsgate Wood

Tenantsfield La
LIPPIAT HILL
BA3

Bladdock Gutter
A366
Oldfield House
Orestone Cottage

Rockley Ford Farm
RUCKLEY FORD
Pond Farm
Faulkland Farm
Oldfield Cottage
Limestone Cottage

THE GREEN
Lower Farm
Faulkland

GROVE LA
BISHOP ST
POND COTTS
Chapel Farm

HIGH ST
PH
Horsepond Farm

FULWELL CL
FULWELL LA
1 GREENWAY
2 CHURCHWAY
3 LANSDOWN VIEW

TURNER'S TWR
PARK LA
CHICKNELL LA

A366 Radstock (A362)

72 A B 73 C D 74 E F

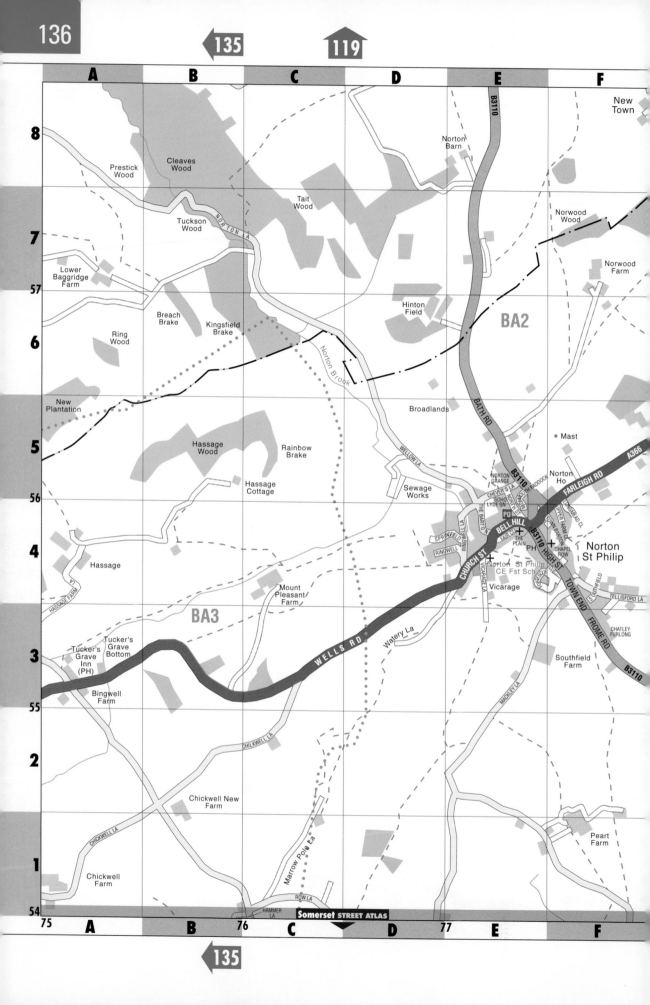

A B C D E F

New Town

B3110

8

Prestick Wood

Cleaves Wood

Norton Barn

Tait Wood

Norwood Wood

7

Tuckson Wood

NORTON LA

57

Lower Baggridge Farm

Breach Brake

Kingsfield Brake

Norwood Farm

Ring Wood

Hinton Field

BA2

6

Norton Brook

New Plantation

Broadlands

Mast

5

Hassage Wood

Rainbow Brake

WELLOW LA

BATH RD

A366

Norton Grange

Norton Ho

FARLEIGH RD

56

Hassage Cottage

Sewage Works

CHEVER'S LA

SOHO

LYDE GN

B3110

NORTH ST

SOUTH PADDOCK

UPPER FARM CL

LONGMEAD CL

4

Hassage

HASSAGE FARM LA

Mount Pleasant Farm

SPRINGFIELD

RINGWELL LA

THE BARTON

PO

BELL HILL

FAIRCRS

THE PLAIN

PH

FAIRCLOSE

B3110 HIGH ST

TOWN BARTON

CHAPEL ROW

Norton St Philip

BA3

RINGWELL

Norton St Philip CE Fst Sch

VICARAGE LA

RESCUE ST

TOWN END

TELLISFORD LA

S SOUTHFIELD

Vicarage

WELLS RD

Watery La

FROME RD

CHATLEY FURLONG

3

Tucker's Grave Inn (PH)

Tucker's Grave Bottom

Southfield Farm

B3110

Bingwell Farm

55

MACKLEY LA

CHILKWELL LA

2

Chickwell New Farm

Peart Farm

1

CHICKWELL LA

Chickwell Farm

MARROW POLE LA

ROW LA

HAMMER LA

Somerset STREET ATLAS

54

75 A B 76 C D 77 E F

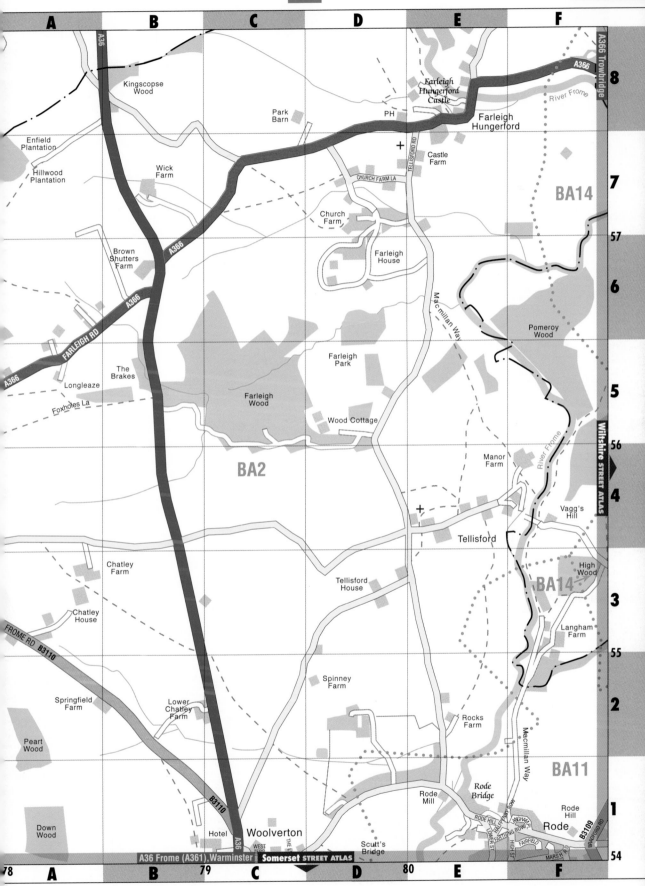

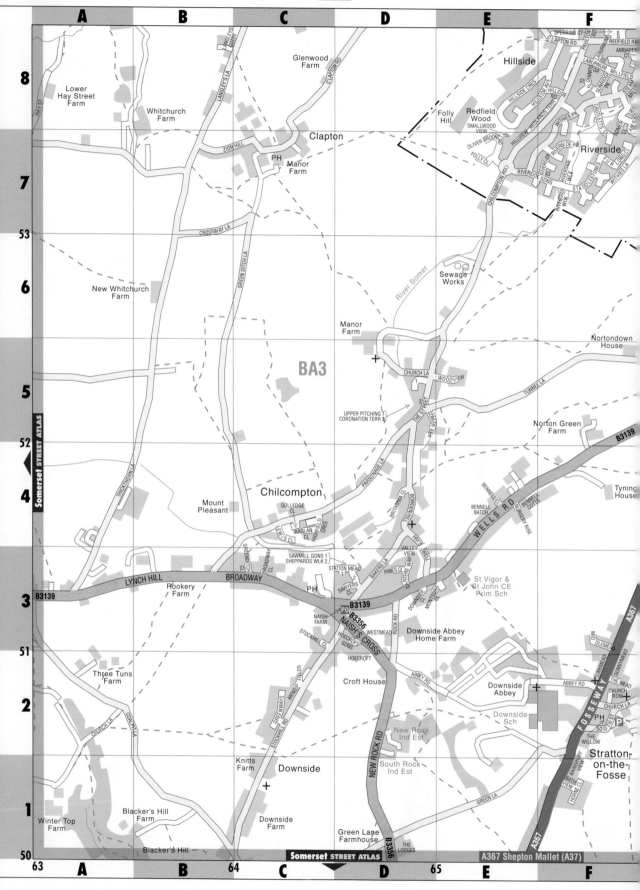

BA3

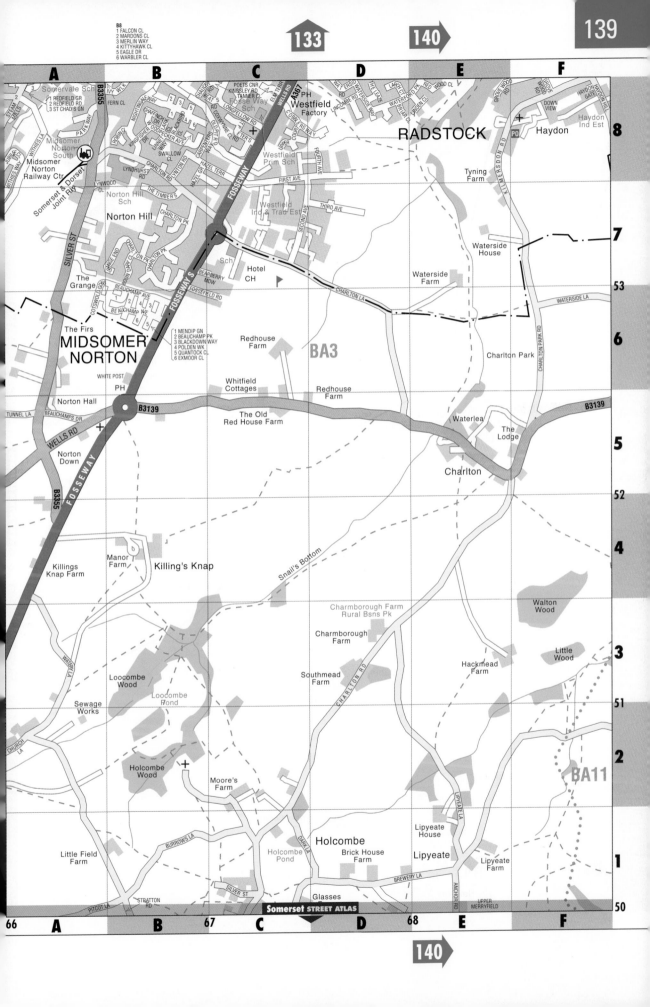

B8
1 FALCON CL
2 MARDONS CL
3 MERLIN WAY
4 KITTYHAWK CL
5 EAGLE DR
6 WARBLER CL

Somervale Sch
1 REDFIELD GR
2 REDFIELD RD
3 ST CHAD'S GN

WITHIES LA
STEAM MILLS

Midsomer Norton South

Midsomer Norton Railway Ctr

Somerset & Dorset Joint Rly

SILVER ST

B3355

PARK WAY

FERN CL

IVY WLK

NIGHTINGALE WAY

ROBINS

KINGFISHER DR

CHAFFINCH CL

WOODPECKER AVE

LINNET CL

SWALLOW CL

CHARLTON RD

Norton Hill Sch

The Timbers

LYNDHURST RD

LYNWOOD

Norton Hill

SPACE END

CHARLTON PK

CHARLTON PK

CLAY

DRUID

CHARLTON RD

COTSWOLD CLS

BEAUCHAMP AVE

BEAUCHAMP AVE

The Grange

The Firs

MIDSOMER NORTON

1 MENDIP GN
2 BEAUCHAMP PK
3 BLACKDOWN WAY
4 POLDEN WK
5 QUANTOCK CL
6 EXMOOR CL

WHITE POST

PH

Norton Hall

BEAUCHAMPS DR

Norton Down

TUNNEL LA

WELLS RD

B3355

FOSSEWAY

Killings Knap Farm

Manor Farm

Killing's Knap

CHALICE WAY

POETS CNR
KINGSLEY RD
TANNER CL

MEAD

RD

LONGFELLOW RD

CHAUCER'S

ELM TERR

WELLS RD

A367

FOSSEWAY

FOXMINE CL RD

CARPENTERS

HAZEL TERR

HAZEL GR

XYNTON RD

Fosse Way Sch

PH

Westfield Factory

COBBLERS WAY

Westfield Prim Sch

Westfield Ind & Trad Est

FIRST AVE

FOURTH AVE

THIRD AVE

SECOND AVE

Sch

Hotel

CH

BEARBERRY MDW

FOSSEFIELD RD

Redhouse Farm

BA3

Whitfield Cottages

The Old Red House Farm

Redhouse Farm

B3139

CHARLTON LA

WATERFORD CL

RED WOOD CL

GROVE WOOD RD

WATERSIDE WAY

LINCOMBE RD

LINDEN CL

THE LEAZE

HADOW

GATE

HILL

DOWN VIEW

HAYDON HILL

+

PO

Haydon

Haydon Ind Est

KILMERSDON RD

GROVE WOOD RD

RADSTOCK

Tyning Farm

Waterside House

Waterside Farm

53

Waterside LA

WATERSIDE LA

6

Charlton Park

CHARLTON PARK RD

Waterlea

The Lodge

5

Charlton

52

B3139

Snail's Bottom

Walton Wood

4

Charmborough Farm Rural Bsns Pk

Charmborough Farm

CHARLTON RD

Hackmead Farm

Little Wood

3

51

Loocombe Wood

Loocombe Pond

Southmead Farm

2

BA11

Sewage Works

CHURCH LA

WATER LA

Holcombe Wood

+

Moore's Farm

Lipyeate House

LIPYEATE LA

Lipyeate

ANCHOR RD

Lipyeate Farm

Little Field Farm

BURROWS LA

Holcombe Pond

SILVER ST

Holcombe

DARK LA

Brick House Farm

BREWERY LA

Glasses

UPPER MERRYFIELD

1

50

PITCOT LA

STRATTON RD

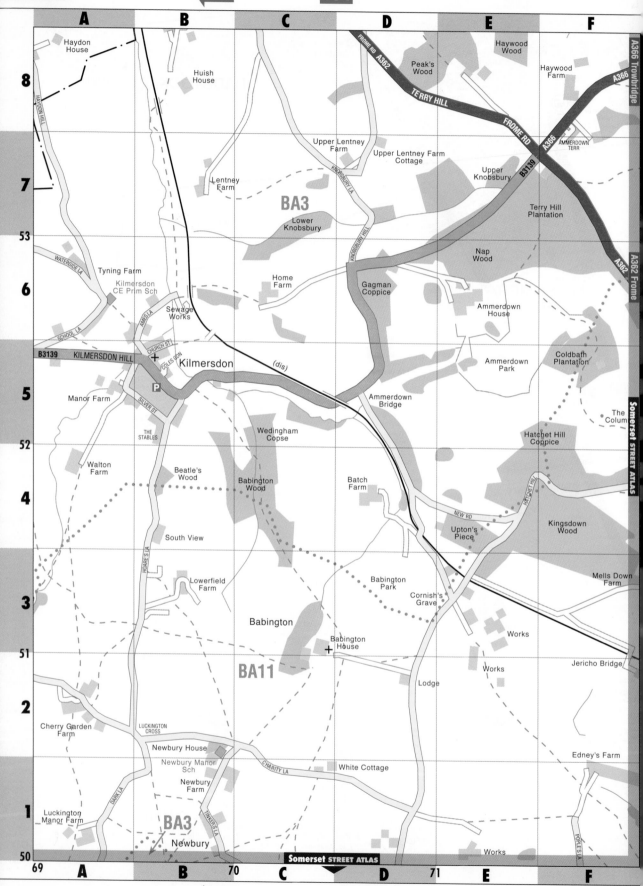

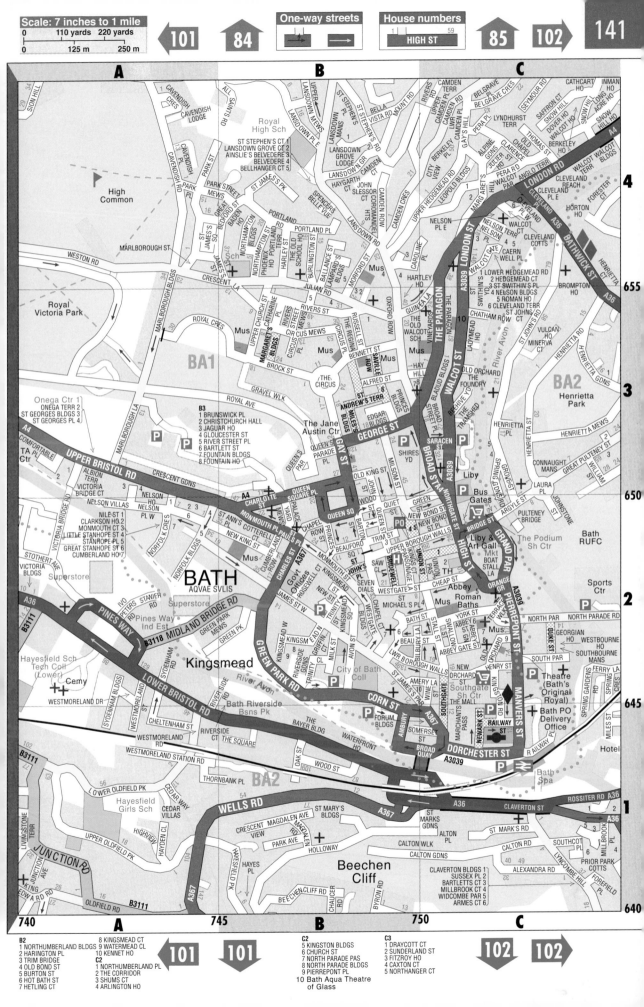

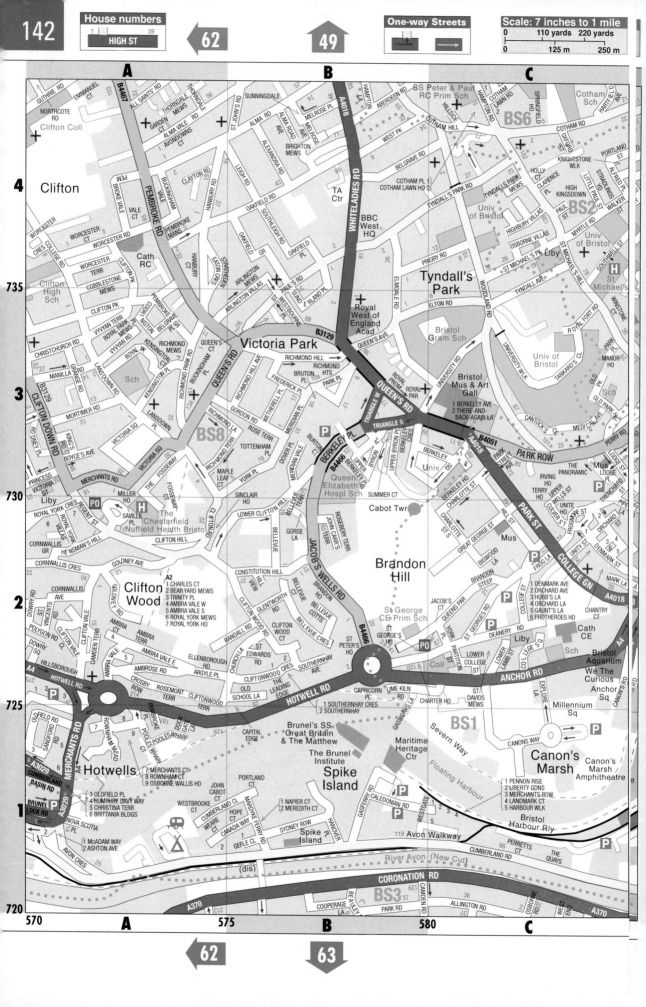

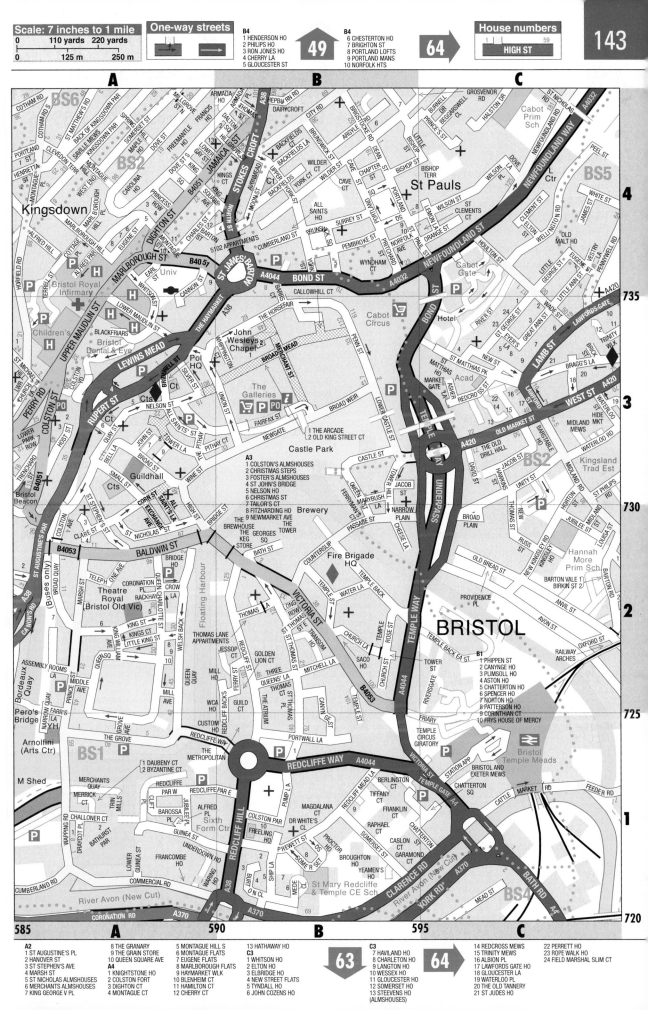

Index

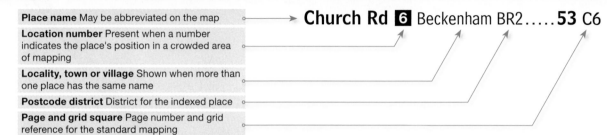

Place name May be abbreviated on the map
→ **Church Rd** 6 Beckenham BR2.....**53** C6

Location number Present when a number indicates the place's position in a crowded area of mapping

Locality, town or village Shown when more than one place has the same name

Postcode district District for the indexed place

Page and grid square Page number and grid reference for the standard mapping

Cities, towns and villages are listed in CAPITAL LETTERS

Public and commercial buildings are highlighted in magenta   **Places of interest** are highlighted in blue with a star★

Abbreviations used in the index

Acad	**Academy**	Comm	**Common**	Gd	**Ground**	L	**Leisure**	Prom	**Promenade**
App	**Approach**	Cott	**Cottage**	Gdn	**Garden**	La	**Lane**	Rd	**Road**
Arc	**Arcade**	Cres	**Crescent**	Gn	**Green**	Liby	**Library**	Recn	**Recreation**
Ave	**Avenue**	Cswy	**Causeway**	Gr	**Grove**	Mdw	**Meadow**	Ret	**Retail**
Bglw	**Bungalow**	Ct	**Court**	H	**Hall**	Meml	**Memorial**	Sh	**Shopping**
Bldg	**Building**	Ctr	**Centre**	Ho	**House**	Mkt	**Market**	Sq	**Square**
Bsns, Bus	**Business**	Ctry	**Country**	Hospl	**Hospital**	Mus	**Museum**	St	**Street**
Bvd	**Boulevard**	Cty	**County**	HQ	**Headquarters**	Orch	**Orchard**	Sta	**Station**
Cath	**Cathedral**	Dr	**Drive**	Hts	**Heights**	Pal	**Palace**	Terr	**Terrace**
Cir	**Circus**	Dro	**Drove**	Ind	**Industrial**	Par	**Parade**	TH	**Town Hall**
Cl	**Close**	Ed	**Education**	Inst	**Institute**	Pas	**Passage**	Univ	**University**
Cnr	**Corner**	Emb	**Embankment**	Int	**International**	Pk	**Park**	Wk, Wlk	**Walk**
Coll	**College**	Est	**Estate**	Intc	**Interchange**	Pl	**Place**	Wr	**Water**
Com	**Community**	Ex	**Exhibition**	Junc	**Junction**	Prec	**Precinct**	Yd	**Yard**

Index of towns, villages, streets, hospitals, industrial estates, railway stations, schools, shopping centres, universities and places of interest

510–Ale

5102 Apartments BS1 143 B4

A

Abbey Church Yd 10
 BA1.............141 C2
Abbey Cl BS31.........81 F6
Abbey Ct
 Bath BA2.............102 B7
 Bristol BS4............64 F5
Abbeydale BS36......37 E6
Abbeyfield Ho BS37...28 C1
Abbey Gate St BA1...141 C2
Abbey Gdns BS22....105 E8
Abbey Gn BA1........141 C2
Abbey Ho 5 BS37.....39 D7
Abbey La
 Hinton Charterhouse
 BA2.............120 A4
 Thornbury BS35.......15 D6
Abbey Mews GL12.....11 F4
Abbey Pk BS31........81 F6
Abbey Rd
 Bristol BS9...........48 F7
 Chilcompton BA3.....138 D2
 Stratton-on-t-F BA3...138 F2
Abbey St
 Bath BA1............141 C2
 Kingswood GL12......11 F5
Abbey View
 Bath BA2............102 B5
 Radstock BA3........134 A3
Abbey View Gdns BA2 102 B5
Abbeywood Dr BS9....48 C5
Abbeywood Pk BS34...36 C2
Abbey Wood Ret Pk
 BS34.............36 C2
Abbot Alphege Acad
 BATH BA1............84 E4
 Charlcombe BA1......84 D4
Abbots Ave BS15......65 C4
Abbotsbury Rd BS48...59 D1
Abbots Cl BS14........80 A3
Abbot's Cl BS22.......89 A3
Abbotsford Rd BS6....49 B1

Abbots Horn BS48.....59 D2
ABBOTSIDE...........9 F2
ABBOTS LEIGH........62 A8
Abbots Leigh Rd BS8..62 C7
Abbots Rd BS15.......65 C2
Abbots Way
 Bristol BS9...........49 E6
 Longwell Green BS30...65 F2
Abbotswood
 Bristol BS15..........65 D7
 Yate BS37............39 D7
Abbotswood Cl BS31..81 D3
Abbotswood Prim Sch
 BS37.............39 D6
Abbott Rd BS35.......22 A5
Abbotts Farm Cl BS39 132 D5
Aberdeen Rd BS6.....142 B4
Abingdon Gdns BA2...118 D8
Abingdon Rd BS16.....51 A3
Ableton Ct BS35......22 A6
Ableton La
 Hallen BS10..........34 A8
 Severn Beach BS35....22 A5
Ableton Wlk BS9......48 C5
Abon Ho BS9..........48 C4
Abraham Cl BS5.......64 B8
Abraham Fry Ho BS15. 65 E7
Abrahams Cl BS4......79 F7
ABSON...............53 D2
Abson Rd
 Pucklechurch BS16....53 C3
 Wick BS30...........67 C8
Acacia Ave
 Bristol BS16..........51 D4
 Weston-s-M BS23....105 B8
Acacia Cl BS5.........51 D3
Acacia Ct BS31.......81 C4
Acacia Gr BA2.......101 C3
Acacia Mews 5 BS16. 51 D4
Acacia Rd
 Bristol BS16..........51 D4
 Radstock BA3.......133 E1
Access 18 BS11.......33 D3
Accommodation Rd
 BS24.............121 E6
Acer Cres BS32........24 E5
Acer Village BS14......80 C7
Aconite Cl BS22.......89 B5
Acorn Dr BS16........52 C8

Acorn Gr BS13........78 E6
Acorns The BS37......27 B5
Acraman's Rd 7 BS3..63 C4
Acresbush Cl BS13....79 A5
Acton Rd BS16........51 A3
ACTON TURVILLE.....42 F6
Acton Turville Rd GL9..42 B4
Adams Cl BA2........134 D8
Adams Ct 5 BS8......62 F6
Adams Hay 6 BS4.....64 D1
Adams Land BS36.....38 C7
Adastral Rd BS24....106 D4
Adderly Gate BS16....52 B7
Addicott Rd BS23....104 E6
Addiscombe Rd
 Bristol BS14..........80 B5
 Weston-s-M BS23....104 E4
Addison Rd BS3.......63 E3
Adelaide Pl
 Bristol, Fishponds BS16.. 50 F4
 12 Bristol, Upper Easton
 BS5.............64 B8
Adelaide Terr 1 BS16.. 51 A4
Adelante Cl BS34......37 A4
Admiral Cl BS16.......50 E7
Admiral's Wlk BS20....45 B5
Adryan Ct 6 BS5......64 C7
Aelfric Mdw BS20.....45 F4
Aesop Dr BS31.......81 C3
Agate St BS3..........63 B3
Aiken St BS5..........64 B6
Ainslie's Belvedere
 BA1.............141 B4
Aintree Dr BS16.......37 F1
Air Balloon Ct 1 BS5..65 A7
Air Balloon Hill Jun & Inf
 Schs BS5...........65 A7
Air Balloon Rd BS5....65 A7
Airoh End BS24.......105 B4
Airport Rd BS14.......80 A8
Airport Rdbt BS24....105 E7
Airport View Cvn Pk
 BS24.............105 D7
Aisecome Way BS22..105 C6
Akeman Way BS11....47 C8
Alanscourt BS30......66 B5
Alard Rd BS4..........79 F7
Albany BS23...........87 F1
Albany Ct 6 BA1.....101 B6

Albany Gate BS34.....36 E5
Albany Rd
 Bath BA2............101 C6
 Bristol BS6...........49 F1
Albany St BS15........65 C8
Albany Way BS30......66 C5
Albemarle Row 10 BS8 62 F6
Albemarle Terr 7 BS8. 62 F6
Albert Ave
 Peasedown St John
 BA2.............134 C7
 Weston-s-M BS23....104 E6
Albert Cres BS2.......64 B5
Albert Ct BS23.......104 E6
Albert Gr BS5.........64 F8
Albert Gr S BS5.......64 F8
Albert Ho BS1........143 B2
Alberton Rd BS16......50 F6
Albert Par BS5........64 D8
Albert Park Pl BS6.....49 F1
Albert Pk BS6.........49 F1
Albert Pl
 Bath BA2............102 C1
 1 Bristol, Bedminster
 BS3.............63 C3
 Bristol, Eastfield BS9...49 A7
 Portishead BS20......45 D4
Albert Quadrant BS23 104 E8
Albert Rd
 Bristol, Hanham BS15..65 D5
 Bristol, St Philip's Marsh
 BS2.............64 A4
 Bristol, Staple Hill BS16. 51 E4
 Clevedon BS21.......57 E3
 Keynsham BS31......81 E5
 Portishead BS20......45 D5
 Severn Beach BS35....22 A6
 Weston-s-M BS23....104 E6
Albert St BS5.........64 C8
Albert Terr
 Bath BA2............101 C6
 Bristol BS16..........50 F4
Albion Bldgs BA1....101 D7
Albion Cl BS16.........51 F5
Albion Pl
 Bath BA1............141 A3
 16 Bristol BS2.......143 C3
Albion Rd BS5.........50 B1
Albion St 6 BS5.......64 C8

Albion Terr
 Bath BA1............141 A3
 Bristol BS34..........24 B1
Alburys BS40..........92 D3
Alcina Way BS31......81 C2
ALCOMBE.............86 F7
Alcove Rd BS16........50 F3
Alden Ho BS36........37 D4
Aldercombe Rd BS9...48 C8
Alder Ct BS14.........80 B5
Alderdown Cl BS11....48 A8
Alder Dr BS5..........50 E1
Alderley Rd BA2......101 B4
Aldermoor Way BS30.. 65 E4
Alderney Ave BS4.....64 F4
Alders The BS16......37 B1
Alder Terr BA3.......133 E2
ALDERTON.............31 F2
Alderton Rd
 Bristol BS7...........49 E8
 Burton SN14.........43 D6
Alder Way BA2.......118 D8
ALDWICK.............110 D7
Aldwick Ave BS13.....79 C3
Aldwick La BS40......110 C7
Alec Ricketts Cl BA2..100 F5
Alexander Bldgs 12
 BA1.............85 B1
Alexander Ct 4 BS3...63 A3
Alexander Hall BA2...120 C6
Alexander Ho 5 BS23 104 F4
Alexander Hosea Prim Sch
 GL12.............18 B5
Alexander Mews 5
 BS23.............104 E7
Alexander Pl BA2....120 C6
Alexander Rd BS31....81 C2
Alexander Way BS49..91 B7
Alexandra Apartments
 BS6.............49 C3
Alexandra Cl BS16....51 D4
Alexandra Ct
 Bristol BS16..........50 F4
 Clevedon BS21.......57 E4
Alexandra Gate BS8..142 B4
Alexandra Gdns BS16. 51 D4
Alexandra Par BS23..104 E7
Alexandra Pk
 Bristol, Cotham BS6....49 C2

Ale–Ave 145

Alexandra Pk *continued*
Bristol, Ridgeway BS16 . . **50** F4
Paulton BS39 . . . . **132** E5
Alexandra Pl
Bath BA2 . . . . **102** C1
Bristol BS16. . . . . **51** D4
Alexandra Rd
Bath BA2 . . . . **141** C1
Bristol BS8. . . . . **142** B4
Bristol, Eastfield BS10. . . **49** C8
Bristol, Hanham BS15 . . . **65** D5
Bristol, Highridge BS13 . . **78** F7
Clevedon BS21. . . . . **57** E4
Frampton Cotterell BS36 **38** D7
Alexandra Terr BS39. . . . **132** E5
Alexandra Way BS35 . . . . **8** B3
Alford Rd BS4 . . . . **64** C2
Alfred Ct 4 BS23 . . . . . **104** E7
Alfred Hill BS2. . . . . **143** A4
Alfred Lovell Gdns 7
BS30. . . . . **66** A4
Alfred Par BS2. . . . . **143** A4
Alfred Pl BS2 . . . . **142** C4
Alfred Rd
Bristol, Westbury Park
BS6 . . . . **49** A4
Bristol, Windmill Hill BS3 **63** D3
Alfred St
Bath BA1 . . . . **141** B3
Bristol, Moorfields BS5 . . **64** D8
Bristol, Newton BS2. . . . . **64** A6
Weston-s-M BS23 . . . . . **104** E8
Algars Dr BS37 . . . . **26** E3
Algiers St BS3 . . . . **63** D3
Alison Gdns BS48 . . . . . . **76** A7
Allanmead Rd BS14 . . . . . **80** B8
Allans Way BS24 . . . . . . **105** F7
Allengrove La SN14 . . . . **31** C3
Allens La BS25. . . . . **125** F8
Aller BS24 . . . . **105** B2
Aller Par BS24 . . . . **105** B2
Allerton Cres BS14 . . . . . **80** B4
Allerton Gdns BS14 . . . . . **80** B5
Allerton Rd BS14. . . . . **80** B4
Allfoxton Rd BS7. . . . . . . **50** A3
All Hallows Ct 11 BS5 . . **64** B8
All Hallows Rd BS5. . . . . . **64** B8
Allington Dr BS30. . . . . . . **65** F4
Allington Gdns BS48 . . . **75** C8
Allington Rd BS3. . . . . . **142** C1
Allison Ave BS4 . . . . **64** E4
Allison Rd BS4. . . . . **64** E3
Allotment La
Keynsham BS31. . . . . **81** B2
Keynsham BS31. . . . . **81** B2
All Saints Cl BS30 . . . . . . **66** A3
All Saints' Ct BS1 . . . . . **143** A3
All Saints East Clevedon CE Prim Sch BS21 . . . . **57** H4
All Saints Ho BS2 . . . . . **143** B4
All Saints La BS21. . . . . . **57** H4
All Saints' La BS1 . . . . . **143** A2
All Saints Pl BA2. . . . . . . **102** E4
All Saints Rd BA1 . . . . . **141** B4
All Saints' Rd
Bristol BS8. . . . . **142** A4
Weston-s-M BS23 . . . . . . **87** E1
All Saints' St BS1 . . . . . **143** A3
Alma Cl BS15 . . . . **65** E8
Alma Ct BS8 . . . . **49** B1
Alma Rd
Bristol BS8. . . . . **142** B4
Bristol, Kingswood BS15 **51** E1
Alma Road Ave BS8 . . . **142** B4
Alma St
Bristol BS8. . . . . **49** B1
Weston-s-M BS23 . . . . . **104** E7
Alma Vale Rd BS8 . . . . . **142** A4
Almeda Rd BS5 . . . . **65** A6
Almond Cl BS22. . . . . **89** A1
ALMONDSBURY **24** B5
Almondsbury Bsns Ctr
BS32. . . . . **24** D3
Almondsbury CE Prim Sch
BS32. . . . . **24** A4
Almondsbury Intc BS32. **24** E4
Almond Way BS16. . . . . . **51** F5
Almorah Rd BS3 . . . . **63** E3
Almshouses SN14. . . . . . . **69** E8
Alonzo Pl BS21 . . . . **57** F4
Alpha Ctr The BS37 . . . . **27** C3
Alpha Rd BS3. . . . . **63** D4
Alpine Cl BS39. . . . . **132** F4
Alpine Gdns BA1. . . . . . . **141** C4
Alpine Rd
Bristol BS5. . . . . **50** C1
Paulton BS39 . . . . **132** F4
Alsop Rd 4 BS15 . . . . . . **51** D1
Alton Pl BA2. . . . . **141** C1
Alton Rd BS7 . . . . **49** F5
Altringham Rd BS5. . . . . **64** D8
Alverstoke BS14 . . . . **79** F7
ALVESTON **15** B4
ALVESTON DOWN. **14** F5
Alveston Hill BS35 . . . . . **15** A6
Alveston Rd BS32 . . . . . . **14** D3
Alveston Wlk BS9 . . . . **48** B7
Alwins Ct 2 BS30. . . . . . **65** F4
Ambares Ct BA3 . . . . . . **138** F8
Amberey Rd BS23. . . . . **104** F5
Amberlands Cl BS48 . . . **76** A7
Amberley Cl
Bristol BS16. . . . . **51** D7
Keynsham BS31. . . . . **81** E4
Amberley Gdns 3
BS48. . . . . **59** D1
Amberley House Sch
BS8. . . . . **49** A1
Amberley Rd
Bristol, Kingswood
BS16 . . . . **51** D7
Bristol, Patchway BS34 . . **36** B8
Amberley Way GL12. . . . **18** B4
Amble Cl BS15. . . . . **65** F7
Ambleside Ave BS10 . . . **35** B2
Ambleside Rd BA2 . . . . **101** C2
Ambra Ct BS8 . . . . **142** A2
Ambra Terr BS8 . . . . **142** A2
Ambra Vale BS8. . . . . . . **142** A2
Ambra Vale E BS8 . . . . . **142** A2
Ambra Vale S 5 BS8 . . **142** A2
Ambra Vale W 4 BS8. . **142** A2
Ambrose Rd BS8 . . . . . . **142** A2
Ambury BA1. . . . . **141** B1
Amercombe Wlk BS14. . **80** D7
American Mus in Britain★
BA2. . . . . **103** A5
Amery La BA1 . . . . **141** C2
AMESBURY **115** F2
Amesbury Dr BS24 . . . . **122** B6
Ames La BA3 . . . . **140** B6
Ammerdown Terr BA3 **140** F7
Anchor Cl BS5 . . . . **64** F6
Anchor Ho BS4 . . . . **64** B2
Anchor La BA2. . . . . **118** D5
Anchor Rd
Bath BA1 . . . . **84** B1
Bristol BS1. . . . . **142** C2
Bristol, Kingswood BS15 **52** A2
Anchor Way BS20 . . . . . . **47** D4
Ancliff Sq BA15 . . . . . . **120** E4
Andalusia Acad BS2. . . **143** C4
Andereach Cl BS14. . . . . **80** B8
Andover Rd BS4 . . . . **63** F2
Andrew Millman Ct
BS37. . . . . **27** F1
Andruss Dr BS41 . . . . **78** D2
Angels Gd BS4. . . . . **64** F6
Angers Rd BS4. . . . . **64** A4
Anglesea Pl 15 BS8 . . . . **49** A2
Anglo Terr BA1. . . . . **141** C4
Animal Farm Adventure Pk★ TA8. . . . . **121** B2
Ankatel Cl BS23. . . . . . . **105** A5
Annandale Ave BS22 . . . **88** E1
Annie Scott Cl 2 BS16 . **51** A4
Anson Cl BS31 . . . . **82** D2
Anson Rd
Locking BS24 . . . . **106** B6
Weston-s-M BS22 . . . . . . **88** D4
Anstey Rd BS37 . . . . **27** D6
Ansteys Cl BS15. . . . . **65** B5
Anstey's Ct BS15. . . . . . . **65** C5
Anstey's Rd BS15 . . . . . . **65** C5
Anstey St BS5. . . . . **50** B1
Anthea Rd BS5. . . . . **50** E2
Antona Ct BS11 . . . . **47** D7
Antona Dr BS11. . . . . **47** D7
Antrim Rd BS9. . . . . **49** B6
Anvil Rd BS49. . . . . **74** F1
Anvil St BS2 . . . . **143** C2
Apex Ct BS32 . . . . **24** D3
Apollo Pk BS37 . . . . **27** C3
Apperley Cl BS37 . . . . . . **39** E8
Appleby Wlk BS4 . . . . . . **79** D7
Applecroft BA2 . . . . **134** E6
Appledore 4 BS22. . . . . . **88** F2
Appledore Cl BS14 . . . . . **80** B8
Apple Farm La BS24. . . . **89** C1
Applegate BS10. . . . . **35** B3
Appleridge La GL13 . . . . . **3** C4
Appletree Ct BS22 . . . . . **89** B2
Apple Tree Dr BS25. . . . **125** A8
Appletree Mews BS22 . . **89** B2
Applin Gn BS16 . . . . **52** C6
Appsley Cl BS22 . . . . **88** C1
Apseleys Mead BS32 . . . **24** C2
Apsley Cl BA1. . . . . **101** B7
Apsley Garden Apartments
BS6. . . . . **49** E2
Apsley Mews BS8 . . . . . . **49** A2
Apsley Rd
Bath BA1 . . . . **101** A7
Bristol BS8. . . . . **49** A1
Apsley St BS5. . . . . **50** C3
Arbutus Dr BS9 . . . . **48** C8
Arbutus Wlk BS9. . . . . **34** D1
Arcade The BS1 . . . . **143** B3
Arcadius Way BS31. . . . . **81** F8
Arch Cl BS41. . . . . **61** F1
Archer Ct
Bristol BS30. . . . . **65** F3
Clevedon BS21. . . . . **57** F4
Archer Wlk BS14. . . . . . . **80** E6
Arches The
Bath BA2 . . . . **101** A6
1 Bristol BS5 . . . . **64** B7
Archfield Ct BS6 . . . . **49** C1
Archfield Rd BS6. . . . . . . **49** C1
Archgrove BS41. . . . . **61** F1
Archway St BA2. . . . . . . **102** B5
Ardagh Ct BS7 . . . . **49** F7
Arden Cl
Bristol BS32. . . . . **36** E6
Weston-s-M BS22 . . . . . . **88** F3
Ardenton Wlk BS10 . . . . **35** A3
Ardern Cl BS9 . . . . **48** B8
Ardmore BS8 . . . . **62** D7
Argus Ct 4 BS3. . . . . **63** C2
Argus Rd BS3 . . . . **63** C3
Argyle Ave
Bristol BS5. . . . . **50** C2
Weston-s-M BS23 . . . . . **104** F4
Argyle Dr BS37 . . . . **27** E4
Argyle Pl BS8. . . . . **142** A2
Argyle Rd
Bristol BS2. . . . . **143** B4
Bristol, Chester Park
BS16 . . . . **51** B2
Clevedon BS21. . . . . **57** F6
Argyle St
Bath BA2 . . . . **141** C2
5 Bristol, Eastville BS5 . **50** C2
6 Bristol, Southville BS3 **63** C4
Argyle Terr BA2 . . . . **101** C6
Arkells Ct GL12 . . . . **18** A6
Arley Cotts 5 BS6 . . . . . **49** D1
Arley Ct 4 BS6 . . . . **49** D1
Arley Hill BS6. . . . . **49** D1
Arley Pk BS6. . . . . **49** D1
Arley Terr BS5 . . . . **50** E1
Arlingham Way BS34. . . . **23** F1
Arlington Ho 4 BA1 . . **141** C2
Arlington Mans BS8. . . **142** B4
Arlington Rd
4 Bath BA2 . . . . **101** D5
Bristol BS4. . . . . **64** D5
Arlington Villas BS8 . . . **142** B3
Armada Ho BS2. . . . . **143** A4
Armada Pl BS1 . . . . **143** B4
Armes Ct BA2. . . . . **141** C1
Armidale Ave 4 BS6 . . . **49** E1
Armidale Cotts 5 BS6 . **49** E1
Armoury Sq BS5 . . . . **64** A8
Armstrong Cl BS35. . . . . **15** D7
Armstrong Ct BS37. . . . . **27** C3
Armstrong Dr BS30 . . . . **66** B5
Armstrong Way BS37. . . **27** B3
Arnall Dr BS10. . . . . **34** F1
Arncliffe BS10 . . . . **49** C8
Arneside Rd BS10. . . . . . **35** C1
Arnold Ct BS37 . . . . **28** B1
Arnold Rd BS16. . . . . **52** B3
Arnolds Field Trad Est
GL12. . . . . **18** A5
Arnold's Way BS49. . . . . **74** A2
Arnolfini (Arts Ctr)★
BS1 . . . . **143** A1
Arnor Cl BS22 . . . . **89** A4
Arno's St BS4. . . . . **64** A3
ARNO'S VALE **64** B4
Arrowfield Cl BS14. . . . . **80** A2
Artemesia Ave BS22. . . **105** E8
Arthur Ball Way BS10 . . **21** F2
Arthurs Cl BS16. . . . . **52** C6
Arthur Skemp Cl BS5. . . **64** B7
Arthur St
7 Bristol, Moorfields
BS5 . . . . **64** C8
Bristol, St Philip's Marsh
BS2 . . . . **64** A5
Arthurswood Rd BS13 . . **79** A4
Arundel Cl BS13 . . . . **79** B5
Arundel Ct BS7 . . . . **49** D3
Arundell Ct BS23. . . . . . **104** E8
Arundell Rd BS23 . . . . . . **87** E1
Arundel Rd
Bath BA1 . . . . **85** A1
Bristol BS7. . . . . **49** D3
Clevedon BS21. . . . . **57** F3
Arundel Wlk BS31. . . . . . **81** D5
Ascension Ho BA2 . . . . **101** D4
Ascot Cl BS16. . . . . **37** F1
Ascot Rd BS10 . . . . **35** E2
Ashbourne Cl 1 BS30. . **66** C6
Ash Brook BS39. . . . . . . **115** D1
Ashbrooke House Sch
BS23. . . . . **104** D6
Ashburton Rd BS10 . . . . **35** C1
Ashbury Dr BS22 . . . . **88** B2
Ash Cl
Bristol, Hillfields BS16. . . **51** C3
Bristol, Little Stoke BS34 **36** D7
Weston-s-M BS22 . . . . . . **89** D2
Winscombe BS25. . . . . . **108** A1
Yate BS37. . . . . **27** D3
Ashcombe Cres BS30. . . **66** D6
Ashcombe Ct 1 BS23 . **104** F7
Ashcombe Gdns BS23 . **105** A8
Ashcombe Park Rd
BS23. . . . . **88** A1
Ashcombe Pl 4 BS23 . **104** F7
Ashcombe Prim Sch
BS23. . . . . **105** A7
Ashcombe Rd BS23 . . . **104** F7
Ashcott BS14 . . . . **79** F7
Ashcroft BS24 . . . . **105** B2
Ashcroft Ave BS31 . . . . . **81** D5
Ashcroft Rd BS9 . . . . **48** C7
Ash Ct BS14 . . . . **80** A6
Ashdene Ave BS5 . . . . . . **50** D3
Ashdene Rd BS23 . . . . . **105** A8
Ashdown Ct BS9 . . . . **48** F8
Ashdown Rd BS20. . . . . . **45** A6
Asher La BS2 . . . . **143** C3
Ashes La BA2. . . . . **120** A4
Ashey La BS40 . . . . **110** A5
Ashfield Pl BS6 . . . . **49** F1
Ashfield Rd BS3. . . . . **63** B3
Ashfield Terr 9 BS3. . . . **63** B3
Ashford Dr BS24 . . . . . . **105** A1
Ashford Rd
Bath BA2 . . . . **101** D4
Bristol BS34. . . . . **36** A7
Redhill BS40. . . . . **93** E4
Ashford Way BS15 . . . . . **66** A7
Ash Gr
Bath BA2 . . . . **101** C4
Bristol BS16. . . . . **51** D3
Clevedon BS21. . . . . **57** G4
Weston-s-M BS23 . . . . . **104** E2
ASHGROVE. **134** D8
Ashgrove
Peasedown St John
BA2 . . . . **134** D8
Thornbury BS35. . . . . **8** C1
Ashgrove Ave
Abbots Leigh BS8. . . . . . . **62** B7
Bristol BS7. . . . . **49** F4
Ashgrove Cl BS7 . . . . **49** F4
Ashgrove Ct BA2 . . . . . **134** D8
Ashgrove Rd
Bristol, Ashley Down
BS7 . . . . **49** F4
Bristol, Bedminster BS3 . **63** B3
Ash Hayes Dr BS48. . . . . **59** E1
Ash Hayes Rd BS48. . . . . **59** F1
Ash La BS32 . . . . **23** D2
Ashland Rd BS13. . . . . . . **79** A4
Ashleigh Cl
Paulton BS39 . . . . **132** E6
Weston-s-M BS23 . . . . . **105** A8
Ashleigh Cres BS49 . . . . **91** B8
Ashleigh Rd
Weston-s-M BS23 . . . . . **105** A8
Yatton BS49 . . . . **91** B8
Ashley BS15 . . . . **65** F8
Ashley Ave BA1 . . . . **101** C7
Ashley Cl
Bristol BS7. . . . . **49** F4
Winscombe BS25. . . . . . **125** A7
Ashley Court Rd 2 BS7 **49** F2
Ashley Ct 1 BS2. . . . . . . **49** F1
ASHLEY DOWN **49** E4
Ashley Down Jun & Inf Schs BS7. . . . . **49** F5
Ashley Down Rd BS7 . . . **49** F4
Ashley Green BA15. . . . **103** F1
Ashley Grove Rd
7 Bristol BS2. . . . . **49** F2
1 Bristol BS2. . . . . **50** A1
Ashley Hill BS6, BS7 . . . . **49** F2
Ashley Ho BS34 . . . . **23** F1
Ashley La BA15 . . . . **120** F7
Ashley Par BS2 . . . . **49** F2
Ashley Pk BS6 . . . . **49** F3
Ashley Rd
Bathford BA1, SN13. . . . . **86** D2
Bristol BS6. . . . . **49** E1
Clevedon BS21. . . . . **57** D1
Ashley St BS2. . . . . **50** A1
Ashley Terr 1 BA1 . . . . **101** C7
Ashley Trad Est 6 BS2 . **49** F2
Ashman Cl BS5 . . . . **64** A8
Ashman Ct 1 BS16 . . . . . **50** E3
Ashmans Ct BA1 . . . . . . **101** B6
Ashmans Gate BS39. . . . **132** E5
Ashmans Yd BA1. . . . . . **101** B6
Ashmead BS39. . . . . **114** E1
Ashmead Ho 12 BS5. . . . **64** C7
Ashmead Way 8 BS1 . . **62** F5
Ash Rd
Banwell BS29. . . . . **106** E4
Bristol BS7. . . . . **49** E5
Ash Ridge Rd BS32. . . . . **24** B3
Ashton BS16. . . . . **37** C1
Ashton Ave BS1. . . . . . . **142** A1
Ashton Cl BS21 . . . . **57** D1
Ashton Court Estate★
BS41. . . . . **62** C4
Ashton Cres BS48 . . . . . . **59** D1
Ashton Dr BS3 . . . . **62** F2
ASHTON GATE **62** F4
Ashton Gate Prim Sch
BS3. . . . . **63** A4
Ashton Gate Rd BS3. . . . **63** A4
Ashton Gate Stadium (Bristol City FC) BS3. . **62** F3
Ashton Gate Terr 4
BS3. . . . . **63** A4
Ashton Gate Trad Est
BS3. . . . . **62** E3
Ashton Gate Underpass
BS3. . . . . **62** F3
Ashton Hill BA2. . . . . . . **100** A7
Ashton Park Sch BS3. . . **62** E3
Ashton Rd
Bristol BS3. . . . . **62** D2
Bristol, Ashton Gate BS3. **62** F4
Bristol, Bower Ashton
BS3 . . . . **62** D3
Ashton Rise BS3 . . . . **62** F2
ASHTON VALE **62** F2
Ashton Vale Prim Sch
BS3. . . . . **62** F2
Ashton Vale Rd BS3 . . . . **62** E3
Ashton Vale Trad Est
BS3. . . . . **62** F1
Ashton Way BS31 . . . . . . **81** E6
Ash Tree Cl BS24 . . . . . **122** C6
Ash Tree Ct BA3. . . . . . . **133** E1
Ashvale Cl BS48. . . . . **60** A2
Ashville Pk BS35. . . . . . . **15** B7
Ashville Rd BS3 . . . . **63** A4
Ashways Ho BS39 . . . . . **114** E1
Ashwell Cl BS14 . . . . **80** E6
Ashwicke BS14 . . . . **80** A6
Ashwicke Rd SN14 . . . . . **70** B3
Ash Wlk BS10. . . . . **35** B3
Ashwood BS40. . . . . **129** F4
Aspects L Pk BS15 . . . . . **65** E5
Aspen Cl SN14. . . . . **70** F6
Aspen Dr BS10. . . . . **35** B5
Aspen Park Rd BS22 . . **105** E8
Assembly Rooms★
BA1. . . . . **141** B3
Assembly Rooms La
BS1. . . . . **143** A2
Astazou Dr BS24 . . . . . . **105** B4
Aster Cres BS16. . . . . **52** D8
Aston Ho 4 BS1 . . . . . . **143** B1
Astry Cl BS11 . . . . **34** A1
Atchley St 18 BS5 . . . . . **64** B7
Athena Ct 3 BS7 . . . . . . **49** F4
Atherston BS30 . . . . **66** D5
Athlone Wlk BS4. . . . . . . **63** E1
Atholl Cl BS22 . . . . **88** F3
Atkins Cl BS14 . . . . **80** E6
Atlantic Rd
Bristol BS11. . . . . **47** C8
Weston-s-M BS23 . . . . . . **87** C1
Atlantic Rd S BS23 . . . . . **87** C1
Atlantic View Ct BS23 . . **87** C1
Atlas Cl BS5 . . . . **51** A2
Atlas Rd BS3. . . . . **63** E3
Atlas St BS2 . . . . **64** B5
Atlay Ct BS49 . . . . **74** B1
Atrium The
Bristol BS1. . . . . **143** B2
Bristol BS2. . . . . **143** C2
Attewell Ct BA2. . . . . . . **101** F4
Atwell Dr BS32. . . . . **24** B1
Atwood Dr BS11 . . . . **34** B2
Atyeo Cl BS3. . . . . **62** E1
Aubretia Rd BS16 . . . . . . **52** E7
Aubrey Ho 10 BS3. . . . . . **63** B3
Aubrey Meads BS30 . . . . **82** E8
Aubrey Rd BS3. . . . . **63** B3
Auburn Ave BS30 . . . . . . **66** B3
Auburn Rd BS6 . . . . **49** B1
Auckland Cl BS23 . . . . . **104** F3
Auden Mead BS7 . . . . . . **50** A8
Audley Ave BA1. . . . . . . **101** D7
Audley Cl
Bath BA1 . . . . **101** D7
Rangeworthy BS37 . . . . . **27** A8
Audley Gr BA1 . . . . **101** C7
Audley Lodge BA1 . . . . **101** D7
Audley Park Rd BA1. . . **101** C7
Audrey Wlk BS9. . . . . **49** D7
Augusta Pl BA1 . . . . **101** D7
Augustine's Cl BS20. . . . **44** E4
Augustus Ho BS15 . . . . . **65** B6
Aurelius Cl BS31 . . . . **81** F8
AUST **13** A6
Austen Dr BS22 . . . . **89** B4
Austen Gr BS7 . . . . **50** A8
Austen Ho BS7. . . . . **50** A8
Austen Pl BS11 . . . . **47** E7
Aust La BS9 . . . . **49** A8
Aust Rd
Northwick BS35. . . . . **12** D3
Olveston BS35 . . . . **13** F5
Autumn Mews BS24. . . **106** A8
Avalon Cl BS49. . . . . **74** A1
Avalon Ho BS48. . . . . **59** C1
Avalon La BS5 . . . . **65** B6
Avalon Rd BS5. . . . . **65** B6
Avebury Rd BS3. . . . . **62** F2
Avening Cl BS48 . . . . **76** A8
AVENING GREEN. **10** D8
Avening Rd BS15. . . . . . . **65** A8
Avenue Pl BA2. . . . . **102** B1
Avenue The
Backwell BS48. . . . . **76** A7
Bath, Bushey Norwood
BA2 . . . . **102** E5
Bath, Combe Down BA2 **102** C1
Bristol, Ashley Down BS7 **49** E3
Bristol, Clifton BS8 . . . . . **49** A1
Bristol, Crew's Hole BS5 . **64** F8
Bristol, Frenchay BS16 . . **36** E1

Avenue The *continued*
Bristol, Little Stoke BS34 . . 36 C6
Bristol, Patchway BS34 . . 24 B2
Bristol, Sneyd Park BS9 . . 48 E3
Clevedon BS21 . . . . 57 G6
Keynsham BS31 . . . . 81 E6
Timsbury BA2 . . . . 116 B2
Weston-s-M BS22 . . . . . . 89 C3
Winscombe BS25 . . . . . . 125 C8
Yate BS37 . . . . 27 D1
Yatton BS49 . . . . 91 B8
Averay Rd BS16 . . . . 50 C4
Averill Ct BS7 . . . . 57 F4
Avonbank Ind Est BS11 . 47 B7
Avonbridge Trad Est
BS11 . . . . 47 C8
Avon Bsns Pk BS16 . . . . 51 A3
Avon Cl
Bristol BS5 . . . . 64 F6
Keynsham BS31 . . . . 81 F6
Weston-s-M BS23 . . . . . . 104 F2
AVONCLIFF 120 F4
Avoncliff Halt BA15 . . . . 120 F5
Avon Cres
Bristol BS1 . . . . 142 A1
Wickwar GL12 . . . . 18 B6
Avon Ct
Batheaston BA1 . . . . 86 A4
Bristol, Clifton BS8 . . . . . 49 A1
Bristol, Fishponds BS16 . . 51 B5
Avondale Bldgs BA1 . . . . 85 B2
Avondale Bsns Ctr
BS15 . . . . 51 C2
Avondale Ct
Bath BA1 . . . . 101 B7
Bristol BS9 . . . . 48 D3
Bristol, Oldland BS30 . . . . 65 F3
Avondale Rd BA1 . . . . . . 101 B6
Avondown Cl BS10 . . . . . 35 D2
Avondown Ct 5 BS3 . . . . 63 C2
Avondown Ho BA2 . . . . . 101 B5
Avondowns Ct BS8 . . . . . 142 A4
Avon Gorge Ind Est
BS11 . . . . 47 C7
Avon Gorge Nature
Reserve ★ BS8 . . . . 62 E7
Avon Gr BS9 . . . . 48 D2
Avon Hts BA2 . . . . 120 C6
Avon La BS31 . . . . 82 F5
Avonlea
Bristol BS15 . . . . 65 C5
Yate BS37 . . . . 39 D8
Avonlea Ct BS30 . . . . . . 66 A3
Avonleaze BS9 . . . . 48 B5
Avonleigh Ct 4 BS3 . . . . 63 B2
Avonleigh Rd BS3 . . . . . 63 B2
Avonmead BS2 . . . . 143 B4
Avon Meads BS2 . . . . . . 64 C5
Avon Mill La BS31 . . . . . 81 F6
AVONMOUTH 33 D2
Avonmouth CE Prim Sch
BS11 . . . . 47 C8
Avonmouth Rd
Avonmouth BS11 . . . . 33 B1
Bristol BS11 . . . . 47 C8
Avonmouth Sta BS11 . . . 33 B1
Avonmouth Way
Avonmouth BS11 . . . . 33 D1
Bristol BS10 . . . . 34 E3
Avonmouth Way W
BS11 . . . . 33 B1
AVONPARK 120 C6
Avon Pk
Bath BA1 . . . . 101 A7
Bristol BS5 . . . . 64 D7
Avon Prim Sch BS11 . . . 47 D8
Avon Rd
Bristol BS13 . . . . 79 A6
Charfield GL12 . . . . 11 A4
Keynsham BS31 . . . . 81 F5
Pill BS20 . . . . 47 C5
Avon Rise SN14 . . . . 31 E4
Avon Riverside Est
BS11 . . . . 47 B7
Avon Riverside Sta ★
BS30 . . . . 82 E6
Avonside Ind Est BS2 . . . 64 C6
Avonside Rd BS2 . . . . . . 64 C6
Avonside Way BS4 . . . . . 64 C6
Avon Ski Centre ★
BS25 . . . . 108 C3
Avonsmere Residential Pk
BS34 . . . . 36 C3
Avon St
Bath BA1 . . . . 141 B2
Bristol BS2 . . . . 143 C2
Avon Trad Est BS2 . . . . . 64 A5
Avon Vale BS9 . . . . 48 D4
Avonvale Pl BA1 . . . . 85 F3
Avonvale Rd BS5 . . . . . . 64 C7
Avon Valley Bsns Pk
BS4 . . . . 64 E6
Avon Valley Ctry Pk ★
BS31 . . . . 82 D6
Avon Valley Farm Bsns Pk
BS31 . . . . 82 D5

Avon Valley Rly ★
Bitton BS30 . . . . 82 D7
Bristol BS30 . . . . 66 C3
Avon View BS15 . . . . 65 B3
Avon Way
Bristol BS9 . . . . 48 C4
Bristol, Southmead BS10 . 49 D7
Portishead BS20 . . . . 45 C5
Thornbury BS35 . . . . 15 D7
Avonwood Cl BS11 . . . . . 47 E6
Awdelett Cl BS11 . . . . . . 34 B1
AWKLEY 23 E8
Awkley La BS32 . . . . 23 E8
Awkward Hill BS40 . . . . 111 D5
AXBRIDGE 125 B1
Axbridge Bypass BS26 . 125 A3
Axbridge CE Fst Sch
BS26 . . . . 125 C1
Axbridge Ct BS48 . . . . . . 75 E8
Axbridge Moor Dro
BS26 . . . . 125 C1
Axbridge Rd
Bath BA2 . . . . 102 A2
Bristol BS4 . . . . 63 F2
Cheddar BS27 . . . . 125 F2
Axe Cl BS23 . . . . 105 A5
Axe Ct 4 BS35 . . . . 15 C8
Axford Way BA2 . . . . . . 134 D8
Axis BS14 . . . . 79 D5
Aycote Cl BS22 . . . . 88 C2
Ayford La SN14 . . . . 69 F4
Aylesbury Cres BS3 . . . . 63 B1
Aylesbury Rd BS3 . . . . . 63 B1
Aylmer Cres BS14 . . . . . 80 B6
Aylminton Wlk BS11 . . . . 34 B2
Ayr St BA2 . . . . 101 D6
Azalea Rd BS22 . . . . 89 A5
Azelin Ave BS13 . . . . 79 B5

B

BABINGTON 140 C3
Backfield Farm BS37 . . . . 26 F5
Backfields BS2 . . . . 143 B4
Backfields Ct BS2 . . . . . 143 B4
Backfields La BS2 . . . . . 143 B4
Back La
Axbridge BS26 . . . . 125 C2
Chewton Mendip BA3 . . 130 B1
Keynsham BS31 . . . . 81 E6
Kingston Seymour BS21 . 73 A5
Litton BA3 . . . . 130 E2
Marshfield SN14 . . . . 69 F8
Pill BS20 . . . . 47 C5
Pucklechurch BS16 . . . . . 53 C4
Rowberrow BS25 . . . . . . 109 A1
Wickwar GL12 . . . . 18 A5
Back Of Kingsdown Par
BS6 . . . . 49 B1
Back Rd BS3 . . . . 63 A4
Back St
Hawkesbury Upton GL9 . 20 A3
Weston-s-M BS23 . . . . . 104 E7
Back Stoke La BS9 . . . . . 48 F6
BACKWELL 76 B6
Backwell Bow BS48 . . . . 60 C1
Backwell CE Jun Sch
BS48 . . . . 76 C5
Backwell Comm BS48 . . . 76 B8
BACKWELL COMMON . . 76 B8
Backwell Down BS48 . . . . 76 D6
BACKWELL GREEN 76 D8
Backwell Hill BS48 . . . . . 76 B3
Backwell Hill Rd BS48 . . . 76 E5
Backwell Sch BS48 . . . . . 76 B6
Backwell Wlk BS13 . . . . . 78 F8
Backy Hill BA2 . . . . 118 C4
Badenham Gr BS11 . . . . . 47 F8
Baden Hill Rd GL12 . . . . 16 C6
Baden Ho BA1 . . . . 141 B4
Baden Rd
Bristol, Kingswood
BS15 . . . . 66 A7
Bristol, Redfield BS5 . . . . 64 C7
Bader Cl BS37 . . . . 27 D3
Badger Cl BS30 . . . . 65 F3
Badger Rd BS35 . . . . 8 D3
Badger Rise BS20 . . . . . . 44 F3
Badgers Cl BS32 . . . . 24 D3
Badger Sett BS5 . . . . 65 B7
Badgers Holt BS14 . . . . . 80 C6
Badger's La BS32 . . . . . . 23 C3
Badgers Rise BS10 . . . . . 35 E4
Badgers The BS22 . . . . . 89 D3
Badgers Way BS24 . . . . 105 F8
Badgers Wlk BS4 . . . . . . 64 D2
Badgeworth BS37 . . . . . . 39 D6
Badman Cl BS39 . . . . . . 132 D5
BADMINTON 30 F2
Badminton BS16 . . . . 37 C1
Badminton Ct
17 Weston-s-M BS23 . . . 87 C1
Yate BS37 . . . . 27 C2
Badminton Ctr The
BS37 . . . . 27 C2
Badminton Gdns BA1 . . 101 C8

Badminton Rd
Bristol, Downend BS16 . . 51 E7
Bristol, Montpelier BS7 . . 49 F1
Chipping Sodbury BS37 . . 41 B7
Frampton Cotterell BS36,
BS37 . . . . 38 C6
Badminton Road Trad Est
BS37 . . . . 27 B1
Badminton Sch BS9 . . . . 49 A5
Badminton Wlk BS16 . . . 51 E7
Badock's Wood Prim Sch
BS10 . . . . 35 B1
Baggridge Hill BA2 . . . . 135 F7
Baglyn Ave
Bristol BS15 . . . . 51 F3
Mangotsfield BS15 . . . . . 50 F3
Bagnell Cl BS14 . . . . 80 E5
Bagnell Rd BS14 . . . . 80 E5
BAGSTONE 17 A3
Bagstone Rd BS37, GL12 . 17 A2
Bagworth Dr BS30 . . . . . 65 F3
BAILBROOK 85 D3
Bailbrook Gr BA1 . . . . . . 85 C3
Bailbrook La BA1 . . . . . . 85 D3
Baildon Cres BS23 . . . . 105 A4
Baildon Ct 2 BS23 . . . . 104 F4
Baildon Rd BS23 . . . . . . 105 A4
Bailey Cl BS22 . . . . 105 E8
Bailey Ct BS20 . . . . 45 F6
Bailey's Court Prim Sch
BS32 . . . . 36 F6
Baileys Court Rd BS32 . . 36 F6
Baileys Ct BS32 . . . . 36 F6
Baileys Mead Rd BS16 . . 50 C5
Bailiffs' Wall BS26 . . . . 125 C1
Baily Pl BS7 . . . . 50 C8
Bainsbury View BA3 . . . 138 F1
Baker Cl 7 BS21 . . . . . . 57 D1
Baker's Bldgs BS40 . . . . 92 D2
Bakersfield BS30 . . . . . . 66 B3
Bakers Ground BS34 . . . . 37 A5
Bakers La
Chilcompton BA3 . . . . . 138 D3
Lower Langford BS40 . . 109 C8
Bakers Par BA2 . . . . 116 B2
Bakers Pk BS13 . . . . 79 B6
Baker St BS23 . . . . 104 E8
Balaclava Ind Est BS16 . 50 F3
Balaclava Rd BS16 . . . . . 50 F3
Baldwin Chambers 6
BS1 . . . . 143 A2
Baldwin Lofts BS1 . . . . . 143 A2
Baldwin St BS1 . . . . 143 A2
Balfour Rd BS3 . . . . 63 B3
Ballance St BA1 . . . . . . 141 B4
Ballast La BS11 . . . . 33 C2
Balls Barn La BS24 . . . . . 90 A2
Balmain St BS4 . . . . 64 A4
Balmoral Cl BS34 . . . . . . 36 D4
Balmoral Ct BS16 . . . . . . 52 A5
Balmoral Ho BS1 . . . . . 142 C1
Balmoral Mans 3 BS7 . 49 F2
Balmoral Rd
Bristol, Longwell Green
BS30 . . . . 65 F2
Bristol, Montpelier BS7 . . 49 F2
Keynsham BS31 . . . . 81 E4
Balmoral Way BS22 . . . . 88 D2
Baltic Pl BS20 . . . . 47 D4
Balustrade 17 BA1 . . . . . 85 B1
Bamfield BS14 . . . . 80 A6
Bampton 5 BS22 . . . . . . 88 F2
Bampton Cl
Bristol, Emerson's Green
BS16 . . . . 52 C6
Bristol, Headley Park
BS13 . . . . 79 B7
Bampton Croft BS16 . . . . 52 C6
Bampton Dr BS16 . . . . . . 37 D1
Banfield Cl BS11 . . . . 48 A8
Bangor Gr BS4 . . . . 64 F5
Bangrove Wlk BS11 . . . . 47 E8
Banister Gr BS4 . . . . 79 D7
Bank Leaze Prim Sch
BS11 . . . . 34 B2
Bank Pl BS20 . . . . 47 D4
Bank Rd
Avonmouth BS11 . . . . . . 33 D7
Bristol BS15 . . . . 65 D8
Pilning BS35 . . . . 22 E6
Banks Cl BS21 . . . . 73 D8
Bankside BS16 . . . . 51 F4
Bankside Rd BS4 . . . . . . 64 D3
Bannerdown Cl BA1 . . . . 86 B4
Bannerdown Dr BA1 . . . . 86 A4
Bannerdown Rd BA1 . . . . 86 C5
Bannerleigh La BS8 . . . . 62 E6
Bannerleigh Rd BS8 . . . . 62 E6
Bannerman Rd BS5 . . . . . 64 B8
Bannerman Road Com Sch
BS5 . . . . 50 B1
Banner Rd BS6 . . . . 49 E1
Bannetts Tree Cres
BS35 . . . . 15 A5
Bantock Cl BS4 . . . . 79 D6
Bantry Rd BS4 . . . . 79 E8
BANWELL 107 B3
Banwell Caves BS26 . . . 106 E2

Banwell Cl
Bristol BS13 . . . . 79 A8
Keynsham BS31 . . . . 82 A2
Banwell Prim Sch
BS29 . . . . 107 B3
Banwell Rd
Banwell BS26, BS29 . . . 123 E8
Bath BA2 . . . . 118 D8
Bristol BS3 . . . . 63 A3
Locking BS24 . . . . 106 B3
Winscombe BS25, BS29 124 E8
Banyard Rd BS20 . . . . . . 46 E5
BAPTIST MILLS 50 A2
Baptist St BS5 . . . . 50 A1
Baranwheel Ct BS5 . . . . . 64 F6
Barberry Farm Rd
BS49 . . . . 74 B1
Barbour Gdns BS13 . . . . 79 D3
Barbour Rd BS13 . . . . . . 79 D3
Barcroft Cl BS15 . . . . 65 C8
Barker Ct
5 Bristol BS5 . . . . 64 C7
Long Ashton BS41 . . . . . 61 E1
Barkers Mead BS37 . . . . . 27 F4
Barker Wlk BS5 . . . . 50 A1
Barkleys Hill BS16 . . . . . 50 C5
Barlands Ho BS10 . . . . . . 34 F3
Barley Cl
Bristol BS16 . . . . 52 A6
Frampton Cotterell BS36 . 38 C8
Barley Close Com Prim
Sch BS16 . . . . 52 A6
Barley Croft BS9 . . . . 48 F5
Barley Cross BS22 . . . . . 89 A5
Barleyfields BS2 . . . . . . 143 C2
Barley Fields BS35 . . . . . 8 B3
Barley Wood Walled
Garden ★ BS40 . . . . . . 92 F3
Barnabas Cl BS26 . . . . . 125 D2
Barnabas St 9 BS2 . . . . 49 E1
Barnaby Cl BA3 . . . . . . 133 B2
Barnack Trad Est BS3 . . 63 C1
Barnard's Cl BS49 . . . . . 91 C7
Barnard Wlk BS31 . . . . . 81 D4
Barn Cl BS16 . . . . 52 B6
Barn End
East Harptree BS40 . . . . 129 E3
Marshfield SN14 . . . . 70 A8
Barnes Ct BS34 . . . . 36 E3
Barnes St BS5 . . . . 64 D8
Barnfield Way BA1 . . . . . 86 B3
Barn Hill BA2 . . . . 134 F5
Barnhill Cl BS37 . . . . 28 A4
Barnhill Rd BS37 . . . . . . 28 B1
Barn La BS39 . . . . 115 A7
Barn Owl Way BS34 . . . . 36 F5
Barn Pool BS25 . . . . 125 F8
Barns Cl
Barrow Gurney BS48 . . . . 77 E4
Nailsea BS48 . . . . 59 E2
Barns Ground BS21 . . . . 73 E8
Barnstaple Ct BS4 . . . . . 79 E8
Barnstaple Rd BS4 . . . . . 79 E8
Barnstaple Wlk BS4 . . . . 79 F8
Barnwood 4 BS7 . . . . . . 50 C8
Barnwood Ct BS48 . . . . . 59 B1
Barnwood Rd BS37 . . . . . 39 C7
Baron Cl BS30 . . . . 82 E8
Barons Cl BS3 . . . . 62 F3
Barossa Pl BS1 . . . . 143 A1
Barrack's La BS11 . . . . . . 47 D8
Barratt St BS5 . . . . 50 C1
Barrington Cl BS15 . . . . . 51 F2
Barrington Ct
Bristol BS4 . . . . 64 A4
11 Bristol, Knowle BS2 . 63 F4
Bristol, New Cheltenham
BS15 . . . . 51 E1
BARROW COMMON 78 B4
Barrow Court La BS19 . . 77 B5
Barrow Ct
Barrow Gurney BS48 . . . . 77 A5
Tickenham BS21 . . . . 58 F4
BARROW GURNEY 77 E5
Barrow Hill BS30 . . . . . . 67 B5
Barrow Hill Cres BS11 . . 47 C7
Barrow Hill Rd BS11 . . . . 47 D6
Barrow La BS40 . . . . 77 F1
Barrowmead Dr BS11 . . . 47 F7
Barrow Rd
Bath BA2 . . . . 101 C1
Bristol BS2 . . . . 64 A7
Hutton BS24 . . . . 105 E2
Barrow St BS48 . . . . 77 D5
Barrows The
Cheddar BS27 . . . . 126 A1
Weston-s-M BS22 . . . . . 105 A7
BARROW VALE 115 D5
Barrs Court Ave BS30 . . . 66 A5
Barrs Court Prim Sch
BS30 . . . . 65 F5
Barrs Court Rd BS30 . . . . 66 A5
Barrs La GL11 . . . . 5 E4
Barry Cl
Bristol BS30 . . . . 66 C1
Weston-s-M BS24 . . . . . 105 A1
Barry Rd BS30 . . . . 66 C2
Barstaple Ho BS2 . . . . . 143 C3
Barter Cl BS15 . . . . 65 D8

Bartholomew Row
BA2 . . . . 116 B2
Bartholomew Sq BS7 . . . 49 F7
Bartletts Ct BA2 . . . . . . 141 C1
Bartlett's Rd BS3 . . . . . . 63 C2
Bartlett St 6 BA1 . . . . . 141 B3
Bartletts Way BS24 . . . . 106 A4
Bartley Ct BS5 . . . . 64 C7
Bartley St BS3 . . . . 63 D4
BARTON 124 B6
Barton Bldgs BA1 . . . . . 141 B3
Barton Cl
Alveston BS35 . . . . 15 A5
1 Bristol BS4 . . . . 64 F6
Winterbourne BS36 . . . . . 37 E5
Barton Ct BS5 . . . . 64 C6
Barton Dro BS25 . . . . . . 124 D5
Barton Gn BS5 . . . . 64 B7
BARTON HILL 64 C6
Barton Hill Prim Sch
BS5 . . . . 64 B6
Barton Hill Rd BS5 . . . . . 64 B7
Barton Hill Trad Est 10
BS5 . . . . 64 C6
Barton Ho BS5 . . . . 64 C6
Bartonia Gr BS4 . . . . 64 D1
Barton Manor BS2 . . . . . 64 A6
Barton Rd
Bristol BS2 . . . . 143 C2
Winscombe BS26 . . . . . . 124 C6
Barton St
Bath BA1 . . . . 141 B2
Bristol BS1 . . . . 143 A4
Barton The
Barton BS25 . . . . 124 B5
Bleadon BS24 . . . . 122 C6
Bristol BS15 . . . . 65 C4
Compton Martin BS40 . . 129 B7
Corston BA2 . . . . 100 A7
Hawkesbury Upton GL9 . 19 F3
Norton St Philip BA2 . . . 136 E4
Barton Vale
6 Bristol BS2 . . . . 64 A6
Bristol BS2 . . . . 143 C2
Barton Wlk BS7 . . . . 50 B8
Barwick Ho BS11 . . . . . . 47 C7
Barwood Cl BS15 . . . . . . 65 E8
BATCH 121 F3
Batch Bsns Pk BS24 . . . 121 F2
Batches The BS3 . . . . 63 C3
Batchfield La BS16 . . . . . 53 D8
Batch La
Clutton BS39 . . . . 114 F3
Lympsham BS24 . . . . . . 121 F3
Batch The
Backwell BS48 . . . . 76 D1
Batheaston BA1 . . . . 85 F3
Burrington BS40 . . . . . . 110 B3
Butcombe BS40 . . . . . . 111 B8
Chew Magna BS40 . . . . . 96 B3
Churchill BS25 . . . . 108 F4
Compton Martin BS40 . . 129 A6
Farmborough BA2 . . . . . 116 A6
Hinton Charterhouse
BA2 . . . . 119 C1
Saltford BS31 . . . . 82 F3
Yatton BS49 . . . . 91 B7
Bates Cl BS5 . . . . 64 A8
BATH 141 B1
Bath Abbey ★ BA1 . . . . . 141 C2
Bath Acad BA1 . . . . 141 B3
BATHAMPTON 85 F1
Bathampton La BA2 . . . . 85 E1
Bathampton Prim Sch
BA2 . . . . 85 F2
Bath Bldgs BS6 . . . . 49 E1
Bath Bridge Rdbt
BS1 . . . . 143 C1
Bath Chew Valley
Caravan Pk BS39 . . . . 113 C4
Bath Coll BA3 . . . . 133 F2
BATHEASTON 85 F4
Batheaston CE Prim Sch
BA1 . . . . 85 F4
BATHFORD 86 C1
Bathford CE Prim Sch
BA1 . . . . 86 C2
Bathford Hill
Bathford BA1 . . . . 86 B2
Compton Dando BS39 . . . 98 E5
Bathford Manor BA1 . . . . 86 C2
Bath Foyer The BA2 . . . 101 A4
Bath Hill
Keynsham BS31 . . . . 81 F5
Wellow BA2 . . . . 118 C2
Bathings The 1 BS35 . . 15 C8
Bath La GL9 . . . . 19 E2
Bath New Rd BA3 . . . . . 133 F4
Bath Old Rd BA3 . . . . . . 133 F4
Bath Postal Mus ★
BA1 . . . . 141 C2
Bath Race Course ★
BA1 . . . . 84 A4
Bath Rd
Bitton BS30 . . . . 82 B8
Blagdon BS40 . . . . 111 B1
Bristol BS2, BS4 . . . . . . 143 C1
Bristol, Brislington BS4 . . 64 F1

Bath Rd continued
Bristol, Longwell Green
BS30 . . . . **65** F3
Bristol, North Common
BS30 . . . . **66** D6
Bristol, Totterdown BS4. . **64** B4
Bristol, Upper Knowle
BS4 . . . . **64** D2
Bristol, Willsbridge BS30 **66** C1
Chipping Sodbury BS37,
GL9 . . . . **41** C4
Colerne SN14 . . . . **70** E2
Farmborough BA2 . . . . **115** E5
Kelston BA1, BS30. . . . **83** B6
Kingsdown SN13 . . . . . **86** F5
Norton St Philip BA2 . . **136** E5
Paulton BS39 . . . . . . **132** F6
Peasedown St John
BA2 . . . . **134** C7
Saltford BS31 . . . . . . **82** D3
Thornbury BS35 . . . . . **15** B8
Upper Langford BS40 . . **109** D3
Wick BS30 . . . . **67** E4
Bath Spa Sta BA1 . . . . **141** C1
Bath Spa Univ Art and
Design BA1 . . . . **84** E1
Bath Spa University Coll
(Newton Pk Campus)
BA2 . . . . **100** B5
Bath St
Bath BA1 . . . . **141** C2
Bristol BS1 . . . . **143** B2
Bristol, Ashton Gate BS3 **63** A4
Bristol, Staple Hill BS16 . **51** E4
Bathurst Par BS1 . . . . **143** A1
Bathurst Rd BS22 . . . . **105** C8
Bath View BA3 . . . . . . **138** F1
Bathwell Rd BS4 . . . . . **64** A3
BATHWICK **102** B7
Bathwick Hill BA2 . . . . **102** C6
Bathwick Rise BA2. . . . **102** B7
Bathwick St Mary CE Prim
Sch BA2 . . . . **102** C8
Bathwick St BA1, BA2. . **141** C4
Batley St BS30 . . . . . . **66** D4
Batstone Cl BA1 . . . . . **85** B2
Batt Cl BS32 . . . . **24** E5
Battenburg Rd BS5. . . . **65** A8
Batten Ct BS37. . . . . . **28** C1
Batten's La BS5 . . . . . **65** A6
Battens Rd BS5 . . . . . **65** B7
Battersby Way BS10. . . **34** E2
Battersea Rd BS5 . . . . **64** C8
Battery La BS20. . . . . . **45** D7
Battery Rd BS20 . . . . . **45** D6
Battle La BS40 . . . . . . **96** A3
Battle Wk BA1 . . . . . . **84** E4
Battson Rd BS14 . . . . . **80** E4
Baugh Gdns BS16 . . . . **37** E1
Baugh Rd BS16 . . . . . . **37** E1
Baxter Cl BS15 . . . . . . **65** F8
Bayer Bldg The BA2 . . **141** B1
Bay Gdns BS5 . . . . . . **50** C2
Bayham Rd BS4 . . . . . . **64** A3
Bayleys Dr BS15 . . . . . **65** C6
Baynham Ct BS15 . . . . **65** B5
Baynton Ho BS5. . . . . . **64** C7
Baynton Rd BS3. . . . . . **63** A4
Bay Rd BS21 . . . . **57** F6
Bayswater Ave BS6. . . . **49** B3
Bayswater Rd BS7 . . . . **49** F7
Bay Tree Cl BS34 . . . . . **35** F7
Baytree Ct BS22. . . . . . **88** C1
Baytree Rd BS22 . . . . . **88** C1
Bay Tree Rd
Bath BA1 . . . . **85** B2
Clevedon BS21 . . . . . . **57** G1
Baytree Sch BS24 . . . . **106** A8
Bay Tree View BS22. . . **88** D1
Baytree View BS22 . . . **88** D1
Bay Willow Dr BS6 . . . . **49** B2
BEACH **67** C2
Beach Ave
Clevedon BS21. . . . . . **57** E2
Severn Beach BS35 . . . . **22** A7
Beach Ct BS23 . . . . . **104** D6
Beach End Rd BS23 . . **104** C2
Beachgrove Gdns BS16 **51** C4
Beachgrove Rd BS16 . . **51** B4
Beach Hill
Bristol BS30 . . . . **66** F3
Portishead BS20 . . . . . **45** C6
Beach La BS30 . . . . . . **67** C2
Beachlands Pk BS22 . . **88** A4
Beachley Wlk BS11. . . . **47** D7
Beach Mews BS21 . . . . **57** E4
Beach Rd
Severn Beach BS35 . . . . **21** F7
Weston-s-M BS23 . . . . **104** D6
Weston-s-M, Kewstoke
BS22. . . . . **88** A5
Beach Rd E BS20 . . . . . **45** D6
Beach Rd W BS20 . . . . . **45** C6
Beach The BS21 . . . . . . **57** E4
BEACON HILL **84** F1
Beacon La BS16. . . . . . **37** C6
Beaconlea BS15 . . . . . **65** D6
Beacon Rd BA1. . . . . . . **85** A1

Beacon Rise Prim Sch
BS15. . . . . **65** D6
Beaconsfield Cl 6 BS2. **64** B6
Beaconsfield Rd
Bristol, Clifton BS8 . . . . **49** A1
Bristol, Crew's Hole BS5 . **64** E7
Bristol, Kensington Park
BS4 . . . . **64** B3
Clevedon BS21. . . . . . . **57** G3
Weston-s-M BS23 . . . . **104** E7
Beaconsfield St 8 BS5. **64** B6
Beafort Cl BS24 . . . . . **106** C3
Beale Cl BS14 . . . . **80** E6
Beam St BS5 . . . . **64** C7
Bean Acre The BS11. . . **47** D8
Beanhill Cres BS35 . . . **15** A5
Beanwood Pk (Cvn Site)
BS37. . . . . **39** E3
Bearbridge Rd BS13. . . **78** F4
BEAR FLAT **101** F4
Bear Yard Mews 2
BS8. . . . . **142** A2
Beauchamp Ave BA3 . . **139** B6
Beauchamp Pk BA3 . . . **139** B6
Beauchamp Rd BS7 . . . **49** D4
Beauchamps Dr BA3 . . **139** A5
Beauford Sq BA1. . . . . **141** B2
Beaufort Bldgs 7 BS8 . **62** F7
Beaufort Cl BS5. . . . . . **64** D7
Beaufort Cres BS34 . . . **36** E4
Beaufort Ct
Bristol BS16. . . . . **52** A8
Clevedon BS21. . . . . . . **57** E5
Beaufort E BA1 . . . . . . **85** C1
Beaufort Gdns 2 BS48 . **59** D1
Beaufort Ho 11 BS5 . . . **64** B7
Beaufort Hts BS5 . . . . . **64** E7
Beaufort Mews
3 Bath BA1 . . . . **85** C1
11 Bristol BS8 . . . . **62** F7
Chipping Sodbury BS37 . . **28** B1
Beaufort Pl
Bath BA1 . . . . **85** C1
Bristol, Frenchay BS16 . . **37** B1
Bristol, Upper Easton
BS5 . . . . **64** A8
Beaufort Rd
Bristol, Clifton BS8 . . . . **49** A1
Bristol, Horfield BS7 . . . **49** F6
Bristol, Kingswood BS15 . **51** C1
Bristol, Pile Marsh BS5 . . **64** E7
Bristol, Staple Hill BS16 . **51** E5
Bristol, Vinney Green
BS16 . . . . **52** A8
Frampton Cotterell BS36 . **38** A8
Weston-s-M BS23 . . . . **104** F7
Yate BS37 . . . . **27** D2
Beaufort St
2 Bristol, Bedminster
BS3 . . . . **63** C2
4 Bristol, Upper Easton
BS5 . . . . **64** A8
Beaufort Trad Pk BS16 . **53** B5
Beaufort View SN14 . . . **31** E4
Beaufort Villas 8 BA1. . **85** B1
Beaufort W 11 BA1. . . . **85** B1
Beaufort Way BS10. . . . **49** D8
Beauley Rd BS3. . . . . . . **63** B4
Beaumont BA1. . . . . . . **84** F1
Beaumont Cl
Bristol BS30 . . . . **66** A3
Weston-s-M BS23 . . . . **104** F4
Beaumont St BS5 . . . . . **64** A8
Beaumont Terr 6 BS5. . **64** A8
Beau St BA1 . . . . **141** B2
Beaver Cl BS36 . . . . . . **37** F7
Beazer Cl 4 BS16. . . . . **51** D3
Beck Cl BS16 . . . . **52** C7
Becket Ct BS16 . . . . . . **53** B5
Becket Dr BS22 . . . . . . **89** A3
Becket Prim Sch BS22. . **89** A2
Becket Rd BS22 . . . . . . **89** A4
Becket's La BS48. . . . . . **75** E8
Beckford Ct BA2 . . . . . **102** B7
Beckford Dr BA1. . . . . . **84** E4
Beckford Gdns
Bath BA2 . . . . **102** B8
Bristol BS14. . . . . **80** A3
Beckford Rd BA2. . . . . **102** B7
Beckford's Twr & Mus ★
BA1. . . . . **84** D4
Beckhampton Rd BA2 . **101** D5
Beck Ho BS34. . . . . **36** A8
Beckington Rd BS3 . . . . **63** F2
Beckington Wlk BS3 . . . **63** F2
Becks Bsns Pk BS23. . . **105** A7
Beckspool Rd BS16 . . . . **37** C1
Bedford Cres BS7 . . . . . **49** F5
Bedford Ct 9 BA1 . . . . **102** B8
Bedford Rd BS23 . . . . **104** E4
Bedford St
Bath BA1 . . . . **102** B8
6 Bathwick BA2. . . . . . **102** B8
BEDMINSTER **63** C3

BEDMINSTER DOWN . . . **79** B8
Bedminster Down Rd BS3,
BS13. . . . . **63** B1
Bedminster Down Sch
Bristol BS13. . . . . **78** F7
Bristol BS13. . . . . **79** A7
Bedminster Par BS3 . . . **63** D4
Bedminster Pl 9 BS3 . . . **63** D4
Bedminster Rd BS3 . . . . **63** C2
Bedminster Sta BS3. . . . **63** D3
Bedwin BS20 . . . . **44** F4
Beechacres BS35 . . . . . . **8** C1
Beech Ave BA2 . . . . . . **102** E5
Beech Cl
Alveston BS35 . . . . **15** A5
Bristol BS30. . . . . **66** A5
Shipham BS25 . . . . . . **125** F8
Beechcroft BS41 . . . . . . **78** D2
Beech Croft BS14 . . . . . **80** B5
Beechcroft Wlk BS7. . . . **50** A8
Beech Ct BS14 . . . . **80** A5
Beech Dr
Nailsea BS48. . . . . **60** A3
Shipham BS25 . . . . . . **125** E8
BEECHEN CLIFF **141** B1
Beechen Cliff Rd BA2 . . **141** B1
Beechen Cliff Sch
BA2 . . . . **102** A4
Beechen Cliff Villas
BA2 . . . . **141** B1
Beechen Dr BS16 . . . . . **51** B3
Beeches Gr BS4 . . . . . . **64** D2
Beeches Ind Est BS37 . . **27** B2
Beeches The
Bath BA2 . . . . **101** D1
Bristol BS9 . . . . **48** D3
Bristol, Bradley Stoke
BS32 . . . . **36** D8
Bristol, Frenchay BS16 . . **37** B1
Bristol, Oldland Common
BS30 . . . . **66** C2
Bristol, St Anne's BS4 . . . **64** E5
Sandford BS25 . . . . . **108** B4
Beechfield Cl BS41. . . . . **62** C2
Beechfield Gr BS9 . . . . . **48** C8
Beech Gr BA2 . . . . **101** D4
BEECH HILL **39** B7
Beech Ho
Bristol BS16. . . . . **50** C5
Clevedon BS21 . . . . . . **57** F4
Beech Leaze BS35 . . . . . **15** A5
Beechmont Dr BS24. . . **105** A1
Beechmont Cl BS24 . . . **104** F1
Beechmount Ct BS14. . . **80** B8
Beechmount Gr BS14 . . **80** B8
Beech Rd
Bristol BS7. . . . . **49** E5
Saltford BS31. . . . . **82** E3
Shipham BS25 . . . . . . **125** E8
Yatton BS49 . . . . **91** C8
Beech Terr BA3 . . . . . . **133** E1
Beechwood Ave
Bristol BS15. . . . . **65** D5
Locking BS24 . . . . **106** A5
Beechwood Cl BS14 . . . . **80** C8
Beechwood Dr BS20 . . . **44** E5
Beechwood Ho BS16 . . . **51** A4
Beechwood Rd
Bath BA2 . . . . **102** B2
Bristol BS16. . . . . **51** B4
Easton-in-G BS20. . . . . **47** A4
Nailsea BS48. . . . . **59** D2
Portishead BS20 . . . . . **44** E5
Beehive Trad Est BS5. . . **64** E7
Beehive Yd BA1. . . . . . **141** C4
Beek's La SN14, BA1 . . . **69** D5
Bees Ho BS21. . . . . **57** E2
Beesmoor Rd BS36 . . . . **38** B6
Begbrook Dr BS16 . . . . . **50** F6
Begbrook La BS16 . . . . . **50** F6
Begbrook Pk BS16 . . . . . **51** A7
Begbrook Prim Acad
BS16. . . . . **50** F6
Beggar Bush La BS8 . . . **62** B6
Beggarswell Cl BS2 . . . **143** C4
Belfast Wlk BS4. . . . . . . **79** E8
Belfields La BS16 . . . . . . **37** C1
Belfry BS30 . . . . **66** B6
Belfry Ave BS5. . . . . **65** A8
Belgrave Cres BA1 . . . . **141** C4
Belgrave Hill 5 BS8 . . . **49** A2
Belgrave Ho BS8. . . . . . **142** A3
Belgrave Pl
Bath BA1 . . . . **141** C4
Bristol BS8 . . . . **142** A3
Belgrave Rd
Bath BA1 . . . . **85** B1
Bristol BS8 . . . . **142** A4
Weston-s-M BS22 . . . . **105** B8
Belgrave Terr 1 BA1. . . . **85** A1
Bellamy Ave BS13 . . . . . **79** C4
Bellamy Cl BS15 . . . . . . **65** A5
Belland Dr BS14 . . . . . . **79** F4
Bell Ave BS1. . . . . **143** A1
Bella Vista Rd BA1 . . . . **141** B4
Bell Barn Rd BS9. . . . . . **48** D6
Bell Cl
Bristol BS10. . . . . **49** E7
Farmborough BA2 . . . . **115** F6

Belle Ct 7 BS2 . . . . **63** F4
Bellevue BS8 . . . . **142** B2
BELLE VUE **133** B3
Belle Vue BA3. . . . . . . **133** B3
Bellevue Cl BS15 . . . . . **65** E7
Belle Vue Cl BA2 . . . . . **134** D7
Bellevue Cotts
Bristol, Brandon Hill
BS8 . . . . **142** B2
5 Bristol, Eastfield BS9 **49** A7
Bellevue Cres BS8 . . . . **142** B2
Bellevue Ct
Bristol, Brandon Hill
BS8 . . . . **142** B2
6 Bristol, St George
BS5 . . . . **65** A8
Clevedon BS21 . . . . **57** F4
Bellevue Mans BS21. . . **57** F4
Bellevue Pk BS4 . . . . . . **64** D2
Bellevue Rd
Bristol, Kingswood
BS15 . . . . **65** F7
Bristol, St George BS5. . . **65** A8
6 Bristol, Windmill Hill
BS2 . . . . **63** F4
Clevedon BS21 . . . . **57** F4
Belle Vue Rd BS5. . . . . . **50** C1
Bellevue Terr
Bristol BS8 . . . . **142** B2
Bristol, Brislington BS4. . **64** D2
Bristol, Windmill Hill BS2. **63** F4
Bell Field The SN14 . . . . **31** E4
Bellflower Cl BS16 . . . . . **52** D8
Bellhanger Ct BA1 . . . . **141** B4
Bell Hill
Bristol BS16. . . . . **50** C4
Norton St Philip BA2 . . **136** E4
Bell Hill Rd BS5. . . . . . . **64** F8
Bellhorse La BS40. . . . . **129** C5
Bellhouse Wlk BS11. . . . **34** B1
Bellifants BA2 . . . . **116** A6
Bell La BS1. . . . . **143** A3
Bell Language Sch The
BA1 . . . . **101** C8
Bellotts Rd BA2 . . . . . . **101** C6
Bell Pit Brow BS48. . . . . **60** B2
Bell Rd BS36. . . . . **38** C7
Bell Sq
Blagdon BS40. . . . . . . **110** E3
Marshfield SN14 . . . . . . **70** A8
Bellum SN14. . . . . **69** E8
BELLUTON **97** D6
Belluton La BS39. . . . . . **97** D5
Belluton Rd BS4. . . . . . . **64** A3
Belluton Villas BS39 . . . **97** D5
Bell Wlk BS40. . . . . **92** E2
Belmont Dr
Bristol BS34. . . . . **36** E5
Failand BS8 . . . . **61** B3
Belmont Hill BS48. . . . . **61** B1
Belmont Pk BS7 . . . . . . **35** F1
Belmont Rd
Bath BA2 . . . . **102** C1
Bristol, Arno's Vale BS4. . **64** C3
Bristol, Montpelier BS6. . **49** E2
Winscombe BS25 . . . . . **125** A8
Belmont St BS5 . . . . . . **50** B1
Belmont The BS21 . . . . **57** F3
Belmore Gdns BA2 . . . **101** B3
Beloe Rd BS7 . . . . **49** E5
Belroyal Ave BS4. . . . . . **64** F3
Belsher Dr BS15 . . . . . . **66** A6
Belstone Wlk BS4 . . . . . **79** C8
Belton Ct BA1 . . . . **84** B2
Belton Rd
Bristol BS5. . . . . **64** B8
Portishead BS20 . . . . . **45** A6
Belvedere BA1 . . . . **141** B4
Belvedere Cl BS34 . . . . . **36** B5
Belvedere Cres BS22 . . . **88** C1
Belvedere Rd BS6. . . . . . **49** B3
Belvoir Rd
6 Bath BA2 . . . . **101** D5
Bristol BS6. . . . . **49** E2
Bence Ct 3 BS15. . . . . . **65** B5
Bence Rd BS37 . . . . **27** E5
Bences La SN14 . . . . . . **69** F8
Benches La BS40. . . . . . **94** D3
Bendalls Bridge BS39 . **114** C2
Benford Cl BS16 . . . . . . **51** C6
Benleaze Rd BS40. . . . . **130** C2
Bennell Batch BA3 . . . . **138** E4
Bennell Cl BA3. . . . . . . **138** E4
Bennell Cotts BA3. . . . . **138** E4
Bennett La BA1 . . . . **85** A1
Bennett Rd BS5. . . . . . . **64** E7
Bennett's BS37. . . . . **28** A1
Bennett's Rd BA1 . . . . . **85** C3
Bennett St BA1 . . . . . . **141** B3
Bennetts Way BS21 . . . . **57** G2
Bennett Way BS1, BS8 . . **62** F5
Bensaunt Gr BS10. . . . . **35** D4
Bentley Cl BS14. . . . . . . **79** F3
Bentley Rd BS22 . . . . . . **89** B3
Benville Ave BS9. . . . . . **48** C8
Berchel Ho 4 BS3 . . . . . **63** D4
Berenda Dr BS30. . . . . . **66** B3
Beresford Cl BS31. . . . . . **82** E2
Beresford Gdns BA1. . . . **84** A3

Berkeley Ave
Bristol BS8. . . . . **142** C3
Bristol, Bishopston BS7. . **49** D3
Midsomer Norton BA3. . **133** A2
Berkeley Cl
Bristol BS16. . . . . **52** A8
Charfield GL12 . . . . **11** A5
Berkeley Cres
Bristol BS8. . . . . **142** B3
Weston-s-M BS23 . . . . **104** C2
Berkeley Ct
Bath BA2 . . . . **102** C6
Bristol, Bishopston BS7. . **49** D3
Berkeley Ct Bsns Pk
BS5. . . . . **64** B7
Berkeley Gdns BS31 . . . **81** E4
Berkeley Gn BS16 . . . . . **37** B1
Berkeley Gn Rd BS5 . . . **50** D2
Berkeley Gr BS5 . . . . . . **50** C2
Berkeley Ho
Bath BA1 . . . . **141** C4
Bristol BS1. . . . . **142** C3
7 Bristol, Staple Hill
BS16 . . . . **51** D5
Berkeley Pl
Bath BA1 . . . . **141** C4
Bristol, Brandon Hill
BS8 . . . . **142** B3
Bristol, Windmill Hill BS3 **63** D2
Berkeley Rd
Bristol, Bishopston BS7. . **49** D3
Bristol, Kingswood BS15 . **65** D7
Bristol, Mayfield Park
BS16 . . . . **51** B2
Bristol, Staple Hill BS16 . **51** D5
Bristol, Westbury Park
BS6 . . . . **49** B4
Berkeleys Mead BS34 . . **37** A6
Berkeley Sq BS8 . . . . . **142** C3
Berkeley St BS5. . . . . . . **50** C3
Berkeley Way BS16. . . . . **52** B7
Berkshire Rd BS7 . . . . . **49** D3
Berlington Ct BS1. . . . . **143** B1
Bernard Ireland Ho
BA1 . . . . **84** B1
Berners Cl BS4 . . . . **79** D7
Berrow Lodge 7
BS23. . . . . **104** E5
Berrows Mead BS37. . . . **27** A8
Berrow Wlk BS3 . . . . . . **63** E2
Berry Croft 5 BS3 . . . . . **63** D4
Berry Hill Cl BS10 . . . . . **35** D1
Berry La BS7 . . . . **49** F6
BERWICK **34** D6
Berwick Cl BS10 . . . . . . **34** E8
Berwick Cres BS10. . . . . **34** B5
Berwick Dr BS10 . . . . . . **34** E5
Berwick La BS10. . . . . . **34** D7
Berwick Rd BS5. . . . . . . **50** B2
Beryl Gr BS14. . . . . **80** C8
Beryl Rd BS3 . . . . **63** B3
Besom La BS37 . . . . **39** D5
Bethel Rd BS5 . . . . **64** F8
Betjeman Ct 2 BS30. . . **66** A5
Betts Gn BS16 . . . . **52** C7
Bevan Ct BS34. . . . . . . **35** F2
Bevan Rd BS30. . . . . . . **82** E8
Beverley Ave BS16 . . . . . **37** F1
Beverley Cl BS5. . . . . . . **65** B6
Beverley Ct BS7. . . . . . . **49** F8
Beverley Gdns BS9 . . . . **48** D7
Beverley Rd BS7 . . . . . . **49** F8
Beverstone BS15 . . . . . . **65** C8
Beverston Gdns BS11 . . . **34** B2
BEVINGTON **2** F6
Bevington Cl BS34 . . . . . **23** E1
Bevington La GL13 . . . . . . **2** F7
Bevington Wlk BS34. . . . **23** E1
Bewdley Rd BA2 . . . . . **102** B4
Bexley Rd BS16 . . . . **51** B3
BIBSTONE **10** C3
Bibstone BS15 . . . . **66** A8
Bibury Cl
Bristol BS9. . . . . **49** D7
Nailsea BS48. . . . . **60** A1
Bibury Cres
Bristol, Hanham BS15 . . **65** C5
Bristol, Henleaze BS9 . . . **49** D7
Bibury Ho BA1. . . . . **84** B2
Bickerton Cl BS10. . . . . . **34** F3
Bickfield La
Compton Martin BS40 . **129** B8
Ubley BS40 . . . . **111** F2
Bickford Cl BS30 . . . . . . **66** A6
Bickley Cl BS15 . . . . **65** C5
Biddestone Rd BS7 . . . . **35** E1
Biddisham Cl 6 BS48. . . **59** E1
Biddle St BS49 . . . . **91** B7
Bideford Cres BS4 . . . . . **79** F8
Bideford Rd BS22 . . . . . **88** F2
Bidwell Cl BS10 . . . . **35** B3
Bifield Cl BS14 . . . . **80** F5
Bifield Gdns BS14 . . . . . **80** E5
Bifield Rd BS14 . . . . **80** E5
Bignell Cl BS25 . . . . . . **124** F8**

Big Tree Cl BS26 .....124 C3
Bigwood La BS1 ......142 C2
Bilberry Cl BS9 ......48 C8
Bilbie Cl
  Bristol BS10......49 E7
  Chew Stoke BS40......112 E8
Bilbie Rd
  Chew Stoke BS40......112 E8
  Weston-s-M BS22......89 B3
Bilbury La BA1......141 B2
Billand Cl BS13......78 E3
Bilsham La BS35......12 F2
Binces La BA2......99 E3
Bince's Lodge La BA3 .133 F3
Bindon Dr BS10......35 D4
Binhay Rd BS49......91 C7
Binley Gr BS14......80 D5
Binmead Gdns BS13.....79 B4
Birbeck Rd BS9......48 E5
Birchall Rd BS6......49 C4
Birch Ave
  Bleadon BS24......122 C6
  Clevedon BS21......57 G4
Birch Cl
  Bristol BS34......35 E7
  Locking BS24......106 B4
Birch Croft BS14......80 A3
Birch Ct
  Keynsham BS31......81 C4
  Weston-s-M BS22......89 C2
  Yate BS37......27 D2
Birchdale Rd BS14.....80 A8
Birchdene BS48......60 A2
Birch Dr
  Alveston BS35......14 F4
  Churchill BS40......109 A5
  Pucklechurch BS16.....53 B5
Birches The BS48......60 A2
Birch Gr BS20......45 C4
Birch Ho BS16......51 B5
Birchills Trad Est BS4 . 64 F1
Birch Rd
  Bristol, Kingswood
  BS15......51 E3
  Bristol, Southville BS3 . . 63 B4
  Radstock BA3......133 E1
  Yate BS37......27 D2
Birchwood Ave BS23 ..105 A7
Birchwood Ct BS4......64 F6
Birchwood Dr BS8 ......63 B4
Birchwood La BS39 .....97 F2
Birchwood Rd BS4 .....64 F4
Birdale Cl BS10......34 E3
Birdcombe Cl BS48.....59 E3
Birdlip Cl BS48......60 A2
Birds Bush La GL12......18 B1
Birdwell La BS41......61 F1
Birdwell Prim Sch
  BS41......78 A8
Birdwell Rd BS41......61 F1
Birdwood BS15......65 D6
Birgage Rd GL9......19 F2
Birkdale
  Bristol BS30......66 B6
  Yate BS37......39 E8
Birkett Rd BS23......87 B1
Birkin St **5** BS2......64 A6
Birnbeck Ct BS23......104 D7
Birnbeck Rd BS23......87 C1
Biscay Dr BS20......45 F6
Bisdee Rd BS24......105 D2
Bishop Ave BS22......89 A3
Bishop La BS7......49 E4
Bishop Manor Rd BS10 49 D7
Bishop Rd
  Bristol, Bishopston BS7. .49 D4
  Bristol, Emerson's Green
  BS16......52 C6
Bishop Road Prim Sch
  BS7......49 D4
Bishops Cl BS9......48 E3
Bishops Cove BS13......78 F5
Bishops Ct BS9......48 C3
Bishops Knoll BS9 ......48 B3
Bishops Mead BS49......92 A8
Bishops Rd BS49......92 A8
Bishop St
  Bristol BS2......143 B4
  Faulkland BA3......135 D2
BISHOPSTON......49 C3
BISHOP SUTTON......113 D3
Bishop Sutton Prim Sch
  BS39......113 D4
Bishop's Wood BS32 ...24 C6
BISHOPSWORTH......79 A5
Bishopsworth CE Jun Sch
  BS13......78 F6
Bishopsworth Rd BS13 .79 A7
Bishop Terr BS2......143 C4
Bishopthorpe Rd BS10 .49 E7
Bishport Ave BS13 ......79 C5
Bishport Cl BS13......79 B4
Bishport Gn BS13......79 C3
Bisley BS37......39 C7
Bissex Mead BS16......52 B5
Bittern Cl BS22......88 F1

Bitterwell Cl BS36......38 D3
Bittlemead BS13......79 F4
BITTON......82 E7
Bitton Sta* BS30......66 B1
Blackacre BS14......80 C4
Blackberry Ave **5** BS16 50 E5
Blackberry Cl **5** BS37 .. 27 F4
Blackberry Dr
  Frampton Cotterell
  BS36......38 C6
  Weston-s-M BS22......89 A2
Blackberry Hill BS16......50 E5
Blackberry Hill Hospl
  BS16......50 F5
Blackberry La
  Portishead BS20......44 F2
  Winsley BA2......120 C8
Blackberry Way BA3 ...132 F3
Blackbird Cl BA3......139 B8
Blackcurrant Dr BS41 ...77 E8
Blackdown Ct BS14......80 B5
Blackdown Rd BS20......45 B5
Blackdown Way BA3 ...139 B6
Blackfriars BS1......143 A3
Blackfriars Rd BS48......59 B1
BLACKHORSE......52 A7
Blackhorse Cl BS16......52 A8
Blackhorse Ct BS15......65 C8
Blackhorse Hill BS35,
  BS10......35 B8
Blackhorse La BS16......52 A8
Blackhorse Pl BS16......52 A6
Blackhorse Prim Sch
  BS16......52 A8
Blackhorse Rd
  Bristol, Kingswood
  BS15......65 D8
  Bristol, Mangotsfield
  BS16......52 A7
Black La BS26......125 E2
BLACKMOOR
  Chew Stoke......95 C3
  Lower Langford......109 D6
Blackmoor
  Charterhouse BS40 ...127 F4
  Clevedon BS21......57 E1
  Lower Langford BS40 ..109 C6
  3 Weston-s-M BS22....88 F2
Blackmoor Cl BS40......109 C6
Blackmoor Rd BS8......47 E2
Blackmoors La BS3......62 E4
Blackmore Dr BA2......101 C5
Black Nore Point BS20 . . 44 F5
BLACKROCK......97 E8
Blackrock La BS39......97 E7
Black Rock Nature Trail*
  BA5......127 A1
Blackrock Villas BS20 . .45 B1
Blacksmith La BS20 ......85 B6
Blacksmith's La BA1 ...83 B3
Blackswarth Ho **6** BS5 64 D7
Blackswarth Rd BS5......64 D7
Blackthorn Cl BS13......79 D5
Blackthorn Dr
  Bristol BS32......36 D7
  Portishead BS20......45 E5
Blackthorn Gdns BS22.. 89 A1
Blackthorn Rd BS13......79 D5
Blackthorn Sq BS21......57 F1
Blackthorn Terr BS22.... 89 A1
Blackthorn Way BS48 ...60 A2
Blackthorn Wlk BS15.... 51 E2
Bladen Cl **1** BS20......45 E4
Bladud Bldgs BA1......141 C3
BLAGDON......110 E2
Blagdon Cl
  Bristol BS3......63 E2
  Weston-s-M BS24......104 F1
Blagdon La BS40......110 F6
Blagdon Pk BA2......101 A4
Blagdon Prim Sch
  BS40......110 E2
Blagrove Cl BS13......79 C3
Blagrove Cres BS13......79 C3
Blaisdon
  Weston-s-M BS22......105 D7
  Yate BS37......39 E7
Blaisdon Cl BS10......35 A1
Blaise Castle Mus*
  BS10......34 E2
Blaisedell View BS10 ...34 A8
Blaise Hamlet BS11 ......34 D2
Blaise Prim Sch BS10 ...34 F2
Blaise Wlk BS9......48 C6
Blake End BS22......88 E4
Blakeney Gr BS48......75 C8
Blakeney Mills BS37......27 E1
Blakeney Rd
  Bristol BS34......23 E1
  Bristol, Horfield BS7 ....50 A4
Blake Rd BS7......50 B6
Blakes Rd BS35......8 B1
Blanchards BS37......40 D8
Blanchards Cotts BS37 .40 D8
Blandford Cl
  2 Bristol BS9......49 B6
  Nailsea BS48......59 E1
Blandmour Way BS10 ...35 D2
Blands Row BS35......12 B1

BLEADON......122 C7
Bleadon Hill BS23,
  BS24......122 A8
Bleadon Mill BS24......122 C5
Bleadon Rd BS24......122 B7
Blenheim Cl
  Peasedown St John
  BA2......134 D7
  Weston-s-M BS22......89 A2
Blenheim Ct
  10 Bristol, Kingsdown
  BS1......143 A4
  Bristol, Patchway BS32 ..24 D3
Blenheim Dr
  Bristol BS34......36 B4
  Yate BS37......27 D3
Blenheim Gdns BA1......85 A2
Blenheim Rd BS6......49 B3
Blenheim St BS5......50 A1
Blenheim Way BS20......45 E5
Blenman Cl BS16......51 A7
Blethwin Cl BS10......34 F1
Blew Cl BS29......106 C7
Blind La
  Bath BA1......84 C2
  Chew Stoke BS40......112 E8
  Congresbury BS49......91 F6
  Tunley BA2......117 A4
  Yatton BS49......91 F7
BLOOMFIELD
  Bath......101 E3
  Timsbury......116 B4
Bloomfield
  Hallatrow BS39......132 A6
  Weston-s-M BS24......105 A2
Bloomfield Ave
  Bath BA2......101 E4
  Timsbury BA2......116 B3
Bloomfield Cl BA2......116 B3
Bloomfield Cotts BA2 ..134 C7
Bloomfield Cres BA2 ...101 D2
Bloomfield Dr BA2......101 D2
Bloomfield Gr BA2......101 E3
Bloomfield La BS39......132 E5
Bloomfield Park Rd
  BA2......116 B3
Bloomfield Pk BA2......101 E3
Bloomfield Rd
  Bath BA2......101 E3
  Bristol BS4......64 D4
  Timsbury BA2......116 B3
Bloomfield Rise BA2 ...101 D2
Bloomfield Rise N
  BA2......101 D2
Bloomfield Road Link
  BS4......64 C4
Bloomfield Terr BA2.....134 C7
Bloy St BS5......50 C1
Bluebell Cl
  Bristol BS9......48 B6
  2 Goose Green BS37.. 27 F5
  Thornbury BS35......8 D2
Bluebell Dr BS31......81 D3
Bluebell Rd BS22......89 A6
Bluebell Rise BA3......132 F3
Bluebells The BS32......36 F7
Bluebell Way BS16......38 C1
Blueberry Way BS22......88 F1
Blue Falcon Rd BS15 ...51 E1
Blue Iris Rd BS16......52 D8
Blue Water Dr BS24 ...106 D3
Blythe Gdns BS22......89 A3
Boardinghouse La
  BS35......23 C5
Boat La BS24......122 C3
Boat Stall La BA2......141 C2
Bobbin La BA15......120 F4
Bobbin Pk BA15......120 F3
Bodey Cl BS30......66 A5
Bodley Way BS24......105 E7
Bodmin Wlk BS4......79 F8
Bodyce Rd **4** BS35......15 A5
Bofors Twr BS23......105 B4
Boiling Wells La BS2......50 A3
Bolingbroke Way BS34 . 36 B5
Bolton Rd BS7......49 E3
Bond La BS35......14 C8
Bond's La SN14......69 E8
Bond St BS1......143 B4
Bonhill La BS39......113 D5
Bonhill Rd BS39......113 D5
Bonnington Wlk BS7 ...50 B7
Bonville Bsns Ctr BS4 ..64 F2
Bonville Rd BS4......64 F2
Booth Rd BS3......63 C4
Boot La BS3......63 D4
Bordesley Rd BS14......80 A3
Boreal Way **4** BS24 ...105 F7
Borgie Pl BS22......88 F3
Borkley St BS34......36 A7
Borleyton Wlk BS13......78 F4
Borver Gr BS13......79 B4
Boscombe Cres BS16... 51 F7
Boston Rd BS7......49 F6
Botham Cl BS22......89 A4

Botham Dr BS4......64 E1
Bottoms Farm La BS30 . 53 F1
Boucher Pl **2** BS2......50 A2
Boulevard BS23......104 E8
Boulters Rd BS13......79 C4
Boulton's La **6** BS15 ...65 D8
Boulton's Rd **5** BS15.. 65 D8
Boundaries The BS24 ..122 B1
Boundary Cl
  Kingswood G12......11 E4
  Midsomer Norton BA3 . .139 B7
  Weston-s-M BS23......104 E3
Boundary Rd
  Avonmouth BS11......33 D3
  Frampton Cotterell BS36 38 D7
  Weston-s-M BS24......106 A7
Bourchier Gdns BS13...79 B3
BOURNE......110 B4
Bourne Cl
  Bristol BS15......65 B8
  Winterbourne BS36......37 E7
Bourne La
  Blagdon BS40......110 C4
  Bristol BS5......50 B2
  Burrington BS40......110 B4
Bourne Rd BS15......65 A8
Bourneville Rd BS5......64 D8
BOURNSTREAM......5 F2
Bournville Com Inf Sch
  BS23......105 A4
Bournville Jun Sch
  BS23......104 F5
Bournville Rd BS23......104 E5
Boursland Cl BS32......24 D2
BOURTON......89 E6
Bourton Ave BS34......36 C8
Bourton Cl BS34......36 C8
Bourton Combe BS48 ...76 F7
Bourton La
  Cross BS26......124 E3
  Weston-s-M BS22......89 D4
Bourton Mead
  Flax Bourton BS48......76 F8
  Long Ashton BS41......62 A1
Bourton Wlk BS13......79 A8
Bouverie St BS5......64 B8
Boverton Rd BS34......36 B4
Bow Cotts BS20......47 C4
Bowden Cl BS9......48 C8
Bowden Hill BA3......138 D4
Bowden Pl BS16......51 F7
Bowden Rd BS5......50 E1
Bowden Way BS8......61 B3
Bowen Rd BS24......106 C5
BOWER ASHTON......62 E4
Bower Ashton Terr BS3.. 62 E4
Bower Cl BS3......63 A2
Bowerleaze BS9......48 C5
Bower Rd BS3......63 A3
Bower Wlk BS3......63 E3
Bowland Cl BS20......24 D1
Bowland Gr BS20......24 D1
Bowlditch La BA3......133 B4
Bowling Hill BS37......28 A1
Bowling Hill Bsns Pk
  BS37......28 A1
Bowling Rd BS37......40 B8
Bowmead **7** BS4......64 D1
Bowood BS16......37 C1
Bowring Cl BS13......79 C3
Bowsland BS32......24 E2
Bowsland Green Prim Sch
  BS32......24 D2
Bowsland Way BS32......24 D2
Bowstreet La BS35......35 A8
Boxbury Hill BS39......132 F3
Box Bush La BS24......90 C1
Boxhedge Farm La
  BS36......38 E3
Box Rd BA1......86 C3
Box Wlk BS31......81 C4
Boyce Cl BA2......100 F5
Boyce Dr BS2......50 A2
Boyce's Ave BS8......142 A3
Boyd Cl BS30......67 B7
Boyd Rd BS31......82 D3
Brabazon Rd BS34......36 B2
Bracewell Gdns BS10...35 C4
Bracey Dr BS16......51 C6
Brackenbury Dr BS34 ...36 F5
Brackendene BS32......24 E4
Brackenwood Rd BS21.. 57 G6
Bracton Dr BS14......80 A5
Bradeston Gr BS16......51 A7
Bradford Cl BS21......57 E1
Bradford Pk BA2......102 A2
Bradford Rd
  Bath BA2......102 A1
  Bathford BA1......86 B2
  Winsley BA15......120 E7
  Winsley, Avonpark
  BA15......120 D6
Bradhurst St **8** BS5.... 64 B6
BRADLEY......11 F8
Bradley Ave
  Bristol BS11......47 E6
  Winterbourne BS36......37 E5
Bradley Cres BS11......47 E6
Bradley Ct BS16......51 C5
BRADLEY GREEN......11 E7

Bradley Pavilions BS32 24 C2
Bradley Rd
  Bristol BS34......23 F1
  Portbury BS20......46 E5
BRADLEY STOKE......36 F8
Bradley Stoke Com Sch
  BS32......36 E8
Bradley Stoke Way
  BS32......36 E7
Bradstone Rd BS36......37 D5
Bradville Gdns BS41.....77 F8
Bradwell Gr BS10......49 C8
Braemar Ave BS7......35 F1
Braemar Cres BS7......35 F1
Braemor Ct BS9......49 A8
Brae Rd BS25......125 B8
Brae Rise BS25......125 A8
Bragg's La BS2......143 C3
Braikenridge Cl BS21... 57 E1
Braikenridge Rd BS4 ...64 D4
Brainsfield BS9......48 F6
Brake Cl
  Bristol, Bradley Stoke
  BS32......36 E7
  Bristol, Warmley Hill
  BS15......65 F7
Brake The
  Frampton Cotterell
  BS36......38 C5
  Yate BS37......27 C5
Brakewell Gdns BS14...80 A4
Bramble Cl BS16......52 D7
Bramble Dr BS9......48 D3
Bramble La BS9......48 C3
Brambles The
  Bristol BS13......79 C4
  Hinton Charterhouse
  BA2......119 E1
  Keynsham BS31......81 D3
  Weston-s-M BS22......89 D2
Bramble Way BA2......102 B3
Bramblewood BS49......74 B1
Bramblewood Rd BS22 . 88 E3
Brambling Wlk BS16 ....50 F6
Bramley Cl
  Kingswood GL12......11 F4
  Locking BS24......106 A5
  Olveston BS35......14 A3
  Peasedown St John
  BA2......134 D7
  Pill BS20......47 C4
  Sandford BS25......108 A4
  Yatton BS49......91 B7
Bramley Copse BS41 ...77 E8
Bramley Ct **6** BS30 ...65 F4
Bramley Dr BS48......76 A5
Bramley Sq BS49......91 E3
Bramleys The
  Nailsea BS48......75 B8
  Portishead BS20......45 F5
Bramling Ave BS20......46 A6
Brampton Ho **4** BS20 . 45 E4
Brampton Way BS20 ....45 E4
Bramshill Dr BS22......88 F3
Branche Gr BS13......79 D3
Branches Cross BS40.... 92 E3
Branch Rd BA2......119 F2
Brandash Rd BS37......28 C1
Brandon Cotts BS1......142 C2
BRANDON HILL......142 B2
Brandon Ho BS8......142 B2
Brandon St BS1......142 C2
Brandon Steep BS1 ....142 B2
Brandown Cl BS39......114 E1
Brangwyn Gr BS7......50 B6
Brangwyn Sq BS22......88 F2
Branksome Cres BS34.. 36 B3
Branksome Dr
  Bristol BS34......36 B3
  Winterbourne BS36......37 E6
Branksome Rd BS6......49 B3
Bransby Way BS24......106 A8
Branscombe Ct BS3......63 D2
Branscombe Rd BS9 ....48 C4
Branscombe Wlk BS20 . 44 F3
Branwhite Cl BS7......50 E4
BRASSKNOCKER......102 F2
Brassknocker Hill BA2 102 F2
Brassmill Ent Ctr BA1 .101 A7
Brassmill La BA1......101 A7
Brassmill Lane Trad Est
  BA1......101 A7
Bratton Rd BS4......79 D7
Braunton Rd BS3......63 C3
Braydon Ave BS32......36 D7
Brayne Ct BS30......65 F3
Braysdown Cl BA2......134 B1
Braysdown La BA2......134 C7
BREACH......114 F6
Breaches Gate BS32.... 36 F6
Breaches The BS20......47 B5
Breach Hill Comm
  BS40......112 A6
Breach Hill La BS40 ...112 C6
Breach La BS48......74 F7
Breach Rd BS3......63 A3
Breachwood View
  BA2......101 C2
BREAN......121 A5

Brean Down Ave
Bristol BS9 49 B5
Weston-s-M BS23 104 E4
Brean Gdns BS3 63 E2
Brean Rd BS24 121 F1
Brecknock Rd BS4 64 A3
Brecon Cl BS9 49 B6
Brecon Ct BS16 36 D1
Brecon Rd BS9 49 B6
Brecon View BS24 105 A1
Bredon BS37 39 D7
Bredon Cl BS15 65 F7
Bredon Nook Rd BS10 49 C7
Bree Cl BS22 89 A4
Brendon Ave BS23 104 F8
Brendon Cl BS30 66 C4
Brendon Gdns 2 BS48 59 E1
Brendon Rd
Bristol BS3 63 D3
Portishead BS20 45 A5
Brennan Cl BS4 79 F7
Brenner St BS5 50 B2
Brent Cl BS24 105 B2
Brent Rd BS7 49 F5
BRENTRY 35 B2
Brentry Ave 5 BS5 64 B7
Brentry La BS10 35 B3
Brentry Lo BS10 35 A3
Brentry Prim Sch BS10 35 B4
Brentry Rd BS16 50 F3
Brereton Way BS30 66 B4
Brewerton Cl BS10 35 C3
Brewery Ct BS3 63 A4
Brewery Hill BS30 82 F7
Brewery La BA3 139 D1
Brewhouse The BS1 143 B2
Briar Cl
Nailsea BS48 60 A2
Radstock BA3 139 D8
Briar Ct BS20 47 C4
Briarfield Ave BS15 65 C5
Briarlands Office Pk
BS35 15 A2
Briarleaze BS35 14 F2
Briar Mead BS49 74 A1
Briar Rd BS24 105 E3
Briars Ct BA2 101 A4
Briarside Ho BS10 35 D3
Briarside Rd BS10 35 D3
Briars The BS48 75 F7
Briar Way BS16 51 C3
Briar Wlk BS16 51 C3
Briarwood BS9 48 F6
Briarwood Sch BS16 51 B3
Briary Rd BS20 45 C5
Briavels Gr BS6 49 F2
Brick Cotts BS35 6 E1
Brick Hill Way BS34 35 E6
Brick St BS2 143 C3
Bridewell La
Bath BA1 141 B2
Hutton BS24, BS26,
BS29 106 D1
Bridewell St BS1 143 A3
Bridge Access Rd BS35 13 A7
Bridge Bldgs BS39 132 B3
Bridge Cl BS14 80 C4
Bridge Farm Cl BS14 80 A3
Bridge Farm Prim Sch
Bristol BS14 80 A4
Bristol BS14 80 A4
Bridge Farm Sq BS49 91 D4
Bridge Farm Wlk BS16 52 B3
Bridge Gdns BA2 116 A6
Bridge Ho
Alveston BS35 14 F5
11 Bath BA1 85 C1
Bristol BS1 143 A2
9 Clevedon BS21 57 E2
Weston-s-M BS23 104 F6
Bridgeleap Rd BS16 51 F8
Bridge Place Rd BA2 133 E8
Bridge Rd
Bath BA2 101 C5
Bleadon BS24 122 B6
Bristol, Eastville BS5 50 B3
Bristol, Lower Soundwell
BS15 52 A3
Bristol, Shortwood BS16 52 C4
Leigh Woods BS8 62 E6
Weston-s-M BS23 104 F6
Yate BS37 27 A2
Bridge Road Ind Est
BS15 52 A3
Bridges Ct 2 BS16 51 B4
Bridges Dr 3 BS16 51 C6
Bridge St
Bath BA2 141 C2
Bristol BS1 143 A2
Bristol, Eastville BS5 50 D2
Bridge Valley Rd BS8 62 E8
Bridge Way BS36 38 B8
Bridge Wlk BS7 50 A8
BRIDGE YATE 66 E7
Bridgman Gr BS34 36 B3
Bridgwater Ct BS24 105 A3
Bridgwater Rd
Dundry BS41, BS13,
BS48 78 D6
Bridgwater Rd *continued*
Felton BS48 94 A8
Lympsham BS24 122 C4
Weston-s-M BS23, BS24 104 F2
Winscombe BS25 125 A5
Bridle Ave BS14 80 D3
Bridle Way BS35 14 F4
Bridleway Cl BA3 138 E8
Briercliffe Rd BS9 48 D7
Brierly Furlong BS34 36 D3
Briery Leaze Rd BS14 80 A4
Brighton Cres BS3 63 B2
Brighton Mews BS8 142 B4
Brighton Pk 16 BS5 64 B8
Brighton Pl BS15 51 D1
Brighton Rd
Bristol, Patchway BS34 35 F8
Bristol, Redland BS6 49 C1
Weston-s-M BS23 104 E6
Brighton St
12 Bristol BS2 49 E1
7 Bristol BS2 143 B4
Brighton Terr 9 BS3 63 B2
Bright St
Bristol, Kingswood
BS15 65 D8
Bristol, Russell Town BS5 64 B7
Brigstocke Rd BS2 143 B4
Brimbles The BS7 36 B2
Brimbleworth La BS22 89 C3
Brimridge Rd BS25 125 A8
Brimsham Green Sch
BS37 27 D4
Brimsham Park Sh Ctr
BS37 27 F4
Brinkmarsh La GL12 9 D2
Brinkworth Rd BA2 102 B2
Brinkworthy Rd BS16 50 E6
Brinmead Wlk BS13 78 F3
Brins Cl BS34 36 F4
BRINSEA 108 E8
Brinsea Batch BS49 108 E8
Brinsea Green Farm La
BS49 108 F8
Brinsea La BS49 108 F8
Brinsea Rd BS49 91 E2
Brinsham La BS37 28 A6
Brinsmead Cres BS20 47 D4
Briscoes Ave BS13 79 D4
BRISLINGTON 64 E2
Brislington Hill BS4 64 E2
Brislington Ret Pk BS4 64 E1
Brislington Trad Est
BS4 64 F2
BRISTOL 143 C2
Bristol & Anchor Ho
BS5 64 D8
Bristol and Exeter Mews
BS1 143 C1
Bristol Beacon* BS1 143 A3
Bristol Bsns Pk BS16 36 E1
Bristol Cathedral Sch
BS1 142 C2
Bristol Dental Hospl
BS1 143 A3
Bristol Eye Hospl BS1 143 A3
Bristol Gate 1 BS8 62 F5
Bristol Gateway Sch The
BS2 50 A2
Bristol General Hospl
BS1 143 A1
Bristol Gram Sch BS8 142 C3
Bristol Harbour Rly*
BS1 142 C1
Bristol Hill BS4 64 D2
Bristol Hippodrome The*
BS1 142 C2
Bristol Homeopathic Hospl
BS6 142 C4
Bristol Ind Mus* BS1 143 A1
Bristol International
Airport BS48 93 E7
Bristol Old Vic Theatre Sch
BS8 49 A1
Bristol Parkway N BS34 37 A5
Bristol Parkway Sta
BS34 36 E4
Bristol Rd
Bristol BS16 37 C2
Chew Stoke BS40 112 E8
Churchill BS25 109 A5
Congresbury BS49 91 D5
Cromhall GL12 17 B7
Farrington Gurney BS39 131 F5
Frampton Cotterell BS36 26 B3
Keynsham BS31 81 E6
Luckington SN14 31 E3
Newton St Loe BA2 100 D7
Paulton BS39 132 E7
Pensford BS39 97 D6
Portishead BS20 45 E4
Radstock BA3 133 F3
Redhill BS40 94 A3
Thornbury BS35 15 B8
Weston-s-M BS22 89 C2
Whitchurch BS14 80 D3
Winscombe BS25 125 C8
Winterbourne BS16 37 D4
Wraxall BS48 60 D4
Bristol Rd By-pass
BS40 109 C5
Bristol Rd Lower BS23 87 F1
Bristol Royal Hospl for
Children BS1 143 A3
Bristol Royal Infmy
BS2 143 A4
Bristol Southend BS3 63 D2
Bristol Steiner Waldorf
Sch BS6 49 B2
Bristol Temple Meads Sta
BS1 143 C1
Bristol Vale Trad Est
BS3 63 B1
Bristol View BA2 118 C8
Bristol Zoo Gdns* BS8 48 F1
Bristow Broadway
BS11 33 C1
Bristowe Ho BS16 51 B5
Bristowe Lodge BS16 51 C4
Britannia Bldgs BS8 142 A1
Britannia Cl
4 Bristol BS16 37 F1
Chilcompton BA3 138 D4
Britannia Cres BS34 36 D5
Britannia Ct 1 BS16 51 D5
Britannia Ho BS34 35 F2
Britannia Rd
Bristol, Kingswood
BS15 65 C8
Bristol, Lower Easton
BS5 50 C1
Bristol, Patchway BS34 35 E7
Britannia Way BS21 57 E1
British Rd BS3 63 C3
British The BS37 27 B4
Brittan Pl BS20 46 E3
Britten Ct 10 BS30 65 F4
BRITTENS 132 F6
Brittens BS39 132 F6
Britten's Cl BS39 132 F6
Britten's Hill BS39 132 F6
Britton Bottom GL9 20 B1
Britton Gdns BS15 51 C1
Britton Ho BS15 66 B8
Brittons Pass SN14 69 F8
Brixham Rd BS3 63 C1
Brixton Rd BS5 64 B8
Brixton Road Mews 22
BS5 64 B8
Broadbury Rd BS4 79 E8
Broad Cft BS34 35 F6
Broadcroft BS40 95 F3
Broad Croft BS32 24 C2
Broadcroft Ave BS49 74 F1
Broadcroft Cl BS49 74 F1
Broadfield Ave BS15 51 C1
Broadfield Ct BS15 65 C8
Broadfield Rd
Bristol BS4 64 B1
Bristol BS4 80 A8
Broad La
Henfield BS36 38 D5
Westerleigh BS37 39 A4
Yate BS37 27 C4
Broadlands BS21 57 H3
Broadlands Ave BS31 81 D6
Broadlands Dr BS11 34 A1
Broadlands Sch BS31 81 D6
Broadleas BS13 79 C7
Broadleaze BS11 47 E7
Broad Leaze 5 BS34 35 F7
Broadleaze Way BS25 107 F2
Broadleys Ave BS9 49 C7
Broadmead BS1 143 B3
Broadmead La BS31 82 A6
Broad Mead La BS40 95 A3
Broadmead Lane Ind Est
BS31 82 B7
Broadmoor La BA1 84 A3
Broadmoor Pk BA1 84 B2
Broadmoor Vale BA1 84 A3
Broadoak Hill BS41 78 F2
Broadoak Mathematics &
Computing Coll
BS23 104 E3
Broadoak Rd
Churchill BS40 109 A5
Weston-s-M BS23 104 D3
Broad Oak Rd BS13 78 F4
Broad Oaks BS8 62 E6
Broadoak Wlk BS16 51 B4
Broad Plain BS2 143 C2
Broad Quay
Bath BA1 141 C1
Bristol BS1 143 A2
Broad Rd
Blagdon BS40 127 D8
Bristol BS15 51 C1
Broad St
Bath BA1 141 C3
Bristol BS1 143 A3
Bristol, Staple Hill BS16 51 F4
Chipping Sodbury BS37 28 B1
Congresbury BS49 91 D4
Wrington BS40 92 D2
Broadstone La BS21 72 F3
Broadstones BA15 103 E7
Broadstone Wlk BS13 79 D5
Broad Street Pl BA1 141 C3
Broadwalk Sh Ctr BS4 64 B2
Broadway
Bath BA2 102 B6
Chilcompton BA3 138 C3
Locking BS24 106 D4
Saltford BS31 82 D3
Shipham BS25 125 E8
Weston-s-M BS24 105 A2
Yate BS37 27 F2
Broadway Acres BS27 125 F1
Broadway Ave BS9 49 D6
Broadway Cl BA3 138 C3
Broadway Inf Sch
BS37 27 F2
Broadway La BA3 133 B5
Broadway Rd
Bristol, Bishopston BS7 49 D3
Bristol, Bishopsworth
BS13 78 F5
Broadways Dr BS16 50 F7
Broadway The GL11 5 F8
Broad Weir BS1 143 B3
Broad Wlk BS4 64 A2
Brock End BS20 44 F3
Brockeridge Inf Sch
BS36 38 C7
Brockhurst Gdns BS15 65 A8
Brockhurst Rd BS15 65 A8
BROCKLEY 75 C2
Brockley Cl
Bristol BS34 36 C7
Nailsea BS48 59 D1
Weston-s-M BS24 104 F1
Brockley Combe Rd
BS48 76 B1
Brockley Cres BS24 104 F1
Brockley La BS48 75 D4
Brockley Mini Farm
(Open Farm)* BS48 92 F7
Brockley Rd BS31 82 D3
Brockley Way BS49 75 B3
Brockley Wlk BS13 79 A8
Brockridge La BS36 38 C7
Brocks 4 BS4 64 D1
Brocks La BS41 61 F1
Brocks Rd BS13 79 C3
Brock St BA1 141 B3
Brockway BS48 59 F2
Brockwood BA15 120 F7
Brockworth BS37 39 C6
Brockworth Cres BS16 50 F6
Bromfield Wlk BS16 52 B7
Bromley Dr BS16 51 D8
Bromley Farm BS16 37 D1
BROMLEY HEATH 37 D1
Bromley Heath Ave
BS16 51 D8
Bromley Heath Jun & Inf
Schs BS16 51 E8
Bromley Heath Rd
BS16 51 D8
Bromley Heath Rdbt
BS16 37 D1
Bromley Rd
Bristol BS7 49 F5
Stanton Drew BS39 96 F1
Brompton Cl BS15 66 A8
Brompton Ho BA2 141 C4
Brompton Rd BS24 105 A2
Broncksea Rd BS7 35 F1
Bronte Cl BS23 105 B4
Bronte Wlk BS7 50 A8
Brook Cl BS41 62 B1
Brookcote Dr BS34 36 D6
Brook Cotts BA2 100 B7
Brook Ct BS13 79 A6
Brookdale Rd BS13 79 B6
Brook End SN14 31 F5
Brookfield Ave BS7 49 D3
Brookfield Cl BS37 28 C2
Brookfield La 2 BS6 49 D2
Brookfield Pk BA1 84 B2
Brookfield Rd
3 Bristol, Montpelier
BS6 49 D2
Bristol, Patchway BS34 36 B8
Brookfield Wlk
Bristol BS30 66 C3
Clevedon BS21 57 H3
Brook Gate BS3 62 E1
Brook Gdns BS40 109 A5
Brook Hill BS6 49 F1
Brook Ho
Bristol BS34 36 C8
3 Thornbury BS35 15 C8
Brookhouse La SN14 55 B1
Brook La
Bristol, Montpelier BS6 49 F1
Bristol, Stapleton BS16 50 E6
Brookland Rd
Bristol BS6 49 D5
Weston-s-M BS22 105 B7
Brooklands BA2 117 D3
Brooklea BS30 66 B3
Brookleaze BS9 48 C5
Brookleaze Bldgs BA1 85 B2
Brook Lintons BS4 64 D3
Brooklyn BS40 92 D2
Brooklyn Rd
Bath BA1 85 C2
Bristol BS13 79 B8
Brookmead BS35 15 D7
Brook Office Pk BS16 38 B2
Brook Rd
Bath BA2 101 D6
Bristol, Hillfields BS16 51 B4
Bristol, Mangotsfield
BS16 51 F6
Bristol, Montpelier BS6 49 F1
Bristol, Southville BS3 63 D4
Bristol, Speedwell BS5 50 F1
Bristol, Warmley BS15 66 B8
Brookridge Ct 6 BS16 51 D4
Brookridge Ho BS10 34 F3
Brookside
Paulton BS39 132 E6
Pill BS20 47 D3
Winford BS40 94 F7
Brookside Cl
Batheaston BA1 85 F5
Paulton BS39 132 E6
Brookside Dr
Farmborough BA2 115 F6
Frampton Cotterell BS36 38 B8
Brookside Ho BA1 84 B1
Brookside Rd BS4 64 E2
Brook St BS5 64 C7
Brookthorpe BS37 39 D8
Brookthorpe Ave BS11 34 A1
Brookthorpe Ct BS37 39 D8
Brookview Wlk BS13 79 B7
Brook Way BS32 36 D8
Broom Farm Cl BS48 75 E8
Broomground BA15 120 E7
BROOMHILL 50 E6
BROOM HILL 64 F3
Broom Hill BS16 50 E5
Broomhill Inf Sch BS4 64 F3
Broomhill Jun Sch BS4 64 F3
Broomhill La BS39 114 E3
Broom Hill La BS39 132 E8
Broomhill Rd BS4 65 A2
Brooms The BS16 38 A1
Brotherswood Ct BS32 24 D4
Brougham Hayes BA2 101 D6
Brougham Pl 2 BA1 85 C2
Broughton Ho BS1 143 B1
Brow Hill BA2 85 F4
Browne Ct 4 BS8 62 F6
Browney La BA2 118 A5
Browning Ct BS7 50 B8
Brownlow Rd BS23 104 E4
Browns Ct BS23 104 E6
Brown's Folly Nature
Reserve BA15 86 D1
Brow The
Bath BA2 101 B5
Bath, Combe Down BA2 102 C1
Broxholme Wlk BS11 47 F8
Bruce Ave BS5 50 C1
Bruce Rd BS5 50 C1
Brue Cl BS23 105 A5
Brummel Way BS39 132 C6
Brunel Cl
Bristol BS30 66 C7
Weston-s-M BS24 104 F1
Brunel Ct
Portishead BS20 45 D6
Yate BS37 27 C2
Brunel Ho BA2 101 A6
Brunel Lock Rd BS1 62 F5
Brunel Rd
Bristol BS13 79 A8
Nailsea BS48 59 B1
Brunel Way
Bristol BS1, BS3 62 F4
Thornbury BS35 15 B7
Brunswick Pl
1 Bath BA1 141 B3
10 Bristol BS1 62 F5
Brunswick Sq BS2 143 B4
Brunswick St
1 Bath BA1 85 B1
3 Bathwick BA2 102 B8
Bristol BS2 143 B4
Bristol, Redfield BS5 64 C7
Bruton BS24 105 A2
Bruton Ave
Bath BA2 101 F4
Portishead BS20 45 A5
Bruton Avenue Garages
BA2 101 F4
Bruton Cl
Bristol BS5 64 F8
Nailsea BS48 75 E8
Bruton La GL12 11 F5
Bruton Pl BS8 142 B3
Bryansons Cl BS16 50 D6
Bryant Ave BA3 133 D1
Bryant Gdns BS21 57 E1
Bryants Cl BS16 37 C1
Bryant's Hill BS5 65 B6
Brynland Ave BS7 49 E4
Brynland Ct BS7 49 E5

Buckingham Ct BS32....24 D3
Buckingham Dr BS34...36 D5
Buckingham Gdns
  BS16...........51 E6
Buckingham Ho BS34...35 F2
Buckingham Lodge **1**
  BS31............81 F6
Buckingham Par **11**
  BS35............8 B1
Buckingham Pl
  Bristol BS8........142 A3
  Bristol, Mangotsfield
  BS16............51 E6
Buckingham Rd
  Bristol BS4.......64 D5
  Weston-s-M BS24...105 B2
Buckingham St **1** BS3 .63 C2
Buckingham Vale BS8 .142 A4
Buckland Gn BS22....89 A5
Bucklands Batch BS48 .75 F8
Bucklands Dr BS48....76 A8
Bucklands End BS48...75 F8
Bucklands Gr BS48....75 F8
Bucklands La BS48....75 F8
Bucklands View BS48...76 A8
Bucklewell Cl BS11....47 F6
Buckleys Rd BS34....36 A7
BUCKOVER 9 B1
Buckthorn Ct **3** BS37..27 F5
Bude Ave BS5.......65 A8
Bude Cl BS48.......60 B1
Bude Rd BS34.......36 B4
Building of Bath Mus★
  BA1...........141 C3
Bullens Cl BS32.....24 D2
Buller Rd
  Bristol BS4.......64 C2
  Locking BS29.....106 C7
Bullfinch Cl BS34....36 B6
Bull La
  Bristol BS5.......64 F6
  Pill BS20.........47 C4
Bullocks La BS21.....73 C4
Bull's Hill BA2......118 E1
Bully La BS37.......17 D1
Bumper's Batch BA2 .119 A8
Bungalows The BS25..125 C2
Bungay's Hill BA2,
  BS39...........115 E1
Bunting Ct BS22.....88 E1
Burbank Cl BS30......66 A3
Burchells Ave BS15....51 B1
BURCHELLS GREEN....51 B1
Burchells Green Cl
  BS15............51 B1
Burchells Green Rd
  BS15............51 B1
Burchill Cl BS39.....114 F3
Burcombe Cl BS36....38 D6
Burcott Rd BS11.....33 D5
Burden Cl BS32.......36 F6
Burdock Rd BS16....52 D7
Burdock Way BS16....52 D8
Burfoote Gdns BS14...80 E4
Burfoot Rd BS14.....80 E4
Burford Ave BS34....36 C8
Burford Cl
  Bath BA2.........101 B3
  Portishead BS20 ....45 E4
Burford Gr BS11.....47 F5
Burgage BS37.......40 B8
Burghill Rd BS10.....35 A1
Burghley Ct BS36....37 E5
Burghley Rd BS6.....49 E2
Burgis Rd BS14......80 D6
Burledge Comm BS39 .113 B1
Burledge La BS39....113 D1
Burleigh Gdns BA1....101 A8
Burleigh Way GL12....18 B5
Burley Ave BS16.....51 F5
Burley Crest BS16....51 F5
Burley Gr BS16......51 F5
Burlington Ct
  9 Bristol BS6......49 B2
  Portishead BS20 ....45 E6
Burlington Rd
  Bristol BS6.........49 B2
  Midsomer Norton BA3.133 C2
  Portishead BS20 ....45 E7
Burlington St
  Bath BA1.........141 B4
  15 Weston-s-M BS23..104 E8
Burltons The GL12....10 B2
Burnbush Cl BS14....80 E6
Burnbush Prim Sch
  BS14............80 D5
Burnell Dr BS2......143 C4
Burneside Cl BS10....35 C2
BURNETT..........99 B7
Burnett Bsns Pk BS31..82 B1
Burnett Hill BS31.....99 B8
Burnett Ind Est BS40..92 E1
Burney Way BS30....66 A3
Burnham Cl
  Bristol BS15.......51 F1

Burnham Cl continued
  Weston-s-M BS24.....104 F1
Burnham Dr
  Bristol BS15.......51 F1
  Weston-s-M BS24....104 F1
Burnham Rd
  Bath BA2.........101 C6
  Bristol BS11.......47 D6
Burnt House Cotts
  BA2............118 C8
Burnt House Rd BA2..118 D8
BURRINGTON........109 F3
Burrington Ave BS24..104 F1
Burrington CE Prim Sch
  BS40...........109 F3
Burrington Cl
  Nailsea BS48.......59 E1
  Weston-s-M BS24....104 F1
Burrington Combe
  BS40...........127 C8
Burrington Coombe★
  BS40...........110 A1
Burrington La
  Burrington BS40 ....110 A3
  Burrington BS40 ....110 A3
Burrington Rd BS40..128 D2
Burrington Wlk BS13...79 A8
Burrough Way BS36...37 E6
Burrows La BA3......139 B1
Burrows The BS22....89 D3
BURTON..........43 B3
Burton Cl BS1......143 B1
Burton Ct
  Bristol BS8........142 B3
  2 Bristol, Upper Eastville
  BS16............50 E3
Burton Farm Cl SN14...43 B3
Burton Rd GL9......42 F6
Burton St **5** BA1....141 B2
Burwalls Rd BS8.....62 E6
Burycourt Cl BS11....34 A1
Bury Hill BS36......37 F3
Bury Hill La BS37....28 A8
Bury La BS30.......67 F7
Bury The BS24......106 A3
Bury View BA2......99 C5
Bushacre Bsns Pk
  BS22...........105 C8
Bush Ave BS34......36 D5
Bush Ct
  Alveston BS32.......14 F5
  10 Bristol BS2.......63 F4
Bushes La BS37......29 A6
BUSHEY NORWOOD....102 F6
Bush Ind Est BS5.....64 D8
Bushy Combe BA3....132 F3
Bushy Ho BS2......63 F3
Bushy Leas BS16.....50 D8
Bushy Pk BS2.......63 F3
Bushy Rd BS34......36 A7
Bushy Thorn Rd BS40..112 E8
Business Pk The BS13 ..79 E3
BUTCOMBE........111 B8
Butcombe La BS24....105 A2
Butcombe Wlk BS14 ...80 B5
Butham La
  Chew Magna BS40....96 B3
  Chew Magna BS40....96 B4
Buthay La GL12......18 A5
Buthay The GL12.....18 A5
Butlass Cl BS39.....115 D1
Butler Ho BS5......64 F8
Butlers Cl BS5......64 F7
Butlers Wlk **3** BS5....64 F8
Buttercliffe Rise BS41..62 C3
Buttercup Cres BS16 ..52 D7
Buttercup Rd BS35....8 B3
Butterfield Cl
  Bristol BS10.......49 E7
  Frampton Cotterell
  BS36............38 B6
Butterfield Pk BS21...57 E1
Butterfield Rd BS10...49 E7
Buttermere Rd BS23 ..105 A5
Butterworth Ct BS4 ...79 D7
Butt La BS35.......8 C3
Button Cl BS14......80 A6
Butts Batch BS26....124 B3
BUTT'S BATCH 92 D1
Butt's Batch BS40....92 D1
Butt's La SN14......55 B4
Butts Orch BS40.....92 D1
Buxton Wlk BS7.....50 A8
BW Ests BS24......105 A3
Bye Mead BS16......52 B8
Byfield BA2........102 B1
Byfield Pl BA2......102 B1
Byfields BS21.......73 C8
Byron Cl BS24......106 A4
Byron Ct BS23......104 F8
Byron Pl
  Bristol BS8.......142 B3
  Bristol, Staple Hill BS16 .51 E4
Byron Rd
  Bath BA2.........101 F4
  Locking BS24......106 A4
  Weston-s-M BS23...105 A4

Byron St
  Bristol, Moorfields BS5 ..64 C7
  5 Bristol, St Pauls BS2 ..50 A1
Byways Cvn Pk BS21...57 E1
Byzantine Ct BS1.....143 A1

C

Cabot Cl
  Bristol BS15.......65 C7
  Saltford BS31.......82 D2
  Yate BS37.........27 F1
Cabot Ct BS7.......35 F1
Cabot Gn BS5......64 B7
Cabot Ho **6** BS35....15 C8
Cabot Pk BS11......33 D6
Cabot Prim Sch BS2 ..143 C4
Cabot Rise BS20....45 A5
Cabot Twr★ BS8.....142 B2
Cabot Way
  Bristol BS8........62 F5
  Pill BS20.........47 D3
  Weston-s-M BS22....89 A3
Cabstand BS20......45 D6
Cadbury Camp La BS20 59 D6
Cadbury Camp La W
  BS21............58 C5
Cadbury Farm Rd BS49 91 C7
Cadbury Gdns BS30...66 B6
Cadbury Halt BS20...44 F1
CADBURY HEATH....66 B5
Cadbury Heath Prim Sch
  BS30............66 B6
Cadbury Heath Rd
  BS30............66 B5
Cadbury Ho **5** BS20..45 E4
Cadbury La BS20....44 F1
Cadbury Rd
  Keynsham BS31.....82 A2
  Portishead BS20....45 D4
Cadbury Sq BS49....91 E3
Cadby Ho BA2......101 A6
Caddick Cl BS15.....51 F2
Cade Cl
  Bristol, Kingswood
  BS15............65 F6
  Bristol, Stoke Gifford
  BS34............36 E5
Cadet Dr BS24......105 B4
Cadogan Gr BS48....76 B6
Cadogan Rd BS14....80 A8
Caen Rd BS3.......63 D3
Caernarvon Rd BS31...81 C4
Caern Well Pl BA1....141 C4
Caine Rd BS7.......49 F7
Cains Cl BS15......65 E6
Cairn Cl BS48......60 A1
Cairn Gdns BS36.....37 E4
Cairns' Cres **12** BS2...49 F1
Cairns Ct BS6......49 C4
Cairns Rd BS6......49 C4
Cairo Ct **18** BS23....87 C1
Caitlin Ct BS14.....80 D6
Cala Trad Est BS3....62 F3
Calcott Rd BS4......64 A3
Caldbeck Cl BS10....35 D2
Calder Cl BS31......82 A4
Caldicot Cl
  Bristol, Lawrence Weston
  BS11............34 C2
  Bristol, Willsbridge BS30 66 B2
Caledonian Mews BS8..62 F6
Caledonia Rd
  Bath BA2.........101 D6
  Bristol BS1.......142 B1
Caledonia Pl BS8....62 F7
California Rd BS30...66 B3
Callicroft Prim Sch
  BS10............35 F8
Callicroft Rd BS34....36 A7
Callington Rd BS4....64 D1
Callowhill Ct BS1....143 B3
Calluna Cl BS22.....89 A5
Calton Gdns BA2....141 C1
Calton Rd BA2......141 C1
Calton Wlk BA2.....141 B1
Calves Gdn BS34....35 F7
Camberley Dr BS36...37 F8
Camberley Rd BS4....79 D8
Camberley Wlk BS22..105 E8
Camborne Rd BS7....50 A7
Cambrian Dr BS37....27 E3
CAMBRIDGE BATCH...77 C8
Cambridge Cres BS9...49 A7
Cambridge Gr BS40...92 D2
Cambridge Gr BS21...57 F5
Cambridge Pk BS6....49 B3
Cambridge Pl
  Bath BA2.........102 B5
  Weston-s-M BS23....104 D8
Cambridge Rd
  Bristol BS7........49 E4
  Clevedon BS21.......57 F5
Cambridge Sq
  8 Bristol, Redfield
  BS5............64 C7
  Bristol, Windmill Hill BS3..63 F4
Cambridge Terr BA2...102 B5

Cam Brook Cl BA2...133 D8
Cambrook Ho BS39..131 F8
Camden Cres BA1....141 B4
Camden Ct BA1......141 B4
Camden Rd
  Bath BA1.........85 A1
  Bristol BS3.......142 B1
Camden Row BA1....141 B4
Camden Terr
  Bath BA1.........141 C4
  Bristol BS3.......142 A2
  Weston-s-M BS23...104 E7
CAMELEY.........131 C8
Cameley CE Prim Sch
  BS39...........114 E1
Cameley Cl BS39....131 E8
Cameley Gn BA2....100 F6
Cameley La BS39....130 F7
Cameley Rd BS39....131 C8
Camelford Rd BS5....50 D1
Camellia Dr BS32....24 D5
Cameron Wlk BS7....50 C6
Cameroons Cl BS31...81 E4
CAMERTON.........133 E8
Camerton Cl BS31....82 E3
Camerton Hill BA2...133 E8
Camerton Rd
  Bristol BS5.......50 D1
  Timsbury BA2......116 E1
Camomile Wlk BS20...45 F5
Campbell Ct BS11....33 F1
Campbell Farm BS11...33 F1
Campbell Farm Dr
  BS11............33 F1
Campbell St BS2.....49 E1
Campian Wlk BS4....79 D6
Campion Cl
  Thornbury BS35.......8 D2
  4 Weston-s-M BS22...105 D7
Campion Dr BS32....24 D2
Camp La SN14......55 C4
Camplins BS21......57 E1
Camp Rd
  Bristol BS8........62 F7
  Oldbury-on-S BS35....7 D6
  Weston-s-M BS23....87 C1
Camp Rd N BS23....87 B1
Camps La BS37......29 B3
Camp View
  Nailsea BS48.......59 D2
  Winterbourne BS36....37 E4
Camvale BA2.......134 B8
Camview BS39......132 D6
Camwal Ind Est BS2..64 A5
Camwal Rd BS2.....64 A5
Canada Coombe BS24 106 A1
Canada Way BS1.....142 B1
Canal Terr BA2......85 F1
Canal View BA2.....133 E8
Canberra Cres BS24..106 B6
Canberra Gr BS34....36 B4
Canberra Rd BS23...104 F3
Candy Ct BS4......64 D5
Canford La BS9.....48 E3
Canford Rd BS9.....48 F8
Cannan Ct BA2......102 A2
Cannans Cl BS36....37 E7
Cann La BS30.......66 E6
Cannons Gate BS21..73 C8
CANNON'S MARSH...142 C1
Cannon St
  Bristol BS1.......143 A4
  Bristol, Southville BS3..63 C4
Canons Cl BA2......101 B2
Canons Rd BS1.....142 C2
Canon's Rd BS1.....142 C2
Canon St BS5......64 C8
Canons Way BS1.....142 C1
Canons Wlk BS22....88 D2
Canon's Wlk BS15....51 F2
Canowie Rd BS6....49 B3
Cantell Gr BS14.....80 F5
Canterbury Cl
  Weston-s-M BS22....89 B3
  Yate BS37.........27 E3
Canterbury Ct BS16...50 E6
Canterbury Rd BA2...101 D6
Canterbury St **5** BS5..64 B6
Canters Leaze GL12...18 B4
Cantock's Cl BS8....142 C3
Canvey Cl BS10.....49 E7
Canynge Ho **2** BS1..143 B1
Canynge Rd BS8.....62 F8
Canynge Sq BS8.....62 F8
Canynge St BS1.....143 B2
Capel Cl BS15......66 B8
Capell Cl BS22......105 B8
Capel Rd BS11......34 B1
Capenor Cl BS20....45 C4
Capgrave Cl BS4.....65 A3
Capgrave Cres BS4....65 A3
Capital Edge BS8....142 B1
Caple La BS40......112 B5
Cappards Rd BS39...113 D4
Capricorn Pl BS8....142 B2
Capri Villas BS23....87 C2
Caraway Gdns BS5....50 C2
Carberry View BS24..106 A8
Cardigan Cres BS22..105 C8

Cardigan Mews BS9...49 B5
Cardigan Rd BS9....49 B6
Cardill Cl BS13......79 A8
Cardinal Cl BA2.....118 D8
Carditch Dro BS49...108 B8
Carey Developments **1**
  BS21............57 E1
Carey's Cl BS21.....57 H4
Careys Way BS24....105 E7
Carfax Ct BS6......49 A3
Carice Gdns BS21....73 D8
Carisbrooke Lodge BS6 49 A3
Carisbrooke Rd BS4...79 D7
CARLINGCOTT.......117 B1
Carlingcott La
  Carlingcott BA2......117 B1
  Peasedown St John BA2 134 B8
Carlingford Terr BA3 ..134 A2
Carlingford Terrace Rd
  BA3............134 A2
Carlow Rd BS4......79 E8
Carlton Cl BS39.....114 F3
Carlton Ct
  1 Bristol, Ashley Down
  BS7............49 F4
  3 Bristol, Eastfield BS9 49 A7
Carlton Ho **2** BS9...49 A7
Carlton Mans BS23...104 D7
Carlton Pk BS5......64 C8
Carlton St BS23.....104 D7
Carlyle Rd BS5......50 C1
Carmarthen Ct BS37...27 F4
Carmarthen Rd BS9...49 A5
Carnarvon Rd BS6....49 D2
Carnation Rd **6** BS16..52 C7
Carolina Ho BS2.....143 A4
Caroline Bldgs BA2..102 B5
Caroline Cl
  Chipping Sodbury BS37..28 B2
  Keynsham BS31.....81 C4
Caroline Pl BA1.....141 B4
Carousel La BS24....105 E7
Carpenter Cl BS23....105 A7
Carpenters Hill BA2..134 B8
Carpenters La BS31...81 E5
Carpenter's Shop La
  BS16............51 B6
Carpenters Way BA3 ..139 A1
Carre Gdns BS22....88 F4
Carr Ho
  Bath BA2.........101 A6
  3 Bristol BS2......49 F1
Carriage Dr BS10....35 B2
Carrick Ho **8** BS8....62 F6
Carrington Rd BS3....63 A3
Carroll Ct BS16.....36 E1
Carrs Cl BA2.......101 A6
Carsons Rd BS16....52 B2
Carter Rd BS39.....132 D5
Carters Bldgs **12** BS8..62 F7
Carters Way BA3....138 D3
Carter Wlk BS32....36 D8
Cartledge Rd **6** BS5...50 C1
Cary Ct **2** BS2.....49 F1
Casey Cl BS4......79 F7
Cashmore Ho **9** BS5..64 B7
Caslon Ct BS1......143 B1
Cassell Rd BS16.....51 C5
Cassey Bottom La BS5..65 D3
Casson Dr BS16.....50 E8
Castle Batch Com Prim
  Sch BS22.........89 A5
Castle Cl
  Bristol BS10.......34 C2
  Flax Bourton BS48....76 F7
Castle Coombe BS35...8 C1
Castle Cotts SN14....55 E2
Castle Ct
  Bristol BS34.......37 A4
  Bristol, Arno's Vale BS4..64 C4
  Thornbury BS35......8 B1
Castle Farm La BS41...78 B2
Castle Farm Rd BS15..65 C2
Castlegate Ho BS4....64 E3
Castle Gdns BA2.....101 E3
Castle Hill BS29.....107 C2
Castle La SN14......55 E2
Castlemead Sh Ctr
  BS22...........89 A4
Castle Prim Sch BS31 .81 D4
Castle Rd
  Bristol, Kingswood
  BS15............51 D2
  Bristol, Oldland Common
  BS30............66 D3
  Clevedon BS21.......57 G6
  Pucklechurch BS16...53 C6
  Weston-s-M BS22....88 B1
Castle Sch Sixth Form Ctr
  The BS35.........8 B1
Castle Sch The BS35 ...8 B2
Castle St
  Bristol BS1.......143 B3
  Thornbury BS35......8 B1
Castle View **2** BS24..105 F4
Castle View Rd BS21..57 F5
Castlewood Cl BS21...57 F4
Caswell Hill BS20....46 B1

Caswell La BS20 . . . . . . **46** B2
CATBRAIN **35** B6
Catbrain Hill BS10 . . . . **35** B6
Catbrain La BS10 . . . . . **35** B6
Catchpot La BS37 . . . . . **41** A6
Catemead BS21 . . . . **73** C8
Cater Dr BS37 . . . . **27** D6
Cater Rd BS13 . . . . **79** B6
Catharine Pl BA1 . . . . . **141** B3
Cathcart Ho **6** BA1 . . . . **85** A1
Cathedral Church of The
  Holy & Undivided
  Trinity★ BS1 . . . .**142** C2
Cathedral Wlk BS1 . . . .**142** C1
Catherine Ct **14** BS6 . . . . **49** E1
Catherine Hill BS35 . . . **13** F2
Catherine Mead St BS3 **63** D4
Catherine St BS1 . . . . . **47** C8
Catherine Way BA1 . . . . **86** A5
Cathorn La BS48 . . . . . . **77** C6
Catley Gr BS41 . . . . **62** B2
Cato St BS5 . . . . **50** B2
Catsbrain La BS5 . . . . . . **8** D5
Cattistock Dr BS5 . . . . . **65** A6
Cattle Market Rd BS1 . .**143** C1
Cattybrook Rd BS16 . . . . **52** D6
Cattybrook Rd N BS16 . . **52** D6
Cattybrook St
  7 Bristol BS5 . . . . **64** B7
  23 Bristol BS5 . . . . **64** B8
Caulfield Rd BS22 . . . . . **89** B4
Causeway BS48 . . . . **59** B3
Causeway The
  Congresbury BS49 . . . . **91** D4
  Frampton Cotterell BS36 **38** D7
  Yatton BS49 . . . . **91** C7
Causeway View BS48 . . . **59** C2
Causley Dr BS30 . . . . . . **66** A5
Cautletts Cl BA3 . . . . . .**138** F8
Cavan Wlk BS4 . . . . **63** D1
Cave Cl BS16 . . . . **51** D6
Cave Ct BS2 . . . .**143** B4
Cave Dr BS16 . . . . **51** D6
Cave Gr BS16 . . . . **52** B7
Cavell Ct BS21 . . . . **57** E1
Cavendish Cl
  Saltford BS31 . . . . **82** D2
  Tormarton GL9 . . . . . . **41** E2
Cavendish Cres BA1 . . .**141** A4
Cavendish Gdns BS9 . . . **48** C4
Cavendish Lodge BA1 . .**141** A4
Cavendish Pl BA1 . . . . .**141** A4
Cavendish Rd
  Bath BA1 . . . .**141** A4
  Bristol, Henleaze BS9 . . **49** A5
  Bristol, Patchway BS34 . . **35** F8
Caveners Ct BS22 . . . . . **88** B1
Caversham Dr BS48 . . . . **60** A2
Caves Cotts BS16 . . . . . **51** E7
Cave St BS2 . . . .**143** B4
Caxton Ct **4** BA2 . . . . .**141** C3
Cecil Ave BS5 . . . . **50** F1
Cecil Rd
  Bristol, Clifton BS8 . . . . **62** F8
  Bristol, Kingswood BS15 **65** D8
  Weston-s-M BS23 . . . . . **87** C1
Cedar Ave BS22 . . . . **88** C1
Cedar Cl
  Bristol, Oldland BS30 . . **66** B4
  Bristol, Patchway BS34 . . **35** F7
  Long Ashton BS41 . . . . . **61** F1
Cedar Ct
  Bristol BS9 . . . . **48** C4
  Bristol, Combe Dingle
    BS9 . . . . **48** D7
  Bristol, Mangotsfield
    BS16 . . . . **51** E6
  Bristol, Westbury on T
    BS9 . . . . **48** F8
Cedar Dr BS31 . . . . **81** D4
Cedar Gr
  Bath BA2 . . . .**101** D3
  Bristol BS9 . . . . **48** D5
Cedar Hall BS16 . . . . . . **51** C8
Cedarhurst Rd BS20 . . . **44** E4
Cedarn Ct BS22 . . . . **88** B4
Cedar Pk BS9 . . . . **48** D5
Cedar Row BS11 . . . . . . **47** F6
Cedars The
  Bristol BS9 . . . . **48** D3
  Chew Stoke BS40 . . . . .**112** D8
Cedars Way BS36 . . . . . . **37** D5
Cedar Terr BA3 . . . .**133** D1
Cedar Villas BA2 . . . . . .**141** A1
Cedar Way
  Bath BA2 . . . .**141** A1
  Nailsea BS48 . . . . **60** A2
  Portishead BS20 . . . . . . **45** C4
  Pucklechurch BS16 . . . . **53** C5
Cedern Ave BS24 . . . . .**106** C3
Cedric Cl BA1 . . . .**101** C7
Cedric Rd BA1 . . . .**101** C8
Celandine Cl BS35 . . . . . **8** D2
Celandine Ct **5** BS37 . . **27** F5
Celestine Rd BS37 . . . . . **27** E4
Celia Terr BS4 . . . . **64** F6
Cello Cl BS31 . . . . **82** B4
Celtic Way BS24 . . . . . .**122** B7
Cemetery Rd BS4 . . . . . . **64** A3

Cennick Ave BS15 . . . . . **51** E1
Centaurus Rd BS34 . . . . **35** D7
Central Ave
  Bristol BS15 . . . . **65** C5
  Dyer's Common BS35 . . . **22** D2
  Severn Beach BS10 . . . . **22** A3
Central Pk BS14 . . . . . . **80** B7
Central Trad Est BS4 . . **64** B4
Central Way
  Bristol BS10 . . . . **49** E8
  Clevedon BS21 . . . . **57** G1
Centre Dr BS29 . . . . . .**106** E4
Centre Quay BS20 . . . . . **45** E7
Centre The
  Keynsham BS31 . . . . **81** F5
  10 Weston-s-M BS23 . .**104** E7
Centre Walk Ave GL9 . . . **30** F2
Ceres Cl BS30 . . . . **65** F2
Cerimon Gate BS34 . . . . **36** E5
Cerney Gdns BS48 . . . . . **60** A2
Cerney La BS11 . . . . **47** E5
Cerutti Cl BS39 . . . . . .**132** D6
Cesson Cl BS37 . . . . **40** C8
Chadleigh Gr BS4 . . . . . **79** D7
Chaffinch Ave BS31 . . . . **81** C3
Chaffinch Dr BA3 . . . . .**139** B8
Chaffins The BS21 . . . . . **57** G2
Chaingate La BS37 . . . . . **27** A6
Chakeshill Cl BS10 . . . . . **35** C3
Chakeshill Dr BS10 . . . . **35** C4
Chalcombe Cl BS34 . . . . **36** C8
Chalcroft Ho **2** BS3 . . . . **63** A4
Chalcroft Wlk BS13 . . . . **78** E4
Chalet The BS10 . . . . **34** F3
Chalfield Cl BS31 . . . . . . **82** A2
Chalfont Rd BS22 . . . . .**105** C8
Chalford Cl BS37 . . . . . . **39** D8
Chalk Farm Cl BS39 . . . . **97** A7
Chalks Rd BS5 . . . . **64** D8
Chalks Rd BS40 . . . . **96** B3
Challender Ave BS10 . . . **34** F2
Challoner Ct BS1 . . . . . .**143** A1
Challow Dr BS22 . . . . . . **88** B2
Champion Rd
  Bitton BS30 . . . . **82** E8
  Bristol BS15 . . . . **52** A2
Champneys Ave BS10 . . **34** F3
Champs Sur Marne
  BS32 . . . . **36** E8
Chancel Cl
  Bristol BS9 . . . . **48** D3
  Nailsea BS48 . . . . **59** D1
Chancellor's Pound
  BS40 . . . . **93** D3
Chancery Cl BS48 . . . . . **64** B7
Chandag Inf Sch BS31 . . **82** A4
Chandag Jun Sch BS31 **82** A4
Chandag Rd BS31 . . . . . **82** A4
Chandler Cl BA1 . . . . . . **84** B1
Chandos BS6 . . . . **49** C2
Chandos Ct BS23 . . . . .**104** D6
Chandos Ho **7** BA1 . . .**141** B2
Chandos Rd
  Bristol BS6 . . . . **49** C1
  Keynsham BS31 . . . . **81** E7
Chandos Trad Est BS2 . **64** A5
Channel Ct BS22 . . . . . . **88** B3
Channel Hts BS24 . . . .**104** F1
Channel Rd BS21 . . . . . . **57** G5
Channel View Cres
  BS20 . . . . **45** B5
Channel View Farm La
  BS49 . . . . **92** A7
Channel View Rd BS20 . **45** B5
Channon's Hill BS16 . . . **50** F4
Chantry Cl BS48 . . . . . . **59** C1
Chantry Ct BS1 . . . .**142** C2
Chantry Dr BS22 . . . . . . **89** A4
Chantry Gr BS11 . . . . . . **34** C2
Chantry La BS16 . . . . . . **37** F1
Chantry Mead Rd BA2 **101** E3
Chantry Rd
  Bristol BS8 . . . . **49** B1
  Thornbury BS35 . . . . **8** B2
Chapei Way BS10 . . . . . . **49** D8
Chapel Barton
  7 Bristol BS3 . . . . **63** B2
  Nailsea BS48 . . . . **59** C2
Chapel Cl
  Bristol BS15 . . . . **66** B8
  Chew Stoke BS40 . . . . .**112** E8
  Farrington Gurney BS39 **131** F4
  Nailsea BS48 . . . . **59** C2
  Winford BS40 . . . . **95** A6
Chapel Ct
  8 Bath BA1 . . . .**141** B2
  Bristol, Brentry BS10 . . . **35** D3
  Bristol, St Philip's Marsh
    BS2 . . . . **64** A5
  Clandown BA3 . . . .**133** E4
  Clevedon BS21 . . . . **57** F3
Chapel Field BA2 . . . . .**134** E8
Chapel Gdns BS10 . . . . . **35** A1
Chapel Green La BS6 . . . **49** B2
Chapel Hill
  Backwell BS48 . . . . **76** D7
  Clevedon BS21 . . . . **57** F3
  Newport GL13 . . . . **4** B7

Chapel Hill continued
  Ubley BS40 . . . .**111** C5
  Wrington BS40 . . . . **92** D3
Chapel La
  Acton Turville GL9 . . . . . **43** A6
  Bristol, Clay Hill BS5 . . . **50** D3
  Bristol, Fishponds BS16 . **51** A4
  Bristol, Frenchay BS16 . . **51** C7
  Bristol, Lawrence Weston
    BS11 . . . . **34** C2
  Bristol, Warmley BS15 . . **66** B8
  Chew Stoke BS40 . . . . .**112** D8
  Chipping Sodbury BS37 . . **41** A7
  Claverham BS49 . . . . . . **91** F3
  Cleeve BS49 . . . . **92** B7
  Hillesley GL12 . . . . **19** E8
  Hinton SN14 . . . . **54** C5
  Thornbury BS35 . . . . **9** A1
  Winford BS40 . . . . **95** A6
Chapel Lawns BA3 . . . .**133** E4
Chapel Orch BS37 . . . . . **27** C2
Chapel Pill La BS20 . . . . **47** E4
Chapel Rd
  Bristol, Bishopsworth
    BS13 . . . . **79** A6
  Bristol, Hanham BS15 . . **65** C5
  Clandown BA3 . . . .**133** E4
  Oldbury-on-S BS35 . . . . . **7** C5
Chapel Row
  Bath BA1 . . . .**141** B2
  Bathford BA1 . . . . **86** C2
  Clandown BA3 . . . .**133** E4
  Luckington SN14 . . . . . . **31** E4
  Norton St Philip BA2 . . .**136** F4
  Pill BS20 . . . . **47** C4
Chapel St
  Bristol BS2 . . . . **64** A5
  Thornbury BS35 . . . . **15** B8
Chapel Way BS4 . . . . **64** E6
Chaplains Wood BS20 . . **44** E5
Chaplin Rd BS5 . . . . **50** B1
Chapter St BS2 . . . . . .**143** B4
Chapter Wlk BS6 . . . . . . **49** B3
Charbon Gate BS34 . . . . **36** F5
Charborough Ct
  Bristol BS34 . . . . **35** F2
  Bristol BS34 . . . . **36** A2
Charborough Rd BS34 . . **35** F2
Charborough Road Prim
  Sch BS34 . . . . **35** F2
Charbury Wlk BS11 . . . . **47** E5
Chard Cl BS48 . . . . **75** D5
Chard Ct BS14 . . . . **80** B6
Chard Rd BS21 . . . . **57** G1
Chardstock Ave BS9 . . . **48** D8
Char Dyke Dr BS39 . . . .**114** E1
CHARFIELD **11** B4
Charfield **4** BS15 . . . . . **66** A8
CHARFIELD GREEN **11** B5
CHARFIELD HILL **10** F5
Charfield Prim Sch
  GL12 . . . . **10** F5
Charfield Rd
  Bristol BS10 . . . . **35** D1
  Kingswood GL12 . . . . . . **11** E5
Chargrove
  2 Bristol BS30 . . . . . . **66** C6
  Yate BS37 . . . . **39** D7
Charis Ave BS10 . . . . . . **49** C7
Charity La BA11 . . . . . .**140** C1
CHARLCOMBE **84** E3
Charlcombe La BA1 . . . . **84** F3
Charlcombe Pk BS20 . . . **44** F3
Charlcombe Rise BA1 . . **84** F2
Charlcombe View Rd
  BA1 . . . . **85** A2
Charlcombe Way BA1 . . **84** F2
Charlcome Rise BS20 . . **44** D3
Charlecombe Ct BS9 . . . **48** F6
Charlecombe Rd BS9 . . . **48** F6
Charlecote BA1 . . . . **84** F1
Charles Ave BS34 . . . . . . **36** E4
Charles Cl BS35 . . . . **8** C3
Charles Ct **1** BS8 . . . . .**142** A2
Charles England Ho **1**
  BS34 . . . . **35** F7
Charles Pl BS8 . . . .**142** A4
Charles Rd
  Bristol BS34 . . . . **36** B3
  Yate Rocks BS37 . . . . . . **27** E5
Charles St
  Bath BA1 . . . .**141** B2
  Bristol BS1 . . . .**143** A4
Charles Wesley Ct BS5 . **65** A6
Charleton Ho **8** BS2 . .**143** C3
Charlock Cl **3** BS22 . . .**105** D7
Charlock Rd BS22 . . . . .**105** D7
Charlotte St S BS1 . . . .**142** C2
Charlotte St
  Bath BA1 . . . .**141** B2
  Bristol, Brandon Hill
    BS1 . . . .**142** C3
CHARLTON **139** E5
Charlton Ave
  Bristol BS34 . . . . **35** F2
  Weston-s-M BS23 . . . . .**104** D4
Charlton Bvd BS34 . . . . **36** A7

Charlton Comm BS10 . . **35** D4
Charlton Ct BS34 . . . . . . **23** F1
Charlton Dr BS48 . . . . . . **60** C7
Charlton Gdns BS10 . . . **35** D4
Charlton La
  Bristol BS10 . . . . **35** A3
  Radstock BA3 . . . .**139** D6
Charlton Leaze BS10 . . . **35** A4
Charlton Mead Ct BS10 **35** D4
Charlton Mead Dr BS10 **35** D4
Charlton Park Rd BA3 **139** F6
Charlton Pk
  Keynsham BS31 . . . . **81** D5
  Midsomer Norton BA3 . .**139** B8
Charlton Pl BS10 . . . . . . **35** D4
Charlton Rd
  Bristol, Brentry BS10 . . . **35** C3
  Bristol, Kingswood BS15 **51** D1
  Holcombe BA3 . . . .**139** D3
  Keynsham BS31, BS14 . . **81** C3
  Midsomer Norton BA3 . .**139** B8
  Weston-s-M BS23 . . . . .**104** D4
Charlton St **17** BS5 . . . . **64** B7
Charlton View BS20 . . . . **45** C5
Charmborough Farm Rural
  Bsns Pk BA3 . . . .**139** D3
Charminster Rd BS16 . . **51** B3
Charmouth Ct BS3 . . . . **63** D1
Charmouth Rd BA1 . . . .**101** B7
Charnell Rd BS16 . . . . . . **51** E4
Charnhill Brow BS16 . . . **52** A4
Charnhill Cres BS16 . . . **51** F4
Charnhill Dr BS16 . . . . . **51** F4
Charnhill Ridge BS16 . . **52** A4
Charnhill Vale BS16 . . . . **51** F4
Charnwood BS16 . . . . . . **52** A4
Charnwood Rd BS14 . . . **80** B4
Charter Ho BS1 . . . .**142** B2
CHARTERHOUSE **127** C4
Charterhouse Cl BS48 . . **59** F1
Charterhouse Rd BS5 . . **64** D8
Charter Rd BS22 . . . . . .**105** B8
Charter Wlk BS14 . . . . . **80** A6
Chartley BS9 . . . . **48** D2
Chasefield La **1** BS16 . . **51** B4
Chase La GL12 . . . . **18** C6
Chase Rd BS15 . . . . **51** D2
Chase The BS16 . . . . **51** C3
Chatcombe BS37 . . . . . . **39** E7
Chatford Ho BS8 . . . . . . **62** F8
Chatham Pk BA2 . . . . . .**102** C6
Chatham Row BA1 . . . . .**141** C3
Chatley Furlong BA2 . .**136** F3
Chatsworth Pk BS35 . . . **8** C3
Chatsworth Rd
  Bristol, Arno's Vale BS4 . **64** C4
  Bristol, Hillfields BS16 . . **51** B3
Chattenden Ho BS9 . . . . **48** F3
Chatterton Gn BS14 . . . **79** F3
Chatterton Ho **5** BS1 . .**143** B1
Chatterton Rd BS37 . . . **27** D1
Chatterton Sq BS1 . . . .**143** C1
Chatterton St BS1 . . . . .**143** C1
Chaucer Rd
  Bath BA2 . . . .**101** F4
  Midsomer Norton BA3 . .**139** B8
  Weston-s-M BS23 . . . . .**105** A4
Chaundey Gr BS13 . . . . . **79** B5
Chavenage BS15 . . . . . . **52** A1
Cheapside BS2 . . . .**143** C4
Cheapside St **8** BS3 . . . **63** F4
Cheap St BA1 . . . .**141** C2
Cheddar Cl BS48 . . . . . . **75** D5
Cheddarcoombe La
  BS25 . . . .**108** D1
Cheddar Gorge★ **126** E1
Cheddar Gr BS13 . . . . . . **79** A8
Cheddar Grove Prim Sch
  BS13 . . . . **79** A8
Cheddar Gr Prim Sch
  BS13 . . . . **79** A8
Cheddar Rd BS26 . . . . .**125** E2
Chedworth
  Bristol BS15 . . . . **51** F3
  Yate BS37 . . . . **39** B7
Chedworth Cl BA2 . . . .**102** F3
Chedworth Rd BS7 . . . . **50** A6
Cheers St BS5 . . . . **50** F1
Cheese La BS2 . . . .**143** B2
Chelford Gr BS34 . . . . . . **36** B8
Chelmer Gr BS31 . . . . . . **81** F4
Chelmsford Wlk BS4 . . . **64** F5
Chelscombe BA1 . . . . . . **84** B1
Chelscombe Cl BA1 . . . . **84** E4
Chelsea Cl BS31 . . . . **82** A5
Chelsea Ho BA1 . . . .**141** C4
Chelsea Pk BS5 . . . . **64** C8
Chelsea Rd
  Bath BA1 . . . .**101** C7
  Bristol BS5 . . . . **50** B1
Chelsfield BS48 . . . . **76** A4
Chelston Rd BS4 . . . . . . **79** D7
Chelswood Ave BS22 . .**105** C8
Chelswood Gdns
  BS22 . . . .**105** D8
Cheltenham Cres **2**
  BS6 . . . . **49** D1
Cheltenham La BS6 . . . . **49** D2

Cheltenham Rd BS6 . . . . **49** E1
Cheltenham St BA2 . . . .**141** A1
CHELVEY **75** D5
Chelvey Batch BS48 . . . **75** F3
Chelvey La BS48 . . . . . . **75** E4
Chelvey Rd BS48 . . . . . . **75** D5
Chelvey Rise BS48 . . . . . **60** A1
Chelvy Cl BS13 . . . . **79** D3
CHELWOOD **115** A8
Chelwood BS31 . . . .**104** F8
Chelwood Dr BA2 . . . . .**101** D1
Chelwood Rd
  Bristol BS11 . . . . **47** D7
  Saltford BS31 . . . . **82** E4
Chelwood Rdbt BS39 . .**114** E8
Chepstow Pk BS16 . . . . . **37** F1
Chepstow Rd BS4 . . . . . **79** D8
Chepstow Wlk BS31 . . . . **81** D5
Chequers Cl BS30 . . . . . **66** C3
Chequers Ct BS34 . . . . . **37** A5
Cherington
  Bristol BS15 . . . . **65** B5
  Yate BS37 . . . . **39** D6
Cherington Rd
  Bristol BS10 . . . . **49** D7
  Nailsea BS48 . . . . **60** A2
Cheriton Pl
  Bristol, Eastfield BS9 . . . **49** B7
  Bristol, Warmley BS30 . . **66** C6
Cherry Ave BS21 . . . . . . **57** G2
Cherry Banks BS16 . . . . **38** C1
Cherry Cl BS49 . . . . **91** B8
Cherry Ct **12** BS1 . . . . .**143** A4
Cherry Garden La BS30 . **66** B2
Cherry Garden Prim Sch
  BS30 . . . . **66** C2
Cherry Garden Rd BS30 **66** C1
Cherry Gdns BS30 . . . . . **66** C1
Cherry Gr
  Bristol BS16 . . . . **52** A6
  Yatton BS49 . . . . **91** B8
Cherry Hay BS21 . . . . . . **57** F1
Cherry La **4** BS1 . . . . .**143** B4
Cherry Orchard La
  4 Bristol BS5 . . . . **64** F8
  Luckington SN14 . . . . . . **31** C5
Cherry Rd
  Chipping Sodbury BS37 . . **28** A1
  Long Ashton BS41 . . . . . **61** F1
  Nailsea BS48 . . . . **59** D1
Cherry Tree Cl
  Bristol BS16 . . . . **51** C2
  Keynsham BS31 . . . . **81** C4
  Radstock BA3 . . . .**133** E1
Cherrytree Cres BS16 . . **51** C2
Cherrytree Ct BS16 . . . . **53** C5
Cherry Tree Ct BS21 . . . **73** C2
Cherrytree Rd BS16 . . . . **51** C2
Cherry Wood BS30 . . . . **66** B2
Cherrywood Rd BS22 . . **88** F2
Cherrywood Rise BS22 . **88** F2
Chertsey Rd BS6 . . . . . . **49** B1
Cherwell Cl BS35 . . . . . . **15** C7
Cherwell Rd BS31 . . . . . **82** A4
Chescombe Rd BS49 . . . **91** B7
Chescombe Rd N BS22 .**105** B8
Chesham Rd S BS22 . . .**105** B8
Chesham Way BS15 . . . . **51** D1
Cheshire Cl BS37 . . . . . . **27** E3
Chesle Cl BS20 . . . . **44** E3
Cheslefield BS20 . . . . . . **44** E3
Chesle Way BS20 . . . . . . **44** E3
Chesley Hill BS30 . . . . . . **66** F7
Chessel Cl BS32 . . . . **24** C2
Chessel Ct **6** BS3 . . . . . **63** B2
Chessel Dr BS34 . . . . . . **36** A7
Chessell Ave BS35 . . . . . **22** C7
Chessel Mews **8** BS3 . . **63** C3
Chessel St BS3 . . . . **63** B3
Chessington Ave BS14 . . **80** B5
Chester Cl BS24 . . . . . .**106** A8
Chester Ct **4** BS5 . . . . . **64** C7
Chesterfield Ave BS6 . . **49** E2
Chesterfield Bldgs
  BS8 . . . .**142** B3
Chesterfield Cl BS29 . .**106** F3
Chesterfield Ho
  Bristol BS10 . . . . **34** F1
  Midsomer Norton BA3 . .**133** B1
Chesterfield Hospl
  BS8 . . . .**142** A2
Chesterfield Rd
  Bristol, Mangotsfield
    BS16 . . . . **51** E5
  Bristol, Montpelier BS6 . **49** E2
Chestermaster Cl BS32 **24** A5
CHESTER PARK **51** B2
Chester Park Jun & Inf
  Schs BS16 . . . . **51** A3
Chester Park Rd BS16 . . **51** B2
Chester Pk BS5 . . . . **50** E1
Chester Rd BS5 . . . . **50** E1
Chesters BS30 . . . . **66** A4
Chester St BS5 . . . . **50** B2
Chesterton Dr BS48 . . . . **60** A2
Chesterton Ho **6** BS2 **143** B4

Chestertons The BA2 . . 102 F8
Chestnut Ave
Axbridge BS26 . . . . 125 C2
Weston-s-M BS22 . . . . . 89 A1
Chestnut Barn Ind Est
BS24 . . . . 90 D3
Chestnut Chase BS48 . . 60 A3
Chestnut Cl
Acton Turville GL9 . . . . 43 A6
Banwell BS29 . . . . 107 A3
Bristol BS14 . . . . 80 F5
Congresbury BS49 . . . . 91 D4
Paulton BS39 . . . . 132 E6
Radstock BA3 . . . . 133 E1
Chestnut Ct
Bristol BS13 . . . . 79 A7
Bristol, Hillhouse BS16 . 52 A5
Chestnut Dr
Chipping Sodbury BS37 . 28 A1
Claverham BS49 . . . . . . 74 F1
Thornbury BS35 . . . . 8 C1
Chestnut Gr
Bath BA2 . . . . 101 C4
Clevedon BS21 . . . . 57 G4
Westwood BA15 . . . . . 120 F4
Chestnut Ho BS13 . . . . . 79 D3
Chestnut Pk BS24 . . . . 122 B7
Chestnut Park Est GL12 . 11 F4
Chestnut Park Prim Sch
BS49 . . . . 73 F2
Chestnut Pk G12 . . . . . . 11 F4
Chestnut Rd
Bristol, Lower Soundwell
BS15 . . . . 51 F3
Bristol, Mangotsfield
BS16 . . . . 51 D6
Long Ashton BS41 . . . . . 62 B2
Chestnut Springs BS37 . 27 B4
Chestnuts The
Cheddar BS27 . . . . 126 A1
Winscombe BS25 . . . . . 125 A7
Chestnut Way BS15 . . . . 51 F3
Chestnut Wlk
Bristol BS13 . . . . 79 A6
Saltford BS31 . . . . 82 E3
Chetwode Cl BS10 . . . . . 35 D3
Chetwood Ho BS5 . . . . . 64 C6
Chevening Cl BS34 . . . . 36 D4
Chever's La BA2 . . . . . 136 E5
Cheviot Dr BS35 . . . . . . 15 E8
Cheviot Way BS30 . . . . . 66 C5
Chew Cotts BS31 . . . . . . 81 F5
Chew Court Farm BS40 . 96 B3
Chew Hill BS40 . . . . 96 A4
Chew La BS40 . . . . 95 F1
CHEW MAGNA 96 C4
Chew Magna Prim Sch
BS40 . . . . 96 B3
Chew Rd BS40 . . . . 95 C5
Chew St BS40 . . . . 96 A3
CHEW STOKE 112 D8
Chew Stoke CE Prim Sch
BS40 . . . . 112 D8
Chewton Cl BS16 . . . . . . 51 B3
CHEWTON KEYNSHAM . 81 E2
Chewton Rd BS31 . . . . . 81 F2
Chew Valley Lake Nature
Trails ★ BS39 . . . . 113 B7
Chew Valley Lake Visitor
Ctr ★ BS39 . . . . 113 A7
Chew Valley Sch BS40 . . 95 F1
Cheyne Rd BS9 . . . . 48 D6
Chichester Ho BS4 . . . . . 64 F6
Chichester Pl BA3 . . . . 134 A2
Chichester Way
Weston-s-M BS24 . . . . 106 A8
Yate BS37 . . . . 27 D3
Chickwell La BA3 . . . . . 136 A1
CHILCOMPTON 138 C4
Chilcompton Rd BA3 . . 138 E7
Chilkwell La BA3 . . . . . 136 C2
Chillwood Cl BS37 . . . . . 26 E3
Chillyhill La BS40 . . . . . 95 F2
Chiltern Cl
Bristol BS14 . . . . 80 B4
Bristol, Warmley BS30 . . 66 C5
Chiltern Pk BS35 . . . . . . 15 E8
Chilton Ct **7** BA1 . . . . . . 85 B1
Chilton Rd
Bath BA1 . . . . 85 B1
Bristol BS4 . . . . 80 A8
Chilwood Cl BS37 . . . . . 26 E3
Chimes The BS48 . . . . . . 75 C8
Chimney Steps BS2 . . . 143 C2
Chine The BS16 . . . . 50 D5
Chine View BS16 . . . . . . 51 F8
Chiphouse Rd BS15 . . . . 51 F3
Chippenham Rd
Doynton BS30 . . . . 68 D6
Marshfield SN14 . . . . . . 69 C7
Marshfield SN14 . . . . . . 70 A8
Chipperfield Dr BS15 . . . 51 F1
Chipping Cross BS21 . . . 73 C8
Chipping Edge Est
BS37 . . . . 28 C1
CHIPPING SODBURY . . . 28 D1

Chipping Sodbury Sch
BS37 . . . . 40 B8
Chippings The BS16 . . . . 50 D5
Chipping The GL12 . . . . 11 F4
Chisbury St BS5 . . . . 50 C3
Chittening Ind Est
BS11 . . . . 33 D7
Chittening Rd BS11 . . . . 33 E7
Chivers St BA2 . . . . 102 A2
Chock La BS9 . . . . 49 A7
CHOLWELL 114 D2
Cholwell Cotts BS39 . . 114 D2
Christchurch Ave BS16 . 51 D5
Christ Church CE Inf Sch
BS16 . . . . 51 D5
Christ Church CE Jun Sch
BS16 . . . . 51 D5
Christ Church CE Prim Sch
BS8 . . . . 142 A3
Christ Church CE Prim Sch
BS3 . . . . 63 A3
Christ Church CE Prim Sch
BS23 . . . . 104 E8
Christ Church Cl **1**
BS48 . . . . 59 E2
Christchurch Hall **2**
BA1 . . . . 141 B3
Christ Church Hanham CE
Prim Sch BS15 . . . . . . 65 B4
Christchurch La BS16 . . 51 D5
Christ Church Path S **12**
BS23 . . . . 104 E8
Christchurch Rd BS8 . . 142 A3
Christian Cl BS22 . . . . . 89 A3
Christina Terr BS8 . . . . 142 A1
Christmas St **7** BS1 . . 143 A3
Christmas Steps **3**
BS1 . . . . 143 A3
Christmas Tree BS34 . . . 35 D6
CHRISTON 123 D7
Christon Hill BS26 . . . . 123 B8
Christon Rd
Banwell BS29 . . . . 107 A1
Loxton BS26 . . . . 123 C6
Christon Terr BS23 . . . 104 F2
Christ the King RC Prim
Sch BS35 . . . . 8 D1
Christy Cl BS36 . . . . 38 B6
Chubb Cl BS30 . . . . 65 F5
Church Ave
Bristol BS9 . . . . 48 E4
3 Bristol, Upper Easton
BS5 . . . . 50 B1
Bristol, Warmley BS30 . . 66 D7
Falfield GL12 . . . . 9 E7
Church Cl
Bathampton BA2 . . . . . . 85 F2
Bathford BA1 . . . . 86 B2
Bristol BS10 . . . . 34 E2
Clevedon BS21 . . . . 57 C2
Frampton Cotterell BS36 . 38 B8
Portishead BS20 . . . . . . 45 D5
Yatton BS49 . . . . 91 C7
Church Cnr BS24 . . . . . 122 B1
Church Cotts
Monkton Combe BA2 . . 119 E8
Newton St Loe BA2 . . . 100 B6
Church Ct
8 Bristol BS16 . . . . . . 51 D3
Midsomer Norton BA3 . 133 A1
Redhill BS40 . . . . 93 D3
Churchdown Wlk BS11 . 47 E5
Church Dr
Bristol BS5 . . . . 64 E8
Congresbury BS49 . . . . 91 D4
CHURCHEND 10 F3
Churchend La GL12 . . . . 10 F3
Church Farm Bsns Pk
BA2 . . . . 100 A7
Churchfarm Cl BS37 . . . 27 F3
Church Farm Cl BA2 . . . 99 B1
Church Farm La BA2 . . 137 D7
Church Farm Rd BS16 . . 52 C6
Churchfields The Village
Sch BA15 . . . . 103 E7
Church Hayes Cl BS48 . . 75 E8
Church Hayes Dr BS48 . 75 E8
Church Hill
Bristol BS4 . . . . 64 E2
Burton SN14 . . . . 43 B3
Freshford BA2 . . . . 120 B5
Oldbury-on-S BS35 . . . . . 7 B5
Olveston BS35 . . . . 13 F3
Radstock BA3 . . . . 134 C3
Timsbury BA2 . . . . 116 B2
Church Hill Ho BS4 . . . . 64 E2
Church Ho BS7 . . . . 49 F8
CHURCHILL 108 F5
Churchill Ave BS21 . . . . 57 E2
Churchill Bsns Pk
BS23 . . . . 105 A7
Churchill CE VA Prim Sch
BS40 . . . . 109 A5
Churchill Cl
Bristol BS30 . . . . 66 A5
5 Clevedon BS21 . . . . 57 E2
Churchill Com Sch & Sixth
Form Ctr BS25 . . . . . . 108 D5
Churchill Dr BS9 . . . . . . 48 D7

Churchill Gate BS25 . . 108 F4
Churchill Gdns BS37 . . . 27 E4
Churchill Gn BS25 . . . . 108 C5
CHURCHILL GREEN . . . 108 D5
Churchill Rd
Bristol BS4 . . . . 64 C4
Weston-s-M BS23 . . . . 105 A7
Churchill Sch & Sixth Form
Ctr BS25 . . . . 108 D5
Church La
Axbridge BS26 . . . . 125 C2
Backwell BS48 . . . . 76 C5
Badminton GL9 . . . . 30 E5
Bath BA2 . . . . 102 C4
Batheaston BA1 . . . . . . 85 F4
Bishop Sutton BS39 . . . 113 D4
Bitton BS30 . . . . 82 E7
Bristol, Bromley Heath
BS16 . . . . 37 F1
Bristol, Clifton Wood
BS8 . . . . 142 B2
Bristol, Dundry Hill BS14 . 80 B3
Bristol, Henbury BS10 . . 34 E2
Bristol, Southville BS3 . . 63 D3
Chew Stoke BS40 . . . . 112 D8
Chilcompton BA3 . . . . . 138 D5
Chipping Sodbury BS37 . 41 B8
Churchill BS25 . . . . . . 108 D5
Clutton BS39 . . . . 114 E3
Compton Bishop BS26 . 124 B3
Compton Dando BS39 . . 98 D6
Cromhall GL12 . . . . 10 A1
Downside BA3 . . . . 138 A2
East Harptree BS40 . . . 129 E4
Farmborough BA2 . . . . 116 A6
Farrington Gurney BS39 132 A4
Flax Bourton BS48 . . . . 76 F7
Frampton Cotterell BS36 . 38 C6
Hambrook BS16 . . . . . . 37 E2
Hutton BS24 . . . . 105 E2
Limpley Stoke BA2 . . . . 120 A5
Long Ashton BS41 . . . . . 62 C2
Loxton BS26 . . . . 123 D4
Lympsham BS24 . . . . . 122 B1
Marshfield SN14 . . . . . . 70 A8
Midsomer Norton BA3 . 133 A1
Monkton Combe BA2 . . 119 E8
Nailsea BS48 . . . . 59 C1
Paulton BS39 . . . . 132 E6
Portbury BS20 . . . . 46 E3
Rangeworthy BS37 . . . . 16 F1
Stratton-on-t-F BA3 . . . 138 F2
Tickenham BS21 . . . . . . 59 C4
Timsbury BA2 . . . . 116 B2
Wickwar GL12 . . . . 18 A6
Winscombe BS25 . . . . . 124 E6
Winterbourne BS36 . . . . 37 C6
Yatton BS49 . . . . 91 C7
Churchlands Rd **8** BS3 . 63 B2
Churchland Way BS22 106 B8
Church Lane End BS48 . 76 F8
Church Leaze BS11 . . . . 47 D6
Church Mdws BS14 . . . . 80 C4
Church Par BS4 . . . . 64 E2
Church Path Rd BS20 . . 47 C4
Church Pl BS20 . . . . 47 C4
Church Rd
Abbots Leigh BS8 . . . . . 62 A8
Almondsbury BS32 . . . . 24 A5
Alveston BS35 . . . . 15 A1
Bath, Combe Down BA2 102 C1
Bath, Weston Park BA1 . 84 C1
Bitton BS30 . . . . 82 E7
Bristol BS9 . . . . 48 D3
Bristol, Bedminster BS3 . 63 C3
Bristol, Bishopsworth
BS13 . . . . 79 A6
Bristol, Filton BS34 . . . . 36 A3
Bristol, Frenchay BS16 . . 51 C7
Bristol, Hanham BS15 . . 65 B5
Bristol, Horfield BS7 . . . 49 E5
Bristol, Kingswood BS15 . 65 E8
Bristol, Moorfields BS5 . 64 C8
Bristol, Stoke Gifford
BS34 . . . . 36 E4
Bristol, Upper Soundwell
BS16 . . . . 51 E3
Bristol, Westbury on Trym
BS9 . . . . 49 A7
Doynton BS30 . . . . 54 A1
Dundry BS41 . . . . 78 D2
Easter Compton BS35 . . 23 A1
Easton-in-G BS20 . . . . . 47 A4
Frampton Cotterell BS36 38 C8
Leigh Woods BS8 . . . . . 62 D6
Luckington SN14 . . . . . . 31 F4
Lympsham BS24 . . . . . 122 B1
Oldbury-on-S BS35 . . . . . 7 B5
Peasedown St John BA2 134 B8
Pensford BS39 . . . . 97 A7
Pilning BS35 . . . . 22 B7
Redhill BS40 . . . . 93 D3
Severn Beach BS35 . . . . 22 A6
Thornbury BS35 . . . . 8 B8
Tormarton GL9 . . . . 41 D2
Weston-s-M BS22 . . . . . 88 E2
Whitchurch BS14 . . . . . . 80 C4
Wick BS30 . . . . 67 B6

Church Rd continued
Winford BS40 . . . . 95 A7
Winscombe BS25 . . . . 124 E7
Winterbourne BS36 . . . . 37 E4
Yate BS37 . . . . 27 E3
Yate BS37 . . . . 27 F2
Yatton BS49 . . . . 91 C7
Church Rd N BS20 . . . . . 45 D5
Church Rd S BS20 . . . . . 45 D4
Church Rise BS40 . . . . . 95 A7
Church Row BA3 . . . . . 138 F2
Churchside BS16 . . . . . . 51 B7
Church Sq
Clutton BS39 . . . . 114 E2
Midsomer Norton BA3 . 133 A1
Church St
Banwell BS29 . . . . 107 B3
6 Bath BA1 . . . . 141 C2
Bathford BA1 . . . . 86 B2
Bath, Weston Park BA1 . 84 B1
Bath, Widcombe BA2 . . 102 B4
Blagdon BS40 . . . . 110 F2
Bristol BS1 . . . . 143 B2
Bristol, Lower Easton
BS5 . . . . 50 B1
Bristol, Russell Town BS5 64 B6
Kilmersdon BA3 . . . . . 140 B5
Norton St Philip BA2 . . 136 E4
Paulton BS39 . . . . 132 D6
Pensford BS39 . . . . 97 D4
Radstock BA3 . . . . 133 F2
Woolley BA1 . . . . 84 F6
CHURCH TOWN 76 C5
Church Town BS48 . . . . 76 C5
Church View
Almondsbury BS32 . . . . 23 F4
6 Bristol BS15 . . . . . . 65 E8
Bristol, Filton BS34 . . . . 36 A3
Bristol, Staple Hill BS16 . 51 D5
Hillesley GL12 . . . . 19 D8
Newport GL13 . . . . 4 C8
Thornbury GL13 . . . . 8 E7
Wraxall BS48 . . . . 60 B2
Churchward Cl BS15 . . . 65 B5
Churchward Rd
Weston-s-M BS22 . . . . . 89 B3
Yate BS37 . . . . 27 B3
Churchway BA3 . . . . . . 135 D1
Churchways BS14 . . . . . 80 C4
Churchways Ave BS7 . . . 49 E6
Churchways Cres BS7 . . 49 E6
Church Wlk
Pill BS20 . . . . 47 C4
Wrington BS40 . . . . 92 D2
Churston Ct BS14 . . . . . 80 A3
Cicil Rd **1** BS15 . . . . . . 65 D8
Cider Mill La BS16 . . . . . 52 A2
Circle The BA2 . . . . 101 B3
Circuit 32 BS5 . . . . 64 B8
Circular Rd BS9 . . . . 48 E2
Circus Mews BA1 . . . . . 141 B3
Circus Pl BA1 . . . . 141 B3
Circus The BA1 . . . . 141 B3
City Academy Bristol The
BS5 . . . . 64 C8
City Bsns Pk BS5 . . . . . . 64 A8
City Mus & Art Gal ★
BS8 . . . . 142 C3
City of Bath Coll BA1 . . 141 B2
City of Bristol Coll
BS1 . . . . 143 A2
City of Bristol Coll, Ashley
Down Ctr BS7 . . . . 49 F4
City of Bristol Coll,
Bedminster Ctr BS3 . . 63 E2
City of Bristol Coll,
Downend Ctr BS16 . . . 52 A8
City of Bristol College
Lawrence Weston Ctr
BS11 . . . . 34 B1
City of Bristol Coll (Folly
La Ctr) BS2 . . . . 64 A6
City of Bristol Coll
(Hartcliffe Ctr) BS13 . . 79 D4
City of Bristol Coll
(Kingswood Ctr) BS15 65 E8
City of Bristol Coll,
Parkway Transport Tech
Ctr BS34 . . . . 36 D3
City Rd BS2 . . . . 143 B4
City View
Bath BA1 . . . . 141 C4
Bristol BS4 . . . . 64 A3
Clamp The BS30 . . . . . . 66 C3
Clanage Rd BS3 . . . . 62 E4
Clanders Batch BS40 . . 110 D3
CLANDOWN 133 E4
Clandown Rd BS39 . . . . 132 F4
Clan Ho BA2 . . . . 102 C7
CLAPTON 138 C7
Clapton Dro BS20 . . . . . 45 D1
CLAPTON IN
GORDANO 45 E1
Clapton La BS20 . . . . . . 45 E2
Clapton Rd
Midsomer Norton BA3 . 132 D1
Stone GL13 . . . . 2 B8

CLAPTON WICK 58 E6
Clapton Wlk BS9 . . . . . . 48 C5
Clara Cross La BA2 . . . 101 E1
Clare Ave BS7 . . . . 49 C3
Clare Gdns BA2 . . . . . . 101 D1
Claremont Ave BS7 . . . . 49 D3
Claremont Bldgs BA1 . . 85 A1
Claremont Cres BS23 . . 87 B1
Claremont Ct BS9 . . . . . 49 C5
Claremont Gdns
Clevedon BS21 . . . . 57 G1
Hallatrow BS39 . . . . . . 132 B7
4 Nailsea BS48 . . . . . 59 D1
Claremont Hall BS21 . . . 57 G4
Claremont Pl **12** BA1 . . 85 A1
Claremont Rd
Bath BA1 . . . . 85 B1
Bristol BS7 . . . . 49 D3
Claremont Specl Sch
BS9 . . . . 49 C5
Claremont St BS5 . . . . . 50 B1
Claremont Terr **10** BS5 . 64 D7
Claremont Wlk BA1 . . . . 85 A1
Clarence BS24 . . . . 105 E2
Clarence Ave BS16 . . . . 51 E5
Clarence Ct **3** BS15 . . . 51 B1
Clarence Gdns BS16 . . . 51 E5
Clarence Grove Rd
BS23 . . . . 104 E5
Clarence Ho **2** BS15 . . 51 B1
Clarence Pl
Bath BA1 . . . . 101 B4
Bristol BS2 . . . . 142 C4
Clarence Rd
Bristol BS1 . . . . 143 B1
Bristol, Kingswood BS15 51 B1
Bristol, Newton BS2 . . . 64 A7
Bristol, Staple Hill BS16 . 51 E5
Clarence Rd E BS23 . . . 104 E5
Clarence Rd N BS23 . . . 104 D5
Clarence Rd S BS23 . . . 104 D5
Clarence St BA1 . . . . . . 141 C4
Clarence Terr BA2 . . . . 102 D5
Clarendon Mews BS16 . 51 B8
Clarendon Rd
Bath BA2 . . . . 102 B2
Bristol BS6 . . . . 49 C2
Weston-s-M BS23 . . . . 104 F8
Clarendon Villas BA2 . . 102 B5
Clare Rd
Bristol, Cotham BS6 . . . 49 D1
Bristol, Kingswood BS15 51 C2
Bristol, Lower Easton
BS5 . . . . 50 B2
Clare St
Bristol BS1 . . . . 143 A2
Bristol, Moorfields BS5 . 64 C8
Clare Wlk BS35 . . . . 8 B2
Clark Cl BS48 . . . . 60 B2
Clark Dr
Bristol BS16 . . . . 50 F7
Yate Rocks BS37 . . . . . . 27 D6
Clarken Cl BS48 . . . . . . 59 E1
Clarken Coombe BS41 . 62 B3
Clarke St BS3 . . . . 63 D4
Clarkson Ave BS22 . . . . 88 C1
Clarkson Ho BA1 . . . . . 141 A2
Clark St BS5 . . . . 64 A8
Clarks Way BA2 . . . . . . 101 C2
Clatworthy Dr BS14 . . . 80 A3
Claude Ave BA2 . . . . . . 101 C5
Claude Terr BA2 . . . . . . 101 C5
Clavell Rd BS10 . . . . 34 F2
CLAVERHAM 74 E1
Claverham Cl BS49 . . . . 91 D7
Claverham Dro BS49 . . . 74 D5
Claverham Pk BS49 . . . . 91 F8
Claverham Rd
Bristol BS16 . . . . 51 A5
Yatton BS49 . . . . 91 E8
CLAVERTON 103 B5
Claverton Bldgs BA2 . . 141 C1
Claverton Ct BA2 . . . . . 102 E4
CLAVERTON DOWN . . . 102 F3
Claverton Down Rd
BA2 . . . . 102 F3
Claverton Dr BA2 . . . . . 102 F3
Claverton Hill BA2 . . . . 103 A4
Claverton Lodge BA2 . . 102 C5
Claverton Pumping Sta ★
BA2 . . . . 103 C5
Claverton Rd BS31 . . . . 82 E2
Claverton Rd W BS31 . . 82 D3
Claverton St BA2 . . . . . 141 C1
Clay Bottom BS5 . . . . . . 50 E2
Claydon Gn BS14 . . . . . 79 F3
Clayfield BS37 . . . . 27 E5
Clayfield Rd BS4 . . . . . . 64 E3
CLAY HILL 50 E2
Clay Hill BS5 . . . . 50 E2
Clayhill Dr BS37 . . . . . . 27 F5
Clay La
Bitton BS30 . . . . 82 B8
Bristol, Little Stoke BS34 36 C7
Bristol, Willsbridge BS30 66 D1
Thornbury BS35 . . . . 8 E1
Claymore Cres **1** BS15 . 51 B1
Claypiece Rd BS13 . . . . 79 A4
Clay Pitch BS37 . . . . 29 E3

Claypit Hill BS37 . . . . . . **40** B7
Claypit Rd BS41 . . . . **79** B1
Clay Pit Rd BS6 . . . . **49** A3
Claypool Rd BS15 . . . . . . **65** E7
Claysend BA2 . . . . **100** D5
CLAYS END **100** D6
Clays End La BA2 . . . . . . **100** D6
Clayton Cl BS20 . . . . **45** E4
Clayton Rd
  Bristol BS3 . . . . **63** A1
  Clifton BS8 . . . . **63** A4
Clayton St
  Avonmouth BS11 . . . . . **33** A1
  21 Bristol BS5 . . . . . . **64** B8
Cleave St BS2 . . . . **50** A1
CLEEVE **92** B8
Cleeve Ave BS16 . . . . . . **51** E7
Cleeve Ct BS16 . . . . **51** D7
Cleevedale BA2 . . . . . . **102** A1
Cleeve Dr BS49 . . . . **92** B8
Cleeve Gdns BS16 . . . . . **51** D7
Cleeve Gn BA2 . . . . **101** A6
Cleeve Gr BS31 . . . . **81** D5
Cleeve Hill
  Bristol BS16 . . . . **51** D7
  Ubley BS40 . . . . **128** E8
Cleeve Hill Extension
  BS16 . . . . **51** E6
Cleeve Hill Rd BS40 . . . **92** C7
Cleeve La BS30 . . . . **53** D1
Cleeve Lawns BS16 . . . . **51** D7
Cleeve Lodge Cl BS16 . . **51** E6
Cleeve Lodge Rd BS16 . . **51** E6
Cleeve Park Rd BS16 . . . **51** E7
Cleeve Pl BS48 . . . . **60** A1
Cleeve Rd
  Bristol BS4 . . . . **64** B3
  Bristol, Frenchay BS16 . . **51** C8
  Bristol, Mangotsfield
  BS16 . . . . **51** E6
  Yate BS37 . . . . **27** E1
Cleeves Ct BS30 . . . . . . **65** F2
Cleeve Wood Pk BS16 . . **51** C7
Cleeve Wood Rd BS16 . . **51** D7
Clematis Rd BS16 . . . . . . **38** D1
Clement St BS2 . . . . **143** C4
Clermont Cl BS34 . . . . . . **35** F8
Cleve Ct
  3 Bristol, Clifton Wood
  BS8 . . . . **62** F6
  Bristol, Filton BS34 . . . . **36** B4
Clevedale BS16 . . . . **51** D7
Clevedale Ct BS16 . . . . . **51** D7
CLEVEDON **57** D3
Clevedon Court★ BS21 **58** A4
Clevedon Craft Ctr★
  BS21 . . . . **58** A1
Clevedon Hospl BS21 . . **57** G3
Clevedon La BS21 . . . . . **59** C7
Clevedon Min Rly★
  BS21 . . . . **57** D3
Clevedon Pier★ BS21 . **57** E4
Clevedon Rd
  Bristol BS7 . . . . **49** D4
  Flax Bourton BS48 . . . . . **60** F2
  Midsomer Norton BA3 . . **133** A2
  Nailsea BS48 . . . . **60** B4
  Portishead BS20 . . . . . . **45** D3
  Tickenham BS21 . . . . . . **59** B4
  Weston-s-M BS23 . . . . **104** E6
  Wraxall BS48 . . . . **60** D6
Clevedon Sch BS21 . . . . **57** H5
Clevedon Terr BS6 . . . . . **143** A4
Clevedon Wlk **2** BS48 . . **59** E2
Cleve House Sch BS4 . . **64** B3
Cleveland Cl BS35 . . . . . **15** E8
Cleveland Cotts BA1 . . . **141** C4
Cleveland Ct BA2 . . . . . **102** C6
Cleveland Pl BA1 . . . . . . **141** C4
Cleveland Pl E BA1 . . . . **141** C4
Cleveland Pl W BA1 . . . . **141** C4
Cleveland Reach BA1 . . **141** C4
Cleveland Row BA1 . . . . **102** B8
Cleveland Terr BA1 . . . . **141** C4
Cleveland Wlk BA2 . . . . **102** C6
Cleve Rd BS34 . . . . **36** A4
Clevewood Ho BS16 . . . . **51** C7
Clewson Rise BS14 . . . . **79** F3
Cliff Court Dr BS16 . . . . **51** B7
Cliffe Dr BA2 . . . . **120** A6
Clifford Gdns BS11 . . . . **47** E6
Clifford Ho BS23 . . . . . **104** D6
Clifford Rd BS16 . . . . . . **51** C4
Cliff Rd BS22 . . . . **88** A2
Cliffs The
  Charterhouse BA5 . . . . **127** A1
  Cheddar BS27 . . . . **126** E1
Clift House Rd BS3 . . . . **63** A4
Clift House Spur BS3 . . **62** F4
CLIFTON **142** A4
Clifton Arc BS8 . . . . **142** A3
Clifton Ave BS23 . . . . . **104** E5
Clifton Cl **1** BS8 . . . . . . **62** F7
Clifton Coll BS8 . . . . . . **142** A4
Clifton College Prep Sch
  BS8 . . . . **48** F1
Clifton Ct **10** BS21 . . . . . **57** E2
Clifton Down BS8 . . . . . **62** F7
Clifton Down Rd BS8 . . **142** A3

Clifton Down Sh Ctr **11**
  BS8 . . . . **49** B1
Clifton Down Sta BS8 . . **49** B1
Clifton High Gr BS8 . . . . **48** E5
Clifton High Sch BS8 . . **142** A4
Clifton Hill BS8 . . . . **142** A2
Clifton Metro **10** BS8 . . . **49** B1
Clifton Park Rd BS8 . . . . **62** F8
Clifton Pk BS8 . . . . **142** A3
Clifton Pl BS5 . . . . **64** A8
Clifton Rd
  Bristol BS8 . . . . **142** A2
  Weston-s-M BS23 . . . . **104** E5
Clifton St
  Bristol, Bedminster BS3 . **63** C3
  Bristol, Upper Easton
  BS5 . . . . **64** A8
  Portishead BS20 . . . . . . **45** C2
Clifton Suspension
  Bridge★ BS8 . . . . . . **62** E7
Clifton Suspension Bridge
  Rd BS8 . . . . **62** F7
Clifton Vale BS8 . . . . . . **142** A2
Clifton Vale Cl BS8 . . . . **142** A2
Clifton View
  Bristol, Bedminster Down
  BS13 . . . . **63** A1
  1 Bristol, Windmill Hill
  BS3 . . . . **63** F4
CLIFTON WOOD **142** A2
Cliftonwood Cres BS8 **142** A2
Clifton Wood Ct BS8 . . **142** B2
Clifton Wood Rd BS8 . **142** B2
Cliftonwood Terr BS8 . **142** A2
Clift Pl BS1 . . . . **143** A1
Clift Rd BS3 . . . . **63** A4
Clinton Rd BS3 . . . . **63** C2
Clive Rd BS14 . . . . **80** C8
Clockhouse Mews
  BS20 . . . . **45** D6
Cloisters BS8 . . . . **62** F8
Cloisters Ct BS36 . . . . . **37** E6
Cloisters Rd BS36 . . . . . **37** F6
Cloisters The BS6 . . . . . **49** C3
Clonmel Rd BS4 . . . . . . **63** D1
Closemead BS21 . . . . . . **57** F1
Close The
  Bristol BS16 . . . . **36** F1
  Bristol, Henbury BS10 . . **35** A5
  Bristol, Little Stoke BS34 . **36** C6
  Bristol, Patchway BS32 . . **24** C1
  Bristol, Upper Soundwell
  BS16 . . . . **51** D3
  Frampton Cotterell BS36 . **38** C6
  Portishead BS20 . . . . . . **44** F1
  Thornbury BS35 . . . . **15** B8
Clothier Rd BS4 . . . . . . **64** F2
Cloud Hill Ind Est
  BS39 . . . . **132** A8
Clouds Hill Ave BS5 . . . **64** F8
Clouds Hill Rd BS5 . . . . **64** F8
Clovelly Cl BS5 . . . . **64** F8
Clovelly Rd
  Bristol BS5 . . . . **64** F8
  Weston-s-M BS22 . . . . . **89** A2
Clover Cl
  Clevedon BS21 . . . . **57** H3
  Paulton BS39 . . . . **132** E4
Clover Ct **2** BS22 . . . . **105** D7
Cloverdale Dr BS30 . . . . **66** A3
Clover Ground BS9 . . . . **49** B7
Clover Hill Way
  Barrow Gurney BS48 . . . **77** F7
  Bristol BS48 . . . . **78** A6
Cloverlea Bsns Ctr
  BS36 . . . . **38** C3
Cloverlea Rd BS30 . . . . **66** C5
Clover Leaze BS32 . . . . **36** D4
Clover Rd
  Lyde Green BS16 . . . . . **52** C8
  Thornbury BS35 . . . . **8** B4
  Weston-s-M BS22 . . . . . **89** A6
CLUTTON **114** E3
CLUTTON HILL **115** B4
Clutton Hill BS39 . . . . . **115** B4
Clutton Prim Sch
  BS39 . . . . **114** E3
Clyde Ave BS31 . . . . . . **81** F4
Clyde Ct **2** BS3 . . . . . . **63** C3
Clyde Gdns
  Bath BA2 . . . . **101** B6
  Bristol BS5 . . . . **65** B6
Clyde Gr BS34 . . . . **35** F2
Clyde Ho **7** BS35 . . . . . **15** C8
Clyde La BS6 . . . . **49** C2
Clyde Mews **3** BS6 . . . **49** C2
Clyde Rd
  Bristol, Redland BS6 . . . **49** B2
  Bristol, Totterdown BS4 . . **64** A3
  Frampton Cotterell BS36 . **38** B8
Clydesdale Cl BS14 . . . . **80** A6
Clyde Terr
  Bristol, Bedminster BS3 . **63** C3
  Bristol, Totterdown BS4 . . **64** A3
Clynder Gr BS21 . . . . . . **57** G6
Clyntonville BS22 . . . . . **88** A4
Coach House La BS5 . . . **64** E8
Coach House Mews
  BS23 . . . . **87** D1

Coalbridge Cl BS22 . . . . **88** F2
Coaley Rd BS11 . . . . . . **47** D5
COALPIT HEATH **38** D6
Coalpit La BA3 . . . . . . **138** A2
Coalpit Rd BA1 . . . . **86** A4
Coalsack La BS36 . . . . . **38** B3
Coalville Rd BS36 . . . . . **38** D7
Coape Rd BS14 . . . . **80** F5
Coast Cvn Pk BS21 . . . . **44** B1
Coates Est BS48 . . . . . . **59** F3
Coates Gr BS48 . . . . . . **60** A2
Coates Wlk BS4 . . . . . . **79** D6
Cobblestone Mews
  BS8 . . . . **142** A4
Cob Ct BS34 . . . . **36** C3
Cobden Ctr The BS16 . . **38** B2
Cobden St BS5 . . . . **64** C7
Coberley BS15 . . . . **65** C6
Cobhorn Dr BS13 . . . . . **78** F4
Cobley Croft BS21 . . . . **73** C8
Cobourg Rd BS6 . . . . . . **49** F2
Cobthorn Way BS49 . . . **91** E5
Coburg Villas **10** BA1 . . **85** A1
Cock And Yew Tree Hill
  BS40 . . . . **95** A2
Cockers Hill BS39 . . . . . **98** C5
Cock La SN14 . . . . **54** D5
Cock Rd BS15 . . . . **65** F6
Cockshute La
  Greenways GL11 . . . . **4** D8
  Greenways GL13 . . . . **2** D8
CODRINGTON **40** C2
Codrington Pl BS8 . . . **142** A3
Codrington Rd BS7 . . . **49** D3
Cody Ct **2** BS15 . . . . . . **65** B5
Cogan Rd BS16 . . . . **51** E3
Cogsall Rd BS14 . . . . . . **80** F6
Coity Pl BS21 . . . . **57** E4
Coker Rd BS22 . . . . **89** B2
Colbourne Rd BA2 . . . . **101** D1
Colburn Ct BS7 . . . . **49** F7
Colchester Cres BS4 . . . **79** D7
COLD ASHTON **68** F6
Coldharbour La
  Bristol BS16 . . . . **50** E8
  Weston-s-M BS23 . . . . **104** D3
Coldharbour Rd BS6 . . . **49** B4
Coldpark Gdns BS13 . . . **78** E5
Coldpark Rd BS13 . . . . . **78** E5
Coldrick Cl BS14 . . . . . . **79** F3
Colebrook Rd BS15 . . . . **65** C8
Coleford Rd BS10 . . . . . **35** D1
Colehouse La BS21 . . . . **73** C8
Colemead BS13 . . . . **79** B5
Cole Rd BS2 . . . . **64** B6
Coleridge Ct **10** BS3 . . . **63** C3
Coleridge Ho BS34 . . . . **24** A1
Coleridge Rd
  Bristol BS5 . . . . **50** C3
  Clevedon BS21 . . . . **57** E3
  Weston-s-M BS23 . . . . **105** A4
Coleridge Vale Rd E **1**
  BS21 . . . . **57** F2
Coleridge Vale Rd N
  BS21 . . . . **57** E2
Coleridge Vale Rd S
  BS21 . . . . **57** F2
Coleridge Vale Rd W **2**
  BS21 . . . . **57** E2
COLERNE **70** E6
Colesborne Cl BS37 . . . **39** E8
Coles Gdns BA3 . . . . . **140** B5
Coleshill Dr BS13 . . . . . **79** B5
COLEY **130** C4
Coley Hill BS40 . . . . . . **130** D5
Coley Narrow BS40 . . . **130** C3
Coley Rd BS40 . . . . . . **130** B4
Colin Rd BS35 . . . . **8** C1
Collard Ho **2** BS16 . . . . **50** F4
College Ave BS16 . . . . . **51** A5
College Ct
  Bristol BS8 . . . . **142** A4
  Bristol, Fishponds BS16 . **51** A5
College Fields BS8 . . . . **62** F8
College Gn BS1 . . . . . . **142** C2
College Mews BS9 . . . . **49** A7
College Park Dr BS10 . . **34** F1
College Rd
  Bath BA1 . . . . **84** E1
  Bristol, Clifton BS8 . . . . **62** F8
  Bristol, Fishponds BS16 . **51** A5
  Bristol, Westbury on Trym
  BS9 . . . . **49** A7
College Sq BS1 . . . . . . **142** C2
College St BS1 . . . . . . **142** C2
College View **17** BA1 . . **85** A1
College Way BS34 . . . . . **36** A4
Collet Cl BS22 . . . . **89** C4
Collett Cl BS15 . . . . **65** B5
Collett Ho BS36 . . . . . . **37** D4
Collett Way BS37 . . . . . **27** C3
Collier Cl BA2 . . . . **133** D8
Colliers Break BS16 . . . **52** B3
Colliers Gdns
  Backwell BS48 . . . . **75** F7
  Bristol BS16 . . . . **51** B5
Colliers La BA1 . . . . **84** F4
Colliers Rise BA3 . . . . **134** A3
Colliers Way BA3 . . . . **139** F8

Colliers Wlk **4** BS48 . . . **59** E2
Colliery La BA2 . . . . . . **134** D5
Collingwood Ave BS15 . **51** E1
Collingwood Cl
  Saltford BS31 . . . . **82** E2
  Weston-s-M BS22 . . . . . **88** E4
Collingwood Rd **4** BS6 . **49** B1
Collin Rd BS4 . . . . **64** D4
Collins Ave BS34 . . . . . . **36** C6
Collins Dr BS35 . . . . **22** C3
Collinson Rd BS13 . . . . . **79** B5
Collins St BS11 . . . . **47** B8
Collum La BS22 . . . . **88** E6
Colne Gn BS31 . . . . **82** A4
Coln Sq BS35 . . . . **15** C8
Colombo Cres BS23 . . . **104** E3
Colston Ave BS1 . . . . . **143** A3
Colston Cl
  Bristol BS16 . . . . **51** D3
  Winterbourne BS36 . . . . **37** E4
Colston Ct BS7 . . . . **49** D3
Colston Dale BS16 . . . . **50** D4
Colstone Ct **3** BS16 . . . **50** E3
Colston Fort **2** BS2 . . . **143** A4
Colston Hill BS16 . . . . . **50** D4
Colston Mews BS6 . . . . **49** E1
Colston Par BS1 . . . . . **143** B1
Colston Rd BS5 . . . . **50** C1
Colston's Almshouses **1**
  BS1 . . . . **143** A3
Colston's Prep Sch
  BS16 . . . . **50** D5
Colston's Sch BS16 . . . **50** C4
Colston St
  Bristol BS1 . . . . **143** A3
  Bristol, Upper Soundwell
  BS16 . . . . **51** D3
Colston Yd BS1 . . . . . . **143** A3
Colthurst Dr BS15 . . . . . **65** E5
Colthurst Mews BS2 . . . **64** B4
Colts Gn BS37 . . . . **40** E8
COLT'S GREEN **40** E8
Colts Ground **6** BS7 . . . **50** C8
Columbus Ho BA2 . . . . **102** D8
Colwyn Rd **2** BS5 . . . . . **50** C1
Colyton **11** BS22 . . . . . . **89** A2
Colyton Ct BS3 . . . . **63** D1
Combe Ave BS20 . . . . . **45** C6
COMBE DOWN **102** B1
Combe Down CE Prim Sch
  BA2 . . . . **102** B1
Combe Down CEVC Prim
  Sch BA2 . . . . **102** B1
Combe Fields BS20 . . . . **45** C6
Combe Gr BA1 . . . . **101** B8
COMBE HAY **118** D4
Combe Hay La BA2 . . . **118** B6
Combe La BS39 . . . . . . **132** B6
Combe Pk BA1 . . . . . . **101** C8
Combe Rd
  Bath BA2 . . . . **102** B1
  Portishead BS20 . . . . . **45** D5
Combermere BS35 . . . . . **15** D8
Combe Road Cl **3**
  BA2 . . . . **102** B1
Combeside BA2 . . . . . . **102** A3
Combe Side BS48 . . . . . **76** A7
Combe The BS40 . . . . . **109** F2
Combfactory La **18** BS5 . **64** B8
Comb Paddock BS9 . . . . **49** B7
Comfortable Pl BA1 . . . **141** A3
Commercial Rd BS1 . . . **143** A1
Commercial Way BS22 . **89** B2
Common (East) The
  BS32 . . . . **24** C1
Commonfield Rd BS11 . **34** C1
Common La
  Aust BS35 . . . . **13** A6
  Churchill BS25 . . . . . . **108** B5
  Easton-in-G BS20 . . . . . **47** B2
Commonmead La BS37 . **40** F8
Common Mead La
  BS16 . . . . **37** A1
Common Rd
  Bristol BS15 . . . . **65** B3
  Winterbourne BS36 . . . . **37** F7
Common The
  Bristol, Frenchay BS16 . . **51** B4
  Bristol, Patchway BS32 . . **24** C1
  Olveston BS35 . . . . **13** F3
Como Ct BS20 . . . . **45** C6
COMPTON BISHOP . . . **124** A3
COMPTON COMMON . . **98** C5
COMPTON DANDO **98** D6
Compton Dr
  Bristol BS9 . . . . **48** C7
  Weston-s-M BS24 . . . . **105** E7
Compton Gn BS31 . . . . . **81** E4
COMPTON
  GREENFIELD **34** F8
Compton La BS26 . . . . **125** B1
Compton Lodge **3** BS6 . **49** B1
COMPTON MARTIN . . . **129** A7
Compton St BS5 . . . . . . **64** C7
Comrade Ave BS25 . . . **125** E8

Comyn Wlk BS16 . . . . . . **51** A5
Concorde Dr
  Bristol BS10 . . . . **35** B1
  Clevedon BS21 . . . . **57** D1
Concorde Ho BS34 . . . . **35** F2
Concorde Rd BS34 . . . . **35** F7
Condor Cl BS22 . . . . . . **105** D8
Condor Ho BS7 . . . . **50** C7
Condover Rd BS4 . . . . . **65** A3
Conduit Pl **2** BS2 . . . . . **50** A1
Conduit Rd BS2 . . . . **50** A1
Cone The BS10, BS34 . . **35** C6
Coneygree BS13 . . . . . . **78** F6
Conference Ave BS20 . . **45** F5
Conference Cl BS20 . . . **45** F4
Congleton Rd BS5 . . . . . **64** D8
CONGRESBURY **91** E4
CONHAM **65** A5
Conham Hill BS15 . . . . . **65** A5
Conham Ho BS15 . . . . . **65** A5
Conham Rd BS4, BS5,
  BS15 . . . . **64** F5
Conifer Cl
  Bristol BS16 . . . . **51** D6
  Frampton Cotterell BS36 **26** A1
Conifer Way BS24 . . . . **105** E5
Coniston Ave BS9 . . . . . **48** E6
Coniston Cl BS30 . . . . . **66** D6
Coniston Cres BS23 . . . **104** F4
Coniston Prim Sch
  BS34 . . . . **23** F1
Coniston Rd BS34 . . . . . **23** F1
CONKWELL **103** C1
Conkwell BA15 . . . . . . **103** C2
Connaught Mans BA2 . **141** C3
Connaught Pl BS23 . . . **104** D8
Connaught Prim Sch
  BS4 . . . . **79** E8
Connaught Rd BS4 . . . . **79** E8
Connection Rd BA2 . . . **101** A6
Constable Cl BS31 . . . . **81** F6
Constable Dr BS22 . . . . **88** F3
Constable Rd BS7 . . . . . **50** B6
Constantine Ave BS34 . . **36** F5
Constitution Hill BS8 . **142** B2
Contemporis BS8 . . . . **142** A3
Convent Cl BS10 . . . . . . **34** D3
Convocation Ave BA2 . **102** E5
Conway Gn BS31 . . . . . . **82** A3
Conway Rd BS4 . . . . **64** C4
Conygar Cl BS21 . . . . . . **57** H5
Conygre Gn BA2 . . . . . **116** C2
Conygre Gr BS34 . . . . . **36** C3
Conygre Rd BS34 . . . . . **36** B3
Conygre Rise BA2 . . . . **115** F6
Cook Cl BS30 . . . . **66** C4
Cooke's Dr BS35 . . . . . . **23** A1
Cooks Bridle Path
  BS48 . . . . **93** D8
Cooks Cl BS32 . . . . **24** D3
Cook's Folly Rd BS9 . . . **48** D3
Cooks Gdns BS48 . . . . . **60** A2
Cooks Hill
  Clutton BS39 . . . . **114** E3
  Clutton BS39 . . . . **114** E3
Cooks La BS36 . . . . **38** D3
Cook's La
  Banwell BS29 . . . . **107** A4
  Clevedon BS21 . . . . **58** B2
Cooksley Rd BS5 . . . . . . **64** C8
Cook St BS11 . . . . **47** C8
Cookworthy Cl **2** BS5 . . **64** B6
Coombe Ave BS35 . . . . . **8** B2
Coombe Bank Mews
  BS23 . . . . **87** D1
Coombe Bridge Ave
  BS9 . . . . **48** D6
Coombe Brook La BS5 . **50** E2
Coombe Cl BS10 . . . . . . **34** D3
Coombe Dale
  Backwell BS48 . . . . **94** A8
  Bristol BS9 . . . . **48** C6
COOMBE DINGLE **48** C8
Coombe Gdns BS9 . . . . **48** E6
Coombe Ho **4** BS15 . . . **65** E8
Coombe La
  Bristol BS9 . . . . **48** E6
  Compton Bishop BS26 . . **124** B4
  East Harptree BS40 . . . **129** E4
  Easton-in-G BS48 . . . . . **47** A2
Coomb End BA3 . . . . . **133** F3
Coombend Ho BA3 . . . **133** F3
Coombend Rise BA3 . . **133** F3
Coombe Rd
  Bristol BS5 . . . . **50** C2
  Nailsea BS48 . . . . **59** E1
  Weston-s-M BS23 . . . . . **87** E1
Coombes Way BS30 . . . . **66** D4
Coombe The
  Blagdon BS40 . . . . **110** C3
  Compton Martin BS40 . . **129** A6
Coombe Way BS10 . . . . **34** D3
Coombe Rocke BS9 . . . . **48** D6
COOMB'S END **41** A6
Cooperage La BS3 . . . . **142** B1
Cooperage Rd BS5 . . . . **64** D7

Co-operation Rd BS5 . .50 C1
Cooper Rd
  Bristol BS9............48 F7
  Thornbury BS35........15 B7
Coopers Dr BS37....27 F5
Coots The BS14......80 E6
Copeland Dr BS14....80 B5
Cope Pk BS32........24 C5
Copford La BS41......62 B1
Copley Ct BS15......65 E5
Copley Gdns
  Bristol BS7............50 B6
  Weston-s-M BS22......88 F2
Coppack Ho **6** BS21...57 E2
Copperfield Dr BS22...88 F4
Coppice End Cnr
  BS24...............122 C2
Coppice Mews BS21....57 E4
Coppice The
  Bristol, Bradley Stoke
    BS32..............36 E7
  Bristol, Highridge BS13..78 E4
Copse Cl BS24.......105 A1
Copse Cnr BS24......122 C2
Copse End BS25.....107 F2
Copseland BA2......102 D5
Copse Rd
  Bristol BS4...........64 B3
  Clevedon BS21........57 E4
  Keynsham BS31.......82 C4
Copse The BS22......89 D2
Copthorne Cl BS14....80 B5
Copthorn La BS40....109 F6
Coralberry Dr BS22...88 F1
Corbet Cl BS11......34 C2
Corbett Cl **1** BS37....27 F4
Corbett Ho **11** BS5....64 C7
Cordwell Wlk BS10...49 D7
Corey Cl **6** BS2......49 F1
Corfe Cl BS48.......59 D1
Corfe Cres BS31.....81 E4
Corfe Pl BS30.......66 B1
Corfe Rd BS4........79 D7
Coriander Dr BS34....37 A7
Coriander Wlk BS5....50 C2
Corinthian Ct **9** BS1..143 B1
Corinum Cl BS16.....52 C6
Corker's Hill **9** BS5...64 F6
Cork Pl BA1.........101 D7
Cork St BA1.........101 D7
Cork Terr BA1.......101 D7
Cormorant Cl BS22....88 F1
Corner Croft BS21....57 F1
Cornfield Cl BS32....24 C1
Cornfields The BS22...88 F5
Cornhill Dr BS14.....80 A7
Cornish Gr BS14.....80 E6
Cornishmen's Rd BA1..84 E4
Cornish Rd BS14.....80 E6
Cornish Wlk BS14....80 E6
Cornleaze BS13......79 A5
Corn St
  Bath BA1...........141 B2
  Bristol BS1.........143 A3
Cornwall Cres BS37...27 F3
Cornwallis Ave
  Bristol BS8.........142 A2
  Weston-s-M BS22......88 F4
Cornwallis Cres BS8...62 F6
Cornwallis Gr BS8....142 A2
Cornwallis Ho BS8....142 A2
Cornwall Rd BS7.....49 D4
Coromandel Hts BA1..141 B4
Coronation Ave
  Bath BA2...........101 C4
  Bristol BS16.........51 A4
  Keynsham BS31.......81 D4
Coronation Cl BS30...66 A5
Coronation Est BS23..104 F3
Coronation Pl BS1...143 A2
Coronation Rd
  Banwell BS29........107 A3
  Bath BA1...........101 D7
  Bleadon BS24.......122 C6
  Bristol BS3.........142 B1
  Bristol, Cadbury Heath
    BS30..............66 B5
  Bristol, Mangotsfield
    BS16..............51 E5
  Bristol, Warmley BS15..66 A7
  Weston-s-M BS22......88 E2
Coronation Terr BA3..138 D5
Corondale Rd BS22...105 D8
Corpus Christi RC Prim
  Sch BS23...........104 D6
Corridor The **2** BA1..141 C2
Corsley Wlk BS4.....79 F8
CORSTON...........100 B7
Corston BS24........105 A4
Corston Dr BA2......100 B6
Corston La BA2......100 A8
Corston View BA2....101 C2
Corston Wlk BS11....47 D7
Cossham Cl BS35.....8 C2
Cossham Memorial Hospl
  BS16..............51 C2

Cossham Rd BS5.....64 D7
Cossham St BS16.....52 B5
Cossham Wlk BS5.....51 A1
Cossington Rd BS4....79 F8
Cossins Rd BS6......49 B3
Costers Cl BS35......15 A5
Costiland Dr BS13....78 F6
Cote Bank Ho BS9....49 B8
Cote Dr BS9.........49 A4
Cote House La BS9....49 A5
Cote La BS9.........49 A5
Cote Lea Pk BS9.....49 B7
Cote Paddock BS9....48 F4
Cote Pk BS9.........48 E6
Cote Rd BS9.........49 A4
COTHAM...........49 C1
Cotham Brow BS6.....49 C1
Cotham Gardens Prim Sch
  BS6...............49 D1
Cotham Gdns **15** BS6..49 B1
Cotham Gr BS6.......49 D1
Cotham Gram Sch
  (Charnwood Annex)
  BS6...............49 C1
Cotham Hill BS6.....49 C1
Cotham Lawn Ho BS6.142 C4
Cotham Lawn Rd
  Bristol BS6...........49 C1
  Bristol BS6.........142 C4
Cotham Pk BS6......49 C1
Cotham Pk N BS6.....49 C1
Cotham Pl BS6......142 C4
Cotham Rd BS6......142 C4
Cotham Rd S BS6.....143 A4
Cotham Sch BS6.....142 C4
Cotham Side BS6.....49 D1
Cotham Vale BS6.....49 C1
Cotman Wlk
  Bristol BS7...........50 B6
  1 Weston-s-M BS22...88 F2
Cotrith Gr BS10......34 E3
Cotswold Cl **3** BS20...45 E4
Cotswold Ct
  Bristol BS16.........36 E1
  Chipping Sodbury BS37..28 B1
Cotswold Ed Ctr The
  BS34..............35 F2
Cotswold Gdns BA3...139 A6
Cotswold La BS37....41 A8
Cotswold Rd
  Bath BA2...........101 E4
  Bristol BS3.........63 D3
  Chipping Sodbury BS37..40 B8
Cotswold View
  Bath BA2...........101 B5
  Bristol, Filton BS34....36 A3
  Bristol, Kingswood BS15 51 D2
  Charfield GL12.......11 B5
  Wickwar GL12........18 B6
Cotswold Way SN14...69 A6
Cottage Gdns BS5....65 A7
Cottage Pl
  3 Bath BA1.........85 C2
  Bristol BS2.........143 A4
Cottages The BS40...92 D2
Cotterell Ct BA1.....141 B2
Cottington Ct BS15...65 E5
Cottisford Rd BS5....50 B4
Cottle Gdns BS14....80 F6
Cottle Rd BS14......80 F6
Cottles La BA15.....120 F6
Cottongrass Rd BS16..52 D7
Cotton Mead BA2....100 B7
Cotton Mill La BS5....64 C6
Cottonwood Dr BS30..66 A3
Cottrell Ave BS15....51 C2
Cottrell Rd BS5......50 C3
Coulson Dr BS22.....89 B3
Coulson Ho **2** BS7....49 F4
Coulson's Cl BS14....80 A3
Coulson's Rd BS14....80 A3
Coulson Wlk BS15....51 C2
Council Hos
  Bleadon BS24.......122 B5
  Kingston Seymour BS21..73 C3
  Wick St L BS22.......89 B8
Council Hos The BS40..111 B8
Council Houses BS24...90 C3
Council Houses The
  BS39..............130 E6
Counterpool Rd BS15..65 C7
Countership BS1.....143 B2
Countership Gdns BS14 80 C6
Countess Wlk BS16...50 D6
County Bridge BA3...133 F2
County St BS4.......64 A4
County Way BS34....37 A4
Court Ave
  Bristol BS34.........36 F5
  Yatton BS49.........91 C7
Court Cl
  Backwell BS48........76 C5
  Bristol BS7...........49 E7
  Portishead BS20......45 D4
Court Cotts BS37....29 D6
Court-de-Wyck Prim Sch
  BS49..............74 F1
Court Dr BS25.......108 B4
Courtenay Cres BS4...79 D7

Courtenay Rd BS31...82 B2
Courtenay Wlk BS22..89 A3
Court Farm Gdns BS30.65 E2
Court Farm Park★
  BS29..............106 F5
Court Farm Rd
  Bristol BS14.........79 F3
  Bristol, Longwell Green
    BS30..............65 E2
Courtfield Gr BS16...51 A4
Court Gdns
  Batheaston BA1.......86 A4
  Yate BS37............39 E8
Court Hay BS20......47 A4
Court Hill BS39......98 D5
Court Ho BS26.......125 B2
Court La
  Bathford BA1.........86 A2
  Clevedon BS21........58 A3
  Shipham BS25.......125 F8
  Wick BS30............67 B6
Courtlands
  Bristol BS32.........24 C1
  Keynsham BS31.......81 E5
Courtlands La BS3....62 E4
Court Mdw GL13......3 E3
Courtmead BA2......118 F7
Court Mead GL13.....3 E3
Courtney Prim Sch
  BS15..............65 F7
Courtney Rd BS15....65 E7
Courtney Way BS15...66 A7
Court Pl BS22.......88 F2
Court Rd
  Bristol, Horfield BS7...49 F6
  Bristol, Kingswood BS15 65 D7
  Bristol, Oldland Common
    BS30..............66 C3
  Frampton Cotterell BS36..37 F8
  Weston-s-M BS22.....88 A5
Courtside Mews BS6...49 C1
Court View BS30.....67 C6
Court View Cl BS32...24 A5
Courtyard The BS40..129 E6
Courville Cl BS35....15 A4
Cousins Cl BS10.....34 D3
Cousins La BS5......64 F8
Cousins Mews BS4....64 F6
Cousins Way BS16....52 B8
Couzens Cl BS37.....28 B2
Couzens Pl BS34.....36 F5
Coventry Wlk BS4....64 F6
Cow Barton BS7......50 C8
Cowdray Rd BS4.....79 D7
COWHILL..........7 B3
Cowhorn Hill BS30...66 C4
Cow Leaze BS36.....38 B6
Cowleaze La BS40....129 C6
Cowler Wlk BS13.....78 F4
Cowling Dr BS14.....80 C5
Cowling Rd BS14.....80 D5
Cowper Rd BS6......49 C1
Cowper St BS5.......64 C7
Cowship La GL12.....17 D6
Cowslip Cres BS16...52 C8
COWSLIP GREEN....110 B8
Cowslip La BS26.....123 D3
Cowslip Way G12.....11 B5
Cox Ct BS30.........65 F4
Coxgrove Hill BS16...52 F7
Coxley Dr BA1.......85 B2
Cox's Gn BS40.......92 E1
COX'S GREEN.......92 E1
Coxway BS21........57 H2
Coxwynne Ct BA3....139 C8
CRAB HOLE.........123 E2
Crabtree Cl BS41....78 D1
Crabtree La BS41....78 D2
Crabtree Wlk BS5....50 D2
Cradock Cl BS30.....66 B4
Craftes Ct BS5......50 E1
Cranberry Wlk BS9...48 C8
Cranbourne Chase
  BS23..............88 A1
Cranbourne Rd BS34..35 F7
Cranbrook Rd BS6....49 C3
Crandale Rd **3** BA2...101 D5
Crandell Cl BS10.....34 F4
Crane Cl BS15.......66 B8
Cranesbill Cres G12...11 B5
Cranford Cl BS22....88 D1
Cranford Ct **1** BS9...49 B6
Cranham BS37.......39 C7
Cranham Cl BS15....51 F2
Cranham Dr BS34....24 C1
Cranham Rd BS10....49 C8
Cranhill Rd BA1.....101 D8
Cranleigh BA2......118 F8
Cranleigh Court Inf Sch
  BS37..............27 D3
Cranleigh Court Rd
  BS37..............27 D2
Cranleigh Gdns BS9...48 E4
Cranleigh Rd BS14...80 B5
Cranmoor Gn BS35...22 D6
Cranmoor La BS49....73 D2
Cranmore BS24......105 A2
Cranmore Ave BS31...81 E6
Cranmore Cres BS10..35 D1

Cranmore Pl BA2....118 E8
Cranside Ave BS6....49 C4
Cransley Cres BS9....49 C7
Crantock Ave BS13...79 B8
Crantock Dr BS32....24 B5
Crantock Rd BS37....27 D1
Cranwell Gr BS14....80 A5
Cranwell Rd
  Locking BS24.......106 C5
  Locking BS24.......106 C5
Cranwells Pk BA1...101 D8
Crates Cl BS15......65 E8
Craven Cl BS30......65 F5
Craven Way BS30....65 F5
Crawford Cl **1** BS21..57 D1
Crawl La BA3.......133 C4
Craydon Gr BS14....80 D4
Craydon Rd BS14....80 D5
Craydon Wlk BS14...80 D5
Create Ctr★ BS1.....62 F5
Crediton **5** BS22....89 A2
Crediton Cres BS4....63 F1
Crescent Gdns BA1...141 A3
Crescent La BA1.....141 B4
Crescent Place Mews
  BA2...............101 D1
Crescent Rd BS16....51 C6
Crescent The
  Backwell BS48........76 A6
  Bristol BS16.........36 F1
  Bristol, Frenchay BS16..36 F1
  Bristol, Henleaze BS9...49 C6
  Bristol, Sea Mills BS9...48 C6
  Bristol, Upper Soundwell
    BS16..............51 D3
  Farrington Gurney BS39 132 B3
  Lympsham BS24......122 C5
  Olveston BS35.......14 D4
  Stanton Drew BS39....96 F1
  Weston-s-M BS22.....88 B1
  Wick BS30............67 C7
Crescent View BA2...141 B1
Crescent View Cl BS22.88 B1
Creslands Ind Units
  BS24..............105 A3
Cresswell Cl BS22....89 A2
Crest The
  Bristol BS4..........64 C2
  West Kington SN14....56 F3
Creswicke Ave BS15...65 C5
Creswicke Ho **12** BS1..143 A3
Creswicke Rd BS4....79 E7
Crewkerne Cl BS48...60 B1
CREW'S HOLE.......64 E7
Crew's Hole Rd BS5...64 E7
CRIBBS CAUSEWAY...35 D6
Cribbs Causeway Ctr
  BS34..............35 A6
Cribbs Causeway Ret Pk
  BS10..............35 C6
Cribbs Cswy BS10....35 A6
Cribb's La BS40......93 D1
Crickback La
  Chew Magna BS40....96 A2
  Chew Magna BS40....96 A3
Cricket Field Gn BS48.59 D2
Cricket La BS10......49 A8
Cricklade Ct BS48....60 A1
Cricklade Rd BS7....49 E4
Cripps Rd BS3.......63 C3
Crispin La **4** BS35....8 B1
Crispin Way BS15....51 F2
Crockerne CE Prim Sch
  BS20..............47 C4
Crockerne Dr BS20...47 C3
Crockerne Ho BS20...47 C4
CROCOMBE........116 C3
Crocombe BA2......116 C3
Crocombe La BA2....116 C3
Crocus Rd BS16.....52 D7
Croft Ave BS16......50 C4
Croft Cl BS30........82 D8
Crofters Wlk BS32...36 D8
Crofton Ave BS7.....49 F6
Crofton Fields BS36...37 E6
Crofton Mews BS15...65 E7
Croft Rd BA1........85 B1
CROFTS END........50 F1
Crofts End Ind Est BS5 50 E1
Crofts End Rd BS5....50 E1
Croft The
  Backwell BS48........76 A7
  Bristol, Mangotsfield
    BS16..............51 F5
  Bristol, Oldland Common
    BS30..............66 C3
  Clevedon BS21........57 H4
  Hutton BS24.........105 E3
  Monkton Combe BA2...102 E1
  Westwood BA15......120 F3
Croft View BS9......49 C6
Crokeshall Wlk BS11..34 A1
Cromer Ct BS21......57 F5
Crome Rd BS7.......50 B7
Cromer Rd
  Bristol BS5..........50 C2
  Weston-s-M BS23.....104 E5
CROMHALL........10 A1
Cromhall La GL12.....9 D1

Cromwell Ct BS15....65 E5
Cromwell Dr BS22....89 A4
Cromwell Rd
  Bristol, Montpelier BS6..49 E2
  Bristol, St George BS5...65 A8
Cromwells Hide BS16..50 E5
Cromwell St BS3.....63 C3
Cromwell View BS6...49 E2
Crookes La BS22.....88 A4
Croomes Hill BS16...51 D6
Cropthorne Rd BS7...36 A1
Cropthorne Road S
  BS7...............50 A8
Crosby Hall BS23....104 D8
Crosby Row BS8.....142 A2
CROSS.............124 E2
Crosscombe Dr BS13..79 B3
Cross Combe Wlk BS13.79 B3
Cross Cotts GL13.....2 C3
Cross Elms La BS9....48 E5
Cross Field **9** BS34...35 F7
Crossfield Rd BS16...51 E3
Cross Hands Rd BS35..22 D7
Cross La BS26.......125 A2
Cross Lanes BS20....47 C4
Crossleaze Rd BS15...65 C3
Crossley Cl BS36.....37 F7
Crossley Farm Bsns Ctr
  BS36..............37 E7
Crossman Ave BS36...37 E5
Crossman Rd BS37...27 D6
Crossman Wlk BS21...57 H2
Cross Moor Dr BS26..125 B1
Cross Moor Dro BS26..124 E1
Cross Moor Rd BS26..125 B1
Crosspost La BA2....99 B4
Cross St
  Bristol BS15.........51 D1
  Keynsham BS31.......81 F7
  3 Weston-s-M BS23..104 E2
Cross The BS40......129 F4
Cross Tree Gr BS32...36 D8
Crossway La BA3.....138 B7
CROSSWAYS.........8 F2
Crossways GL11......4 F8
Crossways Cvn Pk
  BA2...............117 F5
Crossways Jun & Inf Schs
  BS35..............8 D1
Crossways La
  Combe Hay BA2......118 A5
  Crossways BS35.......8 E2
Crossways Rd
  Bristol BS4..........64 A1
  Thornbury BS35.......8 D1
Cross Wlk BS14......80 A6
Crowe Hill BA2......120 B5
Crowe La BA2.......120 B5
CROWELL BROOK....5 F6
Crow La
  Bristol BS1.........143 A3
  Bristol, Henbury BS10...34 F2
Crowley Way BS11....33 B1
Crow Mdw GL12.....11 F4
Crowndale Rd BS4...64 A3
Crown Gdns BS30....66 B7
Crown Glass Pl **5** BS48 59 E2
Crown Hill
  Bath BA1...........84 C1
  Bristol BS5..........64 F8
  Winford BS40........95 A5
Crown Hill Wlk BS5...50 F1
Crown Ho
  Bristol BS1.........143 A3
  Nailsea BS48........59 C1
Crown Ind Est BS30...66 C7
Crown La BS16.......51 D3
Crownleaze BS16.....51 D3
Crown Rd
  Bath BA1...........84 B1
  Bristol, Upper Soundwell
    BS15..............51 D2
  Bristol, Warmley BS30...66 C6
Crown Way BS30.....66 C7
Crows Gr BS32.......24 D3
Crowther Pk BS7.....50 A4
Crowther Rd BS7....50 A4
Crowthers Ave BS37..27 E3
Crowther St BS3.....63 B3
Croydon Ho **1** BS5....64 B8
Croydon St BS5......64 B8
Cruikshank Gr BS24..106 B5
Crunnis The BS32....36 E6
Crusader Ho **4** BS1..143 A2
Crusty La BS20.......47 C5
Crystal Way BS32....36 E8
Cuck Hill BS25......125 E7
Cuckoo La
  High Littleton BS39...115 B3
  Winterbourne BS36....37 F3
  Wraxall BS48........60 A6
Cuffington Ave BS4...64 D4
Culleysgate La BS30...67 F6
Cullimore's La BA1....83 C4
Culvert BS39........98 D6
Culver Cl BS30......101 B2
Culverhay BS39......98 D6
Culverhill Rd BS37...28 A1
Culverhill Sch BS37..39 D7
Culver La BS40......129 F3

Culvers Cl BS31 81 E6
Culvers Rd BS31 81 E6
Culver St BS1 142 C2
Culvert Ave BS37 27 B1
Culvert The BS32 36 D8
Culverwell Rd BS13 79 A4
Culvery La BS39 97 D4
Cumberland Basin Rd BS8 62 F5
Cumberland Cl BS1 142 A1
Cumberland Gr 5 BS6 49 F2
Cumberland Ho BA1 141 A2
Cumberland Pl 6 BS8 62 F6
Cumberland Rd BS1 142 B1
Cumberland Row BA1 141 B2
Cumberland St BS2 143 B4
Cumbria Cl BS35 8 E1
Cunningham Gdns BS16 51 B5
Cunnington Cl BS30 66 B1
Curland Gr BS14 80 B5
Curlew Cl BS16 50 F6
Curlew Gdns BS22 88 F1
Curlew Pl BS20 45 F6
Currells La BS40 77 B1
Curtis La BS34 37 A4
Cussons St BA2 102 C8
Custom Cl BS14 80 A7
Custom Ho BS1 143 A1
Cutler Rd BS13 78 F6
Cutters Row BS3 63 E4
Cuttsheath Rd GL12 16 C8
Cutts Heath Rd BS35 9 A1
Cygnet Cres BS22 88 F1
Cylde Pk BS6 49 B2
Cynder Way BS16 38 A1
Cynthia Rd BA2 101 D5
Cypress Ct BS9 48 D3
Cypress Gdns BS8 62 E6
Cypress Gr BS9 49 C6
Cypress Terr BA3 133 D1
Cypress Wlk SN14 70 F6
Cyrus Ct BS16 52 B7

D

Dabinett Dr BS25 108 A4
Daffodil Way BS16 52 D8
Dafford's Bldgs BA1 85 C2
Dafford St BA1 85 C2
Daglands The BA2 133 E8
Dahlia Gdns BA2 102 B7
Daines Ct 4 BS16 50 E3
Dairy Cl BS49 74 A2
Dairycroft BS2 143 B4
Dairy Hill BA2 135 B5
Daisy Bank BA2 102 B4
Daisy Green La GL12 5 D2
Daisy Rd BS5 50 C2
Dakin Cl BS4 63 E1
Dakota Dr BS14 80 A4
Dalby Ave BS3 63 D4
Daldry Gdns BS35 14 A3
Dale St BS5 64 F8
Daley Cl BS22 89 B3
Dalkeith Ave BS15 51 C1
Dalrymple Rd 10 BS2 49 E1
Dalston Rd BS3 63 B4
Dalton Sq BS2 143 B4
Dalwood 12 BS22 89 A2
Dame Court Cl BS22 88 F4
Damery La
Stone GL13 3 F3
Woodford GL13 4 A4
Damery Works GL13 4 B3
Dampier Rd BS3 63 A3
Damson Cl BS36 38 A3
Damson Rd BS22 105 E7
Danbury Cres BS10 35 C1
Danbury Wlk BS10 35 C1
Danby Ho BS7 50 A5
Danby St BS7 50 C8
Dancey Mead BS13 78 F6
Dandy's Mdw BS20 45 E4
Daneacre Rd BA3 134 A3
Dane Cl BA15 120 E7
Dane Rise BA15 120 E7
Dangerfield Ave BS13 78 F6
Daniel Cl BS21 57 H3
Daniel Mews BA2 102 B7
Daniel St BA2 102 B7
Dapps Hill BS31 81 F5
Dapwell La BS14, BS31 81 A1
Dark La
Backwell BS48 76 B5
Banwell BS29 107 C2
Bathampton BA2 85 F1
Blagdon BS40 110 E3
Chew Magna BS40 95 F3
Freshford BA2 120 B5
Holcombe BA3 139 C1
Kilmersdon BA11 140 A1
Darley Cl BS10 34 D3
Darlington Mews BA2 102 B7
Darlington Pl BA2 102 B6
Darlington Rd BA2 102 B8
Darlington St BA2 102 B7
Darmead BS24 89 B1
Darnley Ave BS7 49 F6
Dart Cl BS35 15 B8
Dartmoor St BS3 63 B3
Dartmouth Ave BA2 101 C5
Dartmouth Cl BS22 89 A2
Dartmouth Wlk BS31 81 D4
Dart Rd BS21 57 F1
Daubeny Cl BS16 51 B5
Daubeny Ct BS1 143 A1
Davenport Cl BS30 66 A2
Daventry Rd BS4 63 F1
Davey St BS2 49 F1
Davey Terr 8 BS2 49 F1
Davids Cl BS35 15 A4
David's La BS35 15 A4
Davidson Rd BS10 35 D2
David's Rd
Bristol BS14 80 C6
Thornbury BS35 8 C1
David St BS2 143 C3
David Thomas Ho BS6 49 E2
Davies Dr BS4 64 F5
Davin Cres BS20 47 C3
Davis Cl BS30 65 F5
Davis Ct BS35 8 C2
Davis La BS21 73 F8
Davis St BS11 47 B8
Davron Ct BS3 63 E4
Dawes Cl BS21 57 F1
Dawes Ct 2 BS8 62 F6
Dawley Cl BS36 37 E7
Dawlish Rd BS3 63 D2
Dawn Rise BS15 52 A1
Daws Ct BS16 51 B4
Day Cres BA2 100 F6
Day House La GL12 19 C8
Day's Rd BS2 64 A6
Days Road Commercial Ctr BS2 64 A7
Deacon Cl BS36 37 E5
Deacons Cl BS22 88 E2
Deacons Ct BS22 88 C1
Deadmill La BA1 85 C3
Dean Ave BS35 8 C2
Dean Cl
Bristol BS15 65 B4
Weston-s-M BS22 89 B3
Dean Cres
8 Bristol BS3 63 C4
1 Bristol BS3 63 D4
Dean Ct BS37 27 C3
Deanery Cl BS15 66 B8
Deanery Rd
Bristol BS1 142 C2
Bristol, Warmley BS15 66 B8
Deanery Rd Rdbt BS15 66 B8
Deanery Wlk BA2 120 C6
Deanhill La BA1 84 A2
Dean La BS3 63 C4
Deanna Ct BS16 51 E6
Dean Rd
Avonmouth BS11 33 C5
Yate BS37 27 C3
Dean's Ct BS1 142 C2
Dean's Dr BS5 51 A2
Deans Mead BS11 48 A8
Dean St
Bristol BS2 143 B4
Bristol, Southville BS3 63 C4
Deans The BS20 45 B4
Debecca's La BS20 47 B4
De Clifford Rd BS11 34 C2
Deep Coombe Rd BS3 63 A2
Deep Pit Rd BS5 50 F2
Deep St BS1 143 A3
Deerhurst
Bristol BS15 51 E3
Yate BS37 39 C8
Deering Cl BS11 34 B1
Deerleap BS25 125 F8
Deer Mead BS21 57 D1
Deer Pk BS35 8 B3
Deerswood BS15 52 A2
Delabere Ave BS16 51 B5
Delapre Rd BS23 104 D3
De La Warre Ct 11 BS4 64 F6
Delius Gr BS4 79 D7
Dell The
Bristol, Bradley Stoke BS32 36 E7
Bristol, Oldland Common BS30 66 C5
Bristol, Westbury on T BS9 48 F5
Nailsea BS48 59 D2
Weston-s-M BS22 88 E4
Delvin Rd BS10 49 C8
De Montalt Pl BA2 102 B1
Denbigh St BS2 49 F1
Dene Cl BS31 81 F3
Dene Rd BS14 80 C4
Dening Gdns BS5 50 F1
Denleigh Cl BS14 80 A4
Denmark Ave BS1 142 C2
Denmark Pl BS7 49 E3
Denmark Rd BA2 101 D6
Denmark St BS1 142 C2
Denning Ct BS22 89 B4
Dennisworth BS16 53 B5
Dennor Pk BS14 80 B7
Denny Cl BS20 45 A5
Denny Isle Dr BS35 22 A6
Denny La BS40 96 B1
Denny View BS20 45 A5
Dennyview Rd BS8 61 F8
Denston Dr BS20 45 E4
Denston Wlk BS13 79 A7
Denton Patch BS16 52 B7
Dentwood Gr BS9 48 B8
Denys Ct BS35 14 A3
Derby Rd BS7 49 E3
Derby St BS5 64 D7
Derek Mead Way BS29 106 C7
Derham Cl BS49 91 B8
Derham Cres BS37 27 E6
Derham Ct BS49 91 B8
Derham Pk BS49 91 B8
Derham Rd BS13 79 A5
Dermot St 11 BS2 49 F1
Derricke Rd BS14 80 F6
Derrick Rd BS15 65 D8
Derry Rd BS3 63 B2
Derwent Cl BS34 36 A8
Derwent Ct BS35 15 D8
Derwent Gr BS31 82 A5
Derwent Rd
Bristol BS5 50 F1
Weston-s-M BS23 105 A5
Devaney Cl BS4 64 F5
Deveron Gr BS31 82 A4
De Verose Ct BS15 65 E4
Devil's La GL12 11 A2
Devon Gr BS5 64 C8
Devon Rd BS5 50 C1
Devon Road Trad Est 1 BS5 50 C1
Devonshire Bldgs
Bath BA2 101 F4
Bristol BS3 63 E4
Devonshire Ct BS23 104 E4
Devonshire Dr BS20 44 F5
Devonshire Mews BA2 101 F3
Devonshire Pl BA2 101 F4
Devonshire Rd
Bathampton BA2 85 E1
Bristol BS6 49 B4
Weston-s-M BS23 104 E4
Devonshire Villas BA2 101 F3
Dewfalls Dr BS32 24 D1
Dial Hill Rd BS21 57 F4
Dial La
Bristol BS16 51 D6
Felton BS40 77 D1
Diamond Batch BS24 89 B1
Diamond Rd BS5 64 F7
Diamond St BS3 63 C3
Diamonite Ind Pk BS16 51 A3
Diana Gdns BS32 36 E8
Dibden Cl BS16 52 A8
Dibden La BS16 52 B7
Dibden Rd BS16 52 A7
Dickens Cl BS7 50 A8
Dickenson Rd BS23 104 E6
Dickenson's Gr BS49 91 E3
Dickinsons Fields BS3 63 D2
Didsbury Cl BS10 34 F1
Dighton Ct 3 BS2 143 A4
Dighton Gate BS34 36 E5
Dighton St BS2 143 A4
Dillon Ct 18 BS5 64 D7
Dinder Cl BS48 75 E8
DINGHURST 108 E4
Dinghurst Rd BS25 108 E4
Dingle Cl BS9 48 C6
Dingle Ct BS13 78 F7
Dingle Rd BS9 48 D7
Dingle The
Bristol BS9 48 D7
Winterbourne BS36 37 F3
Yate BS37 27 F4
Dingle View BS9 48 C7
Dinglewood Cl BS9 48 D7
Dingley La BS37 27 F5
DINGS THE 64 A6
Dings Wlk 4 BS2 64 A6
Dipland Gr BS40 110 F2
Dirac Rd BS7 49 F4
District Ctr BS32 36 D8
Dixon Bsns Ctr BS4 64 F2
Dixon Cl 1 BS15 65 D5
Dixon Gdns BA1 84 F1
Dixon Rd BS4 64 F2
Dobunni Cl BS14 80 D3
Dock Gate La BS8 142 A1
DODINGTON 40 F5
Dodington Ash BS37 41 B2
Dodington La BS37 40 D5
Dodington Rd
Chipping Sodbury BS37 40 B7
Yate BS37 39 F7
Dodisham Wlk BS16 51 B6
Dogwood Rd BS32 24 D5
Doleberrow BS25 108 F3
Dolebury Warren Nature Reserve★ BS40 109 A3
DOLEMEADS 102 B5
Dolemoor La
Congresbury BS49 91 C3
Puxton BS49 91 A4
Dolman Cl BS10 34 F3
Dolman Ct BS37 27 D1
Dolphin Sq BS23 104 D7
Dominion Rd
Bath BA2 101 A6
Bristol BS16 50 F3
Donald Rd BS13 78 F7
Donal Early Way BS7 49 E8
Doncaster Rd BS10 49 C8
Doncombe Hill SN14 70 F7
Doncombe La SN14 70 F7
Donegal Rd BS4 63 D1
Dongola Ave BS7 49 E4
Dongola Rd BS7 49 E4
Don John Ho BS5 64 E8
Donnington Wlk BS31 81 D4
Donns Cl BS34 36 A7
Doone Rd BS7 49 F8
Dorcas Ave BS34 36 F5
Dorchester Cl 6 BS48 59 D1
Dorchester Rd BS7 50 A7
Dorchester St BA1 141 C1
Dorester Cl BS10 35 C4
Dorian Cl BS7 49 E7
Dorian Rd BS7 49 E7
Dorian Way BS7 49 E8
Dormeads View 6 BS24 105 F7
Dormer Cl BS36 38 D6
Dormer Rd BS5 50 B3
Dorset Cl BA2 101 D6
Dorset Gr 10 BS2 50 A2
Dorset Ho BA2 101 D3
Dorset Rd
Bristol, Kingswood BS15 51 D1
Bristol, Westbury on Trym BS9 49 B6
Dorset St
Bath BA2 101 D6
6 Bristol BS3 63 B3
Dorset Way BS37 28 A3
Double Hill BA2 134 F7
Doudney Ct BS3 63 E4
Douglas Ct 3 BS23 104 F5
Douglas Rd
Bristol, Horfield BS7 49 F7
Bristol, Kingswood BS15 65 D7
Weston-s-M BS23 104 F5
Douglas Road Ind Pk BS15 65 D7
Doulton Way BS14 80 B5
Dovecote BS37 39 E7
Dovedale BS35 15 D8
Dove La
Bristol BS2 143 C4
Bristol, Russell Town BS5 64 C7
Dovercourt Rd BS7 50 A6
Dover Ho BA1 141 C4
Dover Pl
5 Bath BA1 85 A1
Bristol BS8 142 B3
Dover Place Cotts BS8 142 B3
Dovers La BA1 86 C2
Dovers Pk BA1 86 C2
Dove St S BS2 143 A4
Dove St BS2 143 A4
Doveswell Gr BS13 79 A4
Dovetail Dr BS23 105 A7
Dovey Ct BS30 66 C5
Dowdeswell Cl BS10 34 F3
Dowding Cl BS37 28 C2
Dowding Rd BA1 85 B1
Dower Ho The BS16 50 E7
Dowland 13 BS22 89 A2
Dowland Gr BS4 79 D6
Dowling Rd BS13 79 D3
Down Ave BA2 102 A1
Down Cl BS20 44 F4
DOWNEND 51 E8
Downend Comp Sch BS16 51 F7
Downend Park Rd BS16 51 D5
Downend Pk BS7 49 F5
Downend Rd
Bristol, Fishponds BS16 51 C5
Bristol, Horfield BS7 49 F5
Bristol, Kingswood BS15 51 D1
Down Farm Ho BS36 37 D6
Downfield
Bristol BS9 48 C7
Keynsham BS31 81 D5
Downfield Cl 1 BS35 15 A5
Downfield Dr BS36 38 B8
Downfield Lodge BS8 49 A1
Downfield Rd BS8 49 A1
Down La BA2 85 F1
Downland Cl 5 BS48 59 D1
Downleaze
Bristol, Downend BS16 51 D8
Portishead BS20 45 A5
Stoke Bishop BS9 48 F3
Down Leaze 2 BS35 15 A5
Downleaze Dr BS37 40 B8
Downleaze Rd BS9 48 F3
Downman Rd BS7 50 A5
Down Rd
Alveston BS35 15 A5
Marshfield SN14 56 C2
Portishead BS20 44 F4
Winterbourne BS36 37 F4
Downs Cl
3 Alveston BS35 15 A5
Weston-s-M BS22 88 F1
Downs Cote Ave BS9 48 F6
Downs Cote Dr BS9 48 F6
Downs Cote Gdns BS9 49 A6
Downs Cote Pk BS9 49 A6
Downs Cote View BS9 49 A6
Downs Ct BS9 49 B6
DOWNSIDE
Chilcompton 138 C1
Nailsea 76 D1
Downside BS20 45 C5
Downside Abbey★ BA3 138 E2
Downside Cl
Bathampton BA2 85 F1
Bristol BS30 65 F5
Chilcompton BA3 138 D3
Downside Rd
Backwell BS48 93 E8
Bristol BS8 49 A1
Weston-s-M BS23 104 F4
Downside Sch BA3 138 E2
Downs Pk E BS6 49 A4
Downs Pk W BS6 49 A4
Downs Rd
Bristol BS9 49 A6
Dundry BS41 78 D2
Downs Sch The BS48 60 C8
Downs The
Portishead BS20 45 B4
Wickwar GL12 17 F7
Downsview Ct BS8 49 A1
Downsway BS39 132 D6
Down The
Alveston BS35 14 F5
Tockington BS32 14 D3
Downton Rd BS4 63 D1
Down View
Bristol BS7 49 F3
Radstock BA3 139 F8
Dowry Pl 3 BS8 62 F5
Dowry Rd BS8 142 A2
Dowry Sq BS8 142 A2
Dowsell Way BS37 27 E6
DOYNTON 54 A1
Doynton La SN14, BS30 54 B3
Doynton Mill BS30 53 F1
Dragon Ct BS5 50 E1
Dragonfly Cl BS15 65 D7
Dragon Rd BS36 37 D5
Dragons Hill Cl BS31 81 F5
Dragons Hill Ct BS31 81 F5
Dragons Hill Gdns BS31 81 F5
Dragonswell Rd BS10 35 A2
Dragon Wlk BS5 50 F1
Drake Ave BA2 101 F2
Drake Cl
Saltford BS31 82 D2
Weston-s-M BS22 88 F4
Drake Rd BS3 63 A3
Drakes Way BS20 45 B5
Dram La BS5 65 A6
Dramway Rdbt BS16 52 D6
Dransfield Way BA2 101 C4
Draper Ct 3 BS5 64 C7
Draycot Pl BS1 143 A1
Draycott Ct 1 BA2 141 C3
Draycott Rd BS7 49 F5
Draydon Rd BS4 79 D8
Drayton BS24 105 A2
Drayton Cl BS14 80 B8
Drayton Rd BS9 48 C8
Drifton Hill SN14 56 F7
Dring The BA3 133 E2
Drive The
Bristol BS14 80 C6
Bristol, Henleaze BS9 49 B5
Churchill BS25 108 E4
Keynsham BS31 81 E6
Shipham BS25 125 E8
Stanton Drew BS39 96 F1
Weston-s-M BS23 104 F8
Drove Ct BS48 59 E3
Drove Rd
Congresbury BS49 91 D3
Weston-s-M BS23 104 F5
Drovers Way BS37 28 B2
Drove The BS20 46 D6
Drove Way BS24, BS25 107 E7
Druetts Cl BS10 49 E6
Druid Cl BS9 48 E5
Druid Hill BS9 48 E5
Druid Rd BS9 48 D4
Druids Garth BA2 85 D1
Druid Stoke Ave BS9 48 D5
Druid Woods BS9 48 C5

Drumhead Way The
  BS25 . . . . 125 E8
Drummond Ct BS30 . . . . 65 F4
Drummond Rd
  Bristol, Fishponds BS16 . . 50 F3
  Bristol, St Pauls BS2 . . . . 49 E1
Drumway The BS31 . . . . . 82 B4
Dr White's Cl BS1 . . . . . 143 B1
DRY HILL 45 C6
Dryleaze
  Keynsham BS31 . . . . 81 E7
  Yate BS37 . . . . 27 E5
Dryleaze Rd BS16 . . . . . 50 F6
Drysdale Cl BS22 . . . . . . 88 D1
Dubbers La BS5 . . . . 50 D6
Dublin Cres BS9 . . . . 49 B6
Duchess Rd BS8 . . . . 49 A1
Duchess Way BS16 . . . . . 50 D6
Duchy Cl BA3 . . . . 133 E5
Duchy Rd BA3 . . . . 133 E5
Ducie Cl GL12 . . . . 10 E2
Ducie Ct BS16 . . . . 51 E4
Ducie Rd
  Bristol, Russell Town
  BS5 . . . . 64 B7
  Bristol, Staple Hill BS16 . . 51 E4
Ducie Rd Bsns Pk 6
  BS5 . . . . 64 B7
Duckett Fields BS10 . . . . 49 D7
DUCKHOLE 8 C5
Duck La
  Churchill BS40 . . . . 109 A8
  Kenn BS21 . . . . 74 A6
Duckmoor Rd BS3 . . . . . . 63 A3
Duckmoor Road Ind Est
  BS3 . . . . 63 A3
Ducks La BS22 . . . . 89 A8
Duck St
  Churchill BS25 . . . . 108 C5
  Tytherington GL12 . . . . . 16 C5
Dudley Cl BS31 . . . . 81 E4
Dudley Ct 3 BS30 . . . . . 65 F4
Dudley Gr BS7 . . . . 50 A8
Dugar Wlk BS6 . . . . 49 C3
Duke St BA2 . . . . 141 C2
Dukwick La SN14 . . . . . . 67 A3
Dulverton Rd BS7 . . . . . . 49 D4
Dumaine Ave BS34 . . . . . 36 E5
Dumfries Pl BS23 . . . . . 104 E5
Dumpers La BS40 . . . . . . 96 B2
Duncan Gdns BA1 . . . . . . 84 A3
Duncan Ho BS8 . . . . 142 A4
Duncombe La BS15 . . . . . 51 B2
Duncombe Rd BS15 . . . . . 51 B1
Dundas Cl BS10 . . . . 34 E2
Dundonald Rd BS6 . . . . . 49 B3
Dundridge Gdns BS5 . . . . 65 A6
Dundridge La BS5 . . . . . . 65 A6
DUNDRY 78 D2
Dundry CE Prim Sch
  BS41 . . . . 78 D2
Dundry Cl BS15 . . . . 65 D6
DUNDRY HILL 80 B3
Dundry La
  Dundry BS41 . . . . 78 C3
  Winford BS40 . . . . 95 A7
Dundry View BS4 . . . . 64 A1
Dunedin Way BS22 . . . . . 89 C4
Dunford Rd BS3 . . . . 63 D3
Dungarvon Rd BS24 . . . . 105 F7
Dunkeld Ave BS34 . . . . . . 35 F2
Dunkerry Rd BS3 . . . . 63 D3
DUNKERTON 117 E4
Dunkerton Hill BA2 . . . . 117 E2
Dunkerton La
  Combe Hay BA2 . . . . . . 118 B4
  Dunkerton BA2 . . . . 117 F3
Dunkery Cl BS48 . . . . 59 E1
Dunkery Rd BS23 . . . . . . 87 F1
DUNKIRK 20 B1
Dunkirk Rd BS16 . . . . 50 F3
Dunlin Dr BS20 . . . . 45 F6
Dunmail Rd BS10 . . . . 35 C2
Dunmore St 3 BS2 . . . . 63 F4
Dunmurry BS9 . . . . 48 D3
Dunsdown La SN14 . . . . . 55 B5
Dunsford Pl BA2 . . . . . . 102 B6
Dunster Cres BS24 . . . . 105 A2
Dunster Ct BS25 . . . . . . 125 A8
Dunster Gdns
  Bristol BS30 . . . . 66 B2
  5 Nailsea BS48 . . . . . . 59 E1
Dunster Ho BA2 . . . . . . 102 A2
Dunster Rd
  Bristol BS4 . . . . 79 F8
  Keynsham BS31 . . . . 81 E4
Dunsters Rd BS49 . . . . . . 74 F1
Durban Rd BS34 . . . . 35 F8
Durban Way BS49 . . . . . . 74 B1
Durbin Park Rd
  BS21 . . . . 57 F5
Durbin Wlk BS5 . . . . 64 A8
Durcott La BA2 . . . . 133 D8
Durdham Ct BS6 . . . . 49 A3
Durdham Pk BS6 . . . . 49 A3
Durham Gr BS31 . . . . 81 D4

Durham Rd
  11 Bristol BS2 . . . . 50 A2
  Charfield GL12 . . . . 11 A5
Durleigh Cl BS13 . . . . . . 79 A7
Durley Hill BS31 . . . . 81 C7
Durley La BS31 . . . . 81 D7
Durley Pk BA2 . . . . 101 E4
Durnford Ave BS3 . . . . . . 63 A4
Durnford St BS3 . . . . 63 A4
Durnhill BS40 . . . . 128 F7
Dursley Cl BS37 . . . . 27 E1
Dursley Rd BS11 . . . . 47 E5
Durston BS24 . . . . 105 A2
Durville Rd BS13 . . . . 79 B6
Durweston Wlk BS14 . . . 80 C8
Dutton Cl BS14 . . . . 80 D6
Dutton Rd BS14 . . . . 80 D6
Dutton Wlk BS14 . . . . 80 D6
Dye House Rd GL12 . . . . . 11 F5
Dyers Cl BS13 . . . . 79 D4
DYER'S COMMON 22 C3
Dyer's La BS37 . . . . 27 A4
Dylan Thomas Ct 4
  BS30 . . . . 66 A5
Dymboro Ave BA3 . . . . . 132 F1
Dymboro Cl BA3 . . . . 132 F1
Dymboro Gdns BA3 . . . . 132 F1
Dymboro The BA3 . . . . . 132 F1
DYRHAM 54 D4
Dyrham BS16 . . . . 37 C1
Dyrham Cl
  Bristol, Henleaze BS9 . . . 49 D6
  Bristol, Kingswood BS15 . . 65 F8
  Pucklechurch BS16 . . . . . 53 C4
  Thornbury BS35 . . . . 8 C3
Dyrham Par BS34 . . . . . . 36 C8
Dyrham Rd BS15 . . . . 65 F8
Dyrham View BS16 . . . . . 53 C4
Dyson Cl BS49 . . . . 91 B8**

E

Eagle Cl BS22 . . . . 105 D8
Eagle Cres BS16 . . . . 53 C5
Eagle Dr
  Bristol BS34 . . . . 35 E8
  5 Radstock BA3 . . . . . 139 B8
Eagle Pk BA1 . . . . 85 F5
Eagle Rd
  Batheaston BA1 . . . . 85 F5
  Bristol BS4 . . . . 64 D2
Eagles The BS49 . . . . 91 B8
Eagles Wood BS32 . . . . . 24 D3
Eagles Wood Bsns Pk
  BS32 . . . . 24 C3
Eamoth Ground BS34 . . . 35 E6
Earlesfield BS48 . . . . 59 C1
Earlham Gr BS23 . . . . . . 105 A7
Earl Russell Way BS5 . . . 64 B7
Earlsmead BS16 . . . . 50 E4
Earl St BS1 . . . . 143 A4
Earlstone Cl BS30 . . . . . . 66 A4
Earlstone Cres BS30 . . . . 66 A4
EARTHCOTT GREEN 25 D5
Earthcott Rd BS35 . . . . . 15 F1
Easedale Cl BS10 . . . . . . 35 D2
Eastbourne Ave 15 BA1 . 85 B1
Eastbourne Rd 9 BS5 . . 64 B8
Eastbury Cl BS35 . . . . 8 C1
Eastbury Rd
  Bristol BS16 . . . . 51 A4
  Thornbury BS35 . . . . 8 C1
East Cl BA2 . . . . 101 A5
EAST CLEVEDON 57 H3
East Clevedon Triangle
  BS21 . . . . 57 H3
Eastcliff BS20 . . . . 45 E7
Eastcombe Gdns BS23 . . 87 F1
Eastcombe Rd BS23 . . . . 87 F1
Eastcote Pk BS14 . . . . . . 80 B5
Eastcourt Rd BS39 . . . . 131 F8
Eastcroft BS40 . . . . 110 E2
East Croft BS9 . . . . 49 C7
Eastcroft Cl BS40 . . . . . 110 E2
East Ct BS3 . . . . 62 F3
Eastdown Pl BA3 . . . . . . 133 E5
Eastdown Rd BA3 . . . . . 133 D5
EAST DUNDRY 79 A1
East Dundry La BS41 . . . . 79 A1
East Dundry Rd BS13,
  BS14 . . . . 79 F2
EAST END
  Blagdon 110 E2
  Marshfield 70 A8
  Nailsea 60 A1
EASTER COMPTON 23 A2
Easter Ct BS37 . . . . 27 B1
Eastermead La BS29 . . . 107 C3
Eastern Ho BS23 . . . . 87 E1
EASTERTOWN 122 D2
Eastertown BS24 . . . . . . 122 D1
EASTFIELD 49 B7
Eastfield BS9 . . . . 49 B7
Eastfield Ave BA1 . . . . . . 84 B2
Eastfield Dr BS37 . . . . . . 27 E4
Eastfield Gdns BS23 . . . . 87 F1
Eastfield La BS35 . . . . . . 12 E3

Eastfield Pk BS23 . . . . . . 87 F1
Eastfield Rd
  Bristol, Eastfield BS9 . . . . 49 B7
  Bristol, Montpelier BS6 . . 49 D2
  Bristol, Westbury on Trym
  BS9 . . . . 49 A7
  Hutton BS24 . . . . 105 E2
East Fields Rd BS16 . . . . 50 D8
Eastfield Terr BS9 . . . . . . 49 B7
Eastgate Office Ctr BS5 . 50 B3
Eastgate Ret Pk BS5 . . . . 50 B3
East Gr BS6 . . . . 49 F1
EAST HARPTREE 129 E4
East Harptree CE VA Prim
  Sch BS40 . . . . 129 F4
EAST HEWISH 90 B6
East Hill BS9 . . . . 49 B7
East Hill Cl BS9 . . . . 49 B6
Eastlake Cl BS7 . . . . 50 B7
Eastland Ave BS35 . . . . . . 8 C2
Eastland Rd BS35 . . . . 8 C2
Eastlea BS21 . . . . 57 D1
East Lea Rd BA1 . . . . . . 101 A8
Eastleigh Cl BS16 . . . . . . 51 E4
Eastleigh Rd
  Bristol, Brentry BS10 . . . . 35 D1
  Bristol, Staple Hill BS16 . . 51 E3
Eastley Cl GL12 . . . . 9 E7
Eastlyn Rd BS13 . . . . 79 B8
East Mead BA3 . . . . 133 B2
Eastmead Ct BS9 . . . . . . 48 E4
Eastmead La BS9 . . . . . . 48 E4
Eastnor Rd BS14 . . . . 80 A3
Easton Bsns Ctr BS5 . . . 64 B8
Easton CE Prim Sch
  BS5 . . . . 64 A8
Easton Ct BA3 . . . . 131 E1
Easton Gdns BA1 . . . . . . 85 F5
Easton Hill Rd BS35 . . . . . 8 D1
Easton Ho 9 BA1 . . . . . 85 C1
EASTON-IN-
  GORDANO 47 A4
Easton Rd
  Bristol, Newton BS5 . . . . 64 A7
  Bristol, Upper Easton
  BS5 . . . . 64 B8
  Pill BS20 . . . . 47 C4
Easton Way BS5 . . . . 64 A8
Eastover Cl BS9 . . . . 49 A8
Eastover Gr BA2 . . . . . . 101 C1
Eastover Rd BS39 . . . . . 115 D1
East Par BS9 . . . . 48 C6
East Park Dr BS5 . . . . 50 C4
Eastpark Trad Est BS5 . . 50 D1
East Pk BS5 . . . . 50 C2
East Priory Cl BS9 . . . . . . 49 A7
East Ridge Dr BS13 . . . . . 78 F5
EAST ROLSTONE 90 B1
East Shrubbery 3 BS6 . . 49 B2
East St
  Avonmouth BS11 . . . . . . 33 A1
  Banwell BS29 . . . . 107 C3
  Bristol, Southville BS3 . . . 63 D4
EAST TWERTON 101 D6
East View BS16 . . . . 51 F6
EASTVILLE 50 C3
Eastville BA1 . . . . 85 B1
Eastway BS48 . . . . 59 E3
East Way BA2 . . . . 101 A5
Eastway Cl BS48 . . . . 59 D2
Eastway Sq BS48 . . . . . . 59 E3
Eastwell La BS25 . . . . . . 124 E6
East Wlk BS37 . . . . 27 E1
Eastwood
  Bath BA2 . . . . 102 F6
  Sherborne BS40 . . . . . . 130 B2
Eastwood Cl BS39 . . . . . 115 C1
Eastwood Cres BS4 . . . . 64 F4
East Wood Pl BS20 . . . . . 45 E7
Eastwood Rd BS4 . . . . . . 64 F4
Eastwoods BA1 . . . . 86 B3
Eaton Cl
  Bristol BS14 . . . . 80 E5
  Bristol, Fishponds BS16 . . 51 B4
Eaton Cres BS8 . . . . 142 A4
Eaton St 14 BS3 . . . . . . 63 C3
Ebden Lo 15 BS22 . . . . . 89 A4
EBDON 89 B6
Ebdon La BS22 . . . . 89 C5
Ebdon Rd BS22 . . . . 88 F4
Ebenezer La BS9 . . . . 48 E5
Ebenezer St BS5 . . . . 64 D7
Ebenezer Terr BA2 . . . . 141 C1
Eccleston Ho 1 BS5 . . . 64 B6
Eckweek Gdns BA2 . . . . 134 D8
Eckweek La BA2 . . . . . . 134 E8
Eckweek Rd BA2 . . . . . . 134 D8
Eclipse Ct 1 BS16 . . . . . 51 C4
Eclipse Office Pk 2
  BS16 . . . . 51 C4
Eddington Ct BS23 . . . . 104 D7
Eden Croft BS22 . . . . . . 105 E8
Eden Gr BS7 . . . . 36 A1
Eden Office Pk BS20 . . . . 47 E4
Eden Park Cl BA1 . . . . . . 86 A4
Eden Park Dr BA1 . . . . . . 86 A4
Eden Terr BA1 . . . . 85 B2
Eden Villas 4 BA1 . . . . . 85 C2
Edgar Bldgs BA1 . . . . . . 141 B3

Edgarley Ct BS21 . . . . . . 57 E5
Edgecombe Ave BS22 . . . 88 D2
Edgecombe Cl BS15 . . . . . 51 F1
Edgecombe Mews BA1 . . 84 B1
Edgecorner La SN14 . . . . 43 A3
Edgecumbe Rd BS6 . . . . . 49 D2
Edgefield Cl BS14 . . . . . . 79 F3
Edgefield Rd BS14 . . . . . . 79 F3
Edgehill Rd BS21 . . . . 57 F6
Edgeware Rd
  Bristol, Southville BS3 . . . 63 C4
  Bristol, Staple Hill BS16 . . 51 D4
Edgewood Cl
  Bristol BS14 . . . . 80 B8
  Bristol, Longwell Green
  BS30 . . . . 66 A3
Edgeworth BS37 . . . . 39 C6
Edgeworth Rd BA2 . . . . 101 C2
Edinburgh Pl 1 BS23 . . 104 E8
Edinburgh Rd BS31 . . . . . 81 E4
Edington Gr BS10 . . . . . . 35 A2
Edmund Cl BS16 . . . . 51 D6
Edmund Ct BS16 . . . . 53 B6
Edna Ave BS4 . . . . 64 E3
Edward Bird Ho BS7 . . . . 50 B6
Edward Cl BS31 . . . . 81 F4
Edward Parker Rd BS16 . 50 F8
Edward Rd
  Bristol, Kingswood
  BS15 . . . . 65 E8
  Bristol, Totterdown BS4 . . 64 B4
  Clevedon BS21 . . . . 57 G5
Edward Rd S BS21 . . . . . 57 G5
Edward Rd W BS21 . . . . . 57 G6
Edwards Ct 17 BS5 . . . . 64 D7
Edward St
  Bath, Bathwick BA2 . . . . 102 B7
  Bath, Lower Weston
  BA1 . . . . 101 C7
  Bristol, Eastville BS5 . . . . 50 D2
  Bristol, Moorfields BS5 . . 64 C7
Edwin Short Cl BS30 . . . . 82 E8
Effingham Rd BS6 . . . . . . 49 E2
Egerton Brow BS7 . . . . . . 49 E4
Egerton Ct BS7 . . . . 49 E4
Egerton Rd
  Bath BA2 . . . . 101 E4
  Bristol BS7 . . . . 49 D4
Eggshill La BS37 . . . . 27 D1
Eglin Croft BS13 . . . . 79 B4
Egret Dr BS49 . . . . 73 F2
Eighteen Acre Dr
  Bristol BS34 . . . . 35 F6
  Little Stoke BS34 . . . . . . 36 A7
Eighth Ave
  Bristol BS14 . . . . 80 A7
  Bristol, Filton BS7 . . . . . . 36 B1
Eirene Terr BS20 . . . . 47 D4
ELBERTON 14 A6
Elberton BS15 . . . . 66 A8
Elberton Rd
  Bristol BS9 . . . . 48 B7
  Elberton BS35 . . . . 13 F5
Elborough Ave BS24 . . . . 91 B8
Elborough Gdns BS24 . . 106 C3
Elbridge Ho 3 BS2 . . . . 143 C3
Elbury Ave BS15 . . . . 51 C2
Elbury View GL12 . . . . 11 B5
Elderberry Way BS32 . . . 24 E5
Elderberry Wlk
  Bristol BS10 . . . . 35 C3
  Weston-s-M BS22 . . . . . . 88 F1
Elderflower Dr BS16 . . . . 38 D1
Elderwood Dr BS30 . . . . . 66 A3
Elderwood Rd BS14 . . . . . 80 B7
Eldon Pl BA1 . . . . 85 B2
Eldon Terr BS3 . . . . 63 D3
Eldonwall Trad Est BS4 . 64 C5
Eldon Way BS4 . . . . 64 C5
Eldred Cl BS9 . . . . 48 D5
Eleanor Cl BA2 . . . . 101 A5
Eleanor Cotts BA2 . . . . 101 A6
Eleventh Ave BS7 . . . . . . 36 B1
Elfin Rd BS16 . . . . 51 A5
Elgar Cl
  Bristol BS4 . . . . 79 D6
  Clevedon BS21 . . . . 57 G1
Elgin Ave BS7 . . . . 35 F1
Elgin Pk BS6 . . . . 49 B2
Elgin Rd BS16 . . . . 51 B2
Eliot Cl
  Bristol BS7 . . . . 36 A1
  Weston-s-M BS23 . . . . . 105 A3
Elizabeth Cl
  Hutton BS24 . . . . 105 D3
  Thornbury BS35 . . . . 15 D8
Elizabeth Cres BS34 . . . . 36 E4
Elizabeths Mews 12
  BS4 . . . . 64 F6
Elizabeth Way BS16 . . . . 52 B3
Elkstone Wlk BS30 . . . . . 66 C2
Ella Cl BS16 . . . . 51 C6
Ellacombe Rd BS30 . . . . . 65 F2
Ellan Hay Rd BS34 . . . . . 37 A6
Ellbridge Cl BS9 . . . . 48 D5
Ellenborough Cres
  BS23 . . . . 104 E6
Ellenborough Ct BS23 . . 104 E6
Ellenborough Ho BS8 . . 142 A2

Ellenborough Park Rd
  BS23 . . . . 104 E6
Ellenborough Pk N
  BS23 . . . . 104 D6
Ellenborough Pk S
  BS23 . . . . 104 D6
Ellen Ho BA2 . . . . 101 A5
Ellerncroft Rd GL12 . . . . 11 F8
Ellesmere BS35 . . . . 15 C8
Ellesmere Rd
  1 Bristol BS4 . . . . 64 D1
  Weston-s-M BS23 . . . . . 104 D2
Ellfield Cl BS13 . . . . 78 F6
Ellick Rd BS40 . . . . 110 D1
Ellicks Cl BS32 . . . . 24 E2
Ellicott Rd BS7 . . . . 49 F5
Ellinghurst Cl BS10 . . . . . 35 A2
Elliott Ave BS16 . . . . 37 C1
Elliott Ho BS7 . . . . 50 A3
Ellis Ave BS13 . . . . 79 A8
Ellis Pk BS22 . . . . 89 C4
Elliston Dr BA2 . . . . 101 B4
Elliston La BS6 . . . . 49 C2
Elliston Rd BS6 . . . . 49 C2
Ellsworth Rd BS10 . . . . . . 34 F2
Ellyott Ct 5 BS16 . . . . . 50 E3
Elmbrook BA1 . . . . 101 A8
Elm Cl
  Banwell BS29 . . . . 106 E4
  Bristol BS34 . . . . 36 D7
  Bristol, Lawrence Weston
  BS11 . . . . 33 F1
  Chipping Sodbury BS37 . . 28 A1
  Nailsea BS48 . . . . 59 C1
  Star BS25 . . . . 108 D1
  Yatton BS49 . . . . 91 B7
Elmcroft Cres BS7 . . . . . . 50 A4
Elm Ct
  Bristol BS14 . . . . 80 A6
  Bristol, Redland BS6 . . . . 49 B2
  Keynsham BS31 . . . . 81 C4
Elmdale Cres BS35 . . . . . . 8 C1
Elmdale Gdns 4 BS16 . . 51 A4
Elmdale Rd
  Bristol BS8 . . . . 142 B3
  Bristol, Bedminster BS3 . . 63 B2
Elm Farm BS48 . . . . 60 A2
Elmfield BS15 . . . . 65 E6
Elmfield Cl BS15 . . . . 65 E6
Elmfield Rd BS9 . . . . 49 A8
Elmfield Sch for Deaf
  Children BS10 . . . . 49 B8
Elm Gr
  Bath, Larkhill BA1 . . . . . . 85 C2
  Bath, The Oval BA2 . . . . 101 C4
  Locking BS24 . . . . 105 F4
Elmgrove Ave 10 BS5 . . . 64 B8
Elmgrove Dr BS37 . . . . . . 27 F2
Elmgrove Pk 1 BS6 . . . . 49 D1
Elmgrove Rd
  Bristol, Fishponds BS16 . . 50 E3
  Bristol, Redland BS6 . . . . 49 D1
Elmham Way BS24 . . . . . 89 B1
Elm Hayes BS13 . . . . 78 F6
Elm Hayes Rd BS34 . . . . . 35 F7
Elmhirst Gdns BS37 . . . . 28 A2
Elmhurst Ave BS5 . . . . . . 50 D3
Elmhurst Est
  Batheaston BA1 . . . . 86 A4
  Bathford BA1 . . . . 86 A4
Elmhurst Gdns BS41 . . . . 77 F8
Elmhurst Rd BS24 . . . . . 105 E2
Elmhyrst Rd BS23 . . . . . 104 F8
Elming Down Cl BS32 . . . 36 D6
Elm La BS6 . . . . 49 B2
Elmlea Ave BS9 . . . . 48 F5
Elmlea Jun & Inf Schs
  BS9 . . . . 48 F5
Elmleigh Ave BS16 . . . . . 52 B5
Elmleigh Cl BS16 . . . . 52 B5
Elmleigh Rd BS16 . . . . . . 52 B5
Elm Lodge Rd BS48 . . . . . 60 B2
Elmore
  Bristol BS15 . . . . 51 F2
  Yate BS37 . . . . 39 D8
Elmore Rd
  Bristol BS34 . . . . 23 F1
  Bristol, Horfield BS7 . . . . 50 A6
Elm Park Prim Sch
  BS36 . . . . 37 E6
Elm Pk BS34 . . . . 36 A2
Elm Pl BA2 . . . . 101 F4
Elm Rd
  Bristol, Horfield BS7 . . . . 49 E5
  Bristol, Kingswood BS15 . . 65 E5
  Paulton BS39 . . . . 132 E5
Elms Gr BS34 . . . . 24 B1
Elmsleigh Rd BS23 . . . . 104 E4
Elmsley La BS22 . . . . 88 C5
Elms The
  Banwell BS29 . . . . 107 A4
  Bath, Lambridge BA1 . . . . 85 C2
  Bath, Weston Park BA1 . . 84 C1
  Bristol, Frenchay BS16 . . . 37 C1
  Bristol, Henbury BS10 . . . 34 F2
  Tockington BS32 . . . . 14 B2
Elmswood BS23 . . . . 104 F8
Elm Terr BA3 . . . . 139 C8
Elmtree Ave BS16 . . . . . . 52 A7

Elm Tree Ave
Nailsea BS21 ... 59 A4
Radstock BA3 ... 133 D1
Elmtree Cl BS15 ... 51 D1
Elmtree Dr BS13 ... 78 F5
Elm Tree Pk BS20 ... 46 D3
Elm Tree Rd
Clevedon BS21 ... 57 F2
Locking BS24 ... 106 A4
Elmtree Way BS15 ... 51 D1
Elmvale Dr BS24 ... 105 F3
Elm View
Midsomer Norton BA3 .. 133 B1
Temple Cloud BS39 ... 114 E1
Elm Wlk
Portishead BS20 ... 45 C4
Yatton BS49 ... 91 B7
Elm Wood BS37 ... 39 E8
Elsbert Dr BS13 ... 78 E6
Elstree Rd BS5 ... 50 E1
Elton Ho
Bristol, Clifton BS8 ... 142 A3
2 Bristol, Newton BS2 143 C3
Elton La BS7 ... 49 D2
Elton Mans 5 BS7 ... 49 D2
Elton Rd
Bristol BS8 ... 142 C3
Bristol, Bishopston BS7 .. 49 D2
Bristol, Kingswood BS15 51 C1
Clevedon BS21 ... 57 E3
Weston-s-M BS22 ... 89 A4
Elton St BS2 ... 143 C4
Elvard Cl BS13 ... 79 A4
Elvard Rd BS13 ... 79 A4
Elvaston Rd BS3 ... 63 E3
Elwell La BS40, BS41 ... 78 A1
Ely Gr BS9 ... 48 B7
Embassy Rd BS5 ... 50 E1
Embassy Wlk BS5 ... 50 E1
Embercourt Dr BS48 ... 76 A6
Embleton Rd BS10 ... 35 C2
EMERSON'S GREEN ... 52 C6
Emersons Green La
BS16 ... 52 B6
Emersons Green Prim Sch
BS16 ... 52 B7
Emerson Sq BS7 ... 50 A8
Emerson Way BS16 ... 52 C7
Emery Gate BS29 ... 107 B3
Emery Rd BS4 ... 64 F1
Emet Gr BS16 ... 52 B6
Emet La BS16 ... 52 B6
Eminence BS1 ... 143 B1
Emley La BS40 ... 110 B6
Emlyn Cl 6 BS22 ... 89 B4
Emlyn Rd BS5 ... 50 C2
Emma-Chris Way BS34 36 C2
Emmanuel Ct BS8 ... 142 A4
Emmett Wood BS14 ... 80 B3
Empire Cres BS15 ... 65 E4
Empress Menen Gdns
BA1 ... 101 A8
Emra Cl BS5 ... 50 F1
Emra Ho 10 BS5 ... 64 A8
Enderleigh Gdns BS25 108 F4
Enfield Rd BS16 ... 51 A3
ENGINE COMMON ... 27 B5
Engine Common La
BS37 ... 27 C5
Engine La BS48 ... 75 B8
England's Cres BS36 ... 37 E7
ENGLISHCOMBE ... 100 F2
Englishcombe La BA2 101 D3
Englishcombe Rd BS13 79 C3
Englishcombe Rise
BA2 ... 101 A3
Englishcombe Tithe Barn*
BA2 ... 100 F2
Englishcombe Way
BA2 ... 101 E3
Enmore BS24 ... 105 A2
Ennerdale Cl BS23 ... 105 A5
Ennerdale Rd BS10 ... 35 D2
Ensleigh Ave BA1 ... 84 E4
Enterprise Ctr The
BS24 ... 105 A3
Enterprise Trade Ctr
BS4 ... 79 E7
Entry Hill BA2 ... 101 F2
Entry Hill Dr BA2 ... 101 F3
Entry Hill Gdns BA2 ... 101 F3
Entry Hill Pk BA2 ... 101 F2
Entry Rise BA2 ... 101 F1
Epney Cl BS34 ... 23 F1
Epsom Cl BS16 ... 37 F1
Epworth Rd BS10 ... 35 A3
Equinox BS32 ... 24 C3
Erin Wlk BS4 ... 79 D8
Ermine Way BS11 ... 47 C7
Ermleet Rd 1 BS6 ... 49 C2
Ernest Barker Cl 15
BS5 ... 64 B7
Ernestville Rd BS16 ... 50 F3
Ervine Terr BS2 ... 143 C4
Esgar Rise BS22 ... 88 E3
Eskdale BS35 ... 15 D7
Eskdale Cl BS22 ... 105 D8
Esmond Gr BS21 ... 57 F4
Esplanade Rd BS20 ... 45 C7
Essery Rd BS5 ... 50 C2
Esson Rd BS15 ... 51 B1
Estcourt Gdns BS16 ... 50 D5
Estoril BS37 ... 27 F1
Estuary Ho BS20 ... 45 E7
Estune Wlk BS41 ... 62 A2
Etloe Rd BS6 ... 49 A4
Etonhurst BS23 ... 104 D6
Eton La BS29 ... 106 E7
Eton Rd BS4 ... 64 D3
Ettlingen Way BS21 ... 57 H2
Ettricke Dr BS16 ... 51 B5
Eugene Flats 7 BS2 ... 143 A4
Eugene St
Bristol, Kingsdown
BS2 ... 143 A4
Bristol, St Pauls BS2,
BS5 ... 143 C4
Evans Cl BS4 ... 64 F5
Evans Rd BS6 ... 49 B2
Eveleigh Ave BA1 ... 85 D3
Evelyn Rd
Bath BA1 ... 101 B8
Bristol BS10 ... 49 C7
Evelyn Terr 13 BA1 ... 85 A1
Evenlode Gdns BS11 ... 47 F5
Evenlode Way BS31 ... 82 A3
Evercreech Rd BS14 ... 80 B4
Eve Rd BS5 ... 50 B1
Everest Ave BS16 ... 50 E4
Everest Rd BS16 ... 50 E4
Evergreen Cl BS25 ... 107 F1
Ewart Rd BS22 ... 105 C8
Ewell Rd BS14 ... 80 B6
Exbourne 10 BS22 ... 89 A2
Excelsior St BA2 ... 102 B5
Excelsior Terr BA3 ... 133 B1
Exchange Ave BS1 ... 143 A2
Exchange Ct 8 BS15 ... 65 D8
Exeter Bldgs BS6 ... 49 B2
Exeter Rd
Bristol BS3 ... 63 B4
Portishead BS20 ... 45 E4
Weston-s-M BS23 ... 104 E5
Exford Cl BS23 ... 104 F2
Exley Cl BS30 ... 66 D5
Exmoor Cl BA3 ... 139 B6
Exmoor Rd BA2 ... 101 F2
Exmoor St BS3 ... 63 B3
Exmouth Rd BS4 ... 63 F1
Explore La BS1 ... 142 C2
Exton BS24 ... 105 A2
Exton Cl BS14 ... 80 B5
Eyer's La BS2 ... 143 C3
Eyers Rd BS24 ... 105 F7

F

Faber Gr BS13 ... 79 C4
Fabian Dr BS34 ... 36 E5
Factory Rd BS36 ... 37 F7
FAILAND ... 61 C3
Failand Cres BS9 ... 48 C5
Failand La
Easton-in-G BS8 ... 47 A1
Portbury BS20 ... 46 F2
Failand Wlk BS9 ... 48 C6
Fairacre Cl
Bristol BS7 ... 50 B5
Locking BS24 ... 106 B4
Fairacres Cl BS31 ... 81 F5
Fair Ash BS40 ... 129 D7
Fair Cl BA2 ... 136 E4
Faircross La SN14 ... 69 D8
Fairfax St BS1 ... 143 B3
Fairfield
Rode BA11 ... 137 F1
Tunley BA2 ... 117 A3
Fairfield Ave BA1 ... 85 A2
Fairfield Cl
Backwell BS48 ... 76 D7
Marshfield SN14 ... 69 F8
Weston-s-M BS22 ... 88 B1
Fairfield High Sch
Bristol BS5, BS7 ... 50 A3
Bristol BS6 ... 49 F2
Fairfield Mead BS48 ... 76 D7
FAIRFIELD PARK ... 85 A2
Fairfield Park Rd BA1 .. 85 A2
Fairfield Pl BS3 ... 63 B4
Fairfield Pneu Sch
BS48 ... 76 C6
Fairfield Rd
Bath BA1 ... 85 B1
Bristol, Montpelier BS6 .. 49 F2
Bristol, Southville BS3 .. 63 B4
Fairfield Terr
Bath BA1 ... 85 A1
Peasedown St John
BA2 ... 134 C7
Fairfield View BA1 ... 85 A2
Fairfield Way
Backwell BS48 ... 76 C6
Saltford BS31 ... 82 B4
Fairfoot Rd BS4 ... 64 A3
Fairford Cl BS15 ... 51 F2
Fairford Cres BS34 ... 36 C8
Fairford Rd BS11 ... 47 D7
Fair Furlong BS13 ... 79 A4
Fair Furlong Prim Sch
Bristol BS13 ... 79 B4
Bristol BS13 ... 79 B4
Fairhaven BS37 ... 27 F1
Fairhaven Rd BS6 ... 49 C4
Fair Hill BS25 ... 125 F8
Fairlawn BS16 ... 51 D4
Fair Lawn BS30 ... 66 B4
Fairlawn Ave
Bristol BS34 ... 35 F5
Bristol BS34 ... 36 A3
Filton BS34 ... 36 A3
Fairlawn Rd BS6 ... 49 F2
Fairlyn Dr BS15 ... 51 F3
Fairoaks BS30 ... 66 A3
Fairseat Ind Unit
BS40 ... 112 E7
Fairview BS22 ... 88 F4
Fairview Ct BS15 ... 65 D6
Fair View Dr BS6 ... 49 C2
Fairview Ho BS9 ... 48 F8
Fairview Rd BS15 ... 65 F8
Fairway BS4 ... 64 D1
Fairway Cl
Bristol BS30 ... 66 B4
Weston-s-M BS22 ... 88 B2
Yate BS37 ... 28 C2
Fairway Ind Ctr BS34 ... 35 F3
Fairways
Charlcombe BA1 ... 84 E4
Saltford BS31 ... 82 E2
Fairy Hill BS39 ... 98 D6
Fakeham Rd BS24 ... 121 F8
Falcon Cl
Bristol, Patchway BS34 .. 35 E8
Bristol, Westbury on T
BS9 ... 48 F8
Portishead BS20 ... 45 D4
1 Radstock BA3 ... 139 B8
Falcon Cres BS22 ... 105 D8
Falcon Ct BS9 ... 49 A7
Falcondale Rd BS9 ... 48 F7
Falcondale Wlk BS9 ... 49 A8
Falcon Dr BS34 ... 35 E8
Falconer Rd BA1 ... 84 A3
Falcon Rd GL12 ... 11 A5
Falcons Gate BS37 ... 27 C3
Falcon Way BS35 ... 8 D2
Falcon Wlk BS34 ... 23 E1
FALFIELD ... 9 E7
Falfield Rd BS4 ... 64 C3
Falfield Wlk BS10 ... 49 C8
Falkland Rd 4 BS6 ... 49 F2
Fallodon Ct BS9 ... 49 B5
Fallodon Way BS9 ... 49 B5
Fallowfield
Blagdon BS40 ... 110 E2
Bristol BS30 ... 66 D5
Weston-s-M BS22 ... 88 F3
Falmouth Cl BS48 ... 60 A1
Falmouth Rd BS7 ... 49 E4
Fane Cl BS10 ... 35 A3
Fanshawe Rd BS14 ... 80 A7
Faraday Rd 2 BS8 ... 62 F5
Farendell Rd BS16 ... 38 B1
Far Handstones BS30 ... 66 A4
Farington Rd BS10 ... 49 D7
Farlands BS16 ... 53 B6
FARLEIGH ... 76 D7
Farleigh Ct BS48 ... 77 B8
FARLEIGH
HUNGERFORD ... 137 E8
Farleigh Hungerford
Castle* BA2 ... 137 E8
Farleigh La
Cromhall GL12 ... 10 C2
Hinton Charterhouse
BA2 ... 119 F1
Westwood BA2 ... 120 A1
Farleigh Rd
Backwell BS48 ... 76 C6
Clevedon BS21 ... 57 D1
Keynsham BS31 ... 81 D4
Norton St Philip BA2 ... 136 F5
Farleigh Rise BA15 ... 86 E1
Farleigh View BA15 ... 120 F3
FARLEIGH WICK ... 103 E4
Farleigh Wlk BS13 ... 79 A8
Farler's End BS48 ... 75 F8
FARLEY ... 44 B1
Farley Cl BS34 ... 36 C7
FARMBOROUGH ... 116 B6
Farmborough CE VA Prim
Sch BA2 ... 115 F6
Farmborough La BA2 .116 E6
Farm Cl
Bristol BS16 ... 52 B6
Weston-s-M BS22 ... 89 C4
Farmcote GL12 ... 19 D8
Farm Ct BS16 ... 51 E7
Farmer Rd BS13 ... 78 E4
Farmers Wlk BS35 ... 8 B4
Farmhouse Cl 7 BS48 ... 59 E2
Farmhouse Ct 1 BS48 ... 59 E1
Farm La
Easter Compton BS35 ... 22 E2
Wellow BA2 ... 118 E1
Farm Lees GL12 ... 11 A6
Farm Rd
Bristol BS16 ... 51 E7
Hutton BS24 ... 105 E2
Weston-s-M BS22 ... 88 B1
Farmwell Cl BS13 ... 79 B5
Farnaby Cl BS4 ... 79 C7
Farnborough Rd BS24 106 C4
Farndale BS5 ... 65 A6
Farndale Rd BS22 ... 105 D8
Farne Cl BS9 ... 49 B5
Farrant Cl BS4 ... 79 D6
Farrier Wy BS14 ... 80 D3
Farringford Ho BS5 ... 50 D2
Farrington Fields
BS39 ... 132 C3
Farrington Fields Trad Est
BS39 ... 132 C3
FARRINGTON
GURNEY ... 132 A3
Farrington Gurney By-Pass
BS39 ... 132 A3
Farrington Gurney CE Prim
Sch BS39 ... 132 A4
Farrington Rd BS39 ... 132 C5
Farrington Way BS39 .. 132 A3
Farrs La BA2 ... 102 B2
Farr's La BS1 ... 143 A2
Farr St BS11 ... 47 B8
Farthing Combe BS26 125 D2
Farthing Row BA11 ... 137 E1
FAULKLAND ... 135 E2
Faulkland La BA2, BA3 135 C4
Faulkland Rd BA2 ... 101 D5
Faulkland View BA2 ... 134 E7
Faversham Dr BS24 ... 105 A1
Fawkes Cl BS15 ... 66 B8
Featherbed La
Chew Stoke BS40 ... 95 A3
Clutton BS39 ... 114 C6
Oldbury-on-S BS35 ... 7 B6
Featherstone Rd 4
BS16 ... 50 F4
Fedden Village BS21 ... 44 F5
Feeder Rd BS2 ... 64 A5
Felix Rd BS5 ... 64 B8
Felstead Rd BS10 ... 35 E1
Feltham Ct BS34 ... 35 F2
Feltham Rd BS16 ... 53 C6
Feltmakers La BS37 ... 27 B6
FELTON ... 94 D8
Felton Gr BS13 ... 79 A8
Felton La BS40 ... 94 E7
Felton St BS40 ... 94 C7
Fenbrook Cl BS16 ... 37 B1
Feniton 6 BS22 ... 89 A2
Fennel Dr BS34 ... 37 A7
Fennel La BS26 ... 125 B2
Fennell Gr BS10 ... 35 A2
Fenners BS22 ... 89 B4
Fenns La BS41 ... 61 E1
Fenshurst Gdns BS41 ... 77 F8
Fenswood Cl BS41 ... 61 F1
Fenswood Ct BS41 ... 61 E1
Fenswood Mead BS41 .. 61 E1
Fenswood Rd BS41 ... 61 E1
Fenton Cl BS31 ... 82 D3
Fenton Ct BS7 ... 49 D4
Fenton Rd BS7 ... 49 D4
Ferenberge Cl BA2 ... 116 A6
Fermaine Ave BS4 ... 64 F3
Fernbank Ct 2 BS6 ... 49 C2
Fernbank Rd BS6 ... 49 C2
Fernbrook Cl BS16 ... 37 B1
Fern Cl
Bristol BS10 ... 35 B3
Midsomer Norton BA3 .. 133 B1
Ferncliffe BS8 ... 62 E7
Ferndale Ave BS30 ... 66 A3
Ferndale Cl BS32 ... 24 D7
Ferndale Rd
Bath BA1 ... 85 C3
Bristol BS34 ... 36 A2
Portishead BS20 ... 45 D6
Ferndene BS32 ... 24 C2
Ferndown BS37 ... 27 E1
Ferndown Cl BS11 ... 48 A7
Ferndown Grange BS9 . 49 B6
Ferney Leaze La BS39 .115 C3
Fern Gr
Bristol BS32 ... 36 D8
Nailsea BS48 ... 75 C8
Fernhill BS32 ... 24 C7
Fernhill Ct
Bristol BS11 ... 34 B1
Tockington BS32 ... 24 C7
Fernhill La BS11 ... 34 B1
Fernhurst Rd BS5 ... 50 F1
Fern Lea BS24 ... 122 B6
Fernlea Gdns BS20 ... 47 B4
Fernlea Rd BS22 ... 105 C7
Fernleaze BS36 ... 38 C6
Fernleigh Ct 1 BS6 ... 49 B2
Fern Lodge BS23 ... 104 D6
Fern Rd BS16 ... 51 D5
Fernside BS48 ... 76 A7
Fern St BS2 ... 49 F1
Fernsteed Rd BS13 ... 78 F6
Fernville Est BS21 ... 57 E2
Ferry Ct BA2 ... 102 B6
Ferry La
Bath BA2 ... 102 B6
Lympsham BS24 ... 122 C3
Ferryman's Ct BS2 ... 143 B2
Ferry Rd BS15 ... 65 D1
Ferry St BS1 ... 143 B2
Ferry Steps Ind Est BS2 64 A4
Fersfield BA2 ... 102 B3
Feynman Way Central
BS16 ... 52 C8
Feynman Way N BS16 .. 38 C1
Fiddes Rd BS6 ... 49 C4
Fiddlers Wood La BS32. 36 E8
Fielders The BS22 ... 89 B4
Fieldfare BS16 ... 38 A2
Fieldfare Ave BS20 ... 46 A6
Fieldfare Cl BS31 ... 81 C3
Fieldfare Gdns BS49 ... 73 F2
Field Farm Cl BS34 ... 36 F4
Fieldgardens Rd BS39 114 F1
Field Grove La BS30 ... 82 C8
Fielding Ho BA2 ... 101 A6
Fielding's Rd BA2 ... 101 C6
Fieldins BA15 ... 120 E7
Field La
Bristol BS30 ... 65 F3
Dyrham SN14 ... 54 F6
Littleton-u-S BS35 ... 14 A8
Tytherington BS35 ... 15 E3
Field Marshal Slim Ct 24
BS2 ... 143 C3
Field Rd BS15 ... 51 C1
Fields The BS22 ... 89 D2
Field View 9 BS5 ... 64 A8
Field View Dr BS16 ... 51 C6
Fieldway BS25 ... 108 B4
Fiennes Cl BS16 ... 51 E4
Fifth Ave
Bristol BS14 ... 80 B7
Bristol, Filton BS7 ... 36 A1
Fifth Way BS11 ... 33 E2
Filby Dr BS34 ... 36 C8
Filer Cl BA2 ... 134 D8
FILTON ... 36 B3
Filton Abbey Wood Sta
BS34 ... 36 B1
Filton Ave
Bristol, Filton BS34 ... 36 B3
Bristol, Horfield BS7,
BS34 ... 50 A7
Filton Avenue Jun & Inf
Schs BS7 ... 50 A7
Filton Coll BS34 ... 36 A4
Filton Coll (WISE Campus)
BS34 ... 36 D3
Filton Gr BS7 ... 49 F6
Filton High Sch BS34 ... 36 D3
Filton Hill Prim Sch
BS34 ... 36 B4
Filton La BS34 ... 36 D2
Filton Rd
Bristol, Frenchay BS16 .. 36 F2
Bristol, Harry Stoke BS34 36 D2
Bristol, Horfield BS7 ... 49 F8
Filton Rdbt BS34 ... 36 A2
Filton Road Avon Ring Rd
BS16 ... 37 C1
Filwood Broadway BS4. 79 E8
Filwood Ct BS16 ... 51 B3
Filwood Dr BS15 ... 65 F8
Filwood Ho BS15 ... 65 F8
FILWOOD PARK ... 79 E8
Filwood Rd BS16 ... 51 A3
Finch Cl
Thornbury BS35 ... 8 C2
Weston-s-M BS22 ... 105 E8
Finches The BS20 ... 45 F6
Finch Rd BS37 ... 40 A8
Finisterre Par BS20 ... 45 F6
Finmere Gdns BS22 ... 89 A4
Fircliff Pk BS20 ... 45 D7
Fireclay Rd BS5 ... 64 D6
Fire Engine La BS36 ... 38 D7
Fire Station La BS11 ... 33 B2
Firework Cl BS15 ... 66 B8
Firfield St BS4 ... 64 A4
Firgrove Cres BS37 ... 28 A2
Firgrove La BA2 ... 117 B1
Fir La BS40 ... 127 B5
Fir Leaze BS48 ... 59 B1
Fir Rd SN14 ... 70 F6
Firs Ct BS31 ... 81 C4
First Ave
Bath BA2 ... 101 E4
Bristol BS14 ... 80 A7
Bristol, St Anne's BS4 ... 64 E5
Portbury BS20 ... 46 E5
Radstock BA3 ... 139 C8
First Field Way BS34 ... 35 E6
Firs The
Bath BA2 ... 102 B1
Bristol BS16 ... 51 E6
Limpley Stoke BA2 ... 120 A5
First Way BS11 ... 33 C1
Fir Tree Ave
Paulton BS39 ... 132 F4

Fir Tree Ave continued
Weston-s-M BS24 . . . . . . .105 E4
Fir Tree Cl BS34 . . . . 35 F7
Fir Tree La BS5 . . . . 65 A7
Fisher Ave BS15 . . . . 52 A1
Fisher Rd BS15 . . . . 52 A1
Fishers Mead BS41 . . . . . . 61 E1
FISHPONDS 51 A5
Fishponds Rd BS5 . . . . 50 D3
Fishponds Trad Est
BS5 . . . . 50 E2
Fishpool Hill BS10 . . . . . . 35 B4
Fitchett Wlk BS10 . . . . 34 F3
Fitzgerald Rd BS3 . . . . 63 F3
Fitzgerald St BS34 . . . . . . 35 F5
Fitzharding Ho 8
BS1 . . . . .143 A3
Fitzharding Rd BS20 . . . . . 47 E3
Fitzroy Circ BS20 . . . . 45 F6
Fitzroy Ho 3 BA2 . . . . . .141 C3
Fitzroy Rd BS16 . . . . 51 B2
Fitzroy St BS4 . . . . 64 A4
Fitzroy Terr 7 BS6 . . . . . . 49 B2
Five Acre Dr BS16 . . . . 51 A7
Five Arches Cl BA3 . . . . .133 D2
Five C Bsns Ctr BS21 . . . . 57 D1
Flagstaff Rd BS26 . . . . . .123 D7
Flamingo Cres BS22 . . . .105 E8
Flat The BS39 . . . . .114 D5
Flatts La BS39 . . . . .115 C4
Flatwoods Cres BA2 . . . .102 F3
Flatwoods Rd BA2 . . . . . .102 F3
FLAX BOURTON 76 F7
Flax Bourton CE Prim Sch
BS48 . . . . 76 F8
Flax Bourton Rd BS8 . . . . 61 B3
Flaxman Cl BS7 . . . . 50 B6
FLAXPITS 37 E5
Flaxpits La BS36 . . . . 37 E5
Fletcher Rd BS37 . . . . 27 C6
Florence Brown Com Sch
BS4 . . . . 79 D8
Florence Gr BS22 . . . . . .105 B8
Florence Pk
Almondsbury BS32 . . . . . 24 C5
Bristol BS6 . . . . 49 B4
Florence Rd BS16 . . . . 51 E3
Florida Terr BA3 . . . . . . .133 C2
Flowerdown Bridge
BS22 . . . . .105 D7
Flowerdown Rd BS24 . .106 D4
Flowers Hill BS4 . . . . 64 E1
Flowers Hill Cl BS4 . . . . . 64 E1
Flowers Hill Trad Est
BS4 . . . . 64 E1
Flowerwell Rd BS13 . . . . . 79 B5
Fogarty Park Rd 2
BS15 . . . . 65 D5
Folleigh Cl BS41 . . . . 62 B2
Folleigh Dr BS41 . . . . 62 B2
Folleigh La BS41 . . . . 62 B2
Folliot Cl BS16 . . . . 51 A7
Folly Bridge Cl BS37 . . . . 27 D2
Folly Brook Rd BS16 . . . . 38 B1
Folly Cl BA3 . . . . .138 E7
**Folly Farm Nature
Reserve**★ BS39 . . . . . .114 B5
Folly La
Bristol BS2 . . . . 64 A6
Shipham BS25 . . . . .125 E7
Weston-s-M BS23 . . . . . .104 E1
Folly Rd
Latteridge BS37 . . . . 26 A5
North Corner BS37 . . . . . 25 F4
Folly The
Bristol BS16 . . . . 51 F7
Cold Ashton SN14 . . . . . . 68 F6
Paulton BS39 . . . . .132 F6
Saltford BS31 . . . . 82 F2
Fontana Cl BS30 . . . . 66 B3
Fonthill Prim Sch BS10 . 35 E2
Fonthill Rd
Bath BA1 . . . . 84 E2
Bristol BS10 . . . . 35 D2
Fonthill Way BS30 . . . . . . 66 C2
Fontmell Ct BS14 . . . . . . 80 D7
Fontwell Dr BS16 . . . . . . 37 F1
Footes La BS36 . . . . 38 B7
Footshill Cl BS15 . . . . 65 C6
Footshill Dr BS15 . . . . . . 65 C7
Footshill Rd BS15 . . . . . . 65 C6
Forde Cl BS30 . . . . 65 F5
Fordell Pl BS4 . . . . 64 A3
Ford La
Bristol BS16 . . . . 52 B6
Ford Rd
Peasedown St John
BA2 . . . . .134 D8
Wellow BA2 . . . . .118 F1
Ford St BS5 . . . . 64 C6
Forefield Pl BA2 . . . . . . .141 C1
Forefield Rise BA2 . . . . .102 B4
Forefield Terr BA2 . . . . .102 A4
Forelands BS22 . . . . 87 B1
Forest Ave BS16 . . . . 51 B3
Forest Dr
Bristol BS10 . . . . 35 C3

Forest Dr continued
Weston-s-M BS23 . . . . . . 88 A1
Forest Edge BS15 . . . . . . 65 C4
Forester Ave BA2 . . . . . .102 B8
Forester Ct BA2 . . . . . . .141 C4
Forester La BA2 . . . . . . .102 B8
Forester Rd
Bath BA2 . . . . .102 B8
Portishead BS20 . . . . 45 D4
Forest Hills BS32 . . . . 24 B5
Forest Rd
Bristol, Fishponds BS16 . . 51 B4
Bristol, Kingswood BS15 . 65 D7
Forest Wlk
Bristol, Fishponds BS16 . . 51 B4
Bristol, Kingswood BS15 . 65 D7
Forge End BS20 . . . . 46 E3
Forgetmenot Way BS16 . 38 C1
Fortescue Rd BA3 . . . . . .133 F2
Fortfield Rd BS14 . . . . 80 B5
Forth Ave BS20 . . . . 45 F6
FORTHAY 5 E5
Forty Acre La BS35 . . . . . . 15 B3
Forum Bldgs BA1 . . . . . .141 C1
Foss Ct 8 BS5 . . . . 64 F8
Fosse Barton BS48 . . . . . 59 D2
Fosse Cl BS48 . . . . 59 C2
Fossedale Ave BS14 . . . . 80 C6
Fossefield Rd BA3 . . . . . .139 B6
Fosse Gdns BA2 . . . . . . .118 D8
Fosse Gn BA3 . . . . .133 E4
Fosse La
Batheaston BA1 . . . . 86 A4
Clandown BA3 . . . . .133 D3
Nailsea BS48 . . . . 59 D2
Fosseway
Clandown BA3 . . . . .133 E4
Clevedon BS21 . . . . 57 E2
Midsomer Norton BA3 . .139 A5
Radstock BA3 . . . . .139 C8
Fosse Way BS48 . . . . 59 C2
Fosseway Cl BA2 . . . . . . .134 C7
Fosse Way Cotts BA3 . . .133 D2
Fosseway Ct BS8 . . . . . . .142 A2
Fosse Way Est BA2 . . . . .101 D1
Fosseway Gdns BA3 . . . .133 D1
Fosseway S BA3 . . . . . . .139 B7
Fosse Way Sch BA3 . . . .139 C8
Fosseway The BS8 . . . . . .142 A2
Foss La
Norton BS22 . . . . 88 D6
Oldbury-on-S BS35 . . . . . . 7 E6
Foster's Almshouses 4
BS1 . . . . .143 A3
Foster St BS5 . . . . 50 B2
Foundry Cotts BA2 . . . . .116 B4
Foundry La BS5 . . . . 50 F2
Foundry The BA1 . . . . . .141 C3
Foundry Yd BS5 . . . . 50 F2
Fountain Bldgs 7
BA1 . . . . .141 B3
Fountain Ct
Bristol BS32 . . . . 24 C3
2 Yate BS37 . . . . 39 D7
Fountaine Ct 3 BS5 . . . . 50 C2
Fountain Ho 8 BA1 . . . . .141 B3
Fountain La BS25 . . . . . .125 B7
Fountains Dr BS30 . . . . . . 65 F6
Four Acre Ave BS16 . . . . . 51 E8
Four Acre Cres BS16 . . . . 37 E1
Four Acre Rd BS16 . . . . . . 51 E8
Four Acres BS13 . . . . 78 E4
Four Acres Cl
Bristol BS13 . . . . 78 E4
Nailsea BS48 . . . . 75 E8
Four Acres Prim Sch
BS13 . . . . 78 E4
Four Seasons Sq BS37 . . 27 E1
Fourth Ave
Bristol BS14 . . . . 80 B7
Bristol, Filton BS7 . . . . . . 36 A1
Radstock BA3 . . . . .139 D8
Fourth Way BS11 . . . . 33 E1
Fowey Cl BS48 . . . . 76 A8
Fowey Rd BS22 . . . . 89 A4
Fox and Hounds La
BS31 . . . . 81 F5
Fox Ave BS37 . . . . 27 D2
Foxborough Gdns BS32 . 24 D2
Fox Cl
Bristol BS4 . . . . 64 F5
Hawkesbury Upton GL9 . . 19 F3
Thornbury BS35 . . . . 8 D3
Foxcombe Rd
Bath BA1 . . . . .101 B7
Bristol BS14 . . . . 80 B4
FOXCOTE 134 F4
Foxcote BS15 . . . . 65 F7
Foxcote Ave BA2 . . . . . . .134 C7
Foxcote Rd BS3 . . . . 63 A3
Foxcroft Cl BS32 . . . . 36 F6
Foxcroft Rd BS5 . . . . 64 D8
Fox Ct BS30 . . . . 65 F3
Fox Den Rd BS34 . . . . . . 36 D3
Foxe Rd BS36 . . . . 38 B8
Foxfield Ave BS32 . . . . . .24 D2
Foxglove Cl
Bristol BS16 . . . . 50 E5
Thornbury BS35 . . . . 8 D2

Foxglove Cl continued
Weston-s-M BS22 . . . . . .89 A5
Foxglove Rd 2 BS16 . . . 52 C7
FOX HILL 102 A2
Fox Hill BA2 . . . . .102 A2
Foxhill Ho BA2 . . . . .102 A1
FOX HILLS 134 A1
Fox Ho
Bristol, Broom Hill BS4 . . 64 E3
Bristol, Victoria Park
BS8 . . . . .142 A3
Foxholes La BS32 . . . . . . 14 C1
Foxhol La G12 . . . . 10 D1
Fox La BS25 . . . . .125 A7
Fox Rd BS5 . . . . 50 B1
Foye Ho BS8 . . . . 62 E6
Fraley Rd BS9 . . . . 49 A7
FRAMPTON
COTTERELL 38 B7
**Frampton Cotterell CE
Prim Sch** BS36 . . . . . . 38 A8
Frampton Cres BS16 . . . . 51 C4
Frampton Ct
8 Bristol, Longwell Green
BS30 . . . . 65 F4
16 Bristol, Pile Marsh
BS5 . . . . 64 D7
FRAMPTON END 38 D8
Frampton End Rd BS37 . 26 D2
France La GL9 . . . . 20 B2
Frances Greeves Ct
BS10 . . . . 34 F1
Frances Mews 12 BS3 . . 63 C4
Francis Fox Rd 7
BS23 . . . . .104 E7
Francis Gr BA2 . . . . .102 A2
Francis Ho BS2 . . . . .143 A4
Francis Pl BS30 . . . . 65 F4
Francis Rd
Bristol, Bedminster BS3 . 63 C2
Bristol, Westbury on Trym
BS10 . . . . 49 C8
Yate Rocks BS37 . . . . 27 E6
Francis Way BS30 . . . . . . 66 D6
Francombe Gr BS10 . . . . 49 E6
Francombe Ho BS1 . . . . .143 A1
Frankcom Ho BA2 . . . . .102 B7
Frankford Mans 7
BS23 . . . . 87 C1
Frankland Cl BA1 . . . . . . 84 B1
Frankley Bldgs BA1 . . . . 85 B1
Frankley Terr 6 BA1 . . . . 85 B1
Franklin Ct BS1 . . . . . . .143 B1
Franklin's Way BS49 . . . . 74 F1
Franklyn Ct 6 BS16 . . . . 50 E3
Franklyn La 10 BS2 . . . . . 49 F1
Franklyn St BS2 . . . . 49 F1
Franklyn Terr BS39 . . . . .132 A4
Fraser Cl BS22 . . . . 88 F4
Fraser St 5 BS3 . . . . 63 D3
Frayne Rd BS3 . . . . 63 A4
Frederick Ave BA2 . . . . .134 C7
Frederick Pl BS8 . . . . . . .142 B3
Fredericks Way SN14 . . . 43 B3
Fredrick St BS4 . . . . 64 A4
Freeland Bldgs 1 BS5 . . 50 C2
Freeland Pl BS8 . . . . 62 F6
Freelands BS21 . . . . 73 C8
Freeling Ho BS1 . . . . . . .143 B1
Freemans La BS48 . . . . . 77 B2
Freemantle Gdns BS5 . . 50 C3
Freemantle Ho BS2 . . . .143 A4
Freemantle Rd BS5 . . . . . 50 C3
Freestone Rd BS2 . . . . . . 64 A6
Freeview Rd BA2 . . . . . .101 A5
Freezinghill La BS30 . . . . 68 B4
Fremantle La 9 BS6 . . . . 49 D1
Fremantle Rd BS6 . . . . . . 49 D1
Fremantle Sq BS6 . . . . . . 49 D1
FRENCHAY 51 B8
Frenchay CE Prim Sch
BS16 . . . . 51 B7
Frenchay Cl BS16 . . . . . . 51 B7
Frenchay Hill BS16 . . . . . 51 C7
Frenchay Park Rd BS16 . 50 F6
Frenchay Rd
Bristol BS16 . . . . 51 C6
Weston-s-M BS23 . . . . . .104 E4
Frenchay Village Mus★
BS16 . . . . 51 A8
French Cl
Nailsea BS48 . . . . 59 F3
Peasedown St John
BA2 . . . . .134 D7
Frenchfield Rd BA2 . . . . .134 D7
FRESHFORD 120 B5
Freshford Church Sch
BA2 . . . . .120 B5
Freshford La BA2 . . . . . .120 A4
Freshford Sta BA2 . . . . .120 C5
Freshland Way BS15 . . . . 65 B8
Freshmoor 6 BS21 . . . . . 57 H3
Friar Ave BS22 . . . . 88 E3
Friars Ho 4 BS37 . . . . . . 39 D7
Friary BS1 . . . . .143 C1
Friary Cl
Clevedon BS21 . . . . 57 E5
Westwood BA15 . . . . . .120 E4

Friary Grange Pk . . . 37 E6 BS36
Friary Rd
Bristol BS7 . . . . 49 D4
Portishead BS20 . . . . 45 B5
Friary Wood La BA2 . . . .120 B2
Friendly Row BS20 . . . . . 47 C5
Friendship Gr 2 BS48 . . 59 F2
Friendship Rd
Bristol BS4 . . . . 64 A2
Nailsea BS48 . . . . 59 F3
Friezewood Rd BS3 . . . . . 63 A4
Fripp Cl BS5 . . . . 64 B6
Frith La BS25 . . . . 90 C4
Frobisher Ave BS20 . . . . . 45 B5
Frobisher Cl
Portishead BS20 . . . . 45 A5
Weston-s-M BS22 . . . . . .88 E4
Frobisher Rd BS3 . . . . . . 63 A3
Frog La
Bristol BS1 . . . . .142 C2
Felton BS40 . . . . 94 C8
Frampton Cotterell BS36 38 E7
North Nibley GL11 . . . . . . 5 C5
Ubley BS40 . . . . .111 D1
Winford BS40 . . . . 94 F5
Frogmore St BS1 . . . . . .142 C2
Frog La BS40 . . . . 94 F5
Fromebank Jun Sch
BS37 . . . . 27 D3
Frome Ct BS35 . . . . 15 C8
Frome Glen BS36 . . . . . . 37 E4
Frome Old Rd BA3 . . . . .134 A2
Frome Pl 1 BS16 . . . . . . 50 E5
Frome Rd
Bath BA2 . . . . .101 D1
Chipping Sodbury BS37 . 28 C1
Norton St Philip BA2 . . .136 F3
Radstock BA3 . . . . .134 B2
Radstock BA3 . . . . .140 E8
Fromeside Pk BS16 . . . . . 51 B7
Frome Terr BS16 . . . . 50 E5
Frome Valley Rd BS16 . . 50 F6
Frome View BS36 . . . . . . 38 B7
Frome Villas BS16 . . . . . . 51 C7
Frome Way BS36 . . . . 37 E5
Front Home Cl BS34 . . . . 35 E6
Front St BS25 . . . . .108 E4
Froomshaw Rd BS16 . . . . 51 A7
FROST HILL 91 C6
Frost Hill BS49 . . . . 91 D7
Frost & Reed Ho 3
BS5 . . . . 64 F8
Fry Ct 2 BS3 . . . . 63 C4
Fry's Bottom
Breach BS39 . . . . .114 F7
Chelwood BS39 . . . . . . .115 A6
Fry's Cl BS16 . . . . 50 D4
Fry's Hill BS15 . . . . 51 E2
Fry's Hill BS4 . . . . 64 D2
Frys House of Mercy 10
BS1 . . . . .143 B1
Fry's La BS40 . . . . .109 F3
Frys Leaze BA1 . . . . 85 B2
Fry's Well BA3 . . . . .138 D3
Fryth Ho BS48 . . . . 60 D3
Fryth Way BS48 . . . . 59 C2
Fuchsia Rd BS16 . . . . 52 D8
Fuddlebrook Cotts
SN14 . . . . 69 F6
Fulford Rd BS13 . . . . 79 C5
Fulford Wlk BS13 . . . . . . 79 B5
Fullens Cl BS22 . . . . .105 D7
Fuller Rd BA1 . . . . 85 C2
Fullers Cl BS22 . . . . .125 A6
Fullers Way BA2 . . . . . . .118 D8
Fullwell Cl BA3 . . . . .135 D1
Fulmar Cl BS35 . . . . 8 D2
Fulmar Rd BS22 . . . . 88 F1
Fulwell La BA3 . . . . .135 D1
Furber Ct BS5 . . . . 65 B6
Furber Rd BS5 . . . . 65 B6
Furber Ridge BS5 . . . . . . 65 B6
Furber Vale BS5 . . . . 65 B6
Furland Rd BS22 . . . . 88 C2
Furlong Cl BA3 . . . . . . .138 F7
Furlong Pl BS26 . . . . . . .125 C1
Furlong The BS6 . . . . 49 D6
Furnace Way BS49 . . . . . 91 E4
Furnleaze BS39 . . . . .114 E3
Furnwood BS5 . . . . 65 A6
Furze Cl BS22 . . . . 88 B2
Furze Rd
Bristol BS16 . . . . 51 C3
Weston-s-M BS22 . . . . . . 88 A3
Furzewood Rd BS15 . . . . 65 F8
Fussell Ct BS15 . . . . 65 F8
Fylton Croft BS14 . . . . . . 80 B3

G

Gable Cl BS35 . . . . 23 A2
Gable Rd 8 BS5 . . . . 50 A1
Gables Cl BS29 . . . . .107 B3
Gadshill Dr BS34 . . . . . . 36 E5
Gadshill Rd BS5 . . . . 50 C2
Gages Cl BS15 . . . . 65 F7
Gages Rd BS15 . . . . 65 F7
Gainsborough Ct BA1 . . 84 B1

Gainsborough Dr BS22 . 88 F3
Gainsborough Gdns
BA1 . . . . .101 C8
Gainsborough Mews
BS10 . . . . 35 B2
Gainsborough Rd BS31 . 81 F5
Gainsborough Sq BS7 . . 50 B7
Galingale Way BS20 . . . . 45 F5
Gallagher Ret Pk
Bristol BS30 . . . . 65 E4
Weston-s-M BS23 . . . . . .105 A5
Galleries The BS1 . . . . . .143 B3
Gallivan Cl BS34 . . . . 36 B8
Galway Rd BS4 . . . . 63 E1
Gambril La GL12 . . . . 9 F5
Gander Cl BS13 . . . . 79 B5
Gannet Rd BS22 . . . . 88 F1
Garamond Ct BS1 . . . . .143 B1
Garden Cl
Bristol BS9 . . . . 48 C5
Weston-s-M BS22 . . . . . . 88 E2
Garden Ct BS8 . . . . .142 A4
Gardeners Wlk BS41 . . . 62 B1
Gardens Rd BS21 . . . . . . 57 E4
Gardens The
Bristol, Frenchay BS16 . . 36 F1
3 Bristol, Upper Soundwell
BS16 . . . . 51 D3
Gardner Ave BS13 . . . . . . 78 F7
Gardner Rd BS20 . . . . . . 45 D6
Garfield Ct BS5 . . . . 64 F8
Garfield Rd BS5 . . . . 65 A8
Garfield Terr 1 BA1 . . . . 85 C2
Garland Ho 7 BS21 . . . . 57 E2
Garner Ct 4 BS22 . . . . . 89 B4
Garnet St BS3 . . . . 63 B3
Garnett Pl BS16 . . . . 51 F7
Garonor Way BS20 . . . . . 46 F5
Garre Ho BA2 . . . . .100 F5
Garrett Dr BS32 . . . . 36 D7
Garrick Rd BA2 . . . . .100 F5
Garsdale Rd BS22 . . . . . .105 D8
Garston Cotts BS40 . . . .110 E3
Garston La BS40 . . . . . . .110 E3
Garstons
Bathford BA1 . . . . 86 D2
6 Clevedon BS21 . . . . . 57 F5
Wrington BS40 . . . . 92 E1
Garstons Cl
Backwell BS48 . . . . 75 F6
Wrington BS40 . . . . 92 E2
Garstons Orch BS40 . . . . 92 D1
Garstons The BS20 . . . . . 45 D4
Garth Rd BS13 . . . . 79 A8
Garton Ho 3 BS16 . . . . . 51 D5
Garvey Ho 14 BS5 . . . . . 64 C7
Gascoigns Way BS34 . . . 36 A7
Gaskins The BS7 . . . . . . 50 A5
Gas La BS2 . . . . 64 A6
Gassons BA2 . . . . .134 C2
Gaston Ave BS31 . . . . . . 81 F6
Gastons The BS11 . . . . . 48 A8
Gasworks La BS1 . . . . . .142 B1
Gatcombe Dr BS34 . . . . . 36 E4
Gatcombe Farm Ind Est
BS40 . . . . 92 D3
Gatcombe La BS48 . . . . . 77 C8
Gatcombe Mill La BS48 61 C1
Gatcombe Rd BS13 . . . . . 79 B5
Gatehouse Ave BS13 . . . 79 A5
Gatehouse Cl BS13 . . . . . 79 A5
Gatehouse Cl BS13 . . . . . 79 B5
Gatehouse Ctr The
BS13 . . . . 79 B5
Gatehouse Way BS13 . . . 79 A5
Gatesby Mead BS34 . . . . 36 E5
Gateway Terr BS20 . . . . . 45 E6
Gathorne Cres BS37 . . . . 27 D2
Gathorne Rd BS3 . . . . . . 63 B4
Gatton Rd BS2 . . . . 50 A1
Gaunts Cl BS20 . . . . 44 F4
GAUNT'S EARTHCOTT . . 25 B5
Gaunts Earthcott La
BS32 . . . . 25 B5
Gaunt's La BS1 . . . . .142 C2
Gaunts Rd BS37 . . . . 40 B8
Gauting Rd BS34 . . . . . . 35 E6
Gay Ct BA1 . . . . 85 E3
Gay Elms Prim Sch
BS13 . . . . 79 A4
Gay Elms Rd BS13 . . . . . 79 A4
Gayner Rd BS7 . . . . 36 A1
Gay's Hill BA1 . . . . .141 C4
Gays Rd BS15 . . . . 65 D4
Gay St BA1 . . . . .141 B3
Gaywood Ho 7 BS3 . . . . 63 B3
Gazelle Rd BS24 . . . . . . .105 B3
Gazzard Cl BS36 . . . . 37 E7
Gazzard Rd BS36 . . . . . . 37 E7
GEE MOOR 65 F6
Gee Moors BS15 . . . . 65 F6
Gefle Cl BS1 . . . . .142 B1
Geldof Dr BA3 . . . . .133 A2
Gentian Cl BS16 . . . . 52 C8
Geoffrey Cl BS13 . . . . . . 78 E6
George Cl BS48 . . . . 76 D7
George Ct 12 BS6 . . . . . 49 B2
George & Dragon La 11
BS5 . . . . 64 D7

George Holmes Wy
BS16 . . . . 50 E8
George Jones Rd BS2 . . 64 A6
George La SN14 . . . . 55 E1
Georges Bldgs BA1 . . . . 85 C3
Georges Ho BA2 . . . . . . 102 B6
George's Pl BA2 . . . . . . 102 B6
George's Rd BA1 . . . . . . 85 A1
Georges Sq BS1 . . . . . . 143 B2
George St
Bath BA1 . . . . 141 B3
Bath, Bathwick BA2 . . . 102 B6
Bristol BS5 . . . . 64 C8
Portishead BS20 . . . . . . 45 C2
Weston-s-M BS23 . . . . 104 E7
Georgian Ho BA2 . . . . . 141 C2
Georgian House (Mus)★
BS1 . . . . 142 C2
Georgian View BA2 . . . 101 C2
Gerald Rd BS3 . . . . 63 A3
Gerrard Rd BS23 . . . . . 104 F8
Gerrard Bldgs BA2 . . . 102 B7
Gerrard Cl BS4 . . . . 79 D7
Gerrish Ave
Bristol, Moorfields BS5 . . 64 C8
Bristol, Staple Hill BS16 . 51 F5
Gibbet La BS14 . . . . 80 D1
Gibbets Brow BS40 . . . 129 A3
Gibbs Ct 15 BS5 . . . . . . 64 D7
Gibbsfold Rd BS13 . . . . 79 C4
Gibbs La BS37 . . . . 40 B4
GIBB THE 43 F3
Gibson Rd BS6 . . . . 49 D1
Giffard Ho BS34 . . . . . . 36 C6
Gifford Cl BS37 . . . . . . 27 A8
Gifford Cres BS34 . . . . . 36 C6
Gifford Ct BS34 . . . . . . 36 D2
Gifford Rd BS10 . . . . . . 34 F4
Giffords Pl BS13 . . . . . . 79 A7
Gilbeck Rd BS48 . . . . . . 59 C2
Gilbert Rd
Bristol, Kingswood
BS15 . . . . 51 D1
Bristol, Moorfields BS5 . . 64 C8
Gilberyn Dr BS22 . . . . . 89 A3
Gilda Cl BS14 . . . . 80 C5
Gilda Cres BS14 . . . . . . 80 B6
Gilda Par BS14 . . . . 80 C5
Gilda Sq W BS14 . . . . . . 80 B5
Gillard Cl BS15 . . . . 65 B8
Gillard Rd BS15 . . . . . . 65 B8
Gill Ave BS16 . . . . 51 B6
Gillebank Cl BS14 . . . . . 80 D5
Gillham Ho 4 BS7 . . . . 49 D2
Gillingham Hill BS5 . . . . 65 A8
Gillingham Terr 3 BA1 . 85 B1
Gillingstool BS35 . . . . . 15 C8
Gillingstool Prim Sch
BS35 . . . . 15 B8
Gill Mews BS22 . . . . . . 89 B4
Gillmore Cl BS22 . . . . . 88 D1
Gillmore Rd BS22 . . . . . 88 D1
Gillray Cl BS7 . . . . 50 B6
Gillson Cl BS24 . . . . . . 105 D2
Gilpin Cl BS15 . . . . 51 F1
Gilroy Cl BS30 . . . . 66 B3
Gilslake Ave BS10 . . . . . 35 B3
Gilton Ho BS4 . . . . 64 E2
Gimblet Rd BS22 . . . . . 89 B4
Gingell's Gn 4 BS5 . . . 65 A8
Gipsy Patch La BS34 . . 36 C6
Glades The BS5 . . . . . . 50 E2
Gladstone Ct
Bath BA2 . . . . 102 C2
Bristol BS16 . . . . 51 E4
Gladstone Dr BS16 . . . . 51 E3
Gladstone La BS36 . . . . 38 C7
Gladstone Pl BA2 . . . . . 102 C2
Gladstone Rd
Bath BA2 . . . . 102 C2
Bristol BS14 . . . . 80 B6
2 Bristol, Kingswood
BS15 . . . . 51 D1
Gladstone St
Bristol, Bedminster BS3 . 63 B3
Bristol, Kingswood BS16 . 51 D3
13 Bristol, Pile Marsh
BS5 . . . . 64 D7
Midsomer Norton BA3 . 133 A8
Glaisdale Rd BS16 . . . . 51 A5
Glamis BS24 . . . . 105 E7
Glanville Dr BS39 . . . . 130 E6
Glanville Gdns BS15 . . 65 E7
Glass House La BS2 . . . 64 B5
Glastonbury Cl
Bristol BS30 . . . . 65 F5
Nailsea BS48 . . . . 60 B1
Glastonbury Way BS22 . 89 A2
Glebe Ave BS20 . . . . . . 45 E4
Glebe Cl BS41 . . . . 62 C2
Glebe Field BS32 . . . . . 24 A5
Glebe Ho
Bath BA2 . . . . 102 B5
Portishead BS20 . . . . . . 45 E4
Weston-s-M BS22 . . . . . 88 F3
Glebe Inf Sch The
BS49 . . . . 91 C4
Glebelands BA3 . . . . . 133 D1
Glebelands Rd BS34 . . . 36 A3

Glebe Rd
Bath BA2 . . . . 101 B4
Bristol BS5 . . . . 64 E8
Clevedon BS21 . . . . 57 E2
Long Ashton BS41 . . . . . 62 C2
Portishead BS20 . . . . . . 45 E4
Weston-s-M BS23 . . . . 104 E8
Glebes The BS5 . . . . . . 64 E8
Glebe The
Freshford BA2 . . . . . . 120 B4
Hinton Charterhouse
BA2 . . . . 119 D2
Pilning BS35 . . . . 22 C7
Timsbury BA2 . . . . . . 116 B3
Wrington BS40 . . . . . . 92 D2
Glebe Wlk BS31 . . . . . . 81 C4
Gledemoor Dr BS36 . . . 38 D7
Glena Ave BS4 . . . . 64 B2
Glenarm Rd BS4 . . . . . . 64 E2
Glenarm Wlk BS4 . . . . . 64 E2
Glen Ave BS8 . . . . 61 F8
Glenavon Ct BS9 . . . . . . 48 C5
Glenavon Pk BS9 . . . . . 48 C5
Glen Brook BS9 . . . . . . 48 D4
Glenburn Rd BS15 . . . . 51 B1
Glencairn Ct BA2 . . . . . 102 B6
Glencoe Bsns Pk
BS23 . . . . 105 A7
Glencoyne Ct 1 BS10 . . 35 C2
Glencoyne Sq BS10 . . . . 35 C2
Glencroft Way BS22 . . . 88 E3
Glendale
17 Bristol BS8 . . . . 62 F6
Bristol, Downend BS16 . . 51 E8
Bristol, Hillfields BS16 . . 51 C3
Glendare St BS5 . . . . . . 64 C6
Glendevon Rd BS14 . . . 80 A3
Glendower Ho BS8 . . . . 62 F7
Glen Dr BS9 . . . . 48 D5
Gleneagles BS37 . . . . . 27 E1
Gleneagles Cl
Nailsea BS48 . . . . 60 A1
Weston-s-M BS22 . . . . . 88 F3
Gleneagles Dr BS10 . . . 34 D3
Gleneagles Rd BS30 . . . 66 B6
Glenfall BS37 . . . . 39 D7
Glenfrome Prim Sch
BS5 . . . . 50 B4
Glenfrome Rd BS2 . . . . 50 B3
Glen Hospl The BS6 . . . 49 A2
Glen La BS4 . . . . 64 D2
Glen Park Gdns BS5 . . . 65 A8
Glen Pk
Bristol, Eastville BS5 . . . 50 C2
Bristol, St George BS5 . . 65 A8
Glenroy Ave BS15 . . . . . 51 B1
Glenside Cl BS16 . . . . . 51 C7
Glenside Hospl Mus★
BS16 . . . . 50 E5
Glenside Pk 3 BS16 . . . 50 E5
Glen The
Bristol, Hanham BS15 . . 65 B4
Bristol, Redland BS6 . . . 49 B3
Saltford BS31 . . . . 82 F1
Weston-s-M BS22 . . . . . 88 B2
Yate BS37 . . . . 27 C2
Glentworth Ct 19 BS23 . 87 C1
Glentworth Rd
Bristol BS8 . . . . 142 B2
Bristol, Redland BS6 . . . 49 C2
Glenview Ho BA2 . . . . . 134 D8
Glenview Rd BS4 . . . . . . 64 D2
Glenwood BS16 . . . . . . 51 C3
Glenwood Dr BS30 . . . . 66 B4
Glenwood Mans BS23 . . 87 D1
Glenwood Rd BS10 . . . . 49 C7
Glenwood Rise BS20 . . . 44 F5
Glen Yeo Terr BS49 . . . 91 C4
Glevum BS16 . . . . 52 C7
Glider Ave BS24 . . . . . 105 B4
Gloster Ave BS5 . . . . . . 50 D3
Gloucester Cl BS34 . . . . 36 D5
Gloucester Ho 11 BS2 . 143 C3
Gloucester La 18 BS2 . 143 C3
Gloucester Pl 2 BS2 . . 143 B3
Gloucester Rd
Almondsbury BS32,
BS35 . . . . 24 C6
Avonmouth BS11 . . . . . 33 A1
Bath BA1 . . . . 85 C3
Bristol BS32 . . . . 24 A3
Bristol, Bishopston BS7 . 49 E4
Bristol, Patchway BS34 . 36 B7
Bristol, Staple Hill BS16 . 51 D3
Stone GL13 . . . . 3 F3
Thornbury BS35 . . . . . . 8 C3
Upper Swainswick BA1 . 85 A7
Gloucester Rd N BS7,
BS34 . . . . 36 A4
Gloucester Row
6 Bristol BS8 . . . . 62 F7
Kingswood GL12 . . . . . 11 F8
**Gloucestershire Cty
Cricket Club★** BS7 . . 49 F4
Gloucester St
4 Bath BA1 . . . . 141 B3
5 Bristol BS2 . . . . . . 143 B4
9 Bristol, Clifton BS8 . 62 F7
Bristol, Eastville BS5 . . . 50 D3

Gloucester St continued
Weston-s-M BS23 . . . . 104 D7
Gloucester Terr 12 BS35 . 8 B1
Glovers Field BS25 . . . 125 F7
Glyn Vale BS3 . . . . 63 E1
Gnome Rd BS24 . . . . . 105 C5
Goddard Dr BS22 . . . . . 89 B4
Goddard Way BS10 . . . . 35 A1
Godfrey Ct 7 BS4 . . . . . 65 F4
Godwin Dr BS48 . . . . . . 59 C3
Goffenton Dr BS16 . . . . 51 B6
Goldcrest Rd BS37 . . . . 39 F7
Goldcrest Way
Dyer's Common BS35 . . . 22 C3
Portishead BS20 . . . . . . 45 F6
GOLDEN HILL 49 D5
Golden Hill BS6 . . . . . . 49 C5
Golden La GL12 . . . . 11 F4
Golden Lion Ct BS1 . . . 143 B2
Goldenrod Rd BS16 . . . . 52 D8
Golden Valley BS30 . . . 67 C6
Golden Valley La
Bitton BS30 . . . . 82 E8
Upton Cheyney BS30 . . . 66 F2
Golden Valley Prim Sch
BS48 . . . . 59 F2
Goldfinch Way BS16 . . . 53 C4
Goldney Ave
Bristol BS8 . . . . 142 A2
Bristol, Warmley BS30 . . 66 C7
Goldney Ct BS39 . . . . . 114 F1
Goldney Ct 7 BS16 . . . . 50 E3
Goldney Rd BS8 . . . . . 142 A2
Goldney Way BS39 . . . . 114 F1
Goldsbury Wlk BS11 . . . 34 A1
GOLD'S CROSS 113 E6
Golf Club La BS31 . . . . . 82 E2
Golf Course La BS34 . . . 35 F3
Golf Course Rd BA2 . . . 102 D6
Golledge Cl BA3 . . . . . 138 C4
Gooch Ct BS30 . . . . 66 C3
Gooch Way BS22 . . . . . 89 B3
Goodeve Pk BS9 . . . . . . 48 D3
Goodeve Rd BS9 . . . . . . 48 D3
Goodhind St BS5 . . . . . 64 A8
Goodneston Rd BS16 . . . 51 A3
Goodrich Cl BS37 . . . . . 27 B1
Gooding Hill BS11 . . . . . 34 A1
Good Shepherd Cl BS7 . 49 C4
Goodwin Dr BS14 . . . . . 79 F4
Goodwood Gdns BS16 . . 37 F1
Goold Cl BA2 . . . . 100 A8
Goolden St BS4 . . . . . . 64 A3
Goosard La BS39 . . . . . 132 E8
Goose Acre BS32 . . . . . 36 F6
Goosefoot Rd BS16 . . . . 52 D7
Goose Gn
Bristol BS30 . . . . 52 C1
Frampton Cotterell BS36 . 38 C8
Yate BS37 . . . . 27 E3
GOOSE GREEN
Bristol 52 C1
Yate 27 E3
Goose Green Way BS37 . 27 E4
Gooseham Mead BS49 . 91 D4
Gooseland Cl BS14 . . . . 79 F3
Goosey La BS22 . . . . . . 89 C2
Gordano Ct BS20 . . . . . 45 E5
Gordano Gate Bsns Pk
BS20 . . . . 45 E5
Gordano Gdns BS20 . . . 47 B4
Gordano Rd BS20 . . . . . 46 D7
Gordano St BS20 . . . . . 45 D3
Gordano Way BS20 . . . . 46 F5
Gordon Ave BS5 . . . . . . 50 E1
Gordon Bldgs BA3 . . . 134 A3
Gordon Cl BS5 . . . . 50 E1
Gordon Rd
Bath BA2 . . . . 102 B5
Bristol BS8 . . . . 142 B3
14 Bristol, St Pauls BS2 . 49 F1
Bristol, Whitehall BS5 . . 50 D1
Peasedown St John
BA2 . . . . 134 D8
Weston-s-M BS23 . . . . 104 F7
Gore Rd BS3 . . . . 63 A3
Gore's Marsh Rd BS3 . . 63 A2
Gores Pk BS39 . . . . . . 115 B2
Gorham Cl BS11 . . . . . . 34 C2
Gorlands Rd BS37 . . . . . 28 C1
Gorlangton Cl BS14 . . . 80 A7
Gorse Cover Rd BS35 . . 22 A7
Gorse Hill BS16 . . . . . . 51 C3
Gorse La
Bristol BS8 . . . . 142 B2
Cold Ashton BS30, SN14 . 68 D7
Gosford Mans 6 BS23 . 87 C1
Gosforth Cl BS10 . . . . . 35 B1
Gosforth Rd BS10 . . . . . 35 B1
Goslet Rd BS14 . . . . . . 80 E5
Goss Barton BS48 . . . . . 59 D1
Goss Cl BS48 . . . . 59 C1
Goss La BS48 . . . . 59 C1
Goss View BS48 . . . . . . 59 C1
Gotley Rd BS4 . . . . 64 D2
Gott Dr BS4 . . . . 64 D5
Goulston Rd BS13 . . . . . 79 A5
Goulston Wlk BS13 . . . . 79 A5

Goulter St BS5 . . . . 64 B6
Gournay Ct BS39 . . . . . 132 A3
Gourney Cl BS11 . . . . . . 34 B2
Governors Ho 2 BA2 . 101 D6
Gover Rd BS15 . . . . 65 C3
Govier Way BS35 . . . . . 22 C4
Grace Cl
Chipping Sodbury BS37 . 28 C1
Yatton BS49 . . . . 91 B8
Grace Ct BS16 . . . . 51 D6
Grace Dr
Bristol BS15 . . . . 66 A8
Midsomer Norton BA3 . 133 A4
Gracefield Sch BS16 . . . 51 C5
Grace Park Rd BS4 . . . . 64 D1
Grace Rd
Bristol BS16 . . . . 51 C5
Weston-s-M BS22 . . . . . 89 B4
Gradwell Cl BS22 . . . . . 89 B3
Graeme Cl BS16 . . . . . . 51 A4
Graham Rd
3 Bristol, Bedminster
BS3 . . . . 63 C3
Bristol, Downend BS16 . . 51 F6
21 Bristol, Upper Easton
BS5 . . . . 50 B1
Weston-s-M BS23 . . . . 104 E7
Grainger Ct BS11 . . . . . 47 E7
Grain Loft The 9 BS1 . 143 A2
Graitney Cl BS49 . . . . . 92 A8
Grampian Cl BS30 . . . . 66 C4
Granary The 8 BS1 . . . 143 A2
Granby Ct 18 BS8 . . . . . 62 F6
Granby Hill BS8 . . . . . . 62 F6
Grandmother's Rock La
BS30 . . . . 67 D2
Grand Par BA2 . . . . . . 141 C2
Grand Pier★ BS23 . . . 104 D7
Granfield Gdns BS40 . . 109 A5
Grange Ave
Bristol, Hanham BS15 . . 65 D5
Bristol, Little Stoke
BS34 . . . . 36 C6
Grange Bsns Pk The
BS24 . . . . 90 A5
Grange Cl
Bristol, Patchway BS32 . 24 C2
Bristol, Stoke Gifford
BS34 . . . . 37 A4
Weston-s-M BS23 . . . . 104 E1
Grange Cl N BS9 . . . . . . 49 B6
Grange Court Rd BS9 . . 49 A6
Grange Ct
Bristol BS15 . . . . 65 D5
Bristol, Henleaze BS9 . . 49 B6
Bristol, Westbury on Trym
BS9 . . . . 49 A8
Grange Dr BS16 . . . . . . 51 C6
Grange End BA3 . . . . . 139 B7
Grange Farm Rd BS49 . 74 A1
Grange Pk
Bristol, Frenchay BS16 . . 51 C8
Bristol, Westbury on Trym
BS9 . . . . 49 B6
Grange Rd
Bristol BS8 . . . . 142 A3
Bristol, Bishopsworth
BS13 . . . . 79 A5
Saltford BS31 . . . . 82 C3
Weston-s-M BS23 . . . . 104 E1
**Grange Sch & Sports Coll
The** BS30 . . . . 66 B3
Grange The
Bath BA1 . . . . 84 C1
Bristol, Coombe Dingle
BS9 . . . . 48 D7
Bristol, Sneyd Park BS9 . 48 F3
Flax Bourton BS48 . . . . 76 F7
Limpley Stoke BA2 . . . 120 B5
Grangeville Cl BS30 . . . 66 B3
Grangewood Cl 4
BS16 . . . . 51 C6
Granny's La BS15 . . . . . 65 E6
Grantham Ct 1 BS15 . . . 65 C8
Grantham Ho BS15 . . . . 51 C1
Grantham La BS15 . . . . 65 C8
Grantham Rd BS15 . . . . 51 C1
Grantson Cl BS4 . . . . . . 64 E2
Granville Cl BS15 . . . . . 65 B3
Granville Rd BA1 . . . . . . 84 E4
Granville St BS5 . . . . . . 64 C6
Grasmere Cl BS10 . . . . . 49 A8
Grasmere Dr BS23 . . . . 104 F4
Grassington Dr BS37 . . 40 A8
Grass Meers Dr BS14 . . 80 A4
Grassmere Gdns BS30 . 66 D6
Grassmere Rd BS49 . . . 91 B8
Gratitude Rd BS5 . . . . . 50 C1
Gravel Hill BS40 . . . . . 112 B7
Gravel Hill Rd N BS37 . . 28 A6
Graveney Cl BS4 . . . . . . 64 D1
Gray Cl BS10 . . . . 34 E2
Grayle Rd BS10 . . . . . . 35 A2
Grayling Ho BS9 . . . . . . 48 F7
Gray Rd BS4 . . . . 36 E6
Grays Hill BA2 . . . . . . 135 B5
Great Ann St BS2 . . . . 143 C3
Great Bedford St BA1 . 141 B4
Great Brier Leaze BS34 . 35 E7

Great Britain S.S.★
BS1 . . . . 142 B1
Great Brockeridge BS9 . 48 F6
Great Clover Leaze BS7 . 50 B8
Great Copsie Way 3
BS7 . . . . 50 C8
Great Dowles BS30 . . . . 66 A4
Great George St
Bristol, Brandon Hill
BS1 . . . . 142 C2
Bristol, St Pauls BS2 . . 143 C3
Great Hayles Rd BS14 . . 80 A6
Great Leaze BS30 . . . . . 66 A4
Great Mdw BS34 . . . . . . 37 A6
Great Meadow Rd BS32 . 36 F6
Great Park Rd BS32 . . . 24 C3
Great Pease Pk BS34 . . . 35 F6
Great Pulteney St
BA2 . . . . 141 C3
Great Stanhope St
BA1 . . . . 141 A2
GREAT STOKE BS34 . . . . 37 A5
Great Stoke BS34 . . . . . 37 A5
Great Stoke Way
Bristol, Great Stoke
BS34 . . . . 37 A5
Bristol, Harry Stoke BS34 36 D3
Greatstone La BS40 . . . 94 F5
Great Swanmoor Cl
BS34 . . . . 36 C3
Great Western Bsns Pk
BS37 . . . . 27 B3
Great Western Ct BS34 . 36 F4
Great Western La BS5 . . 64 C6
Great Western Rd BS21 . 57 F2
Great Wood Cl BS13 . . . 79 C4
Greenacre BS22 . . . . . . 88 B2
Green Acre Rd BS14 . . . 80 A3
Greenacres
Bath BA1 . . . . 84 B3
Bristol BS9 . . . . 48 E7
Midsomer Norton BA3 . 132 E1
Greenacres Park Homes
BS36 . . . . 38 E5
Greenbank Ave E BS5 . . 50 C1
Greenbank Ave W BS5 . . 50 C1
Greenbank Gdns BA1 . . 84 B1
Greenbank Rd
Bristol, Hanham BS15 . . 65 D5
Bristol, Lower Easton
BS5 . . . . 50 D2
Bristol, Southville BS3 . . 63 A4
Greenbank View
Bristol, Kingswood
BS15 . . . . 65 E7
Bristol, Lower Easton
BS5 . . . . 50 D2
Green Cl
Bristol BS7 . . . . 50 A8
Paulton BS39 . . . . 132 E6
Green Cotts BA2 . . . . . 102 C2
Green Croft BS5 . . . . . . 51 A1
Green Ct BS35 . . . . 14 A2
Greendale Rd
Bristol, Lower Knowle
BS3 . . . . 63 E3
Bristol, Redland BS6 . . . 49 B3
Green Dell Cl BS10 . . . . 34 D3
Greenditch Ave BS13 . . 79 C5
Greenditch Cl BA3 . . . . 138 C3
Green Ditch La BA3 . . . 138 B6
Greenditch St BS35 . . . 13 D1
Greendown BS5 . . . . . . 65 A7
Greendown Pl BA2 . . . . 102 A1
Green Dragon Rd BS36 . 37 D5
Greenfield Ave BS10 . . . 49 D8
Greenfield Cres BS48 . . 59 E3
Greenfield Ct BS10 . . . . 35 D1
Greenfield Pk BS20 . . . . 45 C3
Greenfield Pl BS23 . . . 104 C8
Greenfield Prim Sch
BS4 . . . . 79 C7
Greenfield Rd BS10 . . . . 35 D1
Greenfields Ave BS29 . 107 A3
Greenfields Way BS23 . 105 B4
Greenfield Wlk BA3 . . . 133 A3
Greenfinch Lodge BS16 . 50 E6
Greengage Cl 6 BS22 . 105 E8
Greenhaven 5 BS5 . . . 50 C1
Greenhayes BS37 . . . . . 40 C8
GREENHILL 133 A3
Greenhill BS35 . . . . 15 A4
Green Hill BS35 . . . . . . 15 A4
Greenhill Cl
Nailsea BS48 . . . . 59 D2
Weston-s-M BS22 . . . . . 89 A3
Greenhill Croft BS25 . . 108 B4
Greenhill Down BS35 . . . 15 A5
Greenhill Gdns BS35 . . . 15 A4
Greenhill Gr BS3 . . . . . . 63 A2
Greenhill La
Alveston BS35 . . . . 14 F4
Bristol BS11 . . . . 34 C1
Sandford BS25 . . . . . . 108 B4
Greenhill Par 5 BS35 . . 15 A5
Greenhill Pl BA3 . . . . . 133 A3

Greenhill Rd
Alveston BS35 . . . . .15 A5
Midsomer Norton BA3 .133 A3
Sandford BS25 . . . . .108 B4
Greenhouse La
Nempnett Thrubwell
BS40 . . . . .111 C6
Regil BS40 . . . . .94 D1
Green La
Avonmouth BS11 . . . . . . .33 B1
Bristol BS11 . . . . .47 B8
Butcombe BS40 . . . . . . .111 A7
Failand BS8 . . . . .61 C4
Farrington Gurney BS39 131 F6
Felton BS40 . . . . .94 C3
Hinton Charterhouse
BA2 . . . . .119 E1
Marshfield SN14 . . . . . . .69 E8
Priddy BS40 . . . . .128 B7
Rangeworthy BS37, GL12 17 B2
Severn Beach BS35 . . . . .22 B8
Stratton-on-t-F BA3 . . . .138 C1
Tytherington GL12 . . . . . .16 B8
Winsley BA15 . . . . .120 F6
Winterbourne BS36 . . . . .37 C7
Greenland Rd BS22 . . . .88 D1
Greenlands Rd BA2 . .134 C8
Greenlands Way BS10 . .34 F4
Greenleaze BS4 . . . . . . .64 B1
Greenleaze Ave BS16 . . .37 D1
Greenleaze Cl BS16 . . . .37 D1
Greenmore Rd BS4 . . . . .64 B2
Greenore BS15 . . . . . . .65 C7
Green Paddock BS34 . . .35 E6
Green Park Mews
BA1 . . . . .141 A2
Greenpark Rd BS10 . . . .35 E1
Green Park Rd BA1 . . . .141 B2
Green Park Station
BA1 . . . . .141 B2
GREEN PARLOUR 134 D2
Green Parlour Rd BA3 134 D1
Green Pastures Rd
BS48 . . . . .60 B2
Green Patch La BA2 . .115 E7
Green Pk BA1 . . . . .141 B2
Greenridge BS39 . . . . .114 F3
Greenridge Cl BS13 . . .78 E4
Green Sands Rd [3]
BS34 . . . . .35 F7
Greensbrook BS39 . . . .114 F3
Green's Hill BS16 . . . . . .50 E3
Green Side BS16 . . . . . .52 A6
Greenside Cl BS10 . . . .34 D3
Greenslade Gdns BS48 .59 D3
Greensplott Rd BS11 . . .33 E7
Green St
Bath BA1 . . . . .141 C2
Bristol BS3 . . . . .63 F4
Shoscombe BA2 . . . . . .134 E5
Green The
Backwell BS48 . . . . .76 A5
Bath BA2 . . . . .101 D1
Bristol, New Cheltenham
BS15 . . . . .51 E2
Bristol, Stoke Gifford
BS34 . . . . .36 E4
Chipping Sodbury BS37 . .41 A8
Cromhall GL12 . . . . .17 B8
Faulkland BA3 . . . . . . .135 D2
Hinton Charterhouse
BA2 . . . . .119 F1
Iron Acton BS37 . . . . . . .26 D4
Locking BS24 . . . . .106 A4
Luckington SN14 . . . . . .31 E4
Olveston BS35 . . . . .14 A2
Pill BS20 . . . . .47 D4
Wick BS30 . . . . .67 B5
Winscombe BS25 . . . . .125 A7
Green Tree Rd BA3 . . . .133 B3
GREENVALE 116 B1
Greenvale BA2 . . . . . . .116 B1
Greenvale Cl BA2 . . . . .116 B1
Greenvale Dr BA2 . . . . .116 B1
Greenvale Rd BS39 . . .132 D5
Greenview BS30 . . . . . .66 A2
Greenway BA3 . . . . . . .135 C1
Greenway Bush La
BS3 . . . . .63 B4
Greenway Ct BA2 . . . . .101 F4
Greenway Dr BS10 . . . .49 D8
Greenway Farm BS30 . .67 E5
Greenway Ho [10] BS6 . . .49 B2
Greenway La
Bath BA2 . . . . .102 A4
Cold Ashton SN14 . . . . .68 D5
Greenway Pk
Bristol BS10 . . . . .49 D8
[3] Clevedon BS21 . . . . .57 H3
Greenway Rd BS6 . . . . .49 B2
Greenways
Bristol BS15 . . . . .52 A1
Chilcompton BA3 . . . . . .138 C2
Greenways Rd [4] BS37 .27 E3
Greenway The BS16 . . .51 C3
Greenwell La BS40 . . . .109 C7

Greenwich Apartments
BS6 . . . . .49 C3
Green Wlk BS4 . . . . .64 A1
Greenwood Cl BS7 . . . . .49 E7
Greenwood Dr BS35 . . . .14 F4
Greenwood Rd
Bristol BS4 . . . . .64 A1
Weston-s-M BS22 . . . . . .88 E2
Gregory Cl BS30 . . . . . . .66 A6
Gregory Mead BS49 . . . .74 A1
Gregorys Gr BA2 . . . . . .118 D8
Gregorys Tyning BS39 .132 F6
Greinton BS24 . . . . . . .105 A2
Grenville Ave BS24 . . . .106 A4
Grenville Chapel [5]
BS8 . . . . .62 F5
Grenville Cl BS5 . . . . . . .64 F8
Grenville Pl [7] BS1 . . . . .62 F5
Grenville Rd BS6 . . . . . .49 E3
Greve Ct [5] BS30 . . . . . .65 F4
Greville Rd BS3 . . . . . . .63 B4
Greville St BS3 . . . . .63 C4
GREYFIELD 115 C2
Greyfield Comm BS39 .115 C2
Greyfield Rd BS39 . . . . .115 C2
Greyfield View BS39 . . .114 F1
Grey Gables BS35 . . . . .14 A3
Grey Hollow BS40 . . . . .129 F4
Greylands Rd BS13 . . . . .78 F7
Greystoke Ave BS10 . . . .35 C1
Greystoke Bsns Ctr
BS20 . . . . .45 D4
Greystoke Gdns BS10 . . .49 A8
Greystones BS16 . . . . . .37 E1
Grib La BS40 . . . . .110 F2
Griffen Rd BS24 . . . . . .105 E7
Griffin Cl BS22 . . . . .89 B2
Griffin Ct BA1 . . . . .141 B2
Griffin Ho BS21 . . . . .73 D8
Griffin Rd BS21 . . . . .57 G3
Griggfield Wlk BS14 . . . .80 A7
Grimsbury Rd BS15 . . . .66 A7
Grindell Rd BS5 . . . . . . .64 D7
Grinfield Ave BS13 . . . . .79 C4
Grinfield Ct BS13 . . . . . .79 C4
Grittleton Rd BS7 . . . . . .49 E8
GROSVENOR 85 C1
Grosvenor Bridge Rd
BA1 . . . . .85 C1
Grosvenor Ct [2] BS6 . . .49 B1
Grosvenor Pk BA1 . . . . .85 C1
Grosvenor Pl BA1 . . . . . .85 C1
Grosvenor Rd
Bristol BS2 . . . . .49 F1
Bristol BS2 . . . . .143 C4
Grosvenor Terr BA1 . . . .85 C2
Grosvenor Villas [9]
BA1 . . . . .85 B1
Grove Ave
Bristol BS1 . . . . .143 A1
Bristol, Coombe Dingle
BS9 . . . . .48 C7
[3] Bristol, Fishponds
BS16 . . . . .50 F4
Grove Bank BS16 . . . . . .37 C1
Grove Ct BS9 . . . . .48 E5
Grove Dr BS22 . . . . .88 C1
Grove Hall BS4 . . . . .64 D2
Grove Ho BA2 . . . . .102 B6
Grove Ind Est The BS34 .36 B8
Grove Jun Sch BS48 . . . .75 D8
Grove La
Faulkland BA3 . . . . . . .135 D2
Hinton SN14 . . . . .54 C6
Weston-s-M BS23 . . . . .104 D8
Grove Leaze BS11 . . . . .47 D6
Grove Mews The BS36 . .37 E7
Grove Orch BS40 . . . . . .110 E2
Grove Park Ave BS4 . . . .64 D2
Grove Park Ct BS23 . . . .87 D1
Grove Park Rd
Bristol BS4 . . . . .64 D2
Weston-s-M BS23 . . . . . .87 D1
Grove Park Terr BS16 . . .50 F4
Grove Pk
Bristol, Brislington BS4 . .64 D2
Bristol, Redland BS6 . . . .49 C2
Grove Rd
Banwell BS29 . . . . .106 E4
Bristol, Coombe Dingle
BS9 . . . . .48 D8
Bristol, Fishponds BS16 . .50 F4
Bristol, Redland BS6 . . . .49 A2
Weston-s-M BS23 . . . . .104 D8
Weston-s-M, Milton BS22 88 C1
Grovesend Rd BS35 . . . .15 D8
Grove St BA2 . . . . .141 C3
Groves The BS13 . . . . . .79 D4
Grove The
Bath BA1 . . . . .84 C1
Bristol BS1 . . . . .143 A1
Bristol, Oldland BS30 . . .66 A4
Bristol, Patchway BS34 . .36 B7
Hallatrow BS39 . . . . . . .132 B7
Rangeworthy BS37 . . . . .27 A8
Winscombe BS25 . . . . .107 F1
Wraxall BS48 . . . . .60 C3
Grove View BS16 . . . . . .50 E6
Grove Wood Rd BA3 . . .133 F1

Guardian Ct [8] BS8 . . . .62 F7
Guernsey Ave BS4 . . . . .64 F4
Guernsey Rd BS25 . . . .124 F7
Guest Ave BS16 . . . . . . .52 B7
Gug The BS39 . . . . .115 C2
Guild Ct BS1 . . . . .143 B2
Guildford Rd BS4 . . . . . .64 E6
Guildhall The ★
Bath BA1 . . . . .141 C2
Bristol BS1 . . . . .143 A3
Guinea La
Bath BA1 . . . . .141 C3
Bristol BS16 . . . . .51 A4
Bristol, Fishponds BS16 . .51 A5
Guinea St BS1 . . . . .143 A1
Gullen BS2 . . . . .135 A6
Gulliford's Bank BS21 . .57 H2
Gullimores Gdns BS13 . .79 B4
Gullivers Pl BS37 . . . . . .40 A8
Gullock Tyning BA3 . . . .133 B1
Gullons Cl BS13 . . . . . . .79 A6
Gullon Wlk BS13 . . . . . . .78 F5
Gullybrook La [3] BS5 . . .64 B6
Gully La BS35 . . . . .8 E7
Gully The BS36 . . . . .37 F7
Gumhurn La BS35 . . . . . .22 E7
Gunning Cl BS15 . . . . . . .65 D6
Gunter's Hill BS5 . . . . . . .65 A6
Guthrie Rd BS8 . . . . . . .142 A4
Gwilliam St BS3 . . . . . . .63 D3
Gwyn St BS2 . . . . .49 E1
Gypsy La
Keynsham BS31 . . . . . . .99 B8
Marshfield SN14 . . . . . . .69 F7
Gypsy Moth La BS24 . . .105 C5

H

Haberfield Hill BS8 . . . . .47 E2
Haberfield Ho [1] BS8 . . .62 F6
Hacket Hill BS35 . . . . . . .15 F8
Hacket La BS35 . . . . .15 F8
Haddrell Ct BS35 . . . . . . .14 F5
Hadley Ct BS30 . . . . .66 B6
Hadley Rd BA2 . . . . .102 B2
Hadrian Cl BS9 . . . . .48 C4
Hadrians Wlk BS16 . . . . .52 C6
Hadwells Rd [7] BS34 . . .35 F7
Haig Cl BS9 . . . . .48 B7
Hailwood Rd [3] BS15 . . .65 D5
Halbrow Cres BS16 . . . . .51 C5
Haldon Cl BS3 . . . . .63 D1
Hale Cl BS15 . . . . .65 D4
Hales Horn Cl BS32 . . . . .36 D6
Half Acre Cl BS14 . . . . . .80 A3
Halfacre La BS14 . . . . . . .80 B4
Halfpenny Row BA11 . . .137 E1
Halfway Gdn BS34 . . . . . .35 E7
Half Yd BS40 . . . . .109 D8
Halifax Rd BS37 . . . . .27 D4
Hallam Ct BS21 . . . . .57 E4
Hallam Rd BS21 . . . . .57 E4
Hallards Cl BS11 . . . . .47 F8
HALLATROW 132 B7
Hallatrow Bsns Pk
BS39 . . . . .132 A6
Hallatrow Rd BS39 . . . . .132 C6
HALLEN 34 C5
Hallen Cl
Bristol, Emerson's Green
BS16 . . . . .52 C6
Bristol, Henbury BS10 . . .34 D3
HALL END 17 D2
Hall End La BS37 . . . . . . .17 D2
Hallen Dr BS9 . . . . .48 C7
Hallen Ind Est BS10 . . . .34 A7
Hallen Rd BS10 . . . . .34 D4
Halletts Way BS20 . . . . . .45 D5
Halliwell Rd BS20 . . . . . .44 D4
Hall La
Cold Ashton BA1 . . . . . . .68 B3
Horton BS37 . . . . .29 E5
Halls Gdns BS34 . . . . . . .37 A4
Halls Rd BS15 . . . . .65 D8
Hall St BS3 . . . . .63 C2
Hall The BS20 . . . . .44 F5
Halsbury Rd BS6 . . . . . . .49 B4
Halstock Ave BS16 . . . . .50 F3
Halston Dr BS2 . . . . .143 C4
Halswell Gdns BS13 . . . .79 B4
Halswell Rd BS21 . . . . . . .57 F1
Halt End BS14 . . . . .80 C3
Halwyn Cl BS9 . . . . .48 D5
HAM 132 F5
Hamble Cl BS35 . . . . .15 C8
Hambledon Ho BS6 . . . .142 C4
Hambledon Rd BS22 . . . .89 C4
HAMBROOK 37 C3
Hambrook La BS34 . . . . .37 A3
Hambrook Prim Sch
BS16 . . . . .37 D3
Ham Cl BS39 . . . . .114 F1
Ham Farm La BS16 . . . . .52 B6
Ham Gn BS20 . . . . .47 D3
Ham Gr BS39 . . . . .132 E5
HAM GREEN 47 E4
Ham Hill BA3 . . . . .133 F3
Hamilton Ct [11] BS1 . . .143 A4

Hamilton Ho BA1 . . . . . .84 E3
Hamilton Rd
Bath BA1 . . . . .84 E2
Bristol, Southville BS3 . . .63 B4
Bristol, Upper Easton
BS5 . . . . .64 B8
[8] Weston-s-M BS23 . . .87 C1
Hamilton Terr BA2 . . . . .134 F5
Ham La
Bishop Sutton BS39 . . . .113 C5
Bristol BS16 . . . . .50 E6
Doynton BS30 . . . . .53 E1
Dundry BS41 . . . . .78 D3
Farrington Gurney BS39 131 F5
Kingston Seymour BS21 . .73 B2
Oldbury-on-S BS35 . . . . . .7 C7
Paulton BS39 . . . . .132 E5
Wraxall BS48 . . . . .60 B4
Yatton BS49 . . . . .74 A3
Hamlet The BS48 . . . . . . .60 A3
Ham Link BS40 . . . . . . .109 F3
Ham Rd BS24, TA8 . . . . .121 B3
Hams La BS26 . . . . .123 C3
Hams Rd BS31 . . . . .81 F7
HAMWOOD 123 C7
Ham Wood Cl BS24 . . . .105 B2
Hanbury Cl BS15 . . . . . . .65 D5
Hanbury Ct BS8 . . . . . . .142 A4
Hanbury Rd BS8 . . . . . . .142 A4
Handel Ave [2] BS5 . . . . .64 D7
Handel Cossham Ct [3]
BS15 . . . . .51 C1
Handel Rd BS31 . . . . .81 E5
Handford Way BS30 . . . . .66 B2
Hanford Ct BS14 . . . . . . .80 D7
Hang Hill BA2 . . . . .135 A6
HANHAM 65 C4
Hanham Abbots Jun Sch
BS39 . . . . .132 A6
Hanham Bsns Pk BS15 . .65 B5
HANHAM GREEN 65 C3
Hanham High Sch BS15 65 C4
Hanham La BS39 . . . . . . .132 F7
Hanham Lodge BS15 . . . .65 D7
Hanham Mills BS15 . . . . .65 D7
Hanham Rd BS15 . . . . . . .65 D7
Hanham Way BS48 . . . . .59 B2
Hanna Cl BA2 . . . . .101 B6
Hannah More Cl BS40 . .92 E2
Hannah More Inf Sch
BS48 . . . . .75 D8
Hannah More Prim Sch
BS2 . . . . .143 C2
Hannah More Rd BS48 .75 C8
Hannay Rd BS27 . . . . . .126 B1
Hanover Cl BS22 . . . . . . .89 A4
Hanover Ct
Bath BA1 . . . . .85 B2
Bristol, Filton BS34 . . . . .36 A3
Radstock BA3 . . . . .134 C2
Hanover Ho
Bristol BS2 . . . . .64 A7
Portishead BS20 . . . . . . .45 B5
Hanover Pl
Bath BA1 . . . . .102 B8
[4] Bathwick BA2 . . . . .102 B8
Bristol BS1 . . . . .142 B1
Hanover St
[2] Bath BA1 . . . . .85 B1
[2] Bristol BS1 . . . . . . .143 A2
Bristol, Russell Town BS5 64 B8
Hanover Terr [5] BA1 . . .85 B1
Hansford Cl BA2 . . . . . .101 E1
Hansford Mews BA2 . . .101 F1
Hansford Sq BA2 . . . . . .101 E1
Hanson's Way [4] BS21 . .57 E2
Hans Price Cl [18] BS23 104 E8
Hans Price Ho [13]
BS23 . . . . .104 E8
Hantone Hill BA2 . . . . . .102 F8
Happerton La BS20 . . . . .47 E2
Hapsburg Cl BS22 . . . . . .89 A4
Harbour Cres BS20 . . . . .45 E5
Harbour Ho BS8 . . . . . . .142 A1
Harbour Rd BS20 . . . . . .45 D6

Harbour Road Trad Est
BS20 . . . . .45 F6
Harbours Edge BS8 . . . .142 B2
Harbour Wall BS9 . . . . . .48 B4
Harbour Way BS1 . . . . . .142 C1
Harbour Wlk BS1 . . . . . .142 C1
Harbury Rd BS9 . . . . .49 C7
Harbutts BA2 . . . . .85 F1
Harcombe Hill BS36 . . . . .37 E4
Harcombe Rd BS36 . . . . .37 D5
Harcourt Ave BS5 . . . . . .65 A6
Harcourt Cl BS31 . . . . . . .82 E2
Harcourt Gdns BA1 . . . . .84 B2
Harcourt Hill BS6 . . . . . . .49 C3
Harcourt Rd BS6 . . . . . . .49 B3
Hardenhuish Rd BS4 . . .64 D5
Harden Rd BS14 . . . . . . .80 E5
Harding Dr BS29 . . . . . .106 C7
Harding Rd BS16 . . . . . . .36 F2
Hardings La BA2 . . . . . . .99 A1
Hardings Row BS2 . . . . . .64 B4
Hardington Dr BS31 . . . . .82 A2
Hardwick Cl
Bristol, Broom Hill BS4 . .64 E3
Bristol, North Common
BS30 . . . . .66 D5
Hardwicke BS37 . . . . . . .39 C7
Hardwick Rd BS20 . . . . . .47 C5
Hardy Ave BS3 . . . . .63 A4
Hardy Ct BS30 . . . . .65 F5
Hardy La BS32 . . . . .14 A1
Hardy Rd BS3 . . . . .63 B2
Harebell Rd BS16 . . . . . . .52 D8
Hareclive Prim Sch
BS13 . . . . .79 C4
Hareclive Rd BS13 . . . . . .79 C4
Harefield Cl BS15 . . . . . . .65 C2
Harescombe BS37 . . . . . .39 E7
Harewood Ho BS6 . . . . . .49 A3
Harewood Rd BS5 . . . . . .51 A1
Harford Cl BS9 . . . . .48 C7
Harford Dr BS16 . . . . .37 C1
Harford Sq BS40 . . . . . . .96 B3
Harington Pl [2] BA1 . . . .141 B2
Harlech Way BS30 . . . . . .66 B2
Harleston St [1] BS5 . . . . .64 A8
Harley Ct [3] BS8 . . . . . . .62 F7
Harley La BS21 . . . . .58 C6
Harley Mews [2] BS8 . . .62 F7
Harley Pl [4] BS8 . . . . . . .62 F7
Harley St BA1 . . . . .141 B4
Harmer Cl BS10 . . . . .34 D3
Harmony Dr BS20 . . . . . . .44 F4
Harnhill Cl BS13 . . . . .79 B4
Harolds Way BS15 . . . . . .65 C6
Harpsichord Way
BS31 . . . . .82 B2
Harptree BS24 . . . . .105 A2
Harptree Cl BS48 . . . . . . .75 D8
Harptree Ct [5] BS30 . . . .66 A4
Harptree Gr BS3 . . . . .63 B2
Harptree Hill BS40 . . . . .129 B5
Harptree La BA3 . . . . . . .130 C1
Harrier Path [3] BS22 . . .105 E8
Harriets Yd BS31 . . . . . . .81 F5
Harrington Ave BS14 . . . .80 E6
Harrington Cl BS30 . . . . . .82 E8
Harrington Gr BS14 . . . . .80 E6
Harrington Rd BS14 . . . . .80 E6
Harrington Wlk BS14 . . . .80 E6
Harris Barton BS36 . . . . .38 B7
Harris Ct BS30 . . . . .65 F4
Harris Gr BS13 . . . . .79 B3
Harris La BS8 . . . . .61 F8
Harrison Cl BS16 . . . . . . .52 B6
Harrowdene Rd BS4 . . . . .64 B3
Harrow Rd BS4 . . . . .64 D3
HARRY STOKE 36 E4
Harry Stoke Rd BS34 . . . .36 E2
Hart Cl BS20 . . . . .47 E4
HARTCLIFFE 79 E4
Hartcliffe Engineering
Com Coll BS13 . . . . . . .79 E4
Hartcliffe Rd BS4 . . . . . . .79 E8
Hartcliffe Way BS3, BS4,
BS13 . . . . .79 C4
Hartcliffe Wlk BS4 . . . . . .79 F8
Hartfield Ave BS6 . . . . . .142 C4
Hartgill Cl BS13 . . . . .79 B3
Hartington Pk BS6 . . . . . .49 C2
Hartland [14] BS22 . . . . . .89 A2
Hartland Ho BS5 . . . . . . .64 C6
Hartley Cl BS37 . . . . .28 C1
Hartley Ho BA1 . . . . .141 B3
Harts Croft BS37 . . . . . . .27 F4
Hart's La BS39 . . . . .132 B7
Harts Paddock BA3 . . . .132 F3
Harvest Cl BS32 . . . . .24 C1
Harvest La BS22 . . . . . . .106 C3
Harvest Way
Thornbury BS35 . . . . .8 B3
Weston-s-M BS22 . . . . . .89 A5
Harvey Cl BS22 . . . . .89 A4
Harvey's La [6] BS5 . . . . .64 F8
Harwood Gn BS22 . . . . . .88 E4
Harwood Ho [14] BS5 . . .64 B7
Harwood Sq BS7 . . . . . . .49 E5
Haselbury Gr BS31 . . . . . .82 E2
Haskins Ct [4] BS30 . . . . .66 A4

Haslemere Ind Est
BS11..............................33 C2
Hassage Farm La BA3 .136 A3
Hassage Hill BA2 ......135 E7
Hassell Dr BS2............64 A7
Hastings Cl BS3..........63 C1
Hastings Rd BS3..........63 C1
Hatches La BS24 ....121 E3
Hatchet Hill BA3, BA11 140 E4
Hatchet La BS34 ....36 E4
Hatchet Rd BS34 ....36 E5
Hatchmere BS35..........15 D8
Hatfield Bldgs BA2....102 B5
Hatfield Rd
   Bath BA2..................101 C1
   Weston-s-M BS23 ....105 A8
Hathaway Ho 13 BS2 ..143 A4
Hatherley BS37 ....39 E7
Hatherley Rd BS7 ....49 E4
Hathway Wlk BS5......64 A8
Hatters' La BS37 ....28 C1
Hatton Rd BS7..............50 C8
Haugh BA15..................103 D2
Havage Dro BS24 ......107 D8
Haven The BS15............51 E1
Haversham Cl BS22 ......88 D1
Haverstock Rd BS4......64 A4
Haviland Gr BA1..........84 B3
Haviland Ho 7 BS2 ..143 C3
Haviland Pk BA1..........84 B2
Havory BA1....................85 C1
Havyat Rd BS40 ....109 E8
Havyat Road Trad Est
BS40..............................92 E1
HAVYATT GREEN....109 F7
Hawarden Terr BA1 ......85 B1
Hawburn Cl BS4............64 D2
Haweswater BS10........35 B2
Haweswater Cl BS30 ....66 B6
Hawke Rd BS22 ....88 E4
HAWKESBURY............19 D2
Hawkesbury CE Prim Sch
GL9..............................19 F3
Hawkesbury Grange
GL9..............................20 A2
Hawkesbury Rd
   Bristol BS16................50 E3
   Hillesley GL12............19 D6
HAWKESBURY UPTON..20 A3
Hawkesley Dr BS34......36 D6
Hawkesworth Rd BS37 27 C3
Hawkfield Bsns Pk
BS14..............................79 D5
Hawkfield Cl BS14 ....79 D5
Hawkfield Rd BS13......79 D5
Hawkfield Way BS14....79 D5
Hawkins Cl BS30..........66 C5
Hawkins Cres BS32......36 E8
Hawkins St BS2..........143 C3
Hawkley Dr BS32..........24 D3
Hawkridge Dr BS16......53 C5
Hawksmoor Cl BS14....80 A6
Hawksmoor La BS16 ....50 E8
Hawksworth Dr
   Bristol BS15................65 B5
   Weston-s-M BS22 ......89 C4
Haw La BS35..................14 B3
Hawley's La G12..........10 D2
Hawthorn Ave BS15....65 B5
Hawthorn Cl
   Bristol BS34................35 E7
   Charfield GL12............11 A4
   Portishead BS20 ....44 F5
Hawthorn Coombe
BS22..............................88 E3
Hawthorn Cres
   Thornbury BS35............8 C2
   Yatton BS49..................74 A2
Hawthorne Cl BS16 ....53 C5
Hawthorne Gdns BS16 51 F4
Hawthorne Rise BS10 ..35 C2
Hawthorne St BS4........64 A3
Hawthornes The BS16..51 F4
Hawthorn Gdns BS22....88 D2
Hawthorn Gr BA2........102 A1
Hawthorn Hill BS22 ......88 E4
Hawthorn Hts BS22 ......88 D3
Hawthorn Pk BS22........88 E3
Hawthorn Rd BA3......134 B2
Hawthorns La BS31......81 E5
Hawthorns The BS21....57 E3
Hawthorn Way
   Bristol BS34................36 E5
   Lyde Green BS16........52 C8
   Nailsea BS48..............60 A2
Haybob Rd BS35............8 B3
Hayborw Way BS39 ..132 E4
Haybow BS24................89 E2
Haycombe BS14 ....79 F6
Haycombe Dr BA2......101 A4
Haycombe La BA2 ....101 A3
Haycroft La GL13..........4 C6
Haycroft Rd BS34........36 A3
Hayden Cl BA2..........141 A1
Haydock Cl BS16..........37 F1
HAYDON........................139 F8
Haydon Ct 12 BS8......49 A2
Haydon Gate BA3......139 F8
Haydon Gdns BS7........50 B5

Haydon Hill BA3 ......140 A8
Haydon Ind Est BA3 ..139 F8
Hayeley Dr BS32 ....36 E6
Hayes Cl BS2................64 A7
Hayes Ct BS34..............36 A7
Hayesfield Pk BA2 ....141 B1
Hayesfield School Tech
   Coll (Upper) BA2......141 A1
Hayesfield Sch Tech Coll
   (Lower) BA2..............101 D6
Haye's La GL9..............30 F2
HAYES PARK............133 A2
Hayes Park Rd BA3...132 F2
Hayes Pl BA2..............141 B1
Hayes Rd BA3............132 F1
Hayes Way BS34..........36 A6
Hayeswood Farm
BA15..............................103 F5
Hayeswood Rd BA2 ..115 E3
Hayfield SN14..............70 A8
Hay Fields BS35............8 C3
Haygarth Ct BA1......141 B4
Hay Hill BA1..............141 B3
Hay La BS40................94 D6
Hay Leaze BS37..........27 D4
Hayleigh Ho BS13......79 C4
Haymarket The BS1 ..143 A3
Haymarket Wlk 9
BS1..............................143 A4
Haynes Ho 3 BS16......51 F4
Haynes La BS16............51 D5
Hay St
   Farrington Gurney
   BA3..........................138 A8
   Marshfield SN14..........70 A8
Hayter Ct BS10............35 D3
Haythorn Ct BS16........51 F5
Haythorne Ct 8 BS16..50 E3
Haytor Pk BS9..............48 D6
Hayward Cl BS21..........57 E1
Hayward Ind Est 1
BS16..............................51 D3
Hayward Rd
   Bristol, Russell Town
   BS5..........................64 C7
   Bristol, Staple Hill BS16..51 D3
Haywood Cl BS24 ....105 A1
Haywood Gdns BS24 ..105 B1
Hazel Ave BS6..............49 B2
Hazel Barrow BS40 ..129 A4
Hazelbury Dr BS30......66 C6
Hazelbury Rd
   Bristol BS14................80 C7
   Nailsea BS48..............59 D1
Hazel Cl BS37..............27 F5
Hazel Cote Rd BS14....80 B4
Hazel Cres BS35............8 D1
Hazeldene Rd
   Bristol BS34................36 A7
   Weston-s-M BS23 ....105 A4
Hazel Gdns BS35..........15 A4
Hazel Gr
   Bath BA2..................101 D4
   Bristol BS7................50 A4
   Midsomer Norton BA3..139 B8
Hazelgrove BS36..........37 E5
Hazel La BS32, BS35....14 E3
Hazell Cl BS21..............57 G1
Hazel St BS14................79 E5
Hazel Terr BA3............139 C8
Hazelton Rd BS7..........49 D3
Hazel Way BA2............118 D8
Hazelwood Ct BS9......48 D3
Hazelwood Rd BS9......48 D3
Hazleton Gdns BA2 ..102 F3
Head Croft BS48..........77 B8
Headford Ave BS5........65 B7
Headford Rd BS13........63 D1
Headington Cl BS15....65 D4
Headley Ct BS13..........79 B6
Headley La BS13..........79 B7
HEADLEY PARK........79 B6
Headley Park Ave BS13 79 B7
Headley Park Prim Sch
BS13..............................79 B6
Headley Park Rd BS13..79 A7
Headley Rd BS13..........79 A6
Headley Wlk BS13......79 B7
Healey Dr SN14..........54 C6
Heart Meers BS14........80 B5
Heath Cl BS36..............37 C6
Heathcote Dr BS36......38 D7
Heathcote La BS36......38 D7
Heathcote Rd
   Bristol, Chester Park
   BS16..........................51 B2
   Bristol, Staple Hill BS16 51 B2
Heathcote Wlk BS16....51 C2
Heath Ct BS16..............51 D7
HEATH END..................17 B8
Heather Ave BS36........38 B6
Heather Cl BS15..........65 B8
Heatherdene BS14......79 F7
Heather Dr BA2..........118 D8
Heather Rd BS16..........52 C7
Heathfield Cl
   Bath BA1....................84 A3
   Keynsham BS31..........81 C5
Heathfield Cres BS14..80 B4

Heathfield Rd BS48......59 E3
Heathfields BS16..........51 D8
Heathfield Way BS48....59 E2
Heathgate BS49............91 B8
Heathgates BS23......104 D4
Heath Gdns
   Bristol BS16................51 D8
   Frampton Cotterell BS36 38 C5
Heath House La BS7,
BS16..............................50 B4
Heath Rd
   Bristol, Downend BS16..51 D8
   Bristol, Eastville BS5....50 B3
   Bristol, Hanham BS15 ..65 A4
   Nailsea BS48..............59 F3
Heath Ridge BS41........62 A2
Heath Rise BS30..........66 B5
Heath St BS5................50 C3
Heath The BS9..............48 E3
Heath Wlk BS16............51 D7
Hebden Rd BA15........120 F3
Heber St BS5................64 C7
Hebron Ct BS3..............63 C3
Hebron Rd BS3..............63 C3
Hedgemead Cl BS16....50 D5
Hedgemead Ct BA1 ...141 C4
Hedgemead View BS16 50 D5
Hedgerows 2 BS32......24 D1
Hedgers Cl BS3............63 A2
Hedges Cl 3 BS21......57 D1
Hedges The BS22........89 C3
Hedwick Ave BS5........64 E7
Hedwick St BS5............64 E7
Heggard Cl BS13..........79 A5
Helens Rd BS25..........108 B4
Heligan Wlk BS24......105 E7
Hellier Wlk BS13..........79 C3
Helston Rd BS48..........60 A1
Hemmings Par 4 BS5..64 B7
Hemming Way BS24....105 E5
Hemplow Cl BS14........80 D7
Hempton Field Dr BS34 36 A7
Hempton La BS32........24 B2
Henacre Rd BS11..........47 F8
HENBURY......................34 E2
Henbury Court Prim Sch
BS10..............................34 F3
Henbury Gdns BS10....34 E2
Henbury Hill
   Bristol BS9..................34 F1
   Bristol BS9..................48 F8
Henbury Ho BA2........102 E4
Henbury Rd
   Bristol BS9..................48 F8
   Bristol, Hanham BS15 ..65 B5
   Bristol, Henbury BS10 ..34 F2
   Bristol, Westbury on Trym
   BS9..........................49 A8
Henbury Sch BS10......34 E3
Hencliffe Rd BS14........80 D7
Hencliffe Way BS15....65 B3
Henderson Ho 1 BS2 143 B4
Henderson Rd BS15....65 B5
Hendre Rd BS3..............63 A2
Heneage La GL12 ....9 F8
HENFIELD....................38 D3
Henfield Bsns Pk BS36 38 D2
Henfield Cres BS30......66 B3
Henfield Rd BS36..........38 C4
Hengasson La BS39 ..113 E6
Hengaston St BS3........63 B2
HENGROVE..................80 B6
Hengrove Ave BS14....80 B8
Hengrove Com Arts Coll
BS14..............................80 B7
Hengrove La BS14........80 B8
Hengrove Rd BS4........64 A2
Hengrove Way BS14....79 E6
Hen La BS40..................94 E3
HENLEAZE..................49 C6
Henleaze Ave BS9........49 A5
Henleaze Gdns BS9 ....49 A5
Henleaze Jun & Inf Schs
BS9..............................49 C5
Henleaze Park BS9......49 C6
Henleaze Park Dr BS9..49 C6
Henleaze Pk BS9..........49 C5
Henleaze Rd BS9........49 B6
Henleaze Terr BS9 ......49 B7
Henley Gr BS9..............49 B5
Henley Grove Ct BS9 ..49 B5
Henley La BS49............91 D7
Henley Lodge BS49 ....91 D7
Henley Pk BS49............91 C7
Henley View BS14......118 D1
Hennessy Cl BS14......79 F3
Henrietta Ct BA2........141 C4
Henrietta Gdns BA2 ..141 C3
Henrietta Mews BA2 ..141 C3
Henrietta Pl BA2........141 C3
Henrietta Rd BA2......141 C3
Henrietta St
   Bath BA2..................141 C3
   Bristol BS2................143 A4
   5 Bristol, Lower Easton
   BS5..........................50 B1
Henrietta Villas BA2 ..141 C3

Henry Butt Ho 11
BS23..............................104 E8
Henry Corbett Rd
BS16..............................50 F8
Henry Shute Rd
   Lockleaze BS16............50 E8
   Lockleaze BS16............50 F8
Henry St
   Bath BA1..................141 C2
   Bristol BS3..................63 F4
Henry Williamson Ct 1
BS30..............................66 A5
Henshaw Cl BS15........51 C2
Henshaw Rd BS15........51 C2
Henshaw Wlk BS15......51 C2
Hensley Gdns BA2 ....101 E4
Hensley Rd BA2..........101 E3
Hensman's Hill BS8 ..142 A2
Hepburn Rd BS2........143 B4
Herald Cl BS9..............48 D5
Herapath St BS5..........64 C6
Herbert Cres BS5........50 D3
Herbert Gdns BA2......115 E5
Herbert Rd
   Bath BA2..................101 D5
   Clevedon BS21............57 F4
Herbert St
   Bristol, Moorfields BS5..64 C8
   Bristol, Southville BS3..63 D4
Hercules BS34..............36 D6
Hercules Wy BS31........81 C3
Hereford Rd BS2..........50 A2
Hereford St BS3............63 D3
Heritage Cl BA2........134 D8
Heritage The BA2 ....133 E8
Herkomer Cl BS7 ....50 B7
Herluin Way BS22,
BS23..............................105 B6
Hermes Cl BS31..........82 D2
Hermitage Cl BS11......47 E7
Hermitage Rd
   Bath BA1....................84 E1
   Bristol BS16................51 E5
Hermitage Wood Rd
BS7..............................50 C8
Hern La BS48................77 E5
Heron Cl BS22............105 E8
Heron Ct BS21..............57 E2
Heron Gdns BS20........45 E4
Heron Rd BS5................50 B1
HERONS GREEN......112 C3
Herons Green La
BS40..............................112 C4
Herons Moor Acad
BS24..............................106 A8
Heron Way BS37..........40 A8
Heron Wlk BS31..........44 B1
Herridge Cl BS13..........79 B4
Herridge Rd BS13........79 B4
Hersey Gdns BS13........78 E3
Hesding Cl BS15..........65 C3
Hestercombe Cl BS24 105 E7
Hestercombe Rd BS13 79 B6
Hester Wood BS37......27 F4
Hestia Cl BS31..............81 C3
Hetling Ct 10 BA1......141 B2
HEWISH..........................90 C5
Hewish Ct BS23..........104 E8
Hewland Ct BS11........34 C2
Hexagon The BA2......101 E1
Heyford Ave BS5..........50 B4
Heyron Wlk BS13..........79 B4
Heywood Rd BS20........47 C4
Heywood Terr BS20......47 C4
Hibbs Cl SN14..............69 F8
Hickory La BS32............24 D5
Hicks Ave BS16............52 B8
HICKS GATE..................81 B8
Hidcote Mews BS24....105 E7
Hide Mkt BS2..............143 C3
Higgs Cl BS37..............27 E5
High Acre BS39..........132 F4
Higham St 4 BS2........63 F4
High Bannerdown
   Batheaston BA1..........86 B4
   Shockerwick BA1........86 B5
Highbury Cotts 7 BA1 85 A1
Highbury Ct 15 BS23 ..87 C1
Highbury Farm Bsns Pk
BS39..............................132 A8
Highbury Par BS23......87 C1
Highbury Pl BA1..........85 A1
Highbury Rd
   Bristol, Bedminster BS3 63 C2
   Bristol, Horfield BS7....49 F7
   Hallatrow BS39..........132 B7
   Weston-s-M BS23 ......87 C1
Highbury Terr 9 BA1..85 A1
Highbury Villas
   8 Bath BA1................85 A1
   Bristol BS2................142 C4
High Cnr BS10..............34 F1

Highcroft
   3 Bristol BS30..........66 C6
   Weston-s-M BS23 ......87 F1
Highdale Ave BS21......57 G3
Highdale Cl BS14........80 B4
Highdale Ct BS21 ....57 F3
Highdale Rd BS21........57 F3
High Down Jun & Inf Schs
BS20..............................45 A4
High Elm BS15..............65 E6
Highett Dr BS5..............50 A1
Highfield Ave BS15......65 D5
Highfield Cl BA2........101 B5
Highfield Cres BA3....138 C4
Highfield Dr BS20........44 E3
Highfield Gdns BS30 ..66 C2
Highfield Gr BS7..........49 D5
Highfield La
   Compton Martin BS40 129 B6
   East Harptree BS40....130 A3
   Horton BS37, GL9........29 C7
Highfield Rd
   Chipping Sodbury BS37 28 A1
   Keynsham BS31............81 F2
   Peasedown St John
   BA2........................134 C8
   Weston-s-M BS24......105 A1
Highfields
   Clandown BA3..........133 E4
   Hawkesbury Upton GL9..19 F2
   Stanton Drew BS39......96 F1
High Fields BA3..........133 D2
Highfields Cl BS34 ......36 F3
High Gr BS9..................48 B7
Highgrove St BS4........64 A4
Highgrove Wlk BS24 ..106 A8
High Kingsdown BS2 ..142 C4
High La BS36................37 C8
Highland Cl BS22 ....88 E2
Highland Cres 3 BS8 ..49 A2
Highland Pl 13 BS8......49 A2
Highland Rd BA2........101 B5
Highlands Dr GL11........5 E4
Highlands La BS24......106 A8
Highland Sq 4 BS8......49 A2
Highlands Rd
   Long Ashton BS41........62 A2
   Portishead BS20 ....45 B5
Highland Terr 3 BA2 ..101 D6
Highleaze Rd BS30......66 C4
High Leaze Rd 8 BS34 35 F7
HIGH LITTLETON........115 C1
High Littleton CE VA Prim
   Sch BS39..................115 C1
High Mdws BA3..........132 F1
Highmead Gdns
   Bishop Sutton BS39....113 D3
   Bristol BS13................78 E4
Highmore Ct BS7..........50 B7
Highmore Gdns BS7....50 C7
Highnam Cl BS34........24 B1
High Pk
   Bristol BS14................64 B1
   Paulton BS39..............132 D6
High Point Ho 1 BS15 51 C1
HIGHRIDGE
   Bristol..........................78 F7
   Dundry........................78 D3
Highridge Cres BS13 ..78 F5
Highridge Gn BS13......78 E6
Highridge Inf Sch BS13 78 F6
Highridge Pk BS13......78 F6
Highridge Rd
   Bristol, Bedminster BS3 63 B2
   Bristol, Withywood BS13,
   BS41..........................78 E4
Highridge Wlk BS13....78 E6
High Six Gdns BS34 ....35 F6
High St
   Axbridge BS26..........125 B2
   Badminton GL9............30 E2
   Banwell BS29............107 A2
   Bath BA1..................141 C2
   Bathampton BA2........85 F1
   Batheaston BA1..........85 F3
   Bathford BA1..............86 D2
   Bath, Twerton BA2....101 B6
   Bath, Weston BA1........84 B1
   Bitton BS30................82 E8
   Blagdon BS40............110 E3
   Bristol BS1................143 A2
   Bristol, Clifton BS8......49 A2
   Bristol, Jefferies Hill
   BS15........................65 C5
   Bristol, Kingswood BS15 65 E8
   Bristol, Lower Easton
   BS5..........................50 B1
   Bristol, Oldland Common
   BS30..........................66 D4
   Bristol, Shirehampton
   BS11..........................47 E6
   Bristol, Staple Hill BS16..51 D4
   Bristol, Warmley BS15 ..66 B8
   Bristol, Westbury on Trym
   BS9..........................49 A7
   Chew Magna BS40......96 A3

High St continued
Chipping Sodbury BS37 . . **28** B1
Claverham BS49 . . . . **74** F1
Congresbury BS49 . . . . . . **91** D4
Doynton BS30 . . . . **53** F1
East Harptree BS40 . . . **129** F5
Faulkland BA3 . . . . **135** D1
Freshford BA2 . . . . **120** B5
Hawkesbury Upton GL9 . . **19** F3
High Littleton BS39 . . . . **115** D1
Hillesley GL12 . . . . **19** D8
Hinton Charterhouse
BA2 . . . . **119** C1
Iron Acton BS37 . . . . **26** D4
Keynsham BS31 . . . . **81** E6
Kingswood GL12 . . . . **11** F4
Marshfield SN14 . . . . **69** F8
Midsomer Norton BA3 . . **133** B1
Nailsea BS48 . . . . **59** F3
Norton St Philip BA2 . . . **136** E4
Paulton BS39 . . . . **132** E5
Paulton, Plummer's Hill
BS39 . . . . **132** E6
Pensford BS39 . . . . **97** E4
Portbury BS20 . . . . **46** E3
Portishead BS20 . . . . **45** D5
Saltford BS31 . . . . **82** F3
Thornbury BS35 . . . . **15** B8
Timsbury BA2 . . . . **116** B2
Tormarton GL9 . . . . **41** D1
Wellow BA2 . . . . **118** D1
Weston-s-M BS23 . . . . . **104** D8
Weston-s-M, Worle BS22 **88** E2
Wick BS30 . . . . **67** D6
Wickwar GL12 . . . . **18** A5
Winford BS40 . . . . **95** A7
Winterbourne BS36 . . . . . **37** D2
Woolley BA1 . . . . **84** F6
Wrington BS40 . . . . **92** D2
Yatton BS49 . . . . **91** C8
High View BS20 . . . . **45** A4
Highview Rd BS15 . . . . . . **51** F2
Highwall La BS14, BS31 . **80** F1
Highway BS37 . . . . **27** F2
Highwood Bsns Pk
BS34 . . . . **35** E7
Highwood La BS10,
BS34 . . . . **35** D7
Highwood Pk Cvn Site
BS34 . . . . **35** E6
Highwood Rd BS34 . . . . . **35** F7
Highworth Cres BS37 . . . **39** D8
Highworth Rd BS4 . . . . . **64** D6
Hildesheim Bridge
BS23 . . . . **104** F7
Hildesheim Cl BS23 . . . **104** F6
Hildesheim Ct **9**
BS23 . . . . **104** E7
Hilhouse BS9 . . . . **48** C6
HILL **2** D3
Hill Ave
Bath BA2 . . . . **101** F1
Bristol BS3 . . . . **63** E3
Hillbrook Rd **5** BS35 . . **15** D8
Hill Burn BS9 . . . . **49** C6
Hillburn Rd BS5 . . . . . . **65** A8
Hill Cl BS16 . . . . **52** B8
Hillcote BS24 . . . . **122** B8
Hillcrest
Peasedown St John
BA2 . . . . **134** C7
Pensford BS39 . . . . **97** E3
Thornbury BS35 . . . . **8** B1
Hill Crest BS4 . . . . **64** B1
Hillcrest Cl BS48 . . . . . . **59** E1
Hillcrest Dr BA2 . . . . . **101** C4
Hillcrest Prim Sch BS4 **64** A3
Hillcrest Rd
Nailsea BS48 . . . . **59** E1
Portishead BS20 . . . . . . **44** E4
Hillcroft Cl
Bristol BS15 . . . . **65** E4
Weston-s-M BS22 . . . . . . **88** A2
Hill Ct BS39 . . . . **132** E6
Hilldale Rd BS48 . . . . . . **76** B5
Hill Dr BS8 . . . . **61** C3
Hillend BS22 . . . . **88** E3
Hill End Dr BS10 . . . . . . **34** D3
HILLESLEY **19** E8
Hillesley CE Prim Sch
GL12 . . . . **19** E8
Hillesley Rd GL12 . . . . . **11** F4
HILLFIELDS **51** B3
Hillfields Ave BS16 . . . . **51** C3
Hillfields Prim Sch
BS16 . . . . **51** C2
Hill Gay Cl BS20 . . . . . . **44** F4
Hill Gr BS9 . . . . **49** C6
Hillgrove St BS2 . . . . . **143** B4
Hillgrove Terr BS23 . . . **104** D1
HILLHOUSE **52** A5
Hill House Rd BS16 . . . . **51** F5
Hillier's La BS25 . . . . . **108** D4
Hill La
Chipping Sodbury BS37 . . **41** B7
Clevedon BS21 . . . . **58** C4

Hill La continued
Portishead BS20 . . . . . . **44** F1
Rowberrow BS25 . . . . . . **109** A1
Thornbury BS35, GL13 . . . . **2** A2
Hill Lawn BS4 . . . . **64** D3
Hillmead BS40 . . . . **109** A5
Hillmer Rise BS29 . . . . **106** F3
Hill Moor BS21 . . . . **57** G2
Hillpath BS29 . . . . **107** B2
Hill Pk BS49 . . . . **91** E5
Hill Rd
Clevedon BS21 . . . . **57** F4
Dundry BS41 . . . . **78** D2
Sandford BS25 . . . . **108** A3
Weston-s-M BS23 . . . . . **104** F8
Weston-s-M, Worle BS22 **88** E2
Hill Rd E BS22 . . . . **88** E2
Hill's Barton BS13 . . . . . **63** A1
Hillsborough BS8 . . . . . **142** A2
Hillsborough Ho BS23 **105** A4
Hillsborough Rd BS4 . . . **64** C4
Hills Cl BS31 . . . . **82** A5
Hillsdon Rd BS9 . . . . . . **48** F8
HILLSIDE **138** E8
Hillside
Axbridge BS26 . . . . **125** C2
Bristol BS6 . . . . **142** C4
Bristol, Mangotsfield
BS16 . . . . **52** A5
Burton SN14 . . . . **43** A4
Portbury BS20 . . . . **46** D3
Hillside Ave
Bristol BS6 . . . . **65** C8
Midsomer Norton BA3 . . **138** F8
Hillside Cl
Frampton Cotterell
BS36 . . . . **38** C7
Paulton BS39 . . . . **132** F6
Hillside Cres BA3 . . . . . **138** E8
Hillside Ct BS5 . . . . **65** B7
Hillside Fst Sch BS22 . . **88** E2
Hillside Gdns
Bishop Sutton BS39 . . . **113** C3
Weston-s-M BS22 . . . . . . **88** B1
Hillside Ho **6** BS6 . . . . **49** D1
Hillside La BS36 . . . . . . **38** C7
Hillside Rd
Backwell BS48 . . . . **76** A4
Bath BA2 . . . . **101** D4
Bleadon BS24 . . . . **122** B8
Bristol BS5 . . . . **65** A7
Clevedon BS21 . . . . **57** F3
Long Ashton BS41 . . . . . **62** B2
Midsomer Norton BA3 . . **138** F8
Portishead BS20 . . . . . . **44** D4
Hillside St BS4 . . . . **64** A4
Hillside View
Midsomer Norton BA3 . . **133** A3
Peasedown St John
BA2 . . . . **134** C2
Hillside W BS24 . . . . . . **105** F2
Hill St
Bristol BS1 . . . . **142** C2
Bristol, Kingswood BS15 . **65** F8
Bristol, St George BS5 . . . **64** F8
Bristol, Windmill Hill BS3 . **63** F4
Hill The
Almondsbury BS32 . . . . . **24** B4
Freshford BA2 . . . . **120** C5
Hilltop Gdns
Bristol, St George BS5 . . . **65** A7
Bristol, Upper Soundwell
BS16 . . . . **51** D2
Hill Top La BS40 . . . . . . **94** B3
Hilltop Rd BS16 . . . . . . **51** D2
Hill Tops BS34 . . . . **35** F6
Hilltop View BS5 . . . . . **65** A7
Hillview
Midsomer Norton BA3 . . **138** E7
Timsbury BA2 . . . . **116** B1
Hill View
Bristol BS8 . . . . **142** B2
Bristol, Blackhorse BS16 **52** A8
Bristol, Filton BS34 . . . . **36** A3
Bristol, Henleaze BS9 . . . **49** C6
Bristol, Upper Soundwell
BS16 . . . . **51** D2
Farrington Gurney BS39 **132** B3
Marksbury BA2 . . . . **99** B1
Priston BA2 . . . . **117** A5
Hillview Ave BS21 . . . . . **57** F2
Hill View Cl BS30 . . . . . **66** C4
Hill View Ct
Bristol BS16 . . . . **51** C5
Weston-s-M BS22 . . . . . **105** D8
Hill View Cvn Pk BS40 . . **77** B1
Hillview Gdns BS40 . . . . **94** C8
Hill View Ho **2** BS15 . . **51** C1
Hill View Park Homes
BS22 . . . . **105** D8
Hillview Rd
Loxton BS26 . . . . **123** C4
Pucklechurch BS16 . . . . . **53** C5
Hill View Rd
Bath BA1 . . . . **85** B2
Bristol BS13 . . . . **79** A8
Weston-s-M BS23 . . . . . **105** A7
Hillyfield Rd BS13 . . . . . **79** A6

Hillyfields BS25 . . . . . **125** B8
Hillyfields Way BS25 . . **125** A8
Hilton Ct **5** BS5 . . . . . . **64** B8
Hinckley Cl BS22 . . . . . . **89** C4
Hind Pitts BS25 . . . . . . **125** F7
HINTON **54** D6
Hinton BS24 . . . . **105** A2
HINTON BLEWETT **130** F6
Hinton Blewett Rd
Hinton Blewett BS39 . . . **130** E8
Sutton Wick BS39 . . . . . **113** E1
**HINTON
CHARTERHOUSE** . . . **119** E1
Hinton Cl
Bath BA2 . . . . **100** F6
Saltford BS31 . . . . **82** E3
Hinton Dr BS30 . . . . **66** C6
Hinton Hill BA2 . . . . . . **119** A1
Hinton La **13** BS8 . . . . . **62** F6
Hinton Rd
Bristol, Fishponds BS16 . . **51** A4
Bristol, Lower Easton
BS5 . . . . **50** C1
Hinton Villas BS5 . . . . **119** E1
Hippisley Dr BS26 . . . . **125** D2
Hiscocks Dr BA2 . . . . . **101** E4
Hitchen Cl SN14 . . . . . . **69** F8
Hitchings Leaze BS34 . . **36** A7
Hither Bath Bridge BS4 **64** C1
Hither Gn BS21 . . . . **57** H2
Hither Green Ind Est
BS21 . . . . **57** H2
Hither Mead BS36 . . . . . **38** B6
Hoare's La BA11 . . . . . **140** B3
Hobart Rd BS23 . . . . . . **104** F3
Hobbiton Rd BS22 . . . . . **89** A4
Hobbs Ct **1** BS48 . . . . . **59** F2
Hobbs La
Barrow Gurney BS48 . . . . **77** E3
Bristol BS30 . . . . **52** B1
Hobb's La BS1 . . . . **142** C2
HOBB'S WALL **115** E5
Hobhouse Cl BS9 . . . . . . **49** C7
Hobwell La BS41 . . . . . . **62** C2
Hockeys La BS16 . . . . . . **51** A4
Hockley Ct BA1 . . . . **84** D1
Hoddon La BS16 . . . . . . **53** D5
Hodshill BA2 . . . . **118** F6
Hoecroft BA3 . . . . **138** D8
Hoecroft Gdns BA3 . . . . **138** D3
Hogarth Mews BS22 . . . **89** A3
Hogarth Wlk
Bristol BS7 . . . . **50** C7
Weston-s-M BS22 . . . . . . **89** A3
Hogues Wlk BS13 . . . . . **79** B4
Holbeach Way BS14 . . . . **80** A2
HOLBROOK COMMON . . **67** B8
Holbrook Cres BS13 . . . . **79** C4
Holbrook La BS30 . . . . . **67** B7
Holcombe BS14 . . . . **80** A5
Holcombe Cl BA2 . . . . . . **85** F1
Holcombe Gn BA1 . . . . . **84** B2
Holcombe Gr BS31 . . . . . **81** D5
Holcombe La BA2 . . . . . . **85** F1
Holcombe Vale BA2 . . . . **85** F1
Holdenhurst Rd BS15 . . . **51** C1
Holders Wlk BS41 . . . . . **77** F8
Holford Cl BS48 . . . . **59** E1
Holford Ct BS14 . . . . . . **80** B5
Holland Rd
Bath BA1 . . . . **85** B1
Clevedon BS21 . . . . **57** D1
Holland St BS23 . . . . . . **105** A8
Hollidge Gdns **3** BS3 . . **63** D4
Hollies La BA1 . . . . **86** A6
Hollies The
Bristol BS15 . . . . **65** E6
Midsomer Norton BA3 . . **133** A1
Hollis Ave BS20 . . . . . . **45** C3
Hollis Cl BS41 . . . . **78** A8
Hollis Cres BS20 . . . . . . **45** C3
Hollis Gdns SN14 . . . . . **31** E4
Hollister's Dr BS13 . . . . **79** D4
Holloway BA2 . . . . **141** B1
Holloway Hill SN14 . . . . **56** F7
Holloway Rd BS35 . . . . . **22** C4
HOLLOW BROOK **113** C6
Hollowbrook La BS39,
BS40 . . . . **113** D6
Hollow La BS22 . . . . **88** F3
Hollow Marsh La BA3,
BS39 . . . . **131** B4
Hollowmead BS49 . . . . . **91** E8
Hollow Mead **6** BS34 . . **35** F7
Hollowmead Cl BS49 . . . **91** F8
Hollow Rd
Almondsbury BS32 . . . . . **24** A4
Bristol BS15 . . . . **65** E8
Shipham BS25 . . . . **125** F8
Hollows The BS36 . . . . . **38** D2
Hollow The
Bath BA2 . . . . **101** B4
Dunkerton BA2 . . . . . . **117** D4
Hollway Cl BS14 . . . . . . **80** E5
Hollway Rd BS14 . . . . . . **80** E5

Hollybrook Pk BS15 . . . **51** B2
Hollybush Cl
Acton Turville GL9 . . . . . **43** A6
Winsley BA15 . . . . **120** E7
Hollybush La
Bristol BS9 . . . . **48** E5
Bristol BS9 . . . . **48** F5
Holly Cl
Alveston BS35 . . . . **14** F4
Bristol BS5 . . . . **51** A2
Nailsea BS48 . . . . **60** A3
Pucklechurch BS16 . . . . . **53** C5
Weston-s-M BS22 . . . . . . **89** A1
Holly Cres BS15 . . . . . . **51** E1
Holly Ct BS2 . . . . **142** C4
Holly Dr
Bath BA2 . . . . **118** D8
Colerne SN14 . . . . **70** F6
Holly Gdns BS34 . . . . . . **36** A7
Holly Gn BS15 . . . . **52** A1
Holly Gr BS16 . . . . **51** C3
Hollyguest Rd BS15 . . . . **65** E6
Holly Hill BS37 . . . . **26** C3
Holly Hill Rd BS15 . . . . . **51** F1
Holly Ho BS11 . . . . **34** C2
Holly La BS21 . . . . **57** H6
Hollyleigh Ave BS34 . . . **35** F2
Holly Lodge Cl BS5 . . . . **51** A2
Holly Lodge Rd BS5 . . . . **50** F2
Hollyman Wlk **5** BS21 . **57** H3
Hollymead La BS9 . . . . . **48** E4
Holly Mews **4** BS37 . . . **27** F5
Hollyridge BS14 . . . . . . **80** C6
Holly Ridge BS20 . . . . . **45** A5
Hollywood La BS10,
BS35 . . . . **35** A7
Hollywood Rd BS4 . . . . . **64** D2
Holmdale Rd BS34 . . . . . **36** C3
Holmes Ct BS9 . . . . **49** B5
Holmesdale Rd BS3 . . . . **63** E3
Holmes Gr BS9 . . . . **49** B5
Holmes Hill Rd BS5 . . . . **64** F8
Holmes St BS5 . . . . **64** B6
Holm La BS35 . . . . **13** B2
Holmlea BS20 . . . . **45** F5
Holmoak Rd BS31 . . . . . **81** C4
Holm Rd BS24 . . . . **105** E2
Holms Rd BS23 . . . . . . **105** A5
Holmwood BS15 . . . . . . **65** C5
Holmwood Cl BS36 . . . . . **37** D6
Holmwood Gdns BS9 . . . **49** B8
Holroyd Ho BS3 . . . . **63** D3
Holsom Cl BS14 . . . . . . **80** F6
Holsom Rd BS14 . . . . . . **80** F6
Holstein Ave BS25 . . . . **124** F7
Holst Gdns BS4 . . . . **79** D7
Holton Rd BS7 . . . . **50** A6
Holtsdown La BA1 . . . . . **85** F7
Holwell La BS39 . . . . . . **132** E4
Holybrook Trad Est
BS15 . . . . **51** B2
Holy Cross RC Prim Sch
BS3 . . . . **63** C4
Holy Family RC Prim Sch
BS34 . . . . **36** B8
Holymead Inf Sch BS4 . . **64** D2
Holymead Jun Sch BS4 **64** D3
Holyrood Cl BS34 . . . . . **36** D4
Holy Trinity Prim Sch
BS32 . . . . **24** C2
Holy Well Cl BS4 . . . . . . **64** E6
Homeapple Hill BS30 . . . **66** F6
Homeavon Ho BS31 . . . . **81** F5
Home Cl
Bristol BS10 . . . . **35** E2
Wrington BS40 . . . . **92** E3
Home Farm Cl BA2 . . . . **134** B7
Home Farm Ct BS22 . . . . **89** C3
Home Farm Rd BS8 . . . . **62** B8
Home Farm Way BS35 . . **23** A1
Homefield
Congresbury BS49 . . . . . **91** E3
Locking BS24 . . . . **106** A5
Thornbury BS35 . . . . **15** D8
Timsbury BA2 . . . . **116** B2
Yate BS37 . . . . **27** E3
Homefield Cl
Locking BS24 . . . . **106** A5
Saltford BS31 . . . . **82** E3
Winscombe BS25 . . . . . **107** F1
Home Field Cl BS16 . . . . **52** B6
Homefield Dr BS16 . . . . . **51** A6
Homefield Ind Est
BS24 . . . . **106** A5
Homefield Rd
Pucklechurch BS16 . . . . . **53** B5
Saltford BS31 . . . . **82** E3
Homeground
Bristol BS16 . . . . **52** B6
Clevedon BS21 . . . . **57** H2
Home Ground
Bristol, Eastfield BS9 . . . **49** B4
Bristol, Shirehampton
BS11 . . . . **47** D7
Homelea Pk E BA1 . . . . **101** A7
Homelea Pk W BA1 . . . **101** A7

Home Leas Cl **1** BS7 . . **50** C8
Homeleaze Rd BS10 . . . . **35** D3
Homemead BA2 . . . . . . **100** A8
Home Mead
Bristol, Cadbury Heath
BS30 . . . . **66** A4
Bristol, Filwood Park BS4 **79** E7
Homemead Dr BS4 . . . . . **64** D1
Home Orch
Chew Stoke BS40 . . . . . **112** D8
Yate BS37 . . . . **27** D2
Homer Wk BS31 . . . . **81** C3
Homestead BS20 . . . . . . **44** E3
Homestead Cl BS36 . . . . **38** D5
Homestead Gdns BS16 . . **51** B8
Homestead Rd BS34 . . . . **36** A3
Homestead The
Clevedon BS21 . . . . **57** E3
Keynsham BS31 . . . . **81** D4
Homestead Way BS25 . **125** A8
Honeyborne Way GL12 . . **18** B5
Honey Garston Cl BS13 . **79** B4
Honey Garston Rd BS13 **79** B4
HONEY HALL **108** C7
Honeyhall La BS49 . . . . **108** D7
Honey Hill Rd BS15 . . . . **65** F8
Honeylands BS20 . . . . . . **45** C3
Honeymead BS14 . . . . . . **80** C6
Honey Pens Cres BS7 . . . **50** B8
Honeysuckle Cl BS32 . . . **24** E2
Honey Suckle La BS16 . . **50** E5
Honeysuckle Pl BS24 . . **106** A8
Honeysuckle Rd BS16 . . **52** D7
Honey Way BS15 . . . . . . **65** F8
Honeywick Cl BS3 . . . . . **63** C2
Honister Ho BS34 . . . . . . **36** A8
Honiton **9** BS22 . . . . . . **89** A4
Honiton Rd
Bristol BS16 . . . . **51** A3
Clevedon BS21 . . . . **57** G1
HOOK **116** D2
Hook Hill BA2 . . . . **116** D2
Hook La BA3, BS39 . . . . **130** E4
Hooks Batch BS40 . . . . **110** C4
Hooper Rd BS14 . . . . . . **80** D5
Hoopers Wlk BS30 . . . . . **65** E3
Hoover's La BS36, BS37 . **26** C2
Hopechapel Hill **11**
BS8 . . . . **62** F6
Hope Cote Lodge BA2 **102** C1
Hope Cotts BS21 . . . . . . **73** B2
Hope Ct BS1 . . . . **142** B1
Hope Rd
Bristol BS3 . . . . **63** C2
Yate BS37 . . . . **27** A2
Hope Sq BS8 . . . . **62** F6
Hope Terr BA3 . . . . **133** B1
Hopetoun Rd BS2 . . . . . **49** F3
Hopewell Gdns BS11 . . . **47** F7
HOPEWELL HILL **51** D1
Hopkin Cl BS35 . . . . **15** D7
Hopkins Ct **13** BS6 . . . . **49** B1
Hopkins St BS23 . . . . . **104** E8
Hopland Cl BS30 . . . . . . **66** B3
Hopp's Rd BS15 . . . . **65** D7
Hopton Wy BA1 . . . . **84** E4
Horesham Gr BS13 . . . . . **79** C5
HORFIELD **49** F6
Horfield CE Prim Sch
BS10 . . . . **49** D7
Horfield Ct BS7 . . . . **49** E4
Horfield Rd BS2 . . . . . . **143** A4
Horley Rd BS2 . . . . **50** A4
Hornbeam Ho **5** BS6 . . . **51** C6
Hornbeams The BS16 . . . **37** B1
Horne Cl BA3 . . . . **138** F1
Horn's La BS26 . . . . **125** B2
HORSECASTLE **74** A2
Horsecastle Cl BS49 . . . . **74** A1
Horsecastle Farm Rd
BS49 . . . . **74** A1
Horsecombe Brow
BA2 . . . . **102** A1
Horsecombe Gr BA2 . . . **102** A1
Horsecombe Vale
BA2 . . . . **102** A1
Horsecroft Gdns BS30 . . **66** A6
Horsefair The BS1 . . . . **143** B3
Horse La BS35 . . . . **8** D3
Horseleaze La BS25 . . . **108** C1
Horse Leaze Rd BS7 . . . . **50** C8
Horsepool La BS30 . . . . . **67** F8
Horsepool Rd BS13 . . . . . **78** E3
Horse Race La BS8 . . . . . **61** A6
Horseshoe Ct BS36 . . . . . **38** D7
Horseshoe Dr BS9 . . . . . **48** C4
Horseshoe La BS37 . . . . . **28** B1
Horseshoe Wlk **1** BS14 **102** B5
Horse St BS37 . . . . **28** C1
Horse World ★ BS14 . . . . **80** D3
Horsford Rd GL12 . . . . . **11** B5
Horstmann Cl **2** BA1 . **101** A7
Hortham La BS32 . . . . . . **24** E5
HORTON **29** B6
Horton CE Prim Sch
BS37 . . . . **29** C5
Horton Court ★ BS37 . . . **29** C5
Horton Hill BS37 . . . . . . **29** C5
Horton Ho BA2 . . . . **141** C4

Horton Rd
Chipping Sodbury BS37 . . **28** C2
Chipping Sodbury, Little
Sodbury End BS37 . . . . . **28** D4
Horton St BS2 . . . . **143** C3
Horwood Ct 🔳 BS30 . . . **66** A4
Horwood La GL12 . . . . . . **18** B4
Horwood Rd BS48 . . . . . . **59** F1
Hosey Wlk BS13 . . . . **79** A5
Hospital Rd BS48 . . . . . **77** F7
Host St BS1 . . . . **143** A3
Hot Bath St 🔳 BA1 . . . **141** B2
Hottom Gdns BS7 . . . . . . **50** A7
Hot Water La BS5 . . . . . **52** A3
Hotwell Hts BS8 . . . . . **142** A2
Hotwell Rd BS8 . . . . . . **142** B1
HOTWELLS **142** A1
Hotwells Ho BS8 . . . . . **142** A2
Hotwells Prim Sch BS8 . **62** F6
Houlgate Way BS26 . . **125** B1
Houlton St BS2 . . . . . . **143** C4
Hounds Cl BS37 . . . . **28** B1
Hounds Rd BS37 . . . . **28** B1
HOUNSLEY BATCH **95** A3
Howard Ave BS5 . . . . . . **64** E8
Howard Cl BS31 . . . . **82** D3
Howard Rd
Bristol, Southville BS3 . . **63** C4
Bristol, Staple Hill BS16 . **51** D4
Bristol, Westbury Park
BS6 . . . . **49** B4
Thornbury BS35 . . . . **8** C2
Howard St BS5 . . . . **50** D1
Howard Wlk BS30 . . . . . . **66** D7
Howecroft Ct BS9 . . . . . **48** E4
Howecroft Gdns BS9 . . . **48** E4
Howells Mead BS16 . . . . **52** B7
Howes Cl BS30 . . . . **66** A6
Howett Rd 🔳 BS5 . . . . **64** C7
Howgrove Hill La BS40 . **94** C2
How Hill BA2 . . . . **101** A6
Howitt Way 🔳 BS24 . . **105** F7
HOWLEY **5** E1
Howsmoor La
Bristol, Lyde Green
BS16 . . . . **52** C8
Bristol, New England
BS16 . . . . **52** B8
Hoylake BS37 . . . . **39** E8
Hoylake Dr BS30 . . . . . . **66** B6
Huckford La BS36 . . . . . . **38** A4
Huckford Rd BS36 . . . . . . **37** E5
Huckley Way BS32 . . . . . **36** F6
Hudds Hill Gdns 🔳 BS5 **64** F8
Hudd's Hill Rd BS5 . . . . **64** F8
Hudd's Vale Rd BS5 . . . . **64** E8
Hudson Ave BS10 . . . . . . **34** B8
Hudson Cl BS37 . . . . **39** F8
Hughenden Rd
Bristol, Clifton BS8 . . . . **49** A2
Bristol, Horfield BS7 . . . **49** E5
Weston-s-M BS23 . . . . **105** A8
Hughes Gdns BS7 . . . . . . **50** A8
Huish Ct BA3 . . . . **134** B2
Hulbert Cl BS4 . . . . **65** A2
Hulse Rd BS4 . . . . **64** D1
Humberstan Wlk BS11 . **47** C6
Humber Way BS11 . . . . . . **33** D5
Humphry Davy Way 🔳
BS8 . . . . **62** F5
Humphrys Barton BS4 . . **64** F5
Hungerford Cl BS4 . . . . . **80** E8
Hungerford Cres BS4 . . . **64** E1
Hungerford Gdns BS4 . . **80** E8
Hungerford Rd
Bath BA1 . . . . **101** C7
Bristol BS4 . . . . **80** E8
Hungerford Terr BA2 . . **118** D1
Hungerford Wlk BS4 . . . **64** E1
Hung Rd BS11 . . . . **47** E5
HUNSTRETE **98** D2
Hunstrete Rd BA2 . . . . **115** F7
Hunters Cl BS15 . . . . . . **65** C5
Hunters Dr BS15 . . . . . . **51** F1
Hunters Mead GL9 . . . . . **20** A2
Hunters Rd BS15 . . . . . . **65** C5
Hunters Rd E BS15 . . . . **65** C4
Hunters Rest Miniature
Rlwy ★ BS34 . . . . **115** A5
Hunter's Way BS34 . . . . . **36** B3
HUNTINGFORD **10** F8
Huntingham Rd BS13 . . . **78** F4
Huntley Gr BS48 . . . . . . **60** A1
Hunts Ground Rd BS34 . **36** F4
Hunts La BS7 . . . . **49** E6
Hunt's La BS49 . . . . **91** E8
Hurle Cres BS8 . . . . **49** B1
Hurle Rd BS8 . . . . **49** B1
Hurlingham Rd BS7 . . . . **49** F2
Hurn La BS31 . . . . **82** A3
Hurn Rd BS21 . . . . **57** H2
Hursley Hill
Bristol BS14, BS39 . . . . . **97** D8
Whitchurch BS14 . . . . . . **80** D1
Hursley La BS14 . . . . **80** E1
Hurston Rd BS4 . . . . **79** D7
Hurst Rd
Bristol BS4 . . . . **79** F8
Weston-s-M BS23 . . . . **105** A6

Hurst Wlk BS4 . . . . **79** F8
Hurstwood Rd BS16 . . . . **51** D5
HUTTON **105** E2
Hutton CE Prim Sch
BS24 . . . . **105** E2
Hutton Cl
Bristol BS9 . . . . **48** E7
Keynsham BS31 . . . . **82** A2
Hutton Hill BS24 . . . . . **105** F2
Hutton Moor La BS22,
BS24 . . . . **105** C6
Hutton Moor Pk BS24 . **105** C6
Hutton Moor Rd BS22 . **105** C7
Hutton Moor Rdbt
BS22 . . . . **105** C7
Huyton Rd BS5 . . . . **50** E3
Hyacinth Cl BS16 . . . . . . **52** D7
Hyacinth Way BS16 . . . . **52** D7
Hyatts Wood Rd BS48 . . **76** E1
Hyde Apartments BS6 . . **49** C3
Hyde Ave BS35 . . . . **8** B3
Hyde's La SN14 . . . . **69** A6
Hydes The BS31 . . . . **81** F6
Hyde The BS21 . . . . **73** C8
Hyland Gr BS9 . . . . **48** F8
HYSTFIELD **3** B5

I

ICELTON **89** C8
Ida Rd 🔳 BS5 . . . . **64** C8
Iddesleigh Rd BS6 . . . . . **49** B3
Idstone Rd BS16 . . . . **51** B4
Idwal Cl BA2 . . . . **134** C8
Iford Cl BS31 . . . . **82** E3
Iford Fields BA15 . . . . . **120** E2
Iford Hill BA15 . . . . **120** E2
Iford La BA2, BA15 . . . . **120** C3
IKB Academy BS31 . . . . . **82** A5
Ilchester Cres BS13 . . . . **63** B1
Ilchester Rd BS13 . . . . . . **79** B8
Iles Cl BS15 . . . . **65** D4
Ilex Ave BS21 . . . . **57** G2
Ilex Cl BS13 . . . . **78** F6
Ilex La BS25 . . . . **107** F1
Ilminster BS24 . . . . **105** A2
Ilminster Ave BS4 . . . . . **79** F8
Ilminster Ave E-ACT Acad
BS4 . . . . **79** F8
Ilminster Avenue Prim Sch
BS4 . . . . **80** A8
Ilminster Cl
Clevedon BS21 . . . . **57** G2
Nailsea BS48 . . . . **75** D8
Ilsyn Gr BS14 . . . . **80** D7
Imber Court Cl BS14 . . . **80** B8
Imperial Arc 🔳 BS3 . . . **63** D4
Imperial Pk BS13 . . . . . . **79** C6
Imperial Rd
Bristol BS14 . . . . **80** C8
🔳 Bristol, Clifton BS6 . . **49** B1
Imperial Wlk BS14 . . . . . **64** B1
Inchalloch 🔳 BA1 . . . . . **85** A1
Inclosures The 🔳
BS22 . . . . **105** F8
INGLESBATCH **117** C8
Ingleside Rd BS15 . . . . . **51** C1
Inglestone Rd GL12 . . . . **18** B5
Ingleton Dr BS22 . . . . . . **89** A4
Ingmire Rd BS5 . . . . **50** B3
INGST **13** C4
Ingst Hill BS35 . . . . **13** B3
Ingst Rd BS35 . . . . **13** D4
Inkerman Cl BS7 . . . . . . **49** E7
Inman Ho BA1 . . . . **141** C4
INMAN'S BATCH **95** A5
Inn Cotts BS11 . . . . **48** A7
Inner Down The BS37 . . **14** D3
Inner Elm Terr BA3 . . . . **133** C1
Innicks Cl BS40 . . . . **111** D1
Innocks Est GL11 . . . . **5** D4
Instow 🔳 BS22 . . . . **89** A2
Instow Rd BS4 . . . . **79** E8
Instow Wlk BS4 . . . . **79** E8
International Helicopter
Mus ★ BS24 . . . . **105** E5
International Trad Est
BS11 . . . . **33** B2
Interplex 16 BS21 . . . . . **24** C3
Inverness Rd BA2 . . . . . **101** C6
IO Ctr BS11 . . . . **33** F5
Ipswich Dr BS4 . . . . **64** E6
Irby Rd BS3 . . . . **63** A3
Irena Rd BS16 . . . . **50** F3
Ireton Rd BS3 . . . . **63** B3
IRON ACTON **26** D4
Iron Acton CE Prim Sch
BS37 . . . . **26** E4
Iron Acton Way BS37 . . . **27** B3
Ironchurch Rd BS11 . . . . **33** C5
Iron Hogg La GL12 . . . . . . **9** C3

Ironmould La
Bristol BS4 . . . . **65** A1
Keynsham BS31 . . . . **81** A8
Irving Cl
Bristol BS16 . . . . **51** E4
Clevedon BS21 . . . . **57** H3
Irving Ho BS1 . . . . **142** C3
I.S.F. Rd BS11 . . . . **33** C3
Island Copsie BS7 . . . . . **50** B8
Island Gdns BS16 . . . . . . **50** C4
Island The BA3 . . . . **133** A1
Island Trad Pk BS11 . . . **33** C1
Isle Of Rhé GL11 . . . . **5** C5
Isleys Ct BS30 . . . . **65** F3
Islington Rd BS3 . . . . . . **63** C4
Ison Hill Rd BS10 . . . . . . **34** D3
ITCHINGTON **15** F2
Itchington Rd
Alveston BS35, GL12 . . . **15** F4
Tytherington GL12 . . . . . **16** B4
Ivo Peters Rd BA2 . . . . **141** A2
Ivor Rd BS5 . . . . **64** C8
Ivy Ave BA2 . . . . **101** C4
Ivy Bank Pk BA2 . . . . . **101** F2
Ivybridge 🔳 BS22 . . . . . **89** A2
Ivy Cl BS48 . . . . **59** D1
Ivy Ct BS20 . . . . **44** F5
Ivy Gr BA2 . . . . **101** C4
Ivy House Cotts BS29 . **106** D7
Ivy La
Bristol BS16 . . . . **51** A3
Weston-s-M BS24 . . . . **106** A8
Ivy Lodge 🔳 BS9 . . . . . **49** A7
Ivy Pl BA2 . . . . **101** C4
Ivy Terr BS37 . . . . **39** B4
Ivywell Rd BS9 . . . . **48** E3
Ivy Wlk
Banwell BS29 . . . . **106** E4
Midsomer Norton BA3 . **139** B8
IWOOD **92** A3
Iwood La BS40 . . . . **92** A2

J

Jack Knight Ho BS7 . . . . **49** F5
Jack Price Cl BS13 . . . . . **79** C3
Jackson Cl BS35 . . . . **22** D7
Jacob Ct BS2 . . . . **143** C3
Jacobs Bldg The BS8 . . **142** B2
Jacob's Ct BS1 . . . . **142** C2
Jacob Mdw BS20 . . . . . . **45** F4
Jacob St
Bristol BS2 . . . . **143** B3
Bristol BS2 . . . . **143** C3
Jacob's Wells Rd BS8 . . **142** B2
Jaguar Ho 🔳 BA1 . . . . **141** B3
Jamaica St BS2 . . . . **143** B4
James Cl BS16 . . . . **51** E4
James Counsell Way
BS16 . . . . **36** F2
James Rd BS16 . . . . **51** E3
James St W BA1 . . . . . . **141** B2
James St
Bristol BS5 . . . . **143** C4
Bristol, Baptist Mills BS2 **50** A2
Janes Gr BA2 . . . . **102** A2
Jane St BS5 . . . . **64** B7
Jarrets Rd BS10 . . . . **35** D2
Jarvis St BS5 . . . . **64** B6
Jasmine Cl BS22 . . . . **89** A1
Jasmine Ct 🔳 BS23 . . **104** E8
Jasmine Gr BS11 . . . . . . **34** C2
Jasmine La BS49 . . . . **74** F2
Jasmine Way BS24 . . . . . **89** A1
Jasper St BS3 . . . . **63** B3
Jays The GL12 . . . . **16** B6
Jay View BS23 . . . . **105** A5
JEFFERIES HILL **65** C5
Jefferies Hill Bottom
BS15 . . . . **65** B5
Jeffery Ct BS30 . . . . **66** B6
Jeffreys Ct 🔳 BS16 . . . **50** E3
Jekyll Cl BS16 . . . . **50** E8
Jellicoe Ave BS16 . . . . . . **50** E8
Jellicoe Ct BS22 . . . . **88** E4
Jena Ct BS31 . . . . **82** D3
Jenkinson Wy G12 . . . . . . **9** E8
Jenner Bvd BS16 . . . . . . **38** C1
Jenner Cl BS37 . . . . **40** D8
Jennings Ct 🔳 BS3 . . . . **63** A4
Jersey Ave BS4 . . . . **64** F4
Jesmond Rd
Clevedon BS21 . . . . **57** E3
Weston-s-M BS22 . . . . . **89** C4
Jesse Hughes Ct BA1 . . **85** C2
Jessop Cres BS10 . . . . . . **35** A1
Jessop Ct BS1 . . . . **143** B2
Jessop Underpass BS3 . **62** F4
Jews La
Bath BA2 . . . . **101** C6
Churchill BS25 . . . . **108** F4
Jim O'Neil Ho BS11 . . . . **47** D7
Jinty La BS16 . . . . **52** B2
Jobbins Cl BS37 . . . . **40** A8
Jocelin Dr BS22 . . . . **88** F4
Jocelyn Rd BS7 . . . . **49** F7
Jockey La BS5 . . . . **65** A7

John Cabot Acad BS15 . **65** C7
John Cabot Ct BS1 . . . . **142** A1
John Carr's Terr BS8 . . **142** B2
John Chiddy Cl BS15 . . . **65** C3
John Cozens Ho 🔳
BS2 . . . . **143** C3
John James Ct BS7 . . . . **50** B7
John Repton Gdns
BS10 . . . . **35** B2
John Slessor Ct BA1 . . **141** B4
Johnson Dr BS30 . . . . . . **65** F5
Johnson Rd BS16 . . . . . . **52** C5
Johnsons La BS5 . . . . . . **50** D1
Johnsons Rd
Bristol BS5 . . . . **50** C1
🔳 Bristol, Moorfields
BS5 . . . . **64** C8
John St
Bath BA1 . . . . **141** B3
Bristol BS1 . . . . **143** A3
Bristol, Baptist Mills BS2 **50** A2
Bristol, Two Mile Hill
BS5 . . . . **65** C8
Johnstone St BA2 . . . . **141** C2
John Wesley Ct 🔳
BS16 . . . . **51** D5
John Wesley Rd BS5 . . . **65** B6
John Wesleys Chapel ★
BS1 . . . . **143** B3
Jones Cl BS35 . . . . **74** A1
Jonny Ball La BS2 . . . . **143** A3
Jordan Wlk BS32 . . . . . . **36** D8
Jorrocks Ind Est BS37 . . **39** C4
Joyce Cl BS7 . . . . **50** A8
Joy Hill BS8 . . . . **62** F6
Jubilee Cres BS16 . . . . . . **52** A6
Jubilee Ct
Bristol BS4 . . . . **64** D4
Weston-s-M BS23 . . . . **104** F8
Jubilee Dr
Failand BS8 . . . . **61** B4
Thornbury BS35 . . . . **8** D1
Jubilee Gdns BS37 . . . . . **28** A2
Jubilee Ho BS34 . . . . **36** C8
Jubilee La
Churchill BS40 . . . . **109** A6
Cromhall GL12 . . . . **17** B7
Jubilee Path BS22 . . . . . **88** C1
Jubilee Pl
Bristol BS1 . . . . **143** A1
Bristol, Woodstock BS15 . **65** F7
Clevedon BS21 . . . . **57** F1
Jubilee Rd
Axbridge BS26 . . . . **125** C2
Bristol, Baptist Mills BS2 **50** A1
Bristol, Crew's Hole BS5 . **64** F7
Bristol, Staple Hill BS15 . **51** E3
Bristol, Upper Knowle
BS4 . . . . **64** C2
Radstock BA3 . . . . **133** D1
Weston-s-M BS23 . . . . **104** E7
Jubilee St BS2 . . . . **143** C2
Jubilee Terr BS39 . . . . . **132** E6
Jubilee Way
Avonmouth BS11 . . . . . . **33** B2
Elberton BS35 . . . . **14** B8
Weston-s-M BS22 . . . . . **89** C3
Julian Cl BS9 . . . . **48** E3
Julian Ct BS9 . . . . **48** E3
Julian Rd
Bath BA1 . . . . **141** B3
Bristol BS9 . . . . **48** E3
Julier Ho BA1 . . . . **141** C4
Julius Cl BS16 . . . . **52** C6
Julius Pl BS31 . . . . **81** F8
Julius Rd BS7 . . . . **49** D3
Junction Ave BA2 . . . . **141** A1
Junction Rd
Bath BA2 . . . . **141** A1
Bristol BS4 . . . . **64** C4
Junction Way BS15,
BS16 . . . . **52** B3
Juniper Ct 🔳 BS5 . . . . . **50** C2
Juniper Pl BS22 . . . . **88** F4
Juniper Way BS34 . . . . . **37** A7
Jupiter Rd BS34 . . . . **35** E7
Justice Ave BS31 . . . . . . **82** E3
Justice Rd BS16 . . . . **51** A3
Jutland Rd BS11 . . . . **33** B1

K

Karelean Ct BS10 . . . . . . **35** D3
Karen Cl BS48 . . . . **76** A4
Karen Dr BS48 . . . . **76** A5
Kathdene Gdns BS7 . . . . **49** F3
Katherine Cl GL12 . . . . . **11** A5
Katherine Lady Berkeley's
Sch GL12 . . . . **11** F6
Kaynton Mead BA1 . . . **101** B7
Keats Cl BS7 . . . . **50** A8
Keats Ho 🔳 BS23 . . . . **104** F4
Keats Rd BA3 . . . . **139** C8
Keble Ave BS13 . . . . **78** F5
Keeds La BS41 . . . . **61** F1
Keedwell Hill BS41 . . . . . **61** F1
Keel Cl BS5 . . . . **64** F6

Hor–Ken 163

Keel's Hill BA2 . . . . **134** C8
Keene's Way BS21 . . . . . **57** E2
Keen's Gr BS35 . . . . **22** C7
Keepers Hill BA2 . . . . . **100** C5
Keepers La BS7 . . . . **49** F3
Keeper's La BA2 . . . . **99** C3
Keep The
Bristol BS30 . . . . **66** D5
Weston-s-M BS22 . . . . . **89** A3
Keg Store The BS1 . . . . **143** B2
Keinton Wlk BS10 . . . . . **35** A2
Kelbra Cres BS36 . . . . . . **38** B6
Kellaway Ave BS7 . . . . . **49** D5
Kellaway Cres BS9 . . . . . **49** D6
Kellaway Ct BS6 . . . . **49** D5
Kellaway La BA2 . . . . . . **102** A5
Kellways BS48 . . . . **76** A4
Kelso Pl BA1 . . . . **101** D7
Kelso Villa BA1 . . . . **101** D7
KELSTON **83** C3
Kelston Cl
Saltford BS31 . . . . **82** D4
Yate BS37 . . . . **39** D7
Kelston Gdns
Bristol BS10 . . . . **49** D8
Weston-s-M BS22 . . . . . **89** B5
Kelston Gr BS15 . . . . **65** E6
Kelston Hill La BA1 . . . . **83** B4
Kelston Rd
Bath BA1 . . . . **83** E1
Bristol BS10 . . . . **49** D8
Keynsham BS31 . . . . **81** D5
Weston-s-M BS22 . . . . . **89** B5
Kelston View BA2 . . . . **101** A5
Kelston Wlk BS16 . . . . . . **51** C4
Kelting Gr BS21 . . . . **57** H2
Kemble Cl
Bristol BS15 . . . . **65** E6
Nailsea BS48 . . . . **60** A1
Kemble Gdns BS11 . . . . . **47** F5
Kemble Ho BS34 . . . . **23** F1
Kemperleye Way BS32 . **36** D7
Kempe's Cl BS41 . . . . **62** A2
Kempe Way BS24 . . . . . **105** E2
Kempthorne La BA2 . . . **101** E1
Kempton Cl
🔳 Bristol BS16 . . . . **37** F1
Thornbury BS35 . . . . **8** B3
Kencot Wlk BS13 . . . . . . **79** B3
Kendall Gdns BS16 . . . . . **51** D4
Kendall Rd BS16 . . . . **51** D4
Kendal Rd BS7 . . . . **50** A7
KENDLESHIRE **38** A4
Kendon Dr BS10 . . . . **49** D7
Kendon Way BS10 . . . . . **49** D8
Kenilworth BS37 . . . . **39** F8
Kenilworth Cl BS31 . . . . **81** D4
Kenilworth Ct
🔳 Bath BA1 . . . . **102** B8
🔳 Bathwick BA1 . . . . . **102** B8
Kenilworth Dr BS30 . . . . **66** B2
Kenilworth Rd BS6 . . . . . **49** C1
Kenmare Rd BS4 . . . . **63** E1
Kenmeade Cl BS25 . . . . **125** E8
Kenmore Cres BS7 . . . . . **35** E1
Kenmore Dr BS7 . . . . **35** E1
Kenmore Gr BS7 . . . . **35** E1
KENN **73** F7
Kennard Cl BS15 . . . . **65** C7
Kennard Rd BS15 . . . . . . **65** C8
Kennard Rise BS15 . . . . . **65** C8
Kennaway Rd BS21 . . . . **57** G2
Kenn Bsns Pk BS21 . . . . **73** E8
Kenn Court
Bristol BS4 . . . . **79** E7
Kenn Court BS4 . . . . **79** E7
Kennedy Ho BS37 . . . . . . **27** F1
Kennedy Way BS37 . . . . **27** F1
Kennel Dr GL9 . . . . **30** E2
Kennel La BS26 . . . . **123** E3
Kennel Lodge Rd BS3 . . **62** E4
Kenn Est BS21 . . . . **73** E5
Kenneth Rd BS4 . . . . **64** D2
Kennet Pk BA2 . . . . **85** E1
Kennet Rd BS31 . . . . **82** A4
Kennet Way 🔳 BS35 . . . **15** D8
Kennford 🔳 BS22 . . . . . **88** F2
Kennington Ave
Bristol, Bishopston BS7 . **49** F4
🔳 Bristol, Two Mile Hill
BS15 . . . . **51** D1
Kennington Rd BA1 . . . **101** B7
Kennion Rd BS5 . . . . **65** A7
Kennmoor Cl BS30 . . . . . **66** A6
Kenn Moor Dr BS21 . . . . **57** G1
KENN MOOR GATE **74** F4
Kennmoor Rd BS21 . . . . **74** A6
Kenn Moor Rd BS49 . . . **74** B1
Kenn Rd
Bristol BS5 . . . . **65** A7
Clevedon BS21 . . . . **73** F6
Kenn St BS21 . . . . **73** F7
Kensal Ave BS3 . . . . **63** E3
Kensal Rd BS3 . . . . **63** E3
Kensington BS24 . . . . . **105** E7
Kensington Apartments
BS6 . . . . **49** C3

Kensington CI BS35 . . . . . 8 B2
Kensington Ct
  Bath BA1 . . . . .85 B2
  Bristol BS8 . . . . .142 A3
Kensington Gdns BA1 . .85 B1
Kensington Ho **5** BS5. .65 A8
KENSINGTON PARK 64 C3
Kensington Park Rd
  BS4. . . . . .64 C2
Kensington Pk **12** BS5. .50 A1
Kensington Pl
  Bath BA1 . . . . .85 B1
  8 Bathwick BA2 . . . .102 B8
  Bristol BS8 . . . . .142 A3
Kensington Rd
  Bristol, Redland BS6 . . . .49 C1
  3 Bristol, St George
    BS5 . . . . .65 A8
  7 Bristol, Staple Hill
    BS16 . . . . .51 D4
  Weston-s-M BS23 . . . . .104 F5
Kent Ave BS37 . . . . .27 F3
Kent CI BS34. . . . . .36 D4
Kent Mews BS16 . . . . . . .50 E7
Kenton Ho BS34 . . . . . . .23 F1
Kenton Mews BS9. . . . . .49 C5
Kent Rd
  Bristol BS7 . . . . .49 E4
  Congresbury BS49. . . . . .91 D5
Kents Gn BS15. . . . . .51 E2
Kentshare La BS40 . . . . .95 B6
Kent St
  Bristol BS3 . . . . .63 C3
  Cheddar BS27 . . . . .126 B1
Kent Way BS22. . . . . .89 B4
Kenwood CI BS15 . . . . . .51 F1
Keppel CI BS31 . . . . .82 D2
Kerry Rd BS4 . . . . .63 E1
Kersteman Rd BS6 . . . . .49 C3
Kestrel CI
  Bristol BS34. . . . . .35 E8
  Chipping Sodbury BS37 . .39 F8
  Thornbury BS35. . . . . . . .8 D2
Kestrel Dr
  Pucklechurch BS16 . . . . .53 C4
  Weston-s-M BS22 . . . . . .88 E1
Kestrel Rd G12. . . . . .11 A5
Keswick Wlk BS10 . . . . .35 C2
Ketch Rd BS3 . . . . .63 F3
Kewhaven Bglws BS22 . .88 B4
Kew Rd BS23 . . . . .87 E1
Kewside BS22 . . . . .88 B4
KEWSTOKE. 88 B4
Kewstoke Prim Sch
  BS22. . . . . .88 B3
Kewstoke Rd
  Bath BA2 . . . . .102 A2
  Bristol BS9 . . . . .48 E4
  Weston-s-M BS22 . . . . . .88 C3
Kew Wlk BS4 . . . . .80 C8
Keyes Path BS22 . . . . . . .88 F4
KEYNSHAM 81 E3
Keynsham By-Pass
  BS31. . . . . .81 E7
Keynsham Hospl BS31. .81 F4
Keynsham Prim Sch
  BS31. . . . . .81 D5
Keynsham Rd BS30,
  BS31. . . . . .82 A8
Keynsham Sta BS31 . . . .81 F6
Keys Ave BS7 . . . . .49 F7
Kidney Hill
  Westerleigh BS37 . . . . . .39 A3
  Westerleigh BS37 . . . . . .39 A3
Kielder Dr BS22. . . . . . . .88 F3
Kilbirnie Rd BS14 . . . . . .80 A3
Kilburn Ct **17** BS5 . . . .64 B8
Kilburn St **19** BS5 . . . .64 B8
Kildare BA2 . . . . .102 B2
Kildare Rd BS4 . . . . .63 D1
Kilkenny La BA2 . . . . . .118 B8
Kilkenny Pl BS20. . . . . . .45 C6
Killcott Rd GL12 . . . . . . .19 E8
KILLING'S KNAP 139 B4
KILMERSDON. 140 B5
Kilmersdon CE Prim Sch
  BA3. . . . . .140 A6
Kilmersdon Hill BA3 . .140 A5
Kilmersdon Rd
  Bristol BS13. . . . . .79 B4
  Radstock BA3. . . . . .139 E8
Kilminster CI BS34. . . . .36 D7
Kilminster Rd BS11 . . . .47 D7
Kiln CI BS15 . . . . .51 B2
Kiln Ct BS5 . . . . .64 B8
Kiln Pk BS23. . . . . .105 A6
Kilve BS24. . . . . .105 A2
Kilvert CI BS4. . . . . .64 D5
Kimberley Ave BS16. . . .51 C5
Kimberley CI BS16 . . . . .51 F7
Kimberley Cres BS16. . .51 C5
Kimberley Rd
  Bristol, Fishponds BS16. .51 C5
  Bristol, Kingswood BS15 .51 D1
  Clevedon BS21. . . . . . . .57 E2

Kinber CI BA1 . . . . .84 A3
Kinema Ho BS4 . . . . . . .64 C4
King Alfred Way BA15 .120 D7
Kingcott Mill Farm Cvns
  BS48. . . . . .77 B8
King Dick's La **7** BS5. .64 F8
KINGDOWN 94 D5
Kingdown Rd BS40. . . . .94 C5
King Edward CI BS14. . .80 A6
King Edward Rd BA2 . .101 D5
King Edward's Pre-Prep
  Sch BA1 . . . . .101 C8
King Edwards Sch
  BA1 . . . . .101 C8
King Edward's Sch
  BA2 . . . . .102 C7
Kingfisher CI
  Bristol BS32. . . . . .24 E2
  Thornbury BS35. . . . . . . .8 D2
Kingfisher Ct BA2. . . . .120 C6
Kingfisher Dr
  Bristol BS16. . . . . .50 E6
  Midsomer Norton BA3. .139 B8
Kingfisher Rd
  Chipping Sodbury BS37 . .40 A8
  Portishead BS20 . . . . . . .46 A6
  Weston-s-M BS22 . . . . .105 F8
King George's Rd
  Bath BA2 . . . . .101 C6
  Bristol BS13. . . . . .78 F5
  Bristol BS13. . . . . .78 F5
King George V Pl **1** BS1 .143 A2
King John's Hunting
  Lodge★ BS26. . . . . . .125 C2
King John's Rd BS15 . . .51 B2
King La
  Clutton BS39 . . . . .114 F4
  Horton BS37 . . . . .29 A7
King Rd
  Bristol BS4. . . . . .64 C1
  Churchill BS49 . . . . .108 E6
King Road Ave BS11. . . .33 B2
Kingrove Cres BS37. . . .40 C8
Kingrove La BS37 . . . . . .40 C7
Kings Ave BS15 . . . . .65 B4
King's Ave BS6, BS7 . . . .49 C4
Kings Chase BS15. . . . . .65 D8
Kingscote BS37 . . . . .39 D6
Kingscote Pk BS5. . . . . .65 B6
Kingscourt CI BS14 . . . .80 A4
Kings Croft BS41. . . . . . .61 E1
Kings Ct
  Bath BA1 . . . . .141 B2
  Bristol BS1. . . . . .143 A2
  Bristol, Little Stoke
    BS34 . . . . .36 C6
  Bristol, St Pauls BS1 . . .143 B4
  Bristol, Southville BS3. . .63 C4
  2 Bristol, Withywood
    BS13. . . . . .78 F4
  8 Nailsea BS48. . . . . .59 E2
KINGSDOWN
  Bathford. 86 F3
  Bristol 143 A4
Kingsdown Gr SN13. . . .86 F3
Kingsdown Par BS6 . . .143 A4
Kingsdown View **15**
  BA1 . . . . .85 A1
Kings Dr
  Bristol, Hanham BS15 . .65 B4
  Bristol, Stoke Gifford
    BS34 . . . . .37 A4
King's Dr BS7. . . . . .49 C4
Kingsfield BA2. . . . . . . .101 C3
Kingsfield La
  Bristol, Longwell Green
    BS15 . . . . .65 E5
  Bristol, Mount Hill BS30 .65 E4
Kingsfield Rdbt BS15. . .65 E5
Kings Fields BS37. . . . . .27 A8
Kingsfield Sch BS15. . . .66 A8
King's Forest Prim Sch
  BS15. . . . . .51 F2
Kingsgate BS37 . . . . .39 E8
KINGSGATE PARK 39 F8
King's Head La BS13. . . .78 F7
Kingshill BS48 . . . . .59 C2
Kingshill CE Prim Sch
  BS48. . . . . .59 D3
Kingshill Gdns BS48. . . .59 C1
Kingshill Ho BS4. . . . . . .64 B1
Kingshill La BS40 . . . . .112 C4
Kingshill Rd BS4. . . . . . .64 B1
Kingsholme Ct BS23 . . .87 E1
Kingsholme Rd BS15 . . .51 D1
Kingsholm Rd BS10. . . .49 D8
King's La
  Clevedon BS21. . . . . . . .57 F5
  6 Weston-s-M BS23. . .104 E8
Kingsland CI **1** BS2. . .64 A6
Kingsland Rd BS2. . . . . .64 A6
Kingsland Road Bridge **3**
  BS2. . . . . .64 A6
Kingsland Trad Est
  Bristol BS2. . . . . .143 C3
  Bristol, Newton BS2. . . . .64 A7
Kingsleigh Ct BS15. . . . .65 F7
Kingsleigh Gdns BS15 . .65 F7
Kingsleigh Pk BS15 . . . .65 F7

Kingsley Ho
  Bristol BS2. . . . . .143 C2
  Bristol, Westbury on Trym
    BS9. . . . . .49 A8
Kingsley Pl **1** BS3 . . . .63 C4
Kingsley Rd
  Bristol, Lower Easton
    BS5. . . . . .50 C1
  Bristol, Montpelier BS6 . .49 D2
  Clevedon BS21. . . . . . . .57 F2
  Radstock BA3. . . . . .133 C1
  Weston-s-M BS23 . . . . .104 F3
Kingsmarsh Ho **3**
  BS5. . . . . .64 B7
KINGSMEAD. 141 A2
Kingsmead BS48. . . . . . .59 C2
Kingsmead Ct **12** BA1 .141 B2
Kingsmead N BA1. . . . .141 B2
Kingsmead Rd BS5. . . . .51 A1
Kingsmead Sq BA1. . . .141 B2
Kingsmead St BA1 . . . .141 B2
Kingsmead W BA1 . . . .141 B2
Kingsmill BS9 . . . . .48 D5
Kings Oak Mdw BS39. .114 E2
King's Parade Ave **1**
  BS8. . . . . .49 B1
King's Parade Mews
  BS8. . . . . .49 A1
Kings Park Ave BS2 . . . .64 C6
King Sq BS2 . . . . .143 A4
Kings Square Ave BS2. .143 A4
Kings Quarter
  Apartments **14** BS2 .143 A4
Kings Rd BS40 . . . . .92 D1
King's Rd
  Bristol BS8. . . . . .142 A3
  Bristol, Kensington Park
    BS4. . . . . .64 C3
  Clevedon BS21. . . . . . . .57 F5
  Portishead BS20 . . . . . . .44 F4
Kings Sq BS30 . . . . .82 D8
King St
  Avonmouth BS11 . . . . . .33 A1
  Bristol BS1. . . . . .143 A2
  Bristol, Lower Easton
    BS5. . . . . .50 C1
  Bristol, St George BS15. .65 B8
Kingston Ave
  Clevedon BS21. . . . . . . .57 G3
  Saltford BS31. . . . . .82 C3
Kingston Bldgs **5**
  BA1 . . . . .141 C2
Kingston CI BS16 . . . . . .52 A7
Kingston Dr
  Bristol BS16. . . . . .52 A7
  Nailsea BS48 . . . . .75 C8
Kingston La BS40 . . . . . .94 F8
Kingston Mead BS40 . . .94 F7
Kingston Rd
  Bath BA1 . . . . .141 C2
  Bristol BS3. . . . . .63 C4
  Nailsea BS48 . . . . .75 C8
KINGSTON SEYMOUR . .73 C2
Kingston Way BS48 . . . .75 C8
Kingstree St BS4. . . . . . .64 A4
KINGSWAY 101 C3
Kingsway
  Bath BA2 . . . . .101 C3
  Bristol, Little Stoke BS34 .36 C6
  Bristol, St George BS5. . .65 B7
  Portishead BS20 . . . . . . .44 F4
Kingsway Ave BS15 . . . .65 B8
Kingsway Cres BS15. . . .65 C8
Kingsway Pk BS30 . . . . .66 B6
Kingsway Sh Prec BS5 . .65 B7
Kingswear **3** BS22. . . .89 A2
Kingswear Rd BS3 . . . . .63 D2
Kings Weston Ave
  BS11. . . . . .47 E8
Kingsweston Down Nature
  Res★ BS9, BS11. . . . . . .34 C1
Kings Weston La
  Avonmouth BS11 . . . . . .33 E3
  Bristol BS11. . . . . .48 A8
Kings Weston Rd BS11,
  BS10. . . . . .34 C1
Kingsweston Sch BS11 .48 A8
Kings Wlk BS13. . . . . . . .78 E7
KINGSWOOD
  Bristol 65 E8
  Wotton-under-Edge. 11 E4
Kingswood Abbey
  Gatehouse★ GL12. . . . .11 F5
Kingswood Douglas Ind Est
  BS15. . . . . .65 D7
Kingswood Foundation Est
  BS15. . . . . .65 C7
Kingswood Hertiage
  Mus★ BS30. . . . . .66 B6
Kingswood Hts BS15 . . .51 D1
Kingswood Ind Est
  BS30. . . . . .65 F4
Kingswood Prep Sch
  BA1 . . . . .84 E1
Kingswood Prim Sch
  GL12. . . . . .11 F5
Kingswood Rd GL12. . . .19 D8
Kingswood Sch BA1. . . .84 E2

Kingswood Sch Upper
  Sports Fields
  BATH BA1. . . . . .84 D4
  Charlcombe BA1 . . . . . . .84 D4
Kingswood Trad Est
  BS15. . . . . .51 D1
KINGTON 7 E1
Kington La BS35. . . . . . . .7 E1
Kington Rd BS35 . . . . . . .7 E3
Kingwell View BS39. . . .115 D2
King William Ave BS1 .143 A2
King William St 63 B4
Kinsale Rd BS14 . . . . . . .80 C7
Kinsale Wlk BS4 . . . . . . .63 E1
Kinvara Rd BS4. . . . . . . .79 E8
Kipling Ave BA2. . . . . . .101 F4
Kipling Rd
  Bristol BS7. . . . . .36 B1
  Radstock BA3. . . . . .133 C1
  Weston-s-M BS23 . . . . .105 A3
Kirkby Rd BS11 . . . . .34 A1
Kirkstone Gdns BS10. . .35 C2
Kirkstone Ho BS34 . . . . .36 A8
Kirtlington Rd BS5. . . . .50 B3
Kite Hay CI BS16. . . . . . .50 E5
Kites CI BS32 . . . . .24 C2
Kite Wlk **2** BS22. . . . .105 E8
Kitland La BS40 . . . . . . .109 C8
Kitley Hill BA3 . . . . .133 C4
Kittyhawk CI **4** BA3. . .139 B8
Knapp La GL12. . . . . . . .10 B3
Knapp Rd BS35 . . . . .8 D1
Knapps CI BS25 . . . . . . .124 F8
Knapps Dr BS25. . . . . . .124 F8
Knapps La BS5. . . . . .50 E2
KNAPP THE 8 F3
Knapp The BS37 . . . . . . .27 F5
Kneller CI BS11 . . . . .48 A8
KNIGHTCOTT 106 F3
Knightcott BS29 . . . . . .106 F3
Knightcott Gdns BS29 .106 F3
Knightcott Ind Est
  BS29. . . . . .106 E3
Knightcott Pk BS29 . . .107 A3
Knightcott Rd
  Abbots Leigh BS8. . . . . .61 F8
  Banwell BS29. . . . . .106 F3
Knighton Rd BS10. . . . . .35 E1
Knightsbridge Pk
  BS13. . . . . .79 E4
Knights CI BS9. . . . . .49 B6
Knightstone CI
  Axbridge BS26. . . . . . . .125 C1
  Peasedown St John
    BA2 . . . . .134 B8
Knightstone Cswy
  BS23. . . . . .104 C8
Knightstone Ct
  Bristol BS5. . . . . .50 D2
  Clevedon BS21. . . . . . . .57 F1
  Weston-s-M BS23 . . . . . .87 D1
Knightstone Gdns
  BS4. . . . . .64 B2
Knightstone Gn BS23. .104 E6
Knightstone Ho
  1 Bristol BS2. . . . . . .143 A4
  Weston-s-M BS23 . . . . .104 D8
Knightstone Lodge
  BS6. . . . . .49 D1
Knightstone Mount
  BS5. . . . . .65 A6
Knightstone Pk **4**
  BS23. . . . . .104 E5
Knightstone Pl
  Bath BA1 . . . . .84 B1
  Bristol BS15. . . . . .65 B2
  7 Weston-s-M BS22. . .88 F2
Knightstone Rd BS23. .104 C8
Knightstone Rise **5**
  BS5. . . . . .64 F8
Knightstone Sq BS14. . .80 C5
Knightstone Wlk BS2. .142 C4
Knightwood Rd BS34. . .36 F5
Knobsbury Hill BA3 . . .140 D6
Knobsbury La BA3 . . . .140 C7
Knole CI BS32 . . . . .23 F4
Knole Ct BS10 . . . . .35 A3
Knole La BS10 . . . . .35 B3
Knole Pk BS32 . . . . .23 F3
Knoll Ct BS9. . . . . .48 D3
Knoll Hill BS9. . . . . .48 D3
Knoll The BS20. . . . . .45 D7
Knovill CI BS11 . . . . .34 B2
KNOWLE. 63 F3
KNOWLE HILL BS40. . . .113 C7
KNOWLE PARK 64 A1
Knowle Park Jun Sch
  BS4. . . . . .64 A1
Knowle Rd BS2 . . . . .63 F3
Knowles Rd BS21 . . . . . .57 E2
Knowsley Rd BS16. . . . . .50 E3
Kyght CI BS15 . . . . .66 A8
Kylross Ave BS14. . . . . . .80 B5
Kynaston Way BS15. . . .65 D4
Kynges Mill CI BS16. . . .51 A7
Kyngstone Ct **10**
  BS16. . . . . .50 D5
Kyrle Gdns BA1 . . . . .85 F3

L

Labbott The BS31. . . . . .81 E5
Laburnum CI BA3. . . . . .138 F8
Laburnum Ct BS23 . . . .105 B7
Laburnum Gr
  Bristol BS16. . . . . .51 B4
  Midsomer Norton BA3. .138 F8
Laburnum Rd
  Bristol BS15. . . . . .65 C5
  Weston-s-M BS23 . . . . .105 B7
Laburnum Terr BA1 . . . .85 F3
Lacey Rd BS14. . . . . .80 F6
Lacock Dr BS30. . . . . . . .65 F5
Ladd CI BS15 . . . . .65 F7
Ladden Ct BS35. . . . . . . .15 C8
Laddon Mead BS37. . . . .27 D4
Ladies Mile BS8. . . . . . . .48 F1
Ladman Gr BS14 . . . . . . .80 E6
Ladman Rd BS14. . . . . . .80 E5
Ladycroft **4** BS21. . . . .57 D1
Ladye Bay BS21. . . . . . . .57 F7
Ladye Wake BS22 . . . . . .88 F4
Ladymead BS20. . . . . . . .45 F5
Ladymeade BS48. . . . . . .76 A7
Ladymead Ho BA1 . . . .141 C3
Ladymead La BS40 . . . .108 F5
Ladysmith Rd BS6. . . . . .49 B4
Ladywell BS40 . . . . .92 D2
Laggan Gdns BA1 . . . . . .84 E1
Laggan Ho BA1 . . . . .84 E1
Lakemead Gdns **3**
  BS13. . . . . .78 F4
Lakemead Gr BS13 . . . . .78 F6
Lake Rd
  Bristol BS10. . . . . .49 C8
  Portishead BS20 . . . . . . .45 D7
Lakeside BS16 . . . . .50 E3
Lakeside CI BS40. . . . . . .111 D5
Lakeside Ct BS24 . . . . . .89 B1
Lake View BS16 . . . . .50 F3
Lake View Rd BS5. . . . . .64 D8
Lakewood Cres BS10. . .49 B8
Lakewood Rd BS10. . . . .49 B8
La Maison BS5. . . . . .51 A2
Lambert Pl BS4 . . . . .79 D4
Lamb Hill BS5 . . . . .64 F7
Lambley Rd BS5 . . . . . . .64 E8
Lambourn CI BS3 . . . . . .63 D3
Lambourne Way BS20. . .45 F5
Lambourn Rd BS31. . . . .82 A4
Lambretta Scooter Mus★
  BS23. . . . . .64 E8
LAMBRIDGE. 85 C2
Lambridge **6** BA1. . . . .85 C1
Lambridge Bldgs **1**
  BA1 . . . . .85 C1
Lambridge Grange **6**
  BA1 . . . . .85 C2
Lambridge Mews **5**
  BA1 . . . . .85 C1
Lambridge Pl BA1. . . . . .85 C1
Lambridge St BA1 . . . . .85 C1
Lambrook Rd BS16. . . . .51 A4
Lamb St BS2 . . . . .143 C3
Lamington CI BS13. . . . .78 F6
Lamont Ho **7** BA1 . . . .85 C1
Lamord Gate BS34 . . . . .36 E5
Lampard's Bldgs BA1 .141 B4
Lampeter Rd BS9 . . . . . .49 A7
Lampley Rd BS21 . . . . . .73 D2
Lampton Ave BS13 . . . . .79 E4
Lampton Gr BS13 . . . . . .79 E3
Lampton Gr BS41. . . . . .61 F1
Lanaway Rd BS16. . . . . .51 B6
Lancashire Rd BS7. . . . .49 E3
Lancaster CI BS34. . . . . .36 D4
Lancaster House Sch
  BS23. . . . . .104 F8
Lancaster Rd
  Bristol BS2. . . . . .50 A4
  Yate BS37. . . . . .27 E3
Lancaster St **10** BS5. . .64 C7
Lancelot Rd BS16 . . . . . .50 E8
Landemann Cir BS23. . .87 C1
Landemann Path **2**
  BS23. . . . . .104 E8
Landmark Ct BS1 . . . . .142 C1
Landrail Wlk BS16. . . . . .50 F6
Landsdown View BA1. . .84 B2
Landseer Ave BS7. . . . . .50 B7
Landseer CI BS22. . . . . .88 F3
Landseer Rd BA2 . . . . . .101 B6
Land The BS36 . . . . .38 C7
Lane End BS40 . . . . .95 C5
Lane End Rd BS34. . . . . .35 E6
Lanercost Rd BS10. . . . .35 C2
Lanesborough Rise
  BS14. . . . . .80 D7
Lanes Dairy BS34 . . . . . .36 A3
Lanes End BS4. . . . . .64 C1
Lane The BS35 . . . . .22 F2
Laneys Dro BS24. . . . . . .105 C3
Langdale Ct BS34 . . . . . .36 A8
Langdale Rd BS16. . . . . .50 F4
Langdon Rd BA2. . . . . . .101 B4
Langdown Ct BS14 . . . . .80 E5
Langfield CI BS10 . . . . . .34 E3

Langford Cl BS39 .....132 D6
Langford Court Cotts
BS40...............109 E5
Langford La BS40.....109 E5
Langford Rd
Bristol BS13..........78 F8
Lower Langford BS40 .109 C6
Weston-s-M BS23......105 A6
Langfords La BS40 ....132 C8
Langford's La BS39...115 D1
Langford Way BS15 ....65 E7
Langham Pl BA11.....137 F1
Langham Rd BS4......64 B2
Langhill Ave BS4......79 D7
Langley Cres BS3......62 E1
Langley Mow BS16.....52 B7
Langleys Cotts BA3 ...138 B8
Langley's La BA3, BS39 132 C1
Langport Gdns BS48 ...75 E8
Langport Rd BS23.....104 E5
LANGRIDGE 84 E7
Langridge La BA1......84 E6
Langsdown Ho **7** BS2. .49 F1
Langthorn Cl BS37......39 E8
Langton Court Rd BS4. .64 D5
Langton Ct **11** BS16....50 E3
Langton Ho **9** BS2....143 C3
Langton Pk BS3........63 C4
Langton Rd BS4.......64 D5
Langton Way BS4......64 F6
LANSDOWN
Bath................84 E1
Upper Langridge 84 B6
Lansdown BS37........39 E8
Lansdown Cl BS15.....51 D2
Lansdown Cres
2 Bath BA1..........84 F1
Timsbury BA2.........116 C2
Lansdown Ct BS23....104 F8
Lansdowne BS16.......37 C1
Lansdowne Ct **8** BS5. .64 A8
Lansdown Gdns BS22...89 B5
Lansdown Gr BA1.....141 B4
Lansdown Grove Ct
BA1................141 B4
Lansdown Grove Lodge
BA1................141 B4
Lansdown Ho
Bath BA1.............84 F1
Bristol BS15..........51 D2
Lansdown Hts BA1.....84 F1
Lansdown La
Bath BA1.............84 B4
Upton Cheyney BS30...67 C1
Lansdown Mans BA1...141 B4
Lansdown Mews **9**
BA1................141 B3
Lansdown Pk BA1.....84 E3
Lansdown Pl
Bristol BS8..........142 A3
High Littleton BS39...115 D1
Lansdown Pl E BA1....141 B4
Lansdown Pl W **1** BA1. 84 F1
Lansdown Rd
Bath BA1.............84 E2
Bristol BS8...........63 A4
Bristol, Kingswood BS15 51 D2
Bristol, Redland BS6 ...49 C1
6 Bristol, Upper Easton
BS5................64 B8
Pucklechurch BS16 ....53 C6
Saltford BS31.........82 E3
Lansdown Terr BS6.....49 D5
Lansdown View
Bath BA2............101 C5
Bristol BS15..........65 F8
Faulkland BA3........135 D1
Timsbury BA2.........116 C2
Tunley BA2...........117 B4
Lanson Roberts Rd
BS35................22 D5
Lanthony Cl BS24.....106 A8
Lapdown La GL9.......41 D1
Laphams Ct **11** BS30...65 F4
Lapwing Cl BS32.......24 D2
Lapwing Gdns
Bristol BS16..........50 F6
Weston-s-M BS22......88 F1
Larch Cl
Churchill BS40........109 A5
Lyde Green BS16.......52 D8
Nailsea BS48..........60 A2
Larch Ct BA3.........139 D8
Larches The BS22......89 A3
Larchgrove Cres BS22. .88 F1
Larchgrove Wlk BS22 ..88 F1
Larch Rd
Bristol BS15..........51 E3
Colerne SN14.........70 F6
Larch Way BS34.......35 E7
Larchwood Ct BA3....134 A3
Lark Cl BA3..........139 B8
Larkfield BS36.........38 D7
LARKHALL............85 C2
Larkhall Pl BA1.......85 C2
Larkhall Terr BA1......85 C2
Larkhill Rd BS24......106 B6
Lark Pl BA1..........101 D7
Lark Rd BS22..........88 F1

Lark Rise BS37.........27 F4
Larks Field BS16.......50 E5
Lark's La BS37.........26 B7
Larksleaze Rd BS30....65 F2
Larkspur Cl BS35.......8 D1
Lasbury Gr BS13.......79 C5
Lascelles Ave BA2.....102 C8
Latchmoor Ho BS13....79 A8
Late Broads BA15.....120 D7
Latimer Cl BS4........64 E4
LATTERIDGE..........26 B6
Latteridge La
Latteridge BS37.......26 A7
Tytherington BS35.....15 F1
Latteridge Rd
Iron Acton BS37.......26 D4
Locking BS24..........26 C6
Latton Rd BS7.........49 F8
Launceston Ave BS15 ..65 B5
Launceston Rd BS15 ...51 B1
Laura Pl BA2.........141 C3
Laurel Dr
Colerne SN14.........70 F6
Lyde Green BS16.......52 C8
Nailsea BS48..........59 F2
Paulton BS39.........132 E5
Weston-s-M BS23.....104 E2
Laurel Gdns
Timsbury BA2.........116 B1
Yatton BS49...........74 B1
Laurel Ho BS25.......125 A8
Laurel St BS15.........65 D8
Laurels The
Bristol, Catbrain BS10 ..35 A6
Bristol, Mangotsfield
BS16................52 A6
Churchill BS25.......108 F4
Weston-s-M BS23.....104 E2
Westwood BA15.......120 F3
Laurel Terr BS49.......74 B1
Laurie Cres BS9........49 D6
Laurie Lee Ct **3** BS30 .66 A5
Lavender Cl
Thornbury BS35........8 D1
Weston-s-M BS22......89 A5
Lavender Ct BS5........50 F1
Lavender Way BS32....36 F7
Lavenham Rd BS37.....27 B2
Lavers Cl BS15.........65 E6
Lavington Cl BS21......57 D1
Lavington Rd BS5......65 B6
Lawford Ave BS34......36 C6
Lawfords Gate BS2....143 C3
Lawfords Gate Ho **17**
BS2................143 C3
Lawford St BS2.......143 C3
Lawn Ave BS16.........51 B5
Lawn Cl **5** BS7.......50 C8
Lawn Rd BS16.........51 B5
Lawnside BS48.........76 B5
Lawns Rd BS37........27 F2
Lawns The
Bristol BS11..........47 E7
Weston-s-M BS22......89 B3
Yatton BS49...........74 A1
Lawnwood Ind Units **14**
BS5................64 B8
Lawnwood Rd **15** BS5 .64 B8
Lawrence Ave BS5......50 B1
Lawrence Cl
Bristol BS15..........52 A2
Weston-s-M BS22......88 E2
Lawrence Dr BS37......27 B2
Lawrence Gr BS9.......49 B5
Lawrence Hill BS5......64 B7
Lawrence Hill Ind Pk
BS5................64 B8
Lawrence Hill Rdbt
BS5................64 A7
Lawrence Hill Sta BS5. .64 B7
Lawrence Mews BS22 ..88 E2
Lawrence Rd
Weston-s-M BS22......88 E2
Wrington BS40........92 A2
LAWRENCE WESTON. .34 A1
Lawrence Weston Rd
Avonmouth BS11.......33 F4
Bristol BS11..........34 A2
Laws Dr BS24.........105 F7
Lawson Cl BS31........82 C2
Laxey Rd BS7.........49 F7
Laxton Cl BS35........14 A3
Laxton Dr GL12........11 F4
Laxton Way BA2......134 D7
Lays Dr BS31..........81 C5
Lays Farm Bsns Ctr
BS31................81 C4
Lays Farm Trad Est
BS31................81 C4
Lays La BS40.........110 D4
Leach Cl BS21.........57 F1
Leader St BS7.........50 C8
Leading Edge The
BS8................142 B2
Leadmine La BS40....127 E4
Leafy Way BS24.......106 B4
Lea Grove Rd BS21.....57 E4
Leaholme Gdns BS14. ..80 A3

Leaman Cl BS37........28 B1
Lea Pound St BS34.....35 F6
Leap Vale BS16........52 A8
Leap Valley Cres BS16 .52 A8
Lear Cl BS30...........66 B5
Lease La BS40........127 E8
Leaze The
Radstock BA3........139 D8
Yate BS37.............27 D2
Leda Ave BS14.........80 A7
Ledbury Rd BS16.......51 C4
Leechpool Way BS37...27 E5
Lee Cl BS34............35 F8
Leedham Rd
Locking BS24.........106 C5
Locking BS24.........106 C5
Leeming Way BS11.....47 C8
Lees Ct BS15..........51 E1
Lees Hill BS15.........51 E2
Leeside BS20..........45 C5
Leewood Rd BS23......87 F1
Leg La BS40...........110 B3
Leicester Sq BS16......51 D3
Leicester St **6** BS3.....63 D4
Leicester Wlk BS4......64 F5
Leigh Cl BA1...........85 A2
Leigh Court Bsns Ctr
BS8................48 A2
Leigh Ct BS9...........48 D3
Leigh La
Cold Ashton BA1.......69 B3
Westerleigh BS37......39 B1
Leigh Rd BS8.........142 B4
Leigh St BS3...........63 A4
Leighton Cres BS24...122 A8
Leighton Rd
Bath BA1.............84 A3
Bristol, Southville BS3 ..63 B4
Bristol, Upper Knowle
BS4................64 B2
Leigh View Rd BS20....45 E7
Leighwood Dr BS48....59 B1
LEIGH WOODS........62 D8
Leigh Woods Forest
Walks★ BS8.........48 C1
Leisure Rd BS15.......65 E5
Lemon La BS2........143 C4
Lena Ave **3** BS5......50 C1
Lena St BS5...........50 C1
Lennox Way BS11.......33 B1
Lenover Gdns BS13.....79 B4
Leonard La BS1.......143 A3
Leonard Rd BS5.......64 D7
Leonards Ave BS5......50 C1
Leonides Ave BS24....105 B4
Leopold Bldgs BA1....141 C4
Leopold Rd BS6........49 E2
Les Brown Ct BS2.....143 C2
Lescren Way BS11......33 D1
Leslie Rise BA15......120 F3
Lester Dr BS22.........89 A3
Lewington Rd BS16.....51 C4
Lewins Mead BS1.....143 A3
Lewin St **9** BS5......64 D7
Lewis Cl
Bristol, Emerson's Green
BS16................52 C5
Bristol, North Common
BS30................66 D5
Chilcompton BA3.....138 C4
Lewisham Gr BS23....105 A8
Lewis Rd BS13.........79 A8
Lewis St BS2...........64 B5
Lewton La BS36........37 E7
LEYHILL..............10 B4
Ley La BS35...........13 F3
Leyland Wlk BS13......78 F4
Leys The BS21.........57 D1
Leyton Vills BS6........49 B2
Liberty Gdns BS1......142 C1
Liberty Ind Pk BS3.....63 A1
Liberty La BS40.......110 E2
Lichfield Rd BS4.......64 E6
Lilac Cl BS10..........35 C1
Lilac Ct BS31..........81 C4
Lilac Dr BS16..........52 C8
Lilac Terr BA1.........133 C2
Lilac Way BS22........89 A5
Lilian Terr BS39.......132 E5
Lillian St **5** BS5......64 C8
Lillington Cl BA3......134 B2
Lillington Rd BA3......134 B2
Lilliput Ave BS37.......40 A8
Lilliput Ct BS37........40 B8
Lillypool Cheese & Cider
Farm★ BS25.........125 F6
Lilstock Ave BS7.......49 F4
Lilton Wlk BS13........63 A1
Lilymead Ave BS4......64 A3
Lime Ave GL9..........42 B8
Limebreach Wood
BS48................59 D3
Limeburn Hill BS40....95 E5
Lime Cl
Bristol BS10..........35 B3
Locking BS24........106 B4

Lime Cl continued
Weston-s-M BS22......89 A1
Lime Croft BS37.......27 F4
Lime Ct BS31..........81 C4
Lime Gr
Alveston BS35.........14 F4
Bath BA2............102 B6
Lime Grove Gdns BA2 .102 B6
Lime Kiln Cl BS34......36 D3
Lime Kiln Ct BS35......15 F3
Lime Kiln Gdns BS32 ..24 D2
Limekiln La BA2......102 F4
Lime Kiln La BS21......57 F3
Limekiln Rd BS37, GL12 .17 C2
Lime Kiln Rd BS1.....142 B2
Limekilns Cl BS31......81 F5
Lime Rd
Bristol, Hanham BS15 ..65 A5
Bristol, Southville BS3 ..63 B4
Lime St BS14..........79 E5
Limes The
Badminton GL9........30 E2
Bristol BS16..........37 B1
Limestone La BS37.....28 A2
Limestone Link BS40 .128 D6
Lime Terr BA3.........133 D1
Lime Tree Gr BS20.....47 D3
Lime Trees Rd BS9.....49 D6
LIMPLEY STOKE.....120 A6
Limpley Stoke Rd
BA15...............120 D6
Lincoln Cl BS31........81 C4
Lincoln Ct BS16........50 D6
Lincoln St BS5.........64 B7
Lincombe Ave BS16....51 D6
Lincombe Rd
Bristol BS16..........51 C6
Radstock BA3........139 D8
Lincott View BA2......101 E1
Linden Ave BS23......105 B8
Linden Cl
Bristol BS14..........80 E6
Bristol, Mayfield Park
BS16................51 A2
Colerne SN14.........70 F6
Radstock BA3........139 E8
Winterbourne BS36.....37 E6
Linden Dr BS32........36 E8
Linden Gdns BA1.....101 D8
Linden Grange BS6.....49 C3
Linden Ho BS16........51 B1
Linden Quarter **13** BS3 .63 C3
Linden Rd
Bristol BS6...........49 B4
Clevedon BS21........57 F4
Lindens The BS22......88 E4
Lindisfarne Cl BA15...120 E6
Lindon Ct **4** BS15.....51 B1
Lindrea St **8** BS3......63 B3
Lindsay Rd BS7........50 A4
Lindsey Cl BS20........44 F4
Linemere Cl BS48......76 D6
Lines Way BS14........80 C3
Lingfield Pk BS16......37 F2
Link La
Burrington BS40......109 F3
Monkton Farleigh BA15 103 F8
Linkmead BA3........138 F2
Link Rd
Bristol BS34..........36 B3
Nailsea BS48..........59 F2
Portishead BS20......45 C5
Yate BS37.............27 F1
Link Sch The BA2......118 E8
Links Ct BS23.........104 D4
Linkside BS21..........57 G6
Links Rd BS23........104 C2
Linley Cl BA2.........101 A5
Linleys The BA1.......101 C7
Linne Ho BA2.........101 A5
Linnell Cl BS7.........50 B6
Linnet Cl
Bristol BS34..........35 E8
Weston-s-M BS22......88 E1
Linnet Gdns BS20......45 F6
Linnet Way
Keynsham BS31.......81 C3
Keynsham BS31.......81 C3
Midsomer Norton BA3 .139 B8
Lintern Cres BS30......66 B6
Lintham Dr BS15.......65 F6
Linton's Wlk BS14.....80 A7
Lion Cl BS48...........59 D2
Lipgate Pl BS20........45 D3
Lippiat Hill BA3.......135 C3
Lippiatt La
Shipham BS25.......125 F8
Timsbury BA2.........116 B3
LIPYEATE............139 E1
Lipyeate La BA3.......139 E2
Lisburn Rd BS4........63 E1
Lisle Rd BS22..........89 B4
Lister Gr BA15........120 F3
Litfield Pl BS8.........62 F7
Litfield Rd BS8.........62 F8
Litt Hill BA3.........130 F2

Little Ann St BS2, BS5. .143 C4
LITTLE BADMINTON. ..30 E5
Little Birch Croft BS14 .80 A3
Little Bishop St BS2...143 B4
LITTLE BRISTOL......11 B3
Little Bristol Cl GL12 ...11 B4
Little Bristol La GL12 ...11 B4
Littlebrook BS39......132 E6
Little Caroline Pl **4**
BS8.................62 F5
Littlecross Ho BS3......63 B4
Littledean BS37........39 E7
Little Dowles BS30.....66 A4
Littlefields Ave BS29...107 B3
Littlefields Rd BS29...107 B3
Littlefields La BS29...107 B3
Little George St
Bristol BS2..........143 C4
Weston-s-M BS23.....104 E7
Little Green La BS35 ...22 A7
Little Halt BS20........44 E4
Little Ham BS21.......73 C8
Little Hayes BS16......51 B6
Little Headley Cl BS13 .79 B7
Little King St BS1.....143 A2
Little La BA2.........116 A6
Little Mdw BS34.......37 A6
Little Mead BS11.......34 B1
Little Mead Cl BS29...105 E3
Little Meadow End
BS48................75 E8
Little Mead Prim Sch
BS10................35 C2
Little Orch BS23......104 D1
Little Paradise BS3.....63 D3
Little Parr Cl BS16.....50 C5
Little Paul St BS2.....142 C4
LITTLE SODBURY.....29 B3
LITTLE SODBURY END. .28 E4
Little Solsbury La BA1. .85 F4
Little Stanhope St
BA1................141 A2
LITTLE STOKE........36 D7
Little Stoke La BS34...36 D6
Little Stoke Prim Sch
BS34................36 D6
Little Stoke Rd BS9....48 E4
Little Stony Leas BS16. .50 D8
Little Thatch Cl BS14...80 C6
LITTLETON............95 C4
Littleton Ct BS34......23 F1
LITTLETON DREW.....43 E5
Littleton Drew La GL9 .43 A6
Littleton La
Wellow BA2.........135 C2
Winford BS40.........95 D5
Littleton Mills BS40....95 D4
Littleton Rd BS3.......63 D2
Littleton St **4** BS5.....50 C1
LITTLETON-UPON-
SEVERN.............13 E8
Little Withey Mead
BS9.................48 F5
Littlewood Cl BS14.....80 B3
Littlewood La BS49.....75 C2
LITTON..............130 F2
Litton BS24...........105 A2
Litton Rd BA3........131 A1
Livingstone Mews **11**
BS3.................63 C3
Livingstone Rd BA2...101 D5
Livingstone Terr BA2 .141 A1
Llanarth Villas **3** BS6 .49 D1
Llewellyn Ct BS9.......49 A8
Llewellyn Way BS22....89 B3
Lobelia Rd BS16........38 D1
Lockemor Rd BS13.....79 F4
Lockes Paddock BS22. .89 C3
Lock Gdns BS13.......78 E7
LOCKING............106 A4
Locking Farm Ind Est
BS24...............106 A5
Locking Head Dro
Locking BS24.........105 F5
Locking BS24.........106 A6
Weston-s-M BS24.....106 A8
Locking Moor Rd
Locking BS24.........106 B5
Weston-s-M BS22.....105 D8
Locking Parklands
BS24...............106 B5
Locking Prim Sch
BS24...............106 B4
Locking Rd BS22, BS23 105 B7
Locking Road Bsns Pk
BS23...............105 A7
Lockingwell Rd BS31...81 D5
LOCKLEAZE...........50 C7
Lockleaze Prim Sch
BS7.................50 B8
Lockleaze Rd BS7......50 A6
Lockleys Way BS16.....50 D8
Lock's Acre BS35.......15 B5
LOCKSBROOK.........101 B6
Locksbrook Ct **8** BA1 101 B6
Locksbrook Pl **6** BA1 101 C7

Locksbrook Rd
 Bath BA1 . . . . .101 C6
 Weston-s-M BS22 . . . . . . 89 B5
Locksbrook Trad Est **7**
 BA1 . . . . .101 B6
Lockside BS20 . . . . 45 E7
Lockside Sq BS20 . . . . . . 45 E7
Lock's La BS37. . . . . 25 E4
Locks Yd BS3 . . . . 63 B1
Lodge Causeway Trad Ctr
 BS16. . . . . 50 F3
Lodge Cl BS49 . . . . 91 B8
Lodge Cswy BS16 . . . . . . 51 A3
Lodge Ct BS9 . . . . 48 E4
Lodge Dr
 Bristol BS30. . . . . 66 C2
 Long Ashton BS41 . . . . . . 62 B2
 Weston-s-M BS23 . . . . . . 88 A1
Lodge Gdns BS22 . . . . . .101 D1
Lodge Hill BS15 . . . . 51 C2
Lodge La BS48 . . . . 60 B2
Lodge Pl BS1 . . . . .142 C3
Lodge Rd
 Bristol BS15 . . . . 51 C1
 Wick BS30 . . . . 53 B1
 Yate BS37 . . . . 27 A3
Lodgeside Ave BS15. . . . 51 C1
Lodgeside Gdns BS15 . . 51 C1
Lodge St BS1 . . . . .142 C3
Lodges The BS3. . . . . . .138 D1
Lodge The BS40 . . . . 92 E2
Lodge Wlk BS16 . . . . 51 D6
Lodore Rd BS16. . . . . . . 50 F3
LODWAY 47 B5
Lodway BS20 . . . . 47 C4
Lodway Cl BS20. . . . . . . 47 C5
Lodway Gdns BS20 . . . . . 47 C4
Lodway Rd BS4 . . . . 64 C2
Logan Rd BS7 . . . . 49 D3
Logus Ct **14** BS30 . . . . . 65 F4
Lombard St BS3 . . . . 63 D4
Lombardy Cl **5** BS22 . .105 E8
Lomond Rd BS7. . . . . . . 35 F1
Londonderry Farm
 BS30. . . . . 82 A8
London Rd
 Bath BA1 . . . . .141 C4
 Bristol, St Pauls BS2 . . . . 49 F1
 Bristol, Warmley BS30 . . 66 D7
 Wick BS30 . . . . 67 E6
London Rd E BA1 . . . . . . 86 A3
London Rd W BA1. . . . . . 85 E2
London Sq BS20 . . . . . . 45 E7
London St
 Bath BA1 . . . . .141 C4
 Bristol BS15. . . . . 65 D8
Longacre BS21. . . . . 73 B8
Long Acre BA1. . . . . . . .141 C4
Long Acre Ho BA1 . . . . .141 C4
Long Acre Rd BS14. . . . . 80 A3
Long Acres Cl BS9 . . . . . 48 D7
LONG ASHTON 62 A1
Long Ashton Bsns Pk
 BS41. . . . . 62 B1
Long Ashton By-Pass
 Barrow Gurney BS48. . . . 77 D7
 Bristol BS41. . . . . 62 C1
 Bristol BS41. . . . . 78 B8
Long Ashton Rd BS41 . . 62 B2
Long Ave BS21. . . . . 57 D2
Long Barnaby BA3 . . . . .133 A2
Long Beach Rd BS30. . . . 66 B3
Longbottom BS25. . . . .126 A6
Longbrook Trad Est
 BS3. . . . . 62 E3
Long Cl
 Bristol, Fishponds BS16. . 51 C6
 Bristol, Little Stoke BS32 36 E6
Long Croft BS37 . . . . . . 27 D4
Longcross GL12. . . . . . . 10 B1
LONG CROSS. 94 D7
Long Cross
 Bristol, Lawrence Weston
 BS11 . . . . 34 B2
 Bristol, Shirehampton
 BS11 . . . . 47 F8
 Felton BS40 . . . . 94 D7
Longden Rd BS16 . . . . . . 51 F6
Long Down Ave BS7. . . . 50 C8
Longdown Dr BS22. . . . . 89 B4
Long Eaton Dr BS14. . . . 80 B7
Longfellow Ave BA2 . . . .101 F4
Longfellow Rd BA3. . . . .139 C8
Longfield Rd BS7 . . . . . . 49 E3
Longford BS37. . . . . 39 C8
Longford Ave BS10. . . . . 49 D8
Long Fox Manor BS4 . . . 65 A1
Long Ground BS34. . . . . 36 A7
Long Hay Cl BA2 . . . . . .101 B5
LONGHOUSE 117 D5
Long La
 Backwell BS48 . . . . 76 C2
 Felton BS40 . . . . 94 B5
 Wrington BS40. . . . . 93 B2
Longlands Ho **13** BS5. . 64 C7

Long Lease SN14. . . . . . 43 C1
Longleat Cl BS9. . . . . . . 49 C5
Longleaze Gdns BS24 .105 F3
Long Leaze Rd BS34. . . . 35 F7
Long Mdw BS16. . . . . . . 50 D6
Long Mead
 Locklease BS7. . . . . 50 C8
 Yate BS37. . . . . 27 E5
Longmead Ave BS7 . . . . 49 D5
Longmead Cl BA2 . . . . .136 F4
Longmead Croft BS13 . . 78 F4
Longmeadow Rd BS31. . 81 C4
Longmead Rd BS16. . . . . 38 B1
Longmoor Ct BS3 . . . . . . 63 A2
Longmoor Rd BS3 . . . . . . 63 A2
Long Rd BS16. . . . . 52 A5
Longreach BS31. . . . . . . 82 C4
Longreach Gr BS14 . . . . . 80 D6
Longridge Way BS24 . .105 F7
Long Row BS1 . . . . .143 B2
Longs Dr BS37. . . . . 27 C2
Longs View GL12. . . . . . 11 A5
Long-Thorn BS48. . . . . . 75 F6
Longthorne Pl BA2. . . . .101 F2
Long Thorn La BS40. . . .111 E7
Longton Grove Rd **3**
 BS23. . . . . .104 E8
Longton Ind Est BS23 .104 F6
Long Valley Rd BA2. . . .100 F5
Longvernal BA3. . . . . . .132 F1
Longvernal Prim Sch
 Midsomer Norton BA3. .132 E1
 Midsomer Norton BA3. .132 F1
Longway Ave BS13,
 BS14. . . . . 79 F4
LONGWELL GREEN. . . . 65 E3
Longwell Green Prim Sch
 BS30. . . . . 65 F3
Longwell Green Trad Pk
 BS30. . . . . 65 E4
Longwell Ho BS30. . . . . . 65 F3
Longwood BS4 . . . . 65 A2
Longwood Ho BS8 . . . . . . 61 D4
Longwood La BS8, BS41. 61 F4
Long Wood Mead BS7. . 50 C7
Long Wood Rd BS7. . . . . 50 C8
Lons Ct BS30 . . . . 66 C1
Lonsdale Ave BS23. . . . .104 F4
Lonsdale Bsns Ctr BS15 51 C2
Loop Rd BS10 . . . . 52 A3
Lorain Wlk BS10 . . . . . . 34 F2
Lorne Rd BA2. . . . . .101 D6
Lorton Cl BS10. . . . . 35 B1
Lorton Rd BS10. . . . . . . 35 B1
Lotts' Ave BS48 . . . . 76 B5
Lotus Ct BS22. . . . . 88 C1
Loughman Cl **2** BS15. . 65 E8
Louisa St BS2. . . . . .143 C2
Louise Ave BS16 . . . . . . 52 A5
Love La
 Chipping Sodbury BS37. . 40 A8
 Yate BS37. . . . . 28 A4
Lovelinch Gdns BS41. . . 61 F1
Lovell Dr BS39 . . . . .113 C4
Lovell's Hill BS15 . . . . . 65 B5
Lovells Mill BS39. . . . . .113 D4
Lovells The BS20. . . . . . 47 B4
Loveridge Cl BS36. . . . . 38 B7
Loveringe Cl BS10. . . . . 34 F4
Lovers La BA3, BS39 . . .133 A5
Lovers' Wlk BS23 . . . . .104 D8
Loves Hill BA2. . . . . . . .116 A1
Love's La BA2. . . . . .115 F6
Lowbourne BS14. . . . . . 79 F6
LOWER
 ALMONDSBURY 24 A6
Lower Ashley Rd
 Bristol, Baptist Mills BS2,
 BS5. . . . . 50 A1
 13 Bristol, St Pauls BS2 . 49 F1
Lower Batch BS40. . . . . 96 B3
Lower Borough Walls
 BA1 . . . . .141 C2
Lower Bristol Rd
 Bath BA2 . . . . .101 B6
 Clutton BS39. . . . . .114 F4
Lower Burlington Rd
 BS20. . . . . 45 E7
Lower Camden Pl
 BA1 . . . . .141 C4
LOWER CANADA 105 F2
Lower Castle St BS1. . . .143 B3
Lower Chapel La BS36. . 38 C7
Lower Chapel Rd BS15 . 65 C5
Lower Cheltenham Pl
 BS6. . . . . 49 F1
Lower Church La BS2 . .143 A3
Lower Church Rd
 Carlingcott BA2. . . . . . . .117 C1
 Weston-s-M BS23 . . . . .104 D8
LOWER CLAVERHAM . . . 74 F2
Lower Claverham BS49. 74 F3
Lower Clifton Hill BS8 .142 B2
Lower Cock Rd BS15 . . . 65 F7
Lower College St BS1 . .142 C2
Lower Conham Vale
 BS15. . . . . 65 A5

Lower Court Rd BS32. . . 24 A5
Lower Down Rd BS20. . . 45 B5
Lower East Hayes BA1 102 B8
LOWER EASTON 50 D2
Lower Fallow Cl BS14 . . 79 F3
Lower Farm La BA2. . . .100 B7
Lower Gay St BS2. . . . .143 A4
Lower Grove Rd BS16 . . 50 F4
Lower Guinea St BS1. . .143 A1
LOWER HAMSWELL. . . . 68 C3
Lower Hanham Rd
 BS15. . . . . 65 C6
LOWER HAZEL. 14 F3
Lower Hedgemead Rd
 BA1 . . . . .141 C4
Lower High St BS11. . . . 47 D7
Lower Ho BS34 . . . . 36 A3
Lower House Cres
 BS34. . . . . 36 B4
Lowerhouse La GL11 . . . . 5 D5
Lower Kewstoke Rd
 Weston-s-M BS22 . . . . . . 88 E3
 Weston-super-Mare
 BS22 . . . . 88 E3
LOWER KILCOTT 20 A7
Lower Kingsdown Rd
 SN13. . . . . 86 F3
Lower Knole La BS10. . . 35 A3
LOWER KNOWLE. 63 E1
Lower Knowles Rd
 BS21. . . . . 57 E2
Lower Lamb St BS1 . . . .142 C2
LOWER LANGFORD . . .109 C5
Lower La The BA2. . . . . .118 C4
Lower Leaze BS34. . . . . 35 E6
Lower Linden Rd BS21 . 57 F3
Lower Maudlin St BS1 143 A3
Lower Moor Rd BS37. . . 27 C4
LOWER MORTON. 8 C4
Lower Northend BA1. . . 85 F5
Lower Norton La
 Weston-s-M BS22 . . . . . . 88 E4
 Weston-s-M, Norton
 BS22 . . . . 88 C4
Lower Oldfield Pk
 BA2 . . . . .141 A1
Lower Parade Ground Rd
 BS24. . . . . .106 C5
Lower Park Row BS1. . .143 A3
LOWER PEASEDOWN . .134 B8
Lower Queen's Rd
 BS21. . . . . 57 F3
Lower Rd BS39 . . . . . . .130 E6
Lower Redland Mews **2**
 BS6. . . . . 49 B2
Lower Redland Rd BS6. 49 B2
Lower Shockerwick La
 BA1 . . . . 86 D5
Lower Sidney St BS3 . . . 63 A4
LOWER SOUNDWELL. . . 51 F2
Lower St SN14. . . . . 54 D4
Lower Station Rd
 6 Bristol, Ridgeway
 BS16. . . . . 51 A4
 Bristol, Staple Hill BS16 .51 C4
Lower Stoke BA2 . . . . . .120 A8
LOWER STONE 3 C1
Lower Stone Cl BS36. . . 38 C7
LOWER STRODE. 112 A8
Lower Strode BS40. . . . .112 A7
Lower Strode Rd BS21. . 73 A7
LOWER SWAINSWICK . . 85 C3
Lower Thirlmere Rd
 BS34. . . . . 36 A8
Lower Tockington Rd
 BS32. . . . . 14 B1
LOWER WESTON. 101 C7
Lower Whitelands
 BA3. . . . . .134 B3
LOWER WICK. 4 E6
LOWER
 WRITHLINGTON. 134 C3
Lowlis Cl BS10 . . . . 34 F3
Lowry Grove BS7. . . . . . 50 C8
Lowther Rd BS10. . . . . . 35 C2
Low Veale La BS39 . . . . .114 A4
Loxley Gdns BA2. . . . . .101 C4
LOXTON 123 C4
Loxton Dr BA2 . . . . .101 B6
Loxton Rd BS23. . . . . . .104 F2
Loxton Sq BS14. . . . . . . 80 A6
Lucas Cl BS4 . . . . 64 D1
Luccombe Hill BS6. . . . . 49 B2
LUCKINGTON. 31 F4
Luckington Com Sch
 SN14. . . . . 31 E5
Luckington Court Gdns★
 SN14. . . . . 31 F5
Luckington Cross
 BA11. . . . . .140 D2
Luckington Rd
 Acton Turville GL9 . . . . . . 43 A7
 Bristol BS7. . . . . 49 E8
Lucklands Rd BA1. . . . . . 84 C1
Luckley Ave BS13 . . . . . 79 C5
Luckwell Prim Sch BS3 63 A3
Luckwell Rd BS3. . . . . . 63 B3
Lucky La BS3 . . . . 63 D4

Ludlow Cl
 Bristol, St Pauls BS2 . . . .49 F1
 Bristol, Willsbridge BS30 66 B2
 Keynsham BS31. . . . . 81 D5
Ludlow Ct BS30. . . . . . . 66 B1
Ludlow Rd BS7. . . . . 50 A7
Ludwell Cl BS36. . . . . . . 37 D5
Ludwells Orch BS39. . . .132 E5
Luggard's Cross BS21 . . 59 C4
Luke's Cl BS3. . . . . .133 F3
Lullington Rd BS4. . . . . . 64 B2
LULSGATE BOTTOM. . . . 94 A8
Lulsgate Rd BS13. . . . . . 79 A5
Lulworth Cres BS16. . . . 51 F8
Lulworth Rd BS31. . . . . . 81 E4
Lundy Gate BS20. . . . . . 45 F6
Lunty Mead BS48 . . . . . 75 F6
Lupin Cl BS16. . . . . 50 E8
Lurgan Wlk BS4. . . . . . . 63 D1
Lutyens Cl BS16. . . . . . . 50 E8
Luvers La BS40. . . . . . .110 D1
Lux Furlong BS9. . . . . . . 48 B7
Luxton St BS5 . . . . 64 B8
Lwr Station App Rd
 BS1. . . . . .143 C1
Lychgate Pk BS24. . . . . .106 A4
Lydbrook Cl BS37. . . . . . 39 D8
Lyddieth Ct BA15 . . . . . .120 E7
Lyddington Rd BS7. . . . . 49 F8
Lyddon Rd BS22 . . . . . . 89 B3
Lyde Gn BA2. . . . . .136 E5
LYDE GREEN. 52 E8
Lyde Green Prim Sch
 BS16. . . . . 52 C8
Lyde Green Rdbt BS16. . 52 B8
Lydford Wlk BS3. . . . . . . 63 C2
Lydiard Croft BS15. . . . . 65 C4
Lydney Rd
 Bristol, Southmead
 BS10. . . . . 35 D1
 Bristol, Staple Hill BS16 .51 E4
Lydstep Terr BS3. . . . . . 63 C4
LYE CROSS. 93 C1
Lye Cross Rd BS40. . . . . 93 C1
Lyefield Rd BS22 . . . . . . 88 E4
LYE HOLE 93 E2
Lye Hole La BS40. . . . . . 93 D2
Lye Mead BS40 . . . . 95 A6
Lyes The BS49 . . . . 91 D3
Lyme Gdns BA1. . . . . . .101 B7
Lyme Rd BA1 . . . . .101 B7
Lymore Ave BA2. . . . . . .101 C5
Lymore Gdns BA2. . . . . .101 C5
Lymore Terr BA2. . . . . . .101 C4
LYMPSHAM 122 B1
Lympsham CE Fst Sch
 BS24. . . . . .122 B1
Lympsham Gn BA2. . . . .118 D8
Lympsham Rd BS24 . . . .122 B1
Lynbrook BS41. . . . . 61 F1
Lynbrook La BA2. . . . . . .101 F3
Lynch Cl BS22 . . . . 88 F3
Lynch Cres BS25 . . . . . .124 F7
Lynch Ct BS30 . . . . 65 F4
Lynch Hill BA3. . . . . . . .138 A3
Lynchmead BS25. . . . . .125 A7
Lynch The BS25 . . . . . . .124 F7
Lyncombe Hall BA2 . . . .102 A4
LYNCOMBE HILL. 102 A4
Lyncombe Hill BA2. . . . .141 C1
LYNCOMBE VALE. 102 A3
Lyncombe Vale BA2 . . . .102 B4
Lyncombe Vale Rd
 BA2 . . . . .102 A4
Lyncombe Wlk BS16. . . . 51 B2
Lyndale Ave BS9. . . . . . . 48 D5
Lyndale Rd
 Bristol BS5. . . . . 64 D8
 Yate BS37. . . . . 27 D1
Lynde Cl BS13 . . . . 79 B4
Lyndhurst Rd
 Bath BA2 . . . . .101 C6
 Bristol BS9. . . . . 48 F7
 Keynsham BS31. . . . . 81 F3
 Midsomer Norton BA3. .139 B8
 Weston-s-M BS23 . . . . .104 E4
Lyndhurst Terr BA1. . . . .141 C4
Lynfield Pk BA1. . . . . 84 C1
Lynmouth Cl BS22 . . . . . 89 A2
Lynmouth Rd **3** BS2. . 50 A2
Lynn Rd BS16. . . . . 50 D5
Lynton **3** BS15. . . . . . . 66 A8
Lynton Cl BS20 . . . . 45 E4
Lynton Pl **9** BS5. . . . . 64 C8
Lynton Rd
 Bristol BS3. . . . . 63 D2
 Midsomer Norton BA3. .139 B8
Lynton Way BS16. . . . . . 37 B1
Lynwood Cl BA3. . . . . . .139 A8
Lynwood Ct BS13. . . . . . 79 B6
Lynwood Rd BS3. . . . . . . 63 B2
Lynx Cres BS24. . . . . . .105 B2
Lyons Court Rd BS14. . . 80 D7
Lyons Ct BS23 . . . . .104 F7
Lyppiatt Rd BS5. . . . . . . 64 D8
Lyppincourt Rd BS10. . . 35 A3
Lypstone Cl BS24. . . . . .106 A8
Lysander Rd BS10, BS34 35 C6
Lysander Wlk BS34. . . . . 36 E5

Lytchet Dr BS16. . . . . . . 51 F8
Lytes Cary Rd BS31. . . . 82 A3
Lytham Ho BS4 . . . . 64 D1
Lytton Gdns BA2 . . . . . .101 B4
Lytton Gr
 Bristol BS7. . . . . 50 A8
 Keynsham BS31. . . . . 82 A5
Lyveden Gdns BS13. . . . 79 B5
Lyvedon Way BS41. . . . . 62 B1

M

Mabberley Cl BS16. . . . . 52 C5
Macaulay Bldgs BA2. . . .102 C4
Macauley Rd BS7 . . . . . . 50 A8
Macdonald Wlk **8**
 BS15. . . . . 65 D8
Macey's Rd BS13. . . . . . 79 D3
Macfarlane Chase
 BS23. . . . . .105 A5
Machin Cl BS10 . . . . 34 F3
Machin Gdns BS10 . . . . 35 A3
Machin Rd BS10 . . . . . . 35 A3
Macies The BA1. . . . . . . 84 B3
Mackie Ave BS34. . . . . . 36 B2
Mackie Gr BS34. . . . . . . 36 B2
Mackie Rd BS34. . . . . . . 36 B2
Mackley La BA2. . . . . . .136 E3
Macleod Cl BS21. . . . . . 57 C2
Macquarie Farm Cl
 BS49. . . . . 74 A1
Macrae Ct BS15. . . . . . . 65 E8
Macrae Rd BS20. . . . . . . 47 E4
Madam La
 Weston-s-M BS22 . . . . . . 88 F2
 Weston-s-M BS22 . . . . . . 89 A3
 Weston-s-M BS22 . . . . . . 89 A3
Madam's Paddock BS40 96 B3
Madeira Ct BS23. . . . . . .104 C8
Madeira Rd
 Clevedon BS21. . . . . 57 F3
 Weston-s-M BS23 . . . . . . 87 C1
Madeline Rd BS16. . . . . . 50 F2
Madison Cl BS37. . . . . . . 27 D2
Madison Way BS35. . . . . 22 D1
Maesbury BS15. . . . . 65 E6
Maesbury Rd BS31. . . . . 82 A2
Maesknoll La BS14,
 BS39. . . . . 97 B8
Maesknoll Rd BS4 . . . . . 64 A2
Magdalena Ct BS1. . . . .143 B1
Magdalen Ave BA2. . . . .141 B1
Magdalene Pl BS2 . . . . . 49 F1
Magdalene Rd BA3. . . . .134 C2
Magdalen Rd BA2. . . . . .141 B1
Magdalen Way BS22 . . . 89 A3
Magellan Cl BS22 . . . . . 88 F4
Maggs Cl BS10. . . . . 35 C3
Maggs Folly BS39. . . . . .115 D2
Maggs La BA2 . . . . .116 B2
Maggs La
 Bristol BS5. . . . . 50 E2
 Whitchurch BS14. . . . . . . 80 C4
Magnolia Ave BS22. . . . . 89 A1
Magnolia Cl BS22 . . . . . .105 E7
Magnolia Gdns BS32 . . . 24 E5
Magnolia Grange BS22. 88 F1
Magnolia Rd BA3 . . . . . .133 C1
Magpie Bottom La
 Bristol, Kingswood
 BS15. . . . . 65 C6
 Bristol, St George BS5. . . 65 B6
Magpie Cl BS22. . . . . . .105 E8
MAIDEN HEAD. 78 F1
Maidenhead Rd BS13. . . 79 D3
Maiden Way BS11. . . . . . 47 C8
Maidstone Gr BS24. . . . .105 A1
Maidstone St BS3. . . . . . 63 F3
Main Dr BS10. . . . . 34 E1
MAINES BATCH 92 E3
Main Rd
 Bristol BS16. . . . . 52 D5
 Brockley BS49 . . . . 75 D2
 Flax Bourton BS48. . . . . . 76 F7
 Hutton BS24. . . . . .105 E2
Main St BS39 . . . . .132 A4
Main View BS36. . . . . . . 38 D7
Maisemore BS37. . . . . . . 39 E6
Maisemore Ave BS34. . . 24 B1
Maize Cl BS35 . . . . 8 B3
Makin Cl BS30 . . . . 66 C5
Malago Dr BS3 . . . . 63 C2
Malago Rd BS3 . . . . 63 D3
Malago Vale Trad Est
 BS3. . . . . 63 B3
Malago Wlk BS13. . . . . . 78 D4
Malden Mead BS13 . . . . 80 A5
Maldowers La **2** BS5 . 65 A8
Malin Par BS20. . . . . . . 45 F4
Mallard Cl
 Bristol BS32. . . . . 24 D2
 Bristol, Crofts End BS5 . . 50 F1
 Chipping Sodbury BS37. . 40 A8
Mallard Wlk **7** BS22 . .105 E7
Mallet Gr BA2 . . . . .102 A2
Mallow Cl
 Clevedon BS21. . . . . 57 G2
 Thornbury BS35. . . . . 8 D2

Mal–Mel 167

Mallow Rd GL12 11 B5
Mall The
Bath BA1 141 C2
Bristol, Clifton BS8 62 F7
Mall The BS34 35 D6
Malmains Dr BS16 37 B1
Malmesbury Cl
Bristol, Bishopston BS6 49 C4
Bristol, Longwell Green BS30 65 F5
Malpass Dr BS15 65 D4
Maltings Ind Est The BA1 101 B6
Maltings The
Midford BA2 119 C5
Weston-s-M BS22 88 F2
Maltlands BS22 105 D8
Malvern Bldgs BA1 85 A2
Malvern Ct BS5 64 F7
Malvern Dr
Bristol BS30 66 C5
Thornbury BS35 15 D8
Malvern Rd
Bristol, Crew's Hole BS5 64 F7
Bristol, Kensington Park BS4 64 D3
Weston-s-M BS23 104 E5
Malvern Terr 3 BA1 85 A1
Malvern Villas 2 BA1 85 A1
Mamba Gr BS24 105 B4
Manchester Cotts BS22 88 E3
Mancroft Ave BS11 47 F7
Mandy Mdws BA3 132 F1
MANGOTSFIELD 51 F6
Mangotsfield CE Prim Sch BS16 52 B6
Mangotsfield Rd BS16 52 A5
Mangotsfield Sch BS16 52 B4
MANIARDS GREEN 2 C2
Manilla Cres BS23 87 C1
Manilla Pl BS23 87 C1
Manilla Rd BS8 142 A3
Manmoor La BS21 58 A1
Manning Rd BS4 79 F7
Manorbrook Prim Sch BS35 8 C2
Manor Cl
Easton-in-G BS20 47 A4
Farrington Gurney BS39 132 A3
Frampton Cotterell BS36 38 C6
Portishead BS20 45 A5
Tockington BS32 14 C1
Wellow BA2 118 D1
Manor Cl The BS8 62 A8
Manor Coalpit Heath CE Prim Sch The BS36 38 D6
Manor Copse Rd BA3 134 C2
Manor Cotts GL11 5 F5
Manor Court Dr BS7 49 E7
Manor Ct
Backwell BS48 76 A5
Bristol, Fishponds BS16 50 E4
9 Bristol, Upper Easton BS5 50 B1
Locking BS24 106 B4
Weston-s-M BS23 105 A8
Manor Dr BA1 86 C2
Manor Farm
Aust BS35 13 B7
Bristol BS32 36 D8
Manor Farm BS22 88 E5
Manor Farm Cl BS24 105 B2
Manor Farm Cres
Bristol BS32 36 D8
Weston-s-M BS24 105 B2
Manor Farm La
Cowhill BS35 7 A4
Littleton-upon-Severn BS35 6 F4
Manor Farm Rd BS40 127 D4
Manor Gardens Ho BS16 50 F5
Manor Gdns
Farmborough BA2 115 F6
Farrington Gurney BS39 132 A3
Locking BS24 106 A4
Weston-s-M BS22 88 B4
Manor Gr
Bristol BS34 24 B2
Bristol, Mangotsfield BS16 52 A4
Manor Grange BS24 122 B7
Manor Ho
6 Bristol, Lower Easton BS5 50 B1
Bristol, Tyndall's Park BS2 142 C3
Manor House La BS14 80 C6
Manor La
Abbots Leigh BS8 61 F8
Charfield GL12 11 A4
Winterbourne BS36 37 F7
Manor Park Cl BA3 134 C2
Manor Pk
Bath BA1 101 B8
Bristol BS6 49 B3
Radstock BA3 134 C2
Tockington BS32 14 C1
Weston-s-M BS23 104 E1
Manor Pl
Bristol, Frenchay BS16 37 C1
Bristol, Stoke Gifford BS34 37 A4
Manor Rd
Abbots Leigh BS8 61 F7
Bath BA1 84 C1
Bristol, Bishopston BS7 49 E4
Bristol, Bishopsworth BS13 79 A6
Bristol, Fishponds BS16 51 A5
Bristol, Mangotsfield BS16 52 A4
Radstock BA3 134 C2
Rangeworthy BS37 27 A7
Saltford BS31 82 C2
Weston-s-M BS23 105 A8
Wick BS30 67 C5
Manor Terr BA3 134 C2
Manor Valley BS23 88 A1
Manor Villas BA1 84 C1
Manor Way
Chipping Sodbury BS37 28 C2
Failand BS8 61 C4
Manor Wlk BS35 8 B3
Mansbrook Ho 3 BA3 133 A1
Mansel Cl BS31 82 C3
Mansell Rd BS34 35 F6
Manser Rd BS24 106 C5
Mansfield Ave BS23 105 B8
Mansfield Cl BS23 105 B8
Mansfield St BS3 63 C2
Manston Cl BS14 80 C7
Manvers St BA1 141 C1
Manworthy Rd BS4 64 D3
Manx Rd BS7 49 F8
Maple Ave
Bristol BS16 51 C3
Thornbury BS35 8 C1
Maple Cl
Bristol BS14 80 D5
Bristol, Little Stoke BS34 36 C7
Bristol, Oldland BS30 66 B4
Weston-s-M BS23 105 A8
Maple Ct
5 Bristol BS15 51 D1
Bristol BS9 48 F8
9 Weston-s-M BS23 87 C1
Maple Dr BA3 133 E1
Maple Gdns BA2 101 E4
Maple Gr BA2 101 E4
Maple Ho BS2 143 A4
Maple Leaf Ct BS8 142 A3
Mapleleaze BS4 64 D3
Maplemeade BS7 49 C4
Maple Rd
Bristol, Horfield BS7 49 E5
Bristol, St Anne's BS4 64 D5
Mapleridge La BS37 28 D7
Maple Rise BA3 134 B2
Maples The BS48 59 C1
Maplestone Rd BS14 80 A3
Maple Wlk
Keynsham BS31 81 D4
Pucklechurch BS16 53 C5
Mapstone Cl BS16 37 B3
Marbeck Rd BS10 35 B1
Marbled White Cl BS35 8 C3
Marchant's La BA2 119 F4
Marchfields Way BS23 105 A5
Marconi Cl BS23 105 B7
Marconi Rd BS20 44 F5
Mardale Cl BS10 35 C2
Marden Rd BS31 82 A4
Mardon Rd BS4 64 D6
Mardons Cl 2 BA3 139 B8
Mardyke Ferry Rd BS1 142 B1
Margaret Rd 4 BS13 78 F4
Margaret's Bldgs BA1 141 B3
Margaret's Hill BA1 141 C4
Margate St BS3 63 F3
Marguerite Rd BS13 78 F7
Marigold Cl BS16 52 D8
Marigold Wlk BS3 63 A2
Marina Gdns BS16 50 E3
Marindrin Dr BS22 89 B4
Marine Hill BS21 57 E5
Marine Par
Clevedon BS21 57 E4
Pill BS20 47 C5
Weston-s-M BS23 87 B1
Weston-s-M BS23 104 D6
Mariners Cl BS48 76 A6
Mariner's Cl BS22 88 D1
Mariners Dr
Backwell BS48 76 A6
Bristol BS9 48 D4
Mariner's Way BS20 47 C5
Marion Rd BS15 65 B3
Marion Wlk BS5 65 A7
Marissal Cl BS10 34 E3
Marissal Rd BS10 34 E3
Mariston Way BS30 66 C6
Maritime Heritage Ctr★ BS1 142 B1
Marjoram Pl BS32 36 F7
Marjoram Way BS20 45 F5
Market Ave BS22 89 C3
Market Gate BS2 143 C3
Market Ind Est BS49 74 B1
Market La BS23 104 D8
Market Pl
Marshfield SN14 70 A8
Radstock BA3 133 F2
Winford BS40 94 F7
Marketside BS2 64 B4
Market Sq BS16 51 C3
Mark La BS1 142 C2
Marklands BS9 48 E3
MARKSBURY 99 B1
Marksbury Bottom BA2 99 A2
Marksbury CE Prim Sch BA2 99 B2
Marksbury La
Farmborough BA2 116 E7
Priston BA2 117 A6
Marksbury Rd BS3 63 D2
Marlborough Ave 13 BS16 50 E3
Marlborough Bldgs BA1 141 A3
Marlborough Dr
Bristol BS16 37 B1
Weston-s-M BS22 89 B2
Marlborough Flats 8 BS2 143 A4
Marlborough Hill BS2 143 A4
Marlborough Hill Pl BS2 143 A4
Marlborough Ho 15 BS2 143 A4
Marlborough La BA1 141 A3
Marlborough St
Bath BA1 141 A4
Bristol BS2 143 A4
Bristol, Eastville BS5 50 E3
Marlepit Gr BS13 78 F6
Marle Pits 1 BS48 76 A6
Marlfield Wlk BS13 78 E7
Marling Rd BS5 64 F8
Marlowe Ho 3 BS23 104 F4
Marlwood Dr BS10 35 A3
Marlwood Sch BS32 14 F5
Marmaduke St BS3 63 F3
Marmalade La BS4 64 C1
Marmion Cres BS10 34 F3
Marne Cl BS14 80 D5
Marron Cl BS26 125 C2
Marsden Rd BA2 101 B3
Marshacre La BS35 13 F6
Marshall Ho 1 BS16 50 F4
Marshall Wlk BS4 79 D7
Marsham Way BS30 65 F4
Marsh Cl BS36 37 E5
MARSH COMMON 22 E4
Marsh Common Rd BS35 22 E3
MARSHFIELD 69 E8
Marshfield CE Prim Sch SN14 70 B8
Marshfield La BS30 67 D1
Marshfield Path GL9 19 F1
Marshfield Pk BS16 51 C8
Marshfield Rd
Bristol, Frenchay BS16 51 C8
Bristol, Hillfields BS16 51 C4
Tormarton GL9 41 E1
Marshfield Way BA1 85 A1
Marsh La
Bristol, Ashton Vale BS3 63 B2
Bristol, Barton Hill BS5 64 C6
Burton SN14, GL9 43 C4
Easton-in-G BS20 47 A4
Farrington Gurney BS39 132 A3
Portbury BS20 46 F6
Temple Cloud BS39 115 A1
Marsh Lane Ind Est BS20 46 F7
Marsh Rd
Bristol BS3 62 F3
Rode BA11 137 F1
Yatton BS49 91 B8
Marsh St
Avonmouth BS11 47 C8
Bristol BS1 143 A2
Marshwall La BS32 23 E6
Marson Rd BS21 57 F3
Marston Rd BS4 64 B3
Martcombe Rd BS20 47 C2
Martha's Orch BS13 78 E7
Martin Cl BS34 35 E8
Martin Ct 12 BS16 50 E3
Martindale Ct BS22 105 D8
Martindale Rd BS22 105 D8
Martingale Rd BS4 64 D4
Martins Cl BS15 65 C5
Martins Gr BS22 88 E2
Martin's Rd BS15 65 C5
Martin St 2 BS3 63 B3
Martins The BS20 46 A6
Martock BS24 104 F2
Martock Cres BS3 63 C1
Martock Rd
Bristol BS3 63 C2
Keynsham BS31 82 A3
Martor Ind Est SN14 56 A2
Mart The 6 BS23 104 E7
Marwood Rd BS4 79 E8
Marybush La BS2 143 B3
Mary Carpenter Pl 15 BS2 49 F1
Mary Ct BS5 64 D8
Mary Elton Prim Sch BS21 57 D1
Marygold Leaze BS30 66 A4
Mary Seacole Ct 8 BS2 50 A2
Mary St BS5 64 D8
Mascot Rd BS3 63 D3
Masefield Ho BS23 105 A4
Masefield Way BS7 50 A6
Maskelyne Ave BS10 49 D7
Masons View BS36 37 F7
Matchells Cl BS4 64 E6
Materman Rd BS14 80 E5
Matford Cl
Bristol BS10 35 D4
Winterbourne BS36 37 E5
Matford La GL13 3 F4
Matthews Cl BS14 80 F6
Matthew's Rd 17 BS5 64 C7
Maules Gdns BS16 36 F2
Maules La BS16 36 F2
Maunsell Rd
Bristol BS11 34 B2
Weston-s-M BS24 105 E7
Maurice Rd BS6 49 E2
Mautravers Cl BS32 36 D7
Mawdeley Ho 11 BS3 63 C4
Maximus Gdns BS30 81 F8
Max Mill La BS25 124 C8
Maxse Rd BS4 64 B2
Maybank Rd BS37 27 D1
Maybec Gdns BS5 65 A6
Maybourne BS4 65 A2
Maybrick Rd BA2 101 D5
Maycliffe Pk BS6 49 F2
Mayfair Ave BS48 59 F1
Mayfield Ave
Bristol BS16 51 A2
Weston-s-M BS22 88 E1
Mayfield Ct BS16 51 A3
MAYFIELD PARK 51 A2
Mayfield Pk BS16 51 A2
Mayfield Pk N BS16 51 A2
Mayfield Pk S BS16 51 A2
Mayfield Rd BA2 101 D5
Mayfields BS31 81 E5
Mayflower Gdns BS48 60 A2
May Gr GL12 11 B5
Maynard Cl
Bristol BS13 79 C5
4 Clevedon BS21 57 H3
Maynard Rd BS13 79 C5
Maynard Terr BS39 114 F3
Mayors Bldgs BS16 51 B5
May Park Prim Sch BS5 50 C2
Maypole Cl
Clutton BS39 114 E3
Hawkesbury Upton GL9 20 A2
Maypole Ct 1 BS15 65 B5
Mays Cl BS36 38 D7
Maysfield Cl BS20 45 D3
Maysgreen La BS24 90 B3
MAYSHILL 26 E1
May's La BS24 90 C3
Maysmead La BS40 109 C6
May St BS15 51 C1
Maytree Ave BS13 79 B7
Maytree Cl BS13 79 B7
May Tree Cl BS48 59 C1
May Tree Rd BA3 133 E1
Maytrees BS5 50 C2
Mayville Ave BS34 36 A3
Maywood Ave 3 BS16 51 B4
Maywood Cres BS16 51 B4
Maywood Rd BS16 51 C4
Maze St BS5 64 B6
McAdam Way BS1 62 F5
McCrae Rd BS24 106 B5
McLaren Rd BS11 33 B1
Mead Cl
Bath BA2 101 E3
Bristol BS11 47 E6
Mead Ct BS36 37 E6
Mead Ct Bsns Pk BS35 15 B8
Meade Ho BA2 101 A5
Meadgate BS16 52 B7
MEADGATE EAST 116 E2
MEADGATE WEST 116 D2
Mead La
Blagdon BS40 110 E3
Ingst BS35 13 D2
Saltford BS31 82 F4
Sandford BS25 107 E4
Meadlands BA2 100 B7
Meadowbank BS22 88 F3
Meadowbrook Prim Sch BS32 36 E8
Meadow Brown Cl BS35 8 C4
Meadow Cl
Backwell BS48 76 B6
Bristol BS16 51 F7
Farrington Gurney BS39 132 A3
Meadow Cl continued
Nailsea BS48 59 E3
Meadow Court Dr BS30 66 C3
Meadowcroft BS16 52 A8
Meadow Croft BS24 105 B2
Meadow Ct BA1 101 A7
Meadow Dr
Bath BA2 118 D8
Locking BS24 106 B4
Portishead BS20 44 F1
Meadow Gdns BA1 84 A1
Meadow Gr BS11 47 D7
Meadow La BA2 85 D1
Meadowland BS49 74 A1
Meadowland Rd BS10 34 E4
Meadowlands BS22 89 C2
Meadow Mead
Frampton Cotterell BS36 38 B8
Yate BS37 27 E5
Meadow Pk BA1 86 B3
Meadow Pl BS22 89 D3
Meadow Rd
Chipping Sodbury BS37 28 A1
Clevedon BS21 57 G3
Leyhill GL12 10 B4
Paulton BS39 132 F4
Meadows Cl BS20 44 F5
Meadows End BS25 108 D4
Meadowside 2 BS35 15 D8
Meadowside Dr BS14 80 A3
Meadows Prim Sch The BS30 82 D8
Meadow St
Avonmouth BS11 33 A1
Axbridge BS26 125 C2
Weston-s-M BS23 104 E7
Meadows The
Bristol BS15 65 D4
Luckington SN14 31 F4
Meadowsweet Ave BS34 36 B3
Meadowsweet Rd 1 BS16 52 C7
Meadow Vale BS5 51 A1
Meadow View
Frampton Cotterell BS36 38 D7
Radstock BA3 134 A1
Meadow View Cl BA1 101 A8
Meadow Villas 14 BS23 104 E8
Meadow Way BS32 36 E7
Mead Rd
Bristol BS34 36 F5
Chipping Sodbury BS37 28 C1
Portishead BS20 45 C2
Mead Rise BS3 63 F4
Mead St BS4 143 C1
Meads The
Bristol BS16 51 F7
Burton SN14 43 B3
Mead Terr BS40 110 E2
Mead The
Alveston BS35 15 A5
Bristol BS34 36 B4
Clutton BS39 114 E3
Dundry BS41 78 D2
Farmborough BA2 116 A6
Keynsham BS31 81 D3
Paulton BS39 132 D5
Shipham BS25 125 E8
Stratton-on-t-F BA3 138 F2
Timsbury BA2 116 C3
Winsley BA15 120 E7
Mead Vale BS22 105 E8
Mead Vale Prim Sch BS22 88 E1
Meadway
Bristol BS9 48 C6
Farmborough BA2 116 A6
Temple Cloud BS39 114 E1
Mead Way BS35 15 B7
Meadway Ave BS48 59 D2
Mearcombe La BS24 122 F6
Meardon Rd BS14 80 E6
Meare BS24 104 F2
Meare Rd BA2 102 A2
MEARNS 115 E2
Mede Cl BS1 143 B1
Media Ho BS8 142 B3
Medical Ave BS2, BS8 142 C3
Medina Cl BS35 15 C7
Medlar Cl BS10 35 B6
Medway Cl BS31 82 A3
Medway Ct BS35 15 D8
Medway Dr
Frampton Cotterell BS36 38 B7
Keynsham BS31 82 A3
Meere Bank BS11 34 B1
Meetinghouse La BS49 75 A1
Meg Thatcher's Gdns BS5 65 B7
Meg Thatchers Gn BS5 65 B7
Melbourne Dr BS37 28 C1

Melbourne Rd BS7......49 D4
Melbourne Terr **2**
  BS21................57 F2
Melbury Rd BS4......64 A2
Melcombe Ct BA2.....101 D4
Melcombe Rd BA2.....101 D4
Melita Rd BS6.........49 E3
Mellent Ave BS13......79 C3
Mells Cl BS31.........82 A2
Mells La BA3........134 B1
Melrose Ave
  Bristol BS8..........142 B4
  Yate BS37............28 A2
Melrose Cl BS37.......28 A2
Melrose Gr BA2......101 B3
Melrose Pl BS8......142 B4
Melrose Terr BA1......85 A2
Melton Cres BS7.......50 A7
Melville Rd BS6.......49 B1
Melville Terr BS3......63 C3
Melvin Sq BS4.........63 E1
Memorial Cl BS15......65 B4
Memorial Rd
  Bristol BS15.........65 B4
  Wrington BS40........92 E2
Memorial Stadium (Bristol
  Rovers FC)★ BS7....49 F6
Mendip Ave BS22......88 F2
Mendip Cl
  Axbridge BS26........125 D2
  Keynsham BS31.......81 D5
  3 Nailsea BS48......59 E1
  Paulton BS39.........132 E4
  Yatton BS49..........91 B7
Mendip Cres BS16......52 A8
Mendip Ct BS16........36 E1
Mendip Edge BS24.....121 F8
Mendip Fields BA3....138 C2
Mendip Gdns
  Bath BA2.............118 D8
  Yatton BS49..........91 B7
Mendip Gn BA3.......139 B6
Mendip Green Fst Sch
  Weston-s-M BS22......88 E1
  Weston-s-M BS22......88 F2
Mendip Lodge BS25...125 A8
Mendip Rd
  Bristol BS3...........63 D3
  Locking BS24.........106 D4
  Portishead BS20......45 B5
  Weston-s-M BS23.....105 A7
  Yatton BS49..........91 B7
Mendip Rise BS24......106 B4
Mendip View BS30.....67 C7
Mendip View Ave BS16..51 A3
Mendip View Bsns Pk
  BS24................90 C5
Mendip Villas
  Cheddar BS27........126 A1
  Compton Martin BS40..128 F7
Mendip Way BS3......133 D3
Menhyr Gr BS10........35 B3
Menlea BS40..........110 D3
Mercer Ct BS14........80 B8
Merchants Almshouses
  BS1.................143 A2
Merchants Ct BS8.....142 A1
Merchants Quay BS1..143 A1
Merchants Rd
  Bristol BS8..........142 A3
  Bristol, Hotwells BS8...142 A1
Merchants Row BS1...142 C1
Merchant St BS1......143 B3
Merchants The SN14....31 E4
Merchants Trad Pk
  BS2.................64 C6
Mercia Dr BS2........50 A2
Mercier Cl BS37.......27 F2
Meredith Ct BS1......142 A1
Merfield Rd BS4.......64 B2
Meriden BA1.........101 D8
Meridian Pl BS8......142 B3
Meridian Rd BS6.......49 C1
Meridian Vale BS8....142 B3
Meriet Ave BS13.......79 B4
Merioneth St BS3......63 F3
Meriton St BS2........64 B5
Merlin Cl
  Bristol BS9...........48 F8
  1 Weston-s-M BS22..105 E8
Merlin Cres G12.......11 A5
Merlin Ct BS10........49 B7
Merlin Pk BS20........45 A4
Merlin Rd BS10, BS34...35 C6
Merlin Ridge BS16.....53 C4
Merlin Way
  Chipping Sodbury BS37..39 F8
  3 Radstock BA3......139 B8
Merrett Ct BS7........50 B6
Merrick Ct BS1.......143 A1
Merrick Fields BA3...138 C4
Merrimans Rd BS11....47 D8
Merritt Way BS16......52 A3
Merryfield Rd BS24...106 B6
Merryholes La BS12....14 D3
Merryweather Cl BS32..36 D8

Merryweathers BS4.....64 E2
Merrywood Cl **5** BS3..63 C4
Merrywood Ct BS4.....64 B2
Merrywood Rd BS3.....63 C4
Merstham Rd **13** BS2...50 A2
Merton Dr BS24.......106 A8
Merton Rd BS7........49 E5
Mervyn Rd BS7........49 E4
Meryl Ct BS6..........49 B1
Metford Gr BS6........49 B3
Metford Pl BS6........49 C3
Metford Rd BS6.......49 C3
Methwyn Cl BS22.....105 C7
Metropolitan The BS1..143 B1
Mews The BA1........101 A8
Mewswell Dr BS27....126 B1
Michaels Mead BA1....84 B2
Middle Ave BS1......143 B2
Middledown Rd SN14...55 C1
Middleford Ho BS13....79 C4
Middle La
  Bath BA1.............85 B1
  Kingston Seymour BS21..72 F4
Middlemead BA3......138 F3
Middlepiece La BA2,
  BS31................99 B7
Middle Rd BS15........51 F3
Middle St BS40.......129 F4
Middle Stoke BA2.....120 A6
Middleton Rd BS11.....47 F8
Middlewood Cl BA2...101 C2
Middle Yeo Gn BS48....59 D3
MIDFORD.............119 C6
Midford BS24.........104 F2
Midford Hill BA2......119 C5
Midford La BA2.......119 E7
Midford Rd BA2.......119 B7
Midhaven Rise BS22....88 E4
Midland Bridge Rd BA1,
  BA2................141 A2
Midland Mews BS2....143 C3
Midland Rd
  Bath BA1............101 D7
  Bristol BS2..........143 C3
  Bristol, Staple Hill BS16..51 D4
Midland Road Bsns Pk
  BS16................51 D4
Midland St BS2.......143 C2
Midland Terr BS16.....50 F3
Midland Way BS35......15 C7
Midland Way Bsns Pk
  BS35................15 B8
Midsomer Ent Pk BA3..133 C2
MIDSOMER NORTON..133 B3
Midsomer Norton Prim
  Sch BA3.............133 B1
Midsomer Norton South★
  BA3................139 A8
Midsummer Bldgs BA1..85 B2
Milburn Rd BS23.....104 F7
Milbury Gdns BS22.....88 C2
Mildred St BS5........64 C7
Miles Ct BS20.........47 E3
Miles Ct
  Bristol, Cadbury Heath
    BS30..............65 F4
  Bristol, Clifton BS8....49 A1
Miles Rd BS8.........49 A1
Miles's Bldgs BA1....141 B3
Miles St BA2.........141 C1
Milestone Ct BS22.....89 D2
Mile Wlk BS14.........80 A6
Milford Ave BS30......67 B7
Milford St BS3........63 C4
Millard Cl BS10........35 D2
Millards Ct BA3......133 B3
Millards Hill BA3.....133 B3
Millard's Hill BA3....133 C3
Millar Ho BS8.......142 A3
Mill Ave BS1.........143 A2
Millbank Cl BS4.......64 E3
Millbook Ct **3** BS6....49 E1
Millbourn Cl BS15....120 D7
Millbrook Ave BS4.....64 F3
Millbrook Cl BS30.....66 C6
Millbrook Ct BA2.....141 C1
Millbrook Pl BA2.....141 C1
Millbrook Rd BS37.....27 B2
Mill Cl
  Frampton Cotterell
    BS36..............38 C7
  Portbury BS20.......46 D2
Mill Cotts BS31.......82 F2
Mill Cres BS37........39 B4
Millcross BS21........73 C8
Mill Ct **3** BA3......133 A1
Millennium Cl BS36....38 D7
Millennium Prom BS1..142 C1
Miller Cl BS23.......104 F8
Millers Cl BS20.......47 C4
Millers Ct **3** BS15....73 E8
Millers Dr BS30.......66 D5
Millers Rise BS22.....89 A4
Miller Wlk BA2........85 F1
Millfield
  Midsomer Norton BA3..138 F8
  Thornbury BS35.......8 C2

Millfield Dr BS30.....66 C6
Millground Rd BS13....78 F5
Millgrove St N BS2...143 A4
Mill Hill BA2.........118 E1
Millhill La BS35.......12 F5
Mill Ho
  Bristol BS1..........143 A2
  11 Bristol, Baptist Mills
    BS5................50 A1
Millier Rd BS49.......92 B8
Milliman Cl BS13......79 C5
Mill La
  3 Bath BA2......101 B6
  Bathampton BA2......85 F2
  Bitton BS30.........82 E8
  Bristol, Southville BS3..63 D4
  Bristol, Warmley BS30...66 C5
  Butcombe BS40.......111 A8
  Chew Stoke BS40.....112 D8
  Chipping Sodbury BS37..40 E6
  Compton Martin BS40..129 A7
  Congresbury BS49.....91 D4
  Doynton BS30.........53 F1
  Falfield GL12.........9 F7
  Frampton Cotterell BS36..26 B1
  Hambrook BS16........37 D3
  Monkton Combe BA2..119 E8
  Portbury BS20........46 E3
  Priston BA2..........117 A7
  Timsbury BA2.........116 B1
  Tockington BS32......14 B1
  Upton Cheyney BS30...66 F1
  Wrington BS40.......109 F8
Mill Leg BS49.........91 D4
Millmead Ho BS13.....79 C4
Millmead Rd BA2.....101 C5
Millpill Cl BS9.........48 D5
Millpond Prim Sch BS5..50 A1
Millpond St **10** BS5...50 A1
Millpool Ct BS10.......49 B8
Mill Rd
  Radstock BA3.........134 B2
  Winterbourne BS36.....37 D4
Mill Road Ind Est BA3..134 B3
Mill Steps BS36........37 E4
Mill Stream Cl BS26....125 C1
Millward Gr BS16.......51 C4
Millward Terr BS39....132 E6
Milner Gn BS30........66 A5
Milner Rd BS7.........49 F5
Milsom Pl BA1.......141 B3
Milsom St
  Bath BA1............141 B3
  Bristol BS5..........64 A8
MILTON...............88 C2
Milton Ave
  Bath BA2............101 F4
  Weston-s-M BS23.....105 A8
Milton Brow BS22......88 B2
Milton Cl
  Nailsea BS48.........59 E3
  Yate BS37.............27 D2
Milton Ct BS23.......105 A8
Milton Gn BS22........88 C1
Milton Hill BS22.......88 B2
Milton Park Prim Sch
  BS22................88 C1
Milton Park Rd BS22...88 C1
Milton Pk **1** BS5....64 C7
Milton Rd
  Bristol BS7..........49 E6
  Radstock BA3........133 C1
  Weston-s-M BS22, BS23..105 B8
  Yate BS37.............27 D2
Milton Rise BS22.......88 C1
Miltons Cl BS13.......79 D4
Milverton BS24.......104 F2
Milverton Gdns BS6....49 F2
Milward Rd BS31.......81 E6
Mina Rd BS2..........50 A2
Minehead Rd BS4......63 F1
Miners Cl BS41........62 F2
Minerva Ct BA2......141 C3
Minerva Gdns BA2....101 C4
Minett Rd BS37.......27 E5
Minor's La BS10.......34 A8
Minsmere Rd BS31.....82 A4
Minster Ct **1** BS37...39 D7
Minster Way BA2......102 C8
Minton Cl BS14........80 B5
Minto Rd BS2.........50 A2
Minto Road Ind Ctr **9**
  BS2.................50 A2
Mission Rd BS37......27 B4
Mitchell La BS1......143 B2
Mitchell Wlk BS30.....66 D7
Mitford-Slade Ct BS49..91 C7
Mivart St BS5.........50 B2
Mizzymead Cl **1** BS48..59 D1
Mizzymead Rd BS48....59 E1
Mizzymead Rise BS48...59 E1
Modecombe Gr BS10...34 F3
Mogg St BS2..........50 A2
Moles Rd BS40........109 B6
Molesworth Cl BS13....79 A4
Molesworth Dr BS13....79 A4
Mollifriend La BA2....116 B8
Molly Cl BS39.........131 E8
Monarch Cl BS16.......38 A1

Millfield Dr BS30.....66 C6
Monarch Ho **11** BS3...63 B3
Monger Cotts BS39...132 F4
Monger La
  Greenhill BA3.........133 A3
  Midsomer Norton BA3..133 A3
  Paulton BS39.........133 A4
Monica Willis Ho **18**
  BS3.................63 C3
Monk Rd BS7..........49 D4
Monks Ave BS15.......65 B8
Monksdale Rd BA2....101 D4
Monks Hill BS22.......88 B3
Monks Ho **3** BS37....39 D7
Monk's Park Ave BS7...49 E8
Monks Park Way BS7...49 E8
Monkton Ave BS24....105 A2
MONKTON COMBE.....102 F1
Monkton Combe Jun Sch
  (Pre-Prep) BA2......102 C1
Monkton Combe Sch
  BA2................102 E1
MONKTON FARLEIGH..103 F7
Monkton Prep Sch
  BA2................102 C1
Monkton Rd BS15......65 B5
Monmouth Cl BS20.....44 F4
Monmouth Ct
  Bath BA1............141 A2
  Pill BS20............47 C5
Monmouth Hill BS32...23 E4
Monmouth Paddock
  BA2................136 E5
Monmouth Pl BA1....141 B2
Monmouth Rd
  Bristol BS7..........49 D4
  Keynsham BS31.......81 D5
  Pill BS20............47 C5
Monmouth St
  Bath BA1............141 B2
  Bristol BS3..........63 F3
Monsdale Cl BS10......35 A3
Monsdale Dr BS10......35 A2
Montacute Cir **4**
  BS22...............105 F8
Montague Cl BS34......36 E5
Montague Ct **4** BS2..143 A4
Montague Flats **6**
  BS2.................143 A4
Montague Hill BS2....143 A4
Montague Hill S **5**
  BS2.................143 A4
Montague Ho **8** BA1..85 C1
Montague Pl BS6.....143 A4
Montague Rd
  Saltford BS31.........82 D2
  Shoscombe BA2......134 E5
Montague St BS1.....143 A4
Montepelier BS23.....104 F8
Montgomery St BS3....63 F3
MONTPELIER...........49 E2
Montpelier Central **1**
  BS6.................49 E1
Montpelier Ct BS6.....49 E2
Montreaux Ho **2** BS5..65 A7
Mont The **2** BS6.....49 E1
Montroy Cl BS9........49 C6
Montsurs Cl BA3......138 D3
Moon St BS2.........143 B4
Moor Croft Dr BS30....65 F3
Moor Croft Rd BS24...105 E3
Moordell Cl BS37......27 D1
MOOREND............37 E2
Moorend Farm Ave
  BS11................33 E5
Moorend Gdns BS11...47 F7
Moorend Rd BS16......37 D3
Moor End Spout BS48...59 D2
Moorfield Rd BS48.....76 A6
MOORFIELDS..........64 C8
Moorfields Cl BA2....101 D3
Moorfields Ct BS48....59 D2
Moorfields Dr BA2....101 D4
Moorfields Ho
  Bristol BS5..........64 C7
  Nailsea BS48.........59 D2
Moorfields Rd
  Bath BA2............101 D4
  Nailsea BS48.........59 D2
Moor Gn BS26........125 C1
Moor Gr BS11.........48 A8
Moorgrove Ho BS9.....48 C7
Moorham Rd BS25....108 A1
Moorhen Rd
  Kingston Seymour BS49..73 F2
  Kingston Seymour BS49..73 F2
Moorhill St **17** BS5...50 B1
Moorhouse Cl BS10....34 B5
Moor House Cvn Pk
  BS10................34 A4

Moorhouse La BS10....34 B4
Moorings The
  Bath BA2............102 B6
  Pill BS20............47 C4
  Pucklechurch BS16....53 C4
Moor La
  Backwell BS48........75 F6
  Clapton in G BS20.....45 E1
  Clevedon BS21........57 G2
  Clevedon BS21........58 A2
  Hutton BS24.........105 D3
  Tickenham BS21......58 F4
  Tockington BS32......24 A8
  Walton in G BS21......58 C6
  Weston-s-M BS24....105 F7
Moorland Cotts BS26..124 F2
Moorland Pk BS24......90 E5
Moorland Rd
  Bath BA2............101 D5
  Weston-s-M BS23.....104 E4
  Yate BS37............27 D1
MOORLANDS..........101 D3
Moorlands Cl BS48.....59 D2
Moorlands Inf Sch
  BA2................101 D4
Moorlands Jun Sch
  BA2................101 D3
Moorlands Rd
  Bristol, Mayfield Park
    BS16..............51 A2
  Bristol, Ridgeway BS16..50 F3
Moorland St BS26....125 C1
Moorlands The BA2...101 D3
Moorlay Cres BS40.....94 F8
MOORLEDGE..........96 C1
Moorledge La BS39,
  BS40................113 F7
Moorledge Rd BS40....96 B1
Moorpark Ave BS37....27 D1
Moor Pk BS21.........57 G2
Moor Rd
  Banwell BS29........107 B5
  Yatton BS49..........74 B2
Moorsfield BS39......114 F3
Moorside BS49........74 B1
Moorside Ct BS21......57 G2
Moorside Villas BS21...57 G2
MOORSLADE............3 D1
Moorslade La GL12......3 D1
Moravian Ct **4** BS15..65 D8
Moravian Rd BS15.....65 D8
Moravian Rd Bsns Pk
  BS15................65 D8
Morden Wlk BS14......80 D7
Moreton Cl BS14......80 A4
Moreton La BS40......112 E2
Moreton Mans **5** BS23..87 C1
Morford St BA1......141 B4
Morgan Cl
  Saltford BS31.........82 D2
  Weston-s-M BS22......106 B8
Morgan Pl BS48.......77 B8
Morgans Bldgs BS20...59 F8
Morgans Hill Cl BS48...75 D8
Morgan's La BS40....129 F2
Morgan St BS2........49 F1
Morgan Sweet Pl
  BS25...............108 A4
Morgan Way BA2.....134 E7
Morley Ave BS16......52 A4
Morley Cl
  Bristol, Little Stoke
    BS34..............36 C6
  Bristol, Staple Hill BS16..51 D4
Morley Rd
  Bristol, Southville BS3...63 C4
  Bristol, Staple Hill BS16..51 D3
Morley Sq BS7........49 E4
Morley St
  Bristol, Baptist Mills
    BS2...............49 F1
  Bristol, Russell Town BS5..64 B7
Morley Terr
  1 Bath BA2......101 D6
  1 Bristol BS15....51 D1
  Radstock BA3........134 A3
Mornington Rd **14** BS8..49 A2
Morpeth Rd BS4.......79 D8
Morris Cl BA1........86 B3
Morris La BA1........86 B3
Morris Rd BS7........50 A5
Morse Rd BS5.........64 C7
Morston Ct BS22.....105 C2
Mortimer Cl BA1......84 B2
Mortimer Rd
  Bristol BS8..........142 A3
  Bristol, Filton BS34.....36 B2
MORTON...............8 D3
Morton Mill BS35.......8 C1
Morton St
  Bristol BS5..........64 B7
  Thornbury BS35.......8 C1
Morton Way BS35.......8 D1
Moseley Gr BS23.....104 E2
Mosquito End BS23...105 E2
Motorway Distribution Ctr
  BS11................33 C2
Mottershead Ave
  BS24...............106 C5

Mountain Ash BA1 .....84 D1
MOUNTAIN BOWER 56 E3
Mountain Mews 5 BS5 65 A7
Mountain's La BA2....115 E6
Mountain Wood BA1 ...86 C2
Mountbatten Cl
Weston-s-M BS22 ......88 E4
Yate BS37..............27 D3
Mount Beacon BA1 ....85 A1
Mount Beacon Pl 3
BA1 ....84 F1
Mount Cl BS36..........37 F8
Mount Cres BS36 ......37 E5
Mounteney's La GL12 ..18 D7
Mount Gdns BS15......65 D6
Mount Gr BA2 ....101 B3
Mount Haviland BA1 ...84 B3
MOUNT HILL 65 E6
Mount Hill Rd BS15 ....65 D6
Mount Pleasant
Bath BA2 ....102 D1
Hallen BS10...........34 C4
Pill BS20..............47 D4
Radstock BA3.........134 B2
Mount Pleasant Terr
BS3..................63 C4
Mount Rd
Bath BA1 ....141 B4
Bath, Southdown BA2 ..101 B3
Mount The BS49 ....91 C8
Mount View
Bath, Beacon Hill BA1 ...85 A1
Bath, Southdown BA2 ..101 B3
Mow Barton
Bristol BS13...........78 F6
Yate BS37..............27 D2
Mowbray Rd BS14......80 C7
Mowcroft Rd BS13 .....79 D4
Moxham Dr BS13 ......79 C4
Muddy La BS22 ....89 A8
Mud La BS49 ....74 D2
Muirfield
Bristol BS30...........66 A6
Yate BS37..............39 E8
Mulberry Ave BS20.....45 E5
Mulberry Cl
Backwell BS48.........76 A6
1 Bristol BS15........65 E8
Portishead BS20 ....45 F5
Weston-s-M BS22 ......89 A1
Mulberry Ct BS4 ....64 D4
Mulberry Dr BS15.......51 F1
Mulberry Gdns 10 BS16 51 D3
Mulberry La BS24.....122 C6
Mulberry Mews BA1 ....84 C1
Mulberry Rd BS49......91 E3
Mulberry Way BA2 ....102 A2
Mulberry Wlk BS9 .....48 C8
Mule St GL13 ....4 B3
Muller Ave BS7 ....49 F4
Muller Rd BS5, BS7 .....50 B3
Mulready Cl BS7.......50 C6
Mumbleys Hill BS35....14 E7
Mumbleys La
Thornbury, Alveston Down
BS35 ....14 E6
Thornbury, Kington BS35 14 E8
Mundy La BS35 ....8 A1
Munscroft Ct BS23....104 F8
Muntjac Rd BS40......109 B6
Murdoch Sq BS7........49 F8
Murford Ave BS13......79 B4
Murford Wlk BS13 .....79 B4
Murhill BA2 ....120 C6
Murray St 9 BS3 ......63 C4
Musgrove Cl BS11......34 C2
Mus of Bath at Work★
BA1..................141 B4
Mus of Costume★
BA1..................141 B3
Mus of East Asian Art★
BA1..................141 B3
Myrtleberry Mead BS22 89 A5
Myrtle Ct BS3..........63 B4
Myrtle Dr BS11 ....47 E5
Myrtle Farm Rd BS22...88 C4
Myrtle Gdns BS49......91 C8
Myrtle Hill BS20 ....47 C5
Myrtle Rd BS2 ....142 C4
Myrtle St BS3...........63 B3
Myrtles The BS24 .....105 D2
Myrtle Tree Cres BS22..88 A6

N

Nags Head Hill BS5 ....65 A7
NAILSEA 59 E3
Nailsea and Backwell
Station BS48.........75 F7
Nailsea Cl BS13........79 A7
Nailsea Moor La BS48..74 F7
Nailsea Park Cl BS48...59 F2
Nailsea Pk BS48 ....59 F2
Nailsea Sch BS48 ......59 F1
Nailsea Wall BS21......74 C8
Nailsea Wall La BS48...74 E7
Nailsworth Ave BS37...27 E1
NAILWELL............117 D6
Naishcombe Hill BS30..67 C7
Naishes Ave BA2......134 D7
Naish Farm BA3 ....138 D3
Naish Hill BS20 ....45 F1
Naish Ho BA2.........101 A6
Naish La BS48 ....77 D3
Naish's Cross BA3 ....138 D3
Naite The BS35...........7 D6
Nanny Hurn's La BS39 114 A1
Napier Ct BS1 ....142 B1
Napier Ho BS6..........49 B2
Napier Miles Rd BS11 ..48 A8
Napier Rd
Avonmouth BS11 ....33 B1
Bath BA1 ....84 A3
Bristol, Baptist Mills BS5 50 B2
Bristol, Redland BS6 ....49 B2
Napier Sq BS11 ....33 A1
Napier St BS5 ....64 B6
Narroways Rd BS2 .....50 A3
Narrow La BS16........51 E4
Narrow Plain BS2.....143 B2
Narrow Quay BS1.....143 A2
Naseby Wlk BS5 ....50 F1
Nash Cl BS31 ....82 A5
Nash Dr BS7 ....50 C7
Nates La BS40 ....92 F1
Naunton Way BS22.....88 B2
Neads Dr BS30.........66 C5
Neale Way BS11 ....33 C1
Neate Ct BS34 ....36 C8
Neath Rd BS5..........64 D8
Nelson Bldgs BA1.....141 C4
Nelson Ct BS22 ....88 E4
Nelson Ho
Bath BA1 ....141 A3
6 Bristol BS1.........143 A3
8 Bristol, Staple Hill
BS16 ....51 D5
Nelson Par 10 BS3 .....63 D4
Nelson Pl BA1 ....141 C4
Nelson Pl E BA1 ......141 C4
Nelson Pl W BA1......141 A2
Nelson Rd
Bristol BS16...........51 D5
4 Bristol, Staple Hill
BS16 ....51 D4
Nelson St
Bristol BS1...........143 A3
Bristol, Ashton Vale BS3 .63 A2
Nelson Villas BA1 .....141 A2
Nelson Ward Dr BA3 ..134 A1
Nempnett St BS40 ....111 D5
NEMPNETT
THRUBWELL........111 D5
Neston Wlk BS4 ....79 F8
NETHAM..............64 D6
Netham Ct 22 BS5.....64 D7
Netham Gdns 21 BS5...64 D7
Netham Park Ind Est
BS5..................64 D6
Netham Rd BS5........64 D6
Netham View Ind Pk 20
BS5..................64 D7
Netherdale Cvn Site
BS25................125 B6
Netherton Wood La
BS48.................75 A6
Netherways BS21 ......57 D1
Nettlefrith La TA8 ....121 B1
Nettlestone Cl BS10...34 E4
NETTLETON GREEN 43 B1
Nettleton Rd SN14 .....43 B2
Nevalan Dr BS5........65 A6
Neva Rd BS23.........104 E6
Neville Rd BS15........51 E2
Nevil Rd BS7...........49 E4
Newark St BA1 ....141 C1
New Bldgs
Bristol BS16...........50 F4
Peasedown St John
BA2................134 B8
New Bond St BA1.....141 C2
New Bond Street Pl
BA1 ....141 C2
Newbourne Rd BS22 ..105 C8
Newbrick Rd BS34 .....37 A5
NEWBRIDGE 101 B8
Newbridge Cl BS4 .....64 D5
Newbridge Ct BA1 ....101 B7
Newbridge Gdns BA1 .101 A8
Newbridge Hill BA1...101 B7
Newbridge Ho BS9.....48 C4
Newbridge Prim Sch
BA1 ....101 B7
Newbridge Rd
Bath BA1, BA2........101 B7
Bristol BS4...........64 E6
Newbridge Trad Est
BS4..................64 D5
New Bristol Rd BS22 ...89 A2
New Brunswick Ave
BS5..................65 B7
NEWBURY 140 B1
Newbury Rd BS7.......50 A7
New Charlotte St BS3 ..63 D4
New Charlton Way
BS10.................35 A6
NEW CHELTENHAM 51 F1
New Cheltenham Rd
BS15.................51 E1
New Church Rd BS23..104 D2
Newclose La BS40 ....112 D1
Newcombe Dr BS9.....48 C4
Newcombe La BS25...125 B7
Newcombe Rd BS9......48 F7
New Cut Bow BS21.....73 A6
Newditch La BS40......77 C1
Newdown La BS41 .....79 B2
New Ear La BS22.......89 E5
NEW ENGLAND 52 B7
Newent Ave BS15 ......65 B7
Newfields BS40.......127 C8
New Fosseway Rd BS14 80 B6
New Fosseway Sch
BS14.................80 B6
Newfoundland Rd
Bristol BS2...........143 C4
6 Bristol, Baptist Mills
BS2 ....50 A1
Newfoundland St BS2 143 C4
Newfoundland Way
Bristol BS2...........143 C4
Portishead BS20 ....45 E6
Newgate BS1.........143 B3
Newhaven Pl BS20.....44 E4
Newhaven Rd BS20 ....44 D4
New John St 17 BS3....63 C3
New Kings Ct BS7......49 C4
New Kingsley Rd BS2 .143 C2
New King St BA1......141 B2
New La BS35...........15 C5
Newland Dr BS13 ......79 A4
Newland Ho BA1.......84 F1
Newland Hts 12 BS2....49 F2
Newland Rd
Bristol BS13...........79 A3
Weston-s-M BS23 .....104 F6
Newlands Ave BS36....38 C7
Newlands Cl BS20......45 C5
Newlands Gn BS21.....57 G1
Newlands Hill BS20 ....45 C4
Newlands La BS16 .....52 C8
Newlands Rd BS31 .....81 D4
Newlands The BS16 ....51 B7
Newland Wlk BS13.....79 A3
NEWLEAZE............36 B2
Newleaze BS34 ....36 A2
New Leaze BS32 ....24 C3
Newleaze Ho BS34.....36 B2
Newlyn Ave BS9 ....48 D5
Newlyn Way BS37......27 F2
Newlyn Wlk BS4 ....64 B1
Newman Cl BS37.......39 B4
Newmans La BA2 .....116 B2
Newmarket Ave 11
BS1.................143 A3
New Mdws BS14 ....80 A6
New Mills La GL12 .....19 E8
Newnham Cl BS14 .....80 D7
Newnham Pl BS34 .....23 F1
New Oak Prim Sch
BS14.................80 A7
New Orchard St BA1 ..141 C2
New Park Ho BS21 .....57 F5
NEW PASSAGE 12 A1
New Passage Rd BS35..12 A1
New Pit Cotts BA2 ....116 F1
Newpit La BS30.......66 F2
NEWPORT..............4 B8
Newport Cl
Clevedon BS21.........57 E2
Portishead BS20 ....44 F4
Newport Rd BS20 .....47 C5
Newport St BS3........63 E3
Newquay Rd
Bristol BS4...........63 F1
Bristol BS4...........79 F8
New Queen St
Bristol, St George BS15..65 B8
Bristol, Windmill Hill BS3 63 E4
New Rd
Banwell BS29.........106 E4
Bathford BA1..........86 D2
Bristol, Filton BS34 .....35 F3
Bristol, Harry Stoke BS34 36 D3
Churchill BS25........108 F4
Clevedon BS21.........57 F2
Freshford BA2 ....120 B5
High Littleton BS39 ....115 C3
Kilmersdon BA3.......140 E4
Kingswood GL12 ....11 F6
North Nibley GL11.......5 E4
Olveston BS35 ....14 A2
Pensford BS39.........97 D3
Pill BS20..............47 C4
Rangeworthy BS37 .....27 A8
Rangeworthy, Hall End
BS37 ....17 C1
Redhill BS40..........94 A4
Shipham BS25 ....108 E1
Tytherington GL12 ......16 C6
New Rock Ind Est BA3 138 D2
New Rock Rd BA3.....138 D1
Newry Wlk BS4 ....63 E1
New Sandringham Ho 6
BS7..................49 D2
New Siblands Sch BS35 . 8 D1
Newsome Ave BS20 ....47 C4
New St
Bath BA1 ....141 B2
Bristol BS2...........143 C3
Charfield GL12.........11 A6
New Stadium Rd BS5...50 B2
New Station Rd BS16...51 A4
New Station Way BS16 .51 A4
New Street Flats 4
BS2.................143 C3
New Thomas St BS2...143 C2
NEWTON
Bristol 64 A7
Thornbury 8 D6
Newton Cl
Bristol BS15...........52 A1
West Harptree BS40 ...129 E6
Newton Dr BS30 ....66 A5
Newton Gn BS48.......75 C8
Newton Rd
Bath BA2 ....100 F6
Bristol BS30...........66 A5
Weston-s-M BS23 .....104 E6
NEWTON ST LOE......100 D6
Newton's Rd
Weston-s-M BS22 ......88 E3
Weston-s-M BS22 ......88 E4
Newton St BS5.........64 A8
NEWTOWN...........124 D2
Newtown GL12..........11 A5
NEW TOWN
Bishop Sutton 113 D7
Hinton Charterhouse ...136 F8
Paulton..............132 D6
Newtown Chapel
BS39................132 D5
New Tyning La BS37....29 C4
New Walls BS2.........63 F4
New Wlk BS15 ....65 B5
Niblett Cl BS15 ....65 F6
Niblett's Hill BS5 ......65 A6
NIBLEY 27 A1
Nibley Bsns Pk BS37 ...27 A1
NIBLEY GREEN 5 C5
Nibley La BS37.........26 F3
Nibley Rd BS11 ....47 E5
Nicholas La BS5 ....65 A6
Nicholas Rd BS5 ....50 B1
Nicholas St BS3........63 E4
Nicholettes BS30.......66 D5
Nicholls Ct BS36 ....37 E7
Nicholls La BS36.......37 E6
Nichol's Rd BS20.......44 F5
Nigel Pk BS11 ....47 E7
Nightingale Cl
Bristol BS4...........64 E6
Frampton Cotterell BS36 38 A6
Thornbury BS35.........8 D2
Weston-s-M BS22 ......88 E1
Nightingale Ct
Bristol BS4...........64 D3
Weston-s-M BS22 ......88 E1
Nightingale Gdns BS48 59 D2
Nightingale La BS36 ...38 A8
Nightingale Rise BS20..44 F3
Nightingale Way BA3..139 B8
Nile St BA1...........141 A2
Nimbus Rd BS24......105 C5
Nine Tree Hill 16 BS1...49 E1
Ninth Ave BS7 ....36 B1
Nippors Way BS25 ....124 F8
Nithsdale Rd BS23 ....104 E4
Nixon Trad Units
BS24................105 A3
No 1 Royal Cres Mus★
BA1.................141 B3
Noah's Ark Zoo Farm★
BS48.................60 B6
Noble Ave BS30........66 C4
Nomis Pk BS49 ....91 E2
Nordrach La BS40.....128 D5
Nore Gdns BS20 ....45 C6
Nore Park Dr BS20.....44 F5
Nore Rd BS20..........45 A6
Norfolk Ave
Bristol BS2...........143 B4
Bristol, Montpelier BS6 ..49 E2
Norfolk Bldgs BA1 ....141 A2
Norfolk Cres BA1 .....141 A2
Norfolk Gr BS31 ....81 C4
Norfolk Hts 10 BS2....143 B4
Norfolk Pl BS3.........63 C3
Norfolk Rd
Portishead BS20 ....45 E4
Weston-s-M BS23 .....104 F5
Norland Rd BS8.......62 F8
Norley La GL9 ....41 D2
Norley Rd BS7 ....49 F7
Normanby Rd 20 BS5...50 B1
Normandy Dr
Yate BS37.............27 F1
Yate BS37.............39 F8
Norman Gr BS15 ....51 D2
Norman Rd
Bristol, Baptist Mills
BS2 ....50 A2
Bristol, Warmley BS30...66 B8
Saltford BS31.........82 E3
Norman's Cotts BS36...37 D7
Normans The BA2......85 F1
Normans Way BS20 ....46 E7
Normanton Rd 16 BS8..49 A2
Norrisville Rd 8 BS6...49 E1
Northampton Bldgs
BA1 ....141 B4
Northampton Ho BS48 .60 D3
Northampton St BA1 ..141 B4
Northanger Ct 5 BA2 141 C3
Northavon Bsns Ctr
BS37.................27 C3
North Chew Terr BS40..96 B3
North Cnr 8 BS3 ......63 B3
NORTH COMMON......66 D6
North Contemporis
BS8.................142 A3
NORTH CORNER 25 F1
Northcote Ho BS8.....142 A3
Northcote Rd
Bristol, Clifton BS8 .....48 F1
Bristol, Crew's Hole BS5 64 E7
Bristol, Mangotsfield
BS16 ....51 F6
Northcote St 18 BS5....50 B1
North Croft BS30.......66 D4
North Ct BS32 ....24 D3
North Devon Rd BS16 ..51 A5
North Down Cl BS25 ..125 F8
North Down La BS25 ..125 F8
Northdown Rd BA3....133 E5
North Dro BS48 ....59 A2
North East Rd BS35 .....8 C2
North Elm La BS40.....96 B4
NORTHEND 85 F5
NORTH END
Clutton..............114 E5
Yatton................73 F3
North End
Luckington SN14 ....31 E5
Midsomer Norton BA3..133 B2
Northend Ave BS15 ....51 D2
Northend Gdns BS15....51 D2
Northend Rd BS15 .....51 E1
North End Rd BS49.....73 F3
Northern Way BS21 ....57 H3
NORTHFIELD 134 B1
Northfield
Radstock BA3.........134 A3
Timsbury BA2.........116 C3
Winsley BA15.........120 F7
Yate BS37.............39 D8
Northfield Ave BS15....65 D5
Northfield Ho
Bath BA1 ....84 F1
10 Bristol BS3.........63 C4
Northfield La SN14.....55 F1
Northfield Rd
Bristol BS5...........65 B7
Portishead BS20 ....44 E3
Northfields BA1........84 F1
Northfields Cl BA1 .....84 F1
Northgate St BA1 .....141 C2
North Gr BS20 ....47 C4
North Green St 12 BS8 .62 F6
North Hills Cl BS24....105 B2
North La
Bath BA2 ....102 D5
Nailsea BS48..........59 B1
2 Weston-s-M BS23...104 E7
Northleach Wlk BS11...47 F5
North Leaze BS41......62 B2
Northleaze CE Prim Sch
Long Ashton BS41 ......62 B1
Long Ashton BS41 ......62 B1
Northleigh Ave BS22 ...88 C1
North Mdws BA2......134 E8
Northmead Ave BA3...132 F2
Northmead Cl BA3 ....132 F2
Northmead La BS37 ....26 D6
Northmead Rd BA3 ...132 F2
NORTH NIBLEY 5 D4
North Nibley CE Prim Sch
GL11..................5 D5
Northover Ct BS35 .....22 E6
Northover Rd BS9......35 A1
North Par
Bath BA2 ....141 C2
Yate BS37.............27 E2
North Parade Bldgs 8
BA1 ....141 C2
North Parade Pas 7
BA1 ....141 C2
North Parade Rd BA2 .102 B6
North Pk BS15 ....51 E1
North Rd
Banwell BS29.........107 A3
Bath, Bathwick BA2....102 C6
Bath, Combe Down BA2 102 B2
7 Bristol BS3 ....63 A4
Bristol, Montpelier BS6 ..49 E2
Bristol, Stoke Gifford
BS34 ....36 F4
Leigh Woods BS8.......62 D7
Lympsham BS24.......122 D2
Midsomer Norton BA3..133 A1
Thornbury BS35.........8 C2

North Rd continued
Timsbury BA2..........116 C2
Winterbourne BS36......37 F7
Yate BS37.............27 B3
Yate, Engine Common
BS37...............27 B5
Northridge Bsns Ctr
BS37...............27 C2
North Side Rd BS48....93 F8
North Somerset Mus★
BS23...............104 E8
North St
Bristol BS1...........143 B4
Bristol, Downend BS16..51 E5
Bristol, Oldland Common
BS30...............66 C4
Bristol, Southville BS3...63 B3
Nailsea BS48..........59 B1
Norton St Philip BA2..136 E4
Weston-s-M BS23......104 E8
Wickwar GL12.........18 A6
NORTH STOKE........83 C6
North Stoke La BS30...83 B8
Northumberland Bldgs **1**
BA1.................141 B2
Northumberland Pl **1**
BA1.................141 C2
Northumberland Rd
BS6.................49 D2
Northumbria Dr BS9...49 B4
North View
Bristol BS6...........49 A4
Bristol, Mangotsfield
BS16...............51 E5
Bristol, Upper Soundwell
BS16...............51 D4
Midsomer Norton BA3..133 B2
Radstock BA3.........134 B2
North View Cl BA2....101 B5
North View Dr BS29...107 A2
NORTHVILLE.........36 A1
Northville Rd BS7......36 A1
North Way
Bath BA2............101 A5
Bristol BS34..........36 B4
Midsomer Norton BA3..133 A4
NORTH WESTON......45 C2
NORTHWICK.........12 E2
NORTH WICK........96 D8
Northwick Gdns BS39..113 D4
Northwick Rd
Bristol BS7...........49 F8
Chew Magna BS39, BS41 96 D7
Northwick BS35........12 E1
NORTH WIDCOMBE..113 B1
North Wlk BS37........27 C1
Northwoods Wlk BS10..35 D3
North Worle Sh Ctr
BS22...............89 B2
NORTON............88 D4
Norton Cl
Bristol BS15..........65 F7
Chew Magna BS40......96 B3
Norton Farm Rd BS9...34 D3
Norton Grange BA2...136 E5
NORTON HAWKFIELD..96 F6
NORTON HILL.......139 B7
Norton Hill Sch BA3...139 B8
Norton Ho
7 Bristol BS1........143 B1
Bristol, Patchway BS34..23 F1
Norton La
Chew Magna BS39, BS40...............96 D5
Wellow BA2..........136 B7
Weston-s-M BS22......88 C4
Whitchurch BS14.......80 C2
NORTON MALREWARD..97 B7
Norton Rd BS4........64 A3
NORTON ST PHILIP..136 F4
Norton St Philip CE Fst
Sch BA2.............136 E4
NORTON'S WOOD....58 C5
Nortons Wood La BS21..58 A5
Norwich Dr BS4.......64 E6
Norwood Ave BA2....102 E5
Norwood Farm★ BA2..136 F7
Norwood Gr BS20.....44 F5
Notgrove Cl BS22.....88 B2
Nottingham Rd BS7....49 E3
Nottingham St BS3....63 F3
Nova Scotia Pl BS1...142 A1
Nova Way BS11........33 B1
Novers Cres BS4......79 C8
Novers Hill BS4.......79 C8
Novers Hill Trad Est
BS3.................63 C1
Novers La BS4........79 D7
NOVERS PARK......79 D8
Novers Park Cl BS4....63 C1
Novers Park Rd BS4...79 D8
Novers Rd BS4........79 C8
Nowhere La BS48......60 A1

Nugent Hill BS6........49 D1
Nunney Cl BS31.......82 A2
Nupdale La BS35......14 D8
NUPDOWN...........2 A4
Nupdown Rd BS35......1 E5
Nurseries The GL12.....16 B5
Nursery Gdns BS10....35 A3
Nursery Rise BA3.....138 E4
Nursery The BS3......63 B3
Nutfield Gr BS34......36 B2
Nutfield Ho BS34......36 B1
Nutgrove Ave BS3.....63 E3
Nutgrove La BS40.....96 A4
Nuthatch Dr BS16.....50 F6
Nuthatch Gdns BS16...51 A6
Nutwell Rd BS22......88 E2
Nutwell Sq BS22......88 E2
NYE................107 E8
Nye Dro BS24.........107 E8
Nye Rd BS25..........107 F5
Nympsfield BS15......51 E2

O

Oak Ave BA2..........101 C3
Oak Cl
Bristol BS34..........36 D7
Yate BS37............27 D3
Oak Ct
Bristol BS14..........80 A5
Weston-s-M BS22......89 C3
Oakdale Ave BS16.....51 D8
Oakdale Cl BS16......51 D7
Oakdale Ct BS16......51 D7
Oakdale Gdns BS22...88 F2
Oakdale Rd
Bristol BS14..........80 A8
Bristol, Downend BS16..51 E8
Oakdale Wlk BS16.....51 E7
Oakdene Ave BS5.....50 D3
Oak Dr BS20..........45 B4
Oakenhill Rd BS4......64 E2
Oakenhill Wlk BS4.....64 E2
Oakes La GL9.........42 B5
Oakfield Bsns Pk BS15..65 D7
Oakfield Cl BA1......101 D8
Oakfield Gr BS8......142 B4
Oakfield Mans BS8....142 B4
Oakfield Pl BS8......142 B4
Oakfield Rd
Bristol BS8..........142 B4
Bristol, Kingswood BS15..65 D7
Keynsham BS31.......81 F2
Oakford Ave BS23.....104 F8
Oakford La
Batheaston BA1.......86 A8
Marshfield SN14......70 B2
Oak Gr BS20..........47 C5
Oakhanger Dr BS11....34 B1
Oakhill BS24.........105 A2
Oakhill Ave BS30......66 C2
Oakhill Cl BS48......60 B1
Oakhill La BS10......34 C4
Oakhill Rd BA2.......101 F2
Oak Ho BS13..........79 D4
Oakhurst Rd BS9......48 F5
Oak La BS5...........50 F2
Oakland Bsns Pk BS37..27 A3
Oakland Dr BS24.....105 E3
Oakland Rd
Bristol, Crew's Hole
BS5...............64 E8
6 Bristol, Redland BS6..49 B1
Oaklands
Clevedon BS21........57 E4
Paulton BS39........132 E4
Temple Cloud BS39...114 E1
Oaklands Cl BS16.....52 B5
Oaklands Dr
Almondsbury BS32....24 A4
Bristol, Frenchay BS16..51 A7
Bristol, Oldland Common
BS30...............66 C2
Oaklands Rd BS16.....52 A5
Oakleaze BS36........38 D7
Oak Leaze BS34.......35 F6
Oakleaze Rd BS35......8 C1
Oakleigh Ave BS5.....50 D1
Oakleigh Cl BS48......76 B5
Oakleigh Gdns BS30...66 C2
Oakley
Bath BA2............102 E5
Clevedon BS21........73 B8
Oakley Rd BS7........49 F7
Oak Lodge BS37......39 D8
Oakmeade Pk BS4.....64 B2
Oak Rd
Bristol BS7...........49 E5
Colerne SN14........70 F5
Winscombe BS25.....125 A8
Oakridge Cl
Bristol BS15.........66 A7
Winscombe BS25.....125 B7
Oakridge La BS25....125 C6
Oaksey Gr BS48.......60 A1
Oak St BA2..........141 B1
Oaks The
Bristol BS7...........49 E4

Oaks The continued
Nailsea BS48..........60 A2
Winford BS40.........94 F7
Oak Terr BA3.........133 D1
Oak Tree Ave BS16.....53 B4
Oak Tree Cl BS15......65 C3
Oak Tree Wlk BS31....81 D3
Oakwood Ave BS9.....49 C6
Oakwood Dr BS16.....38 C1
Oakwood Gdns BS36...38 E7
Oakwood Pk BS16.....51 A3
Oakwood Rd BS9......49 B6
Oasis Acad Brislington
BS4................80 F8
Oasis Acad Long Cross
BS11...............47 F8
Oatfield BS48.........76 F1
Oatlands Ave BS14....80 A6
Oatley Ho BS9.........49 A5
Oatley Trad Est **6**
BS15...............51 D1
Oberon Ave BS5.......50 E2
Observatory Field
BS25..............125 B8
Observatory The BS22..88 D3
Octavius Rd BS31......81 F8
ODD DOWN.........101 D2
Odeon Bldgs BS23....104 E7
Odins Rd BA2........101 D1
Okebourne Cl BS10....35 B4
Okebourne Rd BS10...35 B4
Okeford Ho BS9.......48 F7
Old Acre Rd BS14.....80 A3
Old Ashley Hill BS6....49 F2
Old Aust Rd BS32.....24 C6
Old Banwell Rd BS24..106 B4
Old Barn La BS40......94 A5
Old Barrow Hill BS11...47 D7
Old Bond St **4** BA1..141 B2
Old Bread St BS2.....143 C2
Old Brewery The BS20..47 C4
Old Brewhouse The
BA1................84 B2
Oldbridge Rd BS14....80 C3
Old Bristol Rd
Ridge BS40..........129 A3
Weston-s-M BS22.....89 A2
Old Bromley Heath Road
BS16...............37 D2
Old Burnett La BS31....99 A7
Oldbury Chase BS30...66 A2
Oldbury Court Dr BS16..51 B6
Oldbury Court Prim Sch
BS16...............51 C7
Oldbury Court Rd BS16..51 A5
Oldbury La
Thornbury BS35........8 B4
Wick BS30............67 D5
OLDBURY NAITE......7 E7
OLDBURY-ON-SEVERN..7 C6
Oldbury-on-Severn Prim
Sch BS35.............7 B5
Old Butchers Yd BS26..125 C2
Old Chapel BA1......141 C4
Old Chapel La BS48....74 F7
Old Chelsea La BS8....61 C4
Old Church Cl BS30....66 D7
Old Church Rd
1 Axbridge BS26.....125 C1
Clevedon BS21........57 E3
Nailsea BS48.........75 D8
Weston-s-M BS23.....104 D2
Old Coach Rd BS26...124 E2
Old Dairy Ct BS21.....57 G3
Old Dairy The BA2....101 D4
OLD DOWN..........14 D4
Old Down Hill BS32....14 B2
Old Down Rd GL9......42 C8
Old Drill Hall The BS2..143 C3
Old England Way BA2.134 E8
Old Farm La BS5......65 B6
Old Ferry Rd BA2.....101 C6
Oldfield BS21.........57 G1
Oldfield Girls Sch BA1..83 F1
Oldfield La BA2......101 E4
OLDFIELD PARK.....101 E4
Oldfield Park Inf Sch
BA2................101 D6
Oldfield Park Jun Sch
BA2................101 C4
Oldfield Park Sta BA2..101 D6
Oldfield Pl BS8.......62 F5
Oldfield Rd
Bath BA2............141 A1
Bristol BS8..........142 A1
Oldfields La BS35.....25 D7
Old Forge Mews BS49..91 D8
Old Forge The BA2...117 B4
Old Forge Way BA2...134 E8
Old Fosse Rd BA2....101 C1
Old Frome Rd BA2....118 D3
Old Gloucester Rd
Alveston BS35........15 B5

Old Gloucester Rd continued
Bristol, Stoke Gifford
BS16...............37 B4
Hambrook BS16.......37 B2
North Corner BS36.....25 D3
Thornbury BS35........9 B2
Old Hill
Winford BS40.........94 D6
Oldhill Farm La BS40...94 D6
Old House The BA2...120 C5
Old Hundred La GL9....41 D2
Old Junction Rd BS23..105 B5
Old King St BA1......141 B3
Old King Street Ct
BS1................143 B3
Old La
Bristol BS16..........52 C6
Farmborough BA2....116 A6
Nailsea BS21.........59 C4
OLDLAND............66 A3
OLDLAND COMMON...66 D3
Oldland Common Sta★
BS30...............66 C3
Oldlands Ave BS16.....38 C6
Old Malthouse The
BS2................143 C4
Old Manor Cl GL12....11 A5
Old Market Rdbt BS2..143 C3
Old Market St BS2....143 C3
Oldmead Wlk BS13....78 E7
Old Midford Rd BA2...119 B7
Old Millard's Hill BA3..133 B3
Old Mill Cl BS37......39 B4
Old Mill Rd BS20......45 D5
Old Mill La BS3.......133 D3
Old Mill Way BS24....106 A8
OLDMIXON..........105 B1
Oldmixon Cres BS24..105 A3
Oldmixon Prim Sch
BS24..............105 A2
Oldmixon Rd BS24...105 B1
Old Mixon Rd BS24...105 C2
Old Newbridge Hill
BA1................101 A8
Old Orchard BA1.....141 C3
Old Orchard St BA1...141 C2
Old Orchard The BS16..52 B5
Old Park Hill BS2.....142 C4
Old Park Rd
Bristol BS11..........47 D7
Clevedon BS21........57 G4
Old Pit Rd
Radstock BA3........139 C8
Yate Rocks BS37......27 C5
Old Pit Terr BA3......133 E4
Old Pk BS2...........142 C3
Old Police Sta The BS4..64 A3
Old Pooles Yd BS4....64 E2
Old Post Office La
BS23..............104 D8
Old Priory Rd BS20....47 B4
Old Quarry BA2......101 D2
Old Quarry Gdns BS15..50 F4
Old Quarry Rd BS11....47 E7
Old Quarry Rise BS11...47 E7
Old Rd
Pensford BS39........97 E3
Radstock BA3........134 C1
Old Rectory Rd GL12...11 F4
Old School Cl BS25...108 F4
Old School Ct SN14....70 A8
Old School Hill BA2...118 F7
Old School Ho BS4.....64 B2
Old School Ho The
BA1................141 B4
Old School House The
BS2................143 C4
Old School La BS24...122 C6
Old Smiths Yd BS15....65 D5
Old Sneed Ave BS9....48 D4
Old Sneed Cotts BS9...48 D4
Old Sneed Pk BS9.....48 D4
Old Sneed Rd BS9.....48 D4
OLD SODBURY......41 B8
Old Sodbury CE Prim Sch
BS37...............41 B8
Old St BS21..........57 G3
Old Station Cl BS40....92 D1
Old Tannery The **20**
BS2................143 C3
Old Tarnwell BS39.....97 B2
Old Tk BA2..........119 F7
Old Vicarage Ct BS14...80 C4
Old Vicarage Gn BS31..81 E6
Old Vicarage Pl BS8....49 A1
Old Vicarage The
Bristol BS13.........78 F6
Bristol, Montpelier BS6..49 F1
Oldville Ave BS21.....57 F2
Old Walcot Sch The
BA1................141 C3
Old Wall BS24........121 D5
Old Water Gdns The
BS40..............110 E2

Old Wells Rd BA2....101 F3
Old Wesleyan Chapel The
BS30...............66 B5
Old Weston Rd
Congresbury BS49.....91 B5
Flax Bourton BS48.....77 B8
Oldwood La BS37......27 B8
Old Work Ho The BS5..64 E8
Olive Gdns BS35.......18 F4
Oliver Brooks Rd BA3.138 E7
OLVESTON..........14 B3
Olveston CE Prim Sch
BS35...............14 A3
Olveston Rd BS7......49 E5
Olympus Cl BS34......36 D6
Olympus Rd BS34.....35 D7
Onega Ctr BA1.......141 A3
Onega Terr BA1......141 A3
Oolite Gr BA2.......101 D1
Oolite Rd BA2.......101 D1
Oram Ct BS30.........65 F4
ORANGE END........19 C4
Orange Gr BA1......141 C2
Orange St BS2.......143 C4
Orchard Ave
Bristol BS1..........142 C2
Midsomer Norton BA3..132 F1
Portishead BS21......58 E4
Thornbury BS35........8 D1
Orchard Bvd BS30.....66 B4
Orchard Cl
Banwell BS29........107 B3
Bishop Sutton BS39...113 C3
Bristol, Kingswood BS15..65 E8
Bristol, Westbury on T
BS9...............48 F5
Charfield GL12.......11 A5
Congresbury BS49.....91 D4
Felton BS40..........94 C8
Flax Bourton BS48.....77 A8
Keynsham BS31........81 D6
Locking BS24........105 F4
Portishead BS20......45 D4
Weston-s-M, Kewstoke
BS22...............88 B3
Weston-s-M, Worle
BS22...............88 F2
Westwood BA15.......120 F3
Winterbourne BS36....37 F5
Wrington BS40........92 D1
Yate BS37............27 B4
Orchard Cotts
11 Bristol BS16.......51 D5
Keynsham BS31........81 B2
Timsbury BA2........116 F1
Orchard Cres BS11....47 D7
Orchard Ct
Bristol BS9...........48 C3
Bristol, Filton BS34....36 A4
19 Bristol, Pile Marsh
BS5...............64 D7
Claverham BS49......74 F1
Yate BS37............27 B3
Orchard Dr
Aust BS35............13 A7
Bristol BS13..........79 A6
Sandford BS25.......108 A4
Orchard End BS40....129 F4
Orchard Gate BS32....24 C2
Orchard Gdns
Bristol BS15..........65 E8
Paulton BS39........132 E6
Orchard Grange BS35...8 B2
Orchard Ho
2 Bristol BS5........64 F8
Weston-s-M BS22......88 F2
Orchard La BA1......142 C2
Orchard Lea
6 Alveston BS35......15 A5
Pill BS20............47 D4
Orchard Lodge BA2...102 F8
Orchard Pk BS14......80 C4
Orchard Pl **1** BS23..104 E7
Orchard Rd
Axbridge BS26.......125 C1
Backwell BS48........76 A6
Bristol, Ashley Down BS7 49 E4
Bristol, Crew's Hole BS5 64 E8
Bristol, Kingswood BS15..65 E8
Clevedon BS21........57 E3
Frampton Cotterell BS36 38 D7
Hutton BS24.........105 E2
Long Ashton BS41.....61 F1
Nailsea BS48.........59 D1
Paulton BS39........132 E6
Pucklechurch BS16....53 B5
Orchard Rise BS35....14 A3
Orchard Sch Bristol
BS7................49 E4
Orchard Sq BS5.......64 D7
Orchard St
Bristol BS1..........142 C2
Weston-s-M BS23....104 E8
Orchards The
Bristol, Kingswood
BS15...............65 F7
Bristol, Shirehampton
BS11...............47 E6
Orchard Terr **5** BA2..101 B6

Orchard The
Banwell BS29........**107** A3
Bath, Combe Down BA2 **102** B1
Bath, Newbridge BA1 .**101** A7
Bristol BS34...........**36** F5
Corston BA2...........**100** B8
Frampton Cotterell BS36 **38** C8
Freshford BA2........**120** C5
Locking BS24.........**106** A5
Pensford BS39.........**97** E4
Pill BS20.............**47** C4
Tytherington GL12...**16** B5
Upper Stanton Drew
  BS39................**97** A2
Orchard Vale
Bristol BS15..........**65** F7
Midsomer Norton BA3 .**132** F1
Orchard Vw G12.......**9** E7
Orchard Way BA2....**134** D7
Orchard Wlk
Churchill BS25.......**108** E4
Kingswood GL12.......**11** F4
Orchid Cl BS16......**52** C7
Orchid Dr BA2.....**101** C1
Oriel Gdns BA1.....**85** C2
Oriel Gr BA2......**101** B4
Orion Dr BS34......**36** D6
Orland Way BS30....**66** A3
Orlebar Gdns BS11..**34** B2
Orme Dr BS21.......**57** F5
Ormerod Rd BS9.....**48** E5
Ormonds Cl BS32....**24** E1
Ormrod Gr BS24....**106** C5
Ormsley Cl BS34....**36** C8
Orpen Gdns BS7.....**50** B5
Orpen Pk BS32......**24** B3
Orpheus Ave BS34...**36** D6
Orwell Dr BS31.....**82** A4
Orwell St BS3......**63** E3
Osborne Ave
Bristol BS7...........**49** F3
Weston-s-M BS23.....**104** F7
Osborne Cl BS34.....**36** D4
Osborne Rd
Bath BA1.............**101** B7
Bristol, Clifton BS8..**49** A1
Bristol, Southville BS3..**63** C4
Severn Beach BS35....**22** A7
Weston-s-M BS23.....**104** F7
Osborne Terr 10 BS3..**63** B2
Osborne Villas BS23.**142** C4
Osborne Wallis Ho
BS8.................**142** A1
Osmond Rd 2 BS24..**105** F7
Osprey Ct BS14......**79** D5
Osprey Gdns BS22...**88** F1
Osprey Pk BS35......**8** D3
Osprey Rd 15 BS5...**64** C7
Ostlings La BA1......**86** B2
Otago Terr 5 BA1....**85** C2
Ottawa Rd BS23....**104** F3
Otterford Cl BS14...**80** B5
Otter Rd 1 BS21.....**57** G1
Otter Way BS35......**8** D3
Ottery Cl BS11......**34** A1
Ottrells Mead BS32..**24** C3
Our Lady of Lourdes RC
Prim Sch BS15......**65** E7
Our Lady of the Rosary RC
Prim Sch BS11......**48** A8
OVAL THE.............**101** C4
Oval The BA2.......**101** C4
OVER..................**23** D2
Over Court Gdns BS34..**35** E6
Overdale
Clandown BA3.........**133** E5
Peasedown St John
  BA2................**116** F3
Over Dr BS34........**35** F7
Overhill BS20.......**47** D4
Over La BS35........**23** D2
Overndale Rd BS16...**51** C6
Overndale Sch BS37...**41** A7
Overnhill Cl BS16...**51** D5
Overnhill Rd BS16...**51** D5
Overnhurst Ct 2 BS16 .**51** D5
Overstables La BS1..**57** F3
Overton 5 BS4......**64** D1
Overton Rd BS6......**49** E2
Owen Dr BS8........**61** B4
Owen Gr BS9.........**49** B5
Owen Henry Ho BS2..**50** A1
Owen St 18 BS5.....**64** B8
Owls Head Rd BS15..**65** E6
Oxbarton BS34.......**36** F5
Oxenhan Ct BS5......**64** D8
Oxen Leaze BS32....**24** E2
Oxford Pl
Bath BA2.............**102** C2
21 Bristol, Clifton BS8..**62** F6
14 Bristol, Upper Easton
  BS5................**50** B1
Weston-s-M BS23.....**104** D7
Oxford Row BA1.....**141** B3
Oxford Sq BS24.....**106** B6
Oxford St
Bristol BS2...........**143** C2
7 Bristol, Redfield BS5..**64** C7
Bristol, The Dings BS2 .**64** A6

Oxford St *continued*
Bristol, Tyndall's Park BS2,
  BS6................**142** C4
Bristol, Windmill Hill BS3..**63** F4
Weston-s-M BS23.....**104** D7
Oxhouse Gdns BS10..**34** E3
Oxhouse Ind Est BS22 .**89** A5
Oxhouse La
Failand BS8..........**61** B6
Winford BS40.........**94** D6
Oxleaze BS13.......**79** D4
Oxleaze La BS41.....**78** E3
Oxleaze Way BS39..**132** D6
Oxleigh Way BS16...**36** F3
Oxney Pl BA2......**134** C7
Oxwick Farm La BS37..**28** A4
Ozenhay BS39......**130** E6
Ozleworth BS15......**66** A8

P

Packgate Rd BS11....**33** F4
Pack Horse La BA2...**118** F7
Pacquet Ho BS20.....**47** D5
Paddock Cl
Bristol BS10..........**24** E2
Bristol, Emerson's Green
  BS16................**52** C6
Paddock Gdn BS14....**79** F4
Paddock Gdns BS35...**15** A5
Paddock Park BS22...**89** B2
Paddock Rd BS35.....**8** B3
Paddocks The
5 Bath BA2.........**102** B1
Bristol BS16..........**38** A1
Sandford BS25........**108** C4
Thornbury BS35........**8** D1
Weston-s-M BS23.....**104** D2
Paddock The
Banwell BS29........**107** A3
Clevedon BS21........**57** F2
Corston BA2..........**100** B7
Portishead BS20.......**45** D4
Paddock Woods BA2..**102** D2
Padfield Cl BA2.....**101** B5
Padleigh Hill BA2...**101** B5
Padmore Ct 7 BS5...**64** D7
Padstow Rd BS4......**79** F8
Pagans Hill BS40.....**95** D2
Page Ct BS16........**51** F4
Page Rd BS16........**51** D4
Page's Ct BS49......**91** C8
Pages Mead BS11....**47** C8
Painswick Ave BS34..**36** B8
Painswick Dr BS37...**27** E1
Paintworks BS4......**64** B4
Palace Yard Mews
  BA1................**141** B2
Palmdale Cl BS30....**66** A3
Palmer Ave BS35.....**22** C3
Palmer Row 7 BS23..**104** E8
Palmers Cl BS30.....**66** A6
Palmer's Elm BS24...**90** B4
Palmers La BA2.....**117** B3
Palmers Leaze BS34..**37** A6
Palmer St BS23.....**104** E8
Palmerston Rd BS6...**49** C4
Palmerston St BS3...**63** C3
Palmer's Way BS24..**105** D2
Palmyra Rd BS3......**63** B2
Pamela Ho 9 BS16...**51** D5
Panoramic The BS1..**142** C3
Pantile The 16 BS3..**63** C3
Paper Mill Gdns BS20..**45** F6
Parade Ct BS5.......**50** F2
Parade The
1 Bath BA2.........**101** B6
Bristol BS34..........**23** F1
Bristol, Bishopsworth
  BS13................**79** A6
Bristol, Shirehampton
  BS11................**47** E6
Chipping Sodbury BS37..**28** A1
Paradise Row BS39...**98** A6
Paragon Ct 13 BS23..**87** C1
Paragon Rd BS23.....**87** C1
Paragon Sch The BA2..**102** A3
Paragon The
Bath BA1.............**141** C4
Bristol BS8...........**62** F6
Parbrook Ct BS14....**80** B5
Parfitt's Hill 8 BS5..**64** F6
Parish Brook Rd BS48..**59** B2
Parish The BS3......**142** B1
Park Ave
Bath BA2.............**141** B4
Bristol BS32..........**24** A2
Bristol, Eastville BS5..**50** D3
Bristol, Rose Green BS5..**64** E8
Bristol, Windmill Hill BS3..**63** E3
Frampton Cotterell BS36..**38** B6
Winterbourne BS36....**37** E7
Yatton BS49...........**74** B4
Park Batch BS40....**110** F3
Park Cl
Bristol, Cadbury Heath
  BS30................**66** B5
Bristol, Kingswood BS15..**65** E7

Park Cl *continued*
Keynsham BS31........**81** D5
Paulton BS39........**132** D5
Park Cnr
Paulton BS39........**132** D6
Sharpstone BA2......**120** A4
PARK CORNER........**120** A4
Park Cres
Bristol, Cadbury Heath
  BS30................**66** B5
Bristol, Frenchay BS16..**37** C1
Bristol, Rose Green BS5..**64** E8
Park Ct 5 BS23....**104** E5
Park Edge BS5.......**64** E8
Park End BS29......**106** E4
Parkers Ave BS30....**67** C7
Parkers Barton BS5..**64** B6
Parkers Cl BS10.....**35** E4
Parker St BS3.......**63** B3
Parkes Rd BS24.....**106** C5
Park Farm Bsns Pk
  BS40................**94** B7
Park Farm Ct 13 BS30..**65** F4
Park Farm Village Gn
  BS36................**38** B6
PARKFIELD...........**53** A7
Parkfield BS26......**125** B1
Parkfield Ave 3 BS5..**64** D7
Parkfield Gdns BS39..**113** D3
Parkfield Rank BS16..**53** A7
Parkfield Rd BS16...**53** A6
Park Gdns BA1......**101** D8
Park Gr BS9.........**49** C5
Park Hill BS11......**47** F6
Park Ho BA2........**101** E4
Parkhouse La BS31..**81** C2
Parkhurst Ave 4 BS16..**51** B4
Parkhurst Rd BS23..**105** A1
Park La
Bath BA1.............**101** D7
Blagdon BS40........**110** F3
Bristol BS2..........**142** C3
Faulkland BA3.......**135** A1
Frampton Cotterell BS36..**38** B6
North Nibley GL11.....**5** E7
Parklands
Bristol BS8..........**142** C4
Bristol, Kingswood BS15..**65** E8
High Littleton BS39...**115** D2
Parklands Ave BS22..**89** A4
Parklands Educate
Together Prim Sch
  BS24................**106** B6
Parklands Rd BS3....**62** E4
Parkland Way BS35...**8** C3
Park Leaze
Bristol BS34..........**23** E1
Kendleshire BS36.....**38** A6
Park Pl
Bath BA1.............**141** A4
Bristol, Kingsdown BS2..**142** B3
Bristol, Upper Eastville
  BS5................**50** E3
Bristol, Victoria Park
  BS2................**142** C3
Weston-s-M BS23.....**104** D8
Park Prim Sch The
Bristol BS15..........**65** E8
Bristol BS30..........**66** E8
Park Rd
Bath BA1.............**101** B7
Bristol BS3..........**142** B1
Bristol, Cadbury Heath
  BS30................**66** B5
Bristol, Kingswood BS15..**65** D8
Bristol, Northville BS7..**36** A1
Bristol, Shirehampton
  BS11................**47** F6
Bristol, Staple Hill BS16..**51** E6
Bristol, Stapleton BS16..**50** D5
Clevedon BS21........**57** F4
Congresbury BS49.....**91** E3
Keynsham BS31........**81** E4
Leyhill GL12..........**10** B4
Paulton BS39........**132** D5
Thornbury BS35........**8** B2
Park Row
Bristol BS1..........**142** C3
Frampton Cotterell BS36..**38** A8
Parkside Ave BS36...**37** E6
Parkside Gdns BS5...**50** B4
Park St
Bath BA1.............**141** A4
Bristol BS1..........**142** C3
Bristol BS5...........**64** A4
Bristol, Crew's Hole BS5..**64** E8
Bristol, Totterdown BS4..**64** A3
Hawkesbury Upton GL9..**20** A2
Iron Acton BS37......**26** D4
Parkstone Ave BS7...**49** F6
Park Street Ave BS1..**142** C3
Park Street Mews
  BA1................**141** A4
Park The
Bristol BS32..........**24** C3
Bristol, Frenchay BS16..**37** B1
Bristol, Kingswood BS15..**65** E8
Bristol, Willsbridge BS30..**66** B1
Keynsham BS31........**81** E6

Park The *continued*
Portishead BS20.......**45** F5
Yatton BS49...........**74** B1
Park View
Bath BA2.............**101** D6
Bristol, Kingswood BS15..**65** E7
Bristol, Southville BS3..**63** C4
Yate BS37............**39** E8
Park View Ave BS35...**8** C2
Park View Ct BS16...**51** E5
Park View Terr BS5..**64** E8
Park Villas BS23....**104** D8
Parkwall Cres BS30..**65** F4
Parkwall Prim Sch
  BS30................**66** A4
Parkwall Rd BS30....**66** A4
Parkway
Bristol BS34..........**37** A4
Timsbury BA2........**116** E2
Park Way
Bristol BS30..........**66** B5
Midsomer Norton BA3..**139** A8
Park Way BS22.......**89** B1
Parkway La BA2.....**116** D3
Parkway N BS34......**37** A4
Parkway Trad Est 10
  BS2................**49** F2
Park Wlk BS20.......**47** D4
Park Wood Cl BS14...**79** F4
Parliament St BS4...**64** A4
Parnall Cres BS37...**27** C2
Parnall Rd BS16.....**51** A3
Parnall Road Ind Est
  BS16................**51** A3
Parnell Rd
Bristol BS16..........**50** E7
Clevedon BS21........**57** F3
Parry Cl BA2.......**101** B4
Parry's Cl BS9......**48** E5
Parrys Gr BS9.......**48** E5
Parry's La BS9......**48** F5
Parslow Barton 4 BS5..**65** A7
Parsonage Cl BS40..**94** F6
Parsonage Cl BS20..**45** D4
Parsonage La
Axbridge BS26.......**125** E2
Bath BA1.............**141** B5
Chilcompton BA3.....**138** C4
Pensford BS39........**97** D6
Winford BS40.........**94** F6
Parsonage Rd BS41..**62** C2
Parson St Prim Sch
  BS3................**63** C2
Parsons Ave BS34....**36** F5
Parsons Gn
Clevedon BS21........**73** C8
Weston-s-M BS22.....**89** A3
Parsons Mead BS48...**76** F7
Parsons Paddock BS14..**80** A7
Parson St BS3......**63** B2
Parson Street Prim Sch
  BS3................**63** C2
Parson Street Sta BS3..**63** B2
Parsons Way BS25..**124** E6
Parsons Wlk BS30...**66** D7
Partis College BA1..**101** A8
Partis Way BA1.....**101** A8
Partition St BS1....**142** C2
Partridge Cl
Weston-s-M BS22.....**88** F1
2 Yate BS37.........**27** F4
Partridge Dr BS16...**51** C6
Partridge Rd BS16...**53** C4
Passage Leaze BS11..**47** D6
Passage Rd
Aust BS35............**12** F7
Bristol, Brentry BS10..**34** F3
Bristol, Westbury on Trym
  BS9................**49** A8
Passage Road Brentry Hill
  BS9, BS10..........**35** A2
Passage St BS2.....**143** B2
Pastoral Rd BS35.....**8** B4
Pastures Ave BS22...**89** C3
Pastures The BA15..**120** E3
Patch Croft BS21....**73** C8
Patch Ct BS16.......**52** A8
Patch Elm La BS37...**26** F7
Patch La BS37.......**27** A8
Patch St BA2.......**102** A2
PATCHWAY...........**24** B2
Patchway Brook BS32..**24** C2
Patchway CE Prim Sch
  BS34................**24** C1
Patchway Com Coll
  BS32................**24** B1
Patchway Sta BS34...**36** C6
Patchway Trad Est
  BS34................**35** E7
Patchwood Rd BS34...**77** F7
Patterson Ho 8 BS1..**143** B1
Paul Alan Ho 21 BS5..**64** C7
Paulman Gdns BS41...**77** F8
Paulmont Rise BS39..**114** E1
Paul's Cswy BS49....**91** D4
Paul St BS2........**142** C4
Paulto' Hill BA3, BS39..**133** B6
PAULTON...........**132** F5
Paulton Dr BS7......**49** C4

Paulton Jun & Inf Sch
  BS39...............**132** E5
Paulton La BS39....**133** D7
Paulton Memorial Hospl
  BS39...............**132** F4
Paulton Rd
Farrington Gurney
  BS39...............**132** B4
Hallatrow BS39......**132** B4
Midsomer Norton BA3..**132** F1
Paultow Ave BS3.....**63** E3
Paultow Rd BS3......**63** E3
Paulwood Rd BS39..**114** E1
Pavey Cl BS13......**79** C4
Pavey Rd BS13......**79** C4
Pavilions The BS4...**64** C1
Pawlett BS24......**105** A2
Pawlett Rd BS13.....**79** C3
Pawlett Wlk BS13...**79** C3
Paxton BS16........**50** E8
Paybridge Rd BS13...**78** F4
Payne Dr BS5........**64** B7
Payne Rd BS24.....**105** D2
Paynes Ho 17 BS23..**104** E8
Paynes Orchard Pk
  BS10...............**35** D5
Paywell La BS40....**127** A5
Peache Ct BS16......**51** E6
Peache Rd BS16......**51** F6
Peacock Rd BS35.....**8** C3
Peacocks La BS15....**65** C7
Pearces Hill BS16...**51** B7
Pearl St BS3........**63** B3
Pearsall Rd BS30....**65** E2
Pearse Cl BS22......**89** B5
Peart Cl BS13......**78** E5
Peart Dr BS13......**78** E4
Pear Tree Ave BS41..**77** E8
Peartree Cl BS13....**79** B4
Peartree Field BS20..**45** F5
Peartree Gdns BS24..**122** C6
Pear Tree Hey BS37..**27** E5
Pear Tree Ind Est
  BS40...............**109** C4
Peartree La
Bristol, Lower Soundwell
  BS15...............**51** F2
Bristol, St George BS5..**65** B6
Pear Tree Leaze BS34..**35** F6
Pear Tree Rd BS32...**24** C2
Pear Tree Way BS16..**52** D8
PEASEDOWN ST
JOHN...............**134** C8
Peasedown St John Prim
Sch BA2...........**134** C7
Peats Hill BS39......**97** F5
Pedder Rd BS21......**57** F1
Peelers Ct 2 BS26..**125** C1
Peel St BS5........**143** C4
Pegasus Lodge BS23..**104** D5
Pegasus Pk BS34.....**36** C6
Pegasus Pl BS25...**107** F4
Pegasus Rd BS34.....**35** D7
Peg Hill BS37.......**27** E4
Pegwell Close BS34..**35** E6
Pelican Cl BS22....**105** F8
Pemberton Ct BS16..**51** C5
Pembery Rd BS3......**63** B3
Pembroke Ave BS11..**47** E6
Pembroke Ct BS21...**57** E4
Pembroke Gate BS8..**49** A1
Pembroke Gr BS8.....**142** A3
Pembroke Ho 1 BS23..**87** C1
Pembroke Lodge BS8..**142** A3
Pembroke Mans BS8..**142** A1
Pembroke Pl BS8....**142** A1
Pembroke Rd
Bristol BS8..........**142** A4
Bristol, Kingswood BS15..**51** E2
Bristol, Shirehampton
  BS11................**47** E6
Bristol, Southville BS3..**63** C4
Portishead BS20.......**44** E4
Weston-s-M BS23.....**104** F4
Pembroke St BS2....**143** B4
Pembroke Vale BS8..**142** A4
Penard Way BS15....**65** F7
Penarth Dr BS24...**105** A1
Pendennis Ave BS16..**51** D4
Pendennis Ho 5 BS16..**51** D5
Pendennis Pk
Bristol, Brislington BS4..**64** D2
1 Bristol, Staple Hill
  BS16...............**51** D4
Pendennis Rd BS16...**51** D5
Pendle Cl BS25....**125** A7
Pendlesham Gdns BS23..**88** A1
Pendock Cl BS30.....**66** C1
Pendock Ct BS16.....**52** B7
Pendock Rd
Bristol BS16..........**51** C6
Winterbourne BS36....**37** E5
Penfield Ct BS2.....**50** A2
Penfield Rd BS2.....**50** A2
Penlea Ct BS11......**47** D7
Pennard BS24......**105** A2

Pennard Ct
Bath BA2 . . . . .101 A6
Bristol BS14 . . . . .80 B5
Pennard Gn BA2 . . . . . .101 A6
Penn Ct BS26 . . . . .125 C1
Penn Dr BS16 . . . . .37 C1
Penn Gdns BA1 . . . . . . .101 A8
Penngrove BS30 . . . . . . .66 A3
Penn Hill La BS31 . . . . . .81 A3
Penn Hill Rd BA1 . . . . . .84 A1
Pennine Gdns BS23 . . . . .88 A1
Pennine Rd BS30 . . . . . . .66 C4
Pennings The BS26 . . . . .125 C2
Pennington Rd GL12 . . . .18 B4
Pennlea BS13 . . . . .79 C7
Penn Lea Ct BA1 . . . . . .101 B8
Penn Lea Rd BA1 . . . . . .101 B8
Pennon Rise BS1 . . . . . .142 C1
Penn St BS1 . . . . .143 B3
Penns The BS21 . . . . .57 G2
PENNSYLVANIA 68 F7
Pennsylvania Vw BA1. . .84 E4
Penn Way BS26 . . . . . . .125 C1
Pennycress BA2 . . . . . . .105 D7
Pennycress Cl BS16 . . . . .52 D8
Pennyquick BA2 . . . . . . .100 D6
Pennyquick Hill BA2 . . .100 F4
Pennyquick View BA2 . .100 F6
Pennyroyal Gr BS16 . . . . .50 E4
Pennywell Ct **3** BS5 . . .64 A8
Pennywell Est **3** BS21 . .57 F2
Pennywell Rd BS2, BS5 . .64 A8
Pen Park Rd BS10 . . . . . .35 D2
Penpole Ave BS11 . . . . . .47 E6
Penpole Cl BS11 . . . . . . .47 D7
Penpole La BS11 . . . . . . .47 E7
Penpole Pk BS11 . . . . . . .47 E7
Penpole Pl BS11 . . . . . . .47 E6
Penrice Cl BS22 . . . . .88 C2
Penrith Gdns BS10 . . . . . .49 D8
Penrose BS14 . . . . .79 F7
Penrose Dr BS32 . . . . . . .36 D7
Pensfield Pk BS10 . . . . . .35 D4
PENSFORD 97 E4
Pensford Ct BS14 . . . . . . .80 D5
Pensford Hill BS39 . . . . . .97 D5
Pensford La BS39 . . . . . . .97 A3
Pensford Old Rd BS39 . . .97 E3
Pensford Prim Sch
  BS39. . . . . .97 D4
Pentagon The BS9 . . . . . .48 B5
Penthouse Hill BA1 . . . . .85 F3
Pentire Ave BS11 . . . . . . .79 A6
Pentland Ave BS35 . . . . . .15 E8
Peony Rd BS16 . . . . .38 C1
Peppershells La BS39 . . . .98 C6
Pepys Cl BS31 . . . . .82 D2
Pera Pl BA1 . . . . .141 C4
Pera Rd BA1 . . . . .141 C4
Percival Rd BS8. . . . . .62 F8
Percival Terr BS3 . . . . . .131 F4
Percy Pl **18** BA1. . . . . . . .85 B1
Percy St **8** BS3 . . . . .63 D4
Percy Walker Ct BS16 . . .51 C6
Peregrine Cl BS22 . . . . . .88 F1
Perfect View BA1 . . . . . . .85 A1
Peritrack La BS23 . . . . . .105 E2
Perrett Ho **22** BS2 . . . . .143 C3
Perretts Ct BS1 . . . . .142 C1
Perrett Way BS20 . . . . . . .47 E4
Perrin Cl BS39 . . . . .131 E8
Perrings The BS48 . . . . . .75 E8
Perrinpit Rd BS36. . . . . . .25 E2
Perrott Rd BS15. . . . . .52 A1
Perry Cl BS36. . . . . .37 D4
Perry Court E-Act Acad
  BS14. . . . . .80 A4
Perrycroft Ave BS13. . . . .79 A6
Perrycroft Rd BS13. . . . . .79 A6
Perrymans Cl
  Bristol BS16. . . . . .51 A6
  Doynton BS30 . . . . .68 A8
PERRYMEAD 102 B3
Perrymead
  Bath BA2 . . . . .102 B3
  Weston-s-M BS22 . . . . .89 B5
Perrymead Ct BA2 . . . . .102 B4
Perrymead Pl BA2 . . . . .102 B4
Perry Mead Rd BS40 . . .130 C5
Perry Rd
  Bristol BS1. . . . . .143 A3
  Long Ashton BS41 . . . . .61 F1
Perrys Lea BS32 . . . . .24 D2
Perry St BS5. . . . . .64 A8
Pesley Cl BS13 . . . . .79 A4
Petercole Dr BS13 . . . . . .79 A6
Peterside BS39 . . . . .131 E8
Peterson Sq BS13 . . . . . . .79 C3
Peter's Terr BS5 . . . . .64 B7
Petersway Gdns BS5 . . . .65 A6
Petherbridge Way BS7 . .50 A5
Petherton Cl BS15 . . . . . .65 E7
Petherton Gdns BS14 . . . .80 B7
Petherton Rd BS14. . . . . .80 B7
Pethick Ho BS4 . . . . .79 F8

Peto Garden at Iford
  Manor The★ BA15 . . . .120 E3
Peto Gr BA15 . . . . .120 F3
Pettigrove Gdns BS15 . . .65 E7
Pettigrove Rd BS15 . . . . .65 E6
PETTY FRANCE 30 A7
Pevensey Wlk BS4 . . . . . .79 D7
Peverell Cl BS10 . . . . .34 F3
Peverell Dr BS10 . . . . .34 F3
Pheasant Row BS49 . . . . .73 F2
Philippa Cl BS14 . . . . . . .80 A7
Philips Ho **2** BS2 . . . . .143 B4
Philip St
  Bristol, St Philip's Marsh
    BS2 . . . . .64 B5
  Bristol, Windmill Hill BS3 63 D4
Phillips Rd BS23 . . . . . . .105 A6
Phillis Hill BS39. . . . . . . .132 F4
Phippen St **1** BS1 . . . . .143 B1
Phipps Barton BS15 . . . . .65 B8
Phipps St BS3 . . . . .63 B4
Phoenix Bsns Pk BS3 . . .63 A2
Phoenix Gr BS6 . . . . .49 C5
Phoenix Ho
  Bath BA1 . . . . .141 B4
  Bristol BS5. . . . . .64 B6
Phoenix Way BS20 . . . . . .45 F6
Piccadilly Pl
  Bath BA1 . . . . .102 B8
  5 Bathwick BA2 . . . . .102 B8
Pickedmoor La BS35 . . . . .7 E5
Pickwick Rd BA1. . . . . . . .85 A2
Picton La BS6 . . . . .49 E1
Picton Mews **6** BS6 . . . .49 E1
Picton St BS6. . . . . .49 E1
Pier Cl BS20 . . . . .45 E7
Pier Rd BS20 . . . . .45 E7
Pierrepont Pl **9** BA1. . .141 C2
Pierrepont St BA1 . . . . . .141 C2
Pigeon House Dr BS13 .79 D4
Pigeon La BS40 . . . . .93 E1
Pigott Ave BS13. . . . . .79 A4
Pilemarsh BS5. . . . . .64 D7
PILE MARSH 64 D7
Pilgrims Way
  Avonmouth BS11 . . . . . .47 C7
  Bristol BS16. . . . . .51 D8
  Chew Stoke BS40. . . . .112 D8
  Weston-s-M BS22 . . . . .88 E3
Pilgrims Wharf BS4 . . . . .64 E7
Pilkington Cl BS34. . . . . . .36 C2
PILL 47 C4
Pill Rd
  Abbots Leigh BS8. . . . . .47 F1
  Pill BS20. . . . . .47 E2
Pill St BS20. . . . . .47 D4
Pill Way BS21 . . . . .57 D2
PILNING 22 D7
Pilning Prim Sch BS35 . .22 E6
Pilning St BS35 . . . . .23 C8
Pilning Sta BS35 . . . . .22 F5
Pimms La BS22 . . . . .88 B3
Pimm's La BS22. . . . . .88 B2
Pimpernel Mead BS32. . .36 E7
Pinchay La BS40 . . . . .95 A5
Pinckney Gn BA15 . . . . .103 E5
Pincots La GL12. . . . . .18 B3
Pine Cl
  Thornbury BS35. . . . . . . .8 C1
  Weston-s-M BS22 . . . . .88 D2
Pinecroft
  Bristol BS14. . . . . .79 F7
  Portishead BS20 . . . . . .44 F6
Pine Ct
  Chew Magna BS40. . . . .96 B3
  Keynsham BS31. . . . . . .81 C4
  Radstock BA3. . . . . . . .134 A2
Pinefield BS9. . . . . .49 B7
Pine Gr BS7 . . . . .36 A1
Pine Grove Pl BS7 . . . . . .49 D3
Pine Hill BS22 . . . . .88 D2
Pine Lea BS24 . . . . .122 B6
Pine Rd BS10 . . . . .35 B3
Pine Ridge Cl BS9. . . . . . .48 C4
Pines Cl BA3. . . . . .138 D3
Pines La BS35 . . . . .14 D3
Pines Rd BS30 . . . . .66 C1
Pines The
  Bristol, Lower Soundwell
    BS15 . . . . .52 A3
  Bristol, Sneyd Park BS9. .48 D3
Pines Way
  Bath BA2 . . . . .141 A2
  Radstock BA3. . . . . . . .134 A2
Pines Way Ind Est
  BA2 . . . . .141 A2
Pinetree Rd BS24 . . . . . .106 D4
Pine Wlk BA3. . . . . .133 E1
Pinewood BS15. . . . . .51 F1
Pinewood Ave BA3 . . . . .132 F1
Pinewood Cl BS9 . . . . . . .49 B7
Pinewood Gr BA3 . . . . . .132 F1
Pinewood Rd BA3. . . . . .132 F1
Pinewood Way SN14 . . . .70 F7
Pinhay Rd BS13. . . . . .79 B6
Pinkers Mead BS16 . . . . .52 C6
Pinkhams Twist BS14. . . .80 A5

Pinnell Gr BS16. . . . . .52 C7
Pioneer Ave BA2 . . . . . . .101 F1
Pioneer Pk BS4. . . . . .64 C5
Pipehouse BA2 . . . . .119 E4
Pipehouse La BA2 . . . . . .119 F4
Pipe La BS1 . . . . .142 C2
Piper Rd BS37 . . . . .27 E3
Pippin Cl BA2. . . . . .134 D7
Pippin Cl **4** BS30 . . . . . .65 F4
Pippins The BS20 . . . . . . .45 F5
Pitchcombe BS37. . . . . . . .39 C7
Pitchcombe Gdns BS9. . .48 D7
Pitching The BA3 . . . . . . .138 D5
Pitch La BS6. . . . . .49 D1
Pitch & Pay La BS9. . . . . .48 E3
Pitch & Pay Pk BS9 . . . . .48 E3
Pitfour Terr BA2 . . . . . . .116 B2
Pithay Ct BS1. . . . . .143 A3
Pithay The
  Bristol BS1. . . . . .143 A3
  Paulton BS39. . . . . . . .132 E6
Pit La
  Backwell BS48. . . . . . . .76 A4
  Ubley BS40 . . . . .111 F5
Pitlochry Cl BS7 . . . . .35 F1
Pitman Ct BA1. . . . . .85 C2
Pitman Ho BA2 . . . . .101 D4
Pitman Rd BS23. . . . . . . .104 E6
Pit Rd BA3. . . . . .133 B1
PITT COURT 5 F5
Pitt Rd BS7 . . . . .49 E5
Pittville Cl BS35. . . . . .8 C3
Pittville Pl **16** BS6. . . . . .49 B1
Pitway Cl BS39. . . . . .131 F4
Pitway La BS39 . . . . .131 E4
Pixash La BS31 . . . . .82 C5
Pixash Works BS31. . . . .82 C5
Pixey Hole La BS40. . . . .111 E3
Pixey Ave BS21 . . . . .57 D2
Pixey Ave Ind Est BS21 .57 E2
Pizey Cl BS21 . . . . .57 D2
Plain The
  Norton St Philip BA2 . .136 E4
  Thornbury BS35. . . . . . . .8 B1
Platts Wood BS16. . . . . . .50 D8
Players Cl BS16 . . . . .37 B3
Playford Gdns BS11 . . . . .47 E8
Plaza The BS2 . . . . .143 C2
Pleasant Ho **4** BS16 . . . .51 D5
Pleasant Pl BA1. . . . . .86 D2
Pleasant Rd BS16 . . . . . . .51 D5
Pleshey Ct BS22. . . . . .88 D2
Plimsoll Ho
  3 Bristol BS1. . . . . . .143 B1
  5 Bristol, Woolcott Park
    BS6 . . . . .49 B1
Ploughed Paddock
  BS48. . . . . .59 D1
Plover Cl
  Weston-s-M BS22 . . . . .88 F1
  Yate BS37. . . . . .27 C2
Plovers Rise BA3. . . . . . .134 A3
Plowright Ho **8** BS15 . . .65 B5
Plumers Cl **4** BS21 . . . . .57 G1
Plumley Cres BS24 . . . . .106 A4
Plumley Ct BS23 . . . . . . .104 D4
PLUMMER'S HILL 132 E6
Plummer's Hill BS5 . . . . .64 E8
Plumpton Ct BS16 . . . . . .37 F1
Plumptre Cl BS39 . . . . . .132 E5
Plumptre Rd BS39 . . . . . .132 E5
Plumtree Ct BS25 . . . . . .108 A1
Plum Tree Rd BS22 . . . . .105 E8
Plunder St BS49 . . . . .92 B7
Podgers Dr BA1 . . . . .84 B2
Podium The BA1. . . . . . .141 C2
Poets' Cl BS5 . . . . .64 D8
Poets Cnr BA3 . . . . .139 C8
Polar Gdns SN14 . . . . . . .31 E4
Polden Cl BS48 . . . . .59 E1
Polden Ho BS3 . . . . .63 D3
Polden Rd
  Portishead BS20 . . . . . .45 B5
  Weston-s-M BS23 . . . . .104 F8
Polden Wk BA3 . . . . .139 B6
Polestar Way BS24 . . . . .106 A8
Pollard Rd BS22 . . . . .105 F8
Polly Barnes Cl 6
  BS15. . . . . .65 B5
Polly Barnes Hill BS15. .65 B5
Polygon Rd BS8. . . . . . . .142 A2
Polygon The
  Avonmouth BS11 . . . . . .33 D1
  16 Bristol BS8 . . . . . . .62 F6
Pomfrett Gdns BS14. . . . .80 E5
Pomphrey Hill BS16. . . . .52 C4
Pond Cotts BA3. . . . . . . .135 D2
Pond Head BS20 . . . . .47 D4
Ponsford Rd BS4. . . . . . . .64 B1
Ponting Cl BS5 . . . . .51 A1
Pool Cnr BS32 . . . . .14 B2
Poole Court Dr BS37 . . . .27 E2
Poole Ho BA2. . . . . .100 F5
Poolemead Rd BA2 . . . . .100 F5
Poole St BS11 . . . . .47 B8
Pooles Wharf BS8. . . . . .142 A1
Pooles Wharf Ct BS8. . . .142 A1
Pool Farm BS37. . . . . .39 D5
Pool Ho BS34. . . . . .36 A8

Pool La BS40 . . . . .95 A2
Pool Paddock BS34. . . . . .35 F6
Pool Rd BS15 . . . . .51 E3
Poor Hill BA2 . . . . .115 F6
Pope's Wlk BA2. . . . . . . .102 B3
Poplar Ave BS9 . . . . .48 D6
Poplar Cl
  Bath BA2 . . . . .101 D4
  Bristol BS30 . . . . .66 C6
Poplar Dr BS16 . . . . .53 B5
Poplar Fields BS30. . . . . .66 D6
Poplar Gardens Ho 3
  BS15. . . . . .65 E8
Poplar La GL12 . . . . .18 B4
Poplar Pl
  Bristol BS16. . . . . .51 A3
  16 Weston-s-M BS23. .104 E8
Powells Acres BS21 . . . . .57 G3
Powis Cl BS22 . . . . .88 C2
Powlett Ct BA2 . . . . .102 B7
Powlett Rd BA2 . . . . .102 B8
Pow's Hill BA3. . . . . .133 D5
Pow's Orch BA3 . . . . . . .133 A1
Pow's Rd BS15. . . . . .65 D7
Poyntz Ct BS30 . . . . .65 F3
Poyntz Rd BS4. . . . . .79 F8
Pratten's La **2** BS16 . . .51 D4
Preacher Cl BS5. . . . . .65 B6
Preachers Wlk BS15 . . . . .65 D5
Preanes Gn BS22. . . . . . . .89 A2
Precinct BS49 . . . . .91 D3
Precinct The BS20. . . . . . .45 D5
Preddy's La BS5 . . . . .65 A6
Prescot Cl BS22. . . . . .88 B2
Prescott BS37 . . . . .39 D8
Press Moor Dr BS30. . . . .65 F4
Prestbury BS37 . . . . .39 D8
Preston Wlk BS4. . . . . . . .64 A1
Prestwick Cl BS4 . . . . . . .64 D1
Pretoria Rd BS34. . . . . . . .35 F8
Prewett St BS1 . . . . .143 B1
Priddy Cl BA2. . . . . .101 B5
Priddy Ct BS14. . . . . .80 B5
Priddy Dr BS14 . . . . .80 B5
Priests Way BS22. . . . . . . .88 D2
Priestwood Cl BS10. . . . .35 A3
Primrose Alley BA2 . . . . .99 D2
Primrose Cl
  Bristol BS32. . . . . .24 D2
  Bristol, St George BS15. .65 C8
Primrose Dr BS35. . . . . . . .8 C2
PRIMROSE HILL 84 D1
Primrose Hill BA1. . . . . . .84 D1
Primrose La
  Bristol BS15. . . . . .51 C1
  Midsomer Norton BA3. .133 B1
Primrose Rd **4** BS16. . . .52 C7
Primrose Terr BS15 . . . . .51 C1
Princes Bldgs BA1 . . . . .141 B3
Prince's Bldgs 19
  BS8. . . . . .62 F6
Princes Ct BS30. . . . . .65 F4
Princes' La BS8 . . . . .62 F6
Princes' Pl BS7 . . . . .49 E3
Prince's Rd BS21. . . . . . . .57 F3
Princess Cl BS31. . . . . . . .81 E4
Princess Gdns BS16. . . . .50 D6
Princess Row BS2. . . . . .143 A4
Princess St
  Bristol, Newton BS2. . . .64 A7
  Bristol, Windmill Hill BS3 63 E4
Princes St BA1. . . . . .141 B2
Prince's St
  Bristol BS2. . . . . .143 C4
  Clandown BA3. . . . . . . .133 C3
Princess Victoria St
  BS8. . . . . .62 F6
Prince St BS1. . . . . .143 A1
Prinknash Ct **6** BS37 . . .39 D7
Prior La BS37. . . . . .27 C2
Prior Park Bldgs BA2. . .102 B5
Prior Park Coll BA2 . . . .102 C2
Prior Park Cotts BA2. . . .141 C1
Prior Park Gdns BA2 . . .102 B5
Prior Park Landscape
  Gdn★ BA2. . . . . .102 C3
Prior Park Rd BA2 . . . . . .102 B4
Priors Hill BA2. . . . . .116 A2
Prior's Hill **12** BS6 . . . . .49 D1
Priors Lea BS37. . . . . .27 E1
Priory Ave BS9. . . . . .49 A7
Priory Cl
  Bath BA2 . . . . .102 B2
  Midsomer Norton BA3. .133 A1
Priory Com Sch BS22 . . .89 B3
Priory Court Rd BS9. . . . .49 A7
Priory Ct
  Bristol, Hanham BS15. . .65 C3
  Bristol, Upper Knowle
    BS4 . . . . .64 B2
Priory Dene BS9 . . . . .49 A7
Priory Farm Trad Est
  BS20. . . . . .46 D3
Priory Gdns
  Bristol, Horfield BS7 . . .49 F8
  Bristol, Shirehampton
    BS11 . . . . .47 D7
  Easton-in-G BS20. . . . . .47 B4
Priory Mews BS23 . . . . . .105 B7
Priory Rd
  Bristol BS8. . . . . .142 C4

Priory Rd *continued*
Bristol, Shirehampton
  BS11 . . . . .47 D6
Bristol, Upper Knowle
  BS4 . . . . .64 B2
Easton-in-G BS20 . . . . .47 B4
Keynsham BS31 . . . . . . .81 E7
Portbury BS20 . . . . .46 D3
Weston-s-M BS23 . . . . .105 A7
Priory Wlk BS20 . . . . .46 D3
PRISTON 117 B5
Priston Cl BS22 . . . . . .89 B5
Priston Hill BA2 . . . . .117 C5
Priston La
Farmborough BA2 . . . . .116 C7
Farmborough BA2 . . . . .116 C8
Priston BA2, BA3 . . . . . .117 C5
Priston Rd BA2 . . . . . .117 D6
Pritchard St BS2 . . . . .143 B4
Pritchard Way BS37 . . .27 D6
Privet Dr BS13 . . . . . . .79 C5
Probyn Cl BS16 . . . . . .51 A7
Pro-Cathedral BS8 . . . .142 B3
Proctor Cl BS4 . . . . . . .64 D1
Proctor Ho BS1 . . . . . .143 B1
Promenade The BS7 . . .49 D2
Prospect Ave BS15 . . . .51 B1
Prospect Cl
Easter Compton BS35 . . .23 A2
Frampton Cotterell BS36 . .37 F8
Winterbourne BS36 . . . . .37 E4
Prospect Cres BS15 . . .51 F2
Prospect Gdns BA1 . . . .85 F5
Prospect Ho BS22 . . . . .88 E3
Prospect La BS36 . . . . .37 F8
Prospect Pl
Bath, Beacon Hill BA1 . . .85 A1
Bathford BA1 . . . . .86 D2
Bath, Weston BA1 . . . . . .84 C2
  1 Bristol, Montpelier
    BS6 . . . . .49 D2
Bristol, Moorfields BS5 . . .64 C8
  9 Weston-s-M BS23 . . .104 E8
Prospect Rd
Bath BA2 . . . . .102 C4
Severn Beach BS35 . . . . .22 A5
Prospect Terr 5 BS3 . . .63 C3
Protheroes Ho BS1 . . . .142 C2
Proud Cross BS40 . . . .129 E4
Providence La BS41 . . . .61 F2
Providence Pl BS2 . . . .143 C2
PROVIDENCE PLACE . . .132 F1
Providence Rise BS41 . . .61 F2
Providence View BS41 . . .62 A1
Prowse Cl BS35 . . . . . . .8 C1
Prowse's La BS26 . . . . .125 A1
Prudham St 7 BS5 . . . .50 C1
PUBLOW 97 F5
Publow La BS39 . . . . . .97 E5
PUCKLECHURCH 53 B5
Pucklechurch CE Prim Sch
  BS16 . . . . .53 C6
Pucklechurch Trad Est
  BS16 . . . . .53 B4
Pudding Pie Cl BS40 . . .109 A5
Pudding Pie La BS40 . . .109 A6
Puffin Cl BS22 . . . . . . .105 F8
PULLENS GREEN 7 C5
Pullin Ct BS30 . . . . . . .66 D4
Pullins Gn 3 BS35 . . . . .8 B1
Pulteney Ave BS2 . . . . .102 B6
Pulteney Bridge BA2 . . .141 C2
Pulteney Gdns BA2 . . . .102 B6
Pulteney Gr BA2 . . . . . .102 B6
Pulteney Mews BA2 . . . .102 B7
Pulteney Rd BA2 . . . . . .102 B6
Pulteney Terr BA2 . . . . .102 B6
Pump La
Bathford BA1 . . . . .86 B2
Bristol BS1 . . . . .143 B1
Redhill BS40 . . . . .93 D2
Tockington BS32 . . . . . . .14 D4
Pump Sq BS20 . . . . . . .47 D5
Purcell Wlk BS4 . . . . . .79 D7
Purdown Rd BS7 . . . . . .49 F5
Purdue Cl BS22 . . . . . . .89 B3
Purdy Ct BS16 . . . . .51 A4
Purlewent Dr BA1 . . . . .84 C1
PURN 122 A7
Purn La BS24 . . . . .122 A8
Purn Rd BS24 . . . . .121 F8
Purn Way BS24 . . . . . . .122 B7
Purple Emperor Rd
  BS35 . . . . .8 C3
Pursey Dr BS32 . . . . . . .36 F6
Purton Cl BS15 . . . . . . .65 E6
Purton Rd BS7 . . . . . . .49 D2
Purving Row BS24 . . . . .122 C1
Purving Row La BS24 . . .122 C1
Puttingthorpe Dr
  BS22 . . . . .105 C7
Puxley Cl BS14 . . . . . . .80 E6
PUXTON 90 D3
Puxton La BS24 . . . . . . .90 D3
Puxton Moor La BS24 . . .90 E2
Puxton Rd BS24 . . . . . . .90 C2
Pye Cnr BS25 . . . . .108 D4
PYE CORNER 37 D3
Pye Croft BS32 . . . . . . .24 E3

Pyecroft Ave BS9 . . . . .49 C7
Pyghtell The SN14 . . . . .31 E5
Pylewell La BS25 . . . . .108 D1
Pylle Hill Cres BS3 . . . .63 F4
Pyne Point BS21 . . . . . .57 E3
Pynes The BS31 . . . . . . .82 B4
Pynne Cl BS14 . . . . .80 F5
Pynne Rd BS14 . . . . . . .80 F5
Pyracantha Wlk BS14 . . .80 A6

Q

QEH Theatre ★ BS8 . . . .142 B3
Quadrangle The BS37 . . .39 C4
Quadrant BS32 . . . . . . .24 B3
Quadrant E BS16 . . . . . .51 C3
Quadrant The BS6 . . . . .49 B3
Quadrant W BS16 . . . . .51 C3
Quadrilles The BS35 . . . .22 A6
Quaker Ct 1 BS35 . . . . .8 B1
Quaker La BS35 . . . . . . .8 B1
Quaker's Cl BS16 . . . . . .51 D8
Quakers' Friars BS1 . . . .143 B3
Quaker's Rd BS16 . . . . .51 E8
Quantock Cl
Bristol BS30 . . . . .66 C5
Midsomer Norton BA3 . . .139 B6
Quantock Ct BS16 . . . . .36 E1
Quantock Rd
Bristol BS3 . . . . .63 D3
Portishead BS20 . . . . . . .45 B5
Weston-s-M BS23 . . . . . .104 E4
Quantocks BA2 . . . . . . .102 A1
Quarries The BS32 . . . . .24 C6
Quarrington Rd BS7 . . . .49 E5
Quarry Bank BS37 . . . . .28 B2
Quarry Barton BS16 . . . .37 C4
Quarry Cl
Bath BA2 . . . . .101 F1
Limpley Stoke BA2 . . . . .120 D6
Quarry Hay BS40 . . . . . .112 D8
Quarry La
Bristol BS11 . . . . .34 C1
Winterbourne BS36 . . . . .37 E4
Quarrymans Ct 1
  BA2 . . . . .102 B1
Quarry Mead BS35 . . . . .14 F5
Quarry Rd
Alveston BS35 . . . . .14 F5
Bath BA2 . . . . .102 D6
Bristol BS8 . . . . .49 A2
Bristol, Frenchay BS16 . . .51 C3
Bristol, Kingswood BS15 . .65 D6
Chipping Sodbury BS37 . . .28 A1
Portishead BS20 . . . . . . .45 C4
Sandford BS25 . . . . .108 A2
Quarry Rise BS24 . . . . .121 F6
Quarry Rock Gdns
  BA2 . . . . .102 D4
Quarry Steps 8 BS8 . . . .49 A2
Quarry The BS11 . . . . . .34 C1
Quarry Vale Cotts 2
  BA2 . . . . .102 B1
Quarry Way
Bristol, Emerson's Green
  BS16 . . . . .38 A1
Bristol, Fishponds BS16 . . .50 E5
Nailsea BS48 . . . . .59 D2
Quays Ave BS20 . . . . . .45 E5
Quayside La 4 BS5 . . . . .64 F6
Quay St BS1 . . . . .143 A3
Quays The BS1 . . . . . . .142 C1
Quebec BA2 . . . . .101 A6
Quedgeley BS37 . . . . . . .39 C8
Queen Ann Rd BS5 . . . . .64 B6
Queen Charlotte St
  BS1 . . . . .143 A2
QUEEN CHARLTON 81 B3
Queen Charlton La
  BS14 . . . . .80 E2
Queen Elizabeth's Hospital
  Sch BS8 . . . . .142 B3
Queen Quay BS1 . . . . . .143 A2
Queens Apartments
  BS8 . . . . .142 C3
Queen's Ave
Bristol BS8 . . . . .142 B3
Portishead BS20 . . . . . . .45 C5
Queenscote BS20 . . . . . .45 F5
Queens Ct BS31 . . . . . . .81 E5
Queen's Ct BS8 . . . . . . .142 B3
Queensdale Cres BS4 . . .64 A1
Queens Down Cl BS4 . . .64 C3
Queensdown Gdns BS4 . .64 C2
Queens Down Gdns
  BS4 . . . . .64 C3
Queens Dr BS15 . . . . . . .65 B4
Queen's Dr
Bath BA2 . . . . .102 A2
Bristol BS7 . . . . .49 C5
Queens Gate BS9 . . . . . .48 D5
Queenshill Rd BS4 . . . . .64 A1
Queensholm Ave BS16 . . .37 E1
Queensholm Cl BS16 . . . .37 E1
Queensholm Cres BS16 . . .37 E1
Queensholm Dr BS16 . . . .37 E1
Queens Mans BS8 . . . . .142 B3

Queens Par BS1 . . . . . .142 C2
Queen's Par BA1 . . . . . .141 B3
Queen's Parade Pl
  BA1 . . . . .141 B3
Queens Pl BA2 . . . . . . .102 B5
Queen Sq
Bath BA1 . . . . .141 B2
Bristol BS1 . . . . .143 A2
Saltford BS31 . . . . .82 F3
Queen Square Ave 10
  BS1 . . . . .143 A2
Queen Square Ho BS1 . . .143 A2
Queen Square Pl BA1 . . .141 B3
Queens Rd
Banwell BS29 . . . . .107 A3
Bristol BS4 . . . . .64 C2
Keynsham BS31 . . . . . . .81 D4
Nailsea BS48 . . . . .59 D1
Portishead BS20 . . . . . . .44 E4
Queen's Rd
Bristol BS8 . . . . .142 B3
Bristol, Ashley Down BS7 . .49 F5
Bristol, Bishopsworth BS13,
  BS41 . . . . .78 F4
Bristol, Cadbury Heath
  BS30 . . . . .66 B4
Bristol, Crew's Hole BS5 . .64 F7
Clevedon BS21 . . . . .57 F3
Pucklechurch BS16 . . . . . .53 B5
Radstock BA3 . . . . .134 B2
Weston-s-M BS23 . . . . . .87 D1
Queen St
Avonmouth BS11 . . . . . .33 A1
Bath BA1 . . . . .141 B2
Bristol BS2 . . . . .143 B3
Bristol, Eastville BS5 . . . .50 D3
Bristol, St George BS15 . . .65 B8
Queensway
Bristol BS34 . . . . .36 D6
Weston-s-M BS22 . . . . . .88 F4
Queens Way BS20 . . . . .44 E4
Queensway Ctr BS22 . . . .89 B2
Queens Wlk BS35 . . . . . . .8 B3
Queen Victoria Rd BS6 . .49 A4
Queen Victoria St BS2 . . .64 A6
Queenwood Ave BA1 . . . .85 A1
Quickthorn Cl BS14 . . . . .80 A6
Quiet St BA1 . . . . .141 B2
Quilter Gr BS4 . . . . .79 D7

R

Raby Mews BA2 . . . . . .102 B7
Raby Pl BA2 . . . . .102 B7
Raby Villas BA2 . . . . . .102 B7
Rackfield Pl BA2 . . . . . .101 B6
Rackham Cl BS7 . . . . . . .50 B6
Rackhay BS1 . . . . .143 A2
Rackley La BS26 . . . . . .124 B2
Rackvernal Ct BA3 . . . . .133 B1
Rackvernal Rd BA3 . . . .133 B1
RADFORD 133 C8
Radford Hill
Camerton BA2, BA3 . . . .133 C7
Timsbury BA2 . . . . .116 C1
Radley Rd BS16 . . . . . . .51 B4
Radnor Bsns Ctr BS7 . . .49 E5
Radnor Rd
Bristol, Horfield BS7 . . . .49 E5
Bristol, Westbury on Trym
  BS9 . . . . .49 B5
RADSTOCK 133 E1
Radstock Mus ★ BA3 . . .133 F2
Radstock Rd BA3 . . . . .133 F2
Raeburn Rd BS5 . . . . . . .65 B6
Rag Hill BA3 . . . . .134 D5
Rag La GL12 . . . . .17 D5
Raglan Cl BA3 . . . . .138 C4
Ragland La BA1 . . . . . . .85 A2
Ragland St BA1 . . . . . . .85 A2
Raglan La
Bristol BS5 . . . . .65 A7
Winford BS40 . . . . .94 E7
Raglan Pl
Bristol BS7 . . . . .49 D3
Thornbury BS35 . . . . .15 B8
  20 Weston-s-M BS23 . . .87 C1
Raglan Rd BS7 . . . . .49 D3
Raglan Terr BA1 . . . . . . .85 A2
Raglan Villas BA1 . . . . . .85 A1
Raglan Wlk BS31 . . . . . .81 D4
Railton Jones Cl BS34 . . .36 E3
Railway Arches BS2 . . . .143 C2
Railway Cotts BS37 . . . . .40 E8
Railway La BA2 . . . . . . .118 D1
Railway Pl BA1 . . . . . . .141 C1
Railway St BA1 . . . . . . .141 C1
Railway Terr
Bristol BS16 . . . . .51 C4
Shoscombe BA2 . . . . . . .134 E4
Railway View Pl BA3 . . . .133 B2
Rainbow Ct BS37 . . . . . .27 B3
Rainham Ct 2 BS23 . . . .87 C1
Rains Batch BS40 . . . . .127 A2
Raleigh Cl BS31 . . . . . . .82 D2
Raleigh Ct 3 BS23 . . . . .104 E5
Raleigh Rd BS3 . . . . . . .63 B4
Raleigh Rise BS20 . . . . . .45 B5

Ralph Allen Dr BA2 . . .102 B3
Ralph Allen Sch BA2 . . .102 E2
Ralph Rd BS7 . . . . .49 F4
RAM HILL 38 D4
Ram Hill BS36 . . . . .38 D4
Ram Hill Bsns Pk BS36 . .38 D5
Ramsay Cl BS22 . . . . . . .88 E4
Ramscombe La BA1 . . . . .85 F6
Ramsey Rd BS7 . . . . . . .49 F6
Rams Leaze BS34 . . . . . .36 A7
Ranchways BS20 . . . . . .44 F4
Randall Cl BS15 . . . . . . .51 F2
Randall Rd BS8 . . . . . . .142 B2
Randolph Ave
Bristol BS13 . . . . .79 B5
Yate BS37 . . . . .27 A4
Randolph Cl BS13 . . . . . .79 B5
Rangers Wlk BS15 . . . . .65 C4
RANGEWORTHY 27 B8
Rangeworthy CE Prim Sch
  BS37 . . . . .16 F1
Rankers La BS39 . . . . . .98 C5
Rannoch Rd BS7 . . . . . . .35 F1
Ranscombe Ave BS22 . . . .88 D2
Ransford BS21 . . . . .57 D1
Raphael Ct BS1 . . . . . . .143 B1
Ratcliffe Dr BS34 . . . . . .36 E5
Rathbone Cl BS36 . . . . . .38 C5
Raven Cl BS22 . . . . .88 E1
Raven Ct BS9 . . . . .48 E8
Ravendale Dr BS30 . . . . .66 B2
Ravenglass Cres BS10 . . .35 D2
Ravenhead Dr BS14 . . . . .80 B8
Ravenhill Ave BS3 . . . . . .63 F2
Ravenhill Rd BS3 . . . . . .63 F3
Ravenscourt Rd BS34 . . . .36 B7
Ravenswood BS30 . . . . . .66 B3
Ravenswood Rd BS6 . . . .49 C1
Ravenswood Sch BS48 . . .59 D3
Rawlins Ave BS22 . . . . . .89 A5
Rawnsley Ho 13 BS5 . . . .50 A1
Rayens Cl BS41 . . . . .61 F1
Rayens Cross Rd BS41 . . .61 F1
Rayleigh Rd BS9 . . . . . . .48 E7
Raymend Rd BS3 . . . . . . .63 E3
Raymend Wlk BS3 . . . . . .63 E2
Raymill BS4 . . . . .65 A2
Raymond Ho BS16 . . . . .51 F4
Raymore Rise BS41 . . . . .61 F1
Raynes Rd BS3 . . . . .63 A3
Rayneswood BS23 . . . . .104 F8
Raysfield Inf Sch BS37 . . .39 F8
Raysfield Jun Sch BS37 . .39 F8
Reade Cl BS15 . . . . .65 D4
Reading Ct BS15 . . . . . . .65 B8
Rearing Unit The BS35 . . .7 E7
Rector's Way BS23 . . . .104 F6
Rectory Cl
Farmborough BA2 . . . . .116 A6
Wraxall BS48 . . . . .60 A2
Yate BS37 . . . . .27 F3
Rectory Dr BS49 . . . . . . .91 C7
Rectory Farm La BA2 . . .100 F2
Rectory Gdns BS10 . . . . .34 E2
Rectory La
Bleadon BS24 . . . . .122 C6
Bristol BS34 . . . . .36 A3
Compton Martin BS40 . . .129 B6
Cromhall GL12 . . . . .17 A8
Timsbury BA2 . . . . .116 B1
Rectory Rd
Easton-in-G BS20 . . . . . .47 B3
Frampton Cotterell BS36 . .38 A8
Rectory Way
Lympsham BS24 . . . . . . .121 F2
Yatton BS49 . . . . .91 C7
Recurium Lodge BS26 . . .125 C2
Redacre BS40 . . . . .93 D3
Red Admiral Way BS35 . . .8 C3
Redcar Ct BS16 . . . . . . .37 F1
Redcatch Rd BS4 . . . . . .63 F2
Redcliff Backs BS1 . . . . .143 B2
Redcliff Cres BS3 . . . . . .63 E4
REDCLIFFE BAY 44 E4
Redcliffe Cl BS20 . . . . . .44 E3
Redcliffe Par E BS1 . . . .143 A1
Redcliffe Par W BS1 . . . .143 A1
Redcliffe Way BS1 . . . . .143 B1
Redcliff Hill BS1 . . . . . . .143 B1
Redcliff Mead La BS1 . . .143 B1
Redcliff St BS1 . . . . .143 B2
Redcroft BS40 . . . . .93 D3
Redcross Mews 14
  BS2 . . . . .143 C3
Redcross St BS2 . . . . . . .143 C3
Redding Pit La BS40 . . . .94 E4
Reddings The
Bristol BS15 . . . . .51 F2
Compton Martin BS40 . . .129 B7
REDFIELD 66 C6
Redfield Edge Prim Sch
  BS30 . . . . .66 D4
Redfield Gr BA3 . . . . . . .139 A8
Redfield Hill BS30 . . . . . .66 E3
Redfield Rd
Bristol BS34 . . . . .36 B7
Midsomer Norton BA3 . . .139 A8
Redford Cres BS13 . . . . .78 F3
Redford La BS16 . . . . . . .53 D4

Pri–Rho **173**

Redford Wlk BS13 . . . . . .78 F3
Redham La BS35 . . . . . . .22 F8
REDHILL 93 D3
Red Hill
Peasedown St John
  BA2 . . . . .116 E1
Redhill BS40 . . . . .93 D2
Redhill Cl BS16 . . . . .50 E3
Redhill Dr BS16 . . . . . . .50 E3
Redhill Farm Bsns Pk
  BS35 . . . . .13 F6
Redhill La BS35 . . . . . . .13 E6
Red House La
Almondsbury BS32 . . . . . .24 B4
Bristol BS9 . . . . .48 E6
REDLAND 49 C3
Redland Ave BS16 . . . . . .46 F6
Redland Court Rd BS6 . . .49 C2
Redland Gr BS6 . . . . . . .49 C2
Redland Green Rd BS6 . . .49 B3
Redland Green Sch
  BS6 . . . . .49 C2
Redland Hill BS6 . . . . . . .49 B2
Redland Pk
Bath BA2 . . . . .100 F6
Bristol BS6 . . . . .49 B2
Redland Rd BS6 . . . . . . .49 C2
Redland Sta BS6 . . . . . . .49 C2
Redlands Terr BA3 . . . . .138 F8
Redland Terr 8 BS6 . . . .49 B2
Red Lodge Bsns Pk
  BS24 . . . . .89 D1
Red Lodge The ★ BS8 . . .142 C3
Redlynch La BS31 . . . . . .81 D2
Red Maids Jun Sch The
  BS9 . . . . .49 A6
Red Maids Sch The
  BS9 . . . . .49 A6
Redpoll Dr BS20 . . . . . . .46 A6
RED POST 134 B7
Red Post Ct BA2 . . . . . .134 B7
Red Rd TA8 . . . . .121 A2
Redshard La BS40 . . . . .109 B7
Redshelf Wlk BS10 . . . . .35 C3
REDWICK 22 B8
Redwick Cl BS11 . . . . . . .34 C2
Redwick Crossroads
  BS35 . . . . .22 C7
Redwick Gdns BS35 . . . . .22 C7
Redwick Rd
Pilning BS35 . . . . .22 C8
Redwick BS35 . . . . .22 B8
Redwing Dr BS22 . . . . . .88 F1
Redwing Gdns BS16 . . . . .50 E6
Redwood Cl
Bristol BS30 . . . . .66 A3
Nailsea BS48 . . . . .60 A2
Radstock BA3 . . . . .139 E8
Redwood Dr BS8 . . . . . . .61 F4
Redwood Ho BS13 . . . . . .79 D3
Redwood La BS48 . . . . . .77 C7
Redwoods The BS31 . . . . .81 D6
Reed Cl BS10 . . . . .49 D6
Reed Ct BS30 . . . . .65 F3
Reedley Rd BS9 . . . . .48 F5
Reedling Cl BS16 . . . . . . .50 E6
Reed Rd BS37 . . . . .27 E5
Reed's Row GL12 . . . . . .19 D7
Reed Way BS22 . . . . .89 C3
Regency Dr BS4 . . . . . . .65 A2
Regent Apartments
  BS6 . . . . .49 C3
Regent Rd BS3 . . . . .63 D4
Regents Cl BS35 . . . . .8 B2
Regents St BS8 . . . . . . .142 A2
Regent St
Bristol, Kingswood
  BS15 . . . . .65 D8
Weston-s-M BS23 . . . . . .104 F2
Regents The BS31 . . . . . .81 F6
REGIL 94 F2
Regil La BS40 . . . . .95 A6
Regil Rd BS40 . . . . .94 F3
Regina The BA1 . . . . . . .141 B3
Remenham Dr BS9 . . . . . .49 B5
Remenham Pk BS9 . . . . .49 B5
Rendcomb Cl BS22 . . . . . .88 B2
Rendle Ho BS16 . . . . . . .51 F4
Rene Rd 12 BS5 . . . . . . .50 B1
Rennison Ct BS23 . . . . .104 E4
Repton Hall BS10 . . . . . .35 B2
Repton Rd BS4 . . . . .64 D3
Retford Ho BA2 . . . . . . .102 E5
Retort Rd BS11 . . . . .33 C3
Retreat The
Radstock BA3 . . . . .134 E3
Weston-s-M BS23 . . . . . .87 C1
Reubens Ct BS22 . . . . . . .88 F3
Reubins The BS5 . . . . . . .51 A2
Reynolds Cl BS31 . . . . . .82 A5
Reynold's Wlk BS7 . . . . . .50 A7
Rhode Cl BS31 . . . . .82 A3
Rhodyate BS40 . . . . . . .110 D2
Rhodyate Hill BS49 . . . . .91 F6
Rhodyate La BS49 . . . . . .92 A7
Rhodyate The BS29 . . . .107 C1

Rhyne Terr BS23 . . . . . .**104** D2
Rhyne View BS48. . . . . .**59** B1
Rialls Ground BS34. . . . **35** F6
Ribblesdale BS35 . . . . . . **15** D8
Richards Cl BS22. . . . . . . **89** B4
Richard Stephens Rd
  BS16. . . . .**50** F8
Richeson Cl BS10 . . . . **34** F2
Richeson Wlk BS10 . . . **34** F2
Richmond Apartments
  BS6. . . . .**49** C3
Richmond Ave
  Bristol, Montpelier BS6 . .**49** F2
  Bristol, Stoke Gifford
  BS34. . . . . **36** E5
Richmond Cl
  Bath BA1 . . . . **84** F1
  Keynsham BS31. . . . . . . **81** D4
  Portishead BS20 . . . .**45** E5
Richmond Ct
  Bristol BS34. . . . . **23** F1
  7 Bristol, Clifton BS8 . . **49** A2
  2 Bristol, Windmill Hill
  BS3. . . . . **63** F4
Richmond Dale 6 BS8 . **49** A2
Richmond Gn BS48. . . . .**59** F1
Richmond Hill
  Bath BA1 . . . . **84** F1
  Bristol BS8. . . . .**142** B3
Richmond Hill Ave
  BS8. . . . .**142** B3
Richmond Hts
  Bath BA1 . . . . **84** F2
  Bristol BS8. . . . .**142** B3
Richmond La
  Bath BA1 . . . . **84** F1
  Bristol BS8. . . . .**142** A3
Richmond Mews BS8..**142** A3
Richmond Park Rd
  BS8. . . . .**142** A3
Richmond Pl BA1 . . . . . **84** F1
Richmond Rd
  Bath BA1 . . . . **84** F1
  Bristol, Mangotsfield
  BS16. . . . .**52** A5
  Bristol, Montpelier BS6 . .**49** F2
  Bristol, Pile Marsh BS5 . .**64** E7
Richmond St
  Bristol BS3. . . . . **63** F4
  Weston-s-M BS23 . . . . .**104** D7
Richmond Terr
  Avonmouth BS11 . . . . **33** B1
  Bristol BS8. . . . .**142** A3
Ricketts La BS22. . . . . . **89** A2
RICKFORD **110** B3
Rickford Cotts BS40. . . **110** B4
Rickford La BS40. . . . . .**110** A3
Rickford Rd BS48 . . . . . . **59** F1
Rickford Rise BS40. . . . .**110** A3
Ricklands The BS40. . . . . **95** A6
Rickyard Rd BS40 . . . . . .**92** E2
Ride The BS15 . . . . **52** A2
RIDGE **129** C5
Ridge Cl BS20 . . . .**45** A4
Ridge Cres BS40 . . . . . .**129** E6
Ridge Green Cl BA2 . . .**118** D8
Ridgehill BS9. . . . . **49** C6
Ridge Jun Sch The
  BS37. . . . .**27** F2
Ridge La BS40 . . . . **129** D5
Ridgemeade BS14 . . . . . . **80** B4
Ridgemount Gdns
  BS14. . . . .**80** B5
Ridge The
  Bristol, Hengrove BS14 . . **80** C5
  Bristol, Shirehampton
  BS11. . . . . **47** E7
  Frampton Cotterell BS36 .**38** C7
  Yatton BS49 . . . . **91** B8
Ridgeview BS41. . . . . **62** B2
Ridgeview Ho BS20 . . . . **45** E3
RIDGEWAY **50** F3
Ridgeway
  Frampton Cotterell
  BS36. . . . .**38** D7
  Nailsea BS48 . . . . **59** C1
  Yate BS37. . . . . **28** A2
Ridgeway Ave BS23 . . . **104** E6
Ridgeway Cl BS40. . . . .**129** E6
Ridgeway Ct
  Bristol BS14. . . . . **80** C5
  Bristol, Henbury BS10 . . . **35** A1
Ridgeway Gdns BS14. . . **80** C5
Ridgeway Ind Ctr BS5. . **50** E2
Ridgeway La BS14 . . . . . **80** B5
Ridgeway Par BS5 . . . . . **50** E3
Ridgeway Rd
  Bristol BS16. . . . . **50** F3
  Long Ashton BS41 . . . . . . **62** A2
Ridgeway The
  Bristol BS10. . . . . **35** A1
  Weston-s-M BS22 . . . . . . **88** B2
Ridgewood BS9. . . . . **48** D3
Riding Barn Hill BS30 . .**67** A6
Ridingleaze BS11 . . . . . . **34** A1
Ridings Cl BS37. . . . . **28** D1

Ridings Federation Yate
  Int Acad The BS37 . . . . **27** E1
Ridings' Federation Yate
  Int Acad The BS37 . . . . **39** E8
Ridings Rd BS36 . . . .**38** C6
Ridings The
  Bristol BS13. . . . . **78** E4
  Frampton Cotterell BS36 .**38** C6
Ridley Ave BS15, BS16. . .**52** B3
Ring Mead BS34 . . . . **36** A6
Ringspit La
  Blackrock BS39. . . . . **97** E8
  Bristol BS14, BS39. . . . . **97** E8
Ringswell SN14 . . . . **70** A7
Ringswell Gdns BA1. . . . **85** B1
Ringwell BA2 . . . .**136** E4
Ringwell La BA2 . . . . . . **136** E4
Ringwood Cres BS10 . . . **35** D1
Ringwood Gr BS23 . . . . . **88** A1
Ringwood Rd BA2. . . . . .**101** C5
Ripley Rd BS5 . . . . **51** A1
Ripon Ct BS16 . . . . **37** F2
Ripon Rd BS4. . . . . **64** E6
Rippleside BS20 . . . . **45** C5
Rippleside Rd BS21 . . . . . **57** G5
Ripple The BS21 . . . . **59** D4
Risdale Rd BS3 . . . . **62** F1
Risdale Ho BS15 . . . . **65** D5
Risedale Rd BS25 . . . . . .**125** A8
Rivendell BS22. . . . . **89** A4
Rivergate BS1 . . . .**143** C2
Riverland Dr BS13 . . . . . . **78** F5
Riverleaze
  Bristol BS9. . . . . **48** C5
  Portishead BS20 . . . . **44** F6
River Mead
  Clevedon BS21. . . . . **73** D8
  Yate BS37. . . . . **27** C3
River Pl BA2 . . . .**101** B6
River Rd
  Chipping Sodbury BS37 . .**28** A1
  Portbury BS20 . . . . **46** E5
RIVERSIDE **138** F7
Riverside BS24, BS29. . .**107** B5
Riverside Bsns Pk
  Bath BA2 . . . .**141** B1
  Bristol BS4. . . . . **64** D6
Riverside Cl
  Bristol BS11. . . . . **47** F5
  Clevedon BS21. . . . . **57** D1
  Midsomer Norton BA3 . .**138** F7
  Weston-s-M BS22 . . . . . . **89** C3
Riverside Cotts
  Bristol BS15. . . . . **65** B1
  Radstock BA3. . . . .**134** A2
Riverside Ct
  Bath BA2 . . . .**141** B1
  2 Bristol BS4. . . . . **64** F6
Riverside Dr BS16. . . . . . **51** C7
Riverside Gdns
  Bath BA1 . . . .**141** B2
  Midsomer Norton BA3 . .**138** F7
Riverside Mews BS4. . . . **64** F6
Riverside Pk BS35. . . . . . **21** F6
Riverside Rd
  Bath BA2 . . . .**141** B2
  Midsomer Norton BA3 . .**138** F7
Riverside Steps BS4. . . . **64** E7
Riverside Way BS15 . . . . **65** C3
Riverside Wlk
  6 Bristol BS5. . . . . **64** F6
  Midsomer Norton BA3 . .**138** F7
Rivers Rd BA1 . . . .**141** C4
Rivers St BA1. . . . .**141** B3
Rivers Street Mews
  BA1. . . . .**141** B3
River St BS2 . . . .**143** C3
River Street Pl 5
  BA1. . . . .**141** B3
River Terr BS31. . . . . **81** F5
River View BS16. . . . . **50** E5
Riverway BS48. . . . . **59** F3
River Wlk BS22 . . . . **89** D2
Riverwood Ho BS16. . . . . **37** C1
Riverwood Rd BS16. . . . . **37** C1
Riviera Cres BS16 . . . . . . **51** E4
Riviera Way BS34 . . . . . . **37** A4
Roach's La GL9 . . . . **30** D2
Road Green GL11 . . . . **5** A7
Road Hill
  Batheaston SN13. . . . . . . **86** E8
  Colerne SN14. . . . . **70** D1
Road Two BS10 . . . . **22** A3
Roath Rd BS20. . . . . **45** D5
Robbins Cl
  Bristol BS32. . . . . **36** F6
  Marshfield SN14 . . . . **69** F8
Robbins Ct BS16 . . . . **52** B6
Robel Ave BS36. . . . . **38** A8
Robert Ct
  Bristol BS16. . . . . **52** B7
  Leigh Woods BS8. . . . . . . **62** D7
Robertson Dr BS4. . . . . . **64** F6
Robertson Rd BS5 . . . . . . **50** C2
Robert St
  Bristol, Baptist Mills
  BS5. . . . . **50** B2
  16 Bristol, Russell Town
  BS5. . . . . **64** B7

Robin Cl
  Bristol BS14. . . . . **80** D6
  Bristol, Brentry BS10. . . . **35** B2
  Midsomer Norton BA3 . .**139** B8
  Weston-s-M BS22 . . . . .**105** E8
Robin Dr BS24 . . . .**105** E2
Robinia Wlk BS14. . . . . . . **80** A7
Robin La BS21 . . . . **57** F5
Robinson Cl BS48 . . . . . . **76** A5
Robinson Dr BS5. . . . . . . **64** A8
Robinson Way BS48. . . . . **76** A5
Robin Way BS37 . . . . **40** A7
Rob-Lynne Ct BS25 . . .**124** F8
Rochester Cl BS24 . . . . .**105** A1
Rochester Rd BS4. . . . . . . **64** F5
Rochfort Ct BA1 . . . .**102** B8
Rock Ave BS48. . . . . **59** C2
Rock Cl BS4. . . . . **64** E2
Rock Cotts BS20 . . . . **47** E4
Rock Hall Cotts BA2 . . .**102** B1
Rockhall Ho
  Bath BA2 . . . .**102** B1
  10 Weston-s-M BS23. . **87** C1
Rock Hall La 4 BA2. . . .**102** B1
ROCKHAMPTON **8** E7
Rockhampton Rhine
  BS35. . . . . **8** B6
Rockhill Est BS31 . . . . . . **81** F4
Rock Ho BS10 . . . . **35** C3
Rockingham Gdns
  BS11. . . . . **48** A8
Rockingham Gr BS23 . . . **88** A1
Rockingham Rdbt BS11 **33** D6
Rock La
  Bath BA2 . . . .**102** B1
  Bristol BS34. . . . . **36** F4
Rockland Gr BS16. . . . . . **50** D5
Rockland Rd BS16 . . . . . . **51** D7
Rockleaze
  Bristol BS9. . . . . **48** E2
  9 Thornbury BS35 . . . . **8** B1
Rockleaze Ave BS9. . . . . **48** E3
Rockleaze Ct BS9. . . . . . . **48** E3
Rockleaze Mans 12
  BS23. . . . . **87** C1
Rockleaze Rd BS9. . . . . . **48** E3
Rockliffe Ave BA2. . . . . .**102** B8
Rockliffe Rd BA2. . . . . . .**102** B8
Rock Rd
  Chilcompton BA3 . . . . . .**138** D2
  Keynsham BS31. . . . . **81** E5
  Midsomer Norton BA3 . .**133** C2
  Wick BS30 . . . . **67** D8
  Yatton BS49 . . . . **91** C7
Rockside Ave BS16. . . . . **51** F8
Rockside Dr BS9. . . . . **49** C6
Rockside Gdns
  Bristol BS16. . . . . **51** F8
  Frampton Cotterell BS36 .**38** C8
Rocks La BS40 . . . . **77** E1
Rock St BS35 . . . . **15** B8
Rockstowes Way BS10. . **35** D3
Rock The BS4 . . . . **64** E3
Rockwell Ave BS11. . . . . . **34** B1
Rockwood Ho BS37 . . . . . **28** A4
Rodborough BS37. . . . . . . **39** C7
Rodborough Way BS15 . .**66** A7
Rodbourne Rd BS10. . . . . **49** E6
RODE. **137** F1
Rode Hill BA11. . . . .**137** E1
Rodfords Mead BS14. . . . **80** A7
Rodford Way BS37 . . . . . . **39** D7
Rodmead Wlk BS13 . . . . . **79** A4
Rodmoor Rd BS20. . . . . . . **45** D6
Rodney BS24 . . . .**105** A2
Rodney Ave BS15 . . . . **65** A8
Rodney Cres BS34. . . . . . **36** A4
Rodney Ho BA2 . . . .**101** A6
Rodney Pl BS8. . . . .**142** A3
Rodney Rd
  Backwell BS48. . . . . **76** A6
  Bristol BS15. . . . . **65** A8
  Saltford BS31. . . . . **82** E2
Rodney Wlk BS15 . . . . **51** A1
Rodway Ct BS16. . . . . **52** A5
Rodway Hill BS16 . . . . . . **52** B3
Rodway Hill Rd BS16. . . . **52** A4
Rodway Rd
  Bristol BS34. . . . . **36** A8
  Bristol, Mangotsfield
  BS16. . . . .**52** A5
  Bristol, Patchway BS34 . .**35** F7
Rodway View BS15 . . . . . **51** F3
Roebuck Cl BS22. . . . . . . **89** A4
Roegate Dr BS4. . . . . **64** E6
Roegate Ho BS5 . . . . **51** A1
Rogers Cl
  Bristol BS30. . . . . **66** B5
  Clutton BS39. . . . .**114** C2
  Yate Rocks BS37. . . . . . . **27** E6
Rogers Ct BS37 . . . . **28** C1
Rogers Wlk BS30 . . . . **66** D7
Rokeby Ave BS6. . . . . **49** C1
ROLSTONE **89** F2
Roman Baths & Pump
  Room The★ BA1 . . . . .**141** C2
Roman Farm Ct BS11. . . **34** C2

Roman Farm Rd BS4 . . . **79** E7
Roman Ho BA1 . . . .**141** C4
Roman Rd
  Bath BA1 . . . .**141** C3
  Bleadon BS24. . . . .**122** C8
  Bristol BS5. . . . . **50** B1
  Sandford BS25. . . . .**107** F4
Roman Way
  Bristol BS15. . . . . **65** D4
  Bristol BS9. . . . . **48** C4
  Paulton BS39 . . . .**132** C6
  Peasedown St John BA2 **134** E7
Roman Wlk
  Bristol, Kensington Park
  BS4. . . . . **64** C3
  Bristol, Stoke Gifford
  BS34. . . . . **36** E5
Romney Ave
  Bristol BS7. . . . . **50** B6
  Lockleaze BS7 . . . . **50** C7
Romo Ct BS16. . . . . **51** C4
Romulus Cl BS31. . . . . . . **81** F7
Ronald Rd BS16. . . . . **50** F6
Ronaldson BS30 . . . . **66** C2
Ronayne Wlk BS16. . . . . . **51** C6
Rookery La
  Pilning BS35. . . . . **23** A6
  Pucklechurch BS30, SN14 **53** F4
Rookery Rd BS4. . . . . **64** A3
Rookery Way BS14 . . . . . . **79** F4
Rooksbridge Wlk BA2 . .**101** B5
Roper's La BS40 . . . . **92** E3
Rope Walk Ho 23 BS2 .**143** C3
Rope Wlk BS48. . . . . **76** A5
Rosary Rdbt The BS16. . **52** D7
Rosary The
  Bristol BS16. . . . . **52** D7
  Harry Stoke BS16 . . . . . . **36** F2
Ros Broomhead Cl
  BS16. . . . . **50** F8
Rose Acre BS10 . . . . **35** A3
Rosebay Mead BS16. . . . . **50** E5
Roseberry Pk BS5. . . . . . . **64** D8
Roseberry Pl BA2 . . . . . .**101** C6
Roseberry Rd
  Bath BA2 . . . .**101** C6
  Bristol BS5. . . . . **64** C7
Rosebery Ave BS2. . . . . . **50** A1
Rosebery Ct 7 BS2. . . . . **50** A1
Rosebery Terr BS8 . . . . .**142** B2
Rose Cl BS36 . . . . **37** F4
Rose Cotts BS22. . . . . **89** C2
Rosedale Ave BS23. . . . .**105** A4
Rosedale Rd BS16. . . . . . . **51** C3
Rose Gdns BS22 . . . . **89** B4
ROSE GREEN. **50** E1
Rose Green Cl BS5. . . . . . **50** E2
Rose Green Rd BS5 . . . . . **50** D2
Rose Hill BA1. . . . . **85** C3
Rose La BS36 . . . . **38** D6
Roseland Cl BA1. . . . . **85** C3
Roselarge Gdns BS10 . . . **35** A2
Rosemary Cl BS32 . . . . . . **36** F7
Rosemary Cres BS20 . . . . **45** F5
Rosemary La
  Bristol BS5. . . . . **50** C2
  Freshford BA2. . . . .**120** B4
Rose Mead BS7 . . . . **50** A7
Rose Meare Gdns BS13. **78** E2
Rosemont Terr BS8. . . . .**142** A2
Rosemount Cl BS15 . . . . . **65** B8
Rosemount La BA2. . . . .**102** B3
Rosemount Rd BS48 . . . . **77** B8
Rosenberg Ho 6 BA1 . .**141** B2
Rose Oak Dr BS36. . . . . . . **38** D7
Rose Oak Gdns BS36 . . . **38** D7
Rose Oak La BS36. . . . . . . **38** D7
Rose Rd BS5. . . . . **64** E7
Rosery Cl BS9 . . . . **49** A8
Rosery The BS16 . . . . **51** C3
Rose Terr
  Bath BA2 . . . .**102** C2
  Bristol BS8. . . . .**142** B3
Rose Tree Ho BS16 . . . . . **51** F4
Rosevear BS2. . . . . **64** A7
Roseville Ave BS30. . . . . . **66** A2
Rosewarn Cl BA2 . . . . . .**101** A4
Rosewell Ct BA1. . . . .**141** B2
Rose Wlk BS16. . . . . **51** C3
Rosewood Ave BS35. . . . . **14** F5
Roshni Gar E 16 BS5. . . **50** B1
Roshni Gar W 15 BS5. . . **50** B1
Rosling Rd BS7. . . . . **49** E6
Roslyn Ave BS22. . . . . **88** C1
Roslyn Rd BS6. . . . . **49** C1
Rossall Ave BS34. . . . . . . **36** C6
Rossall Rd BS4 . . . . **64** D3
Ross Cl BS37 . . . . **28** B1
Rossendale Cl BS22. . . . . **88** F3
Rossiter Grange 5
  BS13. . . . . **78** F4
Rossiter Rd BA2 . . . .**141** C1
Rossiter's La BS5 . . . . **65** A6
Rossiter Wood Ct BS11.**34** B2
Rosslyn Cl 1 BA1. . . . . .**101** B7
Rosslyn Rd BA1. . . . .**101** B7

Rosslyn Way BS35. . . . . . . **8** C3
ROTCOMBE **115** D2
Rotcombe La BS39 . . . . .**115** D2
Rotcombe Vale BS39 . . .**115** D2
Roughcroft La GL13 . . . . . **2** C6
Rounceval St BS37 . . . . . . **28** A1
Roundhill Gr BA2 . . . . . .**101** B3
Roundhill Pk BA2 . . . . . .**101** A4
Roundmoor Cl BS31. . . . . **82** D3
Roundmoor Gdns BS14 **80** D7
Round Oak Rd BS27 . . . .**126** A1
Roundways BS36. . . . . **38** D6
Rousham Rd BS5 . . . . **50** A3
Rowacres
  Bath BA2 . . . .**101** B3
  Bristol BS14. . . . . **79** F6
Rowan Cl
  Bristol BS16. . . . . **51** A2
  Nailsea BS48 . . . . **60** A4
Rowan Ct
  10 Bristol BS5. . . . . **64** B7
  Radstock BA3. . . . .**133** E1
  Yate BS37. . . . . **27** C3
Rowan Dr
  Catbrain BS10 . . . . **35** B5
  Lyde Green BS16. . . . . . . **52** C7
Rowan Ho BS13 . . . . **79** D4
Rowan Pl BS24. . . . . **89** B1
Rowan St BS14 . . . . **79** E5
Rowans The
  Bristol BS16. . . . . **37** B1
  Portishead BS20 . . . . **45** B4
Rowan Tree Ho BS16 . . . **51** F4
Rowan Way
  Bristol BS15. . . . . **65** B3
  Churchill BS40. . . . .**109** A5
Rowan Wlk BS31. . . . . **81** C4
ROWBERROW **109** A1
Rowberrow BS14. . . . . **79** F7
Rowberrow La BS25. . . . .**125** F8
Rowberrow Way BS48. . . **59** E1
Rowdell Ave BS36. . . . . . . **38** A6
Rowland Ave BS16 . . . . . . **50** D4
Rowlands Cl BA1. . . . . **86** B2
Rowlandson Gdns BS7 . **50** B6
Rowley Farm La BA2 . . .**118** D5
Rowley St BS3 . . . . **63** C3
Rownham Cl BS3 . . . . **62** E4
Rownham Hill BS8 . . . . . . **62** E6
Rownham Mead BS8 . . .**142** A1
Row Of Ashes La BS40. . **93** F4
Rows The BS22 . . . . **88** E2
Row The BS35 . . . . **13** A7
Roxburgh BS8. . . . . **62** F8
Royal Albert Rd BS6. . . . **49** A4
Royal Ave BA1 . . . .**141** B3
Royal Cl BS10. . . . . **34** D3
Royal Cres★ BA1 . . . . . .**141** A3
Royal Cres BS23 . . . .**104** D8
Royal Ct BS23. . . . .**104** D4
Royal Fort Rd BS2,
  BS8. . . . .**142** B2
Royal High Sch
  Bath BA1 . . . .**141** B4
  Bath, Lansdown BA1 . . . . **84** F2
Royal National Hospl for
  Rheumatic Diseases
  BA1 . . . .**141** B2
Royal Par
  Bristol BS8. . . . .**142** B3
  Weston-s-M BS23 . . . . .**104** D8
Royal Park Mews BS8 .**142** A3
Royal Pk BS8 . . . .**142** A3
Royal Portbury Dock Rd
  BS20. . . . . **46** E5
Royal Prom BS8 . . . .**142** B3
Royal Rd BS16 . . . . **52** A6
Royal Sands BS23 . . . . .**104** D4
Royal United Hospl
  BA1 . . . .**101** B8
Royal Victoria Pk BS10 . **35** A2
Royal West of England
  Acad★ BS8 . . . .**142** B3
Royal York Cres BS8. . . . **62** F6
Royal York Ho 7 BS8. .**142** A2
Royal York Mews 6
  BS8. . . . .**142** A2
Royal York Villas BS8 . .**142** A2
Royate Hill BS5 . . . . **50** D2
Roycroft Rd BS34. . . . . . . **36** B2
Roy King Gdns BS30. . . . **66** C6
Royston Lodge BS23 . . .**104** D6
Royston Wlk BS10. . . . . . . **35** D2
Rozel Ho 14 BS23 . . . . . . **87** C1
Rozel Rd BS7. . . . . **49** E5
Rubens Cl BS31. . . . . **82** D4
Ruby St BS3 . . . . **63** B3
Ruckley Ford BA3. . . . . . .**135** A2
Ruddymead BS21 . . . . **57** F2
Rudford Cl BS34. . . . . **24** B1
Rudge Cl BS15. . . . . **51** F2
RUDGEWAY **14** F1
Rudgeway Pk BS35. . . . . . **14** F1
Rudgeway Rd BS39 . . . .**132** E4
Rudgewood Cl BS13. . . . . **79** D4
Rudgleigh Ave BS20. . . . . **47** C4
Rudgleigh Rd BS20. . . . . . **47** C4
Rudhall Gn BS22 . . . . **89** B3

Rudhall Gr BS10 . . . . . . 49 E7
Rudmore Pk BA1 . . . 101 A7
Rudthorpe Rd BS7 . . . 49 E5
Ruett La BS39 . . . . . . 132 B4
Ruffet Rd BS36 . . . . . . 38 B4
Rugby Rd BS4 . . . . . . 64 D3
Rugmoor La BS40 . . . . 111 D3
Rumney Penrose Rd
BS16 . . . . 50 F8
Runnymead Ave BS4 . . 64 D2
Runnymede BS15 . . . . 51 E1
Runswick Rd BS4 . . . . 64 C3
Rupert Ho BS2 . . . . . 142 C4
Rupert St
Bristol BS1 . . . . 143 A3
Bristol, Redfield BS5 . . 64 C7
Rusham BS13 . . . . . . 78 F4
Rush Cl BS32 . . . . . . 24 D2
Rushgrove Gdns BS39 113 C4
RUSH HILL 101 B2
Rush Hill
Bath BA2 . . . . 101 C2
Farrington Gurney BS39 131 F3
Rushmead La SN14 . . . . 55 F2
Rushmoor BS21 . . . . . 57 C1
Rushmoor Gr BS48 . . . . 76 A5
Rushmoor La BS48 . . . . 76 A5
Rushton Dr BS36 . . . . . 38 D7
Rushway BS40 . . . . . 109 F4
Rushy BS30 . . . . 66 A4
Rushy Leaze BS4 . . . . . 36 A7
Rushy Way BS16 . . . . . 38 A1
Ruskin Gr BS7 . . . . . . 50 A8
Ruskin Ho BS34 . . . . . . 36 A8
Ruskin Rd BA3 . . . . . 133 C1
Rusling La BS40 . . . . . 94 A1
Russell Ave BS15 . . . . 65 E7
Russell Cl BS40 . . . . . 95 A6
Russell Gr BS6 . . . . . . 49 C5
Russell Rd
Bristol, Chester Park
BS16 . . . . 51 B2
Bristol, Westbury Park
BS6 . . . . 49 B4
Clevedon BS21 . . . . . 57 E3
Locking BS24 . . . . . 106 C6
Russell St BA1 . . . . . 141 B3
RUSSELL TOWN 64 B7
Russell Town Ave BS5 . 64 B8
Russell Town Ind Pk 18
BS5 . . . . 64 C7
Russet CI BS35 . . . . . . 14 A3
Russet Ct GL12 . . . . . . 11 F4
Russets The BS20 . . . . 45 F4
Russett Cl BS48 . . . . . 76 B6
Russett Gr BS48 . . . . . 75 C8
Russett Way BA2 . . . . 134 D7
Russ St BS2 . . . . 143 C2
Rustic Pk BS35 . . . . . . 22 A6
Rustic Way BS35 . . . . . . 8 B4
Rust La BS21 . . . . 73 E4
Rutherford Cl BS30 . . . . 66 A3
Ruthven Rd BS4 . . . . . 79 E8
Rutland Ave BS30 . . . . 66 A2
Rutland Cl BS22 . . . . 105 C8
Rutland Rd BS7 . . . . . 49 E3
Rydal Ave BS24 . . . . 106 A4
Rydal Ho BS34 . . . . . . 36 A8
Rydal Rd BS23 . . . . . 104 F4
Ryde Rd BS4 . . . . 64 B2
Rye Cl BS13 . . . . 78 E6
Ryecroft Ave BS22 . . . . 88 E2
Ryecroft Ct BS36 . . . . . 38 C7
Ryecroft Rd BS36 . . . . . 38 C8
Ryecroft Rise BS41 . . . . 62 B1
Ryedown La BS30 . . . . 66 D2
Ryland Pl 1 BS2 . . . . . 50 A2
Rylestone Cl BS36 . . . . 37 F8
Rylestone Gr BS9 . . . . . 48 F5
Rysdale Rd BS9 . . . . . . 48 F6

S

Sabin Cl BA2 . . . . 101 B3
Sabrina Way BS9 . . . . . 48 C4
Saco Ho
11 Bath BA1 . . . . 141 B2
Bristol BS1 . . . . 143 B2
Sadbury Cl BS22 . . . . . 89 B4
Saddlers Ct BS15 . . . . . 51 D1
Sadlier Cl BS11 . . . . . . 48 A8
Saffron Cl BA1 . . . . . 141 C4
Saffron Ho 10 BS23 . . 104 E8
Saffrons The 7 BS22 . . 89 B4
Sage Cl BS20 . . . . 44 E4
Sages Mead BS32 . . . . 36 E8
St Agnes Ave BS4 . . . . 63 F2
St Agnes Cl BS48 . . . . . 60 A1
St Agnes Gdns BS4 . . . . 63 F2
St Agnes Wlk BS4 . . . . 63 F2
St Aidan's Cl BS5 . . . . . 65 B6
St Aidan's Rd BS5 . . . . 65 B6
St Alban's Rd BS6 . . . . 49 B4
St Aldams Dr BS16 . . . . 53 B5
St Aldwyn's Cl BS7 . . . . 49 F8
St Andrews
Bristol BS30 . . . . 66 B6
Yate BS37 . . . . 27 F1

St Andrew's CE Prim Sch
BA1 . . . . 141 B4
St Andrew's CE Prim Sch
GL12 . . . . 10 A1
St Andrews Cl
Nailsea BS48 . . . . 60 A1
Weston-s-M BS22 . . . . 88 F3
St Andrew's Dr BS4 . . . 91 C4
St Andrew's Dr BS21 . . . 57 C2
St Andrews Gate Rdbt
BS11 . . . . 33 B2
Saint Andrews Mews
BS6 . . . . 49 E3
St Andrew's Par 1
BS23 . . . . 104 F4
St Andrew's Prim Sch
BS49 . . . . 91 C4
St Andrews Rd BS48 . . . 76 B5
St Andrew's Rd
Avonmouth BS11 . . . . . 33 B1
Bristol BS6 . . . . 49 E2
St Andrews Road Sta
BS11 . . . . 33 B1
St Andrew's Terr BA1 . . 141 B3
St Andrews Trad Est
BS11 . . . . 33 C2
St Anne's Ave BS31 . . . 81 D6
St Anne's CE Prim Sch
BS30 . . . . 66 C3
St Anne's CE Prim Sch
BS24 . . . . 90 B5
St Annes Cl 7 BS5 . . . . 64 F6
St Annes Cl BS30 . . . . . 66 B4
St Annes Ct BS4 . . . . . 64 D5
St Annes Ct BS31 . . . . . 81 D6
St Annes Dr BS30 . . . . . 66 C2
St Anne's Dr
Frampton Cotterell
BS36 . . . . 38 C5
Wick BS30 . . . . 67 B7
St Anne's Inf Sch BS4 . . 64 D5
St Anne's Jun Sch BS4 . 64 D5
ST ANNE'S PARK 64 E6
St Anne's Park Prim Sch
BS4 . . . . 64 E5
St Anne's Park Rd BS4 . 64 E5
St Anne's Rd
Bristol, St Anne's Park
BS4 . . . . 64 D6
Bristol, St George BS5 . . 65 B6
St Anne's Terr BS4 . . . . 64 E5
St Ann's Pl BA1 . . . . . 141 B2
St Ann's Way BA2 . . . 102 C6
St Anthony's Cl BA3 . . 133 A2
St Anthony's Dr BS30 . . 67 B7
St Aubin's Ave BS4 . . . . 64 F3
St Aubyn's Ave BS23 . . 104 D2
St Augustines of
Canterbury RC Sch
BS16 . . . . 51 F7
St Augustine's Par
BS1 . . . . 143 A2
St Augustine's Pl 1
BS1 . . . . 143 A2
St Austell Cl BS48 . . . . 76 A8
St Austell Rd BS22 . . . 105 B8
St Barnabas CE Prim Sch
Bristol, Montpelier BS6 . 49 F1
Bristol, North Common
BS30 . . . . 66 C6
Portishead BS20 . . . . . 45 B5
St Barnabas Cl
Bristol, Lower Knowle
BS4 . . . . 63 F1
Bristol, Warmley BS30 . . 66 C7
Midsomer Norton BA3 . 133 B4
St Barnabas Ho BS30 . . 66 C7
St Bartholomew's Rd
BS7 . . . . 49 F3
St Bede's RC Coll BS11 . 34 B2
St Bede's Rd BS15 . . . . 51 D2
St Benedict's RC Prim Sch
BA3 . . . . 139 C7
St Bernadette RC Prim Sch
BS14 . . . . 80 B6
St Bernadette RC Sch
BS14 . . . . 80 B6
St Bernard's RC Prim Sch
BS11 . . . . 47 E6
St Bernard's Rd BS11 . . 47 E6
St Bonaventure's RC Prim
Sch BS7 . . . . 49 D4
St Brelades Gr BS4 . . . . 64 F5
St Brendans Rdbt BS11 33 C1
St Brendan's Sixth Form
Coll BS4 . . . . 65 A1
St Brendan's Way BS11 . 33 B1
St Brenda's Ct BS8 . . . 142 A3
St Briavels Dr BS37 . . . . 39 D8
St Bridges Cl BS22 . . . . 88 A6
St Bridges Ct BS22 . . . . 88 A6
St Cadoc Ho BS31 . . . . 81 F5
ST CATHERINE 69 F1
St Catherine La BA1 . . . 69 D2
St Catherine's Cl BA2 . 102 C6
St Catherines Ct BS4 . . 64 A2
St Catherine's Hosp 11
BA1 . . . . 141 C2

St Catherine's Ind Est
BS3 . . . . 63 D3
St Catherine's Mead
BS20 . . . . 47 D3
St Catherines Pl 7
BS3 . . . . 63 D4
St Catherine's Terr
BS3 . . . . 63 D3
St Chad's Ave BA3 . . . 133 A1
St Chad's Gn BA3 . . . . 139 A8
St Charles Cl BA3 . . . . 133 A2
St Christophers Cl
BA2 . . . . 102 C8
St Christopher's Ct
BS21 . . . . 57 E5
St Christopher's Sch
BS6 . . . . 49 B4
St Clements Ct
Bath BA1 . . . . 84 C1
Bristol, St Pauls BS2 . . 143 C4
5 Bristol, Upper Soundwell
BS16 . . . . 51 D3
Clevedon BS21 . . . . . . 57 E4
Keynsham BS31 . . . . . 81 E4
2 Weston-s-M BS22 . . . 89 A2
St Clements Rd BS31 . . 81 F4
St Cuthberts Dr BS4 . . . 64 F3
St David's Ave BS30 . . . 66 B5
St David's Cl BS22 . . . . 88 B2
St David's Cres BS4 . . . . 64 F6
St David's Ct BS21 . . . . 73 E8
St Davids Mews BS1 . . 142 C2
St Dunstans Cl BS31 . . . 81 E6
St Dunstan's Rd BS3 . . . 63 C2
St Edward's Rd BS8 . . . 142 B2
St Edyth's Rd BS9 . . . . 48 C6
SS Peter & Paul RC Cath★
BS8 . . . . 142 A4
SS Peter & Paul RC Prim
Sch BS8 . . . . 142 C4
St Fagans Ct BS30 . . . . 66 B2
St Francis Dr
Wick BS30 . . . . 67 B7
Winterbourne BS36 . . . 37 F6
St Francis RC Prim Sch
BS48 . . . . 59 F1
St Francis Rd
6 Bristol BS3 . . . . 63 A4
Keynsham BS31 . . . . . 81 D6
St Gabriel's Bsns Pk 24
BS5 . . . . 64 B8
St Gabriel's Rd BS5 . . . 64 B8
ST GEORGE 65 A7
St George CE Prim Sch
BS5 . . . . 142 B2
ST GEORGES ★ 89 D3
St George's★ BS1 . . . . 142 C2
St Georges Ave 10 BS5 . 64 F6
St Georges Bldgs BA1 141 B4
St George's Hill
Bath BA2 . . . . 102 D8
Easton-in-G BS20 . . . . 47 A3
St Georges Ho BS5 . . . . 64 E8
St George's Ho BS8 . . 142 B2
St George's Hts 12 BS5 64 D7
St Georges Ind Est
BS11 . . . . 33 B3
St Georges Pl BA1 . . . 141 A3
St Georges Prim Sch
BS22 . . . . 89 C3
St George's Rd BS1 . . 142 C2
St George's Rd
Keynsham BS31 . . . . . 81 D6
Portbury BS20 . . . . . . 46 E7
St Giles Barton GL12 . . . 19 D8
St Gregory's RC Sch
BA2 . . . . 118 D8
St Gregory's Rd BS7 . . . 49 F8
St Helena Rd BS6 . . . . . 49 B4
St Helens CE Prim Sch
BS35 . . . . 15 A4
St Helens Dr
Bristol BS30 . . . . 66 C2
Wick BS30 . . . . 67 C7
St Helen's Wlk BS5 . . . . 51 A1
St Helier Ave BS4 . . . . . 64 F3
St Hilary Cl BS9 . . . . . . 48 D5
St Ivel Way BS30 . . . . . 66 C6
St Ives Cl BS48 . . . . . . 60 A1
St Ives Rd BS23 . . . . . 105 A5
St James BS24 . . . . . . 105 E7
St James' Barton BS1 . 143 B4
St James Cl BS35 . . . . . . 8 C3
St James Ct BS32 . . . . . 24 C3
St James Pl BS16 . . . . . 52 A5
St James's Ct BS8 . . . . 49 B1
St James's Par BA1 . . . 141 B2
St James's Pk BA1 . . . 141 B4
St James's Sq BA1 . . . 141 A4
St James's St
Bath BA1 . . . . 141 B4
Bristol BS16 . . . . 52 A5
St James St BS23 . . . . 104 D7
St John's BA1 . . . . 101 B8
St John's Bridge 5
BS1 . . . . 143 A3
St John's CE Prim Sch
BS8 . . . . 49 A2

St John's CE Prim Sch
BS31 . . . . 81 E5
St John's CE Prim Sch
BA3 . . . . 133 A1
St John's CE Prim Sch
Peasedown St John
BA2 . . . . 134 B7
Weston-s-M BS22 . . . . 87 D1
St John's Cres
Bristol BS3 . . . . 63 E2
Midsomer Norton BA3 . 133 A2
St Johns Ct
Axbridge BS26 . . . . . 125 B2
Bath BA2 . . . . 141 C3
Bristol BS16 . . . . 51 A3
Bristol, Bedminster BS3 . 63 D2
Keynsham BS31 . . . . . 81 E6
St John's Ho BS5 . . . . . 64 D8
St John's La BS3 . . . . . 63 D2
St John's Mead CE Prim
Sch BS37 . . . . 28 B1
St John's Pl BA1 . . . . . 141 B2
St John's RC Prim Sch
BA2 . . . . 102 B6
St John's RC Prim Sch (Inf)
BA2 . . . . 101 D4
St Johns Rd BA2 . . . . . 116 B1
St John's Rd
Backwell BS48 . . . . . . 76 B5
Bath BA2 . . . . 141 C3
Bath, Lower Weston
BA1 . . . . 101 C7
Bristol, Bedminster BS3 . 63 C3
Bristol, Clifton BS8 . . . . 49 A1
Bristol, Southville BS3 . . 63 D4
Clevedon BS21 . . . . . . 57 F3
St Johns Rd GL9 . . . . . 20 A3
St John's St BS3 . . . . . 63 C3
St John St 2 BS35 . . . . . 8 B1
St Johns Way BS37 . . . . 28 C2
St John the Evangelist CE
Prim Sch
Clevedon BS21 . . . . . . 57 C1
Clevedon BS21 . . . . . . 57 E1
St Joseph's RC Prim Sch
Bristol BS16 . . . . 51 B3
Portishead BS20 . . . . . 45 D3
St Joseph's Rd
Bristol BS10 . . . . 35 B3
Weston-s-M BS23 . . . . 87 E1
St Judes Ho 21 BS2 . . . 143 C3
St Jude's Terr BS22 . . . . 88 C1
St Julian's CE Prim Sch
BA2 . . . . 118 E1
St Julian's Cl BS39 . . . 132 E4
St Julian's Rd BA2 . . . 134 F5
St Katharine's CE Prim Sch
BS40 . . . . 94 A7
St Katherine's Sch
BS20 . . . . 47 E3
St Kenya Ct BS31 . . . . . 81 F5
St Keyna Ct BS31 . . . . . 81 F5
St Keyna Rd BS31 . . . . . 81 E5
St Kilda's Rd BA2 . . . . 101 D5
St Ladoc Rd BS31 . . . . . 81 D6
St Laud Cl BS9 . . . . . . 48 D5
St Leonard's Rd
Bristol, Horfield BS7 . . . 49 E5
Bristol, Lower Easton
BS5 . . . . 50 C2
St Loe Cl BS14 . . . . . . 79 F3
St Lucia Cl BS7 . . . . . . 49 E7
St Lucia Cres BS7 . . . . . 49 E7
St Lukes Cl BS16 . . . . . 52 C7
St Luke's Cres BS3 . . . . 63 F4
St Luke's Ct BS3 . . . . . 63 E4
St Luke's Gdns BS4 . . . . 64 E2
St Luke's Mews BS4 . . . 64 E2
St Luke's Rd
Bath BA2 . . . . 101 F3
Bristol BS3 . . . . 63 E4
Midsomer Norton BA3 . 132 F2
St Luke St 13 BS5 . . . . . 64 B7
St Margarets Cl BS48 . . 76 A5
St Margaret's Cl BS31 . 81 D6
St Margaret's Dr BS9 . . 49 C5
St Margaret's La BS48 . 76 A5
St Margaret's Terr
BS23 . . . . 104 D8
St Mark's Ave 1 BS5 . . 50 B1
St Marks Church Ho 4
BS5 . . . . 50 B1
St Marks Cl BS31 . . . . . 81 E6
St Mark's Ecumenical CE/
Methodist Prim Sch
BS22 . . . . 88 F4
St Marks Gdns BA2 . . . 141 C1
St Mark's Gr 8 BS5 . . . 50 B1
St Mark's Ho 13 BS5 . . 50 B1
St Mark's Rd
Bath BA2 . . . . 141 C1
Bristol BS5 . . . . 50 B1
Midsomer Norton BA3 . 133 A2
Weston-s-M BS22 . . . . 89 A3
St Mark's Sch BA1 . . . . 85 B2
St Mark's Terr 11 BS5 . . 50 B1
St Mark's VA Prim Sch
BS22 . . . . 88 F4
St Martins BS21 . . . . . . 57 E5

St Martin's CE Jun Sch
BS22 . . . . 88 D2
St Martins Cl BS4 . . . . . 64 B1
St Martins Ct BS22 . . . . 88 E3
St Martin's Ct BA2 . . . 101 E1
St Martin's Garden Prim
Sch BA2 . . . . 101 D1
St Martin's Gdns BS4 . . 64 B1
St Martins Hospl BA2 . 101 E1
St Martins Ind Pk BS11 . 33 F5
St Martin's La SN14 . . . 69 F8
St Martin's Pk SN14 . . . 69 F8
St Martin's Rd BS4 . . . . 64 B2
St Martin's Wlk BS4 . . . 64 B1
St Mary CE Prim Sch
BA2 . . . . 102 C2
St Mary Redcliffe CE Prim
Sch BS3 . . . . 63 E4
St Mary Redcliffe CE VC
Prim Sch BS3 . . . . . . 63 E4
St Mary Redcliffe &
Temple Sch BS1 . . . . 143 B1
St Mary's Bldgs BA1 . . 141 B1
St Mary's CE Prim Sch
Radstock BA3 . . . . . . 134 C1
Thornbury BS35 . . . . . . 8 A2
St Mary's CE Prim Sch
Timsbury BA2 . . . . . . 116 C3
Yate BS37 . . . . 27 E2
St Mary's CE VA Prim Sch
BS20 . . . . 46 E3
St Marys Cl
Bristol BS30 . . . . 66 B5
Hutton BS24 . . . . 105 D2
St Mary's Cl
Bath BA2 . . . . 102 B6
Timsbury BA2 . . . . . . 116 C3
St Mary's Ct BS24 . . . . 105 A1
St Mary's Gdns BS40 . . 109 B5
St Mary's Gr BS48 . . . . 75 C8
St Mary's Hospl BS8 . . 142 B3
St Mary's Park Rd BS20 45 C4
St Mary's Pk BS48 . . . . 75 C8
St Marys RC Prim Sch
BS34 . . . . 37 A7
St Mary's RC Prim Sch
BA1 . . . . 84 B1
St Mary's Rd
Bristol BS11 . . . . 47 D6
Hutton BS24 . . . . 105 D2
Leigh Woods BS8 . . . . 62 D6
Portishead BS20 . . . . . 45 C4
St Marys Rise BA3 . . . . 134 C2
St Mary St BS26 . . . . . 125 C2
St Mary St BS35 . . . . . 15 B8
St Marys Way 6 BS35 . . . 8 B1
St Mary's Way BS37 . . . 27 F2
St Mary's Wlk BS11 . . . 47 D6
St Matthew's Ave 11
BS6 . . . . 49 D1
St Matthews Cl BS23 . . 87 D1
St Matthews Hall 20
BS5 . . . . 64 C7
St Matthew's Pl BA2 . . 102 B5
St Matthew's Rd BS6 . . 143 A4
St Matthias & Dr Bell's CE
Prim Sch BS16 . . . . . . 51 A4
St Matthias Ho BS2 . . . 143 C3
St Matthias Pk BS2 . . . 143 C3
St Michael on the Mount
CE Prim Sch BS2 . . . 142 C3
St Michael's Ave
Clevedon BS21 . . . . . . 57 F1
Weston-s-M BS22 . . . . 89 A3
St Michael's CE Jun Sch
BA2 . . . . 101 A6
St Michaels CE Prim Sch
BS36 . . . . 37 E6
St Michael's CE Prim Sch
BS34 . . . . 36 E5
St Michaels Cl BS7 . . . . 49 E4
St Michael's Cl BS36 . . . 37 E7
St Michaels Ct BS15 . . . 65 B8
St Michael's Ct BA2 . . . 119 E8
St Michael's Hill BS2 . . 142 C4
St Michael's Hospl
BS2 . . . . 142 C4
St Michael's Pk BS2 . . 142 C4
St Michael's Pl BA1 . . . 141 B2
St Michaels Rd BA2 . . . 101 A5
St Michael's Rd BA1 . . 101 D7
St Monica Ct BS9 . . . . . 49 A5
St Nicholas Almshouses 7
BS1 . . . . 143 A2
St Nicholas CE Prim Sch
BA3 . . . . 133 F2
St Nicholas' CE Prim Sch
BA3 . . . . 134 A2
St Nicholas Chantry CE
Prim Sch BS21 . . . . . . 57 G3
St Nicholas Chantry CE VC
Prim Sch BS21 . . . . . . 57 E3
St Nicholas Cl BA15 . . 120 D7
St Nicholas Ct BS24 . . . 85 F1
St Nicholas of Tolentine
RC Prim Sch BS5 . . . . 64 A8

St Nicholas Pk 10 BS5. . 50 B1
St Nicholas Rd
  Bristol BS2. . . . . .143 C4
  Weston-s-M BS23 . . . .104 D2
  Whitchurch BS14 . . . . . .80 C4
St Nicholas' Rd BS2. . . . 49 F1
St Nicholas St BS1. . . . .143 A2
St Nicholas Way BS48 . .75 D2
St Oswald's Ct BS13. . . .79 A8
St Oswald's Ct BS6. . . . .49 B3
St Oswald's Rd BS6 . . . .49 B3
St Patricks Ct BS31 . . . .81 E5
St Patrick's Ct BA2. . . .102 B6
St Patrick's RC Prim Sch
  BS5. . . . . .64 D7
ST PAULS 143 C4
St Pauls Ho 13 BS3. . . . .63 D4
St Pauls Pl
  Bath BA1 . . . . .141 B2
  Midsomer Norton BA3. .133 A2
St Paul's RC Prim Sch
  BS37. . . . . .39 E8
St Paul's Rd
  Bristol BS8. . . . . .142 B4
  2 Bristol, Southville BS3 63 D4
  Weston-s-M BS23 . . . .104 E5
St Paul St BS2 . . . . .143 B4
St Peter's Ave BS23 . . . .87 D1
St Peter's CE Prim Sch
  BS20. . . . . .45 D4
St Peter's Cres BS36 . . . 38 B8
St Peters Ct 12 BS3 . . . . 63 D4
St Peter's Ho BS8 . . . . .142 B2
St Peters Lodge BS20 . .45 D4
St Peter's Pl 5 BA2. . . .101 D6
St Peters Rd BS20. . . . . .45 D4
St Peter's Rd BA3. . . . . 139 C8
St Peter's Rise BS13 . . .79 B7
St Peter's Terr 6 BA2. .101 D6
St Peter's Wlk 3 BS9. . .49 B6
St Philips Central BS2. .64 A5
St Philip's CE Prim Sch
  BA2. . . . . .101 D2
St Philips Cswy BS2. . . .64 B5
ST PHILIP'S MARSH. . . .64 B5
St Philips Rd BS2 . . . . .143 C3
St Philips Trad Pk BS2. .64 A4
St Phillips Rd BS2. . . . . .64 A7
St Pias X RC Prim Sch
  BS13. . . . . .79 A5
St Pierre Dr BS30. . . . . .66 B6
St Ronan's Ave BS6 . . . .49 C1
St Saviour's CE Inf Sch
  BA1. . . . . .85 B2
St Saviour's CE Jun Sch
  BA1. . . . . .85 B2
St Saviours Ho BS4 . . . .63 F2
St Saviour's Rd BA1. . . .85 C2
St Saviour's Rise BS36 . 38 B6
St Saviour's Terr 10
  BA1. . . . . .85 B1
St Saviours Way 4
  BA1. . . . . .85 C1
St Stephen's Ave 3
  BS1. . . . . .143 A2
St Stephens Bsns Ctr
  BS30. . . . . .66 C5
St Stephen's CE Jun Sch
  BS15. . . . . .51 D2
St Stephen's CE Prim Sch
  BA1. . . . . .84 F1
St Stephens Cl
  Bristol, Brentry BS10. . . 35 C2
  Bristol, Upper Soundwell
  BS16. . . . . .51 E3
St Stephen's Cl BA1. . . .84 F1
St Stephen's Ct BA1. . . 141 B4
St Stephen's Pl BA1. . . 141 B4
St Stephen's Rd
  Bath BA1. . . . . .141 B4
  Bristol BS16. . . . . .51 D2
St Stephen's St BS1. . . .143 A2
St Swithin's Pl BA1. . . .141 C4
St Swithin's Yd BA1. . . 141 C3
St Teresa's RC Prim Sch
  BS7. . . . . .35 E1
St Thomas Pl BS1. . . . . 143 B2
St Thomas Rd BA3 . . . .133 B2
St Thomas St E BS1. . . 143 B2
St Thomas St BS1. . . . . 143 B2
St Ursula's E-ACT Acad
  BS9. . . . . .49 A6
St Vigor & St John CE
  Prim Sch BA3 . . . . . . .138 E3
St Vincent's Hill 1 BS6 49 A2
St Vincent's Rd BS8 . . .142 A2
St Vincents Trad Est
  BS2. . . . . .64 D6
Saint Way BS34. . . . . . . .37 A4
St Werburgh's Pk BS2. .50 A2
St Werburgh's Prim Sch
  BS2. . . . . .50 A2
St Werburgh's Rd BS2. .49 F2
St Whites Cl BS14. . . . . .80 D3
St Whytes Rd BS4. . . . . .79 D8
St Winifreds Dr BA2. . .102 D2

St Wulfstans Ave BS10. .49 A8
Salcombe Gdns BS22. . .89 A2
Salcombe Rd BS4. . . . . .64 A1
Salem Rd BS36 . . . . .37 F7
Salisbury Ave BS15. . . . .65 B8
Salisbury Dr BS16. . . . . .51 E6
Salisbury Gdns BS16 . . .51 E5
Salisbury Pk BS16. . . . . .51 E6
Salisbury Rd
  Bath BA1 . . . . .85 B2
  Bristol, Mangotsfield
  BS16 . . . . .51 E6
  Bristol, Redland BS6 . . .49 D2
  Bristol, St Anne's BS4 . .64 D5
  Paulton BS39 . . . . .132 F4
  Weston-s-M BS22 . . . . .88 C1
Salisbury St
  Bristol, Pile Marsh BS5. .64 F7
  Bristol, Russell Town BS5 64 B6
Salisbury Terr BS23 . . .104 D7
Sallybarn Cl BS30. . . . . .65 E2
Sally Hill BS20. . . . . .45 E7
Sally In The Wood BA1,
  BA15. . . . . .103 D6
Sally Lunn's Kitchen Mus★
  BA1. . . . . .141 C2
Sallysmead Cl BS13. . . .79 B4
Sallys Way BS36 . . . . . . .37 F7
Salmon Cl BS35. . . . . . . .22 A6
Salmon Mead BS14. . . . .80 D3
Salmons Way BS16. . . . .52 B8
SALTFORD. 82 D2
Saltford CE Prim Sch
  BS31. . . . . .82 E2
Saltford Ct BS31 . . . . . . .82 E3
Salthouse Ct BS21. . . . . .57 D2
Salthouse Farm Pk
  BS35. . . . . .22 A7
Salthouse Rd BS21. . . . . .57 D2
Salthrop Rd BS7. . . . . . . .49 E4
Saltings Cl BS21. . . . . . . .57 D2
Saltmarsh Dr BS11. . . . . .34 A1
Saltwell Ave BS14. . . . . .80 C5
Salway Cl BS40 . . . . .95 E1
Sambourne La BS20. . . . .47 C4
Samian Way BS34. . . . . .36 E5
Sampson House Bsns Pk
  BS10. . . . . .34 D7
Sampsons Rd BS13. . . . .79 D4
Samuel 3 BS5 . . . . .64 C8
Samuel White Rd BS15 .65 C4
Samuel White's Inf Sch
  BS15. . . . . .65 C4
Samuel Wright Cl BS30 66 D5
San Andreas BS34 . . . . .35 E6
Sanctuary Gdns BS9. . . .48 D3
Sanctuary The BS11. . . .47 E4
Sandbach Rd BS4. . . . . .64 D4
Sandbed Rd BS2. . . . . . .50 A2
Sandburrows Rd BS13. .78 F6
Sandburrows Wlk BS13. 78 F6
Sandcroft BS14. . . . . . . .79 F6
Sandcroft Ave BS23 . . .104 D2
Sand Farm La BS22. . . . .88 A6
SANDFORD. 108 A3
SANDFORD BATCH. . . .107 F2
Sandford Cl 2 BS21. . . .57 D1
Sandford Prim Sch
  BS25. . . . . .108 B4
Sandford Rd
  Bristol BS8. . . . . .142 A1
  Weston-s-M BS23 . . . .105 A7
  Winscombe BS25. . . . .107 F1
Sandgate Rd BS4 . . . . . .64 D3
Sand Hill BS4. . . . . .64 C4
Sandholme Cl BS16. . . . .51 E8
Sandholme Rd BS4. . . . .64 D4
Sandhurst BS37. . . . . . . .39 D8
Sandhurst Cl BS34 . . . . .24 B1
Sandhurst Rd BS4. . . . . .64 D4
Sandling Ave BS7. . . . . . .50 A4
Sandmead Rd BS25 . . . .108 A4
Sandown Cl BS16 . . . . . .37 F1
Sandown Rd
  Bristol, Filton BS34 . . . .36 C3
  Bristol, Kensington Park
  BS4. . . . . .64 D4
Sandpiper Dr BS22. . . . .88 F1
Sandpits La GL9 . . . . . . .20 A2
Sand Rd BS22. . . . . .88 B5
Sandringham Ave BS16. 51 E8
Sandringham Ct 2
  BS23. . . . . .104 F5
Sandringham Pk BS16. .51 E8
Sandringham Rd
  Bristol, Kensington Park
  BS4. . . . . .64 D4
  Bristol, Longwell Green
  BS30 . . . . .65 F2
  Bristol, Stoke Gifford
  BS34. . . . . .36 D3
  1 Weston-s-M BS23 . .104 F5
Sands Hill SN14. . . . . . . .54 E3
Sands La BS36. . . . . .25 F1
Sandstone Rise BS36. . .37 E4
Sandwich Rd BS4. . . . . .64 D4
Sandy Cl BS32. . . . . .36 E6
Sandy La
  Aust BS35 . . . . .13 A7

Sandy La continued
  Aust BS35 . . . . .13 A8
  Bristol BS5. . . . . .50 C3
  Easton-in-G BS8. . . . . . .61 A8
  Failand BS8 . . . . .61 C7
  Stanton Drew BS39, BS40 96 E3
Sandyleaze BS9. . . . . . . .48 E7
Sandy Lodge BS37 . . . . .39 E8
Sandy Park Rd BS4. . . . .64 C3
Sarabeth Dr BA2. . . . . .117 A4
Saracen Ave BA1 . . . . .141 C3
Saracens The BS7. . . . . .49 E5
Sarah St BS5 . . . . .64 B7
Sargent St BS3 . . . . .63 E4
Sarum Cl BS16. . . . . .52 C6
Sarum Cres BS10 . . . . . .35 C1
Sassoon Ct BS30. . . . . . .65 F5
Satchfield Cl BS10. . . . . .34 F2
Satchfield Cres BS10. . . 34 F2
Sates Way BS9. . . . . .49 C6
Saunders Rd BS16. . . . . .51 E4
Saunton Wlk BS4. . . . . . .79 E8
Savages Wood BS32. . . .36 E8
Savages Wood Rd
  BS32. . . . . .36 D8
Savernake Rd BS22. . . . .88 F3
Saville Cres BS22. . . . . .105 C8
Saville Gate Cl BS9. . . . .48 F4
Saville Mews BS6. . . . . .143 A4
Saville Pl BS8. . . . . 142 A2
Saville Rd
  Bristol BS9. . . . . .48 F3
  Weston-s-M BS22 . . . .105 C8
Saville Row BA1. . . . . . .141 B3
Savoy Rd BS4. . . . . .64 D4
Savoy The BS11. . . . . . . .47 E6
Saw Cl BA1. . . . . .141 B2
Sawmill Gdns BA3. . . . .138 D3
Saw Mill La 5 BS35. . . . .8 B1
Sawyers Cl
  Chilcompton BA3 . . . . .138 D3
  Wraxall BS48. . . . . .60 A2
Sawyers Ct BS21. . . . . . .57 G3
Saxby Cl
  Clevedon BS21. . . . . . . .57 D1
  Weston-s-M BS22 . . . . .89 B4
Saxon Cl BS14 . . . . .80 D3
Saxon Ct
  Axbridge BS26. . . . . . . .125 C1
  Weston-s-M BS22 . . . . .89 D3
Saxon Rd
  Bristol BS2. . . . . .50 A2
  Weston-s-M BS22 . . . .105 C8
Saxon St BS40 . . . . .109 D6
Saxon Way
  Bristol BS32. . . . . .24 C1
  Bristol BS34. . . . . .24 C1
  Peasedown St John BA2 134 E8
  Winsley BA15. . . . . .120 F7
Sayer Pl BS10. . . . . .49 E7
Says La BS40 . . . . .109 B4
Says Wlk BS30. . . . . .66 D7
SBI Ctr BS15. . . . . .65 B5
Scafell Cl BS23 . . . . .88 A1
Scandrett Cl BS10. . . . . .34 E2
Scantleberry Cl BS16. . .51 D8
Scarf Dr BS24. . . . . .106 C5
Scaurs The BS22. . . . . . .88 F2
School Cl
  Banwell BS29. . . . . .107 B3
  Bristol BS14. . . . . .79 F4
  Bristol, Eastville BS5. . .50 D2
  Bristol, Patchway BS34. .36 C8
  Hillesley GL12 . . . . .19 E8
School Ct BS34 . . . . .37 A5
School La
  Badminton GL9. . . . . . . .30 E2
  Barrow Gurney BS48. . .77 D5
  Batheaston BA1. . . . . . . .85 F4
  2 Bristol BS16 . . . . . . .50 E5
  Chew Stoke BS40. . . . . 112 D8
  Farrington Gurney BS39 132 A4
  Felton BS48. . . . . .94 A8
  Kilmersdon BA3. . . . . . .140 A4
  Rowberrow BS25. . . . . .109 A1
  Wick St L BS22. . . . . . . .89 B7
School of Christ the King
  RC Prim BS4 . . . . .79 E8
School Pl BA2 . . . . 103 B5
School Rd
  Bristol BS15. . . . . .65 C8
  Bristol, Broom Hill BS4 . 64 E3
  Bristol, Cadbury Heath
  BS30 . . . . .66 A4
  Bristol, Oldland Common
  BS30. . . . . .66 C3
  Bristol, Totterdown BS4. .64 D3
  Frampton Cotterell BS36 38 A8
  Wrington BS40. . . . . .92 E2
School View BS48. . . . . .60 B1
School Way BS35. . . . . . .22 A6
School Wlk
  Bristol BS5. . . . . .50 D1
  Yate BS37. . . . . .27 C2
Scobell Rise BS39. . . . . 115 C2
Scop The BS32. . . . . .24 B5
Score La BS40. . . . . .110 E2
Score The BS40 . . . . . . .110 E2

Scotch Horn Cl BS48. . . .59 F2
Scotch Horn Way 5
  BS48. . . . . .59 F2
Scot Elm Dr BS24. . . . . .89 D1
Scot La BS40 . . . . .95 D1
Scotland La BS4, BS14 . .81 A7
Scots Pine Ave 3 BS48. 59 F2
Scott Ct BS30 . . . . .65 F5
Scott Lawrence Cl
  BS16. . . . . .51 A7
Scott Rd BS23 . . . . .105 A4
Scott Way BS37. . . . . . . .39 F8
Scott Wlk BS30 . . . . .66 D7
Scumbrum La BS39 . . . .115 C2
Scythe Way BS35. . . . . . . .8 B3
Sea Bank Rd BS20 . . . . .32 E1
Seabrook Rd BS22 . . . . .88 D1
Seagry Cl BS10 . . . . .35 E1
Sea King Way BS24 . . . .105 C5
SEA MILLS. 48 B6
Sea Mills Inf Sch BS9 . .48 C7
Sea Mills Jun Sch BS9. .48 B5
Sea Mills La BS9. . . . . . .48 C5
Sea Mills Sta BS9. . . . . .48 A4
SeaQuarium★ BS23. . . .104 D6
Searle Court Ave BS4 . .64 E4
Searle Cres BS23 . . . . . .105 A6
Searle Ct BS21. . . . . .57 G2
Seaton Rd BS5. . . . . .50 C1
Seavale Mews BS21. . . . .57 E4
Seavale Rd BS21. . . . . . .57 E4
Seaview Rd
  Portishead, Redcliffe Bay
  BS20. . . . . .44 F4
  Portishead, West Hill
  BS20. . . . . .44 F6
Seawalls BS9. . . . . .48 D2
Seawalls Rd BS9. . . . . . .48 D2
Second Ave
  Bath BA2 . . . . .101 D5
  Bristol BS14. . . . . .80 B7
  Radstock BA3. . . . . .139 C7
Second Way BS11. . . . . .33 D1
Seddon Rd 4 BS2. . . . . .64 B7
Sedgefield Gdns BS16. .37 F1
Sedgemoor Cl BS48. . . .75 E8
Sedgemoor Rd
  Bath BA2 . . . . .101 F2
  Weston-s-M BS23 . . . . .87 F1
Sedgewick Ho BS11. . . .47 E7
Sefton Park Jun & Inf Schs
  BS7. . . . . .49 F3
Sefton Park Rd BS7. . . . .49 F3
Sefton Sq BS24 . . . . . . .106 A8
Selborne Rd BS7. . . . . . .49 F5
Selbourne Cl BA1. . . . . .101 A8
Selbourne Rd BS23 . . . .104 E4
Selbrooke Cres BS16. . .51 C6
Selby Rd BS5. . . . . .50 F1
Selden Rd BS14. . . . . . . .80 E5
Selkirk Rd BS15. . . . . . . .51 C1
Selley Wlk BS13 . . . . . . .79 A5
Selway Ct BA2. . . . . 102 B2
Selwood Cl BS22. . . . . .105 C7
Selworthy BS15. . . . . . . .65 E7
Selworthy Cl BS31. . . . . .81 D5
Selworthy Gdns 4
  BS48. . . . . .59 E1
Selworthy Ho BA2 . . . .101 F2
Selworthy Rd
  Bristol BS4. . . . . .64 B2
  Weston-s-M BS23 . . . .105 A4
Selworthy Terr BA2 . . .101 F2
Seneca Pl 1 BS5. . . . . . .64 D7
Seneca St BS5 . . . . .64 D7
Septimus Bldgs BS14. . .79 D5
Serbert Cl BS20. . . . . . . .45 E5
Serbert Rd BS20 . . . . . . .45 E5
Serbert Way BS20. . . . . .45 E5
Sercombe Pk BS21. . . . .57 G1
Serlo Ct BS22. . . . . .89 A4
Serridge La BS36. . . . . . .38 D4
Serse Cl BS31. . . . . .81 C2
Sevastopol Rd BS7. . . . .49 E7
Seven Acres La BA1. . . . .85 F5
Seven Acres The 3
  BS24. . . . . .105 F7
Seven Dials BA1 . . . . . .141 B2
Seventh Ave
  Bristol BS14. . . . . .80 A7
  Bristol, Filton BS34 . . . .36 B1
Severn Acre Lea BS34 . .35 E6
Severn Ave BS23 . . . . . .104 E5
SEVERN BEACH. 22 B6
Severn Beach Prim Sch
  BS35. . . . . .22 A6
Severn Beach Sta BS35 22 A6
Severn Cl GL12. . . . . . . .11 A4
Severn Dr BS35 . . . . .8 B10
Severn Grange BS10 . . .34 D3
Severn Ho BS10. . . . . . . .34 D3
Severn La GL13. . . . . .2 F8
Severnleigh Gdns BS9. .48 F3
Severnleigh Ho BS9. . . .48 F3
Severnmeade BS20 . . . .44 F5
Severn Rd
  Bristol BS11. . . . . .47 D6
  Hallen BS10. . . . . .34 A7

Severn Rd continued
  Pill BS20. . . . . .47 C5
  Portishead BS20 . . . . . .45 C5
  Severn Beach BS35 . . . .21 F3
  Weston-s-M BS23 . . . .104 E5
Severnside Trad Est
  BS11. . . . . .33 C5
Severn View BS10 . . . . . .34 C1
Severn View Ind Pk
  BS10. . . . . .21 F3
Severn View Rd BS35. . . .8 C2
Severn Way
  Bristol BS34. . . . . .23 F1
  Keynsham BS31. . . . . . .82 A5
Severnwood Gdns
  BS35. . . . . .22 A5
Severus St BS31. . . . . . . .81 F8
Sevier Rd BS26 . . . . 123 C3
Sevier St BS2. . . . . .49 F2
Seville Ct BS20. . . . . .45 E7
Seville Rd BS20. . . . . . . .45 E7
Seward Terr BA3 . . . . . .134 C2
Sewell Ho BS25. . . . . . .125 A8
Seymour Ave BS7 . . . . . .49 E4
Seymour Cl
  Clevedon BS21. . . . . . . .57 G3
  Weston-s-M BS22 . . . . .88 F4
Seymour Pl BS36. . . . . . .38 B6
Seymour Rd
  4 Bath BA1 . . . . .85 A1
  Bristol, Ashley Down BS7 49 E4
  Bristol, Kingswood BS15 .51 E4
  Bristol, Staple Hill BS16 .51 E4
  Bristol, Upper Easton
  BS5. . . . . .50 A1
Seyton Wlk BS34. . . . . . .36 E5
Shackel Hendy Mews
  BS16. . . . . .52 B5
Shackleton Ave BS37. . .39 F8
Shadow Wlk BS24. . . . . 106 C3
Shadwell Rd BS7. . . . . . .49 D3
Shaftesbury Ave
  2 Bath BA1 . . . . .101 C7
  Bristol BS6. . . . . .49 E1
Shaftesbury Cl BS48 . . .75 D8
Shaftesbury Crusade
  BS2. . . . . .64 C4
Shaftesbury Mews 7
  BA2. . . . . .101 D5
Shaftesbury Rd
  Bath BA2 . . . . .101 D5
  Weston-s-M BS23 . . . .105 B8
Shaftesbury Terr
  8 Bristol BS5. . . . . .64 D7
  Radstock BA3. . . . . .134 A3
Shaft Rd
  Monkton Combe BA2 . . 102 E1
  Severn Beach BS35. . . .22 A6
Shakespeare Ave
  Bath BA2 . . . . .101 F4
  Bristol BS7. . . . . .50 A8
Shakespeare Ct BS23. .104 F2
Shakespeare Rd BA3 . .133 C1
Shaldon Rd BS7. . . . . . . .50 A4
Shallowbrooks La SN14 31 F8
Shallows The BS31. . . . .82 F3
Sham Castle La BA2. . . .102 C7
Shamrock Rd BS5. . . . . .50 D3
Shanklin Dr BS34. . . . . . .36 B3
Shannon Ct BS35. . . . . . .15 D5
Shannon Wlk BS20. . . . .45 F6
Shapcott Cl BS4 . . . . . . .64 B1
Shaplands BS9. . . . . .48 F4
Sharland Cl BS9. . . . . . . .48 E3
Sharland Gr BS13. . . . . .79 C4
Sharples Cl BS7. . . . . . . .50 C8
SHARPSTONE 120 A4
Shaw Cl
  Bristol BS16. . . . . .52 B3
  3 Bristol, Upper Easton
  BS5. . . . . .64 B8
Shaw Gdns BS14. . . . . . .80 A8
Shaws Way BA2. . . . . . . 100 F5
Shaymoor La BS34. . . . .23 A4
Shearmore Cl BS7. . . . . .50 A7
Shearwater Ct BS16. . . .50 F6
Sheene Ct Ind Est 12
  BS3. . . . . .63 C3
Sheene Rd BS3. . . . . .63 C3
Sheene Way BS3. . . . . . .63 C3
Sheepfair La SN14 . . . . .69 F8
Sheephouse Cvn Pk
  BS20. . . . . .46 E7
Sheeps Croft BS13 . . . . .79 A5
Sheepwash The BS35. . . .7 D5
SHEEPWAY. 46 B5
Sheepway BS20. . . . . . . .46 B5
Sheepway La BS20. . . . .46 C5
Sheepwood Cl BS10. . . 35 A4
Sheepwood Rd BS10. . . 35 A4
Sheiling Sch BS35. . . . . . .8 B2
Sheldare Barton BS5. . .65 B7
Sheldon Cl BS21. . . . . . . .57 H2
Sheldrake Dr BS16. . . . .50 E6
Shellard Rd BS34. . . . . . .36 A2
Shellards La BS35. . . . . .15 C2
Shellards Rd BS30. . . . . .65 F3
Shelley Ave BS21. . . . . . .57 F2
Shelley Cl BS5. . . . . .64 F8

Shelley Ho BS34 ......24 A1
Shelley Rd
 Bath BA2 ....101 F4
 Radstock BA3........133 C1
 Weston-s-M BS23....105 A4
Shelley Way BS7.....50 A8
Shellmor Ave BS34...24 B1
Shellmor Cl ⑪ BS32..24 D1
Shepherds Cl
 Bristol BS16..........51 E5
 Chipping Sodbury BS37..40 F3
Shepherds Way BS32...89 C2
Shepherds Wlk
 ⑧ Bristol BS32......24 D1
 Bristol BS32..........36 D8
Sheppard Rd BS16...51 C6
Sheppards Gdns BA1...84 E1
Sheppards Wlk BA3...138 D3
SHEPPERDINE......1 D3
Shepperdine Rd BS35...1 D1
Sheppy's Mill BS49...91 D5
Shepton BS24 ....105 A2
Shepton Wlk BS3 .....63 C2
SHERBORNE 130 D3
Sherbourne Ave BS32..36 E7
Sherbourne Cl BS15...51 F2
Sherbourne's Brake
 BS32................36 E6
Sherbourne St BS5....64 E7
Sheridan Rd
 Bath BA2 ....100 F5
 Bristol BS7..........50 A8
Sheridan Way BS30...66 A2
Sherrings The BS34...36 B8
Sherrin Way BS13....78 E3
Sherston Cl
 Bristol BS16..........51 B5
 Nailsea BS48 ....60 A1
Sherston Rd
 Bristol BS7..........49 E8
 Luckington SN14......31 F5
Sherwell Rd BS4......64 E3
Sherwood Cl BS31....81 E5
Sherwood Cres BS22..88 F3
Sherwood Rd
 Bristol BS15..........51 B1
 Keynsham BS31.......81 E5
Shetland Rd BS10.....35 D1
Shetland Way BS48....60 A1
Shickle Gr BA2 ......101 D1
Shield Ct BS15.......65 D5
Shield Ret Ctr BS34...36 A3
Shield Road Prim Sch
 BS7.................36 A1
Shields Ave BS7......36 A1
Shiels Dr BS32........36 D7
Shilton Cl BS15.......65 F7
Shimsey Cl ⑫ BS15...51 C6
Shiners Elms BS49....91 B8
Shingle La BS10......21 F4
SHIPHAM..........125 F7
Shipham CE Fst Sch
 BS25................125 E8
Shipham Cl
 Bristol BS14..........80 B5
 Nailsea BS48 ....75 F8
Shipham Hill BS25....125 F5
Shipham La BS25 ....108 B1
Shipham Rd BS27 ....126 A3
Ship La BS1 ....143 B1
SHIPLATE..........122 F6
Shiplate Rd BS24 ....122 E6
Shipley Mow BS16 ....52 B6
Shipley Rd BS9 ....49 A8
Shipman Ct BS16.....51 E4
Shire Gdns BS11......47 D8
SHIREHAMPTON.....47 E7
Shirehampton Prim Sch
 BS11................47 D6
Shirehampton Rd BS9..48 C6
Shirehampton Sta
 BS11................47 D5
Shire Hill SN14.......56 A7
Shire Way BS37.......39 D6
Shirrreff Ct ⑭ BS6...49 B1
SHOCKERWICK......86 E5
Shockerwick Farm La
 BA1.................86 E6
Shockerwick La BA1...86 D4
Shophouse Rd BA2...101 B5
Shop La GL9 ....30 E2
Shopland Ho ⑧ BS21..52 E2
Shoredutch BS40.....112 C7
Shorland Ho BS8.....49 A1
Shorthill Rd BS37.....39 C4
Short La
 Litton BA3...........130 F2
 Long Ashton BS41....62 A2
Shortlands Rd BS11...34 A1
Short St BS2.........64 A5
Short Way
 Failand BS8 ....61 B4
 Thornbury BS35......15 B7
SHORTWOOD.......52 D4
Shortwood Hill BS16...52 E4
Shortwood La BA3...130 F2
Shortwood Rd
 Bristol BS13..........79 E3
 Pucklechurch BS16...53 A4

Shortwood View BS15..65 F8
Shortwood Wlk BS13...79 E3
SHOSCOMBE.......134 E6
Shoscombe CE Prim Sch
 BA2................134 F5
SHOSCOMBE VALE...134 E5
Showering Cl BS14....80 D5
Showering Rd BS14....80 D5
Shrew Gdns BS35......8 D2
Shrewsbury Bow
 BS24...............106 A8
Shrowle BS40........130 A6
Shrubbery Ave BS23...87 D1
Shrubbery Cotts ④
 BS6.................49 B2
Shrubbery Ct ⑥ BS16..51 D5
Shrubbery Rd
 Bristol BS16..........51 D5
 Weston-s-M BS23.....87 D1
Shrubbery Terr ⑪
 BS23................87 C1
Shrubbery Wlk BS23...87 D1
Shrubbery Wlk W BS23..87 D1
Shubb Leaze BS7.....50 C8
Shums Ct ⑧ BA1....141 C2
Shuter Rd BS13.......78 E5
Sibland BS35.........15 D8
Sibland Cl ⑧ BS35...15 D8
Sibland Rd BS35......15 D8
Sibland Way BS35....15 D8
SIDCOT............125 C7
Sidcot BS4 ....65 A2
Sidcot Dr BS25......125 A7
Sidcot Jun Sch BS25..125 C8
Sidcot La BS25......125 A7
Sidcot Sch BS25......125 B7
Siddeley Cl BS10.....35 D4
Sideland Cl BS14.....80 E6
Sidelands Rd BS16....51 C6
Sidelings The BS40...128 D8
Sidings The
 Bristol, Lower Soundwell
  BS16...............52 B2
 Bristol, Newleaze BS34..36 C2
 Charfield GL12 ....11 B5
 Haywood Village BS23..105 B4
Sidmouth Ct BS3......63 D1
Sidmouth Gdns BS3...63 D2
Sidmouth Rd BS3.....63 E2
Sidney Hill Cottage Homes
 BS25...............108 E4
Signal Rd BS16.......51 F4
Silas Rd BS37........27 E5
Silbury Rd BS3.......62 E2
Silbury Rise BS31.....82 A2
Silcox Rd BS13.......79 C4
Silklands Gr BS9......48 C6
Silverberry Rd BS22...89 A1
Silver Birch Cl BS34...36 D7
Silvercombe ⑪ BS23..104 E5
Silver Ct BS48........59 C2
Silverhill Brake BS35..14 E1
Silverhill Rd BS10.....34 E4
Silverhill Sch BS36....37 C1
Silverlow Rd BS48....59 D2
Silver Mead BS11.....91 D2
Silver Moor La BS29..106 F7
Silver St
 Bristol BS1..........143 A3
 Chew Magna BS40....96 B3
 Congresbury BS49....91 D2
 Holcombe BA3.......139 C1
 Kilmersdon BA3......140 B5
 Midsomer Norton BA3..139 A7
 Nailsea BS48 ....59 D2
 Portishead BS20......44 F1
 ⑦ Thornbury BS35....8 B1
 Wrington BS40........92 E2
Silverstone Way BS31..91 D3
Silverthorne La BS2...64 A6
Silverthorne Wharf
 BS2.................64 B6
Silverton Ct BS4......63 F1
Silverweed Rd BS16...52 D7
Simmons Bldgs BS16..37 C3
Simmonds View BS34..36 F5
Simons Cl BS22.......89 A2
Simon's Cl BS39......132 E5
Simons Mews ⑧ BS23..104 F7
Sinclair Ho
 Bristol BS8..........142 A2
 Bristol, Filton BS34...36 A2
Singapore Rd BS23...104 E3
SINGLE HILL........135 A5
Single Hill BA2......134 F5
SION HILL..........84 E1
Sion Hill
 Bath BA1............84 E1
 Bristol BS8..........62 F7
Sion Hill Pl BA1......84 E1
Sion La BS8..........62 F7
Sion Pl
 Bath BA2............102 B6
 Bristol BS8..........62 F7
Sion Rd
 Bath BA1............84 E1
 Bristol BS3..........63 C3
Sir Bernard Lovell Sch
 BS30...............66 C4

Sir Bernard Lovell Sch
 (annexe) BS30.......66 D5
Sir Bevil Grenville's Mon★
 BA1.................68 A1
Sir John's La
 Bristol BS7..........50 B5
 Bristol, Eastville BS5..50 B4
Siskin Cl BS20........45 F6
Siskin Wlk BS22......105 F8
SISTON............52 F3
Siston Cl BS15.......52 A2
Siston Comm BS15....52 A2
Siston Common BS30..52 B1
Siston Ctr The BS15...52 A2
Siston Hill BS30......52 B1
Siston Hill Rdbt BS15..52 B2
Siston La BS30.......52 F2
Siston Pk BS15.......52 A2
Sixpence BS39.......115 D2
Six Streams BA1......84 B2
Sixth Ave
 Bristol BS14..........80 A7
 Bristol, Filton BS7....36 B1
Sixty Acres Cl BS8....61 B4
Six Ways BS1........57 E4
Skinners Cft BS34.....36 A7
Skinner's Hill BA2...133 F7
Skinners La BS25.....108 F4
Skippon Ct BS15......65 E5
Skylark Ave BS21.....44 B1
Skylark Dr BS31......81 C3
Skylark Gr BS49......73 F2
Skypark Rd BS3......63 C3
Sladacre La BS40.....110 E2
Slade Baker Wy BS16..50 F8
Sladebrook Ave BA2...101 C3
Sladebrook Ct BA2...101 C3
Sladebrook Rd BA2...101 B4
Slade La
 Barrow Gurney BS48...77 C4
 Lympsham BS24.....122 B1
Slade Rd BS20........45 D5
Slades Ct ② BS48....76 A6
Slad The BS35........15 F6
Slate La BS14, BS39...98 B7
Slaughter La BS30....67 D2
Sleep La BS14........80 D3
Slimbridge Cl BS37...39 F7
Sloan St BS5.........64 D8
Sloe Cl BS22.........105 D8
Sloe Way BS34.......36 F3
Slough La SN14.......68 F5
Slymbridge Ave BS10..35 A3
Smallbrook La BS39...98 B6
Smallcombe Cl BA3...133 E5
Smallcombe Rd BA3..133 E5
Small Down End BS25..107 F2
Small La BS16........50 E5
Small St
 Bristol BS1..........143 A3
 Bristol, St Philip's Marsh
  BS2................64 A5
Smallway BS49.......91 D5
Smallwood View BS35..138 E7
Smarts Gn BS37......40 C8
SMART'S GREEN.....40 D8
Smeaton Rd BS1......62 F5
SMITHAM HILL......129 D2
Smitham's Hill BS40..129 D2
Smithcourt Dr BS34...36 D6
Smithmead BS13.....79 B5
Smiths Ct BS34.......36 A8
Smith's Forge Ind Est
 BS49................73 F3
Smoke La BS11.......33 D6
Smythe Croft BS14....80 A3
Smyth Ho BS8........62 E6
Smyth La BS3........63 A3
Smyth Rd BS3........63 A3
Smyths Cl BS11.......33 B1
Smyth Terr ⑧ BS3...63 C4
Snapdragon Way BS16..52 D7
Snatch Rd BS40......111 E2
Snatch La BS40......111 E2
SNEYD PARK.......48 D3
Sneyd Park Ho BS9...48 D3
Snowberry Cl
 Bristol BS32..........36 E8
 Weston-s-M BS22.....89 A1
Snowberry Wlk BS5...50 F1
Snowdon Cl BS16.....50 F4
Snowdon Ho BS16....50 F5
Snowdon Rd BS16....50 F4
Snowdon Vale BS23...88 A1
Snowdrop Cl BS22....89 A5
Snowdrop Dr BS16....52 C7
Snow Hill BA1........85 A1
Snow Hill Ho
 ② Bath BA1........141 C4
 ② Bathwick BA2....102 B8
Soapers La BS35......15 B8
Soaphouse Ind Est BS5..64 E8
Sodbury La BS37......40 A5
Sodbury Rd
 Acton Turville GL9....30 E2
 Wickwar GL12........18 A4
Sodbury Vale BS37....28 B2
Soldiers Rd ④ BS34...35 F7
Solent Way BS35.....5 D7

Solon Ct BS13........78 F5
Solsbury Ct BA1......85 F3
Solsbury View ⑯ BA1..85 A1
Solsbury Way BA1....85 A2
Somer Ave BA3......132 F2
Somerby Cl BS32.....36 D7
Somer Ct BA3.......133 B1
SOMERDALE........81 E7
Somerdale Ave
 Bath BA2............101 D2
 Bristol BS4..........64 A1
 Weston-s-M BS22....105 C8
Somerdale Cl BS22...105 C8
Somerdale Rd BS31...81 F7
Somerdale View BA2...101 C2
Somerford Ct BS10....34 F1
Somer Ho ② BA3....133 B1
Somer La BS3........63 C1
Somer Lea BA3......138 D5
Somermead BS3......63 C1
Somer Rd BA3........132 F2
Somer Ridge BA3....132 F2
Somerset Ave
 Weston-s-M BS22,
  BS24...............106 A8
 Yate BS37............27 F3
Somerset Cl GL12.....11 F4
Somerset Cres BS34...36 F5
Somerset & Dorset Joint
 Rly★ BA3...........139 A4
Somerset Folly BA2...116 B2
Somerset Ho
 Bath BA2............101 D3
 ⑫ Bristol BS2......143 C1
 Portishead BS20......45 D4
Somerset La BA1......84 E1
Somerset Mews
 Portishead BS20......45 D4
 Weston-s-M BS23....104 F6
Somerset Pl BA1......84 E1
Somerset Rd
 Bristol BS4..........64 B3
 Clevedon BS21.......57 G3
 Portishead BS20......44 F5
Somerset Sq
 Bristol BS1..........143 B1
 ⑧ Nailsea BS48.....59 E2
Somerset St
 Bath BA1............141 C1
 Bristol BS1..........143 B1
 Bristol, Kingsdown BS2..143 A4
Somerset Terr BS3....63 D3
Somerset Way BS39...132 E6
Somerton BS24.......105 A2
Somerton Cl BS15.....65 E7
Somerton Rd
 Bristol BS7..........49 E6
 Clevedon BS21.......57 G1
Somervale Rd BA3...133 C1
Somervale Sch BA3...133 A1
Somerville Cl BS31....82 E2
Somerville Ho BS10...49 A8
Somerville Rd BS5...108 A4
Sommerville Rd BS7...49 E3
Sommerville Rd S ⑪
 BS6.................49 F2
Sommerville Way BS30..82 E8
Soper Gdns BS4......79 D7
Sophia Gdns BS22....89 B4
Sopworth Rd SN14....31 E5
Sorbus Cl BS32.......24 E5
Sorrel Cl BS35........8 D2
Sorrel Pl BS16........36 F3
Soundwell Rd BS15,
 BS16................51 D2
Sour Mead BS16......50 D8
Southampton Gdns BS7..49 F3
Southampton Mews
 BS7.................49 F3
South Ave
 Bath BA2............101 D5
 Portishead BS20......45 D6
 Yate BS37............27 E1
Southbourne Gdns BA1..85 B1
Southbourne Mans
 BA2................141 C2
Southbow Ho ⑧ BS3..63 A3
South Bristol Bsns Pk
 BS4.................79 E7
South Bristol Ret Pk
 BS3.................63 A3
South Bristol Trad Pk
 BS3.................62 F3
South Combe BS24...122 B6
Southcot Pl BA2......141 C1
South Croft
 Bristol BS9..........49 C7
 Winscombe BS25.....107 F2
South Ct BS32........24 D3
South Dene BS9......48 E6
SOUTHDOWN.......101 B4
Southdown BS22......88 C2
Southdown Ave BA2...101 B3
Southdown Com Inf Sch
 BA2................101 B3
Southdown Jun Sch
 BA2................101 B3
Southdown Rd
 Bath BA2............101 B4

She–Sou 177

Southdown Rd continued
 Bristol BS9..........48 F8
SOUTHEND.........5 E3
Southend Ho GL12....18 A5
Southend Rd BS23...104 E4
Southernhay
 Bristol BS8..........142 B2
 Bristol, Staple Hill BS16..51 D4
Southernhay Ave BS8..142 B2
Southernhay Cres BS8..142 B2
Southern Way BS21...57 E1
Southey Ave BS15....51 E1
Southey Ct BS15.....51 E1
Southey Rd BS21.....57 F2
Southey St BS2.......49 F2
SOUTHFIELD.......134 A2
Southfield
 Norton St Philip BA2...136 F4
 Radstock BA3.......134 A2
Southfield Ave BS15...51 E1
Southfield Cl
 Nailsea BS48 ....59 E3
 Weston-s-M BS23....104 D2
Southfield Ct BS9.....49 A7
Southfield Rd
 Bristol, Cotham BS6...49 D1
 Bristol, Westbury on Trym
  BS9................49 A7
 Nailsea BS48 ....59 F3
Southfield Rd Trad Est
 BS48................59 F3
Southfield Way BS37...28 A4
Southgate BA1......141 C2
Southgate Sh Ctr BA1..141 C2
South Gloucestershire
 Central Teaching Unit
  BS16...............52 A5
South Gr
 Bristol BS6..........49 C5
 Pill BS20............47 C4
South Green St ⑨ BS8..62 F6
South Hayes BS5.....50 B4
South Hill BS25......107 F2
Southlands
 Bath BA1............84 B1
 Bristol, Clifton BS8...49 A1
 Bristol, Knowle Park BS4..64 B1
 Tytherington GL12....16 B4
Southlands Dr BA2...116 B2
Southlands Way BS49..91 E5
South Lawn BS24....105 F4
South Lawn Cl BS24..105 F4
South Lea Rd BA1....101 A8
Southleaze BS25.....125 A6
Southleigh BS25.....124 F8
Southleigh Mews BS8..142 B4
Southleigh Rd BS8...142 B4
South Liberty La
 Bristol BS3..........63 A1
 ② Bristol BS3......63 B2
South Mdws BS40....92 E2
SOUTHMEAD.......35 D1
Southmead BS25.....125 A8
Southmead Hospl BS10..49 E8
Southmead Rd
 Bristol BS10, BS34....35 E1
 Weston-s-M BS22....105 B7
Southmead Way BS10..49 D8
Southover Cl BS9.....49 A8
Southover Rd BS39...115 D1
South Par
 Bath BA2............141 C2
 Chew Magna BS40....96 B3
 Weston-s-M BS23....104 D8
 Yate BS37............27 E1
South Parade Cotts
 BA2................102 C1
South Parade Mans
 BA2................142 B4
South Rd
 ⑦ Bristol, Bedminster
  BS3................63 C3
 Bristol, Kingswood BS15..65 D8
 Bristol, Redland BS6...49 C2
 Lympsham BS24.....122 B1
 Midsomer Norton BA3..133 B1
 Portishead BS20......45 D7
 Timsbury BA2........116 B2
 Weston-s-M BS23....87 C1
 Woodhouse Down BS32..24 E6
Southridge Hts BS24..122 A8
South Rock Ind Est
 BA3................138 D1
Southsea Rd BS34....36 A8
Southside BS23......104 E8
South Side BS49.....91 E5
Southside Cl BS9.....48 B8
Southside Cres BS22..88 A4
South St
 Bristol BS3..........63 B3
 Stratton-on-t-F BA3..138 F2
SOUTHSTOKE......118 E7
Southstoke La BA2...118 F8
Southstoke Rd BA2...101 F1
South Street Prim Sch
 BS3.................63 B3

South Terr
6 Bristol BS6.........49 B2
Weston-s-M BS23....104 D8
SOUTH TWERTON....101 C5
South View
Bristol BS16............51 E5
Clandown BA3........133 E5
Frampton Cotterell BS36 38 B7
Monkton Combe BA2...102 E1
Paulton BS39........132 E6
Portishead BS20......45 D7
Timsbury BA2.........116 B2
South View Bsns Pk
BS16..................51 F5
Southview Cl BS24....105 E2
South View Cres BS36..38 D6
South View Pl BA3....133 E4
South View Rd BA2...101 D6
South View Rise BS36..38 D6
South View Terr BS49...74 B1
SOUTHVILLE..........63 C4
Southville Pl BS3.......63 D4
Southville Prim Sch
BS3..................63 C4
Southville Rd
Bristol BS3............63 C4
Weston-s-M BS23....104 E4
Southville Terr BA2...102 B4
Southway Ct BS21.....57 F1
Southway Dr BS15.....66 D5
SOUTH WIDCOMBE...130 C6
South Wlk BS37........27 E1
Southwood Ave BS9....48 C8
Southwood Dr BS9.....48 B8
Southwood Dr E BS9...48 C8
Sovereign Sh Ctr
BS23.................104 D8
Spalding Cl BS7.........50 A3
Spaniorum View BS35...22 F2
Spar Rd
Avonmouth BS11......33 D4
Yate BS37..............27 D2
Sparrowbill Way BS34...36 A7
Spartley Dr BS13.......78 F6
Spartley Wlk BS13......78 F6
Speckled Wood Rd BS35 8 C3
Specklemead BS39....132 D5
SPEEDWELL.............51 A2
Speedwell Ave 5 BS5..64 D7
Speedwell Cl BS35......8 D2
Speedwell Ind Est 1
BS21.................57 E2
Speedwell Rd BS5, BS15 51 A1
Speedwell Tech Coll
BS15.................51 A1
Spencer Dr
Midsomer Norton BA3..133 A2
Weston-s-M BS22......89 B3
Spencer Ho 6 BS1....143 B1
Spencers Belle Vue
BA1..................141 B4
Spencers Ct BS35......15 B5
Sperring Ct BA3.......138 F8
Spey Cl BS35..........15 C8
SPIKE ISLAND.........142 B1
Spike Island Artspace★
BS1..................142 B1
Spindleberry Gr BS48...60 A2
Spinners End BS22......89 B4
Spinney Croft BS13.....78 F5
Spinney Rd BS24......106 D4
Spinney The
Bristol BS32...........36 F7
Frampton Cotterell BS36 38 B7
Portishead BS20......45 C4
Weston-s-M BS24....104 F1
Spinnings Dro BS48....76 D2
Spires View 4 BS16....50 E5
Spratts Bridge BS40....96 A3
Sprigg Dr BS20........44 F1
Spring Cres BA2......141 C2
Springfield
Norton St Philip BA2...136 E4
Peasedown St John
BA2..................134 C7
1 Thornbury BS35....15 D8
Springfield Ave
Bristol, Horfield BS7....49 F5
Bristol, Mangotsfield
BS16.................52 A7
Bristol, Shirehampton
BS11..................47 D6
Weston-s-M BS22.....88 D1
Springfield Bldgs
Midsomer Norton
BS39.................132 D2
Radstock BA3........134 A3
Springfield Cl
Bath BA2.............101 B5
Bristol BS16...........52 A7
Cross BS26...........124 F2
Springfield Cotts BS30 .83 A8
Springfield Cres BA3..134 A3
Springfield Gdns
BS29.................107 A3

Springfield Gr BS6......49 C5
Springfield Ho
Bristol BS6...........142 C4
Portishead BS20......45 C4
Springfield Hts BA3...133 E4
Springfield Lawns
BS11..................47 D6
Springfield Pl
Bath BA1..............84 F1
Clandown BA3........133 E4
Springfield Rd
Bristol, Cotham BS6...49 D1
Bristol, Mangotsfield
BS16.................52 A7
Pill BS20..............47 C4
Portishead BS20......45 B5
Springfields BS34.....36 A2
Springfort BS9........48 F3
Spring Gardens Rd
BA2..................141 C2
Spring Gdns
Bath BA2.............141 C2
Bristol BS4............64 A1
Spring Ground Rd
BS39.................132 E5
Spring Hill
Bristol BS2...........143 A4
Bristol, Upper Soundwell
BS15.................51 E2
Weston-s-M BS22.....88 D2
Springhill Cl BS39....132 C6
Spring Hill Dr BS22....88 E1
Spring Ho 2 BS35.....15 C8
Spring La
Bath BA1..............85 B2
Dundry BS41..........79 A1
Springleaze
Bristol, Knowle Park
BS4..................64 A1
Bristol, Mangotsfield
BS16.................52 A7
Springly Ct BS15......66 A8
Spring Rise BS20......45 C3
Spring St BS3..........63 E4
Spring Street Pl BS3...63 E4
Spring Terr BS22.......88 C2
Spring Vale BA1.......85 B2
Spring Valley BS22.....88 C2
Springville Cl BS30.....66 A3
Spring Wood Gdns
BS24.................105 E3
Spruce Way
Bath BA2.............118 E8
Bristol BS34...........35 F7
Weston-s-M BS22....105 E8
Square Leaze BS34.....35 F6
Square The
Alveston BS35..........15 A4
Axbridge BS26........125 C2
Banwell BS29.........107 B3
Bath BA2.............141 B1
Bristol BS1...........143 C2
Bristol, Knowle Park BS4 64 A1
Bristol, Staple Hill BS16 .51 E4
Shipham BS25........125 E7
Temple Cloud BS39...114 E1
Timsbury BA2........116 B2
Wellow BA2...........118 D1
Winscombe BS25.....124 E6
Squire La BS40.......111 C1
Squires Ct BS30........65 F4
Squires Leaze BS35.....8 D2
Squirrel Cres BS35......8 D2
Stabbins Cl BS35......89 B5
Stables The BA3......140 B5
Stable Yd BA2........101 D6
Stable Yd The GL9......30 B7
Stackpool Rd BS3......63 C4
Staddlestones BA3....138 F7
Stadium Rd BS6........49 C5
Stafford Cres BS35......8 B1
Stafford Pl BS23......104 E8
Stafford Rd
Bristol BS2............50 A2
Portishead BS20......45 E4
Weston-s-M BS23....104 F7
Staffords Ct BS30......66 A6
Stafford St BS3........63 D4
Stainer Cl BS4.........79 D7
Stalcombe La BA2......99 B4
Stall St BA1...........141 C2
Stambrook Pk BA1.....86 A5
Stanbridge Cl BS16....51 F6
Stanbridge Prim Sch
BS16.................51 F6
Stanbridge Rd BS16....51 F6
Stanbury Ave BS16....51 C5
Stanbury Rd BS3.......63 E3
Stancombe La BS48....76 E7
Stancombe View GL11...5 D5
Standfast Rd BS10.....34 F3
Standing Cross BA2...117 D7
Standish Ave BS34....24 C1
Standish Cl BS10......34 F1
Standon Way BS10.....35 C2
Stane Way BS11.......47 C7

Stanfield Cl BS7.......50 C6
Stanford Cl BS36.......37 F8
Stanford Pl BS4........79 D7
Stanhope Pl BA1.....141 A2
Stanhope Rd
Bristol BS30...........65 F2
Weston-s-M BS23....104 E3
Stanhope St BS2.......64 A5
Stanier Rd
Bath BA2.............141 A2
Bristol BS15, BS16.....52 B3
Stanley Ave
Bristol, Bishopston BS7..49 E3
Bristol, Filton BS36.....36 B2
Stanley Chase BS5.....50 E2
Stanley Cres BS34......36 B2
Stanley Ct BA3........133 B2
Stanley Gdns BS30.....66 B4
Stanley Gr BS23......104 F7
Stanley Hill BS4........64 A4
Stanley Mead BS32....24 E2
Stanley Park Rd BS16..51 E3
Stanley Pk BS5........50 C1
Stanley Rd
Bristol, Cotham BS6...49 C1
Bristol, Warmley BS15..66 B8
2 Weston-s-M BS23..104 F7
Stanley Rd W BA2....101 B5
Stanley St N 9 BS3....63 C3
Stanley St S BS3.......63 C2
Stanley St 4 BS3......63 C3
Stanley Terr
3 Bristol BS3.........63 C2
Radstock BA3........134 A3
Stanley Villas 11 BA1..85 A1
Stanshalls Cl BS40.....94 C4
Stanshalls Dr BS40.....94 C4
Stanshalls La BS40.....94 C4
Stanshaw Cl BS16......51 A7
Stanshawe Cres BS37..27 E1
Stanshawes Court Dr
BS37.................39 E8
Stanshawes Dr BS37...27 D1
Stanshaw Rd BS16.....51 A7
Stanshaws Cl BS32.....24 C2
Stanton Cl BS15.......51 F1
STANTON DREW......96 F2
Stanton Drew Prim Sch
BS39.................97 A2
**Stanton Drew Stone
Circles**★ BS39.......97 A3
Stanton La BS39.......97 D4
STANTON PRIOR.....99 E2
Stanton Rd
Bristol BS10...........35 E2
Chew Magna BS40.....96 B3
STANTON WICK.....114 D8
Stanton Wick La BS39..97 B1
Stanway BS30..........66 C1
Stanway Cl BA2.......101 D1
Staple Gn BS31........81 D5
Staple Grove Cres BS5.65 E4
STAPLE HILL..........51 E4
Staple Hill Prim Sch
BS16.................51 D4
Staple Hill Rd BS16....51 B4
Staples Cl BS21........57 G1
Staples Gn BS22.......89 B3
Staples Hill BA2......120 C4
Staples Rd BS37.......27 D2
STAPLETON...........50 D4
Stapleton Cl BS16......50 D5
Stapleton Rd
Bristol, Baptist Mills
BS5..................50 B1
Bristol, Eastville BS5....50 C3
Stapleton Road Sta
BS5..................50 B1
STAR.................108 D1
Star Ave BS34.........37 A4
Star Barn Rd BS36.....37 E7
Starcross Rd BS22.....89 A2
Star La
Bristol BS16...........50 F3
Pill BS20..............47 D4
Starling Cl BS22......105 E8
Starrs Cl BS26........125 B2
STARVEALL............20 D4
Starveall Cl BS5.......51 A1
Station App
Pensford BS39.........97 D5
Weston-s-M BS23....104 E7
Station Ave 3 BS16....51 A4
Station Ave S 5 BS16..51 A4
Station Cl
Backwell BS48.........75 F7
Bristol BS15...........66 C8
Chipping Sodbury BS37..40 D8
Congresbury BS49.....91 C4
Station Ct BS5.........64 E8
Station La BS7.........50 A4
Station Lodge 8
BS23.................104 E7
Station Mead BA3....138 D3
Station Rd
Acton Turville GL9.....42 F8
Axbridge BS26........125 C2
Backwell BS48.........76 A6
Bath BA1.............101 C7

Station Rd continued
Blagdon BS40........110 E3
Bristol, Ashley Down BS7 49 F4
Bristol, Filton BS34....36 A3
Bristol, Fishponds BS16..51 A4
Bristol, Henbury BS10...34 F4
Bristol, Montpelier BS6..49 E2
Bristol, Newleaze BS34..36 C2
Bristol, Patchway BS34..36 C7
Bristol, Shirehampton
BS11..................47 D5
Bristol, Shirehampton
BS11..................47 E6
Bristol, Staple Hill BS15.51 F3
Bristol, Upper Knowle
BS4..................64 C3
Charfield GL12.........11 B5
Clevedon BS21.........57 F3
Clutton BS39.........114 F3
Congresbury BS49.....91 C4
Flax Bourton BS48.....77 A8
Frampton Cotterell BS36 38 C5
Freshford BA2........120 C5
Iron Acton BS37.......26 D3
Keynsham BS31........81 E6
Midsomer Norton BA3..133 B2
Nailsea BS48..........59 F2
Pill BS20..............47 C4
Pilning BS35...........22 F4
Portbury BS20.........46 D3
Portishead BS20......45 D6
Sandford BS25........107 F4
Severn Beach BS35....22 A6
Wellow BA2..........118 D1
Weston-s-M BS23....104 E7
Weston-s-M, St Georges
BS22.................89 D2
Weston-s-M, Worle BS22..88 F2
Wickwar GL12.........18 B7
Winterbourne BS36....37 E4
Wrington BS40........92 D2
Yate BS37..............27 C2
Yatton BS49............74 B1
Station Road Bsns Ctr
BS15.................52 A3
Station Road Link BS15 52 A2
Station Road Workshops
BS15.................52 A3
Station Yd BS36.......37 E4
Staunton Fields BS14..80 C4
Staunton La BS14......80 D3
Staunton Way BS14....80 D4
Staveley Cres BS10....35 C2
Staverton Cl BS32.....24 C1
Staverton Way BS15....66 A7
Stavordale Gr BS14....80 B6
Staynes Cres BS15.....65 E8
Steam Mills BA3......138 F8
Steanbridge BS32......36 D6
Stean Bridge Rd BS32..36 E6
Steel Ct BS30..........65 F3
Steel Mills BS31.......81 F4
STEEP HOLM........104 B3
Steevens Ho (Almshouses)
13 BS2...............143 C3
Stella Gr BS3..........63 A2
Stennard Gn BA2.....102 B2
Stephens Dr BS30......65 F5
Stephen St BS5........64 C8
Stepney Rd BS5........50 C1
Stepney Wlk BS5.......50 C1
Stepping Stones The
BS4..................64 E6
Sterncourt Rd BS16....51 A7
Stevens Cres BS3......63 F4
Stevens La BS24......122 C3
Stevens Wlk BS32......36 D8
Steway La BA1.........86 B6
Stibbs Ct BS30........65 F4
Stibbs Hill BS5.........65 A7
Stickland BS21........57 E1
STIDCOT...............16 E6
Stidcote La GL12.......16 E5
Stidcot La GL12........16 D5
Stidham La BS31.......82 B6
Stile Acres BS11.......34 A1
Stilemead La BS40....111 D1
Stileway Bsns Pk BS21 73 B8
Stillhouse La BS3.......63 D4
Stillingfleet Rd BS13...79 C5
Stillman Cl BS13.......78 E4
Stinchcombe BS37.....27 E1
Stirling Cl BS37........27 D4
Stirling Rd BS4........64 C3
Stirling Way BS31......81 E4
Stirtingale Ave BA2...101 C3
Stirtingale Rd BA2....101 C3
Stitchings La BA2.....117 D7
Stitchings Shord La
BS39.................113 C4
STOCK...............109 B8
Stock Hill BS35.........7 C1
Stockhill Cl BA3......138 C3
Stockhill Rd BA3......138 C2
Stock La BS40.........109 A7
Stockmead BS40......109 B5
Stockton Cl
Bristol BS14...........79 F4

Stockton Cl continued
Bristol, Oldland BS30...66 B3
Stock Way N BS48......59 F2
Stock Way S BS48......59 E2
Stockwell Ave BS16....52 A6
Stockwell Cl BS16......51 F7
Stockwell Dr BS16.....52 A6
STOCKWOOD..........80 E4
Stockwood Chambers
BS5..................64 C7
Stockwood Cres BS4...63 F2
**Stockwood Green Prim
Sch** BS14............80 E4
Stockwood Hill BS31...81 C7
Stockwood La
Bristol BS14...........80 E5
Keynsham BS14, BS31..81 B7
Stockwood Mews BS4..64 F5
Stockwood Rd BS4.....64 F1
STOCKWOOD VALE...81 C6
Stockwood Vale BS31..81 C6
Stodelegh Cl BS22.....89 B3
STOKE BISHOP.......48 E5
Stoke Bishop CE Prim Sch
BS9..................48 E5
Stoke Bridge Ave BS34 36 D6
Stoke Cotts BS9........48 E4
Stokefield Cl BS35......8 B1
STOKE GIFFORD......36 F4
Stoke Gr BS9...........48 E6
Stoke Hamlet BS9......48 F6
Stoke Hill
Bristol BS9............48 E3
Chew Stoke BS40.....112 D7
Stoke La
Bristol, Broomhill BS16..50 E7
Bristol, Patchway BS34..36 C8
Bristol, Westbury on T
BS9..................48 F6
Stokeleigh Wlk BS9....48 C5
Stoke Lodge Prim Sch
BS34.................36 C8
Stoke Mdws BS32.....24 D1
Stokemead BS34.......36 C8
Stoke Mead BA2......119 F7
Stoke Paddock Rd BS9..48 D6
Stoke Park Rd BS9.....48 E4
Stoke Park Rd S BS9...48 E3
Stoke Rd
Bristol BS8, BS9.......48 F3
Portishead BS20......45 D5
Stokes Croft BS1.....143 B4
Stokes Ct 1 BS30......66 A4
Stoke View BS34.......36 A3
Stoke View Bsns Pk 6
BS16.................50 F4
Stoke View Rd BS16....50 F3
STONE..................3 F3
Stoneable Rd BA3....134 A3
Stoneage La BA2.....117 B1
STON EASTON........131 E1
Stoneberry Rd BS14...80 B3
STONEBRIDGE.......107 A4
Stonebridge BS21......57 F1
Stonebridge Pk BS5....50 E2
Stonebridge Rd BS23..104 F4
Stonechat Gdns BS16..50 E6
Stonechat Gn BS20....46 A6
Stone Cl BS36.........37 E4
STONE-EDGE BATCH...59 D4
Stonehenge La BS48...59 E4
Stonehill BS15.........65 E4
STONE HILL...........65 E4
Stonehill Ctr BS30.....65 E4
Stonehill Farm BS15...65 C3
Stone Hill View BS15...65 C3
Stonehouse Cl BA2...102 B2
Stonehouse La BA2...102 B2
Stone House Mews
BS37.................28 B1
Stone La BS36.........37 F3
Stoneleigh BS40.......96 B3
Stoneleigh Cres BS4...64 C4
Stoneleigh Ct BA1.....84 E3
Stoneleigh Dr BS30....65 F5
Stoneleigh Ho BS8....142 B3
Stoneleigh Rd BS4.....64 A2
Stoneleigh Wlk BS4...64 A2
Stone Monolith BS34...35 E6
Stone's Cross BA3....133 B2
Stones Ct BS6.........49 B2
Stonewell Dr BS49.....91 D3
Stonewell Gr BS49.....91 D3
Stonewell La BS49.....91 D3
Stonewell Park Rd
BS49.................91 D3
Stoneyard La
Litton BA3...........130 D2
Maniards Green BS35...2 A1
Shepperdine BS35......1 F1
Stoneyfield Cl BS20....47 B3
Stoneyfields BS20......47 B4
**Stoney Littleton Long
Barrow**★ BA2.......135 C7
Stoney Steep BS48.....60 A5
Stoney Stile Rd BS15...15 A5
Stony La GL9...........19 E5
STONY LITTLETON...135 B6
Stormont Cl BS23.....104 F3

Stormont Ct BS24 . . . . . 105 E7
Stothard Rd BS7 . . . . . 50 B7
Stottbury Rd BS7 . . . . . 50 A3
Stoulton Gr BS10 . . . . . 35 A3
Stourden Cl BS16 . . . . . 51 A7
Stourton Dr BS30 . . . . . 65 F4
Stover Rd BS37 . . . . . 27 B2
Stover Trad Est BS37 . . . . 27 B2
Stowborough Cotts
BA2 . . . . 134 C7
Stowell Hill Rd GL12 . . 16 B6
STOWEY 113 F4
Stowey Bottom BS39 . 113 E5
Stowey Crossroads
BS39 . . . . 113 F5
Stowey Pk BS49 . . . . . 91 D7
Stowey Rd BS49 . . . . . 91 C8
Stowey Road BS39 . . . . 113 F2
Stow Hill Rd GL12 . . . 16 B6
Stow Ho BS11 . . . . 47 E5
Stowick Gdns BS11 . . . 34 C2
Stradbrook Ave BS5 . . . 65 B7
Stradling Ave BS23 . . . 104 F5
Stradling Rd BS11 . . . . 34 C2
Stradlings Yd BS2 . . . . 142 C4
Straightmead BA3 . . . . 130 F1
Straight St BS2 . . . . . . 143 C2
Straits Par BS16 . . . . . 51 B5
Stratford Cl BS14 . . . . 79 F3
Stratford Ct BS9 . . . . . 48 F8
Stratford La BS40 . . . . 112 E1
Strathearn Dr BS10 . . . 35 B2
Strathmore Rd BS7 . . . 49 F5
Stratton Cl BS34 . . . . . 36 C7
Stratton La BS22 . . . . . 88 A4
STRATTON-ON-THE-
FOSSE 138 F1
Stratton Pl BS30 . . . . . 65 F2
Stratton Rd BS31 . . . . . 82 E3
Strawberry Cl BS48 . . . 59 D1
Strawberry Field
BS26 . . . . 125 D2
Strawberry Gdns BS48 . 75 D8
Strawberry Hill BS21 . . 57 H4
Strawberry La
Bristol BS5 . . . . 64 E7
Dundry BS13, BS41 . . 78 E3
Strawberry Line BS49 . 108 A8
Strawbridge Rd ⑪ BS5 . 64 B7
Stream Cl BS10 . . . . . . 35 D3
Streamcross BS49 . . . . 74 D1
Streamleaze
Chew Magna BS40 . . . 96 B3
Thornbury BS35 . . . . 15 C8
Streamleaze Ct BS35 . . 15 B8
Streamside
Chew Magna BS40 . . . 96 B3
❶ Clevedon BS21 . . . . 57 H3
Stream Side BS16 . . . . 51 F6
Streamside Rd BS37 . . 28 A1
Streamside Wlk BS4 . . 64 E3
Stream The BS16 . . . . . 37 B2
STREET END 110 E2
Street End BS40 . . . . . 110 D2
Street End La BS40 . . . 110 D2
Street The
Acton Turville GL9 . . . 42 F6
Alveston BS35 . . . . . . 15 B5
Bishop Sutton BS39 . . 113 D4
Burton SN14 . . . . 43 B4
Chew Stoke BS40 . . . 112 D8
Chilcompton BA3 . . . 138 D5
Compton Martin BS40 . 129 B7
Farmborough BA2 . . . 115 F6
Luckington SN14 . . . . 31 E4
North Nibley GL11 . . . . 5 D4
Olveston BS35 . . . . . . 14 A3
Radstock BA3 . . . . . . 133 F2
Stowey BS39 . . . . . . 113 F4
Ubley BS40 . . . . 111 D1
Winford BS40 . . . . . . 94 F1
Stretford Ave BS5 . . . . 64 D8
Stretford Rd BS5 . . . . . 64 D8
Stride Cl BS35 . . . . 22 A6
STRODE 111 E7
Strode Comm BS35 . . . 14 F5
Strode Gdns BS35 . . . . 14 F5
Strode Rd BS21 . . . . . . 57 E2
Strode Way BS21 . . . . . 57 D1
Stroud Rd
Bristol, Patchway BS34 . 35 F8
Bristol, Shirehampton
BS11 . . . . 47 E5
Petty France GL9 . . . . 30 B7
Stroud Way BS24 . . . . 105 E7
Stuart Ho BS23 . . . . . . 87 D1
Stuart Pl BA2 . . . . 101 D6
Stuart Rd BS23 . . . . . 105 A5
Stuart St BS5 . . . . 64 C7
Studland Ct BS9 . . . . . 49 B6
Stumpwell La GL12 . . . . 5 E2
Sturden La BS16 . . . . . 37 C3
Sturdon Rd BS3 . . . . . . 63 A3
Sturmer Cl BS37 . . . . . 27 E4
Sturminster Cl BS14 . . 80 D6
Sturminster Lodge
BS14 . . . . 80 D5
Sturminster Rd BS14 . . 80 D7

Suffolk Ho BA1 . . . . . . 101 C8
Sulis Manor Rd BA2 . . 118 D8
Sullivan Cl BS4 . . . . . . 79 D6
Sumerlin Dr BS21 . . . . 57 H3
Summer Ct BS8 . . . . . 142 B3
Summerfield BS22 . . . . 89 A3
Summerfield Rd BA1 . . 85 A1
Summerfield Terr BA1 . 85 A1
Summer Ground Dr
BS13 . . . . 79 A5
Summerhayes BS30 . . . 66 D5
Summer Hill BS4 . . . . . 64 A4
Summerhill Jun & Inf Schs
BS5 . . . . 64 E8
Summerhill Rd
Bath BA1 . . . . 84 D1
Bristol BS5 . . . . 64 F8
Summerhill Terr BS5 . . 64 F7
Summerhouse BS21 . . . 59 D4
Summer House Way
BS30 . . . . 66 B7
Summer La
Banwell BS29 . . . . . 106 E5
Burton SN14 . . . . 43 F3
Monkton Combe BA2 . 119 D8
Weston-s-M BS22, BS24 . 89 B1
Weston-s-M BS22,
BS24 . . . . 106 C8
Weston-s-M BS29 . . 106 D7
Summer La N BS22 . . . 89 A2
Summerlands BS48 . . . 76 B5
Summerlands Rd
BS23 . . . . 105 B8
Summer Lane Park Homes
BS29 . . . . 106 E4
Summerlays Ct BA2 . . 102 B6
Summerlays Pl BA2 . . 102 B6
Summerlea BA2 . . . . . 117 A5
Summerleaze
Bristol BS16 . . . . 51 C3
Keynsham BS31 . . . . 81 E7
Summer Leaze BS39 . . 113 D4
Summers Dr BS30 . . . . 54 A1
Summers Mead BS37 . . 27 E4
Summers Rd ❹ BS2 . . 50 A1
Summer St ❹ BS3 . . . . 63 C4
Summers Terr ❸ BS2 . . 50 A1
Summer View GL12 . . . 18 B4
Summit Cl BS15 . . . . . . 65 E8
SUNDAYSHILL 9 C8
Sundays Hill BS32 . . . . 24 A4
Sunderland Pl BS8 . . . 142 B3
Sunderland St ❷ BA2 . 141 C3
Sundew Rd BS16 . . . . . 52 D7
Sundridge Pk BS37 . . . 39 E8
Sunfield Rd BS24 . . . . 105 E3
Sunningdale
Bristol BS8 . . . . 142 B4
Yate BS37 . . . . 39 E8
Sunningdale Cl BS48 . . 60 A1
Sunningdale Dr BS30 . . 66 B6
Sunningdale Rd BS22 . 88 F3
Sunnybank
Bath BA2 . . . . 102 B4
Bristol BS16 . . . . 51 E6
Westerleigh BS37 . . . 39 A3
Sunny Bank
Bristol BS15 . . . . 51 B1
Wick BS30 . . . . 67 B7
Sunnybank Ct BS24 . . 89 B1
Sunnybank Way BS24 . 89 B1
Sunnydene BS4 . . . . . . 64 D4
Sunny Hill BS9 . . . . . . 48 C7
Sunnyhill Dr BS11 . . . . 47 E6
Sunnyhill Ho E BS11 . . 47 E6
Sunnyhill Ho W BS11 . . 47 E6
Sunnymead
Bristol BS30 . . . . 66 D6
Keynsham BS31 . . . . 81 E3
Midsomer Norton BA3 . 132 F2
Stratton-on-t-F BA3 . . 138 F2
Sunnymead La BS39 . . 113 D3
Sunnymede Rd BS48 . . 59 D3
Sunny Mount BA3 . . . 133 B2
Sunnyside
Bristol BS9 . . . . 48 E5
Clutton BS39 . . . . . . 115 B4
Farrington Gurney BS39 132 B3
Frampton Cotterell BS36 38 B8
Sunnyside Cres BS21 . . 57 F3
Sunnyside Farm Trad Est
BS20 . . . . 47 C2
Sunnyside Gdns BA2 . . 116 B2
Sunnyside La
Hambrook BS16 . . . . . 37 C2
Yate BS37 . . . . 27 C1
Sunnyside Rd
Clevedon BS21 . . . . . 57 F3
Weston-s-M BS23 . . 104 E6
Sunnyside Rd N BS23 . 104 E6
Sunnyside View BA2 . . 134 C7
Sunnyvale
Camerton BA2 . . . . . 133 E8
Clevedon BS21 . . . . . 57 D1
Sunnyvale Dr BS30 . . . 66 B3
Sunny Wlk BS15 . . . . . 51 B1
Sunridge BS16 . . . . . . 51 D6
Sunridge Cl BA3 . . . . . 138 F8

Sunridge Pk BA3 . . . . 138 F8
Sunrise Gr BS4 . . . . . . 64 D4
Sunset Cl BA2 . . . . . . 134 C7
Surrey Rd BS7 . . . . . . 49 E3
Surrey St BS2 . . . . . . 143 B4
Sussex Pl
Bath BA2 . . . . 141 C1
Bristol BS2 . . . . 49 F1
Sussex St BS2 . . . . . . 64 A6
Sutcliffe Ho BA1 . . . . 102 B8
Sutherland Ave
Bristol BS16 . . . . 51 E7
Yate BS37 . . . . 27 D4
Sutherland Dr BS24 . . 105 D2
Sutherland Pl ❾ BS8 . . 49 A2
Sutton Ave BS4 . . . . . . 64 D4
Sutton Cl BS22 . . . . . 105 E8
Sutton Court BS39 . . . 113 F5
Sutton Hill Rd BS39 . . 113 D4
Sutton La BS40 . . . . . . 93 F1
Sutton Pk BS39 . . . . . 113 D4
Sutton St BA2 . . . . . . 102 B7
SUTTON WICK 113 B2
Swainswick BS14 . . . . 79 F6
Swainswick CE Prim Sch
BA1 . . . . 85 B5
Swainswick BA1, BS5 . . 85 C2
Swainswick La BA1 . . . 85 D5
Swaish Dr ❷ BS30 . . . 66 A4
Swallow Cl BA3 . . . . . 139 B8
Swallow Ct BS14 . . . . . 80 F6
Swallow Dr BS34 . . . . . 35 E8
Swallow Gdns BS22 . . 105 E8
Swallow Pk BS35 . . . . . 8 D3
Swallows Ct BS34 . . . . 36 E4
Swallow St BA1 . . . . . 141 C2
Swallows The BS22 . . . 105 D7
Swallowtail Cl BS35 . . . 8 C3
Swan Cl BS22 . . . . . . 105 E8
Swancombe
Blagdon BS40 . . . . . 110 E2
Clapton in G BS20 . . . 59 E8
Swane Rd BS14 . . . . . . 80 F6
Swan Field BS37 . . . . . 27 F2
Swangrove La GL9 . . . 30 D8
Swan La BS36 . . . . 37 C8
Swanley La GL13 . . . . . 4 B5
Swanmoor Cres BS10 . . 35 A4
Sweetgrass Rd BS24 . 106 A8
Sweets Cl BS15 . . . . . . 51 E2
Sweets Rd BS15 . . . . . 51 E2
Sweetwater La BS35 . . 14 D7
Swift Cl BS22 . . . . 88 F1
Swinhay La GL12 . . . . . 11 B8
Swiss Ct ⑬ BS23 . . . . 104 E7
Swiss Dr BS3 . . . . 62 F2
Swiss Rd
Bristol BS3 . . . . 62 F1
Weston-s-M BS23 . . . 104 F7
Swithins La BS34 . . . . . 35 F7
Sycamore Cl
Bristol, Hanham BS15 . 65 B3
Bristol, Whitehall BS5 . 50 E1
Locking BS24 . . . . . 105 E5
Nailsea BS48 . . . . . . 59 E2
Shipham BS25 . . . . . 125 E8
Weston-s-M BS23 . . 105 A8
Sycamore Ct BS7 . . . . 49 E3
Sycamore Dr
Bristol BS34 . . . . 35 F7
Thornbury BS35 . . . . . 8 C1
Sycamore Ho ❻ BS16 . 51 C6
Sycamore Rd BA3 . . . . 134 B2
Sycamores BS23 . . . . . 87 E1
Sydenham Bldgs BA2 . 141 A2
Sydenham Hill BS6 . . . 49 D1
Sydenham La BS6 . . . . 49 E1
Sydenham Pl ⑮ BS6 . . 49 E1
Sydenham Rd
Bath BA2 . . . . 141 A2
Bristol, Cotham BS6 . . 49 E1
Bristol, Totterdown BS4 . 64 A3
Sydenham Terr BA2 . . 102 C1
Sydenham Way BS15 . . 65 C3
Sydney Bldgs BA2 . . . 102 B6
Sydney Ho BA2 . . . . . 102 B7
Sydney Mews BA2 . . . 102 B7
Sydney Pl BA2 . . . . . . 102 B7
Sydney Rd BA2 . . . . . 102 B7
Sydney Row BS1 . . . . 142 B1
Sydney Wharf BA2 . . . 102 B7
Sylvan Way BS9 . . . . . 48 B7
Sylvia Ave BS3 . . . . . . 63 F3
Symes Ave BS13 . . . . . 79 C4
Symes Pk BA1 . . . . 84 A2
Symington Rd BS16 . . . 51 B5
Syston View BS15 . . . . 66 A8
Syston Way BS15 . . . . 51 D1

T

Tabernacle Rd BS15 . . . 65 C6
Tackley Rd BS5 . . . . . . 50 B3
TADWICK 68 E1
Tadwick La BA1 . . . . . . 85 A6
Tailor's Ct ❾ BS1 . . . . 143 A3
Talbot Ave BS15 . . . . . 51 C1

Talbot Ct BS4 . . . . 64 B2
Talbot Rd BS4 . . . . 64 C2
TALBOT'S END 10 C1
Talgarth Rd BS7 . . . . . 49 F4
Tall Elms Rd BS34 . . . . 36 A7
Tallis Gr BS4 . . . . 79 D6
Tamar Cl BS35 . . . . . . 15 D7
Tamar Dr BS31 . . . . . . 82 A4
Tamar Rd
Bristol BS2 . . . . 64 C6
Weston-s-M BS22 . . . 89 A2
Tamblyn Cl BA3 . . . . . 134 A3
Tamsin Ct BS31 . . . . . . 81 F5
Tamworth Rd BS31 . . . 81 E4
Tanhouse La BS37 . . . . 27 D7
Tankard's Cl BS8 . . . . 142 C3
Tanner Cl BS30 . . . . . . 65 F5
Tanner Ct BS30 . . . . . . 65 F5
Tanner Rd BS29 . . . . . 106 C7
Tanners Ct
Bristol, Frenchay BS16 . 37 B1
❹ Bristol, Two Mile Hill
BS15 . . . . 51 C1
Thornbury BS35 . . . . 15 B8
Tanners La SN14 . . . . . 69 F8
Tanners Wlk
Bath BA2 . . . . 100 F5
Marshfield SN14 . . . . 69 F8
Tanorth Cl BS14 . . . . . 80 A3
Tanorth Rd BS14 . . . . . 79 F3
Tansy La BS20 . . . . . . 45 F5
Tanyard The BS30 . . . . 66 B2
Tapsters BS30 . . . . 66 A4
Tara Cl BS36 . . . . 25 F1
Tarn Ho BS34 . . . . 36 A8
Tarnock Ave BS14 . . . . 80 A7
Tarnwell BS39 . . . . . . 97 A2
Tarragon Pl BS32 . . . . 36 F7
Taunton Rd BS22 . . . . 89 B4
Taunton Wlk BS7 . . . . . 50 A7
Taurus Rd BS34 . . . . . . 36 B5
Taveners Wlk BS48 . . . 59 F3
Taverner Cl BS4 . . . . . 79 D7
Taverners Cl ❻ BS23 . 104 F4
TAVERN SCOTT 95 D1
Tavistock Rd
Bristol BS4 . . . . 63 F1
Weston-s-M BS22 . . . 89 A2
Tavistock Wlk BS4 . . . 63 F1
Tawny Way BS22 . . . . 105 E8
Taylor Cl BS15 . . . . . . 65 F8
Taylor Ct BS22 . . . . . . 89 B4
Taylor Gdns BS13 . . . . 78 F4
Taylors Bank ⑩ BS1 . . 143 A3
Taylors Fields BS29 . . 107 B3
Tayman Cl BS10 . . . . . 49 E6
Tayman Ridge BS30 . . . 82 D8
Taynton Cl BS30 . . . . . 66 D6
Teal Cl
Bristol BS32 . . . . 24 D2
Weston-s-M BS22 . . . 88 F1
Teal Way BS20 . . . . . . 45 F6
Teasel Cl BS16 . . . . . . 52 D8
Teasel Mead BS32 . . . . 36 E7
Teasel Wlk BS22 . . . . 105 D7
Teddington Cl BA2 . . . 101 C4
Teesdale Cl BS22 . . . . 105 D8
Teewell Ave BS16 . . . . 51 E4
Teewell Cl BS16 . . . . . 51 E4
Teewell Ct BS16 . . . . . 51 E4
Teewell Hill BS16 . . . . 51 E4
Teignmouth Rd
Bristol BS4 . . . . 63 F1
Clevedon BS21 . . . . . 57 G3
Telephone Ave BS1 . . 143 A2
Telford Ho
Bath BA2 . . . . 101 D3
Leigh Woods BS8 . . . 62 E7
Telford Wlk BS5 . . . . . 51 A1
TELLISFORD 137 E4
Tellisford La BA2 . . . . 136 F4
Tellisford Rd BA2 . . . . 137 E7
Templar Rd BS37 . . . . . 27 E3
Templars Ct ❷ BS2 . . 105 D7
Templars Way BS25 . . 125 E7
Templeland Rd BS13 . . 78 F5
Temple Rose St BS1 . . 143 B2
Temple St
Bristol BS31 . . . . . . 143 B2
Bristol, Bedminster BS3 . 63 B2
Keynsham BS31 . . . . 81 F5
Temple Trad Est BS2 . . 64 C5
Temple Way BS2 . . . . 143 B2
Temple Way Underpass
. . . . 143 C3

Ten Acre La BA2 . . . . . 117 F6
Ten Acre Ri BS34 . . . . . 35 E6
Tenby Rd BS31 . . . . . . 81 D4
Tenby St BS5 . . . . 64 B7
Tennessee Gr BS6 . . . . 49 C5
Tennis Court Ave
BS39 . . . . 132 D5
Tenniscourt Rd BS15 . . 52 A1
Tennis Court Rd BS39 . 132 D5
Tennis Rd BS4 . . . . 64 A2
Tennyson Ave BS21 . . . 57 D2
Tennyson Cl BS31 . . . . 81 F6
Tennyson Rd
Bath BA1 . . . . 101 D7
Bristol BS7 . . . . 49 E5
Weston-s-M BS23 . . 105 A3
Tenterk Cl BS24 . . . . . 122 B6
Tenth Ave BS7 . . . . . . 36 B1
Tereslake Gn BS10 . . . 35 D4
Terrace The BS25 . . . . 125 E7
Terrace Wlk BA1 . . . . . 141 C2
Terrell Gdns ⑭ BS5 . . . 64 D7
Terrell St BS2 . . . . . . 143 A4
Terris Ct BS34 . . . . 36 E4
Terry Hill BA3 . . . . 140 D8
Terry Ho BS1 . . . . 142 C3
Tetbury Cl BS34 . . . . . 36 C7
Tetbury Gdns BS48 . . . 60 A1
Tetbury Rd BS15 . . . . . 65 B8
Teviot Rd BS31 . . . . . . 82 A4
Tewkesbury Rd ⑫ BS2 . 50 A2
Tewther Rd BS13 . . . . . 79 D3
Teyfant Com Sch BS13 . 79 E4
Teyfant Rd BS13 . . . . . 79 E4
Teyfant Wlk BS13 . . . . 79 E4
Thackeray BS7 . . . . . . 50 A8
Thackeray Ave BS21 . . 57 G4
Thackeray Ho BS23 . . 105 A5
Thackeray Rd BS21 . . . 57 G4
Thames Cl GL12 . . . . . 11 A4
Thames Ho ❾ BS35 . . . 15 C8
Thanet Rd BS3 . . . . . . 63 B2
Thatcher Cl BS20 . . . . . 45 D4
Thatchers Cl BS5 . . . . . 65 B7
Theatre Royal★
Bath BA1 . . . . 141 B2
Bristol BS1 . . . . 143 B3
There-and-Back-Again La
BS1 . . . . 142 C3
Theresa Ave BS7 . . . . . 49 E4
Thermae Bath Spa★
BA1 . . . . 141 B2
Theynes Croft BS41 . . . 62 B1
Thicket Ave BS16 . . . . 51 C3
THICKET MEAD 132 F3
Thicket Mead BA3 . . . 133 A2
Thicket Rd BS16 . . . . . 51 C4
Thicket Wlk BS35 . . . . . 8 C1
Thickthorn La BA3 . . . 138 A4
Thiery Rd BS4 . . . . 64 C2
Thingwall Pk BS16 . . . . 50 E3
Third Ave
Bath BA2 . . . . 101 D5
Bristol BS14 . . . . 80 A6
Bristol, Filton BS7 . . . 36 A1
Radstock BA3 . . . . . 139 D7
Third Way BS11 . . . . . 33 C2
Thirlmere Ct BS30 . . . . 66 D6
Thirlmere Rd
Bristol BS34 . . . . 36 A8
Weston-s-M BS23 . . 105 A4
Thistle Cl BS16 . . . . . . 52 D8
Thistle St ❶ BS3 . . . . . 63 B3
Thomas Ave BS16 . . . . 52 B8
Thomas Cl BS29 . . . . 107 A3
Thomas Ct BS1 . . . . . 143 B2
Thomas La BS1 . . . . . 143 B2
Thomas Lane Apartments
BS1 . . . . 143 B2
Thomas Pring Wlk ❶
BS5 . . . . 51 A1
Thomas St N ⑬ BS2 . . 49 D1
Thomas St
Bath BA1 . . . . 141 C4
Bristol BS2 . . . . 143 B4
❽ Bristol, Russell Town
BS5 . . . . 64 B7
Bristol, St Pauls BS2 . . 49 F1
Thomas Way BS16 . . . . 50 E7
Thompson Rd BS14 . . . 80 E6
Thomson Rd ❼ BS5 . . . 64 B8
Thornbank Pl BA2 . . . 141 A1
THORNBURY 8 E2
Thornbury Dr BS23 . . 104 D2
Thornbury Hospl BS35 . 8 C1
Thornbury Ind Est BS35 15 B8
Thornbury Mus★ BS35 . 15 B8
Thornbury Office Pk
BS35 . . . . 15 B8
Thornbury Rd
Alveston BS35 . . . . . . 15 A5
Weston-s-M BS23 . . 104 D2
Thorn Cl
Weston-s-M BS22 . . . 89 B2
Yate BS37 . . . . 27 D1
Thorndale BS8 . . . . . . 142 A4

Thorndale Cl BS22 . . . .**105** D8
Thorndale Mews BS8. .**142** A4
Thornfield Rd BS35 . . . . **3** A2
Thornhayes Cl BS36. . . . . . **38** A8
Thornhills The BS16 . . . . . **51** B6
Thornleigh Rd BS7. . . . . **49** E5
Thornmarsh Cl BS34 . . . . **37** A3
Thornmead Gr BS10. . . . **35** A2
Thorns Farm BS37 . . . . . . **27** E1
Thornycroft Cl BS7. . . . . **50** B7
Thorpe Lodge **10** BS6 . . **49** D1
Three Brooks La BS32 . . **36** E8
Three Oaks Cl BS16 . . . . . **51** C4
Three Queens' La BS1 **143** B2
Threeways Sch
  Summerfield Site
  BA1 . . . . **84** D1
Three Wells Rd BS13 . . **78** F4
Thresher Cl BS35 . . . . **8** B3
Thrissell St BS5. . . . . **64** A8
Throgmorton Rd BS4. . **79** F8
Thrubwell La BS40. . . . . . **94** B4
Thrush Cl **4** BS22. . .**105** E8
Thurlestone BS14. . . . . . **80** A6
Thurlow Rd BS5 . . . . **50** C2
Thurston's Barton BS5. **50** E1
Thyme Cl BS20. . . . . **45** F5
Tibberton BS15. . . . . **66** A8
Tibbott Rd BS14 . . . . **80** D5
Tibbott Wlk BS14 . . . . . . **80** D5
Tiberius Rd BS31 . . . . . . **81** F7
Tichborne Rd
  Bristol BS5. . . . .**64** C7
  Weston-s-M BS23 . . . . . **87** E1
TICKENHAM. **58** F4
Tickenham CE Prim Sch
  BS21. . . . . **58** E4
Tickenham Hill BS48 . . . **59** E4
Tickenham Rd BS21 . . . . **58** A4
Tide Gr BS11 . . . . **48** A8
Tidenham Way BS34 . . . . **23** F1
Tiffany Ct BS1 . . . .**143** B1
Tiger Moth Rd BS24. . . .**105** C5
Tiledown BS39. . . . .**114** E1
Tiledown Cl BS39 . . . . .**114** F1
Tilley Cl
  Farmborough BA2 . . . . .**116** A5
  Keynsham BS31. . . . .**82** A2
Tilley La BA2. . . . .**116** A5
Tilling Rd BS10 . . . . **49** E7
Tilling Wlk BS10 . . . . . . **49** E7
Tilting Rd BS35 . . . . **8** B2
Timber Dene BS16 . . . . . **50** D4
Timberscombe Wlk
  BS14. . . . . **80** C5
Timbers The BA3. . . . . .**139** B7
TIMSBURY. **116** B1
TIMSBURY BOTTOM. .**116** A1
Timsbury Rd
  Bristol BS3. . . . .**63** E2
  Farmborough BA2 . . . . .**116** B5
  High Littleton BS39 . . . .**115** D1
Timsbury Village
  Workshops BA2 . . . . . .**115** F3
Timsbury Wlk BS3 . . . . . **63** E2
Timsbury Workshop Est
  BA2 . . . .**115** F3
Tindell Ct **12** BS30 . . . . **65** F4
Tinding Dr BS16 . . . . **50** D8
Tinkers La BS48. . . . . **76** F2
Tinker's La
  Compton Martin BS40 . .**129** B7
  Kilmersdon BA11 . . . . . .**140** B1
Tintagel Cl BS31 . . . . **81** D4
Tintern Ave BS5 . . . . **64** D8
Tintern Cl BS30 . . . . **65** F6
Tippetts Rd BS15. . . . . . . **65** D6
Tirley Ho BS34 . . . . **23** F1
Tirley Way BS22. . . . . **88** B2
Titan Barrow BA1. . . . . . **86** C2
Titan Rd BS34 . . . . **36** B5
Tiverton Gdns BS22 . . . . **89** A2
Tiverton Rd **2** BS21. . . **57** G1
Tiverton Wlk BS16 . . . . . **51** A2
Tivoli Ho BS23 . . . .**104** E8
Tivoli La BS23 . . . .**104** E8
Tobias Gdns BS37 . . . . . . **27** D1
TOCKINGTON. **14** C1
Tockington Gn BS32. . . . **14** B2
Tockington La BS32 . . . . **24** A7
Tockington Manor Sch
  BS32. . . . . **14** C2
Tockington Park La
  BS32. . . . . **24** E8
Toddington Cl BS37 . . . . **39** D8
Tog Hill BS30. . . . . **68** B6
Toghill La BS30 . . . . **68** A8
Tolland BS24 . . . .**105** A2
Toll Bridge Rd BA1. . . . . **85** E3
Toll Down Way SN14 . . . **43** A3
Toll House Ct **5** BS3 . . **63** A4
Toll Rd BS23 . . . .**121** F8
Tone Rd BS21. . . . . **57** F1
Top Rd BS25 . . . .**125** F7
Tor Cl BS22. . . . . **89** A2
TORMARTON. **41** E2

Tormarton Cres BS10. . . **34** F4
Tormarton Intc BS37 . . . **41** B1
Tormarton Rd
  Acton Turville GL9 . . . . . **42** E6
  Marshfield SN14 . . . . . . **56** A4
  Marshfield, East End
  SN14 . . . . **70** A8
Tormynton Rd BS22 . . . . **88** E3
Toronto Rd BS7 . . . . **50** A8
Torpoint Rd BS3 . . . . **63** D2
Torrance Cl BS30 . . . . . . **66** D6
Torridge Rd BS31 . . . . . . **82** A4
Torrington Ave BS4 . . . . **79** F8
Torrington Cres BS22 . . . **89** A3
TORTWORTH **10** C7
TORTWORTH GREEN . . **10** C5
Tortworth Prim Sch
  GL12. . . . . **10** C7
Tortworth Rd BS7 . . . . . . **49** E5
Torwood House Sch
  BS6. . . . . **49** A3
Totnes Cl BS22. . . . . **89** A2
Totshill Dr BS13. . . . . **79** E4
Totshill Gr BS13. . . . . **79** E4
Tottenham Pl BS8. . . . . .**142** B3
TOTTERDOWN. **64** A4
Totterdown Bridge Ind Est
  BS2. . . . . **64** A4
Totterdown La BS24. . . .**105** A1
Totterdown Rd BS23 . . .**104** F4
TOTTEROAK. **28** F5
Touching End La SN14. . **69** F8
Touchstone Ave BS34 . . . **36** F5
Tovey Cl BS22. . . . . **88** E4
TOWERHEAD. **107** D4
Towerhead Rd BS29. . . .**107** D3
Tower Hill
  Bristol BS2. . . . .**143** B3
  Locking BS24. . . . .**106** D4
Tower House La BS48 . . . **60** A4
Tower La
  Bristol BS1. . . . .**143** A3
  Bristol, Cadbury Heath
  BS30 . . . . **66** B6
Towerleaze BS9. . . . . **48** D3
Tower Rd
  Bristol BS15. . . . . **51** C1
  Portishead BS20. . . . . . . **45** A4
Tower Rd N BS30. . . . . . . **66** B7
Tower Rd S BS30. . . . . . . **66** B5
Tower St BS1. . . . .**143** B2
Tower The
  Bristol BS1. . . . .**143** B2
  Bristol, Redland BS6 . . . . **49** C3
Tower Wlk BS23 . . . . **87** D1
Town Barton BA2 . . . . . .**136** F4
Town End BA2 . . . .**136** F4
Townsend
  Almondsbury BS32. . . . . . **23** F4
  East Harptree BS40. . . . .**130** A5
TOWNS END. **132** E4
Townsend Cl BS14 . . . . . **80** F5
Townsend La BS32 . . . . . **24** A5
Townsend Rd BS14 . . . . . **80** F5
Townshend Rd BS22. . . . **89** B5
TOWNWELL **10** B2
Townwell GL12. . . . . **10** B2
Tozers Hill BS4 . . . . **64** C2
Tracy Cl BS14 . . . . **79** F7
Trafalgar Ct
  Weston-s-M BS23 . . . . .**104** E7
  12 Weston-super-Mare
  BS23 . . . .**104** E7
Trafalgar Rd BA1. . . . . . **84** B1
Trafalgar Terr **3** BS3. . **63** B2
Trajectus Way BS31 . . . . **81** F7
Tralee Wlk BS4 . . . . **63** D1
Tramshed The BA1 . . . . .**141** C3
Tramway Rd BS4. . . . . . . **64** C3
Tranmere Ave BS10 . . . . **35** A4
Tranmere Gr BS10 . . . . . **35** A3
Transom Ho BS1. . . . . . .**143** B2
Tranton La GL13 . . . . **2** C4
Tratman Wlk BS10 . . . . . **34** F3
Travers Cl BS4 . . . . **79** D6
Travers Wlk BS34 . . . . . . **36** F5
Trawden Cl BS23. . . . . . . **88** A1
Tredegar Rd BS16. . . . . . **51** B3
Treefield Pl **5** BS2. . . . **50** A2
Treefield Rd BS21. . . . . . **57** F2
Tree Leaze BS37 . . . . **27** F2
Treetops Cvn Pk BS16 . . **51** A8
Tregarth Rd BS3 . . . . **62** F1
Trelawn Cl BS22 . . . . **89** D2
Trelawney Ave BS5. . . . . **64** D8
Trelawney Pk BS4. . . . . . **64** D3
Trelawney Rd BS6. . . . . . **49** C1
Trelissick Gdns **3**
  BS22. . . . .**105** F8
Trellick Wlk BS16 . . . . . . **50** E8
Tremes Cl SN14 . . . . **69** F8
Tremlett Mews **3**
  BS22. . . . . **89** B4
Trenchard Rd
  Locking BS24. . . . .**106** D4
  Saltford BS31. . . . . **82** D3
Trenchard St BS1. . . . . .**142** C3
Trench La BS32 . . . . **24** E2
Trendlewood Pk BS16. . . **50** E5

Trendlewood Way
  BS48. . . . . **60** A1
Trenleigh Dr BS22. . . . . . **89** A2
Trent Dr BS35. . . . . **15** D7
Trent Gr BS31. . . . . **82** A4
Trentham Cl **7** BS2 . . . **50** A2
Trescothick Cl BS31 . . . . **81** E6
Trescothick Dr BS30. . . . **66** D4
Tresham Cl BS32. . . . . . . **24** D2
Trevanna Rd BS3. . . . . . . **62** F1
Trevelyan Rd BS23 . . . .**104** F7
Trevelyan Wlk
  Bristol, Henbury BS10. . . **34** F3
  Bristol, Stoke Gifford
  BS34 . . . . **37** A5
Treverdowe Wlk BS10 . . **34** D3
Trevethin Cl BS15 . . . . . . **65** D7
Trevisa Gr BS10. . . . . **35** C4
Trewartha Cl BS23 . . . .**104** F8
Trewartha Pk BS23 . . . .**104** F8
Trewint Gdns BS4 . . . . . . **79** F8
Triangle Ct **2** BA2 . . . .**101** D5
Triangle Ctr The BS21 . . **57** F3
Triangle E BA2 . . . .**101** D5
Triangle N BA2 . . . .**101** D5
Triangle S BS8. . . . .**142** B5
Triangle The
  Clevedon BS21. . . . . **57** F3
  Paulton BS39 . . . .**132** E6
  Portishead BS20 . . . . . . **45** B5
  Wrington BS40 . . . . **92** D2
Triangle Villas **1** BA2 .**101** D5
Triangle W
  Bath BA2 . . . .**101** D5
  Bristol BS8. . . . .**142** B3
Trident Cl BS16 . . . . **38** A1
Trim Bridge **3** BA1 . . .**141** B2
Trim St BA1. . . . .**141** B2
Trinder Rd BS20 . . . . **47** B4
Trinity CE Prim Sch
  GL9. . . . . **43** A6
Trinity CE VC Prim Sch
  BA3. . . . .**134** A4
Trinity Cl BA1. . . . .**141** B2
Trinity Coll BS9 . . . . **48** E4
Trinity Ct
  5 Bristol BS15 . . . . . . **65** E8
  Bristol, Horfield BS7 . . . **49** E5
  Nailsea BS48. . . . . **59** C1
Trinity La BS37 . . . . **28** C2
Trinity Mdws BS37 . . . . . **28** C2
Trinity Mews **15** BS2. . .**143** C3
Trinity Pl
  3 Bristol BS8 . . . .**142** A2
  4 Weston-s-M BS23. . . **87** C1
Trinity Rd
  Bath BA2 . . . .**102** B2
  Bristol BS2. . . . . **64** A7
  Nailsea BS48. . . . . **59** C1
  Weston-s-M BS23 . . . . . **87** C1
Trinity St
  Bath BA1. . . . .**141** B2
  Bristol BS2. . . . . **64** A7
Trinity Wlk
  Bristol BS2. . . . .**143** C3
  Bristol, Newton BS2. . . . . **64** A7
Trin Mills BS1. . . . .**143** A1
Tripps Cnr BS49. . . . . **91** D7
Tripps Row BS41. . . . . . . **62** A1
Trollope's Hill BA2 . . . .**103** A1
Troon BS37. . . . . **39** E8
Troon Dr BS30. . . . . **66** B6
Troopers' Hill Rd BS5 . . **65** A7
Trossachs Dr BA2 . . . . .**102** D8
Trowbridge Rd BS10 . . . **35** C1
Trowbridge Wlk BS10 . . **35** C1
Trubodys Yd BS30 . . . . . **66** E7
Trubshaw Cl BS7. . . . . . . **49** F6
Trumpet La BS5. . . . . **65** B7
Truro Rd
  Bristol BS3. . . . . **63** B3
  Nailsea BS48. . . . . **60** A1
Trym Bank BS9 . . . . **48** C5
Trym Cross Rd BS9. . . . . **48** C5
Trymleaze BS9. . . . . **48** C5
Trym Rd BS9. . . . . **49** A7
Trym Side BS9 . . . . **48** C5
Trymwood Cl BS10 . . . . . **34** F2
Trymwood Par BS9. . . . . **48** D6
T T Trad Est BS1. . . . . . . **28** C1
Tucker's La BS40. . . . . . .**128** E6
Tucker St BS2 . . . .**143** C3
Tuckett Ho BS16 . . . . **51** C7
Tuckett La BS16. . . . . **51** C7
TUCKING MILL. **119** D8
Tucking Mill Cotts
  BA2 . . . .**119** D7
Tuckingmill La BS39 . . . **98** E5
Tuckmill BS21 . . . . **57** D1
Tudor Cl BS30 . . . . **66** C3
Tudor Rd
  Bristol, Hanham BS15 . . . **65** C5
  Bristol, Lower Easton
  BS5 . . . . **50** C1
  Bristol, St Pauls BS2 . . . . **49** F1
  2 Portishead BS20. . . . **45** A4
  Weston-s-M BS22 . . . . . **89** A4
Tuffley Rd BS10. . . . . **49** C8
Tufton Ave BS11 . . . . **48** A8

Tugela Rd BS13 . . . . **78** F7
Tuggy's La BA2 . . . .**119** E1
Tunbridge Cl BS40. . . . . **96** B2
Tunbridge Rd BS40. . . . . **96** B2
Tunbridge Way BS16 . . . **52** A8
TUNLEY. **117** B3
Tunley Hill BA2 . . . .**116** E2
Tunley Rd BA2, BA3. . . .**117** D5
Tunnel La BA3 . . . .**138** F5
Tunstall Cl BS9 . . . . **48** E4
TURLEIGH. **120** F6
Turleigh Hill BA15. . . . .**120** F6
Turley Rd BS5 . . . . **50** D1
Turmo Rd BS23 . . . .**105** B4
Turnberry
  Bristol BS30. . . . . **66** B6
  Bristol BS37. . . . . **39** E8
Turnberry Wlk **3** BS4. . **64** D1
Turnbridge Cl BS10 . . . . **35** D4
Turnbridge Rd BS10. . . . **35** C3
Turnbury Ave BS48. . . . . **60** A1
Turnbury Cl BS22 . . . . . . **88** F3
Turner Cl BS31. . . . . **82** A5
Turner Ct BS22 . . . . **88** F3
Turner Dr BS37 . . . . **27** B1
Turner Gdns BS7. . . . . . . **50** B6
Turners Ct **9** BS30 . . . **65** F4
Turner's Twr BA3. . . . . .**135** A1
Turner Way BS21. . . . . . . **57** D1
Turner Wlk BS30 . . . . . . **66** D7
Turnpike Cl BS37. . . . . . . **27** E2
Turnpike Gate GL12 . . . . **18** B6
Turnpike Rd
  Cross BS26 . . . .**124** E1
  Shipham BS25 . . . .**125** E8
Turtlegate Ave BS13. . . . **78** E4
Turtlegate Wlk BS13 . . . **78** E4
Turville Dr BS7 . . . . **50** A6
Tuscany Ho BS6. . . . . **49** A3
Tutton Way BS21. . . . . . . **57** F1
Tuttors Hill BS27 . . . . . .**126** C1
Tweed Cl BS35 . . . . **15** C8
Tweed Rd BS21 . . . . **57** F1
Tweed Rd Ind Est **2**
  BS21. . . . . **57** F1
Tweeny La BS30. . . . . **66** D6
Twelve O'clock La
  BA2 . . . .**100** B3
Twenty Acres Rd BS10. . **35** B2
TWERTON. **101** A5
Twerton Farm Cl **2**
  BA2 . . . .**101** B6
Twerton Inf Sch BA2 . . .**101** A5
Twickenham Rd BS6 . . . . **49** C5
Twinhoe La BA2. . . . . . .**118** E2
Twinnell Ho **5** BS5 . . . **64** A8
Two Acres Cvn Pk BS21. **44** B2
Two Acres Rd BS14. . . . . **80** A7
Two Mile Ct BS15 . . . . . . **65** C8
TWO MILE HILL. **51** C1
Two Mile Hill Jun & Inf
  Schs BS15. . . . . **65** C8
Twomile Hill Rd BS15 . . **65** B8
Two Stones La BS37. . . . **40** E8
Two Trees BS40 . . . .**127** E8
Twynings The BS15 . . . . **51** E2
Tybalt Way BS34 . . . . . . **36** E5
Tydeman Rd BS20. . . . . . **45** F5
Tyler Cl BS15. . . . . **65** E5
Tyler Gn **2** BS22. . . . . . **89** B4
Tylers Farm BS37 . . . . . . **27** F4
Tyler's La BS16 . . . . **51** D5
Tyler St BS2 . . . . **64** A6
Tylers Way BS37 . . . . **27** F5
Tyndale Ave
  Bristol BS16. . . . . **51** A4
  Yate BS37. . . . . **27** D3
Tyndale Cl GL11. . . . . **5** E4
Tyndale Ct **1** BS6. . . . . **49** B1
Tyndale Mon The★ GL11. **5** E4
Tyndale Rd BS15. . . . . . . **51** E2
Tyndale View BS35 . . . . . **15** B8
Tyndall Ave BS8. . . . . . .**142** C4
Tyndall Ho **5** BS2. . . . .**143** C3
Tyndall Rd BS5. . . . . **64** B8
Tyndalls Ct BS8 . . . .**142** C4
Tyndalls Park Mews
  BS2. . . . .**142** C4
Tyndall's Park Rd BS8 . .**142** C4
Tyndalls Way BS10 . . . . . **49** E8
Tyne Gr BS20 . . . . **45** F6
Tyne Ho **8** BS35 . . . . . . **15** C8
Tyne Rd BS7 . . . . **49** D3
Tyne St BS2. . . . . **50** A2
TYNING
  Radstock **134** B3
  Timsbury **116** A2
Tyning Cl
  Bristol BS14. . . . . **80** A7
  Yate BS37. . . . . **27** E2
Tyning End BA2 . . . .**102** B5
Tyning Hill BA3 . . . .**134** B3
Tyning La BA1 . . . . **85** B1
Tyning Pl BA2 . . . .**102** C2
Tyning Rd
  Bath BA2 . . . .**102** C2
  Bathampton BA2 . . . . . . **85** F2

Tyning Rd continued
  Bristol BS3. . . . . **63** F3
  Peasedown St John
  BA2 . . . .**134** D7
  Saltford BS31. . . . . **82** E2
  Winsley BA15. . . . .**120** F7
Tynings BS39 . . . .**114** D3
Tynings Mews BS23 . . . .**104** E4
Tynings Sch The BS16 . . **51** E4
Tynings The
  Clevedon BS21. . . . . **57** C1
  Portishead BS20. . . . . . . **44** F1
Tynings Way
  Clutton BS39 . . . .**114** E3
  Westwood BA15 . . . . . .**120** F3
Tyning Terr
  14 Bath BA1 . . . . **85** A1
  18 Bath BA1 . . . . **85** B1
Tyning The
  Bath BA2 . . . .**102** B5
  Freshford BA2. . . . .**120** B4
Tynte Ave BS13 . . . . **79** E3
Tyntesfield BS48. . . . . . . **61** A2
Tyntesfield★ BS48 . . . . . **60** F4
Tyntesfield Rd BS13 . . . . **79** A8
Tyrone Wlk BS4 . . . . **79** E8
Tyrrel Way BS34 . . . . **36** E5
Tythe Ct SN14. . . . . **70** A8
TYTHERINGTON **16** C5
Tytherington Rd BS35 . . **16** A4

U

UBLEY. **111** E1
Ubley CE Prim Sch
  BS40. . . . .**111** D1
Ubley Dro BS40 . . . .**128** B7
UBLEY SIDELING. **128** D8
UDLEY. **92** C4
Ullswater Cl
  Bristol BS30. . . . . **66** D6
  Weston-s-M BS23 . . . . .**105** A4
  Yate BS37. . . . . **27** E3
Ullswater Dr BA1 . . . . . . **85** A2
Ullswater Rd BS10 . . . . . **35** C1
Uncombe Cl BS48. . . . . . **76** D7
Underbanks BS20. . . . . . **47** D4
Underdown Ho BS1 . . . .**143** A1
Underhill Ave BA3 . . . . .**132** F2
Underhill Dr BS23. . . . .**104** D1
Underhill La BA3. . . . . .**132** F2
Underhill Rd GL12 . . . . . **11** A5
Under Knoll BA2 . . . . . .**134** A6
Underleaf Way BA2 . . . .**134** D7
Undertown BS40. . . . . . .**129** A7
Undertown La BS40 . . . .**129** A7
Under Tree Rd BA2 . . . .**134** A6
Underwood Ave BS22 . . . **88** B1
Underwood Cl BS35. . . . . **15** A4
Underwood End BS25 . .**108** A4
Underwood Rd BS20 . . . **45** C3
Unicorn Bsns Pk BS4. . . **64** D5
Unicorn Pk BS4. . . . . **64** D5
Union Pas BA1. . . . .**141** C2
Union Pl BS23 . . . .**104** D7
Union Rd **2** BS2 . . . . . . **64** A6
Union St
  Bath BA1 . . . .**141** C2
  Bristol BS1. . . . .**143** B3
  Nailsea BS48. . . . . **59** C1
  Weston-s-M BS23 . . . . .**104** D7
Unite Ho BS1. . . . .**141** C2
Unity Ct BS31 . . . . **82** A5
Unity Rd BS31 . . . . **82** A6
Unity St
  Bristol BS2. . . . .**143** C3
  Bristol, Brandon Hill
  BS1 . . . .**142** C2
  Bristol, Kingswood BS15 **65** C8
University Cl BS9 . . . . . . **48** E4
University of Bristol
  Dorothy Hodgkin Bldg
  BS1. . . . .**143** A4
University Rd BS8. . . . . .**142** C3
University Wlk BS8. . . . .**142** C3
Univ of Bath BA2 . . . . . .**102** C3
Univ of Bristol BS8. . . . .**142** C3
Univ of Bristol Botanic
  Gdns★ BS9 . . . . **48** C4
Univ of Bristol Langford
  House Sch of Veterinary
  Science BS40 . . . .**109** B6
Univ of the West of
  England BS3 . . . . **62** E4
Univ of the West of
  England Faculty of
  Health & Social Care
  BS16. . . . . **50** E5
Univ of the West of
  England Frenchay
  Campus BS16 . . . . **36** C1
Univ of the West of
  England, St Matthias
  Campus BS16 . . . . **51** A5
UPHILL. **104** C2
Uphill Ct BS23 . . . .**104** D2
Uphill Dr BA1. . . . . **85** B2

Uphill Farm Cvn Pk
BS23. . . . . .104 E1
Uphill Prim Sch BS23 .104 D2
Uphill Rd BS7. . . . . 49 F5
Uphill Rd N BS23. . . . . .104 D4
Uphill Rd S BS23. . . . . .104 D2
Uphill Way BS23 . . . . . .104 D1
Upjohn Cres BS13. . . . . 79 D3
Uplands Cl BA2 . . . . . . .119 F7
Uplands Dr BS31. . . . . . 82 F2
Uplands La BS31. . . . . . 81 F1
Uplands Rd
  Bristol BS16. . . . . .51 D3
  Saltford BS31. . . . . .82 F2
Uplands The BS48. . . . . 75 C8
Upper Bath Rd BS35. . . . 15 B8
Upper Belgrave Rd BS8 . 49 A2
Upper Belmont Rd BS7. 49 E3
Upper Berkeley Pl
  BS8. . . . . .142 B3
Upper Bloomfield Rd
  BA2. . . . . .101 D1
Upper Borough Walls
  BA1. . . . . .141 C2
Upper Bristol Rd
  Bath BA1. . . . . .101 D7
  Clutton BS39. . . . . .114 D3
  Weston-s-M BS22. . . . . .88 B1
Upper Byron Pl BS8 . . .142 B3
Upper Camden Pl BA1 141 C4
UPPER CANADA 106 C2
Upper Chapel La BS36. . 38 C7
Upper Cheltenham Pl
  BS6. . . . . .49 E1
Upper Church La
  Bristol BS2 . . . . .142 C3
  Hutton BS24. . . . . .105 D2
Upper Church Rd BS23 .87 D1
Upper Church St BA1 .141 B3
Upper Conham Vale
  BS15. . . . . .65 A5
Upper Cranbrook Rd
  BS6. . . . . .49 B4
Upper East Hayes BA1. .85 F3
UPPER EASTON. 64 B8
UPPER EASTVILLE 50 E3
Upper Farm Cl BA2 . . . .136 F4
Upper Furlong BA2 . . . .116 B3
Upper Green La BS40. . .111 B7
Upper Hedgemead Rd
  BA1. . . . . .141 B4
UPPER HILL. 2 E5
Upper Horfield Prim Sch
  BS7. . . . . .50 A8
Upper Kewstoke Rd
  BS23. . . . . .87 B1
UPPER KILCOTT 20 C5
UPPER KNOWLE 64 B2
Upper Lambridge St
  BA1. . . . . .85 C2
UPPER LANGFORD 109 C3
UPPER LANGRIDGE 84 B7
Upper Lansdown Mews
  BA1. . . . . .84 F1
UPPER LITTLETON 95 C6
Upper Maudlin St BS2 .143 A3
Upper Merryfield BA3 .139 E1
UPPER MORTON 8 E4
Upper Mount Pleasant
  BA2. . . . . .120 A4
Upper Myrtle Hill BS20 47 C4
Upper New Rd BS24. . . .126 A1
Upper Oldfield Pk
  BA2. . . . . .141 A1
Upper Perry Hill BS3. . . 63 C4
Upper Pitching BA3. . .138 D5
UPPER RADFORD
  133 B8
  Withy Mills BS39 . . . . . .133 B7
Upper Rd BS39. . . . . . . .130 E6
Upper Sandhurst Rd
  BS4. . . . . .64 D4
UPPER SOUNDWELL . . . 51 D3
Upper St
  Bristol BS4. . . . . .64 A4
  Dyrham SN14. . . . . .54 D4
Upper Stanton BS39. . . . 97 A2
UPPER STANTON
  DREW 97 B2
Upper Station Rd BS16 51 D4
Upper Stone Cl BS36. . . 38 C7
Upper Strode BS40. . . . .111 F7
UPPER SWAINSWICK. . . 85 B5
Upper Sydney St BS3. . . 63 B3
Upper Terr BS11 . . . . . . 34 B1
Upper Tockington Rd
  BS32. . . . . .14 A2
Upper Town La BS40 . . . 94 C8
Upper Wells St BS1. . . .142 C3
UPPER WESTON. 84 A3
UPPER WESTWOOD. . . .120 C4
UPPER WICK 5 A6
UPPER WRAXALL. 56 E2
Upper York St BS2 . . . .143 B4
Upton BS24. . . . . .105 A2
UPTON CHEYNEY 83 B8
Upton Cotts BS41 . . . . . 95 F8
Upton La BS41. . . . . 96 A8
Upton Rd BS3. . . . . 63 B4

Urchinwood La BS49 . . . 91 F4
Urfords Dr ⬛ BS16. . . . . 51 C6
Usk Ct ⬛ BS35. . . . . 15 C8

V

Valda Rd BS22 . . . . 88 C2
Vale Cres BS22. . . . . 89 C2
Vale Ct BS8. . . . . .142 A4
Vale End BS48. . . . . 59 D1
Vale Foundry La BS3 . . . 62 F2
Vale La BS3. . . . . 79 C8
Vale Mill Way BS24. . . .105 F8
Vale Orch GL13 . . . . 3 F3
Valentine Cl BS14. . . . . 80 B5
Valerian Cl BS11 . . . . . . 47 F6
Valerian St BS16. . . . . . 38 D1
Vale St BS4. . . . . 64 A4
Vale The BS16. . . . . 52 F6
Valetta Cl BS23. . . . . . .104 D3
Vale View BA3 . . . . .134 A2
Vale View Pl ⬛ BA1. . . . 85 B1
Vale View Terr BA1. . . . 85 F3
Valley Cl ⬛ BS48. . . . . . 59 E2
Valley Ct BS20. . . . . 44 E3
Valley Gdns
  Bristol BS16. . . . . .51 F8
  Nailsea BS48. . . . . .59 E2
Valley Rd
  Bristol, Bedminster Down
  BS13 . . . . .79 A8
  Bristol, Mangotsfield
  BS16. . . . . .52 A5
  Bristol, Warmley BS30. . .66 D6
  Clevedon BS21. . . . . .57 H5
  Leigh Woods BS8. . . . . . .62 C7
  Portishead BS20. . . . . . . .45 A2
Valley View
  Chilcompton BA3 . . . . . .138 D3
  Clutton BS39. . . . . .114 C3
Valley View Cl BA1. . . . 85 B3
Valley View Rd
  Bath BA1. . . . . .85 C3
  Paulton BS39. . . . . .132 E6
Valley Way Rd BS48. . . . 59 E3
Valley Wlk BA3 . . . . . . .133 D2
Valls The BS32. . . . . 36 F6
Valma Rocks BS5. . . . . . 65 A6
Valonia Cl BA2 . . . . . . .102 B7
Vanbrugh La BS16. . . . . 50 E7
Van Diemen's La BA1 . . 84 F2
Vandyck Ave BS31. . . . . 81 F6
Vane St BA2 . . . . .102 B7
Vantage Office Pk
  BS34. . . . . .37 A6
Varsity Way BS24 . . . . .106 B6
Vassall Ct BS16. . . . . . . 51 B5
Vassall Rd BS16. . . . . . . 51 B5
Vattingstone Ho BS35 . . 14 F5
Vattingstone La BS35. . . 14 F5
Vaughan Cl BS10. . . . . . 34 F3
Vauxhall Terr ⬛ BS3 . . . 63 A4
Vayre Cl BS37. . . . . 28 C1
Veale The BS24 . . . . . . .122 C6
Vee La BS40. . . . . 94 D8
Vellore La BA2 . . . . . . .102 C7
Velvet Bottom BS40. . . .127 E3
Venns Gate BS27. . . . . .126 A1
Ventnor Ave ⬛ BS5. . . . 64 F8
Ventnor Rd
  Bristol, Filton BS34 . . . . .36 B3
  Bristol, St George BS5. . .50 F1
Venton Ct ⬛ BS15. . . . . 65 B5
Venture The BS4 . . . . . . 63 E1
Venue The BS10. . . . . . . 35 C6
Venus La BS39. . . . . . . .114 E3
Venus St BS49 . . . . 91 E2
Vera Rd BS16. . . . . 50 F2
Verbena Way BS22. . . . . 89 A1
Vereland Rd BS24. . . . . .105 E3
Verlands BS49. . . . . 91 E5
Vernals La GL12. . . . . . . 11 C8
Vernham Gr BA2. . . . . .101 C1
Vernhamwood Cl BA2 101 C1
Vernon Cl BS31. . . . . . . 82 D3
Vernon La BS26. . . . . . .124 B3
Vernon Pk BA2 . . . . . . .101 C6
Vernon St ⬛ BS2 . . . . . . 63 F4
Vernon Terr BA2 . . . . . .101 C6
Vernslade BA1. . . . . 84 A2
Verrier Rd BS5. . . . . 64 C7
Verwood Dr BS30. . . . . . 66 C2
Vian End BS22 . . . . 88 F4
Via Traversus BS31. . . . . 81 F7
Viburnum Rd BS32. . . . . 24 D5
Vicarage Cl BS22. . . . . . 89 A3
Vicarage Cotts ⬛ BS16 51 D5
Vicarage Ct
  Bristol, Jefferies Hill
  BS15 . . . . .65 B5
  ⬛ Bristol, Russell Town
  BS5. . . . . .64 C7
Vicarage Gdns BA2. . . .134 B7
Vicarage La
  Barrow Gurney BS48. . . .77 C6
  Compton Bishop BS26 . .124 B3
  Compton Dando BS39 . . .98 D6
  Hillesley GL12 . . . . .19 D8
  Norton St Philip BA2 . . .136 E4

Vicarage La continued
  Olveston BS35. . . . . .14 B3
Vicarage Rd
  Bristol, Bishopsworth
  BS13 . . . . .79 A6
  Bristol, Hanham BS15 . . .65 B5
  Bristol, Moorfields BS5. . .64 C8
  Bristol, Southville BS3. . .63 B4
  Frampton Cotterell BS36 .38 C6
  Leigh Woods BS8. . . . . . .62 D6
  Pilning BS35. . . . . .22 C7
Vicars Cl BS16. . . . . 51 B4
Victor Ho BS34. . . . . 36 C7
Victoria Art Gall The★
  BA2. . . . . .141 C2
Victoria Ave BS5. . . . . . 64 C7
Victoria Bldgs BA2. . . .101 D6
Victoria Bridge Ct
  BA1. . . . . .141 A3
Victoria Bridge Rd BA1,
  BA2. . . . . .141 A2
Victoria Cl
  Bath BA2. . . . . .101 C5
  Portishead BS20. . . . . . . .45 D5
  Thornbury BS35. . . . . 8 B3
Victoria Cotts BA2. . . . .118 F7
Victoria Cres BS35. . . . . 22 A6
Victoria Ct
  ⬛ Bristol, Cotham BS6. . .49 D1
  Bristol, Redland BS6 . . . .49 A3
  Clevedon BS21. . . . . .57 E3
  Portishead BS20. . . . . . . .45 D5
Victoria Gdns
  Batheaston BA1. . . . . . . .85 F3
  ⬛ Bristol BS6. . . . . .49 D1
Victoria Gr BS3. . . . . . . 63 E4
Victoria Ho
  Bath BA1. . . . . .101 D8
  Keynsham BS31. . . . . . . .81 F4
Victoria Jubilee Homes
  BS40. . . . . .109 C6
Victoria Lodge BS22. . . . 88 E2
Victoria Par BS5 . . . . . . 64 C8
VICTORIA PARK. 142 B3
Victoria Park Bsns Ctr
  BA1. . . . . .101 D7
Victoria Park Com Inf Sch
  BS3. . . . . .63 B3
Victoria Park Com Jun Sch
  BS3. . . . . .63 E3
Victoria Park Ct BS3. . . 63 F3
Victoria Pk
  Bristol, Fishponds BS16. .51 A5
  Bristol, Kingswood BS15 .51 D1
  Weston-s-M BS23. . . . . . .87 D1
Victoria Pl
  Bath, Combe Down
  BA2. . . . . .102 C1
  ⬛ Bath, Lambridge BA1 . .85 C3
  Bristol BS3. . . . . .63 C3
  Paulton BS39. . . . . .132 D5
  Weston-s-M BS23. . . . . .104 D8
Victoria Quadrant
  BS23. . . . . .104 E8
Victoria Rd
  Avonmouth BS11. . . . . . .47 B7
  ⬛ Bath BA2 . . . . .101 D6
  Bristol, Hanham BS15 . . .65 C5
  Bristol, St Philip's Marsh
  BS2 . . . . .64 A5
  Bristol, Warmley BS30. . .66 D5
  Clevedon BS21. . . . . .57 E3
  Saltford BS31. . . . . .82 E3
Victoria Rooms★ BS8 .142 B3
Victoria Sq
  Bristol BS8. . . . . .142 A3
  Portishead BS20. . . . . . . .45 D5
  Weston-s-M BS23. . . . . .104 D7
Victoria St
  Bristol BS1. . . . . .143 B2
  Bristol, Staple Hill BS16 .51 D5
Victoria Terr
  Bath BA2. . . . . .101 D6
  ⬛ Bristol, Clifton BS8. . . .62 F6
  Bristol, St Philip's Marsh
  BS2 . . . . .64 B5
  Paulton BS39. . . . . .132 D5
Victoria Wlk BS6. . . . . . 49 D1
Victor Rd BS3. . . . . 63 C3
Victor St
  ⬛ Bristol, Russell Town
  BS5. . . . . .64 B6
  Bristol, St Philip's Marsh
  BS2. . . . . .64 A4
Vigor Rd BS13. . . . . 79 B5
Village Cl BS37. . . . . . . 27 D1
Village Farm BS35. . . . . 14 A6
Village Rd BA2. . . . . . . .100 C6
Village The BS16. . . . . . 52 C7
Villa Rosa ⬛ BS23. . . . . 87 C1
Villice La BS40. . . . . . . .129 A7
Villiers Rd BS5. . . . . 50 B1
Vilner La BS35. . . . . 15 B7
Vimpany Cl BS10. . . . . . 34 F3
Vimpennys La BS35. . . . 22 E1
Vincent Cl BS11. . . . . . . 34 C2
Vincent Ct ⬛ BS16. . . . . 51 D3
Vine Gdns BS22. . . . . . . 89 A2
Viner's La GL9 . . . . 43 B5

Vinery The BS25. . . . . . .125 A7
Vineyard La GL12 . . . . . 11 F5
Vineyards BA1. . . . . . . .141 C3
Vining Wlk ⬛ BS5 . . . . . 64 B8
VINNEY GREEN 52 A7
Vinney La BS37. . . . . . . 28 F8
Vinny Ave BS16. . . . . . . 52 A7
Vintery Leys BS9. . . . . . 49 B7
Viola Way BS16. . . . . . . 52 D7
Virginia Cl BS37. . . . . . 28 A1
Vivian St BS3. . . . . 63 D3
Vivien Ave BA3. . . . . . . .133 A2
Vowell Cl BS13. . . . . 79 B4
Vowles Cl BS48 . . . . 60 A3
Voyager Cl BS34. . . . . . 37 A4
Vulcan Ho BA2. . . . . . . .141 C3
Vynes Cl BS48. . . . . 60 A1
Vynes Ind Est BS48. . . . 60 A3
Vynes Way BS48. . . . . . 60 A1
Vyvyan Rd BS8. . . . . . . .142 A3
Vyvyan Terr BS8. . . . . . .142 A3

W

Wadehurst Ind Pk BS2 .64 A7
Wade Rd BS37. . . . . 27 A3
Wades Rd BS34. . . . . . . 36 B3
Wade St BS2. . . . . .143 C3
Wadham Dr BS16. . . . . . 37 B1
Wadham Gr BS16 . . . . . 52 B5
Wadham St BS23. . . . . .104 D8
Wagtail Gdns BS22. . . . .105 E8
Wainblade Ct ⬛ BS37. . 27 F5
Wainbridge Cres BS35. . 22 D7
Wainbrook Dr BS5. . . . . 50 D2
Wains Cl ⬛ BS21. . . . . . 57 E2
Wainwright Cl ⬛ BS22. 89 B4
Waits Cl BS29. . . . . .106 F3
Wakedean Gdns BS49. . . 74 A1
Wakeford Rd ⬛ BS16. . . 52 A7
Wakeford Way BS30. . . . 66 D7
Wakehurst Gdns
  BS24. . . . . .105 E7
Walcot Bldgs
  Bath BA1. . . . . .102 B8
  Bath BA1. . . . . .141 C4
  ⬛ Bathwick BA2. . . . . . .102 B8
Walcot Gate BA1. . . . . .141 C4
Walcot Ho BA1 . . . . . . .141 C4
Walcot Par BA1. . . . . . .141 C4
Walcot St BA1. . . . . . . .141 C3
Walcot Terr BA1. . . . . . .141 C4
Waldegrave Rd BA1. . . . 84 E1
Waldegrave Terr BA3. . .134 A3
Walden Rd BS31. . . . . . . 82 A4
Walford Ave BS22. . . . . 89 C3
Waling La BA2. . . . . . . .100 D6
Walker Cl
  Bristol, Downend BS16 . .52 A7
  Bristol, Upper Easton
  BS5. . . . . .64 B8
Walker Ct BS16. . . . . . . 51 F5
Walkers Dr BS24. . . . . . .105 F7
Walker St BS2. . . . . .142 C4
Walker Way BS35. . . . . . 15 B7
Walk Mill La GL12. . . . . 11 F4
Walk The GL12. . . . . 11 F5
WALLACE. 129 E3
Wallace La BS40. . . . . . .129 E3
Wallace Rd BA1. . . . . . . 85 B1
Wallcroft Ho BS6. . . . . . 49 A3
Wallenge Cl BS39. . . . . .132 F6
Wallenge Dr BS39. . . . . .132 F6
Waller Gdns BA1. . . . . . 84 E4
Walley La BS40. . . . . . . .113 B7
Wallflower Cl BS16. . . . 52 D7
Wall Gn BS26. . . . . .125 C1
Wallingford Rd BS4. . . . 79 D7
Walliscote Ave BS9 . . . . 49 C6
Walliscote Grove Rd ⬛
  BS23. . . . . .104 E7
Walliscote Prim Sch
  BS23. . . . . .104 E7
Walliscote Rd
  Bristol BS9. . . . . .49 C6
  Weston-s-M BS23. . . . . .104 D6
Walliscote Rd S BS23. .104 D4
Wallis Est BS2. . . . . 49 F3
Wallscourt Rd BS34. . . . 36 B2
Wallscourt Rd S BS34. . 36 B1
Wallsend La SN14. . . . . 55 C5
Wallshut Wood BS7. . . . 50 C8
Wally Court Rd BS40. . . .112 E8
Walmsley Terr ⬛ BA1. . 85 B1
Walnut Ave BS37. . . . . . 28 A2
Walnut Bldgs BA3. . . . . .134 A3
Walnut Cl
  Axbridge BS26. . . . . . . .125 C1
  Bristol BS15. . . . . .51 F1
  Easton-in-G BS20. . . . . . .47 A3
  Frampton Cotterell BS36 38 C6
  Keynsham BS31. . . . . . . .81 C4
  Nailsea BS48. . . . . .75 E8
  Thornbury BS35. . . . . 8 D1
  Weston-s-M BS24. . . . . .105 B2
Walnut Cres BS15. . . . . 65 F8

Walnut Dr
  Bath BA2. . . . . .101 E4
  Colerne SN14. . . . . .70 F6
Walnut La BS15. . . . . . . 66 A8
Walnut Tree Cl
  Almondsbury BS32. . . . . .24 A5
  Ubley BS40. . . . . .111 D1
Walnut Tree Ct BS49. . . 91 D4
Walnut Way ⬛ BS16. . . 52 C7
Walnut Wlk
  Bristol BS13. . . . . .79 A6
  Keynsham BS31. . . . . . . .81 C4
Walsh Ave BS14. . . . . . . 80 A7
Walsh Cl BS24 . . . . .105 B2
Walshe Ave BS37. . . . . . 28 C1
Walsingham Rd BS6. . . . 49 E2
Walter Rd BS36. . . . . . . 38 B6
Walter St BS3. . . . . 63 A4
Waltham End BS24. . . . .106 A4
Walton BS24. . . . . .105 A2
Walton Ave BS4. . . . . . . 64 D5
Walton Bay House Park
  Homes BS21. . . . . .44 B1
Walton Cl
  Bristol BS30. . . . . .66 C1
  Keynsham BS31. . . . . . . .81 D4
Walton Cres BS40. . . . . . 94 F8
Walton Cross BS37. . . . . 58 B7
Walton Heath BS37 . . . . 27 F1
WALTON IN GORDANO. . 58 B7
Walton Rd
  Bristol BS11. . . . . .47 D6
  Clevedon BS21. . . . . .57 H4
Walton Rise BS9. . . . . . 49 A7
WALTON ST MARY 57 G5
Walton St
  Bristol BS5. . . . . .50 B1
  Portishead BS20. . . . . . . .44 A1
Walton in G BS21. . . . . . 58 A8
Walwyn Cl BA2 . . . . . . .101 A6
Walwyn Gdns BS13. . . . 79 C3
Wansbeck Rd BS31. . . . . 82 A4
Wansbrough Rd BS22. . . 89 B6
Wanscow Wlk BS9 . . . . 49 B6
Wansdyke Bsns Ctr
  BA2. . . . . .101 D4
Wansdyke Ct BS14. . . . . 80 B5
Wansdyke Prim Sch
  BS14. . . . . .79 F4
Wansdyke Rd BA2. . . . .101 D1
Wansdyke Way BS14 . . . 80 D3
Wansdyke Workshops
  Keynsham BS31. . . . . . . .82 A6
  Peasedown St John
  BA2. . . . . .134 D6
WAPLEY 39 E4
Wapley Hill BS37. . . . . . 39 E4
Wapley Rank BS37. . . . . 39 D5
Wapley Rd BS37. . . . . . . 40 B3
Wapping Rd BS1. . . . . . .143 A1
Warbler Cl ⬛ BA3. . . . . .139 B8
Warden Rd BS3. . . . . . . 63 C4
Wardour Rd BS4. . . . . . . 79 D8
Ware Ct BS36. . . . . 37 D5
Wareham Cl BS48. . . . . . 59 D1
Warend Hill GL11 . . . . . 5 F6
Waring Ho BS1. . . . . . . .143 A1
WARLEIGH 103 C6
Warleigh Dr BA1. . . . . . 86 A3
Warleigh La BA1. . . . . . .103 C5
Warleigh Manor BA1. . .103 C6
Warleys La BS24 . . . . . . 89 C1
Warman Cl BS14. . . . . . 80 F6
Warman Rd BS14 . . . . . 80 F6
Warmington Rd BS14. . . 80 C8
Warminster Rd
  Bristol BS2. . . . . .50 A2
  Claverton BA2, BA3. . . . .103 B5
WARMLEY 66 B7
WARMLEY HILL. 65 E8
Warmley Park Sch
  BS30. . . . . .66 B7
WARMLEY TOWER 66 B6
Warne Pk BS23. . . . . . . .105 A6
Warner Cl
  Bristol BS15. . . . . .65 F6
  Cleeve BS49. . . . . .92 A7
Warne Rd BS23 . . . . . . .105 A6
Warns The BS30. . . . . . . 66 A4
Warren Cl
  Bristol BS32. . . . . .24 D3
  Hutton BS24. . . . . .105 D2
Warren Croft GL11. . . . . 5 E4
Warren Gdns BS14. . . . . 80 F5
Warren La BS41. . . . . . . 77 E8
Warren Rd BS34. . . . . . . 36 B3
Warren's Cl BS27 . . . . . .126 B1
Warrens Hill BS27 . . . . .126 B1
Warrens Hill Rd
  BS27. . . . . .126 D4
Warren Way BS37. . . . . . 27 E3
Warrilow Cl BS22. . . . . . 89 B5
Warrington Rd BS4. . . . 64 D2
Warry Cl BS48. . . . . 60 B2
Warth La BS22. . . . . 89 A8
Warwick Ave ⬛ BS5. . . . 50 B1

Warwick Cl
Bristol BS30.........66 B2
Weston-s-M BS22.....105 C8
Warwick Gdns BS39...114 D3
Warwick Pl BS35.......8 A1
Warwick Rd
3 Bath BA1...........101 B7
Bristol, Baptist Mills BS5 50 B1
Bristol, Redland BS6...49 B1
Keynsham BS31........81 D4
Washingpool Hill BS35.14 E1
Washingpool Hill Rd
BS32................14 D2
Washingpool La BS11..33 F7
Washing Pound La
Bristol BS14..........80 B4
Nailsea BS48..........59 B4
Washington Ave BS5...50 C1
Watch Elm Cl BS32....36 E6
Watch House Pl BS20..45 E7
Watch House Rd BS20..47 D4
Watchill Ave BS13......78 F6
Watchill Cl BS13.......78 F6
Watcombe Cl BS22.....88 E1
Watercress Rd BS5.....49 F3
Waterbridge Rd BS13..78 F4
Watercress Cl BS48....60 B2
Waterdale Cl BS9......49 C7
Waterdale Gdns BS9...49 C7
Waterford Cl BS35.....15 D8
Waterford Pk BA3.....133 E1
Waterford Rd BS9......49 B6
Waterfront Ho BA2....141 B1
Waterhouse La BA2...119 F8
Water La
Bristol BS1...........143 B2
Bristol, Hanham Green
BS15...............65 B2
Bristol, Upper Knowle
BS4................64 D2
Bristol, Windmill Hill BS3. 63 F3
Paulton BA3, BS39....133 A4
Pill BS20.............47 C4
Waterloo Bldgs **4**
BA2................101 B6
Waterloo Ho BS20.....47 D5
Waterloo Pl **19** BS2..143 C3
Waterloo Rd
Bristol BS2...........143 C3
Radstock BA3.........134 A2
Waterloo St
Bristol BS2...........143 C3
10 Bristol, Clifton BS8...62 F7
Weston-s-M BS23.....104 E8
Watermead Cl **13** BA1.141 B2
Watermill Cl GL12......9 E9
Watermore Cl BS36....38 C7
Watermore Gdns BS36.38 C8
Watermore Prim Sch
BS36................38 D8
Waters Edge BS20.....45 E7
Watershed Media Ctr★
BS1................143 A2
WATERSIDE.........133 E1
Waterside Cres BA3...133 D1
Waterside Dr BS32.....24 A1
Waterside La BA3......140 A6
Waterside Pk BS20....44 D4
Waterside Rd BA3.....133 D1
Waterside Way BA3...139 D8
Water's La BS9........49 A7
Waters Rd BS15.......65 C8
Water St BS40........129 F4
Watery La
Bath BA2............101 A6
Doynton BS30.........68 A8
Marshfield SN14......69 F6
Nailsea BS48..........59 B2
Stratton-on-t-F BA3...139 A3
Winford BS40..........95 B4
Wathen Rd BS6........49 F3
Watkins Yd BS9........49 A8
WATLEY'S END.......37 F7
Watley's End Rd BS36..37 F7
Watling Way BS11.....47 D7
Watson Ave BS4.......64 D4
Watson's Rd BS30.....65 F3
Watters Cl BS36.......38 D6
Wavell Cl BS37........27 D3
Waveney Rd BS31.....82 A3
Wavering Down Rise
BS26...............125 A3
Waverley Ho BS1......142 C1
Waverley Rd
Backwell BS48........76 A7
Bristol, Cotham BS6...49 C1
Bristol, Shirehampton
BS11...............47 E6
Weston-s-M BS23.....104 F4
Yate BS37............27 B2
Waverley St **9** BS5....50 A1
Waverly Ct BS49......91 D3
Wayacre Dro BS24....121 E6
Waycroft Prim Sch
BS14...............80 E5

Wayfarer Cl BS23.....105 B4
Wayfarer Rd BS10......35 B6
Wayfield Gdns BA1.....85 F4
Wayford Cl BS31.......82 A3
Wayland Ct **7** BS16....51 A4
Wayland Rd BS22......88 E3
Wayleaze
Frampton Cotterell
BS36................38 D7
Wapley BS37..........39 F3
Wayside BS22.........88 D2
Wayside Cl BS36.......38 B7
Wayside Dr BS21.......57 G5
WAY WICK..........89 E1
WCA Ho BS1..........143 A2
Weal Terr BA1.........84 B2
Weal The BA1.........84 C2
Weare Ct BS1.........142 A1
Weatherley Dr BS20...44 F3
Weatherly Ave BA2...101 D2
Weavers Cl GL12......11 F4
Weavers La BS37.......27 B6
Weavers Orch BA2....118 D1
Weavers Way BS37.....38 E2
Webb Cres BS37.......27 E5
WEBBINGTON........123 E4
Webbington Rd BS26..124 C3
Webbs Heath BS30....66 E8
WEBB'S HEATH.......66 E8
Webbs Mead BS40....112 D8
Webbs Wood BS32.....36 F7
Webbs Wood Rd BS32..36 F7
Webb St BS5..........64 A8
Wedgewood Rd BS16...37 D1
Wedgwood Cl BS14....80 B5
Wedgwood Rd BS14...101 A5
Wedlock Way BS3......62 F3
Wedmore Cl
Bath BA2............101 A3
Bristol BS15..........65 F7
Weston-s-M BS23....104 F2
Wedmore Pk BA2.....101 A3
Wedmore Rd
Clevedon BS21........57 D1
Nailsea BS48..........75 E8
Saltford BS31.........82 D4
Wedmore Vale BS3....63 E2
Weedon Cl BS5........50 A2
Weekesley La BA2....116 D1
Weetwood Rd BS49....91 E5
Weight Rd **2** BS5......64 C7
Weind The BS22.......88 D2
Weir La
Abbots Leigh BS8......61 F5
Marshfield SN14......69 F8
Weir Rd BS49.........91 E3
Welland Rd BS31......81 F4
Wellard Cl **1** BS22....89 B4
Well Cl
Long Ashton BS41.....62 B1
Weston-s-M BS24....105 B2
Winscombe BS25.....125 A8
Wellesley Prim Sch
BS37................39 D6
Wellgarth Ct BS4.....64 A2
Wellgarth Rd BS4.....64 A2
Wellgarth Wlk BS4....64 A2
Well House Cl BS9.....48 E3
Wellington Ave BS6...49 E1
Wellington Bldgs BA1..84 B2
Wellington Cres BS7...49 E6
Wellington Ct
11 Bristol BS6.......49 E1
Clevedon BS21........57 E5
Wellington Dr
Bristol BS9...........49 D6
Yate BS37............27 B2
Wellington Hill BS7...49 E6
Wellington Hill W BS9..49 D7
Wellington La BS6.....49 E1
Wellington Mews BS11 47 D5
Wellington Pk BS8.....49 A2
Wellington Pl
Bristol BS16..........37 B1
Weston-s-M BS23....104 D7
Wellington Rd
Bristol BS2...........143 C4
Bristol, Kingswood BS15 51 E2
Yate BS37............27 E3
Wellington Terr
20 Bristol BS8........62 F6
Clevedon BS21........57 F5
Wellington Wlk BS10..49 C7
Well La
Badminton GL9........30 D5
Banwell BS29.........106 E3
Yatton BS49..........91 C8
WELLOW............118 D1
Wellow Brook Ct BA3.133 B3
Wellow Brook Mdw
BA3................133 B2
Wellow La
Hinton Charterhouse
BA2................119 D1
Norton St Philip BA2..136 D5
Peasedown St John
BA2................134 C6
Shoscombe BA2.....134 E6

Wellow Mead BA2.....134 B7
Wellow Rd BA2........135 B8
Wellow Tyning BA2...134 D7
Well Pk BS49..........91 E4
Wells Cl
Bristol BS14..........80 C5
Nailsea BS48..........60 B1
Wellsea Gr BS23......105 B7
Wells Rd
Bath BA2............141 B1
Bristol, Hengrove BS14.80 C7
Bristol, Upper Knowle
BS4................64 B2
Chilcompton BA3.....138 F4
Clevedon BS21........57 F1
Corston BA2..........100 B7
Dundry BS40, BS41...95 F7
Hallatrow BS39......132 B7
Norton St Philip BA2,
BA3................136 C3
Radstock BA3........133 D1
Wells Sq BA3.........133 D1
Wells St BS3..........63 A4
Wellstead Ave BS37...27 C1
Wellsway BA2........101 F3
Wellsway Cl BA2......101 D1
Wellsway Pk BA2.....118 D8
Wellsway Rd BS31.....81 F3
Wellsway Sch BS31....82 A5
Well The BS9..........48 E3
Welsford Ave BS16....50 D4
Welsford Rd BS16.....50 C4
Welsh Back BS1.......143 A2
WELTON.............133 B2
Welton Gr BA3........133 B3
WELTON HOLLOW....133 D2
Welton Prim Sch BA3.133 C1
Welton Rd BA3........133 C2
Welton Vale BA3......133 B3
Welton Wlk BS15......51 C2
Wemberham Cres BS49 74 A1
Wemberham La BS49..90 E8
Wenmore Cl BS16.....37 D1
Wentforth Dr **2** BS15..51 C2
Wentwood Dr BS24...105 A1
Wentworth
Bristol BS30..........66 A6
Yate BS37............27 E1
Wentworth Cl BS22....89 A3
Wentworth Rd BS7....49 D3
Wescott Gr BS11......34 C2
Wesley Ave
Bristol BS15..........65 D5
Radstock BA3........133 C1
Wesley Cl
6 Bristol, Upper Soundwell
BS16...............51 D3
Bristol, Whitehall BS5..50 B1
Wesley Ct BS23.......104 F8
Wesley Dr BS22.......89 A3
Wesley Hill BS15......51 D1
Wesley La BS30.......66 B5
Wesley Pl BS8.........49 A2
Wesley Rd
Bristol BS7...........49 E4
Radstock BA3........133 D1
Wesley St BS3.........63 C3
Wessex Ave BS7......49 F7
Wessex Ct BS7........49 F7
Wessex Ho **10** BS2...143 C3
Wessex Rd BS24......105 B2
Westacre Cl BS10.....35 A2
West Ave BA2.........101 C5
Westaway Cl BS49....91 C7
Westaway Pk BS49....91 D7
Westbourne Ave
Clevedon BS21........57 D2
Keynsham BS31.......81 E5
Westbourne Cl **2** BS16 52 A7
Westbourne Cres BS21.57 D2
Westbourne Ct BS5....64 B8
Westbourne Gr **15** BS3.63 C3
Westbourne Ho BA2..141 C2
Westbourne Pl BS8....142 B3
Westbourne Rd
Bristol, Downend BS16..51 F8
8 Bristol, Upper Easton
BS5................64 B8
Westbourne Terr BS16.51 B7
West Broadway BS9...49 D6
Westbrooke Ct BS1...142 A1
Westbrook Pk BA1....84 A2
Westbrook Rd
Bristol BS4...........80 D4
Weston-s-M BS22.....88 D1
Westbury Court Rd BS9 49 A7
Westbury Cres BS23..104 F2
Westbury Ct BS9......49 A7
Westbury Hill BS9.....49 A7
Westbury La BS9......48 C7
Westbury Mews **6** BS9 49 A7
WESTBURY ON TRYM.48 F7
Westbury-on-Trym CE
Prim Sch BS9........49 A8
WESTBURY PARK....49 A3
Westbury Park Prim Sch
BS6................49 B3
Westbury Pk BS6......49 A4
Westbury Rd BS6......49 A4

Westbury Terr BA2....117 E5
Westbury View BA2...134 E8
West Cl BA2..........101 A5
West Coombe BS9.....48 D6
West Country Water Pk★
BS36................24 F2
Westcourt Dr BS30....66 B4
West Croft
Blagdon BS40.........110 C2
Bristol BS9...........49 C7
Clevedon BS21........57 D2
West Ct BS20.........45 D4
West Dene BS9........48 E6
West Dundry La BS41..78 E2
WESTEND............7 B6
WEST END
Blagdon.............110 C3
Clevedon............57 D2
Nailsea..............74 F7
Wickwar.............17 E5
West End
Bristol BS3..........142 C1
Bristol, Kingsdown BS2 143 A4
Oldbury-on-S BS35....7 C6
West End Farm Cvn Pk
BS24................105 E4
Westend La BS35......7 B6
West End La BS48.....75 A8
Westend Rd GL12......17 E5
West End Trad Est
BS48................59 B1
Westering Cl BS16.....52 A5
WESTERLEIGH.......39 B4
Westerleigh Bsns Pk
BS37................27 B1
WESTERLEIGH HILL..39 D3
Westerleigh Rd
Bath BA2............102 B1
Bristol BS16..........51 F6
Clevedon BS21........57 D2
Henfield BS36.........38 D2
Pucklechurch BS16....53 C7
Westerleigh BS36, BS37 39 B6
Yate BS37............39 C8
Western App Distribution
Pk BS35.............22 B4
Western Approach
Distribution Pk BS35..22 C4
Western Ave BS36.....26 A1
Western Ct
Bristol BS34..........37 A4
Clevedon BS21........57 F3
Western Dr BS14......79 F6
Western Grange BS34..36 A3
Western La BS40.....129 C3
Western Rd BS7.......49 E6
Westex Ho BS23......105 B5
WESTFIELD..........139 C8
Westfield BS21........73 D8
West Field **2** BS34....35 F7
Westfield Cl
Backwell BS48........76 A6
Bath BA2............101 E3
Bristol BS15..........65 D5
Keynsham BS31.......81 C5
Weston-s-M BS23....104 D2
Westfield Cres BS29..107 A3
Westfield Dr BS48.....76 A6
Westfield Ho
Bath BA2............101 E3
Stoke Bishop BS9.....48 F5
Westfield Ind & Trad Est
BA3................139 C7
Westfield La BS34.....36 E3
Westfield Pk
Bath BA1............101 A7
Bristol BS6...........49 B1
Westfield Pk S BA1...101 A7
Westfield Pl BS8......62 F7
Westfield Prim Sch
BA3................139 C8
Westfield Rd
Backwell BS48........76 A6
Banwell BS29........107 A3
Bristol BS9...........49 A8
Weston-s-M BS23....104 D2
Westfield Terr BA3...133 D1
Westfield Way BS32..24 D2
West Garston BS29...107 A3
Westgate BS1.........142 B1
Westgate Bldgs BA1..141 B2
Westgate St BA1......141 B2
West Gr BS6..........49 F1
Westhall Rd BA1......101 D7
WEST HARPTREE....129 E6
West Harptree Rd
BS40...............129 C5
Westhaven Cl BS48....76 A6
Westhaven Sch BS23.104 D2
West Hay Rd BS40....92 C3
WEST HEWISH.......90 A5
WEST HILL
Nailsea..............60 A5
Portishead............45 A5
West Hill
Nailsea BS48.........60 A5
Portishead BS20......45 B5
West Hill Ct BS20.....45 C6

WEST HILL GARDENS .133 E5
Westhill Gdns BS20....45 C5
West Hill Gdns
Radstock BA3........133 D1
Radstock BA3.........133 D1
West Hill Rd BA3......133 D1
WEST KINGTON......56 F7
West La BS40.........94 C8
Westland Ave BS30....66 C4
Westland Distribution Pk
BS24................105 B3
West Lea Rd BA1......84 A1
West Leaze Pl BS32...36 E3
Westleigh Cl
Bristol BS10..........35 E1
Yate BS37............27 C1
Westleigh Pl BS37.....27 C1
West Leigh Inf Sch
BS48................76 A6
Westleigh Pk BS14....80 B8
Westleigh Rd BS10....35 E1
West Links BS23......104 D2
West Links Cl BS22....88 B3
West Littleton Rd
Marshfield SN14......69 F8
West Littleton SN14...55 E2
West Mall BS8.........62 F7
Westmark Way BS22..89 A4
Westmarsh BS35.......7 B5
Westmarsh La BS35....7 B5
Westmead BA3.......138 D2
Westmead Gdns BA1...84 A2
Westmead Ho BS11....33 B1
Westmead Rd BS5.....65 B3
Westminster Cl **1** BS9.49 A7
Westminster Rd BS5...64 D8
Westmoreland Dr
BA2................141 A2
Westmoreland Rd
Bath BA2............141 A1
Bristol BS6...........49 B3
Westmoreland St BA2 141 A2
Westmoreland Station Rd
BA2................141 A1
Westmorland Ho BS6..49 A3
Westmorland Terr
BS37................41 D7
WESTON.............84 B1
Weston All Saints CE Prim
Sch BA1.............84 A2
Weston Ave **4** BS5....64 D7
Weston Bsns Pk BS24.105 E5
Weston Cl BS9........48 C7
Weston Coll BS48.....59 E2
Weston College BS23.104 F2
Weston Coll Univ Campus
BS23................104 F2
Weston Coll (Westcliff)
BS23................87 B1
Weston Cres BS7......49 E6
Weston Ct BS24......105 B3
Weston Dro BS20......58 F8
Weston Euro Pk BS24.105 B4
Weston Express Bsns Pk
BS22................105 C6
Weston Farm La BA1..84 C2
Weston Gateway Tourist
Pk BS24.............89 C7
Weston General Hospl
BS23................104 E2
Westonia BS22........88 E2
Westonian Ct BS9.....48 C4
Weston Ind Est BS24.105 E6
WESTON IN GORDANO .44 A4
Weston La
Bath BA1............101 C8
Christon BS26........123 C7
Weston Lock Ret BA2.101 C6
Weston Lodge
Bath BA1............84 A2
Weston-s-M BS23....104 E8
Weston Milton Sta
BS22...............105 C7
Weston Miniature Rly★
BS23................104 D5
WESTON PARK.......84 C1
Weston Park Ct BA1...84 C1
Weston Pk BA1........84 C1
Weston Pk E BA1......84 C1
Weston Pk W BA1.....84 C1
Weston Rd
Bath BA1............101 D8
Brean TA8...........121 A5
Congresbury BS49....91 B3
Failand BS8..........61 C3
Long Ashton BS41.....77 D8
Weston Ret Pk BS23.105 A6
Westons Brake BS16..38 A1
Westons Hill Dr BS16..38 A1
WESTON-SUPER-
MARE..............104 B8
Weston-Super-Mare Sta
BS23................104 E7
Westons Way BS15....65 F7
Weston Way BS24....105 F2
Weston Wood Rd BS20.45 C3
Westover Cl BS9......34 F1
Westover Dr BS9......35 A1
Westover Gdns BS9...48 F8

Westover Rd
Bristol BS9 35 A1
Bristol BS9 48 F8
Westover Rise BS9 35 A1
West Par BS9 48 C7
West Park Rd BS16 51 E5
West Pk BS8 142 B4
West Point Row BS32 24 C3
Westpoint Trad Est
BS15 65 D7
West Priory Cl BS9 49 A7
West Rd
Lympsham BS24 122 B1
Midsomer Norton BA3 133 A3
Yatton BS49 91 B7
West Ridge BS36 38 C7
West Rocke Ave BS9 48 D6
West Rolstone Rd BS24 90 A1
West Shrubbery 5 BS6 49 B2
West St
Axbridge BS26 125 B2
Banwell BS29 107 B3
Bristol BS2 143 C3
Bristol, Bedminster BS3 63 C3
2 Bristol, Kingswood
BS15 65 D8
Bristol, Oldland Common
BS30 66 C4
Tytherington GL12 16 B5
Weston-s-M BS23 104 D8
West Terr BA2 137 C1
WEST TOWN
Backwell 75 F5
Ubley 111 B6
West Town Ave BS4 64 D1
West Town Dr 2 BS4 64 D1
West Town Gr BS4 80 D8
West Town La BS4,
BS14 64 D1
West Town Lane Prim Sch
BS4 64 C1
West Town Pk BS4 64 D1
West Town Rd
Backwell BS48 76 A5
Bristol BS11 47 C7
West Tyning BA2 99 B1
Westview BS39 132 C5
West View
Alveston BS35 14 F4
Bristol BS16 52 A6
Westview Orch BA2 120 B5
West View Rd
Batheaston BA1 86 A3
Bristol BS3 63 B3
Keynsham BS31 81 E5
Westward BS41 62 B2
Westward Cl BS40 92 D2
Westward Dr BS20 47 C4
Westward Gdns BS41 62 B2
Westward Rd BS13 78 F7
Westway BS48 59 E2
West Way
Bristol BS10, BS34 35 E4
Clevedon BS21 57 E3
Westway Farm BS39 113 C3
WEST WICK 89 C1
West Wick BS24 89 C1
West Wick Rdbt BS22,
BS24 106 B8
West Wlk BS37 27 E1
WESTWOOD 120 E3
Westwood BA2 102 E6
Westwood Ave BS39 115 C2
Westwood Cl 2 BS22 88 F2
Westwood Cres BS4 64 D5
Westwood Rd BS4 80 D8
Westwoods BA1 86 B3
Westwood-with-Iford
Prim Sch BA15 120 F3
Wetherby Ct BS16 37 F1
Wetherby Gr 1 BS16 37 F1
Wetherell Pl BS8 142 B3
Wetlands La BS20 45 C3
Wexford Rd BS4 79 D8
Weymouth Ct BA1 102 B8
Weymouth Rd BS3 63 D2
Weymouth St BA1 102 B8
Wharfedale BS35 15 D8
Wharf La BS20 46 B5
Wharf Rd
5 Bristol BS16 50 F4
Haywood Village BS24 105 B4
Wharfside BS24 121 E3
Wharnecliffe Cl BS14 80 B5
Wharnecliffe Gdns
BS14 80 B5
Whartons 8 BS4 64 D1
Whatley Ct 9 BS8 49 B1
Whatley Rd BS8 49 B1
Wheatear Rd BS49 73 F2
Wheatfield Dr
Bristol BS32 24 D1
Weston-s-M BS22 89 A5
Wheatfield Prim Sch
BS32 24 D1
Wheathill Cl BS31 81 D5
Wheatsheaf La BA2 99 C6
Wheelers Cl BA3 133 D2
Wheelers Dr BA3 133 C2
WHEELER'S HILL 133 C2
Wheelers Patch BS16 52 B5
Wheelers Rd BA3 133 D2
Whinchat Gdns BS16 50 F6
Whippington Ct BS1 143 B3
Whistle Rd BS16 52 B2
Whistley La BS40 129 F6
Whitaker Rd BA2 102 A2
Whitby Rd BS4 64 C4
WHITCHURCH 80 D4
Whitchurch District Ctr
BS14 80 A5
Whitchurch La
Bristol BS14 79 E5
Bristol, Bishopsworth
BS13 79 B5
Bristol, Hartcliffe BS13 79 C5
Dundry BS41 79 C1
Whitchurch Prim Sch
BS14 80 C4
Whitchurch Rd BS13 79 A6
Whitebeam Ct BS5 64 E8
Whitebeam Ho 7
BS16 51 C6
Whitebridge Gdns
BS35 15 C7
Whitebrook La BA2 134 A8
Whitecroft Way BS15 66 A7
WHITE CROSS
Bishop Sutton 113 E1
Hallatrow 131 F6
White Cross BS39 131 F6
Whitecross Ave BS14 80 C6
White Cross Gate
BS39 131 F6
Whitecross La BS29 107 A4
Whitecross Rd
East Harptree BS40 129 F4
Weston-s-M BS23 104 E6
Whitefield Ave
Bristol, Hanham BS15 65 D5
Bristol, Speedwell BS5 51 A1
Whitefield Cl
Batheaston BA1 86 B4
7 Bristol BS16 51 D3
Whitefield Fishponds
Com Sch BS16 50 F4
Whitefield Rd BS5 51 A2
Whitefields BS37 28 C1
Whitegate Cl BS24 122 B6
Whitegates BS36 37 D6
WHITEHALL 50 D1
Whitehall Ave BS5 50 E1
Whitehall Gdns BS5 50 D1
Whitehall Prim Sch
BS5 50 D1
Whitehall Rd BS5 64 C8
Whitehall Trad Est 4
BS5 64 C8
WHITE HILL 134 F6
White Hill BA2 134 F6
Whitehorn Vale BS10 35 C3
White Horse Rd BA15 120 E7
White House Bsns Ctr The
BS15 65 D7
Whitehouse Ctr (PRU)
BS13 79 C5
Whitehouse La
Bristol BS3 63 D4
Litton BA3 130 D3
Pilning BS35 22 C7
Wraxall BS48 60 A6
White House La BS26 123 A3
Whitehouse Pl BS3 63 E4
Whitehouse Rd BS49 91 F8
Whitehouse St BS3 63 E4
Whiteladies Rd BS8 142 B4
Whitelands Hill BA3 134 B3
Whiteleaze BS10 49 C8
White Lodge Pk BS20 45 D6
White Lodge Rd BS16 51 F4
Whitemead Ho 3 BS3 63 A3
Whitemore Ct BA1 86 A4
Whiteoak Way BS48 75 D8
White Ox Mead La
BA2 117 F1
White Ox-mead La
BA2 134 E8
White Post BA3 139 B6
Whitesfield Ct BS48 59 D2
Whitesfield Rd BS48 59 D1
WHITESHILL 37 D3
Whiteshill BS16 37 D3
Whites Hill BS5 65 A6
Whiteshill La SN14 55 D3
White St BS5 143 C4
Whitestown La BS40 128 E3
White Tree Rdbt BS6 49 A4
White Tree Rd BS9 49 B4
Whitewall La BS35 8 F1
WHITEWAY
Bath 101 A4
Bristol 51 A1
Whiteway Cl
Bristol, St Anne's Park
BS4 64 E6
Bristol, St George BS5 65 A8
Whiteway Ct 1 BS5 65 A8
Whiteway Mews BS5 65 A8
Whiteway Rd
Bath BA2 101 A3
Bristol BS5, BS15 51 A1
Whitewells Rd BA1 85 A2
Whitewood Rd BS5 50 F1
WHITFIELD 9 C3
Whitfield Ho 7 BS15 65 D8
Whitfield Rd BS35 8 C2
Whiting Rd BS13 79 A4
Whitland Ave BS13 79 B5
Whitland Rd BS13 79 B5
WHITLEY BATTS 97 F2
Whitley Cl BS37 27 C3
Whitley Mead BS34 36 E3
Whitling St BS40 95 A2
Whitmead Gdns BS13 79 C4
Whitmore Ave BS4 65 A3
Whitson Ho 1 BS2 143 C3
Whitson St BS1 143 A4
Whitsun Leaze BS34 35 F6
Whitting Rd BS23 104 E4
Whittington Dr BS22 88 D2
Whittington Rd BS16 51 C6
Whittock Rd BS14 80 D6
Whittock Sq BS14 80 D7
Whittucks Cl BS15 65 D4
Whittucks Rd BS15 65 C4
Whitwell Rd BS14 80 B8
Whytes Cl BS9 49 A8
WICK 67 D6
Wick CE Prim Sch
BS30 67 B6
Wick Cres BS4 64 D3
Wick Ct BS24 89 B1
Wickets The
Bristol, Filton BS7 35 F1
Bristol, Upper Soundwell
BS15 51 D2
Wicketts The BS7 35 F2
Wickfield BS21 57 E1
Wickham Cl BS37 40 D8
Wickham Ct
Bristol BS16 50 D5
Clevedon BS21 57 E3
Wickham Hill BS16 50 D5
Wickham Theatre★
BS8 142 C3
Wickham View BS16 50 D4
Wick House Cl BS31 82 D3
Wick La
Lympsham BS24 121 E1
Peasedown St John BA2,
BA3 116 F1
Pensford BS39 97 D3
Upton Cheyney BS30 67 A2
WICKLANE 117 A1
Wicklow Rd BS4 79 E8
Wick Rd
Bishop Sutton BS39 113 C3
Bristol BS4 64 D4
Greenways GL13 2 D8
Lympsham BS24 121 D2
Pilning BS35 22 C7
Wick St L BS22 89 B7
Wick Rdbt BS16 38 A2
WICK ST LAWRENCE 89 B7
WICKWAR 18 B5
Wickwar Rd
Kingswood GL12 11 E4
Rangeworthy BS37 17 B1
Yate BS37 28 B5
Wick Wick Cl BS16,
BS36 38 A2
WIDCOMBE 102 C4
Widcombe BS14 80 A6
Widcombe CE Jun Sch
BA2 102 B5
Widcombe Cl 3 BS5 65 A7
Widcombe Cres BA2 102 B5
Widcombe Hill BA2 102 C4
Widcombe Inf Sch
BA2 102 B5
Widcombe Par BA2 141 C1
Widcombe Rise BA2 102 B5
Widcombe Terr BA2 102 B5
Wider Mead 2 BS7 50 C8
Widmore Gr BS13 79 B5
Wight Row BS20 45 F6
Wigmore Gdns BS22 88 D2
Wigton Cres BS10 35 C2
Wilbye Gr BS4 79 D7
Wilcox Cl BS15 65 C6
Wildcountry La BS48 77 E6
Wildcroft Ho BS9 49 B4
Wildcroft Rd BS9 49 B4
Wilder Ct BS2 143 B4
Wilder St BS2 143 B4
Wild Flower Rd BS35 8 B4
Willada Cl BS3 63 B2
William Daw Cl BS29 106 F3
William Herschel Mus★
BA1 141 B2
William Mason Cl 19
BS5 64 B7
Williams Cl BS30 65 F3
Williamson Rd BS7 49 F3
William St
Bath BA2 141 C3
Bristol, Fishponds BS16 51 B3
William St *continued*
8 Bristol, Moorfields
BS5 64 C8
Bristol, Newton BS2 64 A6
Bristol, St Pauls BS2 49 F1
Bristol, Totterdown BS3 63 F4
Bristol, Windmill Hill BS3 63 E4
Williamstowe BA2 102 C1
Willinton Rd BS4 79 F8
Willis Rd
Bristol BS15 51 F2
Fox Hill BA2 102 B2
Williton Cres BS23 104 F3
Willment Way BS11 33 D1
Willmott Cl BS14 79 F3
Willoughby Cl
Alveston BS35 15 A4
Bristol BS13 79 B7
Willoughby Rd BS7 49 E5
Willow Bank BS10 49 C7
Willow Bed Cl BS16 51 B6
Willow Cl
Bath BA2 118 E8
Bristol, Patchway BS34 35 E7
Bristol, Warmley BS30 66 D6
Charfield GL12 11 A4
Clevedon BS21 57 G3
Long Ashton BS41 61 F1
Portishead BS20 45 C4
Radstock BA3 133 E2
Weston-s-M, St Georges
BS22 89 D2
Weston-s-M, Uphill
BS23 104 E2
Wick BS30 67 B6
Willow Ct BS7 50 A7
Willowdown BS22 88 E4
Willow Dr
Bleadon BS24 122 C6
Hutton BS24 105 E2
Weston-s-M BS24 105 E5
Willowfalls BA1 85 E3
Willow Gdns BS22 89 D2
Willow Gn BA2 101 D4
Willow Gr 1 BS16 51 C2
Willowherb Rd
Lyde Green BS16 52 C8
Lyde Green BS16 52 C8
Willow Ho BS13 79 D4
Willow Rd BS15 65 C3
Willow Sh Ctr The
BS16 51 E6
Willows The
Bristol BS16 51 E4
Bristol, Bradley Stoke
BS32 36 D8
Bristol, Frenchay BS16 37 B1
Frampton Cotterell BS36 38 F7
Keynsham BS31 81 E6
Nailsea BS48 59 F3
Yate BS37 27 D2
Willow The BA3 138 F2
Willow Way BS36 38 C6
Willow Wlk
Bristol BS10 35 B3
Keynsham BS31 81 D4
WILLSBRIDGE 66 B1
Willsbridge Hill BS30 66 A2
Willsbridge Ho BS30 66 A2
Willsbridge Mill★ BS30 66 B2
Wills Dr BS5 64 A8
Wills Way BS4 79 D6
Willway St BS3 63 D4
WILMINGTON 100 A1
Wilmington Hill
Englishcombe BA2 100 C2
Marksbury BA2 99 E1
Wilmot Ct BS30 66 A6
Wilmots Way BS20 47 D4
Wilshire Ave BS15 65 D5
Wilson Pl BS2 143 C4
Wilson St BS2 143 C4
Wilton Cl BS10 35 C1
Wilton Ct BS23 104 D7
Wilton Gdns BS23 104 D7
Wiltons BS40 92 D2
Wiltshire Ave BS37 28 A3
Wiltshire Pl BS15 51 E3
Wiltshire Way BA1 85 A2
Wilverley Ind Est BS4 64 E1
Wimbledon Rd BS6 49 C5
Wimblestone Rd BS25 107 F2
Wimborne Rd BS3 63 C1
Winash Cl BS14 80 D7
Wincanton Cl
Bristol BS16 37 F1
Nailsea BS48 60 B1
Winchcombe Cl BS48 76 A8
Winchcombe Gr BS11 47 F5
Winchcombe Rd BS36 38 B8
Winchester Ave BS4 64 D3
Winchester Ct BS16 50 E6
Winchester Rd
5 Bath BA2 101 D5
Bristol BS4 64 D3
Wincombe Trad Est
BS2 64 A4
Wincroft BS30 66 C4
Windcliff Cres BS11 47 E7
Windell St BA2 102 A2
Windermere Ave BS23 104 F4
Windermere Rd BS34 36 A8
Windermere Way BS30 66 D6
Windmill Bsns Pk BS21 73 E8
Windmill Cl
Bristol BS15 65 D5
Bristol BS3 63 E4
Windmill Farm Bsns Ctr
BS3 63 D4
WINDMILL HILL 63 E3
Windmill Hill
Bristol BS3 63 D3
Hutton BS24 106 A2
Windmill La BS10 34 D3
Windmill Rd BS21 73 E8
Windrush Cl BA2 100 F4
Windrush Ct BS35 15 C8
Windrush Gn BS31 82 A4
Windrush Rd BS31 82 A4
Windscreens Ave BS2 64 A7
Windsor Ave
Bristol BS5 65 B6
Keynsham BS31 81 E4
Windsor Bridge Rd BA1,
BA2 101 D7
Windsor Castle BA1 101 D7
Windsor Cl
Bristol BS34 36 E4
Clevedon BS21 57 F2
Windsor Cres BS10 34 C4
Windsor Ct
4 Bath BA1 101 C7
14 Bristol, Clifton BS8 62 F6
Bristol, Downend BS16 51 E7
Wick BS30 67 C7
Windsor Dr
Nailsea BS48 59 E2
Yate BS37 27 D2
Windsor Gr 20 BS5 64 B8
Windsor Pl
5 Bath BA1 101 C7
Bristol, Clifton BS8 62 F6
Bristol, Mangotsfield
BS16 52 A5
Windsor Rd
Bristol, Longwell Green
BS30 65 F2
Bristol, Montpelier BS6 49 E2
Weston-s-M BS22 88 C2
Windsor Terr
Bristol, Clifton BS8 62 F6
Bristol, Windmill Hill BS3 63 F4
Paulton BS39 132 E5
Windsor Villas 3 BA1 101 C7
Windwhistle Circ
BS23 104 F4
Windwhistle La BS23 104 E3
Windwhistle Prim Sch
BS23 104 F3
Windwhistle Rd BS23 104 D3
Windyridge BS16 51 E4
Wineberry Cl BS5 50 D1
Wine St
Bath BA1 141 C2
Bristol BS1 143 A3
Winfield Rd BS30 66 C7
WINFORD 94 F7
Winford Bsns Pk BS40 95 D4
Winford CE Prim Sch
BS40 94 F7
Winford Cl BS20 45 E4
Winford Ct BS6 49 A5
Winford Gr BS13 79 A8
Winford La BS41 78 C1
Winford Rd BS40 95 F3
Winford Terr BS41 78 C5
Wingard Cl BS23 104 D2
Wingard Ct 6 BS23 104 E5
Wingfield Rd BS3 63 E2
Winifred's La BA1 84 E1
Winkworth Pl 4 BS2 49 F1
Winnowing End BS25 108 A3
Winsbury View BA2 99 B1
Winsbury Way BS32 24 D1
WINSCOMBE 124 F7
Winscombe Cl BS31 81 D6
Winscombe Dro
Shipham BS25 125 D6
Winscombe BS25 125 A5
Winscombe Hill BS25 124 F5
Winscombe Rd BS23 105 A7
Winscombe Woodborough
Prim Sch BS25 125 A8
Winsford St 2 BS5 64 A8
Winsham Cl BS14 80 B5
WINSLEY 120 D7
Winsley Bypass BA15 120 E7
Winsley CE VA Prim Sch
BA15 120 E7
Winsley Hill BA2 120 B6
Winsley Rd
Bristol BS6 49 D1
Winsley BA15 120 F7
Winstanley Ho 4 BS5 64 B6
Winstone Ct BS2 142 C3

Winstones Rd
Barrow Gurney BS48....**77** F6
Bristol BS48........**78** A6
WINTERBOURNE.......**37** F6
WINTERBOURNE
DOWN.............**37** F4
Winterbourne Hill
BS36................**37** D5
Winterbourne Int Acad
BS36................**37** D6
Winterbourne Rd BS34..**36** E6
Winterfield Cl BS39...**132** E4
Winterfield Pk BS39...**132** E4
Winterfield Rd BS39...**132** E5
WINTERHEAD........**125** D6
Winters La BS40......**93** D6
Winterstoke Cl **5** BS3..**63** B2
Winterstoke Commercial
Ctr BS23...........**105** A6
Winterstoke Ctr **1** BS3.**63** B4
Winterstoke Ho **1** BS3 **63** A3
Winterstoke Hundred Acad
BS24...............**105** D6
Winterstoke Rd
Bristol BS3..........**63** A2
Weston-s-M BS23, BS24 **105** B4
Winterstoke Underpass
BS3................**62** F4
Wint Hill BS29.......**107** B2
Winton St BS2.......**63** F4
Wisemans Ho BS8....**142** A4
Wishford Mews BA3...**133** C2
Wisley Wlk BS22.....**105** F7
Wistaria Ave BS37....**28** A1
Wisteria Ave BS24....**105** D2
Witchell Rd BS5......**64** C7
Witch Hazel Rd BS13..**79** E3
Witcombe BS37.......**39** C7
Witcombe Cl BS15....**51** F1
Witham Rd BS31......**82** A3
Witherlies Rd BS16....**50** F6
Withey Cl E
Bristol BS9..........**48** F6
Stoke Bishop BS9.....**48** F6
Withey Cl W BS9......**48** F5
Witheys The BS14.....**80** C4
Withies La BA3.......**139** A8
Withies Pk BA3......**138** F8
Withington Cl BS30...**66** C2
Withleigh Rd BS4.....**64** B2
Withy Cl BS48........**59** F3
WITHYDITCH.......**117** C3
Withyditch La BA2....**117** C4
Withy La BS34........**36** A7
WITHY MILLS.......**133** A7
Withymead Rd SN14...**70** A8
Withypool Gdns BS14..**80** B5
Withys The BS20......**47** D4
WITHYWOOD........**79** A4
Withywood Com Sch
BS13................**79** A5
Withywood Gdns **1**
BS13................**78** F4
Withywood Rd BS13...**78** F4
Witney Cl BS31.......**82** D3
Witney Mead BS36....**38** B8
Woburn Cl BS30......**65** F5
Woburn Rd BS5.......**50** B3
Wolferton Rd BS7.....**49** F2
Wolfridge Gdns BS10..**35** A4
Wolfridge La BS35.....**14** F4
Wolfridge Ride BS35...**14** F4
Wolseley Rd BS7......**49** D3
Wolvershill Ind Units
BS29...............**106** C6
Wolvershill Pk BS29..**107** A3
Wolvershill Rd BS29...**106** E6
WONDERSTONE.....**122** D6
Woodacre BS20.......**45** E7
Woodbine Rd BS5.....**64** D8
WOODBOROUGH.....**125** B8
Woodborough Cres
BS25...............**125** A7
Woodborough Ct
BS25...............**125** A8
Woodborough Dr
BS25...............**125** A8
Woodborough Hill Cotts
BA2...............**134** C4
Woodborough La BA3 **134** A4
Woodborough Rd
Radstock BA3........**134** A3
Winscombe BS25......**124** F8
Woodborough St BS5..**50** B1
Woodbridge Rd BS4...**64** A2
Woodbury La BS8......**49** A2
Woodchester
Bristol BS15.........**51** E3
Yate BS37...........**39** E7
Woodchester Rd BS10..**49** C7
Woodcliff Ave BS22...**88** C1
Woodcliff Rd BS22....**88** C1
Woodcote BS15.......**65** D6
Woodcote Rd BS16....**51** B3

Woodcote Wlk BS16....**51** B2
Woodcroft BS39.......**113** C3
Woodcroft Ave BS5....**50** D1
Woodcroft Cl BS4.....**64** E4
Woodcroft Rd BS4.....**64** E4
Wooddene BS25.......**125** A8
Woodend BS15........**65** D6
Woodend Rd BS36....**38** C7
Wood End Wlk BS9....**48** C6
Woodfield Rd BS6.....**49** B2
WOODFORD..........**4** A4
Woodford Cl BS48.....**60** A1
Woodford Ct **2** BS23..**104** E5
Woodford Gn GL13......**3** A4
Woodgrove Rd BS10...**34** D2
Woodhall Cl BS16.....**51** F6
WOODHILL..........**45** D7
Woodhill BS49.......**91** E6
Woodhill Ave BS20....**45** D6
Woodhill Ct BS20.....**45** D6
Woodhill La BS20.....**45** D6
Woodhill Pk BS20.....**45** D7
Woodhill Rd BS20.....**45** D6
Woodhill Views BS48...**59** F3
Woodhouse Ave BS32 ..**24** D7
Woodhouse Cl BS32....**24** D6
WOODHOUSE DOWN ...**24** E5
Woodhouse Gr BS7....**49** E6
Woodhouse Rd BA2...**101** A6
Woodhurst BS23......**105** A7
Woodington Ct **1** BS30 **65** F4
Woodington Rd BS21...**57** E1
Wood Kilns The BS49..**74** A1
Wood La
Axbridge BS26.......**125** D2
Clapton in G BS20....**59** E8
Horton BS37.........**19** A1
Weston-s-M BS23......**87** F1
Woodland Ave BS15...**51** D2
Woodland Cl
Bristol BS15.........**51** C2
Failand BS8..........**61** B4
Woodland Cotts BA2..**120** D6
Woodland Ct
Bristol BS9..........**48** C3
Bristol, Tyndall's Park
BS8................**142** C4
Woodland Glade BS21..**57** G5
Woodland Gr
Bath, Bushey Norwood
BA2...............**102** E5
Bath, Weston Park BA1..**84** C1
Bristol BS9..........**48** D6
Woodland Pl BA2.....**102** D5
Woodland Rd
Bristol BS8.........**142** C4
Leyhill GL12.........**10** B4
Nailsea BS48.........**59** E3
Weston-s-M BS23.....**104** D4
Woodlands
Axbridge BS26.......**125** D2
Bristol BS9..........**48** E3
Bristol, Downend BS16..**51** E6
Bristol, Patchway BS32..**24** B3
Tytherington GL12......**16** B6
Weston-s-M BS23......**87** D1
Woodlands Ct
Bristol, Patchway BS32..**24** B3
Bristol, Shirehampton
BS11...............**47** E5
Woodlands Dr BA2...**120** B6
Woodlands La
Bristol BS32.........**24** C3
Woodhouse Down BS32..**24** E5
Woodlands Pk
Bath BA1............**85** C2
Bristol BS32.........**24** C3
Woodlands Rd
Charfield GL12.......**11** A4
Clevedon BS21.......**57** E4
Portishead BS20......**45** D8
Tytherington GL12.....**16** B6
Woodlands Rise BS16..**51** D6
Woodlands The BA2..**116** F3
Woodland Terr
Bristol, Kingswood
BS15...............**65** E7
Bristol, Redland BS6...**49** B2
Woodland Way
Bristol BS15.........**51** C2
Failand BS8..........**61** B4
Woodleaze BS9.......**48** B6
Wood Leaze BS34.....**35** F6
Woodleigh BS35.......**8** C1
Woodleigh Gdns BS14..**80** C6
Woodmancote BS37...**39** D8
Woodmancote Rd **7**
BS6................**49** E1
Woodmans Cl BS37....**40** B8
Woodmans Rd BS37...**40** C8
Woodmans Vale BS37..**40** C8
Woodmarsh Cl BS14...**80** A4
Wood Mead BS34.....**50** D8
Woodmead La BS30...**54** A1
Woodmill BS49.......**74** A1
Woodnook The BS10...**35** C2

Woodpecker Ave BA3..**139** B8
Woodpecker Cl BS31...**81** C3
Woodpecker Cres BS16 **53** C4
Woodpecker Dr BS22..**105** E8
Wood Rd BS15........**65** D8
Woodsage Cres BS16...**52** D7
Woods Hill BA2......**120** A6
Woodside
Bristol BS9..........**48** D3
Midsomer Norton BA3..**132** E1
Woodside Ave BS24...**105** B2
Woodside Cl BS23.....**105** A8
Woodside Dr BS32.....**24** A4
Woodside Gdns BS20..**44** E5
Woodside Gr BS10.....**34** D3
Woodside Rd
Bristol, Downend BS16..**51** C7
Bristol, Kingswood BS15 **65** C7
Bristol, St Anne's Park
BS4................**64** E6
Clevedon BS21.......**57** G5
Frampton Cotterell BS36 **38** E6
Woodspring BS22......**71** C1
Woodspring Ave BS22..**88** B3
Woodspring Cres BS22 **88** A3
Woodspring Priory★
BS22...............**71** C1
Wood St
Bath BA1...........**141** B2
Bath, Beechen Cliff BA2 **141** B1
Bristol BS34.........**35** F7
Bristol BS5..........**50** A3
WOODSTOCK.........**67** F7
Woodstock Ave BS6...**49** C1
Woodstock Cl BS15....**65** F8
Woodstock Rd
Bristol, Kingswood
BS15...............**65** F7
Bristol, Redland BS6...**49** C2
Weston-s-M BS22.....**105** B8
Woodstock Sch BS10...**34** E2
Woodview
Chilcompton BA3.....**138** E5
2 Clevedon BS21.....**57** H3
High Littleton BS39...**115** D1
Paulton BS39........**132** C5
Woodview Cl BS11.....**47** E7
Woodview Cotts BS39 **132** B7
Woodview Dr BS49....**92** B8
Woodview Terr
Bath BA2...........**100** F6
Nailsea BS48.........**59** F2
Weston-s-M BS23.....**105** A6
Woodward Ave BS37...**27** B1
Woodward Dr BS30....**65** F4
Woodwell Rd BS11....**47** E5
Woodyleaze Dr BS15...**65** D6
Wookey Cl BS48.......**75** F8
Woolcot St BS6.......**49** B2
WOOLCOTT PARK....**49** B1
Wooler Rd BS23......**104** E8
WOOLLARD.........**98** A6
Woollard La
Bristol BS14, BS39....**98** A7
Whitchurch BS14......**80** E1
WOOLLEY..........**84** F5
Woolley La BA1.......**85** A4
Woolley Rd BS14......**80** E5
Woolvers Way BS24..**106** B6
WOOLVERTON.......**137** C1
Wootton Cres BS4.....**64** E6
Wootton Pk BS14, BS4..**64** B1
Wootton Rd BS4......**64** F6
Worcester Bldgs BA1...**85** B2
Worcester Cl
Bristol BS16.........**51** B2
Peasedown St John
BA2...............**134** D7
Worcester Cres BS8...**142** A4
Worcester Gdns BS48..**75** C8
Worcester Pk BA1.....**85** B2
Worcester Pl BA1.....**85** B2
Worcester Rd
Bristol BS8.........**142** A4
Bristol, Kingswood BS15 **51** D1
Worcester Terr
Bath BA1............**85** B2
Bristol BS8.........**142** A4
Wordsworth Ho BS34..**36** A8
Wordsworth Rd
Bristol BS7..........**50** B7
Clevedon BS21.......**57** E2
Weston-s-M BS23.....**105** A3
Workshop La BA2....**100** C6
Worldsend La GL13.....**2** E7
World's End La BS31...**82** C5
WORLE.............**88** F2
WORLEBURY........**88** A2
Worlebury Cl BS22....**88** B3
Worlebury Hill Rd BS22,
BS23...............**88** B2
Worlebury Park Rd
BS22...............**88** A2
Worlebury St Pauls CE VA
Fst Sch BS22.........**88** B3
Worle Com Sch BS22..**88** E1
Worle Ct BS22........**88** F3

Worle Ind Est BS22....**89** B2
Worle Moor Rd BS24..**105** E7
Worle Sta BS22.......**89** B1
Worle Village Prim Sch
BS22...............**88** E2
Wormcliff La SN13....**86** F3
Worrall Mews **10** BS8..**49** A2
Worrall Pl **11** BS8.....**49** A2
Worrall Rd BS8.......**49** A2
Worrel's La BS16, BS36..**37** D3
Worsley St BS5.......**64** D7
Worthing Rd BS34.....**35** F8
Worthings The BS24..**122** B1
Worthy Cl BS15.......**65** F6
Worthy Cres BS24....**122** B1
Worthy La **5** BS23....**104** E8
Worthy Pl **4** BS23....**104** E8
Worthy Rd BS11.......**33** D7
Worthys The BS34.....**37** A6
Wotton Rd
Charfield GL12.......**11** B5
Iron Acton BS37......**26** F5
Kingswood GL12......**11** C5
Wrangle Farm Gn BS21 **57** G2
WRANGLE THE.......**129** A5
Wrangle The **5** BS24..**105** F7
WRAXALL...........**60** C3
Wraxall CE VA Prim Sch
BS48...............**60** B4
Wraxall Gr BS13......**79** A8
Wraxall Hill BS48.....**60** C5
Wraxall Rd BS30......**66** A6
Wrenbert Rd BS16....**51** D5
Wren Cl
Bristol BS16.........**50** E7
Weston-s-M BS22....**105** D8
Wren Dr BS16........**51** A6
Wright Way BS16.....**50** E8
WRINGTON.........**92** E1
Wrington CE Prim Sch
BS40...............**92** E2
Wrington Cl BS34.....**36** C7
Wrington Cres BS13...**79** A7
Wrington Hill BS40....**92** F5
Wrington La BS49.....**91** E5
Wrington Mead BS49...**91** E5
Wrington Rd BS49.....**91** F4
WRITHLINGTON.....**134** C2
Writhlington Ct BA3..**134** C1
Writhlington Sch BA3 **134** C1
Wroughton Dr BS13...**79** D4
Wroughton Gdns BS13 **79** D4
Wroxham Dr BS34.....**36** C8
Wyatt Ave BS13.......**78** F5
Wyatt Cl BS13........**78** F5
Wyatt's Cl BS48.......**59** D2
Wyatts View BS4......**64** E6
Wychwood BS15......**65** E6
Wyck Beck Rd BS10....**35** A3
Wycliffe Rd BS9......**49** B7
Wycliffe Row **9** BS3..**63** F4
Wycombe Gr BS4.....**64** D2
Wycotte Hill BA2.....**118** C6
Wye Croft Cl BS10.....**35** D3
Wye Ct BS35..........**15** C8
Wyedale Ave BS9.....**48** C7
Wykis Ct BS15........**65** E5
Wylington Rd BS36....**38** B6
Wyllie Ct BS22.......**89** A5
Wymbush Cres BS13...**79** C5
Wymbush Gdns BS13...**79** C5
Wyndam Ct BS2......**143** B4
Wyndham Cres
Bristol BS4..........**65** A3
Easton-in-G BS20.....**47** B4
Wyndham Way BS20...**45** E5
Wyndham Way Ret Pk
BS20...............**45** D5
Wynstones The BS15...**65** C7
Wynter Cl BS22.......**89** A3
Wyvern Cl BS23......**104** F7
Wyvern Com Sch
BS23...............**104** F5
Wyvern Mews **5** BS23 **104** F7
Wyvern Villas BS9.....**49** A8

Y

Yadley Cl BS25......**125** A7
Yadley La BS25......**125** A6
Yadley Way BS25....**125** A7
Yanel La BS25.......**108** B5
Yanleigh Cl BS13.....**78** B6
YANLEY............**78** C8
Yanley La BS41, BS13...**78** C7
Yarbury Way BS24....**89** B1
Yard The BS2.........**50** A3
Yarrow Cl **5** BS16....**52** D7
Yarrow Ct BS22.......**89** A5
Yarrow Wlk BS16.....**52** D7
YATE...............**27** C1
Yate Court La BS37....**27** D8
Yate Her Ctr★ BS37...**27** E2
Yate Rd BS37........**26** F3
YATE ROCKS........**27** F6
Yate Rocks BS37......**27** F7

Yate Sta BS37........**27** C2
YATTON............**91** C8
Yatton CE VA Jun & Inf
Schs BS49..........**91** C8
Yatton Cl BS13.......**78** F8
Yatton Inf Sch BS49...**91** C8
Yatton Station BS49...**74** A1
Yeaman's Ho BS1.....**143** B1
Yeates Ct BS21.......**57** G3
Yeatman Cl BS39.....**113** D4
Yelverton Rd BS4.....**64** E1
Yeo Bank La
Icelton BS22.........**89** D7
Kingston Seymour BS21..**72** F1
Yeo Cl BS23.........**105** A5
Yeo Ct
Clevedon BS21.......**57** E2
Congresbury BS49....**91** D4
Yeo La BS41.........**61** F1
Yeolands BS21.......**57** D1
Yeomans Cl BS9......**48** D5
Yeomanside Cl BS14...**80** C5
Yeomans Orch BS40...**92** E3
Yeomead BS48.......**59** F3
Yeomeads BS41.......**61** F1
Yeo Moor BS21.......**57** G2
Yeo Moor Inf Sch BS21 **57** G2
Yeo Moor Jun Sch
BS21...............**57** G2
Yeo Moor Prim Sch
BS21...............**57** E2
Yeo Valley Way BS48...**60** B2
Yeoward Rd BS21.....**57** G1
Yeo Way BS21.......**57** D2
Yewcroft Cl BS14.....**80** A4
Yewtree Batch BS40...**94** A1
Yew Tree Cl
Bishop Sutton BS39...**113** D4
Lower Langford BS40..**109** E6
Nailsea BS48.........**59** C1
Yew Tree Cotts BS40..**110** E3
Yew Tree Ct BS14.....**80** B5
Yew Tree Dr
Bristol BS15.........**51** F3
Weston-s-M BS22....**106** B8
Yew Tree Gdns
Nailsea BS48.........**59** C1
Pill BS20............**47** C4
Sandford BS25.......**108** A4
Yew Tree La
Compton Martin BS40 **129** A7
Kingston Seymour BS21..**73** B1
Yew Tree Pk BS49....**91** D3
Yomede Pk BA1.....**101** A7
York Ave BS7.........**49** F4
York Bldgs
Bath BA1...........**141** B3
Bristol BS3..........**63** E4
York Cl
Bristol, Bromley Heath
BS16...............**37** F1
Bristol, Stoke Gifford
BS34...............**36** D4
Weston-s-M BS22.....**89** A4
Yate BS37...........**27** E4
York Ct BS2.........**143** B4
York Gdns
Bristol BS8..........**62** F6
Winterbourne BS36....**37** F8
York Ho BS8.........**142** A3
York Pl
Bath BA1...........**102** B8
Bristol, Brandon Hill
BS1................**142** C2
Bristol, Victoria Park
BS8................**142** B3
York Rd
Bristol BS2.........**143** C1
Bristol, Lower Easton
BS5................**50** C1
Bristol, Montpelier BS6..**49** E1
Bristol, Staple Hill BS16 **51** E4
Bristol, Windmill Hill BS3 **63** E4
York St
Bath BA1...........**141** C2
Bristol BS2.........**143** B4
Bristol, Baptist Mills BS2 **50** A2
2 Bristol, Clifton BS8..**62** F6
9 Bristol, Redfield BS5..**64** C7
Weston-s-M BS23.....**104** D7
Youngs Ct BS16.......**52** B8
Youngwood La BS48...**75** D7
Yoxter Rd
Charterhouse BA5....**127** F1
Ubley Sideling BS40..**128** B2

Z

Zetland Rd BS6.......**49** D2
Zig Zag BS21.........**57** F4
Zinc Rd BS11.........**33** C3
Zion Hill BA3........**138** B7
Zone The **7** BS5.....**65** A6

LEARNING OBJECTIVES

To work out 'by ear' how to play well-known tunes through the medium of graphic notation, making links between sounds and symbols.

The teacher can help students to identify a tune initially by encouraging them to sing the first few bars. This can then be related to the graphic notation, thus making the link between sound and symbol.

Students can then try to complete one of the melodies 'by ear', listening carefully to whether each note is higher or lower, longer or shorter than the previous note.

Once a tune has successfully been worked out 'by ear', it can be recorded in graphic form. Letter-names may be added below the symbols or students may use staff notation.

When a tune has been worked out correctly 'by ear', the student(s) can be asked to perform it.

Students can use hand signals to indicate size of intervals, note repetition and phrase-shape.

They should be encouraged to perform each piece in an appropriately expressive style.

HOMEWORK ACTIVITIES:

Work out a favourite tune 'by ear' at home and notate it using dot-dash phrases (in a subsequent lesson, other students can be asked to identify it and work it out 'by ear').

BACKGROUND INFORMATION

This activity builds upon the knowledge and skills developed in 'Name that Tune' and 'Dot-Dash Phrases'.

Tunes can be worked out during individual practice and then played again in the lesson. Students can be asked to play the given melodies in different keys.

Transposing 'by ear' is an important tool for the advanced musician, especially for brass players who frequently have to transpose their parts in an ensemble.

Regular playing 'by ear' helps to build confidence in the activity.

TEACHING IN GROUPS

Individual players can be given time within the lesson to complete the melody 'by ear'. Alternatively, students can be encouraged to play the prompt together, and then take turns to work out allocated phrases. This can be either a teacher- or student-led activity.

At a later stage (and depending upon the ability of the students), players can be encouraged to compose an harmonic part to the tune. In the first instance the teacher should model the activity, bringing the attention of students to the importance of certain harmonic and structural features such as cadences, transitional harmonies, and harmonic intervals such as 3rds and 6ths.

DIFFERENTIATION

Less advanced students can work out 'by ear' simple, individual phrases. The teacher and pupil may then perform the melody together, the teacher completing the gaps within the melodic line.

EXTENSION ACTIVITIES

Whilst all students will benefit from transposing memorised melodies into other keys, brass players, in particular, can be encouraged to develop fluency in their most common transpositions. For example, trumpet in C, horn in Eb.

Performing a tune in the relative minor key can help develop an understanding of major/minor key relationships.

➡ 'Transposing Tunes By Ear (Strings Only)'.   © Team World Music Ltd 2004

Whole-Tone Improvising

EXPLORATIONS

- This improvisation activity is for two or more players.

- First, learn and memorise the whole-tone scale of C.

- Practise playing the scale, both ascending and descending, using the example rhythms given. *[CD52]*

- Then, try improvising your own rhythm patterns and perform. *[CD52, CD53]*

- Lastly, improvise rhythm patterns to create a spooky, atmospheric composition. *[CD54]*

WHOLE-TONE SCALE OF C

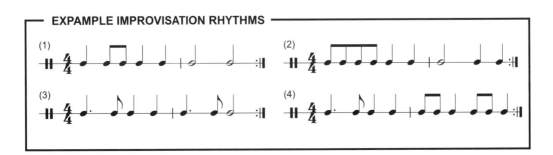

EXPAMPLE IMPROVISATION RHYTHMS

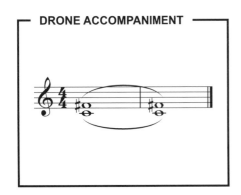

DRONE ACCOMPANIMENT

OSTINATI

EXAMPLE OSTINATO PIANO ACCOMPANIMENT

POINTS TO NOTE ON THE DVD

WHOLE-TONE IMPROVISING:

Please refer to DVD chapter **IMPROVISING WITH RAGAS**.

EXPLORATIONS Recorder Students' Edition

LEARNING OBJECTIVES

To compose by developing musical ideas within given structures and applying instrumental skills in an ensemble context.

The teacher may introduce the scale and explain that, effectively, there are only two different forms of the whole-tone scale, one starting on C and the other on C♯.

Move on to demonstrate the 2-bar 'Listen and Answer' activity. Perform the given examples to the student(s) with the CD accompaniment. Review the 'Listen and Answer' technique. Make links to previous work in this area.

Encourage the students to practise creating 2-bar 'answering' phrases with CD accompaniment. The teacher and student can take turns, if appropriate. To begin with, it may be easier to use simple crotchets and minims for 'answering' phrases. More complicated rhythms can then be introduced when confidence has been gained.

HOMEWORK ACTIVITIES:

Compose a piece of music using the whole-tone scale and perform it, accompanied by an appropriate 'atmospheric' CD track, for example 54.

BACKGROUND INFORMATION

This activity gives students the opportunity to work in a modern idiom, and to explore dissonance in a structured way.

It can be useful if students have had some previous experience with dissonant sound worlds. For example, 'Create-a-Chord' or 'Sound-Scape'.

Some examination syllabuses require students to memorise and perform whole-tone scales. This activity can help to place the scale into a relevant, musical context.

TEACHING IN GROUPS

Depending on the size of the group, percussion instruments could be used for the ostinati, and piano, keyboard or tuned percussion used for the drones.

Students can play a drone when not engaged in 'answering' a 2-bar phrase, and less advanced players can use the notes in the drone for their improvisations.

In order to guarantee that all students participate in the activity for the whole time, the group can copy a 2-bar phrase played by each of the students in turn.

Although students may play a drone or ostinato when not performing a solo or 'answer', they should be advised to 'rest' at any time when they feel that they are lacking in stamina.

DIFFERENTIATION

Less advanced students can attempt the activity drawing upon a limited number of notes from the scale. More advanced students may use the complete scale and extend the range of notes, where appropriate.

EXTENSION ACTIVITIES

Students can apply the 'Listen and Answer' technique to create their own 4-, 8- or 12-bar improvisations.

These can be accompanied by CD track 54 or by a combination of drones and ostinati.

 'Sound Collage'; 'Dodecaphonic Music'.

Composing with Sequence

- In this activity you can learn how to compose an ending for an incomplete melody.

- First, practice the given examples in order to see how a phrase can be 'answered' by another phrase using sequence.

- Then, using this sequence technique, compose endings for each of the incomplete melodies below.

EXAMPLE SEQUENCE PHRASE TECHNIQUE

Try to sing an ending before you play it.

A sequence phrase does not have to be an exact copy.

(4) *Slowly*

(5) *Jolly*

(6) *Allegro*

Now see if you can also complete these melodies by using 'Mirror Technique' or 'Copy and Answer'.

POINTS TO NOTE ON THE DVD

COMPOSING WITH SEQUENCE:

Please refer to DVD chapter **COMPOSING WITH COPY AND ANSWER**.

EXPLORATIONS Recorder Students' Edition

LEARNING OBJECTIVES

To compose by developing musical ideas within simple, given structures and applying instrumental skills.

The teacher may demonstrate the frequent use of sequence in music by playing various examples to the student(s) 'by ear'. For example, 'Do-Re-Me' from 'The Sound of Music'; the chorus section of 'Ding Dong Merrily on High'.

Students can be asked to continue the sequences in examples (1) and (2), in both ascending and descending form. In the first instance this can be approached through clapping and/or singing an ending. The teacher might wish to demonstrate how different endings can be devised by using sequence.

Students should be encouraged to delay writing an ending until they are able to play one fluently on their instrument.

At the end of the process, students can be encouraged to perform the melody, taking heed of the style and marks of expression.

HOMEWORK ACTIVITIES:

Compose complete, original melodies using a combination of imitation, mirror technique and sequence, either with or without a descriptive title.

BACKGROUND INFORMATION

'Composing with Sequence' builds upon the knowledge and skills developed in 'Composing with Copy and Answer'.

Composing an ending for an incomplete melody is part of the aural (or initiative) tests set by some examination boards.

The activity can be approached with a specific aural focus. Students can, for example, experiment with improvised endings, or write an ending before they play it. They could also take turns at improvising, or performing, previously composed endings.

TEACHING IN GROUPS

The whole group can practise clapping, singing or playing the melody up to the point where the notation ends.

Next, each student can be encouraged to clap, sing or play an ending in turn, from the point where the rest of the group stops playing the given prompt. The various outcomes can then be discussed and evaluated.

Students can be asked to try to remember another student's ending and play it.

DIFFERENTIATION

Less advanced students can be encouraged to use only the first three or four notes within a given key and to use only crotchet and minim movement.

More advanced players may draw from any of the notes of the relevant key.

EXTENSION ACTIVITIES

Students can be asked to compose a complete 8- or 16-bar melody, applying the given compositional technique. To begin with, they may use the rhythm of one of the given extracts, changing the pitch of the notes as appropriate, or vice versa.

Some students may find it easier to compose a melody based upon a descriptive theme with which they are familiar. For example a 'Christmas Song' or 'Reggae Tune'.

➡ 'Composing Descriptive Music'; 'Minimalism'.

Listen, Copy and Answer (2)

Echo Mountain

EXAMPLE COPIED PHRASE

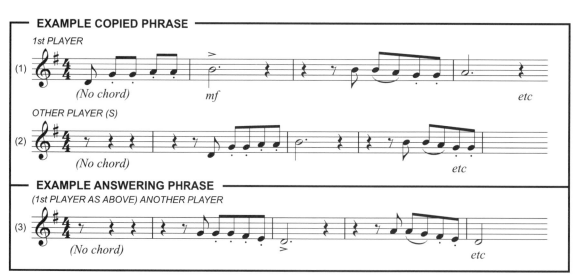

KEYBOARD ACCOMPANIMENT

G	G	D	D	Am⁷	D⁷	G	G⁷	C	C	G	Em	Am	D⁷	G	G

EXPLORATIONS Recorder Students' Edition

POINTS TO NOTE ON THE DVD

LISTEN, COPY AND ANSWER (2):

Please refer to DVD chapter **COMPOSING WITH COPY AND ANSWER**.

LEARNING OBJECTIVES

To repeat with accuracy short, easy rhythmic and melodic phrases by playing back from memory; to improvise rhythmic and melodic phrases freely, or within given structures, individually or as part of a group.

Students can learn to play 'Echo Mountain' in one of three ways:
1) Using the notated melody opposite.
2) Copying the teacher, as in previous 'Listen and Copy' activities.
3) Copying the performance on CD track 55.

When introducing the 'Listen and Answer' form for the first time, students may find it easier to move by step, as indicated in the given examples.

It can also be helpful for students to sing an 'answer' to a phrase, before trying to play it. At a later stage they may try to silently 'finger' a phrase whilst singing it.

In the first instance, the student may find it easier to start an improvised 'answering' phrase on the tonic or dominant note, or on the note which the teacher ended on.

HOMEWORK ACTIVITIES:

(1) 'Answer' a given phrase using just the first three notes of the scale.

(2) Extend those three notes to the first five notes of the scale.

BACKGROUND INFORMATION

This activity builds upon the knowledge and skills developed in 'Listen, Copy and Answer (1)'. In this form of the activity, however, the student(s) must repeat a given phrase, or improvise one, at exactly one bar's length after it has been heard, and while the given phrase is still being played.

This improvisational and compositional device was much used by 19th century composers and, more recently, by writers and performers of pop 'ballads'.

Students will benefit from playing and improvising within rounds before they start this activity, as both tasks require phrases to be played sequentially in an ensemble context.

TEACHING IN GROUPS

To begin with, the whole group can copy each phrase played by the teacher through clapping and singing, at one bar's length. Then, they could copy the rhythm by playing on any given note(s), again at one bar's distance, before attempting an exact 'Listen and Copy' phrase. When performing the 'Listen and Answer' form of the activity, students can take turns at improvising phrases.

DIFFERENTIATION

Less advanced students can improvise with just the first few notes of the scale. The more advanced can use notes drawn from the whole scale.

EXTENSION ACTIVITIES

Students can be asked to compose their own melody in the given key for copying and 'answering', which may then be accompanied by the given chord sequence.

Also, players can be asked to record themselves performing their own melody, and then to use it for improvising as outlined above.

➡ 'Japanese Music'; 'Improvising with Ragas'.

Songs of Persuasion

EXPLORATIONS

- This song composing activity is for one or more players.
- Start by clapping an appropriate 3- or 4-beat pulse whilst saying the words aloud.
- Next, whilst maintaining the pulse, sing the words as a melody, trying to reflect the meaning and mood of the text.
- Then play the melody of your song on your instrument.
- Lastly, perform your song, possibly adding a simple accompaniment.

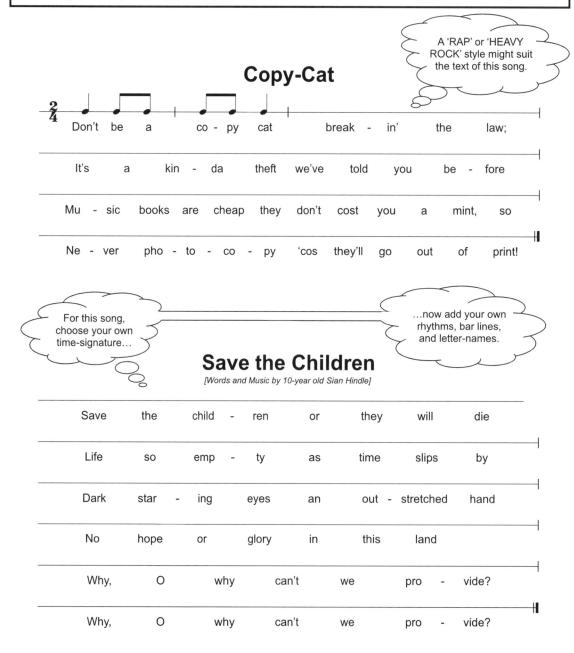

A 'RAP' or 'HEAVY ROCK' style might suit the text of this song.

Copy-Cat

Don't be a co-py cat break-in' the law;

It's a kin-da theft we've told you be-fore

Mu-sic books are cheap they don't cost you a mint, so

Ne-ver pho-to-co-py 'cos they'll go out of print!

For this song, choose your own time-signature…

…now add your own rhythms, bar lines, and letter-names.

Save the Children

[Words and Music by 10-year old Sian Hindle]

Save the child-ren or they will die

Life so emp-ty as time slips by

Dark star-ing eyes an out-stretched hand

No hope or glory in this land

Why, O why can't we pro-vide?

Why, O why can't we pro-vide?

POINTS TO NOTE ON THE DVD

SONGS OF PERSUASION:

Please refer to DVD chapter **MAKE UP A SONG**.

To compose by developing musical ideas within simple, given structures and applying instrumental skills.

This activity, like many others in the EXPLORATIONS series, often requires very little initial input by the teacher, and this can result in a greater feeling of involvement and ownership by the student(s). If necessary, the first song activity ('Copy-Cat') can be used to model the composing process. Students can then work independently on 'Save the Children'. A variety of approaches can be adopted for each song. In the first instance, students may sing improvised phrases using ascending and descending hand-signals to indicate the shape and structure of the verse. They can improvise freely, internalising the text while they do so. Students may record their work using 'dot-dash phrases' and letter names rather than notation.

The teacher can advise on phrase structure by bringing students' attention to compositional devices like imitation and sequence.

Technical suggestions might also be made. For example, would slurring most of a verse be more appropriate than tonguing? Could a mute be used to advantage?

HOMEWORK ACTIVITIES:

Students can be asked to write another verse for their song, or to explore verse/chorus form.

BACKGROUND INFORMATION

This activity builds upon many other previous, related activities, especially 'Composing with Sequence', 'Composing with Copy and Answer' and 'Composing with Mirror Technique'.

Whilst composing songs might normally be associated with classroom music, this activity is one of the many natural ways in which instrumental lessons can be integrated with classroom music lessons.

This can help to ensure that there is some degree of common purpose between classroom music lessons and instrumental lessons, particularly in the areas of composing, improvising and performance. Instrumental teachers and classroom teachers could create opportunities to liaise with each other on these subject areas.

Such an approach can make music lessons more relevant to the student.

TEACHING IN GROUPS

Following the activity instructions (opposite), two students who like working together can co-operate at each stage of the composing process to create a song.

Through this activity, students learn that they can apply their instrumental skills to composing songs.

DIFFERENTIATION

Less advanced students can restrict the range of their song and perhaps rely on simple ascending and descending patterns. More advanced players can be encouraged to use a greater range of notes on their instruments and to consider carefully the musical elements of dynamics, articulation, etc.

EXTENSION ACTIVITIES

Students can be asked to find a poem that interests them and to set it to music.

Alternatively, they might compose a melody and then set words to it, on any subject which interests them.

➡ 'Composing Descriptive Music'.

Tell a Story with Music

EXPLORATIONS

- This descriptive music activity is for two or more players.

- Read through each story and choose one to illustrate with music.

- Then, using a variety of instruments, experiment with scale and arpeggio patterns and sound effects to describe the actions in the text.

- Lastly, perform your story with music, with or without a narrator.

PARACHUTISTS

You are in the park during a Spring festival. You look up and see three parachutists coming down towards you. They seem to fall slowly at first, spiralling round and around, but as they get lower they appear to be falling faster. The first parachutist lands heavily just a few metres from where you are. The second one disappears behind some trees. The third one gets it all wrong and lands in the lake!

BONFIRE NIGHT

It's Bonfire Night and someone lights three rockets. The fuse on the first one burns for a few seconds, then the rocket flies up very quickly and bursts into colour. The second one is damp and only manages to fly up slowly to about twenty metres before it explodes. The third rocket is damaged; it rises to a metre and flies round and round the garden out of control and smashes into a window.

THE HARE AND THE TORTOISE

The hare and the tortoise agree to have a race. Off goes the starting gun! The hare leaps forward at almighty speed; the tortoise, plodding along, is left behind. Far ahead of the tortoise, the hare decides to take a break and drifts off to sleep. The tortoise continues to plod forward, but eventually overtakes the sleeping hare. At the last minute, the hare awakes. Aware of his mistake, he rushes towards the finishing line. But it is too late, the tortoise ambles across the line and wins the race.

JOURNEY INTO SPACE

5, 4, 3, 2, 1... the rockets are ignited and the shuttle blasts upwards towards the sky. Soon the craft reaches the stratosphere, and enters outer space. The shuttle cruises through space and time, beyond the known planets. Months pass, and the crew reach their destination, landing on a strange and bizarre world. Contact is made with alien creatures...

You could notate your story-with-music using a graphic score.

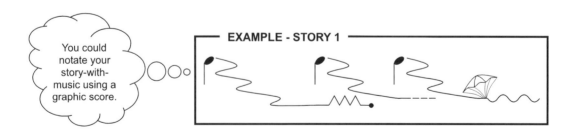

EXAMPLE - STORY 1

POINTS TO NOTE ON THE DVD

TELL A STORY WITH MUSIC:

Please refer to DVD chapters **COMPOSING DESCRIPTIVE MUSIC** and **MAKE UP A SONG**.

LEARNING OBJECTIVES

To compose in different styles, creating and selecting musical ideas by exploring the characteristics of their chosen story line.

To begin, students can read each story aloud and then choose which one(s) they prefer to 'illustrate' with music.

The chosen story can then be discussed in fine detail, and questions posed about how the range of actions and scenes can be represented using melodies, scales, arpeggios and sound effects.

For example, in 'The Hare and the Tortoise', the key action words are 'off goes', 'leaps forward', 'almighty speed', 'plodding along', etc. These would all need different musical representations.

Relevant questions could be:

(1) Would the plodding of the tortoise continue throughout the story?

(2) Would this be represented by a melodic line which captures the nature and movement of the tortoise, or by other means?

(3) How might the erratic nature of the hare be portrayed?

HOMEWORK ACTIVITIES:

(1) Compose a melodic line to represent part of one of the stories.

(2) Make up sound-effects to illustrate part of a story.

BACKGROUND INFORMATION

Telling a story through the medium of music is a way of composing common to all cultures, past and present. In Western musical culture, for example, numerous biblical stories have been expressed musically (e.g. by Bach, Parry, etc), and the musical genres of opera and ballet rely upon the interpretation of a story.

The four short stories in 'Tell a Story with Music' have been devised to highlight the musical elements of pitch, pulse, rhythm, dynamics and texture. They can provide opportunities for creating melodic lines, sound-effects, accompaniments and for exploration of diverse textures.

TEACHING IN GROUPS

Depending upon the size of the group, this activity can be undertaken by the teacher and, say, two students, or by a group of students alone. In either case, it is advisable that the activity should be 'student-led' rather than 'teacher-directed'. This allows students to initiate and develop their own original ideas, whilst the teacher is there to give help and advice, and possibly to be a player in the group.

Students can bring their own, individual strengths to the activity, e.g. by composing a suitable accompaniment with, perhaps, drones and ostinati, by evaluating and refining their work, or by leading a group performance.

The teacher can ensure that all players have an equal opportunity to contribute.

DIFFERENTIATION

There are no prerequisites in terms of ability or age to participate in 'Tell a Story with Music'. The activity can therefore be undertaken by students at any stage. Every opportunity can be taken to give performances of compositions by students.

EXTENSION ACTIVITIES

Students can be asked to compose a piece based upon a story of their choice, or to make up their own story as the basis of a composition.

➡ 'Composing Descriptive Music'.

Sound Collage

EXPLORATIONS Recorder Students' Edition

EXPLORATIONS

- This sound collage is for three or more players.

- The first player plays the phrase in box 1 repeatedly, then, as directed, moves onto box 2, then box 3, and so on.

- The second player joins in with box 1 as the first player starts box 2, and so on, in the manner of a round. Players 3, 4 (etc) start in the same way.

- The sound collage can be brought to a close by a group director at any given moment.

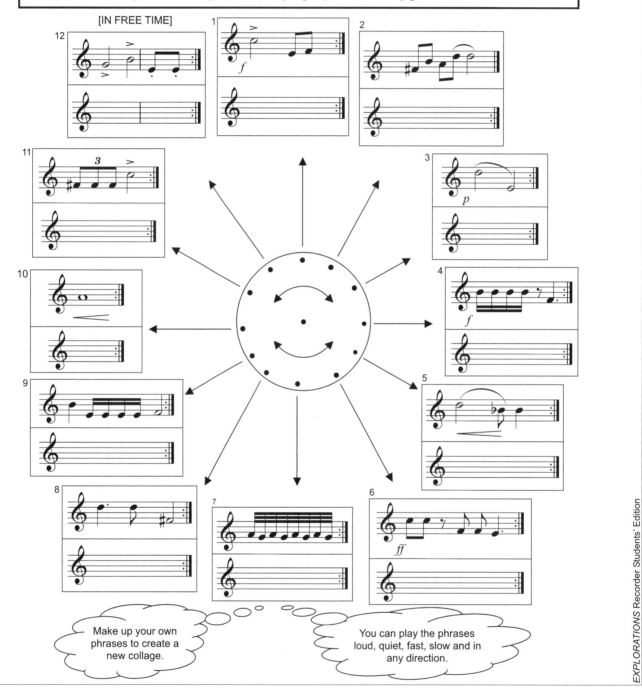

Make up your own phrases to create a new collage.

You can play the phrases loud, quiet, fast, slow and in any direction.

POINTS TO NOTE ON THE DVD

SOUND COLLAGE

- Sound Collage is given a stylistic framework by placing it into a context of film music.

- Students are asked to discuss ways of turning the improvisation into a composition. They decide upon an A-B-C-A structure.

- There appears to be full and interested engagement by all of the students.

LEARNING OBJECTIVES

To compose by developing musical ideas within given structures and applying instrumental skills.

To begin, the teacher and students may play each phrase in turn, to ensure that they present no difficulty to the players (see notes on differentiation concerning less advanced players).

As each phrase must be repeated, a discussion on the 'challenge of repetition' can be helpful. This may cover, for example, the use of dynamics, accents, pace and transposition.

The phrases can be played in any order chosen by the student(s) and/or teacher.

At a later stage, students may improvise their own repeated phrases. In the first instance, these may be based upon the notes and/or rhythms of the given phrases. Alternatively, students can improvise phrases 'freely', without reference to the given phrases.

HOMEWORK ACTIVITIES:

(1) Create original phrases and write them into the manuscript boxes provided.

(2) Record a performance of the given phrases and create original phrases to complement them.

BACKGROUND INFORMATION

This activity builds upon the knowledge and skills developed in 'Create-a-Chord' and 'Sound-Scape'.

Some 20th and 21st century composers have used compositional devices such as 'Sound Collage'. For example, some of the works of Maxwell Davies and Lutoslawski allow performers to contribute towards such a compositional process. The musical outcome is thus dependent on the creativity of the performers, who can subsequently lay a degree of 'ownership' to the music.

At each stage, players can be encouraged to make expressive, musical decisions, either instinctively, or/and by evaluating and revising their work.

TEACHING IN GROUPS

'Sound-Collage' can be either 'student-led' or 'teacher-led'. An assigned group director can use a combination of eye-contact and body movements to indicate when each player should begin and end each phrase. When the activity develops into a sound collage comprising 'free' improvisations by each player, a collective responsibility for starting and ending phrases can be encouraged. 'Sound Collage' can be used to compose a group piece based around a mood, scene or event. Alternatively, students may be asked to find a poem or story that can be musically illustrated.

DIFFERENTIATION

The given phrases indicate the technical starting point of the activity for more advanced players. Less advanced students can create phrases by playing the given rhythms on a more restricted range of notes.

The activity allows virtual beginners to compose with advanced players.

EXTENSION ACTIVITIES

This activity can lead to a discussion on 'aleatoric' and 'atonal' music. Students can be encouraged to listen to film scores and to comment on the use of such music.

➡ 'Minimalism'; 'Dodecaphonic Music'.

Tapas Tarantas

EXPLORATIONS

- This chordal and modal improvisation activity is for one or more players.

- Learn the phrygian mode and the chord sequence and then learn 'Tapas Tarantas'(a 'Tarantas' is a rhythmically free form of flamenco from Spain).

- Next, create your own solo using a mixture of notes from the mode and chords (Remember that this form of music is rhythmically very free).

- Use the first four bars to create an accompaniment and improvise melodic fragments over this using the phrygian mode.

PHRYGIAN MODE

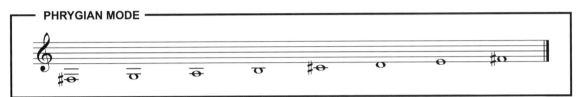

CHORDS

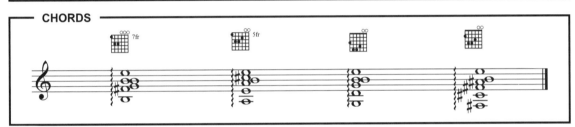

Tapas Tarantas

Leo Turner

POINTS TO NOTE ON THE DVD

TAPAS TARANTAS:

Please refer to DVD chapter **SOUND COLLAGE**.

LEARNING OBJECTIVES

To improvise rhythmic and melodic phrases freely or within given structures, individually or as part of a group.

To begin with, the teacher can perform 'Tapas Tarantas' as an example of Spanish Flamenco style, drawing attention to the freedom of 'time' and the juxtaposition of chords and melodic fragments.

Experiment with short passages from the scale played in various ways, i.e. Slurred or plucked poitecello or sul tasto. Playing the same passage but using different forms of attack, timbre and dynamics can help create the atmosphere for this very emotional music. Students may develop these techniques by using 'Listen and Answer' activities.

Rasgueado is a form of strumming the strokes using various combinations of fingers and thumb. The most basic rasgueado is to use forward strokes starting with the little finger while the thumb rests on an unused bass note.

The melodic fragments can be developed by playing some of the given rhythms on different notes. For example, the semiquaver motif in line 2 can be played with effect a 5th higher.

The characteristic use of downward sequence in this style of music can be explored, both with chords and fragments, as in lines 1 and 3, for example.

HOMEWORK ACTIVITIES:

(1) Learn the mode from memory and subject it to a wide variety of rhythmic and melodic decoration.

BACKGROUND INFORMATION

This activity builds upon the skills acquired in 'Pent-Up Blues' and 'Dorian Jazz', and provides the student with an opportunity to apply modal scales to traditional Spanish Folk music.

Flamenco music and dance originated in Andalucia but is now widely performed throughout the Spanish speaking world. The presence of semitones in the mode between the 1st and 2nd and the 5th and 6th notes gives a flavour of the North African influence in Spanish music, which dates back to Spain's occupation by the Moors in the middle ages.

Rasgueado can be a highly complex technique and the interested student may listen to examples played by the teacher or to recordings of performers such as Paco Pena or Paco de Lucia to appreciate the technical and rhythmic complexities.

GROUP TEACHING STRATEGIES

In the first instance, students can play the chords whilst the teacher performs the melodic fragments or vice versa. At a later stage, the process can be reversed.

Students can each be assigned a melodic fragment to learn (lines 2, 3 and 4). These can be played in turn whilst the remaining students and teacher perform the chords. Then, students can help one another to learn each others' fragments and chords. This can lead to a complete group (or solo) performance.

DIFFERENTIATION

Less advanced students can play one or two notes in each chord (for example upper B and E, which appear in all four chords). Melodic fragments can be based upon crotchet movement.

More advanced students can learn the four chords and melodic fragments and improvise to a technical standard beyond the examples given, if appropriate.

EXTENSION ACTIVITIES

Students can be encouraged to develop other Flamenco-style chord sequences. This may be facilitated by listening to appropriate recordings.

When the related techniques and style have been developed, students can be encouraged to improvise 'freely' using 'Question and Answer'.

 'Improvising with Ragas'.

Salsa Rhythm Round

EXPLORATIONS

- This Salsa rhythm activity is for two or more players.

- Practise the rhythm *[CD58]*, then play it as a round in unison, or in harmony using notes from the chord boxes below *[CD59, CD60, CD61]*. Each chord box lasts for one bar.

- Lastly, perform the rhythm round with the accompaniment. *[CD59, CD60, CD61]*

EXPLORATIONS Recorder Students' Edition

POINTS TO NOTE ON THE DVD

SALSA RHYTHM ROUND:

Please refer to DVD chapter **CARIBBEAN RHYTHM ROUND**.

*Students can be introduced to
the activity by clapping a 4-beat
pulse and speaking the 'word-
rhythms' aloud. To begin with,
this can be done in unison and
then as a round. Students can
then play through the round on
their instruments on any
predetermined note(s).*

*The chords can be introduced
separately, perhaps building
them up from the lowest note.*

*When playing the round using
the chord boxes, students can
move by step in the first
instance. At a later stage, two
(or three) notes in a chord box
may be alternated. For example:*

(etc)

HOMEWORK ACTIVITIES:

*(1) Play the round in simple,
step-wise form with CD track 59.*

*(2) Devise more complex,
alternating patterns of notes
within each box, using
appropriate rhythms.*

┌─BACKGROUND INFORMATION────────

'Salsa Rhythm Round' builds upon all previous 'round'
activities, but here the rhythms are more complex and the pace
much faster. The four CD tracks that offer accompaniments
(58-61) are graded in pace from ♩=106 to ♩=142, in order to give
students the opportunity to work up to effective salsa tempo.

The 'word-rhythms' are an aid to starting the activity only, and are
not intended to be used at the faster tempi (♩=142). The
words become so difficult to articulate at such tempi that it can
be counter-productive for students.

Caribbean and Latin American styles can provide an easy way
into improvisation. The use of 'chord tones' as a staple
improvisational device can simplify the improvisation process.
For example, playing the notes of chords, rather than scales,
limits the number of notes students need to hear and use at any
given moment.

┌─TEACHING IN GROUPS────────────

It is recommended that the two elements of rhythm and
harmony remain separate until players are familiar with both.
The four-part harmony can be effected when three or more
students are present in the lesson. The full harmonic effect can
be successfully realised in a small group if each player in turn
enters on the lowest note and then proceeds upwards by step
through the chords and then descends in the same manner.

The activity can be enhanced by playing with the CD
accompaniment. The addition of dynamics can also improve the
final outcome.

┌─DIFFERENTIATION───────────────

Less advanced students can perform the round by playing any
two adjacent notes, whereas more advanced students may play
all three notes of each chord in every bar, if desired.

┌─EXTENSION ACTIVITIES──────────

Students can be asked to make up their own words, on any
topic, to match the given rhythms. Alternatively, they may
compose new 'word-rhythms' and create their own 'Rhythm
Round'.

 'Minimalism'.

Dorian Jazz

EXPLORATIONS

- This modal jazz activity is for one or more players.
- Practise playing the dorian mode, then learn 'Five Spice Jazz'. *[CD62]*
- Next, decorate the melody using your own improvised jazz rhythms. *[CD63]*
- Finally, perform 'Five Spice Jazz', with rhythmic decorations, playing the theme once at the beginning and once at the end, with the accompaniment. *[CD64]*

DORIAN MODE

Five Spice Jazz

EXAMPLE RHYTHMIC DECORATION

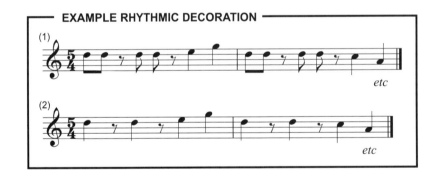

EXAMPLE KEYBOARD ACCOMPANIMENT

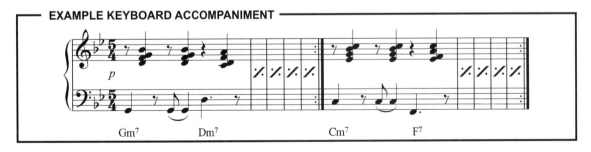

POINTS TO NOTE ON THE DVD

DORIAN JAZZ:

Please refer to DVD chapters **JAZZ ON 3 NOTES** and **JIGS AND REELS**.

EXPLORATIONS Recorder Students' Edition

LEARNING OBJECTIVES

To improvise freely and within given structures, in a jazz style, using rhythmic and melodic decoration.

Students who are not familiar with a 5-beat pulse will benefit from clapping the pulse whilst the teacher performs 'Five Spice Jazz'. They may also benefit from counting the 5-beat pulse aloud.

The teacher can draw students' attention to the structure of the 5-beat pulse, i.e. 1-2-3-1-2 etc.

In the first instance, improvisation can be approached by asking students to clap their own rhythmic decoration of the theme. They may then sing and clap the decorated theme before attempting to play it on their instrument.

At a later stage, students may be encouraged to melodically decorate the theme.

HOMEWORK ACTIVITIES:

(1) Memorise the given scale.

(2) Devise at least two ways to rhythmically decorate 'Five Spice Jazz'.

BACKGROUND INFORMATION

'Dorian Jazz' builds upon the knowledge and skills developed in 'Blues Booster', 'Rhythmic Decoration' and 'Melodic Decoration'.

There is a long tradition among jazz musicians of basing their improvisations and compositions on modes, as well as the 'blues' scale and major scale. The 5/4 time signature has also been used in jazz and it offers the opportunity for complex rhythmic patterns. 'Five Spice Jazz' brings these two strands together, offering scope for improvisation based upon rhythmic and melodic decoration, as well as more 'free' improvisation.

TEACHING IN GROUPS

Within a group context, students can approach improvisation in a variety of ways. Some will internalise the notes as an aural pattern and improvise without the notation whilst others may want to refer to the notation and interpret it in a jazz style. Other students may cognize in terms of finger movements, and so on. The teacher can help to ensure that each approach is accepted, and students may vary their approaches when interacting with others.

DIFFERENTIATION

Less advanced students can improvise using a limited range of notes from the scale. More advanced players may extend their range by adding higher notes, for example.

EXTENSION ACTIVITIES

Students can be asked to compose their own jazz themes based on the Dorian mode. Also, they can be introduced to other modes or encouraged to devise their own modes.

➡ 'Composing Descriptive Music'.

Composing Descriptive Music

EXPLORATIONS

- This descriptive music activity is for one or more players.

- First, read the list of descriptive titles below, and choose one (or more) of them upon which to base your piece of music.

- Then, play through each rhythm grid and find one that is most appropriate to help you compose your chosen piece.

- Next, using notes from a scale of your choice, use your preferred rhythm grid to help with the composition of your piece.

- Lastly, perform your descriptive piece, perhaps adding an accompaniment.

EXAMPLE TITLES

'MOONWALK'   'LULLABY'

'CHINA TOWN'   'SLEIGH RIDE'

'CARIBBEAN STREET PARTY'

'SEA SCAPE'   'THE ELEPHANT'

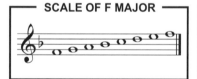

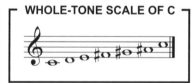

EXAMPLE STARTING POINTS

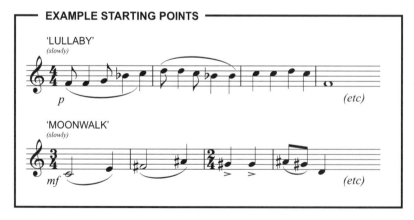

Now make up your own list of descriptive titles and compose another piece of music.

POINTS TO NOTE ON THE DVD

COMPOSING DESCRIPTIVE MUSIC

- The student is given a choice of scales and grids. She decides to use the pentatonic scale because she thinks it 'sounds chinese'.

- The teacher separates the elements of rhythm and pitch by initially playing through the scale, and then playing the rhythm grid on one note.

- Later, she models step-wise movement to the student in order to simplify the improvisational process.

Students often require very little assistance to begin work on the activity. This can lead to a more spontaneous and personal composition by the student.

Clapping through the first line of each rhythm grid, and then playing the same line using the first three or four notes from each scale, in turn, can be helpful. This may suggest a scene or mood to the student.

The teacher may draw the students' attention to compositional devices which have previously been studied. For example, imitation, sequence and mirror technique.

Other scales and modes can be suggested, e.g. minor or Dorian. Different time signatures could also be considered, for example compound time, or 5- or 7-beat pulse.

HOMEWORK ACTIVITIES:

(1) To suggest and perhaps create an accompaniment for a descriptive composition.

(2) Listen to a piece of descriptive music and write down some of its most outstanding features.

BACKGROUND INFORMATION

This activity brings together many strands which have already been introduced, such as 'Make Up a Song', 'Rhythm Grids', 'A Rhythm Round' and 'Sound-Scape'.

In Western musical culture there is a long tradition of describing scenes, moods and places in music. This is different to 'Tell a Story with Music', where a series of events is described in music. Here, the emphasis is upon describing the scene or mood, as in Delius' 'A Walk to the Paradise Garden', rather than a specific sequence of actions.

Students can be asked to discuss the difference between the two approaches to descriptive music and to devise ways of combining both in order to create an original composition.

TEACHING IN GROUPS

Depending upon the size of the group, this activity can be undertaken by the teacher and, say, two students, or by a group of students alone. In either case, it is advisable that the activity should be 'student-led' rather than 'teacher-directed'. This allows students to initiate and develop their own original ideas, whilst the teacher is there to give help and advice, and possibly to be a player in the group.

Students can bring their own, individual strengths to the activity. For example, by composing a suitable accompaniment with drones and ostinati, by evaluating and refining their work, or by leading a group performance.

The teacher can ensure that all players have an opportunity to contribute.

DIFFERENTIATION

Less advanced students can attempt the activity drawing upon a limited number of notes from a scale. More advanced students may use the complete scale and extend the range of notes, where appropriate.

EXTENSION ACTIVITIES

Students can be asked to make a list of example titles and to describe one of them in music. Also, they could be encouraged to devise their own scale and/or time-signature in order to create a composition.

➡ 'Minimalism'.

Japanese Music

JAPANESE 'IN' SCALE

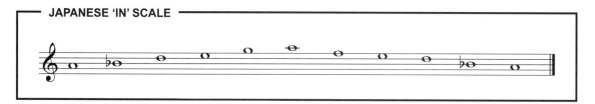

Sakura

EXAMPLE 2-BAR QUESTION AND ANSWER PHRASES

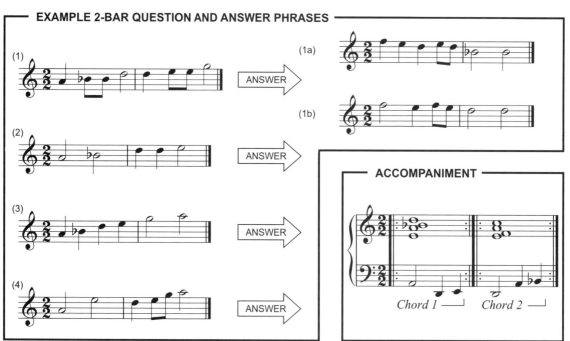

EXPLORATIONS Recorder Students' Edition

© Team World Music Ltd 2004

LEARNING OBJECTIVES

To repeat with accuracy short, easy, rhythmic and melodic phrases by playing back from memory; to improvise melodic phrases freely, or within given structures, individually or as part of a group.

In order to place 'Japanese Music' into its ethnic context, the teacher may consider demonstrating 'Sakura' to the students, accompanied by the relevant CD tracks.

In the first instance, students can be advised to use a limited number of notes and to use step-wise movement when improvising.

Also, improvising by using just the first few notes to begin with avoids the necessity of playing the differing ascending and descending forms.

Because of the differing ascending and descending forms of the scale, students may find it easier to improvise by referring to the notation, rather than playing from memory.

HOMEWORK ACTIVITIES:

(1) Memorise the scale.

(2) Memorise the melody.

(3) Improvise with CD track 66.

BACKGROUND INFORMATION

The purpose of this activity is to provide an opportunity to create music which suggests the sound world of Japanese music.

Students need not be concerned with the complexities of traditional Japanese music. However, the differing ascending and descending forms of this particular 'In' scale make the 'Listen and Copy/Answer' techniques more challenging. Care should be taken, therefore, to progress slowly and carefully with this activity.

Comparisons can be made between the structures of the 'In' scale and the melodic minor, which both have differing ascending and descending forms.

TEACHING IN GROUPS

Depending on the size of the group, tuned percussion instruments could be used for the ostinati, and piano or keyboard used for the drones.

Students can play a drone when not engaged in 'answering' a 2-bar phrase, and less advanced players can use the notes in the drone for their improvisations.

In order to guarantee that all students participate in the activity for the whole time, the group can copy a 2-bar phrase played by each of the students in turn.

Although students may play a drone or ostinato when not performing a solo or 'answer', they should be advised to 'rest' at any time when they feel that they are lacking in stamina.

DIFFERENTIATION

Less advanced students can improvise using just the first three notes of the scale, whilst more advanced players can use the whole scale.

EXTENSION ACTIVITIES

Students can be asked to make up their own scales with differing ascending and descending forms, and to use them for improvising and composition.

➡ 'Improvising with Ragas'.

Minimalism

To compose by developing musical ideas within given structures and applying instrumental skills in an ensemble context.

Introduce the activity by talking about minimalism. Then play CD track 68 and explain that it is made up of layers of different ostinati. The teacher may consider demonstrating some of the phrases, drawing attention particularly to their expressive possibilities.

Step by step, each ostinato can be learnt and related to the given mode.

When experimenting with the superimposition of different ostinati, students should be encouraged to choose and combine patterns to create a unified whole. This can then be discussed, assessed and revised, until a final version is produced.

Students can decide upon the number of times each phrase will be played. Players can 'drop out' and re-enter at given points, or do so randomly. Patterns may be played an octave higher or lower, where appropriate.

HOMEWORK ACTIVITIES:

(1) Practise performing selected ostinati with the CD tracks.

(2) Compose an ostinato using three or more notes from the mode. Draw upon a rhythmic idea given by the teacher.

BACKGROUND INFORMATION

In this activity, students are introduced to the sound world of minimalism. Performance and composing skills are combined to create a minimalist-style composition.

The boxes introduce simple ostinati which can be used as the building blocks for the students' work.

Once they have experimented with the given ideas they can be asked to compose their own.

Students should be encouraged to take control of their creative work. At each stage, players can be encouraged to make expressive, musical decisions, either instinctively, or by evaluating and revising their work.

TEACHING IN GROUPS

'Minimalism' can be either 'student-led' or 'teacher-led'. An assigned group director can use a combination of eye-contact and body movements to indicate when each player should begin and end each phrase. When the activity develops into a sound collage comprising 'free' improvisations by each player, a collective responsibility for starting and ending phrases can be encouraged. 'Minimalism' can be used to compose a group piece based around a mood, scene or event. Alternatively, students may be asked to find a poem or story that can be musically 'illustrated'.

DIFFERENTIATION

The range of ostinati caters for players of different abilities.

Less advanced students can choose to play one ostinato throughout.

More advanced players can change pattern at given moments during the performance, or can use their own ostinati.

EXTENSION ACTIVITIES

Students can go on to compose a complete minimalist piece using their own ostinati patterns alone.

The activity can be performed as part of an informal or formal concert.

Dodecaphonic Music

TONE-ROW

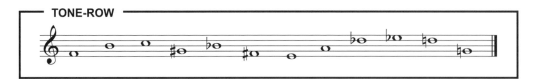

RETROGRADE TONE-ROW

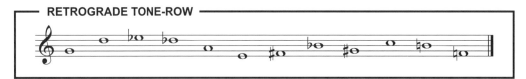

EXAMPLE IMPROVISATIONS

(1) *Freely*

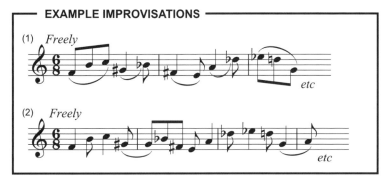

(2) *Freely*

etc

You can play your improvisation in 'strict' or 'free' time.

One or more players can use the tone-row whilst others use the retrograde.

EXAMPLE ACCOMPANIMENT

EXAMPLE KEYBOARD OSTINATO

Try starting your improvisation at different points in the row.

EXPLORATIONS Recorder Students' Edition

POINTS TO NOTE ON THE DVD

DODECAPHONIC MUSIC:

Please refer to DVD chapter **SOUND COLLAGE**.

The teacher can introduce 'Dodecaphonic Music', briefly mentioning the Second Viennese School (Berg, Schoenberg and Webern). It is worth mentioning that this style dates from the early 20th century. CD track 69 may be played as an example of serialism.

Playing the tone-row will illustrate how it is derived from the chromatic scale, with every note occurring only once in the row. Students may then learn the tone-row.

The teacher can then play an example improvisation, such as one of those illustrated. Extend the improvisation and explain that upon completion of the row, the player must return to the first note.

Suggest that students create their own improvisations, drawing upon simple rhythms. In the initial stages it may be helpful to use long, held notes.

Students can be encouraged to use repeated rhythms to create a sense of unity. Once confidence has been gained, students may move onto more complex rhythmic patterns. They may also use notes an octave higher or lower than indicated.

HOMEWORK ACTIVITES:

(1) Practise performing improvisations using the CD backing track. Experiment with using both the tone-row and its retrograde.

(2) Students can learn to play the tone-row from memory and practise improvising without notation.

BACKGROUND INFORMATION

This activity gives the opportunity to work in a modern idiom, explore dissonance, and learn about the compositional technique of serialism.

It can be useful if students have had some experience of playing dissonant music and the chromatic scale, as well as some focused listening to dissonant music, perhaps through the medium of film scores.

Examination syllabuses usually include the requirement to perform chromatic scales from memory. This activity can help to place these scales into a relevant and meaningful context.

TEACHING IN GROUPS

In group situations, students can be encouraged to improvise harmony parts to an improvised melody.

Appointed students could create a counter-melody. The group could also explore creating a dissonant ensemble, experimenting with solos, counter-melodies and harmony parts.

Players may also wish to structure their performance with a clear start, middle and end.

DIFFERENTIATION

Less advanced students can work with a small section of the tone-row, and specific, simple rhythm patterns can be suggested.

Alternatively, students can be encouraged to accompany the teacher, or another player, with a simple ostinato based on three or four notes from the tone-row.

EXTENSION ACTIVITIES

Drawing upon a 12-note chromatic scale, students can progress onto composing their own tone-row as a basis for further improvisation work.

Transposing Tunes 'By Ear'

EXPLORATIONS

- This transposing 'by ear' activity is for one or more players.

- First, learn to play the scales of G, D and A with and without notation.

- Next, pair up the name of each tune (in the left-hand column) with its corresponding rhythm (in the right-hand column).

- Then, work out each tune 'by ear' in the keys of G, D and A, starting on the respective tonic (key-note).

SCALES OF G, D AND A

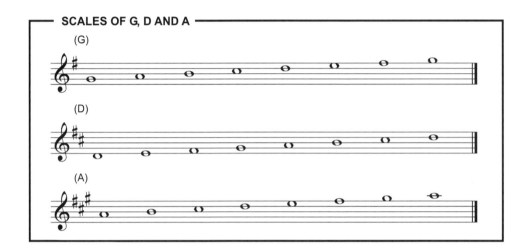

(G)

(D)

(A)

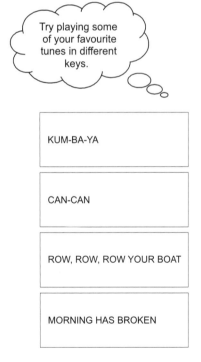

Try playing some of your favourite tunes in different keys.

The dots represent short sounds and the dashes long sounds.

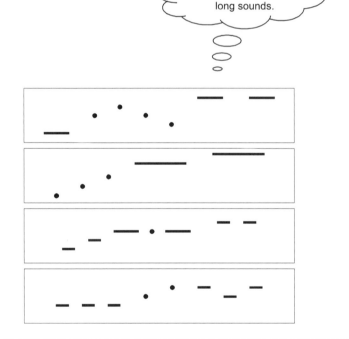

KUM-BA-YA	
CAN-CAN	
ROW, ROW, ROW YOUR BOAT	
MORNING HAS BROKEN	

EXPLORATIONS Violin Students' Edition

POINTS TO NOTE ON THE DVD

TRANSPOSING TUNES 'BY EAR'

- The teacher asks the student to describe the relationship between the dots and dashes and the related melody.

- She gives plain, simple instructions on how to start the activity.

- The student had not previously been introduced to these activities and appears genuinely surprised at her own success.

To work out 'by ear' how to play well-known tunes through the medium of graphic notation, making links between sounds and symbols.

The teacher can help students to identify a tune initially by encouraging them to sing the first few bars. This can then be related to the graphic notation, thus making the link between sound and symbol.

Students can then try to complete one of the melodies 'by ear', listening carefully to whether each note is higher or lower, longer or shorter than the previous note.

Once a tune has successfully been worked out 'by ear', it can be recorded in graphic form. Letter-names may be added below the symbols or students may use staff notation.

When a tune has been worked out correctly 'by ear', the student(s) can be asked to transpose it.

Students can use hand signals to indicate size of intervals, note repetition and phrase-shape.

They should be encouraged to perform each piece in an appropriately expressive style.

HOMEWORK ACTIVITIES:

Work out a favourite tune 'by ear' at home and notate it using dot-dash phrases (in a subsequent lesson, other students can be asked to identify it and work it out 'by ear').

BACKGROUND INFORMATION

This activity builds upon the knowledge and skills developed in 'Name that Tune' and 'Dot-Dash Phrases'.

Tunes can be worked out during individual practice and then played again in the lesson. Students can be asked to play the given melodies in keys other than those specified.

Transposing 'by ear' is an important tool for the advanced musician.

Regular playing 'by ear' helps to build confidence in the activity. Transposing melodies 'by ear' can help to develop an awareness of key relationships.

TEACHING IN GROUPS

Individual players can be given time within the lesson to complete the melody 'by ear'. Alternatively, students can be encouraged to play the prompt together, and then take turns to work out allocated phrases. This can be either a teacher- or student-led activity.

At a later stage (and depending upon the ability of the students), players can be encouraged to compose an harmonic part to the tune. In the first instance the teacher should model the activity, bringing the attention of students to the importance of certain harmonic and structural features such as cadences, transitional harmonies, and harmonic intervals such as 3rds + 6ths.

DIFFERENTIATION

Less advanced students can work out 'by ear' simple, individual phrases. The teacher and pupil may then perform the melody together, the teacher completing the gaps within the melodic line.

EXTENSION ACTIVITIES

Students can be encouraged to transpose a previously memorised melody into another key, for example an examination piece or study.

Performing a tune in the relative minor key can help develop an understanding of major/minor key relationships.

Improvising with Ragas

EXPLORATIONS

- This composing ragas activity is for one or more players.
- First, learn to play the raga ascending and descending, and then memorise it. *[CD70]*
- Next, take turns to improvise 2-bar phrases as in the examples below. Then add the accompaniment. *[CD71]*
- Lastly, compose your own raga based on your improvisations, and perform it, adding the example drones and an ostinato. *[CD71]*

THE RAGA

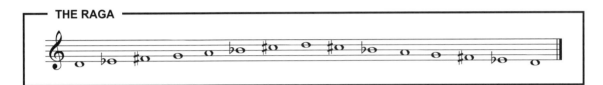

EXAMPLE 2-BAR PHRASES

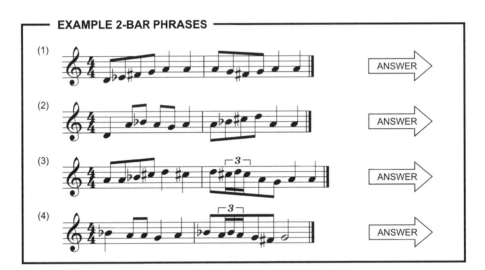

EXAMPLE DRONE AND OSTINATO

KEYBOARD ACCOMPANIMENT

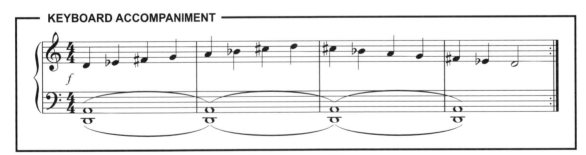

EXPLORATIONS Recorder Students' Edition

POINTS TO NOTE ON THE DVD

IMPROVISING WITH RAGAS

- The raga is introduced by combining the upper halves of two, related examination scales, in order to give the scales a practical, musical relvance.

- The teacher uses both the keyboard and the CD for accompaniment.

- The students appear equally comfortable playing both with, and without, notation.

© Team World Music Ltd 2004

LEARNING OBJECTIVES

To repeat with accuracy short, easy rhythmic and melodic phrases by playing back from memory; to improvise rhythmic and melodic phrases freely, or within given structures, individually or as part of a group.

Students can begin by listening to CD tracks 70 and 71, in order to create the appropriate atmosphere.

The teacher may introduce the scale (raga) by playing it. Explain that there are many types of raga, each with their own mood or character and that they are used to organise melodies in Indian music. The example raga is a popular and well-known form. Encourage the students to learn the raga from memory. This can be done with the aid of CD track 70.

The teacher may then move on to demonstrate the 2-bar 'Listen and Answer' activity. Perform the given examples to the student(s) with the CD accompaniment. Review 'Listen and Answer' technique. Make links to previous work in this area.

The students can be encouraged to practise creating answering 2-bar phrases with the backing track. The teacher and student can take turns, if appropriate. To begin with, it may be easier to use simple crotchets and minims for answered phrases. More complicated rhythms can then be introduced when confidence has been gained.

HOMEWORK ACTIVITIES:

Practise creating different answering phrases accompanied by the CD backing track.

BACKGROUND INFORMATION

The purpose of this activity is to provide an opportunity to create music which suggests the sound world of Indian music. The activity is melodically based but students need not be concerned with the complexities of traditional Indian classical music.

'Improvising with Ragas' can be prepared for a complete performance, perhaps supporting a curriculum topic. This could begin, for example, with 8 bars of drones, to which an ostinato is then added. 'Soloists' can then develop a melodic line, culminating in a loud, climactic finish to the work.

TEACHING IN GROUPS

Depending on the size of the group, percussion instruments could be used for the ostinati, and piano, keyboard or tuned percussion used for the drones.

Students can play a drone when not engaged in 'answering' a 2-bar phrase, and less advanced players can use the notes in the drone for their improvisations.

In order to guarantee that all students participate in the activity for the whole time, the group can copy a 2-bar phrase played by each of the students in turn.

Although students may play a drone or ostinato when not performing a solo or 'answer', they should be advised to 'rest' at any time when they feel that they are lacking in stamina.

DIFFERENTIATION

Less advanced students, not yet able to play the complete raga, can join in by using only the notes they are able to play, and may use simpler rhythms than the more advanced players.

EXTENSION ACTIVITIES

Students can apply the 'Listen and Answer' technique to create their own 4-, 8- or 12-bar improvisations.

These can be accompanied by using CD track 70 or a combination of drones and ostinati.

Jigs and Reels

- This improvisation activity is for one or more players.

- Begin by learning to play 'Emerald Isle' *[CD72]*, then, in the style of the examples given, experiment adding your own rhythmic and melodic decoration *[CD73]*.

- Next, following the chordal structure of the piece and using notes from the chord boxes, practise combining improvised 4-bar phrases to create your own jig melody *[CD74]*. Perform with accompaniment adding decoration of your choice. You may add a harmony part and a drum ostinato.

- Lastly, perform 'Emerald Isle' as a ternary (ABA) form piece. Begin by playing the melody, then improvise for 16 bars, ending with a decorated version of the original theme *[CD75]*.

THE CHORDS

Emerald Isle

EXAMPLE RHYTHMIC AND MELODIC DECORATION

EXAMPLE IMPROVISED 4-BAR PHRASE

KEYBOARD ACCOMPANIMENT

| Am | G | Am | G | Am | Em | Am Em | Am | C | G | Am | Em | Am Em Am | G | Am Em | Am |

─── **POINTS TO NOTE ON THE DVD** ───

JIGS AND REELS

- The teacher builds upon the previous week's work by starting with 'decoration'. The CD is used to provide the appropriate cultural accompaniment.

- The student is asked to choose a rhythmic framework for the improvisation rather than being given one.

- For homework, the student is asked to prepare a complete performance, to include the melody, 'decoration' and improvisation.

EXPLORATIONS Recorder Students' Edition

To make up some variations on a well-known tune, 'by ear', using a range of rhythmic and melodic decorations.

To begin with, the teacher can perform 'Emerald Isle' as an example of a jig/reel. Discuss the dance element and 6/8 metre, and then talk about jigs and reels in relation to Irish or Celtic folk music.

The teacher can then explain that each bar is based upon one of the given chords, with added passing notes. Links can be made to the chord boxes beneath each bar.

Students can be encouraged to experiment with improvising a simple phrase using selected notes from the chords. They can begin by working with easy rhythms like dotted crotchets and dotted minims, using one or two notes from each chord box. Students can then experiment with using quavers and passing notes.

It may be helpful to commit the complete improvisation to memory. Students can then add their own rhythmic and melodic decorations.

Regular practice with the CD accompaniments will nurture confidence.

HOMEWORK ACTIVITIES:

(1) Practise the melody with a CD backing track.

(2) Learn, from memory, a complete improvisation.

BACKGROUND INFORMATION

This activity builds upon the knowledge and skills developed in 'Rhythmic Decoration' and 'Melodic Decoration', and provides the student with an opportunity to apply these in a traditional folk style.

It is important that students should have a good, working knowledge of chordal improvisation by this stage. Relevant, previous activities could include 'Salsa Rhythm Round', 'Caribbean Rhythm Round' and 'Rhythm Grids'.

TEACHING IN GROUPS

When two or more students are present, the 3-part chords can be played. They can be introduced separately, perhaps building up from the lowest note, and then played slowly as a four-chord sequence.

Next, students can play together through the complete chord sequence of 'Emerald Isle', using the given rhythms of the melody. The chord sequence can be used as an accompaniment for a soloist, or as a refrain between solos, and a 'bodhrán' type drum ostinato can be added.

DIFFERENTIATION

Less advanced students can be encouraged to use only dotted crotchet and dotted minim rhythms, for example. They could accompany a student or teacher performing the main theme, drawing upon notes from the chord boxes.

More advanced students can experiment with using step-wise patterns and semiquaver rhythms.

EXTENSION ACTIVITIES

Students can progress to notating their work. They could create an extended improvisation/composition consisting of several sections.

Their work could then be played as part of a formal or informal performance.

DADGBD

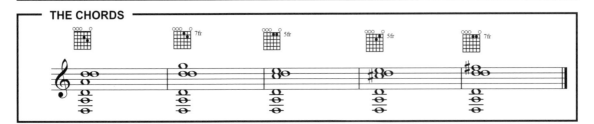

EXPLORATIONS

- This altered guitar tuning activity is for one or more players.

- Retune your guitar to the notes DADGBD, i.e. tune the first and sixth strings down one whole tone.

- Practise the chord shapes and then learn 'DADGBD'. Most of the piece will use these chord shapes. Using these chords, explore different combinations of strumming and picking patterns.

- Explore group arrangements and improvising using the chords, using the CD track to help you.

THE CHORDS

DADGBD

Leo Turner

EXPLORATIONS Classical Guitar Students' Edition

POINTS TO NOTE ON THE DVD

DADGBD:

Please refer to DVD chapter **JIGS AND REELS**.

LEARNING OBJECTIVES

To create some variations on an original tune, 'by ear', using a range of harmonic, rhythmic and melodic decorations.

To begin with, the teacher can perform 'DADGBD' as an example of a jig/reel. Discuss the dance element and 6/8 metre in relation to Irish or Celtic folk music. The teacher could also discuss and demonstrate other altered tunings that are common in folk or contemporary guitar playing.

The teacher can then explain that each bar is based upon one of the given chords, with added passing notes. Links can be made to the notated chords and their shapes on the fretboard.

Students can be encouraged to experiment with improvising a simple phrase using selected notes from the chords. They can begin by working with easy rhythms like dotted crotchets and dotted minims, using one or two notes from each chord. Students can then experiment using quavers and passing notes.

The teacher can lead a discussion on slurring (i.e. 'hammer-ons' and 'pull-offs') and demonstrate the technique. Students may learn the technique by using 'Listen and Copy/Answer' activities.

Regular practice with the CD accompaniments will nurture confidence.

HOMEWORK ACTIVITIES:

(1) Practise the melody with the CD backing track.

(2) Learn, from memory, a complete improvisation.

BACKGROUND INFORMATION

This activity builds upon the knowledge and skills developed in 'Rhythmic Decoration' and 'Melodic Decoration', and provides the student with an opportunity to apply these in a traditional folk style.

It is important that students should have a good, working knowledge of chordal improvisation by this stage. Relevant, previous activities could include 'Salsa Rhythm Round', 'Caribbean Rhythm Round' and 'Rhythm Grids'.

The tablature notation has been added in order to indicate which 'same-pitch' notes are fingered and which are on open strings. The open and fingered 'same-pitch' notes played at the same time produce a 'ringing' effect within the texture.

TEACHING IN GROUPS

In the first instance, students can play the three-note drone while the teacher plays the melody above it. Then students can learn the upper half of each chord whilst the teacher accompanies with the drone. Students should be encouraged to experiment using various percussive and tambour effects to create accompaniments to DADGBD. At a later stage the students can learn DADGBD as a solo and create their own variations.

In performance, students' variations can be played with other group members providing the accompaniment using percussive and tambour effects. Students can be encouraged to experiment with different textures.

DIFFERENTIATION

Less advanced students can be encouraged to use only dotted crotchet and dotted minim rhythms, for example. They could accompany a student or teacher performing the main theme, drawing upon notes from the chord boxes.

More advanced students could create solos using a mixture of chords, slurs and arpeggio patterns. Experiment with another altered tuning such as DGDGBD or DADF#AD.

EXTENSION ACTIVITIES

Students can progress to notating their work. They could create an extended improvisation/composition consisting of several sections.

Their work could then be played as part of a formal or informal performance.

EXPLORATIONS *usage guide*

This quick guide explains which titles in the series integrate and which do not. If you need more detailed information covering which title would suit your specific teaching situation, or have questions regarding content, please visit www.music-tutor.net or email questions to email@music-tutor.net.

EXPLORATIONS	EXPLORATIONS
TRUMPET/CORNET	VIOLIN

EXPLORATIONS	EXPLORATIONS
FLUTE	CLASSICAL GUITAR

EXPLORATIONS instrument specific Students' Editions for all brass, woodwind and string instruments can be used for individual tuition and same-voice group tuition. They generally contain the same activities in friendly keys. They cannot be used in conjunction with each other or in combination with EXPLORATIONS for Wind Band/Orchestra or Classroom Band.

Flute Book + CD	TWM00109	Trombone/Euphonium Bass Clef Book + CD	TWM00125
Oboe Book + CD	TWM00111	F Horn Book + CD	TWM00127
Clarinet Book + CD	TWM00113	Eb Horn Book + CD	TWM00129
Saxophone Eb Book + CD	TWM00115	Tuba Treble Clef Book + CD	TWM00131
Saxophone Bb Book + CD	TWM00117	Tuba Bass Clef Book + CD	TWM00133
Bassoon Book + CD	TWM00119	Classical Guitar Book + CD	TWM00135
Trumpet/Cornet Book + CD	TWM00121	Contemporary Guitar Book + CD	TWM00137
Trombone/Euphonium Treble Clef Book + CD	TWM00123	www.music-tutor.net email@music-tutor.net	

EXPLORATIONS
WIND BAND/ ORCHESTRA

EXPLORATIONS for Wind Band/Orchestra can be used with any group of mixed brass players, woodwind, strings, guitar, and percussion, from quartet/quintet up to full-sized band or orchestra. One edition covering all instruments is available in packs of 10. Includes keyboard supplement and accompaniment CD.

Wind Band/Orchestra 10 pack, Keyboard Supplement + CD   TWM00143   www.music-tutor.net   email@music-tutor.net

---

EXPLORATIONS	EXPLORATIONS
CLASSROOM BAND	CLASSROOM PERCUSSION

EXPLORATIONS
RECORDER

EXPLORATIONS for Classroom Band, Classroom Percussion and Recorder can be used with any mixed group of 'classroom' instruments, including glockenspiel, recorder, keyboard, marimba, guitar, tambourine and triangle, as well as all brass, woodwind and string instruments.

Recorder Book + CD	TWM00139
Classroom Percussion Book + CD	TWM00145
Classroom Band 10 pack, Keyboard Supplement + CD	TWM00142

www.music-tutor.net   email@music-tutor.net

EXPLORATIONS	EXPLORATIONS
VIOLIN	VIOLA

EXPLORATIONS	EXPLORATIONS
CELLO	DOUBLE BASS

EXPLORATIONS for violin, viola, cello and double bass are each instrument specific but all share the same concert pitch activities on same-numbered pages. They can be used in combination for mixed string teaching or for string ensemble work.

Violin Book + CD	TWM00101
Viola Book + CD	TWM00103
Cello Book + CD	TWM00105
Double Bass Book + CD	TWM00107

www.music-tutor.net   email@music-tutor.net

EXPLORATIONS
TEACHERS' EDITION

EXPLORATIONS Teachers' Edition, Audio CD + DVD is for use by teachers of all instruments, classroom music teachers and conductors of any ensemble. It works as a reference book together with any other title from the EXPLORATIONS series.

Teachers' Edition, CD + DVD   TWM00146   www.music-tutor.net   email@music-tutor.net